PERSPECTIVES IN
CONSUMER BEHAVIOR

PERSPECTIVES IN

CONSUMER BEHAVIOR

revised

Harold H. Kassarjian | Thomas S. Robertson

Graduate School of Business Administration | Wharton School of Finance and Commerce
University of California, Los Angeles | University of Pennsylvania

Scott, Foresman and Company
Glenview, Illinois   Brighton, England

Library of Congress Catalog Card Number: 72-93502
ISBN: 0-673-07836-1

To Traute and Diana

Acknowledgments

Albert H. Hastorf and Hadley Cantril, "A Case Study of Differential Perception," *Journal of Abnormal and Social Psychology*, Vol. 49 (1954), pp. 73–79. Copyright 1954 by the American Psychological Association, and reproduced by permission.

"Brand Identification and Perception" by Ralph I. Allison and Kenneth P. Uhl from *Journal of Marketing Research*, Vol. 1 (August 1964), pp. 80–85. Reprinted by permission.

"Buyers' Subjective Perceptions of Price" by Kent Monroe from *Journal of Marketing Research*, Vol. 10 (February 1973), pp. 70–80. Reprinted by permission.

"Preference and Perception Measures in New Product Development: An Exposition and Review" by Alvin J. Silk from *Sloan Management Review*, Vol. 11, No. 1 (Fall 1969). © 1969 by the Industrial Management Review Association, all rights reserved. Reprinted by permission.

"Consumer Rankings of Risk Reduction Methods" by Ted Roselius from *Journal of Marketing*, Vol. 35 (January 1971), pp. 56–61. Reprinted by permission.

"Attribution Theory and Consumer Behavior" by Robert B. Settle was prepared especially for this book.

"Learning and Consumer Behavior" by John A. Howard, from *Marketing Theory* by John A. Howard. © Copyright 1965 by Allyn and Bacon, Inc. Boston, Mass. Reprinted by permission.

"Consumer Brand Choice as a Learning Process" by A. A. Kuehn. Reprinted from the *Journal of Advertising Research*. © Copyrighted 1962, by the Advertising Research Foundation.

"The Impact of Television Advertising: Learning Without Involvement" by Herbert E. Krugman from *The Public Opinion Quarterly*, Vol. 29 (Fall 1965), pp. 349–356. Reprinted by permission of the author and *The Public Opinion Quarterly*.

"Consumer Behavior: A Field Theoretical Approach" by H. H. Kassarjian from *Marketing and the New Science of Planning*, 1968 Fall Conference Proceedings of AMA, pp. 288–289. Reprinted by permission.

"Obesity, Hunger, and Supermarket Shopping Behavior" by Richard E. Nisbett and David E. Kanouse from American Psychological Association *Proceedings*, 1968. Reprinted by permission of the authors and the American Psychological Association.

"Fear Appeals in Marketing—A Social Perspective" by Homer E. Spence and Reza Moinpour from *Journal of Marketing*, Vol. 36 (July 1972), pp. 39–43. Reprinted by permission.

"Personality and Consumer Behavior: A Review" by H. H. Kassarjian from *Journal of Marketing Research*, Vol. 8 (November 1971), pp. 409–418. Reprinted by permission.

"Personality and Innovation Proneness" by Jacob Jacoby from *Journal of Marketing Research*, Vol. 8 (May 1971). Reprinted by permission.

"A Multivariate Analysis of Personality and Product Use" by David L. Sparks and W. T. Tucker from *Journal of Marketing Research*, Vol. 8 (February 1971), pp. 67–70. Reprinted by permission.

"Activities, Interests, and Opinions" by W. D. Wells and D. J. Tigert. Reprinted from the *Journal of Advertising Research.* © Copyrighted 1971, by the Advertising Research Foundation.

"Attitudes and Attitude Change" by George S. Day is an adaptation of the author's chapter "Theories of Attitude Structure and Change" in *Consumer Behavior: Theoretical Sources*, Scott Ward and Thomas Robertson, eds., © 1973. By permission of Prentice-Hall, Inc., Englewood Cliffs, N.J.

"The Search for Attitudinal-Behavioral Consistency" by Martin Fishbein. Reprinted with permission of The Macmillan Company from *Behavioral Science Foundations of Consumer Behavior* by Joel E. Cohen. Copyright © 1972 by the Free Press, a Division of The Macmillan Company.

"A Cognitive Theory View of Brand Preference" by Stewart W. Bither & Stephen J. Miller from the 1969 Fall *Proceedings* of the American Marketing Association, pp. 280–286. Reprinted by permission.

"Consumer Choice Behavior: An Experimental Approach" by Flemming Hansen from *Journal of Marketing Research*, Vol. 6 (November 1969). Reprinted by permission.

"Cognitive Consistency and Consumer Behavior" by Bobby J. Calder was prepared especially for this book.

"Post decision Dissonance at Post Time" by Robert E. Knox and James A. Inkster from *Journal of Personality and Social Psychology*, Vol. 8, No. 4 (1968), pp. 319–323. Reprinted by permission of the authors and the American Psychological Association.

"The Dissonance Model in Post-Decision Product Evaluation" by Joel B. Cohen and Marvin E. Goldberg from *Journal of Marketing Research*, Vol. 7 (August 1970), pp. 315–321. Reprinted by permission.

"The Application of Attitude Immunization Techniques in Marketing" by Stewart W. Bither, Ira J. Dolich, Elaine B. Nell from *Journal of Marketing Research*, Vol. 8 (February 1971), pp. 56–61. Reprinted by permission.

"Reference Groups as Perspectives" by Tamotsu Shibutani from *American Journal of Sociology*, Vol. 60 (May 1955), pp. 560–569. Reprinted by permission of the author and The University of Chicago Press.

"Socially Distant Reference Groups and Consumer Aspirations" by A. Benton Cocanougher and Grady D. Bruce from *Journal of Marketing Research*, Vol. 8 (August 1971), pp. 379–381. Reprinted by permission.

"Effects of Group Pressure Upon the Modification and Distortion of Judgments" by Solomon E. Asch. From *Readings in Social Psychology,* Third Edition, edited by Eleanor E. Maccoby, Theodore M. Newcomb, and Eugene L. Hartley. Prepared by the author from data previously reported in *Groups, Leadership and Men,* ed. H. Guetzkow (Carnegie Press: 1951; Russell & Russell: 1963). Reprinted by permission of Carnegie-Mellon University.

"Consumer Behavior: Conformity and Independence" by M. Venkatesan from *Journal of Marketing Research*, Vol. 3 (November 1966). Reprinted by permission.

"A Test of the Two-Step Flow in Diffusion of a New Product" by Johan Arndt from *Journalism Quarterly*, Vol. 45 (Autumn 1968), pp. 457–465. Reprinted by permission of *Journalism Quarterly.*

"The Effect of the Informal Group Upon Member Innovative Behavior" by Thomas S. Robertson from the *Proceedings* of the 1968 Fall Conference of the American Marketing Association. Reprinted by permission.

"Dimensions of Marital Roles in Consumer Decision Making" by Harry L. Davis from *Journal of Marketing Research*, Vol. 7 (May 1970), pp. 168–177. Reprinted by permission.

"Children's Purchase Influence Attempts and Parental Yielding" by Scott Ward and Daniel Wackman from *Journal of Marketing Research* (August 1972). Reprinted by permission.

Selection 4.9 is from *Beliefs, Attitudes and Human Affairs* by S. L. Bem and D. J. Bem. Copyright 1970 by Wadsworth Publishing Company, Inc. Reprinted by permission of the publisher, Brooks/ Cole Publishing Company, Monterey, California.

"A Woman's Place: An Analysis of the Roles Portrayed by Women in Magazine Advertisements" by Alice E. Courtney & Sarah Wernick Lockeretz from *Journal of Marketing Research*, Vol. 8 (February 1971). Reprinted by permission.

Selection 5.1 is from W. Lloyd Warner, with Marchia Meeker and Kenneth Eells, *Social Class in America*. Harper & Row, Publishers (1960), 6–32. Copyright 1949 by Science Research Associates, Inc., Chicago. Reprinted by permission.

"Social Class and Consumer Behavior" by Sidney J. Levy from *On Knowing the Consumer*, edited by Joseph W. Newman. Copyright © 1966 by John Wiley & Sons. Reprinted by permission.

"Social Class and Commercial Bank Credit Card Usage" by H. Lee Mathews and John W. Slocum, Jr. from *Journal of Marketing*, Vol. 33 (January 1969), pp. 71–78. Reprinted by permission.

"Living Room Styles and Social Attributes: The Patterning of Material Artifacts in a Modern Urban Community" by Edward O. Laumann and James S. House. From *Sociology and Social Research*, Vol. 54, April 1970. Reprinted by permission.

"Low-Income Outlook on Life" (retitled, "Profile in Poverty) by Lola M. Irelan and Arthur Besner from *Low-Income Life Styles*, edited by Lola M. Irelan. Published by U.S. Dept. of Health, Education and Welfare.

Selection 6.1 is from Ralph Linton, The Cultural Background of Personality, Copyright, 1945, D. Appleton-Century Company, Inc. Reprinted by permission of Appleton-Century-Crofts, Educational Division, Meredith Corporation.

"The Silent Language in Overseas Business" by Edward T. Hall from *Harvard Business Review*, (May-June 1960). Copyright © 1960 by the President and Fellows of Harvard College; all rights reserved. Reprinted by permission.

Wayne Dennis, "Uses of Common Objects as Indicators of Cultural Orientations," *Journal of Abnormal and Social Psychology*, Vol. 55 (July 1957), pp. 21–28. Copyright © 1957 by the American Psychological Association, and reproduced by permission.

"The Negro Market" by R. A. Bauer and S. M. Cunningham. Reprinted from the *Journal of Advertising Research*. © Copyrighted 1970, by the Advertising Research Foundation.

"The Role of Blacks in Mass Media" © 1973 by *Journalism Quarterly*. To be published as "The Mass Media and America's Black Citizen" by Waltraud M. Kassarjian, *Journalism Quarterly*, Summer 1973. Reprinted by permission.

"A Theory of Buyer Behavior" by John A. Howard and Jagdish N. Sheth was prepared especially for the first edition of this book. The theory summarized here is treated in greater detail in J. A. Howard and J. N. Sheth, *A Theory of Buyer Behavior* (New York: John Wiley & Sons, Inc., 1969).

"Mathematical Models of Individual Buyer Behavior" by Philip Kotler. Reprinted from *Behavioral Science*, Volume 13, No. 4, 1968, by permission of James G. Miller, M.D., Ph.D., editor, and the author.

"Advertising Management, Consumer Behavior, and Simulation" by F. M. Nicosia. Reprinted from the *Journal of Advertising Research*. © Copyrighted 1968, by the Advertising Research Foundation.

"Information Processing Models of Consumer Behavior" by James R. Bettman from *Journal of Marketing Research*, Vol. 7 (August 1970), pp. 370–376. Reprinted by permission.

Preface

In 1968 the first edition of this book was published. The major impetus for its publication was that we were teaching courses in consumer behavior and felt that adequate text materials were just not available. In the ensuing half a decade, the field of consumer behavior has grown with a vengeance. From an occasional paper or article in the marketing, economics, or psychology literature, we have witnessed an explosion of theories, propositions, concepts, methodologies, and research findings to the point that journal readers and editors are overwhelmed.

There appears to be no end of the deluge in sight. The *raison d'être* of this second edition is no longer the felt need to bring together diverse materials in the field, but rather to present a selection of articles forming a core structure which represents to us the current state of the discipline.

The book is designed to provide the student with an overall view of the subject matter in consumer behavior, rather than a particular model or theoretical position. Few of the articles in the first edition are repeated in this volume; however, the structure of the book has not changed. It has been our experience that the basic structure is meaningful to most students and instructors, so we have tried to present an up-to-date overview of the field without altering the basic set of "propositions."

Each chapter includes an introductory overview, followed by selections from the literature. Whenever possible we have tried to include an article that reviews the literature in each area in order to delineate the present state of knowledge, and to follow that review with a combination of theory-oriented papers, research findings, and applications. The economic view of consumer decision making is not really represented, on the assumption that the reader would already be familiar with much of this material. Similarly, the enormous amount of literature on the process and effects of communication has been largely ignored, since the topic would constitute a book in itself. The emerging topics of consumerism and consumer protection are not fully represented, although we have included selections on this point of view as appropriate. Several good books of readings on these topics are already on the market, and the line had to be drawn somewhere. It was obviously our opinion that the topics in this volume and the reprinted selections made the most sense to students and instructors in a marketing course or course in consumer behavior.

It never ceases to amaze us, in the completion of any work, just how many debts are accrued to colleagues for advice and guidance. Quite important to us were our reviewers: John Myers at Berkeley, Joel Cohen at the University of Illinois, Stewart Bither at Pennsylvania State University, James Myers at the University of Southern California, and Homer Spence at the University of Washington. Masao Nakanishi and James Bettman at UCLA offered critical comments on the text material in several chapters. Marc Slovak was invaluable in his role as a research assistant.

George Day, Bobby Calder, Traute Kassarjian, and Kent Monroe provided us with original material or papers prior to publication elsewhere. And finally, not least important, was the help of Ms. Patricia J. Riley at UCLA and Ms. Mollie Horowits at Wharton.

Harold H. Kassarjian
Thomas S. Robertson

Contents

Introduction: Perspectives   **xii**

Chapter **1**   Perception and Learning

Overview   1
1.1   *Hastorf and Cantril:* A Case Study of Differential Perception   10
1.2   *Allison and Uhl:* Brand Identification and Perception   17
1.3   *Monroe:* Buyers' Subjective Perceptions of Price   23
1.4   *Silk:* Preference and Perception Measures in New Product Development   42
1.5   *Roselius:* Consumer Rankings of Risk Reduction Methods   55
1.6   *Settle:* Attribution Theory and Consumer Behavior   64
1.7   *Howard:* Learning and Consumer Behavior   75
1.8   *Kuehn:* Consumer Brand Choice as a Learning Process   87
1.9   *Krugman:* The Impact of Television Advertising: Learning Without Involvement   104
1.10 *H. Kassarjian:* Consumer Behavior: A Field Theoretical Approach   104

Chapter **2**   Motivation and Personality

Overview   113
2.1   *Nisbett and Kanouse:* Obesity, Hunger, and Supermarket Shopping Behavior   118
2.2   *Spence and Moinpour:* Fear Appeals in Marketing: A Social Perspective   122
2.3   *H. Kassarjian:* Personality and Consumer Behavior: A Review   129
2.4   *Jacoby:* Personality and Innovation Proneness   149
2.5   *Sparks and Tucker:* A Multivariate Analysis of Personality and Product Use   155
2.6   *Wells and Tigert:* Activities, Interests, and Opinions   162

Chapter **3**   Beliefs and Attitudes

Overview   177
3.1   *Day:* Attitudes and Attitude Change   188
3.2   *Fishbein:* The Search for Attitudinal-Behavioral Consistency   210
3.3   *Bither and Miller:* A Cognitive Theory View of Brand Preference   220
3.4   *Hansen:* Consumer Choice Behavior: An Experimental Approach   232
3.5   *Calder:* Cognitive Consistency and Consumer Behavior   247
3.6   *Knox and Inkster:* Postdecision Dissonance at Post Time   264
3.7   *Cohen and Goldberg:* The Dissonance Model in Post-Decision Product Evaluation   270
3.8   *Bither, Dolich, and Nell:* The Application of Attitude Immunization Techniques in Marketing   282

Chapter **4** Social Processes

Overview 292
4.1 *Shibutani:* Reference Groups as Perspectives 299
4.2 *Cocanougher and Bruce:* Socially Distant Reference Groups and Consumer Aspirations 309
4.3 *Asch:* Effects of Group Pressure Upon the Modification and Distortion of Judgments 315
4.4 *Venkatesan:* Consumer Behavior: Conformity and Independence 325
4.5 *Arndt:* A Test of the Two-Step Flow in Diffusion of a New Product 331
4.6 *Robertson:* The Effect of the Informal Group Upon Member Innovative Behavior 342
4.7 *Davis:* Dimensions of Marital Roles in Consumer Decision Making 353
4.8 *Ward and Wackman:* Children's Purchase Influence Attempts and Parental Yielding 368
4.9 *Bem and Bem:* Training the Woman to Know Her Place: The Power of a Nonconscious Ideology 374
4.10 *Courtney and Lockeretz:* A Woman's Place: An Analysis of the Roles Portrayed by Women in Magazine Advertisements 384

Chapter **5** Social Class

Overview 390
5.1 *Warner:* Social Class in America 400
5.2 *Levy:* Social Class and Consumer Behavior 409
5.3 *Mathews and Slocum:* Social Class and Commercial Bank Credit Card Usage 421
5.4 *Laumann and House:* Living Room Styles and Social Attributes: The Patterning of Material Artifacts in a Modern Urban Community 430
5.5 *Irelan and Besner:* Profile in Poverty 441

Chapter **6** Culture and Subcultures

Overview 450
6.1 *Linton:* The Concept of Culture 465
6.2 *Hall:* The Silent Language in Overseas Business 468
6.3 *Dennis:* Uses of Common Objects as Indicators of Cultural Orientations 480
6.4 *Bauer and Cunningham:* The Negro Market 489
6.5 *W. Kassarjian:* The Role of Blacks in Mass Media 504

Chapter **7** Models of Consumer Decision Making

Overview 515
7.1 *Howard and Sheth:* A Theory of Buyer Behavior 519
7.2 *Kotler:* Mathematical Models of Individual Buyer Behavior 541
7.3 *Nicosia:* Advertising Management, Consumer Behavior, and Simulation 560
7.4 *Bettman:* Information Processing Models of Consumer Behavior 572

Name Index 584

Subject Index 596

Introduction

Perspectives

Consumer behavior is an intriguing and complex field of inquiry. Most simply, it is the study of human behavior in the consumer role, and its theoretical basis is primarily that of the behavioral sciences—psychology, sociology, and anthropology.

Human behavior of any form is enormously diverse. There is no single or complete theory of human behavior that is generally accepted, and perhaps there never will be. But we do have a range of theories which are insightful and capable of *improving* our ability to predict behavior. Using them, marketing and social policy programs stand a greater probability of success in meeting human (consumer) needs.

In this introduction we review the basic perspectives from which the study of consumer behavior can be approached, discuss the role of consumer behavior research in our society, and then present an overview of the structure of the book.

Economics Perspective

The elegant simplicity of microeconomic utility theory is one approach toward an understanding of consumer behavior. The essential notion is the principle of utility, or the satisfaction derived from consumption. Consumers will behave in such a way as to maximize utility. This occurs in accord with the following familiar equation.

$$\frac{MU_x}{P_x} = \frac{MU_y}{P_y} = \frac{MU_n}{P_n}$$

Consumers will buy those quantities of products where the marginal utility (additional satisfaction from consuming one more unit) per dollar's worth of any one product equals the marginal utility per dollar's worth of any other product for a given period of time.

The assumptions of this model (as in any model) are critical. It is assumed that the consumer derives satisfaction from consumption, and that he seeks to maximize his satisfaction within the limitations of his income level in relation to a given set of prices. It is further assumed that he acts rationally, and that he is able to judge his tastes and preferences for all products under consideration.[1]

The microeconomic model, although useful to a degree, falls short of satisfactorily explaining consumer behavior because of the difficulties in measuring utility, and because other factors affecting consumer decisions are not included. Nor are the assumptions beyond dispute. For example: Does the consumer truly seek to *maximize* his satisfaction? Research on organizational and individual decision making has indicated that "satisfactory" alternatives are generally the goal rather than "optimal" alternatives. Does the consumer act rationally? What is rationality, and what constitutes an operational definition of the concept? Is it "rational" to buy a high-status car, such as a Cadillac, Lincoln, or Mercedes? We suppose that it might be if it is important to a person's self-concept, and if he feels better owning it than he would owning a Volkswagen. Research on pricing indicates that consumers are not always price sensitive or price knowledgeable, and may even buy the more expensive of two items under the assumption of a price-quality relationship.

Some economists have recognized the limitations of microeconomic theory in explaining consumer actions. Katona (1960) takes into account psychological factors that affect consumer decisions, such as motives and attitudes. These factors are viewed as intervening variables between the product stimuli and the potential response patterns of the individual. He labels his approach "economic psychology." Duesenberry (1949) takes an approach that could be called "economic sociology." His thesis is that consumer behavior theory must recognize the social character of consumption patterns, since many consumer decisions are based upon a desire for esteem in the eyes of others. Veblen (1899), of course, coined the familiar term "conspicuous consumption" to account for this purchase rationale. Although the approaches of Katona and Duesenberry are valuable, they are by no means complete in their explanation of consumer behavior.

Behavioral Science Perspective

The general perspective currently taken in the study of consumer behavior is that of the behavioral sciences—psychology, sociology, and anthropology. In this context, the consumer is viewed as a psychological entity, acting within a social and sociocultural environment.

Of course, it could be interesting to examine consumer behavior at a biological or *physiological* level as well. Using this approach, the researcher would attempt to tie behavior to physiological correlates. For example: The field of genetics is just beginning to scratch the surface of a very exciting body of knowledge. It may well be that genetic structures are related to consumer choice and decision processes. As yet we know very little about blood chemistry or neurological functioning and their relationship to needs and motives. Some day this might help us determine preference for chocolate ice cream over custard pudding.

Psychological Analysis

The psychological level of analysis focuses on the individual as a single behaving entity. His particular values, attitudes, opinions, experiences, needs, and his psychological view of the world—in short, his *cognitions*—govern his responses and actions, including his behavior as a consumer.

Some decisions are highly salient and involving, and may be approached with considerable thought and conflict. Others are nonsalient and noninvolving, and are routinized as much as possible.

If we may think of charity giving as a consumption decision, it may often be a high-involvement decision episode. Sidney J. Levy (1965) describes it this way:

> When people are asked to donate money to a worthy cause, their reactions are not based solely on whether they understand the need. They are being asked to join in a collective action, to give a sign of recognizing a common bond. Their involvement will grow out of many possible motives . . . the feeling to belonging and status; the protection from real or fantasied threat; the enhancement of self-esteem; internalizing group standards in exchange for love and protection received; diverting undue aggressiveness onto real evils.
>
> In more direct and personal terms, this means that people give because of a hierarchy of reasons and goals. The most intense participation and giving usually relate to an emotional awareness due to an afflicted loved one; a wish to be influential in the community; personal anxiety about being sick or deprived; wanting approval in face-to-face relations; and finding it a convenient avenue for demonstrating competence or power-seeking.

Alternatively, brand selection of, say, bread is most often a low-involvement decision. It is simply not very important to the individual's personality or self-concept. Nor is it a socially visible product, so that it is not particularly subject to social influence. Economists might therefore predict that for such a nondifferentiated product, the consumer should purchase the cheapest brand, and that brand loyalties should be minimal. However, this is not generally the case. Consumers are apparently influenced by advertising, and prefer to routinize brand selection to one or two regularly purchased brands, since this simplifies the decision process and avoids the arousal of conflict in purchasing.

The individual's response in the marketplace is also a function of more than the physical properties of the product. In many cases, the individual buys the total symbolic meaning or *brand image* which the item conveys. In other words, consumers often buy products not only for what they *do* but for what they *mean*.

Thus, many consumers objectively know that they cannot tell one popular beer from another in a blindfold test, but they maintain a brand preference anyway. They may simply be willing to play the game and to engage in a suspension of belief that all brands are basically the same. It is simply less cognitively involving to maintain a brand preference: it simplifies decision making; or, brands may have social significance independent of the basic physical product. Chivas Regal scotch has a different social significance in contemporary society than Black & White, for example. And some people almost feel "obligated" to have Jack Daniels bourbon on display at a party.

The ability to create *symbolic* product differentiation for essentially nondifferentiated products is a major zone of contention for marketing today. The social critic sees it as based essentially on advertising, with a concurrent rise in the price of the product and a gain by the marketer of a significant degree of control over the distribution and pricing structure. There is some validity to this argument, although marketers are still essentially providing consumers what they want. Beer, for example, is not really a thirst quencher (if we think of this as the basic function) but is instead a socially defined product. The standard retort to the social critics is represented by the following comments from David K. Hardin (1972), then president of the American Marketing Association:

> Basically, the question centers around whether adding psychic values to a product or service is a legitimate consumer benefit. I think the prevailing governmental view is that it is not a legitimate benefit. One can really quarrel that the imposition of this view is serious intervention in individual rights. If a woman thinks she is more attractive because she uses a certain cosmetic brand and if this, in turn, enhances her confidence and pleasure in the event for which she is using it, is it right to deny this privilege, even though it is a psychological claim which is based on little or no factual product differentiation?

Sociological Analysis

Sociology takes as its basic unit of concern the structure and functioning of *groups*, that is, sets of people who interact over time. For purposes of consumer behavior analysis, the importance of the group as a reference point for consumption decisions must be taken into account. Similarly, it is sometimes helpful to think of the consumer as a group (such as the family) rather than as an individual.

Industrial purchasing decisions are frequently made by a group of individuals. Although a purchasing agent may sign the contract, a financial vice-president may have lent approval, production and engineering may have been involved, and marketing may even have had some influence. The successful salesman under such circumstances may be the one who understands the dynamics of organizational behavior, and is able to plot sociometrically the decision unit and the relative power and influence of each of its members.

In family decision making, the mother may, in some cases, be acting merely as the purchasing agent, or she may be a powerful influence on the decision process. For example: the explicit purpose of advertising to young children is to lead them to request the product from their parents. Whether the parents accede to such requests or dismiss them without consideration is a function of family structure, values, and interaction patterns.

Everyone is familiar with the notion of group influence—the tendency of group members toward conformity. The most noted form of group influence on consumption is status consciousness, or the drive for conspicuous consumption. However, perhaps much more prevalent is the influence of the group as an information source and as a means of defining reality. Leon Festinger has elaborated this notion in his "theory of social comparison processes." Essentially, he reasons that people have a need to evaluate their opinions. In many instances there is no readily available physical reality check on opinions (for example, whether one political candidate is actually better than another). Therefore, "To the extent that objective, non-social means are not available, people evaluate their opinions and abilities by comparison respectively with the opinions and abilities of others" (Festinger, 1954, p. 118).

The group may be an important source of initial awareness and information about an object; it is a particularly important source of advice and idea-testing, especially for the more involving, higher risk consumption decisions.

Sociocultural Analysis

Sociocultural analysis of consumer behavior draws from sociology and cultural anthropology. The unit of analysis is at an aggregate, *social category* level. Here we examine the effects of social class, subcultures, and cultures on consumer actions.

These aggregate social categories influence the individual's cognitive and personality development, and govern the nature and range of his interactions with other people. Just as the probability of going to college or selecting a professional occupation is greater at higher social class levels, so also is there a differential impact of social class, subculture, or culture on life style and consumption patterns.

Multidisciplinary Analysis

Obviously, the study of consumer behavior most often involves multiple levels of analysis. For example: a family's purchase of a sailboat may be the outcome of a complex set of psychological, sociological, and sociocultural factors. The decision may have been influenced by cultural and social class influences, the attitudes and opinions of each family member, the group interaction patterns of the family, and so on.

Consumer behavior analysis is highly interdependent, although for certain types of problems, one level of analysis may be more appropriate than another. Looking at census figures tells us nothing about the income level or spending patterns of any single individual and, in turn, questioning a single person tells us nothing about the income distribution or consumption of the total population.

The Role of Consumer Behavior

The role of consumer behavior as a field of study can be viewed from three distinct vantage points. The traditional view of consumer behavior analysis has been as a imput to marketing decision making. Marketing practitioners have been the primary patrons and users of consumer behavior research. The promise of consumer behavior to marketing managers is that improved understanding of consumer actions will lead to better management decision making, with resulting efficiencies in the marketing program and an improvement in consumer welfare.

An alternative view of consumer behavior theory and research is that it can supply information and insight for social policy decisions involving consumer affairs. The rising tide of consumerism has had an important bearing on the acceptance of this role. Emerging from the latter-day muckrakers such as Rachel Carson and Ralph Nader, and appearing in the political system within state attorney general offices, district attorney offices, and the consumer arms of state and federal government, the pressure for a better appreciation of consumer interests has continued. The consumerist is becoming an important user of consumer behavior research.

Finally, consumer behavior research may be approached directly from the point of view of the consumer, in order to improve information in the marketplace which should result in improved functioning of the market. Consumer behavior has not yet been studied from the point of view of the consumer, for the sake of the consumer, in order to benefit the consumer.[2] Perhaps the consumerist sees this as his role, but until now, consumer protection proposals have largely been based on what is "good" for the consumer from the point of view of his advocate and not based on empirically verified needs.

Structure of the Book

The progression of this book in considering the various behavioral science approaches to consumer behavior generally follows the foregoing structure. We begin with the individual as the unit of analysis (psychological factors) and progress to a consideration of groups (sociological factors) and then subcultures and cultures (sociocultural factors).

Chapters 1–3 are at the individual level of analysis. Chapter 1 and the selections following it cover such topics as perception of reality and differential perception among brands; subjective perception of price; learning theory; and an interesting article on the levels of learning that may occur in television advertising. In addition, the topics of attribution theory and perceptual mapping, as well as perceived risk, are included.

In Chapter 2 we turn our attention to motivation and personality. The selections include a study on the relationship between the amount of supermarket purchases and the time expired since last eating. In addition, an interesting paper discusses the emotion of fear and its influence on behavior change. Finally, three articles examine the issue of personality.

Chapter 3 considers the topics of attitudes and attitude change. Included in this section are a review of the literature and several papers on current approaches to the study of attitudes. Also, we cover the important topic of cognitive dissonance with a review paper and two research studies. One of these involves the behavior of patrons at a race track, and the other a study in which subjects were purposely given bad-tasting coffee altered by chemicals to determine reactions to the purchase of a bad product, a "lemon."

In Chapter 4 the unit of study is the group and its influence on the individual. Discussed here are such topics as reference groups, conformity to others, the diffusion of innovation, and the roles of women. In addition, we have included a paper on the influence of children on their parents and an article on family behavior.

In Chapter 5 we turn to analysis of social class. The selections lead off with Warner's classic paper defining social class and include several research papers comparing consumption differences between members of different social classes.

The influence of cultures and subcultures is covered in Chapter 6. The first selection is a theoretical paper by a renowned anthropologist, followed by a classic article that summarizes the problems of doing business overseas.

This chapter also includes selections on subcultures in U.S. society, discussing consumption differences among racial and other ethnic groups.

Finally, in the last chapter of the book, we turn to global theories of consumer behavior. Several theories have been developed that attempt to package, in one grand structure, the body of knowledge we define as consumer behavior. These four selections perhaps best represent the state of accumulated knowledge.

The fact that the book progresses from the individual to the group, and thence to social class and culture, by no means implies that these various factors can be considered independently or that one is necessarily more important than another. As will be seen, the discussion of one level or factor is often dependent upon corresponding discussions of another. The interdependence of these factors is shown, for example, in the fact that an individual's personality is in part determined by group membership. However, the groups he chooses are often determined by his personality and need-value system. The group may have some influence on an individual's purchases. Once the purchase is consummated, the product in turn may influence his perceptions of similar products, or other people who have bought the same product. The interdependence may go so far as the purchased product's influencing to some degree group membership, as can be seen in the emergence of sports car rally clubs, often limited to one make of car.

This book, then, is about the consumer. We will be examining that subset of his total behavior that involves the exchange process: his purchase of toothpaste, coffee, a political candidate, a TV show, or a magazine to read. Of the forty-eight articles, about ten are considered classics in the field. Almost all of the remainder have been published since the early 1960s, and about one-half have been published since 1970. Consumer behavior is a very new and a very exciting field of study.

Notes

1. An alternative microeconomics approach to this "classical utility" model is the "indifference curve" model, which alters the assumption that the consumer must be able to judge his preferences for all products under consideration. For an excellent basic discussion of these models, see Leftwich (1970), Chapters 4 and 5. For a discussion related to consumer behavior, see Haines (1973).

2. The exception to this statement is the literature in farm economics and home economics. See, for example, *The Journal of Consumer Affairs*.

References

Duesenberry, J. S. *Income, Saving and the Theory of Consumer Behavior*. Harvard University Press, 1949.

Festinger, Leon. "A Theory of Social Comparison Processes." *Human Relations,* Vol. 7 (May 1954), 117–140.

Haines, George H. "Overview of Economic Models of Consumer Behavior." In *Consumer Behavior: Theoretical Sources*, eds. Scott Ward and Thomas S. Robertson. Prentice-Hall, 1973.

Hardin, David K. "Marketing Freedom Periled." *Marketing News,* Vol. 6 (October 1, 1972).

Katona, George. *The Powerful Consumer.* McGraw-Hill, 1960.

Leftwich, Richard H. *The Price System and Resource Allocation.* Holt, Rinehart & Winston, 1970.

Levy, Sidney J. "Humanized Appeals in Fund Raising." *Public Relations Journal* (July 1965).

Veblen, Thorstein. *The Theory of the Leisure Class.* Macmillan, 1899.

1 Perception and Learning

Overview

In this text we have chosen to start our examination of consumer behavior at the individual or "psychological" level—beginning with a discussion of perception and learning.

In responding to a stimulus, say a clock (or perhaps a grumbling stomach) indicating mealtime, the individual reacts in terms of his own personal world. To an urban American, a meal may mean ham and eggs or a steak and martini. To a rural Japanese, it may mean boiled rice, fish, and seaweed.

Similarly, a product or brand may have different meanings to different individuals. A bottle of beer to one consumer may be a cool drink on a hot summer afternoon; to another it may be the cheapest drink one can buy and still see a floor show; and to a third it may be simply immoral.

The decision to consume or not to consume, or to choose one brand over another, is guided by a person's cognitions—what he perceives and what he has learned—and by his beliefs and attitudes on a multiplexity of subjects, including what he feels is good for him, good for others around him, and perhaps even good for his society.

Neoclassical economists characterize the buying process as maximizing utility, on the assumption that each consumer can assign a specific value to each product which might be purchased. This utility is determined subjectively as a function of the consumer's need-value system. A pair of shoes, a new automobile, the usual brand of liquor, or the services of a physician are sought after and paid for in the belief that these products will gratify wants and needs that the consumer feels must be satisfied. In other words, utility is dependent upon perception of the item's level of potential need fulfillment.

Perception

An important beginning, then, toward understanding the consumer decision-making process is knowledge of *perception*. Krech et al. (1962) have

1

grouped principles of perception into two major categories—*stimulus* factors and *personal* factors.

Stimulus Factors

Perception is governed in part by the nature of the physical stimulus itself. For example, if a color advertisement appears in a newspaper, it will be noticed by a larger percentage of readers than if it appeared in black and white. Perception of the color advertisement is not necessarily related to the needs and motivations of the reader, but merely to the fact that the physical stimulus itself is a strong factor in encouraging perception.

Research on stimulus factors has been conducted primarily by experimental psychologists who believe that the perceptual organization of stimuli in the nervous system is related directly to the nature of the physical object (Deutsch and Kraus, 1965). This approach does not necessarily deny the influence of the individual's needs, motivations, and expectations in the perceptual process, but instead emphasizes the importance of the physical object.

Personal Factors

Obviously there is more to perception than merely the stimulus itself impinging upon the neural receptors in the eye, ear, or skin. The individual's needs, moods, memories, experiences, and values modify or screen out the messages he receives from stimuli, so that he perceives what he wants to perceive. This concept of *selective perception* challenges the simple view, sometimes called naïve realism, that representations of objects and events in the external world somehow find their way into the nervous system and eventually into our consciousness.

Today this simpler view of reality is rejected. Numerous studies, primarily from psychology but also within the fields of marketing and consumer behavior, clearly indicate that perception is in part determined by the motivations and need-value systems of the observer as well as the context in which the stimulus appears. Reality is quite personal and is somewhat different for each individual. It is formed by the individual's needs, drives, and past experiences; by what he had learned; by his motives and personality; and by his social and geographic environment. Each of these factors influences how he conceives the world in which he finds himself.

> The cognitive map of the individual is not a photographic representation of the physical world; it is, rather, a partial, personal construction in which certain objects, selected out by the individual for a major role, are perceived in an individual manner. Every perceiver is, as it were, to some degree a nonrepresentational artist, painting a picture of the world that expresses his individual view of reality (Krech et al., 1962).

The first selection in this chapter, by Hastorf and Cantril, is a classic description of several aspects of selective perception. The study was carried out at a time when Dartmouth and Princeton were formidable powers in college football. The authors present an analysis of the perceptions of fans of a particular football game between the two teams. The game was unusually rough, and charged with emotion. The fans of the two teams, sitting in the same stadium on the same Saturday afternoon, saw two different games.

> The data here indicate that there is no such thing as a game existing out there in its own right which people merely observe. The game exists for a person and is experienced by him only in so far as certain happenings have significances in terms of his purpose. Out of all the occurrences going on in the environment, a person selects those that have some significance for him from his own egocentric position in the total matrix.

The selective nature of perception means more than different people having varying values and preferences. As Hastorf and Cantril point out, it is inaccurate and misleading to say that different people merely have different attitudes concerning the same thing.

> For the thing simply is *not* the same for different people whether the thing is a football game, a presidential candidate, Communism, or spinach. We do not simply react to a happening or to some impingement from the environment in a determined way .... We behave according to what we bring to the occasion, and what each of us brings to the occasion is more or less unique. And except for these significances which we bring to the occasion, the happenings around us would be meaningless occurrences, would be inconsequential.

Consumer Implications

In marketing terms, there is no such thing as a product or service which exists by itself in space. For a product to exist, it must exist for a particular consumer with a particular set of needs, values, motivations, and past experiences. Of all the goods and services offered to consumers, only some are relevant to any given consumer, and it is only these of which he will be aware. Deodorant soap, for example, may be just another brand of soap to many people; to some consumers it is an essential aid to social relations; and to others it is an overpriced, overadvertised variation of the basic product, soap. Finally, for many consumers, it does not exist at all, much like thousands of other unknown products on the supermarket's shelves.

In the modern marketplace there is an astonishing array of merchandise, and often the consumer is simply not interested in price or quality—he just wants to possess things. Otherwise, many automobiles, appliances, and high-fashion clothes would not be sold. As Levy (1959) has pointed out, the consumer is often quite vague about the actual price he has paid for something; he has few standards for judging the quality of what he buys and at times winds up not using it. One can only wonder how often workshop drill presses, power jigsaws, and electric paint blenders are really used.

Levy concludes that *people buy things not only for what they can do but also for what they mean.* Often we buy a product or service because of its symbolic meaning above and beyond the actual physical product itself. For example, not pants perhaps were purchased because they implied fashion chic, sexuality, or flouting the values of an older generation, but very seldom for warmth or protection.

> Similarly in a recent study of two cheese advertisements for a certain cheese, one wedge of cheese was shown in a setting of a brown cutting board, dark bread, and a glimpse of a chess game. The cheese wedge was pictured standing erect on its smallest base. Although no people were shown, consumers interpreted the ad as part of a masculine scene, with men playing a game, being served a cheese snack.
> The same cheese was also shown in another setting with lighter colors, a suggestion of a floral bowl, and the wedge lying flat on one of the longer sides. This was interpreted by consumers as a feminine scene, probably with ladies lunching in the vicinity. Each ad worked to convey a symbolic impression of the cheese, modifying or enhancing established ideas about the product (Levy, 1959).

The importance of the symbolic meaning or image of a product in an affluent society probably cannot be overestimated. A created image, combined with our ability to perceive what we want to perceive, is rather neatly pointed out in the selection by Allison and Uhl. In a taste test subjects were not able to discern the taste differences among various brands of beer when labels were removed. But when the various brands were identified, the subjects had clear preferences. That is, the associations the labels evoked in the minds of the subjects influenced their evaluations of taste, aroma, carbonation, and so on.

The use of symbolic meaning by marketers to create product differentiation has been questioned by social critics. It is often to the advantage of firms to spend vast sums on promotion to differentiate commodity products such as bread and aspirin in order to gain market control and pricing latitude. But is it beneficial to consumers or to society? The relative merits of such promotional efforts have been questioned in cases before the Federal Trade Commission.

If consumers cannot distinguish among brands when such identifying characteristics as the logo, distinctive packaging, and promotional associations are removed, one might ask how important price actually is. The selection by Monroe reviews the massive literature in this area. Monroe discusses the influence of odd pricing ($.97 or $1.97 rather than $1.00 or $2.00); the perceived relationship of price and quality; and several other topics. He also introduces the concept of price thresholds—the perceived differences between two prices—and discusses the research on how much of a price change is necessary before a difference is perceived.

Perceptual Mapping

In determining how consumers perceive products, some sophisticated methods have been developed and have been applied in the field of consumer behavior. For example, Stefflre (1965) has claimed that "an individual will behave toward a new thing (say a new product) in a manner that is similar to the way he behaves toward other things he sees the new idea as being similar to." This is a very simple idea but a very powerful one.

Let us, for example, take an imaginary new product, say an electric handkerchief. If the consumer perceives this product as a small electric appliance, he will act toward it as he acts toward other small appliances; he will display somewhat similar values, attitudes, opinions, and behavioral propensities. On the other hand, if he perceives it not as an electrical appliance but rather as being in the class of handkerchiefs or Kleenex, his behavior and his need-value system will be more in line with these classes of products.

To demonstrate the process, Green et al. (1968) asked a group of MBA students to compare six graduate business schools. Using rather complex computer methodology, they were able to create a perceptual map (Figure 1). In this experiment, two-dimensional space appeared to be sufficient, although in more complex situations multidimensional configurations would obviously be necessary. As can be seen, Carnegie and MIT were perceived to be quite similar to each other, and Harvard and Stanford were also perceived as being quite similar to each other, that is, closer in perceptual space. On the other hand, Harvard and MIT were perceived as being quite dissimilar.

The authors labeled the two axes as "quantitative vs. qualitative curriculum" and "high and low prestige." The names given to the dimensions or axes, of course, are not mathematically or statistically determined. They merely represent variables that to the researchers made some sense. In this case, the responses suggested that MIT and Carnegie were perceived to be more quantitative than Harvard and Chicago, so the vertical variable was named to reflect this perception. The horizontal axis reflected the perceived prestige

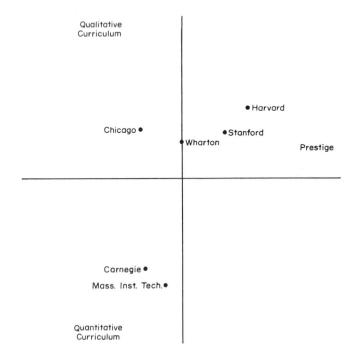

FIGURE 1. Perceptual map of six graduate business schools—simple space.
Source: Green, Carmone, and Robinson, 1968.

of the school, with Harvard and Stanford having the greatest prestige and Chicago and Carnegie the least, in this set of schools.

The implications are clear. If we were to create a new school of business administration, and wanted to compete with Carnegie and MIT, we would design our curriculum to be highly quantitative. If we wanted to compete with Harvard and Chicago, we would design the curriculum to be far more qualitative.

This body of methodology, often termed *perceptual mapping,* has become increasingly popular in the past few years. In fact, several new products have been introduced in the marketplace after using this particular computer technology. The selection by Silk clearly describes the concepts and the basic idea.

Perceived Risk

In addition to product attributes or similarities, still other psychological aspects of products are perceived. For example, the concept of perceived risk has been a topic in consumer behavior literature since about 1960.

Taken from psychology, the concept was first introduced in marketing by Bauer (1960), who claimed much of consumer behavior as involving risk "in the sense that any action of a consumer will produce consequences which he cannot anticipate with anything approximating certainty, and some of which at least are likely to be unpleasant."

Cox (1967, pp. 5–6) has theorized that risk may be perceived by the consumer from any one or more of the following factors:

1. The consumer may be uncertain of his buying goals; i.e., what he really wants.
2. The consumer may be uncertain about which purchase (product, brand, style, etc.) will best match his goals.
3. The consumer may perceive possible adverse consequences if the purchase is made (or is not made), and the result fails to satisfy his buying goals.

As formulated, the concept of perceived risk stresses that consumers generally seek to reduce risk in their decision-making processes. Because perceived risk is a function of both possible *consequences* and the *uncertainty* of these consequences, risk reduction can occur either by reducing the consequences or increasing the certainty of the outcome. Hence, to reduce risk, one can read *Consumer Reports,* turn to experts for advice, become loyal to a well-known brand, etc. Roselius, in a selection in this chapter, discusses his research on the risk-reduction methods used by consumers, and expands on the entire concept of perceived risk.

Attribution Theory

Not only do we perceive quality, brand differences, and degrees of risk, but we also perceive causality. If a housewife buys a cut of beef of particularly high quality, she may attribute the wise purchase to her skill and intelligence as a consumer, to the high repute of the butcher or retail outlet, or perhaps to good luck. A bad purchase may be attributed to bad luck, personal stupidity, the poor quality of mass-produced merchandise, or even to the failures of the capitalist system. Some consumers may even attribute causality to astrological forecasts.

In short, the consumer not only perceives events and occurrences but also perceives causality—what caused a certain event to occur. The attribution of causality can be an important variable in consumer behavior. If a consumer's perception of high quality in products is always attributed to a single manufacturer and poor quality always attributed to, say, imported products, one can see the implications these perceptions would have for that particular consumer in the marketplace.

The selection by Settle in this chapter defines this body of material and reviews some of the work in psychology. On the basis of research in attribution theory, Settle proposes a new classification for goods and services that could have considerable significance for consumer researchers in coming years.

Learning

Before a stimulus object can trigger a reaction, it must first be perceived as existing. But, as we have seen and will see again in various selections in this book, part of the perceptual process is influenced by learning, and much of our behavior is learned.

Hilgard and Bower (1966) define learning as a "process by which an activity originates or is changed through reacting to an encountered situation, provided that the characteristics of the change in activity cannot be explained on the basis of native response tendencies, maturation or temporary states of the organism (e.g., fatigue, drugs, etc.)." Hence, we learn by repetition, by responding, or by problem solving. We learn not only to avoid hot stoves and to jump when a car lurches at us, but we also learn to prefer cucumbers to Mexican chili peppers, to fear walking in a ghetto, and to select Parker pens over brands manufactured in Taiwan.

Learning theories have had a significant influence on the field of consumer behavior. Consumption is, in many ways, a learned response, as witness the Frenchman relishing snails, the American eating corn, and other people eating raw fish, whale blubber, or grasshoppers.

Beyond a definition, however, there is little agreement among psychologists as to what learning is, how it occurs, and what factors facilitate or hinder the learning process. Hilgard and Bower claim that learning theories fall into two major families—*stimulus-response* theories and *cognitive* theories.

Stimulus-Response Theory

The stimulus-response theorist believes that all learning is a chain of responses, not unlike teaching an animal to do tricks by rewarding him for each correct response and withholding the reward or punishing him for each incorrect response. In this manner, either by reward or by mere association of the stimulus and response, habits or behavior patterns are acquired. Stimulus-response theories of learning have been set forth by such psychologists as Pavlov, known for his salivation experiments with dogs; Skinner, who developed the theoretical basis for programed learning; and Hull, who has presented the most comprehensive theory and most tightly controlled experimental evidence.

An example of the stimulus-response view as it applies to consumer behavior can be found in the selection by Howard in this chapter.

More recently, both in psychology and in marketing, still another approach to learning has emerged from S-R conceptualizations. This approach views learning as a probabilistic process, under the assumption that the best predictor of future response (purchase behavior) is the sequence, rhythm, and frequency of past behavior (purchases). Kuehn, in his selection in this chapter, makes perhaps the best statement of this approach and presents an important piece of empirical research using probability theory. Other selections using this theoretical orientation can be found in the last chapter of this book, in which we discuss theoretical positions more fully.

Cognitive Theory

The second major family of learning theories takes the cognitive approach. These theories do not accept the viewpoint that all learning is of a stimulus-response nature but instead borrow more freely from such concepts as memory, expectations, and goal seeking. Cognitive theorists reason that the individual acquires habits not only by repetition of stimulus and response but also by using insight, thinking, and problem-solving techniques. In this view, the central nervous system and the brain become important intermediaries.

This cognitive view, perhaps best represented by the Gestalt psychologists, stresses that what is learned is not merely the acquisition of habits but rather a new cognitive organization. Often in learning one does not merely use trial and error for finding a correct solution, but he thinks, he reorganizes his perceptions, and his cognitive structures change.

From the Gestalt school emerged a point of view that is today referred to as Lewinian field theory. As this school of thought sees it, behavior is a function of the situation which exists at the time behavior occurs; that is, the causes of behavior are forces in the "psychological field" of an individual. This field is the totality of all simultaneously existing facts for the individual, and they are mutually interdependent.

The concept of the psychological field is a fundamental construct in field theory. All events—thinking, planning, buying, consuming—are a function of the field, or life space, which consists of the individual and his environment. To understand behavior, that is, cognitive reorganization, one must understand all of the forces within this life space—the goals, the positive and negative aspects, the forces pushing and pulling the individual in various directions, and the barriers that block his efforts to reach his goals.

Further explanation of field theory is presented in the article by Kassarjian in this chapter. In comparing this article with the ones by Kuehn and Howard, you will see the differences between the approaches of the stimulus-response theorists and the cognitive theorists. The former are concerned with repetitions, rewards, and the acquisition of habits. The latter is concerned with cognitive reorganization and cognitive change.

Low-Involvement Learning

The last article in this chapter is by Herbert Krugman. He discusses learning that occurs upon exposure to television advertising. This situation is quite different from that of a hungry rat who must learn a complex maze before being fed; in TV advertising the viewer is frequently neither listening nor involved. And yet, learning does occur, as unmotivated as it may be.

Krugman claims that in situations of high personal involvement learning can lead to dramatic behavior change. But in consumer behavior, and particularly in advertising, there is low involvement, and the changes that do occur tend to be gradual shifts in perceptual structure, followed by minimal attitude change and perhaps minimal behavior change. It is hard to imagine that people can be strongly involved in the brand of toothpaste or detergent they buy, or the quality of one gasoline producer over another.

There are other theories of learning which cannot be classified as either stimulus-response or cognitive theory. Numerous psychodynamic approaches exist which claim that much of an individual's learning can be explained by an understanding of his need-value system. The discussion of personality theory in Chapter 3 reveals these views of learning in greater detail.

In summary, learning and perception are treated in this book as being among the most basic processes of concern in the study of consumer behavior. Before the individual can react to the world of stimuli impinging upon him, he must first perceive the inputs and learn their relationships. The relevancy and importance of these concepts will emerge as the selections in this chapter are read.

References

Bauer, R. A. "Consumer Behavior as Risk Taking." *Proceedings AMA,* ed. R. S. Hancock (1960), 389–398.

Cox, D. F. *Risk Taking and Information Handling in Consumer Behavior.* Division of Research, Graduate School of Business Administration, Harvard University, 1967.

Deutsch, M., and R. M. Kraus. *Theories of Social Psychology.* Basic Books, 1965.

Green, P. E., F. J. Carmone, and P. J. Robinson. "Nonmetric Scaling Methods: An Exposition and Overview." *Wharton Quarterly* (Winter-Spring 1968), 27–41.

Hilgard, E. R., and G. H. Bower. *Theories of Learning.* 3rd ed. Appleton-Century-Crofts, 1966.

Krech, D., R. S. Crutchfield, and E. L. Ballachey. *Individual in Society.* McGraw-Hill, 1962.

Levy, S. "Symbols for Sale." *Harvard Business Review,* Vol. 37 (July-Aug. 1959), 117–124.

Stefflre, V. "Simulation of People's Behavior Toward New Objects and Events." *American Behavioral Scientist,* Vol. 8 (May 1965), 12–15.

1.1 A Case Study of Differential Perception
ALBERT H. HASTORF, HADLEY CANTRIL

On a brisk Saturday afternoon, November 23, 1951, the Dartmouth football team played Princeton in Princeton's Palmer Stadium. It was the last game of the season for both teams and of rather special significance because the Princeton team had won all its games so far and one of its players, Kazmaier, was receiving All-American mention, had just appeared as the cover man on *Time* magazine, and was playing his last game.

A few minutes after the opening kick-off, it became apparent that the game was going to be a rough one. The referees were kept busy blowing their whistles and penalizing both sides. In the second quarter, Princeton's star left the game with a broken nose. In the third quarter, a Dartmouth player was taken off the field with a broken leg. Tempers flared both during and after the game. The official statistics of the game, which Princeton won, showed that Dartmouth was penalized 70 yards, Princeton 25, not counting more than a few plays in which both sides were penalized.

Needless to say, accusations soon began to fly. The game immediately became a matter of concern to players, students, coaches, and the administrative officials of the two institutions, as well as to alumni and the general public who had not seen the game but had become sensitive to the problem of big-time football through the recent exposures of subsidized players, commercialism, etc. Discussion of the game continued for several weeks.

One of the contributing factors to the extended discussion of the game was the extensive space given to it by both campus and metropolitan newspapers. An indication of the fervor with which the discussions were carried on is shown by a few excerpts from the campus dailies.

For example, on November 27 (four days after the game), the *Daily Princetonian* (Princeton's student newspaper) said:

> This observer has never seen quite such a disgusting exhibition of so-called "sport." Both teams were guilty but the blame must be laid primarily on Dartmouth's doorstep. Princeton, obviously the better team, had no reason to rough up Dartmouth. Looking at the situation rationally, we don't see why the Indians should make a deliberate attempt to cripple Dick Kazmaier or any other Princeton player. The Dartmouth psychology, however, is not rational itself.

The November 30th edition of the *Princeton Alumni Weekly* said:

> But certain memories of what occurred will not be easily erased. Into the record books will go in indelible fashion the fact that the last game of Dick Kazmaier's career was cut short by more than half when he was forced out with a broken nose and a mild concussion, sustained from a tackle that came well after he had thrown a pass.
>
> This second-period development was followed by a third quarter outbreak of roughness that was climaxed when a Dartmouth player deliberately kicked Brad Glass in the ribs while the latter was on his

back. Throughout the often unpleasant afternoon, there was undeniable evidence that the losers' tactics were the result of an actual style of play, and reports on other games they have played this season substantiate this.

Dartmouth students were "seeing" an entirely different version of the game through the editorial eyes of the *Dartmouth* (Dartmouth's undergraduate newspaper). For example, on November 27 the *Dartmouth* said:

> However, the Dartmouth-Princeton game set the stage for the other type of dirty football. A type which may be termed as an unjustifiable accusation.
> Dick Kazmaier was injured early in the game. Kazmaier was the star, an All-American. Other stars have been injured before, but Kazmaier had been built to represent a Princeton idol. When an idol is hurt there is only one recourse—the tag of dirty football. So what did the Tiger Coach Charley Caldwell do? He announced to the world that the Big Green had been out to extinguish the Princeton star. His purpose was achieved.
> After this incident, Caldwell instilled the old see-what-they-did-go-get-them attitude into his players. His talk got results. Gene Howard and Jim Miller were both injured. Both had dropped back to pass, had passed, and were standing unprotected in the backfield. Result: one bad leg and one leg broken.
> The game was rough and did get a bit out of hand in the third quarter. Yet most of the roughing penalties were called against Princeton while Dartmouth received more of the illegal-use-of-the-hands variety.

On November 28 the *Dartmouth* said:

> Dick Kazmaier of Princeton admittedly is an unusually able football player. Many Dartmouth men traveled to Princeton, not expecting to win—only hoping to see an All-American in action. Dick Kazmaier was hurt in the second period, and played only a token part in the remainder of the game. For this, spectators were sorry.
> But there were no such feelings for Dick Kazmaier's health. Medical authorities have confirmed that as a relatively unprotected passing and running star in a contact sport, he is quite liable to injury. Also, his particular injuries—a broken nose and slight concussion—were no more serious than is experienced almost any day in any football practice, where there is no more serious stake than playing the following Saturday. Up to the Princeton game, Dartmouth players suffered about 10 known nose fractures and face injuries, not to mention several slight concussions.
> Did Princeton players feel so badly about losing their star? They shouldn't have. During the past undefeated campaign they stopped several individual stars by a concentrated effort, including such mainstays as Frank Hauff of Navy, Glenn Adams of Pennsylvania and Rocco Calvo of Cornell.

In other words, the same brand of football condemned by the *Princetonian*—that of stopping the big man—is practiced quite successfully by the Tigers.

Basically, then, there was disagreement as to what had happened during the "game." Hence we took the opportunity presented by the occasion to make a "real life" study of a perceptual problem.[1]

Procedure

Two steps were involved in gathering data. The first consisted of answers to a questionnaire designed to get reactions to the game and to learn something of the climate of opinion in each institution. This questionnaire was administered a week after the game to both Dartmouth and Princeton undergraduates who were taking introductory and intermediate psychology courses.

The second step consisted of showing the same motion picture of the game to a sample of undergraduates in each school and having them check on another questionnaire, as they watched the film, any infraction of the rules they saw and whether these infractions were "mild" or "flagrant."[2] At Dartmouth, members of two fraternities were asked to view the film on December 7; at Princeton, members of two undergraduate clubs saw the film early in January.

The answers to both questionnaires were carefully coded and transferred to punch cards.[3]

Results

Table 1 shows the questions which received different replies from the two student populations on the first questionnaire.

Questions asking if the students had friends on the team, if they had ever played football themselves, if they felt they knew the rules of the game well, etc. showed no differences in either school and no relation to answers given to other questions. This is not surprising since the students in both schools come from essentially the same type of educational, economic, and ethnic background.

Summarizing the data of Tables 1 and 2, we find a marked contrast between the two student groups.

Nearly all *Princeton* students judged the game as "rough and dirty"—not one of them thought it "clean and fair." And almost nine-tenths of them thought the other side started the rough play. By and large they felt that the charges they understood were being made were true; most of them felt the charges were made in order to avoid similar situations in the future.

When Princeton students looked at the movie of the game, they saw the Dartmouth team make over twice as many infractions as their own team made. And they saw the Dartmouth team make over twice as many infractions as were seen by Dartmouth students. When Princeton students judged these infractions as "flagrant" or "mild," the ratio was about two "flagrant" to one "mild" on the Dartmouth team, and about one "flagrant" to three "mild" on the Princeton team.

TABLE 1. Data from First Questionnaire

Question	Dartmouth Students (N = 163) (%)	Princeton Students (N = 161) (%)
1. Did you happen to see the actual game between Dartmouth and Princeton in Palmer Stadium this year?		
Yes	33	71
No	67	29
2. Have you seen a movie of the game or seen it on television?		
Yes, movie	33	2
Yes, television	0	1
No, neither	67	97
3. (Asked of those who answered "yes" to either or both of above questions.) From your observations of what went on at the game, do you believe the game was clean and fairly played, or that it was unnecessarily rough and dirty?		
Clean and fair	6	0
Rough and dirty	24	69
Rough and fair[a]	25	2
No answer	45	29
4. (Asked of those who answered "no" on both of the first questions.) From what you have heard and read about the game, do you feel it was clean and fairly played, or that it was unnecessarily rough and dirty?		
Clean and fair	7	0
Rough and dirty	18	24
Rough and fair[a]	14	1
Don't know	6	4
No answer	55	71
(Combined answers to questions 3 and 4 above)		
Clean and fair	13	0
Rough and dirty	42	93
Rough and fair[a]	39	3
Don't know	6	4
5. From what you saw in the game or the movies, or from what you have read, which team do you feel started the rough play?		
Dartmouth started it	36	86
Princeton started it	2	0
Both started it	53	11
Neither	6	1
No answer	3	2
6. What is your understanding of the charges being made?[b]		
Dartmouth tried to get Kazmaier	71	47
Dartmouth intentionally dirty	52	44
Dartmouth unnecessarily rough	8	35
7. Do you feel there is any truth to these charges?		
Yes	10	55
No	57	4
Partly	29	35
Don't know	4	6
8. Why do you think the charges were made?		
Injury to Princeton star	70	23
To prevent repetition	2	46
No answer	28	31

[a]This answer was not included on the checklist but was written in by the percentage of students indicated.

[b]Replies do not add to 100% since more than one charge could be given.

TABLE 2.   Data from Second Questionnaire Checked While Seeing Film

| Group | N | Total Number of Infractions Checked Against | | | |
| | | Dartmouth Team | | Princeton Team | |
		Mean	SD	Mean	SD
Dartmouth students	48	4.3[a]	2.7	4.4	2.8
Princeton students	49	9.8[a]	5.7	4.2	3.5

[a]Significant at the .01 level.

As for the *Dartmouth* students, while the plurality of answers fell in the "rough and dirty" category, over one-tenth thought the game was "clean and fair" and over a third introduced their own category of "rough and fair" to describe the action. Although a third of the Dartmouth students felt that Dartmouth was to blame for starting the rough play, the majority of Dartmouth students thought both sides were to blame. By and large, Dartmouth felt that the charges they understood were being made were not true, and most of them thought the reason for the charges was Princeton's concern for its football star.

When Dartmouth students looked at the movie of the game they saw both teams make about the same number of infractions. And they saw their own team make only half the number of infractions the Princeton students saw them make. The ratio of "flagrant" to "mild" infractions was about one to one when Dartmouth students judged the Dartmouth team, and about one "flagrant" to two "mild" when Dartmouth students judged infractions made by the Princeton team.

It should be noted that Dartmouth and Princeton students were thinking of different charges in judging their validity and in assigning reasons as to why the charges were made. It should also be noted that whether or not students were spectators of the game in the stadium made little difference in their responses.

Interpretation: the Nature of a Social Event

It seems clear that the "game" actually was many different games and that each version of the events that transpired was just as "real" to a particular person as other versions were to other people. A consideration of the experiential phenomena that constitute a "football game" for the spectator may help us both to account for the results obtained and illustrate something of the nature of any social event.[4]

Like any other complex social occurrence, a "football game" consists of a whole host of happenings. Many different events are occurring simultaneously. Furthermore, each happening is a link in a chain of happenings, so that one follows another in sequence. The "football game," as well as other complex social situations, consists of a whole matrix of events. In the game situation, this matrix of events consists of the actions of all the players, together with the behavior of the referees and linesmen, the action on the side-lines, in the grandstands, over the loud-speaker, etc.

Of crucial importance is the fact that an "occurrence" on the football field or in any other social situation does not become an experiential "event" unless and until some significance is given to it: an "occurrence" becomes an "*event*" only when the happening has significance. And a happening generally has significance only if it reactivates learned significances already registered in what we have called a person's assumptive form-world (Cantril, 1950).

Hence the particular occurrences that different people experienced in the football game were a limited series of events from the total matrix of events *potentially* available to them. People experienced those occurrences that reactivated significances they brought to the occasion; they failed to experience those occurrences which did not reactivate past significances. We do not need to introduce "attention" as an "intervening third" (to paraphrase James on memory) to account for the selectivity of the experimental process.

In this particular study, one of the most interesting examples of this phenomenon was a telegram sent to an officer of Dartmouth College by a member of a Dartmouth alumni group in the Midwest. He had viewed the film which had been shipped to his alumni group from Princeton after its use with Princeton students, who saw, as we noted, an average of over nine infractions by Dartmouth players during the game. The alumnus, who couldn't see the infractions he had heard publicized, wired:

> Preview of Princeton movies indicates considerable cutting of impor-tant part please wire explanation and possibly air mail missing part before showing scheduled for January 25 we have splicing equipment.

The "same" sensory impingements emanating from the football field, transmitted through the visual mechanism to the brain, also obviously gave rise to different experiences in different people. The significances assumed by different happenings for different people depend in large part on the pur-poses people bring to the occasion and the assumptions they have of the purposes and probable behavior of other people involved. . . .

In brief, the data here indicate that there is no such "thing" as a "game" existing "out there" in its own right which people merely "observe." The "game" "exists" for a person and is experienced by him only in so far as certain happenings have significances in terms of his purpose. Out of all the occurrences going on in the environment, a person selects those that have some significance for him from his own egocentric position in the total matrix.

Obviously in the case of a football game, the value of the experience of watching the game is enhanced if the purpose of "your" team is accomplished, that is, if the happening of the desired consequences is experienced—i.e., if your team wins. But the value attribute of the experience can, of course, be spoiled if the desire to win crowds out behavior we value and have come to call sports-manlike.

The sharing of significances provides the links except for which a "social" event would not be experienced and would not exist for anyone.

A "football game" would be impossible except for the rules of the game which we bring to the situation and which enable us to share with others the significances of various happenings. These rules make possible a certain repeatability of events such as first downs, touchdowns, etc. If a person is unfamiliar with the rules of the game, the behavior he seeks lacks repeatability and consistent significance and hence "doesn't make sense."

And only because there is the possibility of repetition is there the possibility that a happening has a significance. For example, the balls used in games are designed to give a high degree of repeatability. While a football is about the only ball used in games which is not a sphere, the shape of the modern football has apparently evolved in order to achieve a higher degree of accuracy and speed in forward passing than would be obtained with a spherical ball, thus increasing the repeatability of an important phase of the game.

The rules of a football game, like laws, rituals, customs, and mores, are registered and preserved forms of sequential significances enabling people to share the significances of occurrences. The sharing of sequential significances which have value for us provides the links that operationally make social events possible. They are analogous to the forces of attraction that hold parts of an atom together, keeping each part following its individual, independent course.

From this point of view it is inaccurate and misleading to say that different people have different "attitudes" concerning the same "thing." For the "thing" simply is *not* the same for different people whether the "thing" is a football game, a presidential candidate, Communism, or spinach. We do not simply "react to" a happening or to some impingement from the environment in a determined way (except in behavior that has become reflexive or habitual). We behave according to what we bring to the occasion, and what each of us brings to the occasion is more or less unique. And except for these significances which we bring to the occasion, the happenings around us would be meaningless occurrences, would be "inconsequential."

From the transactional view, an attitude is not a predisposition to react in a certain way to an occurrence or stimulus "out there" that exists in its own right with certain fixed characteristics which we "color" according to our predisposition (Kilpatrick, 1952). That is, a subject does not simply "react to" an "object." An attitude would rather seem to be a complex of registered significances reactivated by some stimulus which assumes its own particular significance for us in terms of our purposes. That is, the object as experienced would not exist for us except for the reactivated aspects of the form-world which provide particular significance to the hieroglyphics of sensory impingements.

Notes

1. We are not concerned here with the problem of guilt or responsibility for infractions, and nothing here implies any judgment as to who was to blame.

2. The film shown was kindly loaned for the purpose of the experiment by the Dartmouth College Athletic Council. It should be pointed out that a movie of a football game follows the ball, is thus selective, and omits a good deal of the total action on the field. Also, of course, in viewing only a film of a game, the possibilities of participation as spectator are greatly limited.

3. We gratefully acknowledge the assistance of Virginia Zerega, Office of Public Opinion Research, and J. L. McCandless, Princeton University, and E. S. Horton, Dartmouth College, in the gathering and collation of the data.

4. The interpretation of the nature of a social event sketched here is in part based on discussions with Adelbert Ames, Jr.

References

Cantril, H. *The "Why" of Man's Experience.* Macmillan, 1950.

Kilpatrick, F. P. (ed.). *Human Behavior from the Transactional Point of View.* Institute for Associated Research, 1952.

1.2 Brand Identification and Perception
RALPH I. ALLISON, KENNETH P. UHL

As a company tries to find the factors accounting for strong and weak markets, typical consumer explanations for both tend to be about the physical attributes of the product. That is, the product quality often becomes both the hero and the culprit, like Dr. Jekyll and Mr. Hyde, but with the hideous reversal coming not by night but by market. The experiment presented in this paper was also designed to give rough measurements of the magnitude of the marketing influences. Unidentified and then labeled bottles of beer were delivered to homes of taste testing participants on successive weeks. The drinkers' taste test ratings provided the data for the study.

The Experimental Design

The principal hypothesis subjected to testing through experimentation[1] was this: "Beer drinkers cannot distinguish among major brands of unlabeled beer either on an overall basis or on selected characteristics." Beer drinkers were identified as males who drank beer at least three times a week.

The test group was composed of 326 drinkers who were randomly selected, agreed to participate in the study, and provided necessary classification data. Each participant in the experiment was given a six-pack of unlabeled beer, identified only by tags bearing the letters A, B, C, D, E, F, G, H, I, or J. The labels had been completely soaked off and the crowns had been wire brushed to remove all brand identification from the 12-oz. brown bottles. Each six-pack contained three brands of beer with individual bottles randomly placed in the pack so no one lettered tag predominated in any one position.[2] There were six different pairs placed among the 326 participants. An effort was made to give each participant a six-pack that contained the brand of beer he said he most often drank. The groups and numbers were placed as follows:

	Place
Group 1 (AB, CD, EF)	53
Group 2 (AB, CD, IJ)	55
Group 3 (AB, CD, GH)	55
Group 4 (AB, EF, IJ)	55
Group 5 (AB, GH, IJ)	54
Group 6 (AB, EF, GH)	54
	326

A and B represented one of the company's beer brands; C and D represented one major regional beer brand; and E and F were one other major brand of regional beer. G and H were one national brand; and I and J were the fifth well-known beer brand used in the experiment. Among these five brands there were some taste differences discernible to expert taste testers.

The lettered tags (one around the collar of each bottle in the six-pack) carried a general rating scale from "1" (poor) through "10" (excellent) on the one side and a list of nine specific characteristics on the reverse side. The specific characteristics, which included after-taste, aroma, bitterness, body, carbonation, foam, lightness, strength, and sweetness, could each be rated as "too much," "just enough," or "not enough." These nine specific characteristics were selected from a much larger field. Their selection was based on both greater agreement on meaning among beer drinkers and on the ability of beer drinkers, in general, to identify and rate them.

One week after the distribution of the unlabeled beer, the empties, nude except for the rating tags, were picked up and new six-packs left behind. This time, however, the bottles were properly labeled with each six-pack containing six different brands of beer (the same five brands plus a sixth brand that was added for the labeled test). In addition, each deposit bottle was tagged, but these tags were identified by the letters K through P. A week after the second placement the empties and rating tags were picked up.

The experiment produced a number of useful findings. More specifically, evidence was available to answer these questions:

1. Could beer drinkers, in general, distinguish among various beers in a blind test?
2. Could beer drinkers identify "their" brands in a blind test?
3. What influence would brand identification have on consumers' evaluations of various beer brands?
4. What influence would brand identification have on consumers' evaluations of specified beer characteristics?

Taste Differences in a Blind Test

The data produced by the experiment indicated that the beer drinkers, as a group, could not distinguish the taste differences among the brands on an overall basis. Table 1 contains the evidence on these ratings. Basically, there appeared to be no significant difference among the various brands at the .05 level.

TABLE 1.   Blind Overall Taste Test—All Participants

Beer Brand	Overall Rating	Significantly Different from Other Brands[a]
AB	65.0	No
CD	64.1	No
EF	63.3	No
GH	63.4	No
IJ	63.3	No

[a]At the .05 level. Source: Carling Brewing Company.

Beer drinkers when asked to rate the nine characteristics listed in Table 2 as "not enough," "just enough," and "too much," indicated a difference that was significant in "just enough" votes for one characteristic on one beer (carbonation of brand CD). Other than the one case, the reported differences among brands were so minor as to be not significant. A second analysis of the data, in which the "just enough" category was treated as a neutral or a zero and the "too much" and "not enough" positions as $+1$ and -1 respectively, in general, substantiated the percentage findings.[3] In addition, this analysis indicated that four of the characteristics—aroma, body, foam, and strength—were rated rather uniformly among the brands as "not enough" and one characteristic—bitterness—received a clear "too much" rating. Based on the overall taste test and the specified characteristics test, the conclusion was that beer drinkers could not distinguish taste differences among the beer brands presented in unlabeled bottles.

TABLE 2. Blind Taste Test—Specific Characteristics (All Participants)

Characteristic	Per Cent Indicating "Just Right" by Beer Brands					Significant Difference Among Brands[a]
	AB	CD	EF	GH	IJ	
After-taste	59	52	57	55	55	No
Aroma	64	68	63	62	62	No
Bitterness	58	54	53	54	54	No
Body	53	58	60	53	57	No
Carbonation	64	70	62	62	65	Only CD
Foam	62	66	63	59	66	No
Lightness	68	63	69	64	69	No
Strength	50	51	56	50	53	No
Sweetness	64	61	59	62	66	No

[a]At the .05 level. Source: Carling Brewing Company.

Could Drinkers Identify "Their" Brands?

The labeled test clearly indicated that beer drinkers would assign "their" brands superior ratings and, accordingly, it was assumed that if participants could identify "their" brands in the blind test that they would respond to them with superior ratings. The general ratings in the nude bottle test, by brand drunk most often, indicated that *none* of the brand groups rated the taste of "their" brand beer superior over all of the other beers (see Table 3). For example, regular drinkers of brand AB, indicated via their ratings that they preferred "their" brand over EF and CD, but they gave virtually similar ratings to brands IJ and GH as they gave to their own brand. Drinkers of the other brands did not rate "their" brands as favorably in the blind comparison tests as did AB drinkers. Drinkers of brand EF rated beer CD significantly above "their" brand. Users of IJ rated all of the comparison brands except CD as equals and CD was rated as poorer tasting. Drinkers of brand GH must not have drunk the brand because they preferred its flavor—they rated two of the four comparison brands as superior in flavor and the other two as no less than equal to "their" brand. And based on the overall taste ratings, the regular drinkers of brand CD could just as well have drunk any of the other comparison brands—there were no significant differences among the assigned ratings.

Based on the data secured from the experiment, the finding appeared to be that most beer drinkers could *not* identify "their" brands of beer in a blind comparison test.

TABLE 3. Users' Loyalty to "Their" Brand (Blind Test)

Brand Drunk Most Often	Taste-Test Ratings by Brand Rated					Own Brand Rated Significantly Higher than All Others[a]
	AB	CD	EF	GH	IJ	
AB	67.0	62.4[b]	57.7[b]	65.0	65.8	No
CD	64.9	65.6	65.4	63.2	63.9	No
EF	68.8	74.5[b]	65.0	62.5	61.4	No
GH	55.4	59.2	68.7[b]	60.0	71.4[b]	No
IJ	68.4	60.5[b]	69.2	62.0	65.6	No

[a]At the .05 level.
[b]Brands significantly different from user's own brand. Source: Carling Brewing Company.

Influence of Brand Identification on Overall Ratings

A number of important findings arose out of comparisons of the data from the nude bottle phase with the labeled bottle phase. The overall ratings for all the brands increased considerably with brand identifications. However, there was also much variation in the amount of increase registered among the various brands. And when beer drinkers were categorized according to the brand most frequently drunk, they consistently rated "their" beer higher than comparison beers in this positive identification taste test. Also, there was much variation in the amounts of increase—some brands received much higher ratings (i.e., overall ratings) from their regular users than did other brands from their regular users. The differences in the ratings were assumed to be due to the presence of labels—the only altered conditions of the experiment.

The data that gave rise to the several statements about the effects of brand identification are examined in more detail below. In the *blind* test, none of the five brands received overall ratings that were sufficiently different from all of the others to be considered statistically significant. However, in the labeled test the differences in all but two of the overall ratings were significant (the ratings assigned to brands EF and IJ were relatively the same). Looking at some of the other figures, brand GH was rated significantly higher than all of the other brands and CD was rated higher than all brands but GH. Other differences that were judged statistically significant can be noted in Table 4. And as can be seen in this table, all five brands in the labeled test were rated significantly higher than the same brands in the blind test. Remember, these were the same brands of beer used in the nude test, but in the labeled test the participants could clearly identify each beer brand.

TABLE 4. Comparison Taste Test—Blind vs. Labeled (Overall Ratings)

Beer Brand	Blind Test	Labeled Test	Significant Difference Between Blind and Labeled Test[a]
AB	65.0	70.6	Yes
CD	64.1	72.9	Yes
EF	63.3	67.8	Yes
GH	63.4	76.9	Yes
IJ	63.3	67.0	Yes
Significant differences between brands	None	Yes[b]	

[a]At the .05 level.
[b]All brands were significantly different from all others at the .05 level except EF and IJ relative to each other. Source: Carling Brewing Company.

The loyalty of the participants toward "their" brands increased when positive brand identification was possible (see Table 5). All of the labeled ratings assigned by regular users were significantly higher than the blind test ratings. In the blind test, participants indicated, at best, very little ability to pick "their" beers and set them off with relatively high overall ratings. For example, the regular drinkers of brand CD in the blind test awarded all of the brands about the same overall rating. However, in the labeled test, the CD drinkers awarded their beer brand an overall rating of 83.6, an 18 point increase over the blind test rating. This change was sufficiently above their overall ratings of all comparison brands to be statistically significant.

The gains in ratings were not uniform from one group to another. In the labeled test, brands GH, CD, and EF picked up more sizable gains than did AB and IJ. Comparison of the data in Table 5 with that in Table 3 will indicate other important rating changes from the blind to the label test.

TABLE 5.   Users' Loyalty to "Their" Brand (Label Test)

Brand Drunk Most Often	Taste-Test Ratings by Brand Rated					Own Brand Rated Signifi- cantly Higher[a]	Blind Test Ratings for Own Brand
	AB	CD	EF	GH	IJ		
AB	(77.3)	61.1	62.8	73.4	63.1	Yes	(67.0)
CD	66.3	(83.6)	67.4	78.3	63.1	Yes	(65.6)
EF	67.3	71.5	(82.3)	71.9	71.5	Yes	(65.0)
GH	73.1	72.5	77.5	(80.0)	67.5	Only over IJ	(60.0)
IJ	70.3	69.3	67.2	76.7	(73.5)	Only over EF	(65.6)

[a]At the .05 level. Source: Carling Brewing Company.

Influence of Brand Identification on Specified Characteristics

The labeled test also produced some changes in ratings of specified characteristics of beer brands. In the blind test with the "just enough" category assigned a zero value, the participants tended to rate all of the beers as not having enough aroma, body, foam, and strength. All but one of the beers were rated on bitterness as "too much," and accordingly, not sweet enough. In the labeled ratings, "aroma" was greatly improved as was "body," "foam," and "strength." However, the ratings on "bitterness" and "sweetness" remained virtually the same as recorded in the nude test.

Conclusions

Participants, in general, did not appear to be able to discern the taste differences among the various beer brands, but apparently labels, and their associations, did influence their evaluations. In other words, product distinctions or differences, in the minds of the participants, arose primarily through their receptiveness to the various firms' marketing efforts rather than through perceived physical product differences. Such a finding suggested that the physical product differences had little to do with the various brands' relative success or failure in the market (assuming the various physical products had been relatively constant). Furthermore, this elimination of the product variable focused attention on the various firms' marketing efforts, and, more specifically, on the resulting brand images.

This experiment also has helped the Company measure and rank its brand image relative to competitive brand images and has offered base comparison marks for similar experiments, both in the same and other markets at later dates. Such information has helped in Company evaluation and competitive marketing efforts. And to the extent that product images, and their changes, are believed to be a result of advertising (i.e., as other variables can be accounted for or held to be homogeneous among the competitive firms), the ability of firms' advertising programs to influence product images can be more thoroughly examined.

Notes

1. The experimental design and the findings outlined are from one market area. However, similar experiments were conducted and similar results were obtained in several other markets.

2. Pretesting gave no evidence of a positional or letter bias; *i.e.*, for participants to drink or rate the beer in any particular alphabetical or spatial order.

3. This three-place neutral center scale is in need of further testing and comparison with four- and five-position scales to help determine the amount of bias it induces.

1.3   Buyers' Subjective Perceptions of Price
KENT B. MONROE

In recent years there has been a growing awareness of the complex role of price as a determinant of a purchase decision. Recent research indicates we know little about how price influences purchase behavior. This article reviews the research on individual response to price and organizes the knowledge obtained from these studies.

The response of interest is individual's perception of price. However, price is only one aspect of the product stimulus confronting a buyer; i.e., the buyer responds to brand name, color, package, size, label, as well as price. The organization of these information cues as purchase decision inputs depends on the perceptual process an individual uses to give meaning to the raw material provided by the external world.

Psychological Pricing: Traditional View

Many basic marketing textbooks provide examples indicating greater demand at particular price points, suggesting that demand falls at prices just above and below the critical price points. Depending on the situation, these psychological prices are referred to as customary prices, odd prices, or price lines. Theoretically, this phenomena indicates that the consumer is perceptually sensitive to certain prices, and departure from these prices in either direction results in a decrease in demand.

Customary pricing excludes all price alternatives except one single price point. The traditional example has been the five-cent candy bar or package of gum. With customary prices, sellers adapt to changes in costs and market conditions by adjusting product size or quality, assuming the buyer would consider paying only one price.

Odd pricing assumes that prices ending with an odd number (e.g., 1, 3, 5, 7, 9), or just under a round number (e.g., 99, 98) increases consumer sensitivity. Evidence justifying such prices has largely been of an anecdotal nature. However, Ginzberg [28] imposed experimental patterns of odd and even prices on selected items in regional editions of a large mail-order catalog. Taking account of all variables influencing demand, he could not discern any generalizable result of the study. More recently, Gabor and Granger [21] concluded that the dominance of pricing below the round figure in some markets may be largely an artifact. That is, if sellers use odd pricing, then some buyers will consider the odd price as the real price and the round figure price as incorrect and respond accordingly. Again, there was no significant evidence supporting the psychological explanation of increased perceptual sensitivity.

Psychological Pricing: A Partial Explanation

Although the research of Ginzberg and Gabor and Granger suggests that buyers tend to expect certain prices after being exposed to them over a period of time, Friedman [19], noting a general consistency in grocery stores' and in suppliers' pricing patterns, offers reasons why certain psychological prices may have their roots in tradition:

1. Multiples of 12 are the most popular number of selling units packed in a case accounting for 74.5% of all test items.
2. Prices ending in 9 or 5 account for as much as 80% of retail food prices.
3. There was extensive multiple-unit pricing with the multiples never dividing evenly into the price.

However, using only odd prices in multiple-unit pricing is inconvenient to the buyer intent on comparing prices. As a recent *Progressive Grocer* study showed, if the multiple is too complicated, the buyer will buy only in quantities most easily calculated [30]. This *Progressive Grocer* finding suggests some discriminating process being applied by the buyer, but only if the comparative method used leads to a conclusion vis-à-vis the particular product offer. Otherwise, the buyer apparently withdraws from the complicated pricing situation.

4. Nearly 50% of all special off-price promotions were in multiples of 5, even-number discounts were more predominant, one-cent discounts were not found, with two-cent and nine-cent discounts very rare.

These findings imply the need to reduce price sufficiently to allow the buyer to perceive a price difference compared to the old price. Given earlier findings on odd number pricing and the rule of 9 and 5, the even-number discounts and the rarity of nine-cent discounts are easily understood.

Ad hoc explanations of traditional pricing practices suggesting critical prices or magical numbers have not been supported by the limited research available. Perhaps there are some logical explanations for these pricing practices based on traditional distribution practices. But, retailers have found some pricing practices work better than others, thereby suggesting there are some buyer behavioral phenomena underlying the observed response patterns.

Price Consciousness

According to economic theory, price is assumed to influence buyer choice because price serves as an indicator of purchase cost. That is, assuming the buyer has perfect information concerning prices and want satisfaction of comparable product alternatives, he can determine a product mix that maximizes his satisfaction for a given budget constraint. However, the extent that buyers are conscious of the prices they pay influences the way prices are perceived and the role price plays in buyer choice.

Using three measures of price consciousness Gabor and Granger [20] surveyed 640 housewives to determine their awareness of grocery prices last paid. The first measure was simply the percentage of prices remembered (82%) irrespective of the correctness of the price named. The researchers also discovered that price consciousness was inversely correlated with social class (income), with the exception of the poor, and that price consciousness was lower for branded items. Second, 57% of the prices were named correctly, with the same general relationship with social class and branded goods. Finally, for a subsample of 184 incorrectly named prices, 52% of the prices differed from the correct price by not more than 10%.

Progressive Grocer also found that price consciousness varied over products [31]. For 60 advertised and price-competitive brand items, the percentage of correct prices named varied from 86% for Coca-Cola to 2% for shortening, and for these items 91% and 34% of the named prices were within 5% of the correct prices.

Explicitly, no research evidence has linked price consciousness with price perception, although these studies did assume that some recollection of the price paid can be taken as evidence of conscious concern for the price of a given item [20, p. 177]. However, Wells and LoSciuto [77], using direct observation, found that concern for price was exhibited by 13%, 17% and 25% of shoppers purchasing cereal, candy, and detergent respectively.

Similar to Wells, Brown [4, 5] hypothesized that shopping behavior would be a better indicator of the ability to perceive price differences than conscious concern for price. His study was based on market basket price indices for 80 items in 27 supermarkets in 5 cities and personal interviews covering price perceptions of supermarkets, store patronage behavior, and patronage motives.

Analysis of the data revealed that shopping variables (number of stores shopped, concern for price, use of a shopping list) were the best discriminators of perceptual validity, which was measured by comparing shoppers' ordinal rankings of stores' price levels with the stores' market basket price indices. Further, price consciousness was a better discriminator of perceptual validity than was price level of the store patronized; very price conscious shoppers were more valid perceivers of price than non-price-conscious shoppers, but for intermediate levels of price consciousness no generalizations were possible. In contrast to Gabor and Granger, Brown was unable to establish significant relationships between perceptual validity and socioeconomic variables.

Brown's findings partially corroborate Gabor and Granger's assumption of a positive relationship between price consciousness and price perception. Both Gabor and Granger and the *Progressive Grocer* study found that for some items the brand influence exhibited dominance over price, thereby suggesting (as Wells did) that price is not of sufficient universal importance to be the primary determinant of choice. Evidence of an inverse relationship between socioeconomic standing and price perception validity found in the Gabor and

Granger study was not found by Brown. Further complicating this relationship is the emerging tendency to find a positive relationship between socioeconomic variables and use of unit price [51]. Who uses price and when is not well documented by research.

The Price-Quality Relationship

Finding some degree of price consciousness among buyers does not necessarily imply that price is used solely as a measure of purchase cost. As Scitovsky [62] has noted, the buyer generally does not have complete information about the quality of alternative product offerings; yet he forms perceptions from the information available. When price information is available and when the buyer is uncertain about product quality, it would seem reasonable to use price as a criterion for assessing quality.

The process of converting explicit and subjective information into perceptions is affected by the buyer's dispositions and his prior experience with the product. Another parameter of the perceptual situation is the symbolic value of the product—its capacity to evoke reactions relevant to a state of affairs it represents [7]. As the Bruner studies [6, 7] have shown, symbolic value leads to perceptual accentuation, i.e., subjectively magnified. Thus, the perceived value of a product may produce an accentuation in the assessed quality of the product. This perceptual accentuation may be positive or negative, and the direction and magnitude of the accentuation will depend on the particular prices and needs involved. Hence, as a criterion for assessing quality, or value, price may serve either to make the product more or less attractive.

Single-Cue Studies

Originally, price-quality studies considered situations where the only differential information available to respondents was price. Initiating these studies, Leavitt [37] asked 30 Air Force officers and 30 male and female graduate students to choose between two differentially priced, lettered, imaginary brands, for four products (moth flakes, cooking sherry, razor blades, and floor wax) and then indicate the "degree of satisfaction" with their choice. Subjects tended to be less satisfied when choosing lower priced brands and also tended to choose the higher-priced brand when (1) price was the only differential information; (2) the products were perceived to be heterogeneous in quality; and (3) the price difference was large. Tull, et al. [74] replicated Leavitt's experiment using table salt, aspirin, floor wax and liquid shampoo and found that the respondents tended to choose the higher-priced brands of products perceived to be heterogeneous.

Distinguishing between the effects of price as an indicator of quality on the perception of product attractiveness or on the perception of purchase offer attractiveness, Olander [53] experimentally tested the effect of price for household textiles on more than 100 young women's perceptions of product attractiveness. When consequences were related to pairwise choices, similar towels were more often preferred when assigned a high price than when assigned a low price.

McConnell [38, 39, 40, 41] tested the hypothesis that product quality perception is a function of price. Sixty married students in each of 24 trials chose one bottle of an identical beer differing only in brand name and price. Analysis revealed that perceived quality was significantly and positively related to price. In an extensive experiment, Shapiro [64] found that for 600 women (1) price was generally an indicator of quality; (2) price could not overcome product preferences; (3) the use of price to judge quality was a generalized attitude; and (4) price reliance varied over products, but was more significant in situations of high risk, low self-confidence, and absence of other cues. Lambert [35, 36] found that for 200 undergraduates the frequency of choosing high-priced brands was positively correlated with perceived variations in product quality and perceived ability to judge quality. Finally, Newman and Becknell [52] found an apparent positive price-quality relationship for ratings of different models of a durable product.

Multi-Cue Studies

A frequent criticism of the single-cue studies is that when price is the only information available, subjects naturally associate price and quality. Although this criticism applies directly to the Leavitt and Tull studies, the other studies cited included other experimentally controlled information, such as actual product samples or promotional information. Generally, when price was the only differential information, a positive price-quality relationship was observed. Moreover, the positive price-quality relationship was enhanced when the products were perceived to be heterogeneous in quality and when the comparative price differences were accentuated.

To overcome the criticism of the single-cue studies, other price-quality studies have experimentally varied other cues in addition to price. Three experiments specifically tested the single-cue, price-quality relationship as a part of the overall experimental design. Using home economics students, housewives, and carpet buyers and salesmen, Enis and Stafford [16, 17] discovered that perception of the quality of carpeting was directly related to price. Although store information did not significantly affect perception of carpet quality, the interactive effect of price and store information was significant. Jacoby, et al. [32] asked 136 adult male beer drinkers to taste and rate four test beers. By experimentally manipulating price, composition differences, and brand image, it was determined that price, except when considered in isolation, did not have a significant effect on quality perception, whereas brand image did. Gardner [27] also found a brand-quality relationship replacing the price-quality relationship in an experiment testing students' perceptions of toothpaste, men's shirts, and men's suits. Moreover, in an earlier experiment using the same product categories, Gardner [26] could find no significant relationship between perceived quality and frequency of purchase or time spent in shopping for the test products.

Although these three studies provide evidence of a positive price-quality relationship, their results do imply that price may not be the dominant cue in quality perception. Unfortunately this diminished saliency of the price cue has not been a generalized finding in other multi-cue studies. Andrews and Valenzi [3] asked 50 female students to rate the quality of sweaters and shoes.

Quality ratings for each product were obtained first for each cue presented separately (price, store name, brand name), then for all 27 variable combinations. The results indicated that the lower the price the greater the influence of brand name, but, in combined quality judgments price was clearly the dominant cue.

Rao [59, 60] using 144 graduate students, experimentally tested the role of price in quality perceptions for electric razors and razor blades. Using the multi-dimensional model of individual differences, he discovered that after accounting for prior product knowledge, personality variables, and brand display, price did not significantly affect perception of product quality. Both prior product knowledge and consumer test information produced significant effects on quality perceptions.

Smith and Broome [67, 68] experimentally tested the effects of price and market standing information on brand preference using 196 student wives and toothpaste, aspirin, green peas, and coffee. Their findings suggest that price and market standing information influence preference of unknown brands, but neither influences preference for known brands. Della Ditta [13] experimentally determined that students used price as an indicator of product attractiveness for table and pocket radios. Moreover, a positive relation between an evaluator's uncertainty about ability to assess product attractiveness and the use of price as an evaluative criterion was discovered.

Finally, using coffee, fabric softener, and spray cologne, Monroe [48] discovered that when housewives had prior differential purchase or use experience, brand attitude overcame the price influence, implying less use of price as a preference decision cue. Departing from previous studies, Monroe disaggregated the data and discovered that when price was the only differential information, the respondents found it very difficult to decide which brand to prefer. In contrast to most previous studies, respondents were permitted to indicate no brand preference for any test situation, and when price was the only differential information, nearly 25% of all responses indicated indifference even when comparative prices were more than 40% apart.

Determining the specific effect price has on buyers' perceptions of quality is complicated by the multitude of research designs and products tested. But throughout the findings surveyed here emerges the suggestion that brand name is important and possibly dominates price for relatively inexpensive grocery products and beverages, whereas for clothing, there is an apparent increasing concern with price, although price may not always dominate the influence of brand name. Perhaps one major disadvantage of experimental research in this area is the difficulty of presenting a wide range of prices to obtain individuals' perceptions of product quality. Only Andrews and Valenzi and Monroe offered a systematic range of prices to the experimental respondents. Also, as suggested in the research reported in the section on differential price thresholds, the range of stimuli (prices) presented does affect respondents' perceptions.

Functional Form of the Price-Quality Relationship

As Gardner [27] has suggested, the research evidence precludes any generalization about a price-quality relationship. The single-cue studies unanimously observed a price-quality relationship but the multi-cue studies often found little direct price-quality relations. In those studies where brand names were a part of the manipulations, the brand influence seemingly dominated the price influence, a result consistent with the price-consciousness studies.

Apart from the issue of generalizability, some of the studies produced evidence on the functional form of the price-quality relationship. McConnell [38, 39] observed a nonlinear relationship—the $1.30 and $1.20 brands of beer were separated by a greater perceptual distance than were the $1.20 and $0.99 brands. Also, Rao [59] observed: (1) that the price-quality relationship was not unidirectional and (2) that brand quality was exponentially related to price.

Noting the implied nonlinear or even discontinuous relationships in some of the previous studies, Peterson [58] estimated the price-quality functional form and discovered a parabolic relationship of the form:

(1) $$\overline{Q}_i = a + bX_i - cX_i^2,$$

where $\overline{Q}_i$ is mean quality rating at the ith price level, X_i is the ith price level, $i = 1, 2, \ldots, n$, and a, b, c are parameters. It should also be noted that the general form of the relationship found by Peterson can also be represented by the exponential form suggested by Rao, except that the exponential form will asymptotically approach an upper limit.

Related to the functional form of the price-quality relationship is the implied demand curve resulting from such a relationship. Although none of these studies specifically examined the price-quality demand relationship, the evidence cited infers that, at least over some range of prices, demand is greater for higher prices, and the demand curve has a positive slope. Other than for such unique situations as inferior and "snob-appeal" goods, economists are understandably reluctant to accept such a possibility, since the positively sloping demand curve for a price-quality relationship is an inference without empirical evidence.

Price-Quality Mapping

How people use price to evaluate quality is suggested by a paradigm developed by Emery [14], in which buyers are hypothesized to categorize the product's price, categorize the assessed quality, and then judge whether the assessed quality is equivalent to the expected quality for the categorized price. His model is shown in Figure 1.

Mapping (a) to (b) and (c) to (d) is done simultaneously. Matching (b) and (c) depends on prior purchase experience with the product. If the line linking (b) and (c) has a negative slope, the item will be judged as high priced, relative to assessed quality, while a positive slope would provide a low price judgment. In either situation, if the value of the slope is perceived to be relatively large, the buyer may refrain from comparing his "standard" price-quality relationship against the one observed.

Absolute Price Thresholds

Research evidence reviewed so far has been directed toward the questions of whether buyers are aware of prices they pay and whether price is used

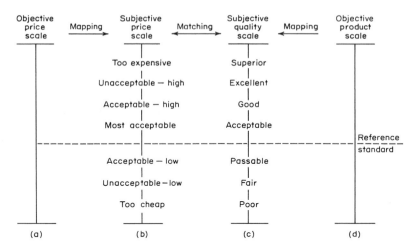

FIGURE 1.   Subjective mapping of price and quality.
Source: (14, p. 104); price categories adapted from (46).

as an indicator of quality, without relating price perception to the perceptual process per se. But it is necessary to determine whether certain perceptual phenomena relating sensory processes to physical stimuli are analogous to price perception. In this section and the next, attention is directed to two perceptual phenomena: absolute and differential thresholds.

Every human sensory process has an upper and lower limit of responsiveness to a stimulus—*absolute thresholds* that mark the transition between response and no response. Within the stimulus set in which responsiveness occurs, the *differential threshold* is the minimum amount of change in a stimulus necessary to produce "just noticeable difference" or JND. In a pricing situation, we are interested in the buyer's ability to discriminate between various product choices (stimuli). Therefore, two questions arise: (1) Do buyers have upper and lower price limits? (2) Given differentially priced products, how do buyers discriminate among choices?

Theoretical Framework

The hypothesis that a buyer has lower and upper price limits for a contemplated purchase has foundation in psychophysics, the study of quantitative relationships between physical objects and corresponding psychological events.

Originating much of the interest in threshold research was Weber's law which suggests that small, equally perceptible increments in a response correspond to proportional increments in the stimulus:

$$(2) \qquad\qquad \Delta S/S = K$$

where S is the magnitude of the stimulus, ΔS is the increment in S corresponding to a defined unitary change in response, and K is a constant.

In judging *differences between two intensities of a stimulus* Weber's law holds only over limited ranges of stimulus intensity. In particular, when stimuli values approach the lower threshold K may become considerably higher, and it also may increase for high stimuli values. Fechner argued that subjective sensation must be measured indirectly by using differential increments, and derived the Weber-Fechner law (see [47] for a complete derivation):

(3) $$R = k \log S + a$$

where R is the magnitude of response, S the magnitude of the stimulus, k a constant of proportionality, and a the constant of integration.

The Weber-Fechner law provides a means of experimentally determining the absolute threshold, because a least squares regression relating R to log S can be fitted from the data. Then the threshold is operationally defined as the stimulus value with a probability of producing a response 50% of the time [12]. The importance of the Weber-Fechner law to pricing is it produces the hypothesis that the relationship between price and an operationally defined response is logarithmic.

Empirical Evidence for Absolute Price Thresholds

The hypothesis of lower and upper price thresholds implies the existence of a range of acceptable prices and that some prices greater than $0 are unacceptable because they are considered to be too low. Stoetzel [70] demonstrated the existence of a range of prices buyers are willing to pay for a radio. Adam [1] then developed a technique for quantifying buyers' attitudes toward price. Interviewing over 6000 people Adam determined upper and lower price thresholds for nylon stockings, an underwear item, children's shoes, men's dress shirts, a gas-lighter, and refrigerators.

Fouilhé [18] extended the work of Stoetzel and Adam to include two household products and package soup and confirmed evidence for a range of acceptable prices. Fouilhé's methodology differed from Stoetzel and Adam in that he actually showed the products to each respondent, including brand name for two of them, and found that the known products had a distinctly narrower acceptable price range.

Gabor and Granger [22, 23] interviewed over 3000 housewives to determine acceptable price ranges for a carpet, nylon stockings, food and 2 household products. Gabor and Granger not only confirmed the acceptable price range hypothesis, but also found that the range shifted downward as income fell. Moreover, as income fell, the upper price threshold dropped less than the lower one, implying that low price was a more potent deterrent to the higher-income groups than was high price to lower-income groups.

Investigating social categorization as a function of acceptance and series range, Sherif [65] found price thresholds for a winter coat using 334 high school white and Indian students to be distinctly lower for the Indian students, particularly as the price stimulus set was lengthened to include higher prices. Monroe [50] adapted psychophysical experimental methodology using college students, and upper and lower price limits were determined for a variety of clothing and personal care items. In a second experiment replicating Sherif's study using high school students, Monroe [46] determined price limits for a sport coat and dress shoes.

Alexis et al. [2] asked 150 housewives to indicate the perceived importance of specific physical attributes and price for five articles of clothing and concluded that "the consumer goes shopping with a 'target' price in mind around which there is an acceptable deviation" [2, p. 28].

Functional Form of the Buy-Response Function

One implication of the price threshold concept is that the probability distribution a buyer will find on acceptable price is bell-shaped (the buy-response function) [23, 45]. Thus, if a buyer's perception follows the normal law, the *cumulative* response function is an S-shaped curve. Further, as hypothesized by the Weber-Fechner law, if equal increments in cumulative responses are produced only when price is increased by a constant proportion, then plotting the logarithm of price against cumulative response to show a uniform response increase will produce a symmetrical ogive.

Adam [1] proposed the logarithmic response function by suggesting that the size of the acceptable price range is proportional to the reference price:

(4) $$\Delta P/P = K$$

where ΔP is the acceptable price range, P is the reference price, and K is the constant of proportionality—essentially Weber's law. As indicated earlier, the logarithmic hypothesis is easily derived from this proportional relationship. In addition, Adam tested for a logarithmic relationship and concluded that the psychological scale of prices followed a logarithmic scale. Fouilhé [18] found that the logarithmic scale "appears to be well established, at least within the limits of the prices shown" [18, p. 90], as did Gabor and Granger [23].

Independently of these efforts, Cooper [10, 11] tested the relationship:

(5) $$Q = k \log P$$

where Q is perceived quality, P price, and k the constant of proportionality. Testing four products, he found a cumulative S-shaped function (ogive) and concluded, "judgments of value ... when compared to objective cash scales follow a relatively stable logarithmic form" [10, p. 119]. In addition, he observed that the value of k varies with the magnitude of price, but is constant for a given product. Finally, Monroe [49] also found logarithmic relationships provided good fits in his psychophysical experiments.

Differential Price Thresholds

Usually a buyer has alternative choices for a contemplated purchase, whose prices may provide cues that facilitate the discrimination process. However, even if the numerical prices are different, it cannot be assumed that the prices are *perceived* to be different. Hence, the problem becomes one of determining the effect of perceived price differences on buyer choice; and the major concern is when and under what circumstances are differentially priced but similar products perceived as different offers? Very little research has been reported on differential thresholds in pricing. This lack of research is surprising because of its practical implications for product line and sale pricing. Thus, the research to be reviewed comes primarily from psychological studies, with pricing implications drawn by analogy.

Weber's Law

Weber's law has often been cited as the basis for inferences about perceived price differences [15, 33, 43, 61, 76], but most writers have ignored other important variables affecting perception of price differences, and simply assumed K to be constant for an individual over all price comparisons. But just as K varies over different physical stimuli and as stimuli values approach minimal or high intensity, so should K vary over different products (similarly priced) and over divergent price levels.

Uhl [75] postulated that behavioral response to price changes depends on exposure to and perception of a price change, and motivation to alter behavior as a result of it. Further, the perception of a retail price change depends on the magnitude of the price change—in (2) the magnitude of ΔS. In the Uhl study, 74% of the experimental price changes were correctly identified, with the 5% deviations correctly identified 64% of the time, and the 15% deviations 84% of the time. Uhl interpreted the data to mean that the larger price changes exceeded the differential price thresholds of greater numbers of respondents.

Uhl also attempted a modified test of Weber's law during the study, hypothesizing that, for example, a 5% change in the price of a 15¢ product should be perceived by more consumers than a 5% change for a 55¢ product. However, the respondents perceived the 5% price deviations better on the higher-priced items.

Finally, Uhl indicated that while perception of price changes was independent of their direction, the dominance of reaction thresholds made respondents more sensitive to price increases. Moreover, 26% perceptual errors due to differential price thresholds and directional errors suggested a significant portion of the respondents were perceptually limited in responding to price changes.

Although not directly concerned with measuring price change perception, Pessemier [55, 56] in his market simulation studies also found price sensitivity to be different for price increases as compared to price decreases. And in a later field experiment he observed that a price change for a specific brand had little short-run effect on demand [57].

As (5) indicates, Cooper [10, 11] tested the Weber-Fechner law relating perceived quality to price. In addition to his findings on the shape of the response function, Cooper found that the value of K varied for different products. The immediate implication is that consumers will be more sensitive to price changes for some products, i.e., have lower differential price thresholds. In other words, for some products, a price increase or decrease may not be perceived, suggesting these products have a relatively high K value, using (2).

Recently Kamen and Toman [33] criticized the attempt of marketing textbook writers to infer analogically that Weber's Law can be applied to a variety of marketing situations. Using a mail survey, they obtained buyer preferences for 36 pairs of gasoline prices and concluded that their data contradicted Weber's Law and, therefore, Weber's Law had been invalidated. Later, Stapel [69] supported Kamen and Toman and suggested that everybody can notice even a one-cent price difference. However, Monroe [47], and Gabor, Granger, and Sowter [25] have indicated there is ample evidence to support the plausibility of Weber's Law applying within a pricing context, particularly when a buyer perceives the entire purchase offer as different. *There is still no valid test of the applicability of Weber's Law to pricing.*

Adaptation-Level Theory

Various researchers have suggested that one determinant of price perception is the price "last paid," or the buyers' notion of a "fair price," relative to the present price level, actual or perceived. This price perception hypothesis has theoretical foundation in Helson's *adaptation-level theory* [29].

Classical psychophysics provided the concept that judgments of stimulus differences are dependent on the magnitude of the standard against which the judgments are made. However, this notion considers the differential threshold to be dependent only on the standard or reference stimulus. Adaptation-level theory provides for a *changing* zero point from which behavioral responses are made and provides an explicit statement of the frame of reference to which behavior is relative.

According to Helson, an individual's behavioral response to stimuli represents modes of adaptation to environmental and organismic forces. These forces are not random, but rather impinge on organisms already adapted to past stimuli, internal as well as external. The pooled effect of three classes of stimuli, *focal, contextual,* and *organic,* determines the adjustment or adaptation level (AL) underlying all forms of behavior. In price perception, focal stimuli are the stimuli the individual is directly responding to, and *contextual* or *background stimuli* are all other stimuli in the behavioral situation providing the context within which the focal stimuli are operative. Adaptation processes result in behavioral responses that are commonly expressed along a continuum ranging from rejection to acceptance with a neutral zone or point of indifference in the transitional region(s).

Perceptual judgment of a stimulus depends on the relationship between the physical value of that stimulus and the physical value of the current AL. In a pricing context, adaptation-level theory suggests that price perception depends on the actual price and the individual's reference price or AL.

Emery [14] has noted some important implications of adaptation-level theory on price perception:

1. Price perceptions are relative to other prices and to associated use-values.
2. There is a "standard price" for each discernible quality level for each product category.
3. The "standard price" serves as an anchor for judgments of other prices.

4. There is a region of indifference about a standard price such that changes in price within this region produce no change in perception.
5. The standard price will be some average of the range of prices for similar products.
6. Buyers do not judge each price singly, but rather each price is compared with the standard price and the other prices in the price range.
7. The standard price need not correspond with any actual price nor the price of the leading brand.

Evidence of a Standard Price

Although the hypothesis of a standard price serving as an AL for price judgments has not been directly tested, evidence does support the plausibility of this hypothesis. Initially, Scitovsky [62] suggested that buyers consider traditional past prices as a product's fair price. When fair and actual prices differ, the judgment of cheap or expensive may be applied. Similarly, Shapiro [63] suggests that price does not indicate quality without a perceptible difference in price from the fair price. Gabor and Granger [22, 23] indicate a buyer will probably decide to purchase if the product's price falls within an acceptable price range whose limits are related to prevailing market prices and the price of the product normally purchased. Data available to Ölander [53] also suggested that a buyer's price judgment is influenced by his perception of prevailing market prices and his perception of the price most frequently charged. McConnell [38, 40, 41], explaining the nonlinearity of perceptual distance between the high-, middle-, and low-priced brands, found evidence that subjects used the high-priced brand as a frame of reference.

Explaining the respondents' lack of success in identifying the price last paid, Uhl [25] observed that in judging a price change consumers use as a reference point the range of prices last paid. Moreover, consumer perception of price changes was related to the importance of the product in the budget and the frequency of product purchase (contextual variables in the AL paradigm). Kamen and Toman [33] advanced the notion consumers have a fair price for a given item. Respondents in Cooper's research [11] believed the standard price provided above average value; average value was judged for products priced 20–30% below current market prices (standard price). Alexis [2] discovered that the consumer goes shopping with a "target price" in mind around which there is an acceptable deviation. Finally, Peterson [58] found that the perceived quality ratings for some subjects appeared to result from an interaction between price and product frame of reference.

Assimilation-Contrast Effects

Several of the pricing studies cited suggest that prevailing range of prices affects the standard or reference price. Since the stimulus range is affected by the extreme or end stimuli values, to explore the influence of price range on perception, attention could be centered on the end prices. In particular, what happens to perceptions when the end prices are varied? Stimuli values used by individuals to make perceptual judgments (AL, end values) are called anchoring stimuli. When an anchor is introduced at or near the end of the stimulus series, the judgment scale is displaced toward the anchor and the new reference point is assimilated into the series. However, when the end reference point is too remote, displacement is away from the anchor and the end point is perceived as belonging to another scale (category)—the contrast effect [66].

Evidence of assimilation-contrast in a pricing context is meager, but, if applicable, the implications are profound. First, the high and low prices in a definable product offering may be more noticeable to a buyer and thus influence his perceptions. These end prices [44], along with the standard price, may accentuate the perceived value for a given product (a bargain), or may diminish the perceived value (too expensive), depending where the product's price lies in the price range. In addition, if either or both end prices are outside the acceptable price range, the reference price cues may increase the ambiguity of the price stimuli.

Second, the perception of a sale price may depend on its position in the price range. Positioning it below other offerings may lead to the perception of a bargain (assimilation effect) or to a disbelief that the sale price is a reduction from the advertised original (contrast effect) [42].

A third consideration is the effect of reducing the range of stimuli by shifting one or both end values toward the stimulus center. Available evidence indicates that respondents then have greater difficulty in discriminating among stimuli, and that this increase in ambiguity leads to assimilation [7, 9, 71, 72]. Thus, as the range of alternative prices narrows, buyers may have greater difficulty in discriminating between choices, leading to a judgment of no price differences (assimilation effect); in these cases it can be expected that other cues (e.g., brand name) will dominate the decision process.

Compounding the selection of an appropriate hypothesis is that concomitant with the price series is a value series (perceived quality), and, as has already been observed, the price and value series may vary concurrently. Value is not a physical stimulus, although it is an important attribute, and efficient discrimination between stimuli in terms of differences in value usually is more important than discrimination in terms of price. Accentuation of price differences may lead to a greater accentuation of perceived value differences [6, 8, 71, 72]. The resultant purchase response in terms of current phenomenology is not predictable.

Sherif's work [65] is the only research evidence available directly testing the assimilation-contrast hypothesis in a pricing context [62, p. 155]:

> When a (price) range exceeded the latitude of acceptance (range of acceptable prices), higher values were assimilated into acceptable categories; but at the same time, a contrast effect occurred, as revealed in the tendency to lump together highly discrepant values into a broad objectionable category. . . . As a result of the interaction between internal anchor and stimulus range, subjects discriminated most keenly among the acceptable values when they were not faced with numerous objectionable items . . . . The results indicate that the range of stimulus values presented for judgment is an important variable in determining whether effects of internal anchors will be detected at all.

Summary and Conclusions

The purpose of this article has been to organize existing research on buyers' subjective perceptions of price, contrasting existing research knowledge and current pricing practices with the unknown knowledge on buyers' price perceptions, and to shake the belief that the inverse price-demand relationship is "one of the best substantiated findings in economics" [54, p. 26]. Although Palda [54] argues that departures from the inverse price-demand relationship—for example, a positive relationship due to quality connotations—are caused by buyers' perceptual changes, the evidence suggests that the perceptual mechanism need not change to infer a positive price-demand relationship.

Findings on the price-quality relationship are mixed, although there are indications that a positive relationship exists, at least over some range of prices for some product categories. Implications of the price-quality relationship on the shape of the demand curve are inconclusive and must be explored directly through empirical studies. There appears to be a general lack of awareness of prices paid for recent purchases. And when buyers do compare prices, the range of prices offered, the reference price, and the end prices may affect judgment, and, therefore, buyers' responses. If the price range and the end prices do affect judgment, the extent that the competitive environment leads to little price variation within alternative purchase choices decreases the likelihood of consumer awareness of prices paid, and increases the likelihood that price changes within the narrow price range are not perceived.

Despite the evidence available from specific effect of price on choice studies, the evidence available from the absolute and differential price threshold research suggests we know very little about how price affects a buyer's perceptions of alternative purchase offers, and how these perceptions affect his response. Perception is one intervening variable between a stimulus and a response, and, as suggested by adaptation-level theory, the stimulus context is indeed an important variable affecting perception. To direct research only to the focus variable, price, and ignore or assume constant the context variables is indeed a grave error. If the ultimate objective is to predict the effect of a pricing decision, then clearly more research is needed on buyers' subjective perceptions of price. Because of the seemingly heavy reliance on the inverse price-demand function by price setters, it should be realized that a number of psychological and other contextual factors may lead to a perception of price by the buyer that is different from the perception assumed by the price setter.

References

1. Adam, D. *Les réactions du consummateur devant le prix*. Paris: SEDES, 1958.

2. Alexis, M., G. Haines, Jr., and L. Simon. "A Study of the Validity of Experimental Approaches to the Collection of Price and Product Preference Data." Paper presented at 17th International Meeting of the Institute of Management Sciences, 1970.

3. Andrews, P. R., and E. R. Valenzi. "Combining Price, Brand, and Store Cues to Form an Impression of Product Quality." Paper presented at Conference of the American Psychological Association, 1971.

4. Brown, F. E. "Price Perception and Store Patronage," *Proceedings AMA* (Fall 1968), 371–376.

5. ——. "Who Perceives Supermarket Prices Most Validly?" *Journal of Marketing Research*, Vol. 8 (February 1971), 110–113.

6. Bruner, J., and C. Goodman. "Value and Need as Organizing Factors in Perception." *Journal of Abnormal and Social Psychology*, Vol. 42 (January 1947), 33–44.

7. —— and A. L. Minturn. "Perceptual Identification and Perceptual Organization." *Journal of General Psychology*, Vol. 53 (July 1955), 21–28.

8. —— and L. Postman. "Symbolic Value as an Organizing Factor in Perception." *Journal of Social Psychology*, Vol. 27 (February 1948), 203–208.

9. Campbell, D., W. Hunt, and N. Lewis. "The Effects of Assimilation and Contrast in Judgments of Clinical Materials." *American Journal of Psychology*, Vol. 70 (September 1957), 347–360.

10. Cooper, P. "Subjective Economics: Factors in a Psychology of Spending." In [73], 112–121.

11. ——. "The Begrudging Index and the Subjective Value of Money." In [73], 122–131.

12. Corso, J. "A Theoretic-Historical Review of the Threshold Concept." *Psychological Bulletin*, Vol. 60 (July 1963), 356–370.

13. Della Bita, A. "An Experimental Examination of Conditions Which May Foster the Use of Price as an Indicator of Relative Product Attractiveness." Unpublished Ph.D. dissertation, University of Massachusetts, 1971.

14. Emery, F. "Some Psychological Aspects of Price." In [73], 98–111.

15. Engel, J., D. Kollat, and R. Blackwell. *Consumer Behavior*. Holt, Rinehart and Winston, 1968.

16. Enis, B., and J. Stafford. "Consumers' Perception of Product Quality as a Function of Various Informational Inputs." *Proceedings AMA* (Fall 1969), 340–344.

17. ——. "The Price-Quality Relationship: An Extension." *Journal of Marketing Research*, Vol. 6 (November 1969), 256–258.

18. Fouilhé, P. "The Subjective Evaluation of Price: Methodological Aspects." In [73], 89–97.

19. Friedman, L. "Psychological Pricing in the Food Industry." In *Prices: Issues in Theory, Practice, and Public Policy*, ed. A. Phillips and O. Williamson. University of Pennsylvania Press, (1967), 187–201.

20. Gabor, A., and C. Granger. "On the Price Consciousness of Consumers." *Applied Statistics*, Vol. 10 (November 1961), 170–188.

21. ———. "Price Sensitivity of the Consumer." *Journal of Advertising Research*, Vol. 4 (December 1964), 40–44.

22. ———. "The Pricing of New Products." *Scientific Business*, Vol. 3 (August 1965), 141–150.

23. ———. "Price as an Indicator of Quality, Report on an Enquiry." *Economica*, Vol. 46 (February 1966), 43–70.

24. ———. "The Attitude of the Consumer to Price." In [73], 132–151.

25. ———, and A. Sowter, "Comments on 'Psychophysics of Prices.'" *Journal of Marketing Research*, Vol. 8 (May 1971), 251–252.

26. Gardner, D. "An Experimental Investigation of the Price-Quality Relationship." *Journal of Retailing*, Vol. 46 (Fall 1970), 25–41.

27. ———. "Is There a Generalized Price-Quality Relationship?" *Journal of Marketing Research*, Vol. 8 (May 1971), 241–243.

28. Ginzberg, E. "Customary Prices." *American Economic Review*, Vol. 26 (June 1936), 296.

29. Helson, H. *Adaptation-Level Theory*. Harper & Row, 1964.

30. "How Multiple-Unit Pricing Helps—and Hurts." *Progressive Grocer*, Vol. 50 (June 1971), 52–58.

31. "How Much Do Customers Know About Retail Prices?" *Progressive Grocer*, Vol. 43 (February 1964), C104–C106.

32. Jacoby, J., J. Olson, and R. Haddock. "Price, Brand Name, and Product Composition Characteristics as Determinants of Perceived Quality." *Journal of Applied Psychology*, Vol. 55 (December 1971), 470–479.

33. Kamen, J., and R. Toman. "Psychophysics of Prices." *Journal of Marketing Research*, Vol. 7 (February 1970), 27–35.

34. ———. "'Psychophysics of Prices': A Reaffirmation." *Journal of Marketing Research*, Vol. 8 (May 1971), 252–257.

35. Lambert, Z. "Price and Choice Behavior." *Journal of Marketing Research*, Vol. 9 (February 1972), 35–40.

36. ———. "Product Perception: An Important Variable in Price Strategy." *Journal of Marketing*, Vol. 34 (October 1970), 68–71.

37. Leavitt, H. "A Note on Some Experimental Findings About the Meaning of Price." *Journal of Business*, Vol. 27 (July 1954), 205–210.

38. McConnell, J. D. "An Experimental Examination of the Price-Quality Relationship." *Journal of Business*, Vol. 41 (October 1968), 439–444.

39. ———. "The Development of Brand Loyalty: An Experimental Study." *Journal of Marketing Research*, Vol. 5 (February 1968), 13–19.

40. ———. "Effect of Pricing on Perception of Product Quality." *Journal of Applied Psychology*, Vol. 52 (August 1968), 331–334.

41. ———. "The Price-Quality Relationship in an Experimental Setting." *Journal of Marketing Research*, Vol. 5 (August 1968), 300–303.

42. McDougall, G. "Credibility of Price-offs in Retail Advertising." Unpublished Ph.D. dissertation proposal, University of Western Ontario, 1970.

43. Miller, R. "Dr. Weber and the Consumer." *Journal of Marketing*, Vol. 26 (January 1962), 57–61.

44. Monroe, K. "A Method for Determining Product Line Prices with End-Price Constraints." Unpublished Ph.D. dissertation, University of Illinois, 1968.

45. ———. "The Information Content of Prices: A Preliminary Model for Estimating Buyer Response." *Management Science*, Vol. 17 (April 1971), B519–B532.

46. ———. "Measuring Price Thresholds by Psychophysics and Latitudes of Acceptance." *Journal of Marketing Research*, Vol. 8 (November 1971), 460–464.

47. ———. "'Psychophysics of Prices': A Reappraisal." *Journal of Marketing Research*, Vol. 8 (May 1971), 248–250.

48. ———. "The Influence of Price and the Cognitive Dimension on Brand Attitudes and Brand Preferences." Paper presented at Attitude Research and Consumer Behavior Workshop, 1970.

49. ———. "Some Findings on Estimating Buyers' Response Functions for Acceptable Price Thresholds." *Proceedings*, American Institute for Decision Sciences, Northeast Conference, 1972.

50. ——— and M. Venkatesan. "The Concept of Price Limits and Psychophysical Measurement: A Laboratory Experiment." *Proceedings AMA*, (Fall 1969), 345–351.

51. ——— and P. LaPlaca. "What Are the Benefits of Unit Pricing?" *Journal of Marketing*, Vol. 36 (July 1972), 16–22.

52. Newman, D., and J. Becknell. "The Price-Quality Relationship as a Tool in Consumer Research," *Proceedings*, American Psychological Association, 78th Annual Conference (1970), 729–730.

53. Ölander, F. "The Influence of Price on the Consumer's Evaluation of Products and Purchases." In [73], 50–69.

54. Palda, K. *Pricing Decisions and Marketing Policy*. Prentice-Hall, 1971.

55. Pessemier, E. "An Experimental Method for Estimating Demand." *Journal of Business*, Vol. 33 (October 1960), 373–383.

56. ———. *Experimental Methods of Analyzing Demand for Branded Consumer Goods*. Economic and Business Study No. 39, Washington State University Press, 1963.

57. ——— and R. Teach. "Pricing Experiments Scaling Consumer Preferences and Predicting Purchase Behavior." *Proceedings AMA* (Fall 1966), 541–557.

58. Peterson, R. "The Price-Perceived Quality Relationship: Experimental Evidence." *Journal of Marketing Research*, Vol. 7 (November 1970), 525–528.

59. Rao, V. "The Salience of Price in the Perception and Evaluation of Product Quality: A Multidimensional Measurement Model and Experimental Test." Unpublished Ph.D. dissertation, University of Pennsylvania, 1970.

60. ———. "Salience of Price in the Perception of Product Quality: A Multidimensional Measurement Approach," *Proceedings AMA* (Fall 1971), 571–577.

61. Roth, E. "How to Increase Room Revenue." *Hotel Management*, Vol. 67 (March 1955), 52ff.

62. Scitovsky, T. "Some Consequences of the Habit of Judging Quality by Price," *Review of Economic Studies*, Vol. 12 (1944–1945), 100–105.

63. Shapiro, B. "The Psychology of Pricing." *Harvard Business Review,* Vol. 46 (July–August 1968), 14ff.

64. ———. "Price as a Communicator of Quality: An Experiment." Unpublished Ph.D. dissertation, Harvard University, 1970.

65. Sherif, C. "Social Categorization as a Function of Latitude of Acceptance and Series Range." *Journal of Abnormal and Social Psychology,* Vol. 67 (August 1963), 148–156.

66. Sherif, M., and C. Hovland. "Judgmental Phenomena and Scales of Attitude Measurement: Placement of Items with Individual Choice of Number of Categories." *Journal of Abnormal and Social Psychology,* Vol. 48 (January 1953), 135–141.

67. Smith, E., and C. Broome. "A Laboratory Experiment for Establishing Indifference Prices Between Brands of Consumer Products." *Proceedings AMA* (Fall 1966), 511–519.

68. ———. "Experimental Determination of the Effect of Price and Market-Standing Information on Consumers' Brand Preferences." *Proceedings AMA* (Fall 1966), 520–531.

69. Stapel, J. "'Fair' or 'Psychological' Pricing?" *Journal of Marketing Research*, Vol. 9 (February 1972), 109–110.

70. Stoetzel, J. "Psychological/Sociological Aspects of Price." In [73], 70–74.

71. Tajfel, H. "Value and the Perceptual Judgment of Magnitude." *Psychological Review*, Vol. 64 (May 1957), 192–204.

72. ———. "Quantitative Judgment in Social Perception." *British Journal of Psychology*, Vol. 50 (February 1959), 16–29.

73. Taylor, B., and G. Wills (eds.). *Pricing Strategy.* Brandon/Systems Press, 1970.

74. Tull, D., R. A. Boring, and M. H. Gonsior. "A Note on the Relationship of Price and Imputed Quality." *Journal of Business,* Vol. 37 (April 1964), 186–191.

75. Uhl, J. "Consumer Perception of Retail Food Price Changes." Paper presented at First Annual Meeting of the Association for Consumer Research, 1970.

76. Webb, E. "Weber's Law and Consumer Prices." *American Psychologist,* Vol. 16 (July 1961), 450.

77. Wells, W., and L. LoSciuto. "Direct Observation of Purchasing Behavior." *Journal of Marketing Research,* Vol. 3 (August 1966), 227–233.

1.4 Preference and Perception Measures in New Product Development
ALVIN J. SILK

The approach to new product development to be discussed here was originally formulated by Volney Stefflre, a psychologist and linguist.[1] Stefflre purports to have developed a methodology, called "market structure analysis," for developing new products that will fit into markets in predetermined ways. More specifically, he claims that his method is capable of yielding [24, p. 252]:

1. Estimates of the share of consumer choices that a brand which does or does not exist will receive when on the market.
2. Estimates of the patterns of substitution and competition among products

or brands currently on the market, and predictions about the patterns that will exist after the introduction of specified new products.
3. Measurements of how closely a product matches the content of its advertising.
4. Indications of the opportunities for new brands in existing markets.
5. A means for the multi-brand firm to "position" new brands so that they will be substitutes for competitor's offerings but not for the firm's existing product line.

Let us begin by looking at the theory behind this methodology which promises so much. The basic premise is quite simple and has been stated by Stefflre as follows: "An individual will behave toward a new thing in a manner that is similar to the way he behaves toward other things he sees the new thing as being similar to" [25, p. 12].

This is hardly a very complex idea, but it is a very powerful and practical one—if, as a hypothesis about human behavior, it can be shown to hold up. Here we have a statement that can be directly applied to the problem of predicting consumer reaction to a new product. In particular, it implies the following: for some product category presently consisting of say, three brands, A, B, and C, if we market a new brand, X, which consumers see as being similar to B, but unlike A and C, then those consumers who previously bought B will be just as likely to buy X as B. In other words, X should attain about one-half of B's previous market share (all other things being equal—price, distribution, promotion, etc.), but the entry of X will not affect the market shares of A and C. There are some additional implications of consequence to this line of reasoning. If we know *why* brands are judged similar or dissimilar—that is, we can identify the attributes or underlying dimensions which consumers use to discriminate or differentiate among available brands—then this knowledge can be used to develop descriptions of new brands which will be perceived as similar or dissimilar to existing brands in predictable ways. Furthermore, Stefflre suggests that the *similarity judgments* which consumers can be asked to make *verbally* with reference to a *description* of a new product can be used to predict the manner in which they would *behave* toward the physical product itself if it were produced and placed on the market.

The foregoing may be summarized by the following set of hypotheses derived by Stefflre from the basic postulate stated previously.

1. *Verbal measures* of consumers' similarity *perceptions* about pairs of items allow prediction of the similarity of their behavior toward these items.
2. *Verbal measures* of similarity *judgments* made in response to descriptions of items allow prediction of the similarity of *behavior* toward the items *themselves.*
3. How items are perceived as similar or dissimilar, using either verbal or nonverbal measures, can vary in different situations, but as long as both measures are obtained in comparable situations, they will still correspond [25, p. 13].

Klahr has suggested an additional related hypothesis: The number of dimensions required to represent the cognitive structure of brand perceptions will be relatively low [see 14].

Previous studies of problem solving indicate that the information processing capacity of humans is limited. Noting this, Klahr conjectured that the cognitive structure of consumers for products could be characterized as a space of relatively low dimensionality—three or fewer dimensions. Alternatively, although a product or brand is a complex bundle of many attributes and qualities, consumers may be expected to pay attention to only a few in evaluating them.

To exploit these propositions for the managerial purposes mentioned previously requires that a series of measurements be obtained. Stefflre has developed a set of techniques which he indicates have proved satisfactory. In 1966, he reported having used this methodology in 12 studies conducted over a five-year period. The studies dealt with a variety of consumer products, including detergents, cigarettes, whiskey, coffee, and automobiles and other durables.[2]

More recently, some published accounts of new product development projects dealing with the problem in a manner that is similar but not identical to Stefflre's approach have appeared [see 7, 22, and 23]. Although not specifically concerned with new product development, several other studies on related aspects of purchasing behavior have been carried out using the same types of perception and preference measurements employed by Stefflre. Of particular importance is the work of Paul Green and his collaborators in this area. Their recent monograph, prepared for the Marketing Science Institute, contains an excellent review of non-metric scaling and related techniques used in analyzing perception and preference data [see 8]. Also presented are the results of several pilot studies on the preference and similarity structures for such diverse objects as business schools, marketing journals, physicians' professional reading habits, women's panties, and computers. This work is an invaluable reference for anyone interested in the procedures used for collecting and analyzing these types of data.

In what follows, we summarize the research program Stefflre has prescribed for the complete development of a new product. Stefflre has made it reasonably clear what steps his approach to this problem entail [see 24], but little in the way of technical detail or data have been publicly reported. The best source of such specific information known to the author is a Harvard case which describes some of Stefflre's work for General Foods on the coffee market [21]. Some materials taken from that source are used here for illustrative purposes.

A Methodology for New Product Development

The sequential procedure advocated by Stefflre for developing a new product is outlined below [based on 24, esp. pp. 267–268]:

1. Define the relevant market in terms of existing patterns of substitution and competition.
2. Determine what products and brands are seen as similar to one another and why through studying small samples of consumers' judgments of similarity and difference.

3. Determine patterns of brand to brand and/or product to product substitution and competition through use of large-scale purchase panel data, when these are available, or through large-scale preference studies when panel data are not available.
4. Determine the relationships between the similarity judgment data and the brand switching or brand preference data.
5. Develop descriptions of possible new brands or products suggested by the results of steps 2 and 3.
6. Insert each description of a potential new product into a large-scale preference study to determine what share of choices it receives and from what existing brands it draws these choices.
7. Build an actual physical product which consumers perceive as matching the new product description and which the results of step 6 indicate will be successful in terms of management objectives.
8. Use similar procedures to determine what brand name, packaging, and advertising copy "fit" the product.
9. Test market.

Defining a Market

Stefflre cautions against making a priori and/or implicit assumptions about what array of products and brands constitutes the relevant market. Patterns of substitution among brands and products are often not at all obvious. As an example, he notes that brandy competes with certain types of whiskies but not others [24, p. 254]. To avoid being misled by one's intuition in this regard, it is highly desirable that some form of data on purchase or usage be examined to determine what is a set of substitute products and brands in the eyes of the consumer. For some product categories, existing information such as that derived from consumer panel data might be helpful. In other instances, a special consumer interview study may be required. At some point, however, judgment must be exercised to determine what range of items constitutes the relevant "market" of alternatives to consider. Defining the market is a crucial step because the set of brands and products identified becomes the inputs or stimuli for the similarity measurements.

Similarity Measurement

Given a set of products and/or brands which one has reason to believe are substitutes for one another and therefore represent competing alternatives, the next step is to determine which ones consumers perceive as similar and why. There are a number of ways of eliciting these similarity judgments. The methods differ in two important ways. First, the measurement may be a simple dichotomous one (similar or dissimilar) or a scale of several degrees of similarity or dissimilarity (most . . . least). A second difference is that the respondent may be either "forced" to make similarity judgments about all possible pairs of objects or, alternatively, he may be presented with one object and asked to indicate which other objects on a list are similar or dissimilar in such a way that he is not forced to make a judgment on all possible pairs of items.

Choice of a similarity measurement technique is not an insignificant problem. If the number of objects being studied is at all large, requiring that judgments be made on all possible pairs can make the interview a long, boring, and highly repetitive task. Stefflre's technique seems to have certain advantages in this regard [for a sample questionnaire, see 21, App. II]. The respondent's attention is first directed toward a particular brand. He is then given a list of other brands and asked to indicate which ones he thinks are similar to the stimulus brand. The procedure is then repeated changing the stimulus brand on each round. By not insisting that respondents make judgments on all possible pairs, the length of time taken and repetitiveness may be reduced. Stefflre's procedure also does not force judgments about brands if the consumer is completely unaware of them. But this is a tricky matter, for we are interested in the content of even vague impressions and do not wish to discourage them. It is the author's own experience that asking consumers to make refined judgments about degrees of similarity or dissimilarity is likely to reduce the reliability of the measures obtained and increase the instance of intransitivities or inconsistent judgments. Studies need to be made of the test-retest reliabilities of these different measures.

The key information obtained from this stage of the research is an overall similarity score for all possible pairs of brands. These scores, obtained by aggregating the similarity judgments of individual respondents in the sample, are arranged in a matrix. The rows and columns of the matrix are formed by the brands and the main diagonal is empty. The cell entries are scores which reflect how similar two particular brands are judged to be by consumers. The manner in which these overall scores are calculated depends upon how the similarity judgments were measured. If, for example, respondents were asked to rate the similarity of each pair of brands on a seven-point scale, then the average for the entire sample (or perhaps some sub-group) would be used in the similarity matrix. For dichotomous measures, Stefflre determines an "index of similarity" which is defined as the ratio of the number of respondents who judge the two brands similar to an expected value. Because respondents do not necessarily make similarity judgments on all possible pairs of brands, brands will differ in the number of times they are judged similar to other brands. Presumably, the better-known brands (e.g., relatively large market share and heavily advertised) will receive more mentions than those less well known. To adjust for this he calculates an expected value in a manner similar to that used in determining a chi-square value for a contingency table. This value represents the number of times one would expect two brands to be judged similar on a chance basis, given the total number of times each was judged similar to all brands considered. Hence, when the value of the index is 1, the actual extent of judged similarity is just equal to that which would be expected by "chance" as defined above.

Analyzing the Structure of Brand Perceptions

Much can be learned from an inspection of a matrix of similarity scores. It is possible to determine which brands are judged to be alike and which are perceived as different. The larger the value of the cell entry, the more similar brands have been judged. In order to get a clear picture of how *all* brands are "positioned" relative to one another in the minds of consumers, the similarity matrix can be analyzed by multidimensional scaling procedures. The basic idea is that consumers' perceptions of different brands may be conceived as a space of some unknown number of dimensions in which individual brands are positioned. The distances between brands reflect their degree of similarity: the more similar two brands are judged to be, the closer together they will be in this perceptual space. Multidimensional scaling techniques utilize similarity data to construct a map of this space.

The problem of multidimensional scaling is that of representing objects geometrically by n points so that their interpoint distances in some sense correspond to the dissimilarities of the n objects.[3] A simple example of multidimensional scaling would be a problem wherein one was given a set of cities and the task was to construct a map where the only information given was the distances between the cities. The technique used by Stefflre was developed by Kruskal.[4] Kruskal views multidimensional scaling as a problem of statistical fitting—the similarities or dissimilarities are given and the task is to find the configuration whose distances fit them "best." To accomplish this, he assumes that distances and dissimilarities are monotonically related. The dissimilarities need only be ordinal or rank-order measures. Kruskal has developed a program which computes that configuration of points (objects) which optimizes goodness of fit for a monotonic relationship between the similarity measures and the interpoint distances. "Goodness of fit" is evaluated by a quantity called "stress" that is *analogous* to a "residual sum of squares" or proportion of unexplained variance. The smaller the stress, the better the fit. For a space of a given number of dimensions, the Kruskal program finds that configuration of points which has minimum stress. The stress would be zero for a perfect relationship (perfect monotone relationship between dissimilarities and distances). The program starts with an arbitrary configuration of points and proceeds iteratively to find the best (minimum stress) configuration in one dimension, then two, and so on up to n-1 dimensions, where n is the number of objects. It is always possible to get a perfect fit of n objects in n-1 dimensions. The lower the dimensionality, the more constrained the solution, and, hence, we are more apt to get poor fits in a small number of dimensions than with a larger number. At each stage the program prints out the minimum stress achieved and the (arbitrary) coordinates of the points and their interpoint distances. The coordinates can be used to plot positioning "maps." Choice of which configuration is the most appropriate representation of the data is a matter of judgment.

Figure 1 shows a three-dimensional map based on similarity data obtained for existing brands and descriptions of possible new brands of coffee [21, App. I]. Note that the location of the axes is purely arbitrary. The meaning of the dimensions is a matter of interpretation, and data on the reasons consumers give for their similarity judgments might be useful for this purpose.[5] Such data or ratings of brands on scales describing various prespecified attributes might be applied to various statistical procedures to try to "explain" the dimensions of this perceptual map.[6] In line with Klahr's hypothesis, it appears from the studies available that relatively few dimensions (2 to 5) are sufficient to obtain good fits of similarity perceptions for consumer products.

A word of caution is in order concerning the evaluation of the goodness of fit obtained from these multidimensional scaling results. Little is known

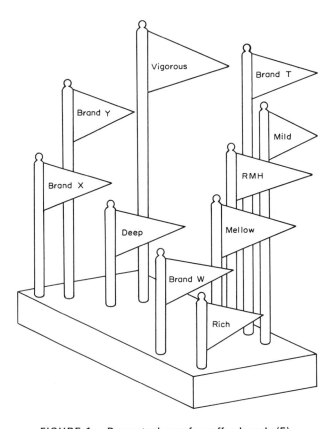

FIGURE 1.   Perceptual map for coffee brands (5).

about the statistical properties of these procedures. That is, no sampling theory has been developed which allows one to make inferences about the likelihood of obtaining a particular result. Klahr has done a most valuable study that bears on this point [see 13]. He applied Kruskal's scaling technique to similarity matrices generated from random numbers and observed the "relative frequency with which apparent structure was erroneously found in the unstructured data." He reports that "For a small number of points (i.e., six or seven) it is very likely that a good fit will be obtained in two or more dimensions when in fact the data are generated by a random process [13, p. 1]. He also presents some estimates which can be used as a rough standard against which the statistical significance of results obtained in a particular study can be evaluated.

The Relationship Between Similarity Perceptions and Brand Switching

Stefflre makes use of very small samples (50 to 100) to obtain his similarity data. The explanation that he gives for being able to do so is that "there appears to be a surprising amount of homogeneity in a population of people about what is similar to what, and much less homogeneity about what is good"

[24, p. 256]. However, other researchers have not consistently found similarity judgments to be markedly homogeneous. For example, after having conducted a number of studies among diverse groups in which similarity data were collected for a broad range of products, Green and Carmone noted that "homogeneity of perception has been the exception rather than the rule" [8, p. 31]. Quite likely, the amount of heterogeneity one observes is affected by the type of similarity measurement used. As mentioned earlier, some methods of obtaining similarity judgments appear to yield more reliable measurements than others. Aside from such methodological matters, it is difficult to see why, in general, perceptions should be homogeneous. Given the variability in what and how consumers learn about products, some heterogeneity in perceptions is to be expected.

To establish the validity of these similarity measures and justify the use of small samples to obtain them, Stefflre has correlated his index of similarity based on verbal responses with a similarity index calculated from brand switching matrices derived from consumer panel data [see 21 for an example]. Brand switching represents a behavioral measure of similarity—consumers will be more likely to switch among brands they regard as similar than among those they view as different. Stefflre reports that the verbal measures of similarity obtained from small samples of consumers have been found to correlate with measures derived from consumer panel data (based on much larger samples) from 0.50 to 0.80 in 12 different studies [24, p. 255]. In the coffee example, correlations of 0.45, 0.64, 0.69, and 0.73 are shown for four different cities [21, p. 31]. Stefflre also notes that the correlations between judged brand similarity and brand switching are about as high as those between switching measures obtained during different time periods.

A strong and simple relationship between similarity judgments may or may not exist. Whereas Doehlert reports high correlation between individuals' similarity judgments and their preferences with respect to automobile colors [see 6], Klahr found only a relatively weak relationship between similarity and preference for cigarettes [see 14]. Other factors besides similarity perceptions can affect brand switching.

Stefflre points out that in addition to "psychological" similarity between brands, overlap in availability and overlap in the audiences of media in which competing brands are advertised account for the patterns of substitution observed in brand switching data [24, p. 256]. Overlaps in availability and advertising increase competition. Stefflre's suggestion that there will be more brand switching among brands advertised in the same media than among those advertised in different ones in intriguing and, in principle, appears to be testable.

If a strong relationship between psychological similarity and brand switching could be assumed to hold generally, it would mean that patterns of brand substitution could be determined in situations where panel data are not available. As well, the cost of estimating market structures from small samples of similarity judgments is likely to be less than the expense involved in securing panel data. Here again, the question of the homogeneity of similarity perceptions is involved. While the correlations Stefflre reports between aggregate measures of similarity and brand switching are encouraging, one would like to see this relationship demonstrated within the same sample.

From this first round of small sample studies, two types of data are obtained: measures of how similar consumers judge existing brands to be and their explanations of why. With the assistance of multidimensional scaling techniques, we are able to develop a picture of how brands currently being sold are positioned relative to one another in the minds of consumers. The qualitative data are used to identify what product features and attributes consumers utilize in making these similarity discriminations and what combination of product features or attributes accounts for each existing brand being positioned as it is in the similarity structure. One goal here may be to identify opportunities for new products that could be developed by combining salient product attributes in some way that would be unique in terms of existing brands and appealing to a substantial proportion of consumers. Alternatively, one might be interested in assessing the potential of some alternative new product ideas identified by other means. That is, similarity information may be helpful at either the "search" or "screen" stages of the new product decision process.

The use of similarity data for either of these two purposes depends a great deal upon the skill and judgment of the investigator. There are certain kinds of formal analysis that can be helpful. For example, if one has similarity and preference measurements for the same people, multidimensional scaling can be used to locate both existing brands and the "ideal" brand for different individuals or market segments.[7] In the Stefflre methodology, what comes out of this and other more informal analyses is a set of descriptions of possible new brands. Developing these descriptions in language that will be meaningful to the consumer is obviously no simple task.

Measuring Preferences for New Product Descriptions

Given a set of descriptions of potential new brands, the next step is to estimate what share of consumers' choices each would receive and for which existing brands the new ones would be substitutes. Stefflre stresses the importance of *not* using aggregate paired comparison data or average ratings of *just* the new product alternatives [24, p. 260]. Using only information about which new product alternatives receive the largest number of choices or highest *average* rating can lead to what Kuehn and Day call the "majority fallacy— . . . assuming that every product must be acceptable to a majority of all consumers if it is to be successful" [18, p. 104]. Instead, what one needs to know is what share of choices a new item would receive if inserted into the array of existing brands. In addition, estimates are needed of the choices which will be drawn from existing brands. This latter information is especially important for the case of a manufacturer who already has a brand on the market and is considering adding another. Clearly, he would like to position a new brand so that it does not compete directly with his present brand but rather steals sales from competitors.

To obtain this information, a large scale preference study would be conducted in which the descriptions of new items along with the names of existing brands are presented and respondents are asked to indicate their preferences.[8] From such a study carried out with a large sample (in the order of 1500 respondents), estimates are obtained of what market share each new product description would secure (if it alone were placed on the market) and how the market shares of existing brands would be affected by its entry. Such estimates allow management to select a new product alternative which will fit into the market in a predictable way and meet its goals with respect to market share and patterns of competition. This assumes, of course, that a new product can be produced which fits the description and that people will behave toward the actual product as they indicated they would when responding to the description in the preference interview.

One means of partially checking such predictions of future brand switching patterns is to conduct another similarity study using a new product description and existing brand names. The similarity judgments should correlate with the preference measurements—again assuming the basic theory is correct.

Development of the Product and Supporting Promotion

The same basic techniques are used to develop the physical product, package, brand name, and advertising copy that will fit the new product description. Working with technical personnel, the researcher attempts to have a product "built" which fits the desired description. Consumer testing becomes a matter of presenting respondents with the actual product and asking them to describe it. The objective here is to develop a product which elicits the desired description from consumers. Next, the actual product is subjected to another preference or quasi-purchase test to see if it performs as did the description it was built to match. Again data are obtained which are used to estimate the new product's expected market share and how existing brands would be affected by its entry into the market. Unsatisfactory performance at any stage leads to a recycling of previous activities. Essentially the same procedures are used to select a name, package design, and advertising messages which match the physical product. When all of this is completed, the product is test marketed as a final check to assure that performance and goals coincide.

Stefflre's views about the role of advertising are worth repeating because they are unusually explicit and are relevant to established as well as new products.[9] He reports having encountered instances where there were marked discrepancies between what advertising said about a brand and how consumers described it and where, as a result, one brand's advertising seemingly helped rather than hindered a competing brand's sales. More specifically, he suggests that for products where repeat purchases are important, advertising should function to:

1. Bring into greater salience the attribute dimensions along which the brand occupies a favorable position;
2. State as euphemistically as possible the undesirable features of the brand which cannot be avoided;
3. Attempt to move the product along those dimensions where advertising is sufficient to place the product in an advantageous position; and
4. "Fit" the product so that, in the consumers' eyes, it does not contradict its advertising and play havoc with repurchase rates [24, p. 262].

Summary

This paper has attempted to summarize and assess briefly a methodology that has been proposed for guiding the development and testing of new products. The approach is based upon a simple yet powerful theory of how people respond to new objects and consists of a series of reasonably well-defined steps. Successful applications have reportedly been realized. Barnett has recently presented an impressive set of results bearing on the predictive power of the methodology [1, p. 164]. Using preference and similarity data obtained with reference to the description of a new consumer packaged good, Stefflre predicted how the product would actually perform in a test market. His pre-test market predictions of the market share that the product would actually achieve and how it would affect sales of existing brands turned out to be quite close to what was later observed in the test market. The approach is theoretically appealing and obviously has great practical value if it is capable of yielding such predictions of new product performance before test marketing. However, as has been noted, there are several methodological questions concerning the procedures used to collect and analyze preference and perception data that are unsettled. Work now in progress may help resolve some of these issues.[10]

It remains to be seen whether the methodology discussed here can be useful for many different types of new products. Most of the work done to date appears to have been in the area of low-priced, frequently purchased consumer goods where a "new product" is often a slight variation of an established product type. Can Stefflre's notions also be applied to a "truly" new product which has no close substitutes? What about the case of industrial products? Answers to these questions must await the outcome of imaginative efforts to adapt the approach to problems of these types. While the specific procedures described here may not be suitable in such situations, the basic concepts of how new objects are perceived may at least suggest an organized way for managers to think about new product planning. Given the vagaries of new product development, even a small step forward is not to be belittled.

Notes

1. This section borrows freely from the writings of Stefflre [24] and [25], and his co-worker, Barnett [2] and [3].

2. See [24, p. 252]. Stefflre also suggests that his methodology may be used to guide the introduction of existing products into new markets and, therefore, is relevant to problems of international marketing. However, this topic will not be considered here.

3. For a good discussion of the basic concepts of multidimensional scaling and a comparison of alternative techniques, see [9].

4. See [16] and [17]. Other approaches have been developed; see [10].

5. See [21], Appendix II, for some examples of verbatim responses obtained with reference to coffee. In that study, two-thirds of all reasons consumers gave for similarity judgments dealt with flavor.

6. See [10] and [12] for some suggested procedures and illustrative applications.

7. See [10] for a discussion of these techniques and some examples.

8. For the details of the procedure, see [21].

9. See [3] for a more detailed discussion of the application of Stefflre's methodology to advertising. His views bear some resemblance to certain other discussions of how advertising operates as an influence process; see [1], [4], and [15].

10. Readers interested in a technical discussion of these problems should consult [10] and [11].

References

1. Amstutz, A. *Computer Simulation of Competitive Market Response.* Cambridge, Mass., MIT Press, 1967.

2. Barnett, N. L. "Beyond Market Segmentation," *Harvard Business Review,* Vol. 47, no. 1 (January–February 1969), 152–166.

3. Barnett, N. L. "Developing Effective Advertising for New Products," *Journal of Advertising Research,* Vol. 8, no. 4 (December 1968), 13–20.

4. "Benton & Bowles, Inc.—Service Bureau Corporation: A Behavioral Simulation Model of the Advertising Communications Process." In: R. D. Buzzell, *Mathematical Models and Marketing Management,* Ch. 9. Boston, Harvard University Graduate School of Business, Division of Research, 1964. Also see: *Proceedings of the Eighth Annual Conference of the Advertising Research Foundation* (October 1962), 52–65.

5. Brown, M. P., Cardozo, R. N., Cunningham, S. M., Salmon, W. J., and Sultan, R. G. *Problems in Marketing,* 4th ed. New York, McGraw-Hill, 1968.

6. Doehlert, D. H. "Similarity and Preference Mapping: A Color Example." In: R. L. King (ed.), *Marketing and the New Science of Planning* (Fall 1968), 250–258. Conference Proceedings. Series No. 28; Chicago, American Marketing Association, 1968.

7. Golby, C. "New Product Development." In: D. Pym (ed.), *Industrial Society,* 426–444. Baltimore, Penguin, 1968.

8. Green, P. E., and Carmone, F. J. "Advertising Perception and Evaluation: An Application of Multidimensional Scaling." Marketing Science Institute Working Paper (August 1968).

9. Green, P. E., and Carmone, F. J. "Multidimensional Scaling: An Introduction and Comparison of Nonmetric Unfolding Techniques," *Journal of Marketing Research,* Vol. 6, no. 3 (August 1969), 330–341.

10. Green, P. E., Carmone, F. J., and Robinson, P. J. *Analysis of Marketing Behavior Using Nonmetric Scaling and Related Techniques.* Philadelphia, Marketing Science Institute, 1968.

11. Green, P. E., Carmone, F. J., and Robinson, P. J. "Nonmetric Scaling Methods: An Exposition and Overview," *Wharton Quarterly,* Vol. 2 (Winter-Spring 1968), 28–41.

12. Green, P. E., Maheshwari, A., and Rao, V. R. "Dimensional Interpretation and Configuration Invariance in Multidimensional Scaling: An Empirical Study," *Multivariate Behavioral Research,* Vol. 4 (April 1969), 159–180.

13. Klahr, D. "A Monte-Carlo Investigation of the Statistical Significance of Kruskal's Nonmetric Scaling Procedure." Paper presented at the International Federation of Information Processing Congress, Edinburgh, 1968.

14. Klahr, D. "A Study of Consumers' Cognitive Structures for Cigarette Brands." Paper presented at the meeting of the Institute of Management Sciences, San Francisco, May 1968.

15. Krugman, H. E. "The Impact of Television Advertising: Learning Without Involvement," *Public Opinion Quarterly,* Vol. 29, no. 2 (Fall 1965), 349–356.

16 Kruskal, J. B. "Multidimensional Scaling by Optimizing Goodness of Fit to a Nonmetric Hypothesis," *Psychometrika,* Vol. 29, no. 1 (March 1964), 1–27.

17. Kruskal, J. B. "Nonmetric Multidimensional Scaling: A Numerical Example," *Psychometrika,* Vol. 29, no. 2 (June 1964), 115–129.

18. Kuehn, A. A., and Day, R. L. "Strategy of Product Quality," *Harvard Business Review,* Vol. 40, no. 6 (November–December 1962), 100–110.

19. Massy, W. F. "A Dynamic Model for Monitoring New Product Adoption." Stanford University Graduate School of Business Working Paper No. 95, March 1966.

20. Massy, W. F. "Stochastic Models for Monitoring New Product Introductions." In: [8], 85–111.

21. "Maxwell House Division." Harvard Business School Case M266. Also in: [10], 439–466.

22. Morgan, N., and Purnell, J. M. "Isolating Openings for New Products in a Multidimensional Space," *Journal of the Market Research Society,* Vol. 11, no. 3 (July 1969), 245–266.

23. Rothman, L. J. "Research for Ranges, Assortments, and Multi-Brand Manufacturers," *Commentary: Journal of the Market Research Society,* Vol. 9, no. 1 (January 1967), 1–11.

24. Stefflre, V. "Market Structure Studies: New Products for Old Markets and New Markets (Foreign) for Old Products." In: [8], 251–268.

25. Stefflre, V. "Simulation of People's Behavior Toward New Objects and Events," *American Behavioral Scientist,* Vol. 8, no. 9 (May 1965), 12–15.

1.5 Consumer Rankings of Risk Reduction Methods

TED ROSELIUS

Buyers often face the dilemma of wanting to purchase a product, and yet they hesitate to buy because it involves taking the risk of suffering some type of loss. When faced with this dilemma, the consumer is confronted with a variety of methods which could be used to reduce the risk of loss. For example, he could rely on his previous success with a brand, study published test results on the product, seek advice from friends, or try a free sample. Thus, the potential buyer can be as uncertain about the best method of reducing the risk as he is about whether to make the purchase. The marketer faces a similar dilemma. Little general information is available to him, for example, about whether buyers have more confidence in brand loyalty than they do in money-back guarantees or major brand image. In turn, public policy makers interested in consumer protection are concerned with creating a wider choice for consumers among the various methods of reducing the risk of a loss.

Since little is known about buyers' relative preferences for methods of reducing risk, the ability to choose from a large number of methods poses problems both for consumers and marketers. Consumer preferences for 11 different methods of reducing the risk associated with various types of loss are presented in this article.

Risk Reduction

When a buyer perceives risk in a purchase he could pursue one of four different strategies of risk resolution: (1) He could reduce perceived risk by either decreasing the probability that the purchase will fail, or by reducing the severity of real or imagined loss suffered if the purchase does fail; (2) he could shift from one type of perceived loss to one for which he has more tolerance; (3) he could postpone the purchase, in which case he would be shifting from one general risk type to another;[1] or (4) he could make the purchase and absorb the unresolved risk.

A risk reliever is a device or action, initiated by the buyer or seller, which is used to execute one of the first two strategies of risk resolution mentioned above. For instance, a buyer might rely on brand loyalty as a way of obtaining a higher probability of purchase success, or he might rely on a guarantee as a way of reducing the severity of money loss in case of purchase failure. Brand loyalty and guarantees are risk relievers; they are methods which relieve risk-related hesitancy to buy by serving as catalysts to facilitate the purchase. It is postulated that buyers have a set of many risk-relieving devices and actions ranging from most preferred to least preferred which they call upon as needed. Perception of risk causes the buyer to select whichever device appears to be best suited for the type of risk involved.

Following Bauer's suggestion to investigate the risk elements of buying,[2] several studies have been conducted on individual methods for relieving risk. While insights were gained about the single method of relief studied, it is difficult to place the results in a comparative perspective with other research. In other words, no reference point exists that shows the attitudinal relationship between, say, free samples and brand loyalty.[3] A researcher may spend valuable time studying a certain method of risk relief which has less significance than other methods would have had in the same situation. Moreover, the researcher may be puzzled by unexpected findings as Cunningham was when his study of "high risk spaghetti buyers" failed to support a hypothesis that had been confirmed by other groups in the study.[4]

The seller faces a trade-off between the cost of offering a risk reliever and the benefits of higher sales volume derived from reducing risk-related hesitancy to buy. The seller's problem is one of deciding which method, out of a wide variety of methods, will serve most effectively for relieving the specific risks his market segment perceives in his product.

The research reported here provides a context within which a wide variety of risk relievers can be viewed simultaneously. This perspective was achieved by having subjects evaluate 11 risk relievers on the basis of how helpful they are for reducing the threat of various kinds of loss; for example, whether guarantees are generally thought to be more helpful than other relievers for reducing the threat of money loss.

Methodology

Data were derived from responses of 472 housewives to a written questionnaire mailed to 1400 households in a commuter suburb of Denver, Colorado. The questionnaire presented several generalized, risky buying situations, each posing a constant threat of some kind of loss. To prevent introducing a product bias, and to make the findings as general as possible, the situations were not related to specific products or purchase methods.

Attitude toward various risk relievers was measured on a five-point scale, reflecting the housewives' opinion as to how helpful each reliever would be for reducing the risk posed in the situation. The scale was anchored at five positions as follows: almost always helpful, usually helpful, sometimes helpful, rarely helpful, almost never helpful.

Eleven methods of risk relief were selected on the basis of their representativeness, applicability to various methods of purchase, and applicability to kinds of products. All relievers were presented for each buying situation and were defined in the questionnaire as follows:

1. *Endorsements:* Buy the brand whose advertising has endorsements or testimonials from a person like you, from a celebrity, or from an expert on the product.

2. *Brand Loyalty:* Buy the brand you have used before and have been satisfied with in the past.
3. *Major Brand Image:* Buy a major, well-known brand of the product, and rely on reputation of the brand.
4. *Private Testing:* Buy whichever brand has been tested and approved by a private testing company.
5. *Store Image:*[5] Buy the brand that is carried by a store which you think is dependable, and rely on reputation of the store.
6. *Free Sample:* Use a free sample of the product on a trial basis before buying.
7. *Money-back Guarantee:*[6] Buy whichever brand offers a money-back guarantee with the product.
8. *Government Testing:* Buy the brand that has been tested and approved by an official branch of the government.
9. *Shopping:* Shop around on your own and compare product features on several brands in several stores.
10. *Expensive Model:*[7] Buy the most expensive and elaborate model of the product.
11. *Word of Mouth:*[8] Ask friends or family for advice about the product.

Attitude about the helpfulness of these 11 relievers was measured and analyzed across four kinds of loss selected to represent the ones which are widely different, easily explained, and commonly suffered. The losses were defined in the questionnaire as follows:

1. *Time Loss:* When some products fail, we waste time, convenience, and effort getting it adjusted, repaired, or replaced.
2. *Hazard Loss:* Some products are dangerous to our health or safety when they fail.
3. *Ego Loss:* Sometimes when we buy a product that turns out to be defective, we feel foolish, or other people make us feel foolish.
4. *Money Loss:* When some products fail, our loss is the money it takes to make the product work properly, or to replace it with a satisfactory product.

Items which respondents had rated on the scale can be ranked by using average scores or by using the gross percent of favorable response from the scales. However, the positive favorable response to an item can be highlighted by using a net percent favorable response. Thus, to rank relievers the number of unfavorable responses (rarely helpful and almost never helpful) was subtracted from the number of favorable responses (usually helpful and almost always helpful). The difference was divided by the total number of responses. The quotient, when multiplied by 100, yields a net percent of favorable response, which the author has labeled "net favorable percentage" (NFP).

The NFP has a continuous range from +100 to −100, reflecting a completely favorable and a completely unfavorable response. This range was divided into seven categories simply to provide qualitative terms which would be consistently descriptive of the general level of preference for using a reliever. (See Table 1.)

TABLE 1.   Qualitative Definition of Preference Level Based on NFP

Range of Net Favorable Percentage	Response is Defined as
+ 100.0 to + 71.5	Extremely Favorable
+ 71.4 to + 42.9	Very Favorable
+ 42.8 to + 14.3	Slightly Favorable
+ 14.2 to − 14.1	Neutral
− 14.2 to − 42.7	Slightly Unfavorable
− 42.8 to − 71.3	Very Unfavorable
− 71.4 to − 100.0	Extremely Unfavorable

The NFP statistic was used to rank the risk relievers for each of four kinds of loss. The rankings yielded by data from all respondents are presented in Table 2.

Findings

Buyer confidence in the helpfulness of each risk reliever provides insights in at least three areas: (1) It is helpful to compare relievers on the basis of the general level of confidence expressed about them; (2) an indication is provided about how well each kind of loss is covered by the relievers studied; and (3) individual relievers can be defined on the basis of the variety of situations to which they can be applied.

As indicated by the NFP values and the rankings of Table 2, brand loyalty and major brand image evoked the most consistently favorable response and were ranked one and two for all types of loss. A Chi-square analysis of the data indicated that response to brand loyalty was significantly more favorable than for all other relievers. Response to major brand image was significantly more favorable than for all relievers except brand loyalty.

Store image, shopping, free sample, word of mouth, and government testing generally evoked a "neutral" or "slightly favorable" response, for all categories but expected hazard loss. Chi-square analysis failed to indicate a consistent pattern of similarity or difference between these relievers.

Endorsements, money-back guarantees, and private testing typically evoked a "slightly unfavorable" response, or "neutral" at best. Chi-square analysis did not uncover a consistent pattern of difference between these relievers.

Buying the most expensive model to relieve risk was consistently the least favored strategy. Chi-square analysis indicated that this reliever evoked a response significantly less favorable than for any other reliever for all loss types.

Some of the risk relievers consistently were rated unfavorably by the respondents. These relievers can be considered to be expensive strategies for manufacturers to pursue. This indicates that a firm could benefit from a complete study of the effectiveness of those relievers that it is currently offering or advertising. Such a study might reveal that a firm may be able to offer equally effective, but less expensive strategies in the reduction of perceived risk.

TABLE 2.   Ranking of Risk Relievers for Four Kinds of Loss Based on Responses from All Buyers

Response Definition	Kind of Loss							
	Time Loss		Hazard Loss		Ego Loss		Money Loss	
	NFP*	Reliever	NFP*	Reliever	NFP*	Reliever	NFP*	Reliever
Extremely Favorable	90.2	Brand Loyalty[a]	92.5	Brand Loyalty	96.0	Brand Loyalty	98.0	Brand Loyalty
Very Favorable	44.1	Major Brand[a]	50.6	Major Brand	62.6	Major Brand	65.4	Major Brand
Slightly Favorable	21.5 19.4 16.3	Store Image Shopping Free Sample	34.4	Gov't. Testing	28.3 27.3 27.3	Store Image Free Sample Shopping	29.7 26.8 19.8	Store Image Free Sample Shopping
Neutral	12.9 − 5.4 − 7.4	Word of Mouth Gov't. Testing Endorsements	0.0 − 1.0 − 3.2 −14.0	Word of Mouth Store Image Shopping Private Test	4.0 − 7.0 − 8.1 − 8.1	Word of Mouth Gov't. Testing Endorsements Money Back Guar.	11.9 6.9 − 1.9 −12.9	Gov't. Testing Word of Mouth Money Back Guar. Endorsements
Slightly Unfavorable	−20.4 −24.7	Money Back Guar. Private Test	−17.2 −33.3	Free Sample Endorsements	−26.2	Private Test	−35.6	Private Test
Very Unfavorable	−65.6	Expensive Model[a]	−47.3	Money Back Guar.			−68.2	Expensive Model
Extremely Unfavorable			−79.5	Expensive Model	−75.8	Expensive Model		

*NFP = ((Number of favorable responses − number of unfavorable responses) ÷ total responses) × 100.

[a] A Chi-square analysis indicated that these findings are significant at the .05 level of confidence.

Relief of Various Loss Types

In general, subjects interpreted a variety of widely different relievers to be applicable for each kind of loss. This would indicate that buyers of products which evoke a certain kind of risk would usually have a variety of ways open to them for relieving their risk tensions. In particular, there is an indication that for time, ego, and money losses a reasonable variety of risk relievers would be available.

For hazard loss, however, choice among risk relievers is somewhat limited. Only three relievers (brand loyalty, major brand image, and government testing) evoked a response that was clearly favorable. Buying in a situation in which none of these three relievers is available would seem to be a fairly common experience, in which case the buyer is forced to absorb the perceived risk of loss if he cannot postpone the purchase.

Special Purpose Methods of Risk Relief

Some buyers were expected more likely to perceive risk in a purchasing situation than others. It was assumed that high perceivers of a loss might have had more or less faith in a particular reliever than did other buyers. To identify respondents who could be defined as high perceivers of each kind of loss, subjects were asked about the relative importance of each kind of loss suffered if a specific product type failed. A buying problem was posed, and answers were collected on a scale anchored at each of its five positions as follows: strongly agree, agree, neutral, disagree, strongly disagree. For instance, high perceivers of money loss were defined as those respondents who "strongly agreed" that there would be an important loss of money to them if the product failed.

In this way, 37.5% of the respondents were defined as high perceivers of time loss and 39.7% were defined as high perceivers of money loss. For hazard and ego loss, those buyers who "agreed" that there would be an important loss were also counted with those who "strongly agreed." For hazard loss, 38.4% of the respondents were defined as high perceivers and 18.1% were defined as high perceivers of ego loss. Some respondents were defined as high perceivers of more than one kind of loss.

High perceivers of risk presumably would have more interest in helpful risk relievers than would respondents who might be defined as medium or low perceivers. Therefore, the response of the high-risk perceivers was compared with that of all other respondents.

Table 3 presents rankings of relievers generated by data from the high-risk perceiver group alone. A Chi-square analysis was used to compare the responses of high-risk perceivers to each reliever across kinds of loss, and to compare their responses with those of all other buyers. Five risk relievers were found to have special meanings; i.e., there are certain relievers which could be defined as special-purpose risk relievers since they would have a different impact according to the buying situation, the kind of loss perceived, and the type of buyer involved.

TABLE 3. Ranking of Risk Relievers for Four Kinds of Loss Based on Response of High-Risk Perceivers

Response Definition	Kind of Loss							
	Time Loss		Hazard Loss		Ego Loss		Money Loss	
	NFP*	Reliever	NFP*	Reliever	NFP*	Reliever	NFP*	Reliever
Extremely Favorable	93.7	Brand Loyalty	89.1	Brand Loyalty	97.5	Brand Loyalty	97.7	Brand Loyalty
Very Favorable	43.7	Major Brand	51.4 43.2	Gov't. Testing Major Brand	62.5 57.5	Major Brand Free Sample	67.5 44.2	Major Brand Free Sample
Slightly Favorable	25.0 18.7 18.7	Word of Mouth Store Image Free Sample			32.5 25.0 22.5	Store Image Word of Mouth Shopping	32.6 25.6 25.6 23.3	Shopping Gov't. Testing Word of Mouth Store Image
Neutral	12.5 12.5 3.1	Gov't. Testing Shopping Endorsements	2.7 −2.7 −8.1 −8.1 −13.5	Private Testing Store Image Free Samples Word of Mouth Shopping	10.0 7.5 7.5 −10.0	Money Back Guar. Endorsements Gov't. Testing Private Testing	9.3 0.0	Money Back Guar. Endorsements
Slightly Unfavorable	−18.7 −28.1	Money Back Guar. Private Testing	−16.2 −40.6	Endorsements Money Back Guar.			−25.6	Private Testing
Very Unfavorable	−62.5	Expensive Model	−67.6	Expensive Model	−72.5	Expensive Model	−58.2	Expensive Model
Extremely Unfavorable								

*NFP = ((Number of favorable responses − number of unfavorable responses) ÷ total responses) × 100.

1. *Major Brand Image:* The high-perceiver group agreed with other buyers on the helpfulness of this reliever in all cases except for the threat of a hazard loss. Since the high-perceiver group rated this reliever significantly less favorably than did other buyers for a hazard loss, there is an indication that the seller of a product which evokes a threat of hazard loss would find that the buyers for whom the hazard loss is most threatening would put less confidence in brand image than would other buyers.

2. *Store Image:* The high-perceiver group felt this reliever to be equally helpful for all losses. However, other buyers expressed a significantly more favorable response toward store image when it was applied to a threatened money loss than they did for other loss types.

    In addition, other buyers did not express as much confidence in the helpfulness of this reliever when applied to a potential time loss. Buyers prone to perceive time loss expressed a significantly less favorable attitude toward store image as a way of relieving threatened time loss than other buyers.

3. *Free Sample:* When buyers who were prone to perceive risk compared this reliever across kinds of loss, they felt free samples to be equally helpful for relieving threats of time and money loss. However, they rated free samples significantly more helpful for relief of ego loss and significantly less helpful for relief of hazard loss.

    High perceivers of risk agreed with other buyers on the helpfulness of free samples, except in the case of a threatened ego loss. High perceivers of ego loss expressed more faith in free samples than did other buyers.

4. *Word of Mouth:* The high-perceiver group felt this reliever to be equally helpful for all kinds of loss except threats of hazard loss. Word of mouth was thought to be significantly less helpful when the threat was of a hazard loss than for other losses.

    High perceivers agreed with other buyers on the helpfulness of word of mouth, if it is used to relieve time and hazard loss. However, buyers prone to perceive ego or money loss felt this reliever to be more helpful than did other buyers.

5. *Government Testing:* The high-perceiver group felt this reliever to be equally helpful for all losses. However, when other buyers compared this reliever across kinds of loss, they indicated government testing to be significantly more helpful for relief of hazard loss than for other loss types.

    The high-perceiver group agreed with other buyers on the helpfulness of the reliever, except in the case of money loss. High perceivers of money loss felt this method of relief to be more helpful than did other buyers.

The above relievers have special meanings, indicating that they would be especially appropriate for a particular type of buyer such as a high-risk perceiver, and also for particular types of loss. Thus, there is an indication that when a manufacturer relies upon any one of these five methods of risk reduction, he should do so with careful thought given to the kind of loss perceived in his product and the relative impact on high versus low perceivers of risk. This would be especially important if subsequent research indicated that the very act of stressing a risk reliever, such as a guarantee, causes some buyers to perceive risk in the purchase.

General Purpose Methods of Risk Relief

The remaining relievers (brand loyalty, private testing, shopping, endorsements, expensive models, and money-back guarantees) did not evoke a significantly different response when each was compared across kinds of loss. Furthermore, there was not a significant difference in response between high perceivers and other buyers with respect to the helpfulness of these relievers for any kind of loss. Therefore, these six relievers have been defined as general-purpose risk relievers. The indication is that if a seller relied on one of these relievers as a method of reducing risk-related hesitancy to buy, he would expect the reliever to have the same impact on those buyers who perceived a greater amount of risk in the purchase as it had on other buyers. These relievers may also be equally effective, or ineffective, regardless of the kind of loss perceived.

Summary

Some relievers may receive a higher or lower rank if associated with certain methods of purchase or with certain types of products, although this question was beyond the scope of this study. However, the results here indicate that buyers generally favor some risk relievers and are relatively unimpressed with others. More important, it was found that buyers prefer some relievers to others depending upon the kind of loss involved, and that the attitude toward relievers can differ between different types of buyers.

Perhaps a seller should first determine the kind of risk perceived by his customers and then create a mix of risk relievers suited for his combination of buyer type and loss type. For example, the fact that endorsements and guarantees evoked a generally unfavorable response indicates that sellers may presently be promoting risk relievers which do not provide any effective reduction in perceived risk for many of their potential customers.

Buyers have preferences which extend over a wide variety of methods of relief. This finding supports the statement that, generally, buyers have a choice open to them for reducing perceived risk. It is also clear from the rankings of the risk relievers that there is a danger of misdirecting research efforts if they were focused on relatively insignificant methods of risk relief—methods which have a neutral or unfavorable meaning to many potential buyers. Thus, future research on risk relief should include a variety of methods for risk reduction, rather than study individual risk relievers in isolation from others.

The makers of public policy relative to consumer protection might consider the findings of this study which have indicated that out of the three relievers that evoked confidence for relieving hazard loss, two of them—brand loyalty and major brand image—probably reduced perceived risk rather than *actual* risk of loss. Perhaps future research should be focused on designing another type of reliever of hazard loss before government testing, the other favored reliever, becomes mandatory on a wider scale.

Notes and References

1. D. T. Popielarz, "An Exploration of Perceived Risk and Willingness to Try New Products," *Journal of Marketing Research,* Vol. IV (November 1967), 368–372.

2. R. A. Bauer, "Consumer Behavior as Risk Taking," in *Dynamic Marketing For a Changing World*, R. S. Hancock, ed. (Chicago, Illinois: American Marketing Association, June 1960), 389–398.

3. This question is also explained in J. N. Sheth and M. Venkatesan, "Risk Reduction Processes in Consumer Behavior," *Journal of Marketing Research*, Vol. V (August 1968), 307–310.

4. S. M. Cunningham, "Perceived Risk as a Factor in the Diffusion of New Product Information," in *Science, Technology, and Marketing*, R. M. Haas, ed. (Chicago, Illinois: American Marketing Association, September 1966), 698–721.

5. Store image and price-quality differences both were discussed recently in J. E. Stafford and B. M. Enis, "The Price-Quality Relationship: An Extension," *Journal of Marketing Research*, Vol. VI (November 1969), 456–458.

6. J. G. Udell and E. E. Anderson, "The Product Warranty as an Element of Competitive Strategy," *Journal of Marketing*, Vol. 32 (October 1968), 1–8.

7. Same reference as footnote 5.

8. Johan Arndt, "The Role of Product-Related Conversations in the Diffusion of a New Product," *Journal of Marketing Research*, Vol. IV (August 1967), 291–295.

1.6 Attribution Theory and Consumer Behavior
ROBERT B. SETTLE

Attribution theory states that the individual will attribute observable events in his environment to underlying causes on the basis of covariance of cause and effect. An effect is attributed to a cause that is present when the effect is observed and absent when the effect is not observed. By attributing effects to causes, the person is able to obtain a stable and meaningful picture of the world around him. If a given effect consistently appears in the presence of a possible cause and never appears in the absence of that particular cause, the individual should be relatively confident that this is the single causal agent. The more frequently the effect is associated with other possible causes, or the less consistent the relationship, the less confident the individual should be that he has identified the unique cause of the effect.

As an example of this principle, assume that the effect to be considered is a remark by another person that a certain movie is very poor. The person receiving this information must now evaluate this effect and its implications for his own behavior. If the process used for this evaluation is the assessment of covariation, as attribution theory suggests, the person might proceed in the following way:

Two possible causes for this effect might be considered. The other person may dislike all kinds of movies, or the movie may be such that it is disliked by all kinds of people. The person making the attribution would then look at the variation in the other person's remarks about other movies and also at the variation in other persons' remarks about this particular movie. If he learns that this person rates all movies as poor, while others rate this movie as good or fair, he would attribute the effect to this person's dislike of movies. If, on the other hand, he finds that this person rates some other movies as good or fair, and if he learns that all other persons rate this movie as poor, he would attribute the effect (the poor rating for this movie by this person) to the movie itself, rather than to the person.

Attribution theory stipulates that the degree of confidence of the individual making the attribution will be a function of the degree of consistency of the relationship between cause and effect. Two experiments were performed, to test the principle of attribution on the basis of covariance and the relationship between consistency and confidence, and to measure the applicability of the theory to consumer information processing and behavior. In the first experiment, Settle, Faricy, and Warren (1971) randomly assigned 90 student subjects (S's) to either one or the other of two groups (conditions). The basic design for presenting the information to the S's and obtaining the responses is presented in Table 1.

TABLE 1.   Design for Presentation of Data Base and Collection of Subjects' Response

Movies	People			
	Alan	Bill	Chet	Dale
	Condition I, Experiments 1 and 2			
Karelia	good	good	good	——
Laconia	fair	fair	fair	——
Mantula	poor	poor	poor	——
Namanga	——	——	——	
	Condition II, Experiments 1 and 2			
Karelia	good	fair	poor	——
Laconia	good	fair	poor	——
Mantula	good	fair	poor	——
Namanga	——	——	——	
	Condition III, Experiment 2 only			
Karelia	good	fair	poor	——
Laconia	fair	fair	fair	——
Mantula	poor	fair	good	——
Namanga	——	——	——	

The S's were given a pack of cards consisting of nine information cards with such statements as, "Alan rated the movie 'Karelia' as *good*," and six question cards, each with two questions, such as, "How do you think Dale will rate the movie 'Karelia'?" and "How certain are you that he will rate the movie that way?" If the S's attributed the effects (the ratings) to the causes (either people or movies) on the basis of covariance as predicted by attribution theory, a given effect should be relatively easy to estimate in the presence of a cause and relatively difficult in the absence of the cause, and these differences should be reflected in the confidence ratings of the S's. In Condition I, for example, if the ratings are attributed to the movies, as expected, the S's should be very confident of their estimates of Dale's ratings, but not for their estimates for the movie "Namanga." The converse would be true for Condition II.

Analysis of variance in mean confidence ratings for high and low consistency treatments indicated that the ratings were significantly higher for high consistency treatments than for low. These results supported the hypothesis that attributions are made on the basis of covariance of cause and effect. While the principles of attribution theory were supported by the study, there appeared to be some question as to whether the S's were actually using the entire data matrix in making an attribution, or simply ordering the data by row or by column and making an estimate by extrapolation.

A second experiment was designed and conducted to determine if the entire data-base matrix was used by the S's to make an attribution of the effect (the ratings) to a cause (either people or movies) (Settle, 1972). The same basic design was employed; however, a third condition was included, as depicted in the lower portion of Table 1. In Condition I, all variance in the information data was between movies, and in Condition II all variance was between raters. In the third condition, there was variance between both movies and raters. It should be noted that the first column and the second row of Condition I are identical to those of Condition III, and that the first row and the second column of Condition II are also identical to those of Condition III.

Comparisons of mean confidence ratings for identical rows or columns, between Condition III and the first two conditions, constituted a test of whether or not the entire data matrix was being used. That is, if only the row or column were used by the S's, ratings should not prove to be significantly different between conditions. If, however, the entire matrix was employed, the differences in the entire matrix would lead to significant differences between identical rows or columns. Analysis of variance in mean confidence ratings indicated significant differences did exist for some such comparisons. These results provide tentative support for the hypothesis that the S's make attributions on the basis of the entire data base matrix.

Attribution and Promotion

Attribution theory states that the individual will attribute observable events to their underlying causes on the basis of covariation of cause and effect. A persuasive message, such as an advertisement, can be regarded as an observable effect by the members of the audience. Principal among the causes to which it might be attributed are (a) the desire of the advertiser to sell his brand of product, or (b) the actual characteristics of the brand being advertised. If the brand is always lauded in every respect by this particular advertiser, and if the message content does not vary over product characteristics, the effect can be seen to covary with the advertiser and would be attributed to the desire to sell his brand of product. If, however, the advertiser claimed that his brand was superior in some respects, although not in others, the effect (the message) can be seen to covary with the characteristics, rather than only with the advertisers.

The message would be attributed to the actual characteristics of the brand, leading to the higher degree of certainty about claims and an increased probability of purchase.

An experiment by Settle and Golden (1972) was designed to measure the effect on credibility of variation in product claims. A three-part questionnaire was designed, pretested, and administered to 120 S's. Each contained five mock advertisements, and below the illustration and copy block of each ad there appeared this sentence: "The (brand name) has been tested against the current leading seller in its price class and compared as follows." Below were listed five product characteristics, three of which were thought to be relatively important to the consumer and two of which were not. To the right of the list were two columns, one labeled with the name of the brand being advertised, and the other labeled Brand X. A check mark indicated superiority for one of the two brands for each product characteristic.

All of the advertisements for each product were identical except for one feature, which constituted the experimental manipulation. Half of the ads for each product claimed superiority for the advertised brand on *all five* product features mentioned, while the other half claimed superiority for *only three* of the five. In the latter group, superiority was disclaimed for two features.

Preceding each ad in the questionnaire, there was a page instructing the subjects to rate the importance of the product characteristics which were to be included in the ad. Following each mock ad was a page containing five questions: "Please indicate how confident you are that the (product characteristic) of the (brand name) is superior to that of the leading seller, Brand X."

Two dependent variables were analyzed. First, the mean confidence ratings for the three product characteristics claimed superior in both conditions were tested for significant differences between conditions. Secondly, the confidence ratings were multiplied by the corresponding importance rating for each product claim, to yield a total expected value for each advertisement. These total expected values were tested for significant differences between conditions.

The results of the experiment indicated that (1) product claims that vary over product characteristics will result in higher confidence ratings for the characteristics claimed to be superior than will claims which do not vary over characteristics; (2) product claims that vary over product characteristics result in total expectancy values approximately equal to those resulting from claims which do not vary over characteristics. In general, the results support the attribution theory principle that effects are attributed to causes on the basis of covariance. The study implies that other configurations of product claims and variation may yield a positive net increase in expectancy value. At least, the study suggests that it would be better for the advertiser to disclaim at least one feature of minor importance than to exclude it from the message entirely. It may prove that one disclaimed product feature would provide enough variation to significantly improve confidence and total expectancy.

Attribution and Information Dependence

The experiments described above indicate that the consumer tends to attribute product information to possible underlying causes, however little is known about the manner in which the consumer subjectively validates the attributions he or she makes. Kelley (1967, p. 197) has identified four criteria used by the individual to validate attributions:

1. *Distinctiveness:* the impression is attributed to the thing if it uniquely occurs when the thing is present and does not occur in its absence.
2. *Consistency over time:* each time the thing is present, the individual's reactions must be the same or nearly so.
3. *Consistency over modality:* his reactions must be consistent even though his mode of interaction with the thing varies.
4. *Consensus:* attributes of external origin are experienced the same way by all observers.

An experimental study was designed to focus on the need for two of these types of information: consistency and consensus (Settle, 1972). Consistency and consensus information were thought to be related to product characteristics. One method of relating the conditions of information dependence and the characteristics of the information sources to products is to classify products so that the conditions of purchase and use are similar within each class. Four product "dimensions" were considered in the study: complexity, social visibility, durability, and multipurpose. These dimensions were hypothesized to be systematically related to information from an expert, information from a close friend, direct personal experience over time, and direct personal experience over modality (ways of interacting or using the product), respectively.

Testing the hypotheses required measurement of the association between the four product classes and the four information sources in terms of the assurance obtained by consumers. A questionnaire containing 96 combinations of 24 products and four information sources was administered to 30 young married women. The products were selected on the basis of five judges' agreement on their status, so that each pair was contrasted on one of the four dimensions and matched on the others. Three pairs contrasted on each dimension were retained. S's were asked to indicate their confidence in a "good" choice for each product, given each information source.

When the data for all four information sources were compiled, the ratings for the product judged low on the contrasted dimension were subtracted from the ratings on the companion product which was judged high on that dimension. This procedure yields difference scores, analogous to scores obtained in the measurement of attitude change. Any "change" can be related to the "treatment" used to obtain it. The treatments in this experiment consisted of the association with a particular information source, and analysis of variance was used to determine the significance of differences in mean scores.

The product pairs contrasted on each dimension, together with their difference scores for the four information sources, are shown in Table 2. The analysis of variance revealed no significant main effects for sources, dimensions, or pairs within dimensions, nor did the design anticipate such main effects. Support of the hypotheses required strong interaction between product dimensions and information sources. This interaction proved to be significant, and the planned comparisons between high-effect and low-effect information

TABLE 2.   Difference Scores

| Product Pairs | Information Sources | | | |
| | Consensus | | Consistency | |
	Expert	Similar	Time	Modality
Products Contrasted on Complexity				
Stereo tuner Living-room chair	+ 1.43	− 0.13	− 0.43	− 0.70
Wristwatch Gold bracelet	+ 0.47	− 0.23	− 0.83	− 0.67
Fondue cooker Serving dish	+ 0.17	− 0.53	− 0.03	− 0.60
Products Contrasted on Visibility				
Skirt Pajamas	− 0.07	+ 0.73	− 0.07	+ 0.27
Cardigan sweater Bathrobe	+ 0.27	+ 0.93	− 0.23	− 0.20
Silverware Cookware	− 0.47	+ 0.13	− 0.30	− 0.27
Products Contrasted on Durability				
Earrings Perfume	+ 0.57	+ 0.13	+ 0.30	+ 0.30
Stereo album Concert tickets	− 1.13	− 0.13	+ 0.70	+ 0.20
Electric hair rollers Salon hair styling	+ 1.07	− 0.20	+ 0.43	− 0.40
Products Contrasted on Multipurpose				
Household detergent Dish detergent	− 0.10	− 0.10	− 0.27	+ 0.47
Electric blender Electric can opener	+ 0.37	+ 0.02	+ 0.47	+ 0.47
Oven toaster Popcorn popper	− 0.33	− 0.07	0.00	+ 0.60

sources for each product dimension indicated significant differences in every case. These results supported the hypotheses.

This experiment indicated that the conditions of a product's purchase and use, reflected in the classification of products according to their status on the four dimensions, are systematically related to the information sources used to validate attributions about the product. For complex products it appears that the consumer is attempting to interpret physical objective reality, and for socially visible products she is attempting to interpret social reality.

Attributional Validation and Personality

The experiment reported above focused on the effects of product differences on preferences for objective versus social information, while ignoring interpersonal differences. It is interesting to note, however, that there were main effects of subjects, indicating that S's did respond in a systematically different manner to the information sources. A study by Settle and Mizerski (1972) was designed to explore more fully these individual differences.

A pair of printed advertisements was produced for each of five products: an automobile, men's clothes, women's clothes, a diamond, and a mouthwash. For each pair, illustrations were the same; however, one ad contained copy which interpreted objective reality (physical or chemical product features), and the other ad contained copy which interpreted social reality (reactions of others toward the product). A questionnaire was constructed which contained (1) The I-O Social Preference Scale (W. Kassarjian, 1962) [see Chapter 2 for a discussion of this concept], (2) five advertisements of either the objective or the social type, and (3) a series of questions following each ad. One question asked, "Based on the information presented in the advertisement, how suitable do you think this brand would be to your own needs and preferences?" A second question asked, "Would you prefer to have additional information on. . . ." The latter question was followed in each case with five pairs of product features, one of which was related to objective features and the other to social features.

The results of this study indicated that preference for objective or social-type advertisements and information was systematically related to the inner-directedness or other-directedness of the subject. The experiment appears to support the hypothesis that attributional information dependence is in part a function of individual personality, as well as the characteristics of the product.

A second experiment dealing with personality and attributional information dependence was conducted by Settle and Carr (1972). In a design similar to that employed above, 66 subjects were scaled on three personality factors: misanthropy (Sullivan and Adelson, 1954), trustworthiness, and variability in human nature (Wrightsman, 1964). The misanthropy construct is a variant of ethnocentrism, with references to minorities in the items replaced by general terms such as "most people." Trustworthiness refers to the extent to which people are seen as moral, honest, and reliable. Variability is the extent to which the person views individuals to be different in basic nature and changeable in nature.

Five pairs of advertisements were prepared for visual presentation in color, and one of each pair presented *direct information* concerning the topic of the ad, while the other contained implicit or explicit *endorsement*. Half of the S's were exposed to each treatment, and all were asked to rate the suitability of the product for *their own* needs and preferences, as well as for those of the *general public.*

Responsiveness to direct versus endorsed information, in terms of their own needs, proved to be in part a function of the S's status in the three personality dimensions. In general, the higher the "trust" scores and the lower the "variability" and the "misanthropy" scores, the more responsive the S's were to the endorsed messages. Response in terms of public suitability showed a similar but much weaker relationship to personality.

The endorsed versus direct treatments used in this study are roughly analogous to the "expert" versus "similar other" sources of information in the *consensus* validation mode referred to earlier. Again, the conclusions from the study indicate that attributional validation and information-source preference are functions of both personality and product characteristics. The previous three experiments provide evidence that these factors can be scaled and measured for their effect on attributional information preference.

Internal-External Locus of Control

The studies cited above indicate that attributions are affected by personality. There is considerable evidence that personality is affected by attributions as well. Some people consistently tend to attribute the things that happen to them during life to causes that are within their own control, such as their own effort, preparation, or skill. Others tend to attribute their outcomes in life to factors beyond their control, such as luck, chance, or strong forces which they can not counteract. The first group perceives an "internal" locus of control, while the second perceives an "external" locus.

It appears that these patterns of attribution can be taught to the child during the development and socialization process. They may be modified or reinforced by personal experience throughout the life of the individual. Phares (1955) did early exploration of locus of control as a generalized personality variable. It was hypothesized that individual perceptions of locus would be generalized to a wide variety of situations and internalized to systematic patterns of attribution. In this research, the concept is viewed as a pervasive and stable personality characteristic which is applicable in a wide variety of circumstances. Battle and Rotter (1963) discovered that locus of control and race were related among black and white children. A study of prison inmates (Lefcourt and Ladwig, 1965) also showed blacks higher on externality than were whites. Lefcourt (1966) concluded ". . . groups whose social position is one of minimal power either by class or race tend to score higher in the external control direction. . . ."

Assume that a white person enters a store to make a purchase, and conducts himself in a hostile manner. He might observe that he received poor service. If, on the next occasion, he conducts himself in a friendly, cordial manner and receives good service, he might observe the covariance between his behavior and the outcomes. But his behavior is under his control, and consequently he perceives the outcomes as under his (internal) control. If, in another example, a black person attempts to make a purchase under both of these same behavioral circumstances, and observes that he receives poor service in both cases, and if in addition he perceives some variance in the quality of service between blacks and whites, he might attribute the outcomes to variance in race. But race is beyond individual control, and consequently the black would become more external in his perceptions of locus of control. Multiply these effects by the thousands of outcomes obtained in daily activity and one can see the likelihood of a generalized pattern of attributions.

Settle, Faricy, and Mizerski (1971) reported a study of consumer locus of control, with these objectives: (1) to measure the degree to which the I-E construct is applicable to marketing, (2) to examine the correlations between perceived locus for marketing effects and those for more general effects, and (3) to test for systematically different perceptions of locus by race, social class, and sex. A consumer I-E scale was constructed, tested, revised, and administered to 162 ninth and tenth grade high school students from an integrated school located in a rural southern community. Each of the 16 items in the scale consisted of a purchase outcome and a choice of two possible causes, one internal and one external. The instrument was balanced on high versus low value outcome, male versus female example, positive versus negative outcome, and internal versus external cause (listed first). A sample item would be as follows:

> Mrs. Miller bought a sweater from a discount store. When she got home and tried it on, it didn't fit very well. The store would not take it back and return her money. If this had happened to you, how would you explain it?
>
> ———You should have checked on return privileges before buying.
>
> ———The store should always tell the customer if the item can't be returned.

In addition to the consumer locus of control scores, a subscale of the Rotter (1966) I-E scale was employed to obtain a measure of general locus, and the S's race, social class, and sex was also recorded. The correlation matrix for the five variables is shown in Table 3.

TABLE 3.   Five-Variable Correlation Matrix[a]

Variable	1	2	3	4	5
1) Consumer locus	1.000	0.405	0.110	0.290	0.537
2) General locus		1.000	0.130	0.167	0.304
3) Sex			1.000	0.118	0.112
4) Social class				1.000	0.346
5) Race					1.000

[a]N = 162

The study indicates that the internal-external locus of control construct is applicable to marketing and consumer behavior, and that there is a significant relationship between general locus and consumer locus of control. It also revealed that blacks are significantly more external than whites for both general and consumer locus of control. Sex and social class did not manifest systematically different locus scores. In earlier studies, sex demonstrated strong differences only in relation to items prone to "socially desirable" responses, and the measure of social class in this study was probably too crude to permit a sensitive measure.

Further analysis of the data indicated that differences in locus between blacks and whites were due almost entirely to attributions of negative outcomes. Blacks tended to attribute negative outcomes to external factors much more often than did whites.

The results of this study, based on junior high school students with little actual market experience, indicates that locus of control is probably in part the result of what the child is taught within the ethnic environment. Ethnic and racial minorities would not be expected to change their patterns of attribution or the behavior patterns based on them suddenly and abruptly, even though the actual marketing and environmental factors were changed or improved. Basic changes in attributional patterns may require one or more generations to be complete.

Internal-External Cue Sensitivity

It has been suggested that some persons may learn to attribute a set of internal cues to one particular "cause" and act accordingly, while others learn to attribute an entirely different set of largely external cues to the same cause, and consequently to exhibit the same behavior. Expressed in terms of labeling, one group may label as "hunger" such internal cues as contractions of the stomach, while another group may label as "hunger" such external factors as the smell of food. Eating behavior would then be the result of sensitivity to different cues for the two groups. Such differentials in cue sensitivity and attributional patterns are not confined to hunger and eating behavior, but have been reported in relation to such diverse concepts as emotion and the interpretation of psychological states.

However, the research on obesity and eating behavior appears to be most germane to marketing and consumer behavior. Studies by Schachter and Gross (1968) and by Nisbett (1968) indicate that obese persons are more sensitive to external cues to eating behavior than are persons of normal weight [see Chapter 2]. The results of this and other such studies of eating behavior indicate the pervasive and fundamental influence on behavior which might result from differences in sensitivity to internal and external cues. It appears that widely different patterns of cues might be attributed to the same cause, and result in similar behavior, depending on the training and experience of the individual.

Summary and Conclusions

The research findings relating attribution theory to consumer behavior can be summarized in the following statements:

1. *Within a given situation,* an observable effect will be attributed to a possible cause on the basis of the covariance of cause and effect.
2. The "information" contained in a persuasive message will be attributed to a cause, importantly affecting the credibility of the source.
3. The consumers' preference for a source of information used to validate an attribution of product value will depend on the characteristics of the product under consideration.
4. Preferences for objective versus social validating information will depend on the personality of the individual consumer.
5. Internal or external patterns of attribution are internalized as a *personality factor,* and subsequently generalized to apply to a wide variety of activity, including consumer behavior.
6. Internal or external patterns of cues or effects are attributed to the same underlying "cause," depending on the experience and training of the individual.

Attribution theory permits the marketer to relate the countless stimuli which invade the senses of the consumer to an extensive repertoire of actions through an understanding of the cognitive processes of the individual.

The attribution process can be viewed at three different levels within the consumer. At the *situational* level, analysis of consumers' perceptions of the covariance of cause and effect can shed light on the meaning the individual obtains from his environment, and the probability of various types of behavior.

At the *personality* level, measurement of locus of control can explain consumer reactions in the market, and inspection of other personality factors can be used to predict information source and content preferences.

At the *sensitivity* level, the consumers' propensity to manifest a particular form of behavior can be explored in the light of previous training and experience.

To date, the research devoted to the attribution process has been confined almost entirely to experimentation in the laboratory, with all its limitations of external validity and generality. Despite the narrow scope and relatively sparse topic content, the findings are encouraging. There appears to be promise for extensive applications of attribution theory to the study of consumer behavior.

References

Battle, E. S., and J. B. Rotter. "Children's Feelings of Personal Control as Related to Social Class and Ethnic Group." *Journal of Personality*, Vol. 31 (1963), 482–490.

Kassarjian, W. M. "A Study of Riesman's Theory of Social Character." *Sociometry*, Vol. 25 (Sept. 1962), 213–230.

Kelley, H. H. "Attribution Theory in Social Psychology." In D. Levine (ed.), *Nebraska Symposium on Motivation*. University of Nebraska Press, 1967.

Lefcourt, H. M., and G. W. Ladwig. "The American Negro: a Problem in Expectancies." *Journal of Personality and Social Psychology*, Vol. 1 (1965), 377–380.

———. "Internal Versus External Control of Reinforcement." *Psychological Bulletin*, Vol. 65, No. 4 (1966), 206–220.

Nisbett, R. E. "Taste, Deprivation, and Weight Determinants of Eating Behavior." *Journal of Personality and Social Psychology*, Vol. 10 (1968), 107–116.

Phares, E. J. *Changes in Expectancy in Skill and Chance Situations*. Unpub. Ph.D. Dissertation, Ohio State Univ., 1955.

Rotter, J. B. "Generalized Expectancies for Internal Versus External Control of Reinforcement." *Psychological Monographs*, American Psychological Association, Vol. 80, No. 1, 1966.

Schachter, S., and L. Gross. "Manipulated Time and Eating Behavior." *Journal of Personality and Social Psychology*, Vol. 10 (1968), 98–106.

Settle, R. B. "The Effect of Information Consistency on the Direction and Confidence of Attributions." Paper presented to the 80th Annual Convention, APA, 1972[a].

————. "Attribution Theory and Acceptance of Information." *Journal of Marketing Research,* Vol. 9 (Feb. 1972[b]), 85–88.

————, and H. L. Carr. "Personality Factors Affecting Attributional Validation." Unpub. paper, Research in Marketing, Univ. of Florida, 1972.

————, and L. L. Golden. "Attributional Confidence and Advertising Claim Consistency," Unpub. paper, Research in Marketing, Univ. of Florida, 1972.

————, and R. W. Mizerski. "Objective Versus Social Reality and Inner/Other Directedness." Unpub. paper, Research in Marketing, Univ. of Florida, 1972.

————, J. H. Faricy, and R. W. Mizerski, "Racial Differences in Consumer Locus of Control." In F. C. Allvine (ed.), *American Marketing Association Combined Conference Proceedings* (Spring and Fall 1971), 629–633.

————, ————, and G. T. Warren. "Consumer Information Processing: Attributing Effects to Causes." In D. M. Gardner (ed.), *Proceedings, 2nd Annual Conference, Association for Consumer Research* (1971), 278–288.

Sullivan, P., and J. Adelson. "Ethnocentrism and Misanthropy." *Journal of Abnormal and Social Psychology,* Vol. 49, 1954.

Wrightsman, L. "Measurement of Philosophies of Human Nature." *Psychological Reports,* Vol. 14, 1964.

1.7 Learning and Consumer Behavior
JOHN A. HOWARD

Common sense suggests the importance of learning[1] in buyer behavior. The increasing volume of industrial research and the consequent new products place demands on the buyer to adapt. Even with given product offerings, changes in such dimensions as price, advertising, and availability require learning. There is very limited evidence, however, of learning theory's being applied in marketing, except for the stochastic learning models discussed below.[2]

Learning theory is an area of psychology with a solid experimental base in laboratory situations involving humans as well as animals. Moreover, much of the whole field of experimental psychology can be subsumed under learning theory, as we do here. In recent years, this body of knowledge about physical, or primary, needs has been extended to the more complex social needs.[3] These extensions are probably very relevant for marketing purposes, although this remains to be shown in a systematic way.

It is important for the marketing specialist to see what possible applications might ultimately take place, even though long in appearing, since his own fundamental research can contribute to these applications. Thus, I have deliberately adopted the policy of citing the most concrete illustrations. The reader, however, must not be misled. Fundamental research must show which, if any, of the following examples cited of potential applications to marketing really are conclusive. Many qualifying issues will not be raised. For an appreciation of the intervening research steps required for direct application to marketing, the reader may consult the standard psychological references, which, of course, do not deal at all with marketing problems (Hilgard, 1956; Hull, 1943, 1951, 1952; Spence, 1956).

The theory's usefulness is not confined to simple learning situations, as we shall see when we move to the more complex conditions.[4] This relevance to social situations is important, because there is evidence that social influences affect buying behavior. Also, it is sometimes alleged that stimulus response-theory is not applicable to purchasing, since physical needs are soon satiated and in the market this satiation is not observed.[5] This view ignores the role of learned needs; for example, all of us, to a greater or lesser extent, learn the drive of social status, which is probably never satiated. . . .

There are three general streams of development in learning theory: a stimulus-response formulation holding only that temporal contiguity of the two elements—stimulus and response—is necessary for learning, a stimulus-response formulation emphasizing reinforcement as a necessary condition, and various cognitive theories. Let us look now at stimulus-response reinforcement theory and, a more recent development in psychology, the application of stochastic models. I emphasize stimulus-response reinforcement theory because of its much greater representation in current research.[6] In addition, it is the most fully worked out theoretical system in psychology, a number of developments suggest that it can be extended to the most complex kinds of behavior, it can probably be integrated with cognitive psychology, which should strengthen both, and the few applications that have been made of the stochastic learning models suggest the importance of learning in many buying situations. . . .

Stimulus-Response Theory

Four central concepts make up the basic theory: *drive* or need, *response, cue,* and *reinforcement.* Drives are strong stimuli which impel action, and are of two kinds: *innate* and *learned.* The first, earlier referred to as "physical" and "primary," are such basic drives as hunger, thirst, pain, cold, and sex. They are physiological. The second, emphasized by the conditions of society such as the drive for social status, are acquired on the basis of innate drives, represent elaborations of them, and serve as a façade behind which the functions of the underlying innate drives are hidden.

Drives impel responses, but cues determine when, where, and how the subject will respond. Cues are what we usually call stimuli, but they are, technically, weak stimuli. Strong stimuli are drives. Here we must distinguish between a cue and a *goal object*. The goal object is the thing being desired (e.g., a brand), and will later be referred to as the *incentive*. The product itself could serve as a cue, such as to a woman walking through a supermarket, but perhaps more often the cue would be something else. Presumably, advertising is often the cue.

What does psychology tell us about the nature of cues? A *change* in an external source of stimulation is a more distinctive cue than is the *absolute* value of that source; for instance, a person is much more likely to note a change in intensity of light than to identify a given level of intensity. Changes, differences, and the direction and size of differences can all serve as cues. Finally, a specific combination of stimuli, called *patterning*, can be a cue. A strong stimulus of either external or internal origin can serve as both a drive and a cue. A light of low intensity, for example, may be the cue for such responses as starting or stopping a car. If the intensity of the light is greatly increased, it becomes painful to our eyes, and thus acquires drive properties.

A response, roughly, is an organism's reaction to a cue. Under responses are grouped a wide range of events, extending from the slight movement of isolated muscle groups to such complex activity as speaking, that is, verbal behavior. A basic problem in learning is to obtain the appropriate response initially, so that it can be rewarded. If the response occurs only infrequently, it is difficult to find an occasion when it occurs and can be rewarded. There are a number of ways in which the response to be connected to a given cue may first be elicited so as to develop a new habit. Eliciting this first response is the key element in many marketing problems, for example, creating a new product or a new market for an existing product. Later, in connection with the concept of generalization, I shall discuss this problem of responses to new objects.

Responses may be arranged in the order of their initial probability of occurrence, which is called the *initial hierarchy of responses*. Learning changes the order of the responses in the hierarchy, and the new one is called the *resultant hierarchy*.

Any event that strengthens the tendency for a response to be repeated is called a *reinforcement*. In common-sense terms, it is a reward. Reinforcement is a process in which the acquisition of a reward or goal object leads frequently to *drive-reduction*. What is reinforced is the tendency to make a particular response in the future to the cue or cues which immediately preceded it. Put another way, what is learned is the *cue-response* association.

Psychologists tend to prefer the term *incentive* to *goal object* or *reward*. The incentive is assumed to bring about reinforcement because it reduces the drive. Reinforcement may be innate—such as food's satisfying hunger—or it may be learned. As indicated earlier, the former is much more likely to lead to satiation. Many of the important incentives in adult human behavior are learned social rewards. One of the most conspicuous examples of a socially learned incentive is money. Obviously, a check or even paper currency satisfies no innate drives directly, yet it functions as a learned reinforcement—we learn to work for money—in the economically advanced societies which are the context of most marketing problems.

In summary, drive impels the subject to respond, and the particular response is elicited by a cue. If there were no drive, no responses would occur. Thus, responses are determined by the combination of drive and cue. If the response is rewarded, or reinforced, the response will be repeated when the drive and cue appear together, and thus we can say we have learning. The essence of learning is this cue-response connection.

Underlying this abbreviated statement of the learning process is the Hullian learning model which, in its simplest form, is:

$$E = D \times K \times H \times V$$

E is "reaction potential," which is roughly equivalent to behavior or response; D is the "initiating drive"; K is the "incentive potential"; H is "habit strength"; and V is the "stimulus-intensity dynamism," the intensity of the cue (Hilgard, 1956, p. 151). Although E is but roughly equivalent to behavior, it will be used here in this way; in the Hullian system, it is an intervening variable that occurs just prior to the response.[7] The concept of "initiating drive," or "drive," has already been discussed. The formula indicates a multiplicative rather than an additive relationship among the independent variables, and the empirical support for a multiplicative relation has been reviewed and is available (Spence, 1956).

Incentive potential is the value of the goal object. For marketing purposes this object is the product. In psychological research, it is usually restricted to some measure of magnitude such as the size or intensity. In an animal experiment, for instance, one, two, or three ounces of a food might represent variation in incentive potential. . . .

Habit strength is a function of the number of previous trials in which a particular response was reinforced. It may be helpful to emphasize here a sometimes confusing distinction. Habit strength is what psychologists mean when they refer to a *learning* principle that is separate from *performance*. Habit strength is said to depend *only* on the number of reinforced responses, whereas performance is a function of habit strength plus the other elements of the behavioral equation shown earlier, namely, D, K, and V. If a person has been reinforced a thousand times for a particular response, his learning or habit strength may be at a very high level. If the value of D (drive), however, were low enough, no response would be observed. Conversely, twenty reinforced trials might provide a relatively low level of learning, but when that low learning factor *(H)* was multiplied by a high level of drive *(D)*, performance might be found to persist at a high level for a substantial period of time.[8]

Finally, stimulus-intensity dynamism refers to the strength of the stimulus.[9] This variable is particularly significant for the study of buyer behavior, because presumably much advertising and personal selling effort could be included as exerting their effect through V. Not all the effect of advertising, however, would be due to V, because it is believed that advertising may directly affect the motivational processes (D) of the buyer. Many of our advertising efforts, for example, are directed toward the status needs of individuals, which is a motivational variable that suggests the D factor in the Hullian model. Hull, however, was referring specifically to the physical intensity of the stimulus; that is, measures of brightness, loudness, voltage. This meaning of intensity should not be confused with such things as an urgent (or "intense") appeal to status needs, and research must still tell us how the two are similar, and how different. Also, advertising tells us about the virtues of one brand over another, and hence, it presumably affects the incentive value (K) of that brand.

Of significance to anyone interested in marketing behavior is the parallelism between this formulation of the Hullian model and the concept of utility in economic theory.[10] Utility theory can be stated as follows:

$$B = f(U) = g(M, I, P)$$

B is behavior; U is the utility concept when risk is incorporated, namely "expected utility"; M is motivational disposition; I is the objective value of the product; P is the subjective probability of the product's having the value the chooser thinks it will. "Motivational disposition" is comparable to "drive," and "objective value" to "incentive potential." Subjective probability is suggestively related to H. Subjective probability in purchasing presumably changes with experience in using the product or under the influence of other uncertainty-reducing influences, such as additional information from any source. As was noted above, H is a function of the absolute number of reinforced trials. Thus, superficially, the three independent variables in each formulation amount to pretty much the same thing. There is no separate counterpart of V, and it is included in the economic model only as a part of the summary concept, U.

In order to make the implications of the basic model more concrete and to relate it to subsequent learning phenomena, drive (D) and incentive potential (K) will be elaborated upon. By taking an example of marketing behavior that closely parallels the laboratory experiments, I hope to show the application of the theory more clearly. Those with only an immediate interest in marketing decisions may not find the hypothetical example useful; more complete and realistic complex applications of the theory will probably be developed in the future. Even now, however, the stochastic learning model applications to be discussed later leave little doubt about the primary role of learning in buying behavior.

In the laboratory, drive has usually been independently measured by depriving the subject of some innate drive-reducing element. The drive could be hunger, and the goal object, food. The nature of the experiment is shown in Table 1 where the respective numbers of hours of food deprivation are given in the left-hand column.

The principle could be applied in a supermarket in which D could be the number of hours since the consumer's last meal and where K is held constant, for example, a can of vegetables of a given size. Records would be maintained on each number of cans purchased at varying drive levels by a sample number of housewives; the mean number of units purchased over a series of trials at each drive level could then be computed, as shown in the right-hand column.

TABLE 1.   Effects of Drive on Buying

Hours Deprivation of Food (Drive)	Mean Number of Units Purchased by Individual
4	4
3	3
2	2
1	1

Table 1 indicates that when a housewife has not eaten for four hours, she may be expected to purchase more units than when she has been deprived of food for only three hours.

It is convenient here to call attention to the concept of threshold, which in the traditional theory of utility and choice has been assumed away. After a person has learned to respond in a particular way, the response will be elicited only if the drive exceeds the minimum level required by the threshold. The concept is accepted in psychology as widely prevalent in human beings, but usually is not the focus of attention in psychological research. Typically, in the report of each study, the "probability of response" for each level of the independent variable is shown, but the reader is left to define what level of probability of response will constitute a "threshold." The highly replicable research that has focused directly on the threshold concept has been mainly in the area of sensation, where the variables are easily measured and probably not too relevant to the marketing situation. This is a very important concept in the attempt to understand buying behavior.

Next, we investigate the consequences for behavior of changing the K value and holding D constant. We might study the behavior of a sample of shoppers who have not eaten for three hours and thus hold drive constant. The results from offering three different sizes of cans, for instance, 6, 12, and 18 oz., with prices proportional to quantities, are shown in Table 2.

TABLE 2.   Effects of Incentive on Buying

Size of Can (Incentive)	Mean Number of Units Purchased
18	60
12	40
6	20

The hypothetical results indicate that with a three-hour food deprivation, the average person, on 100 repeated trials, 20 times purchased a 6 oz. can; 40 times, a 12 oz. can; and 60 times, an 18 oz. can. The interacting effects of both drive and incentive potential can be studied in the same experiment by analysis-of-variance techniques.

In fact, research of this type on buyer behavior need not be confined to the laboratory. There have been enough applications of the R. A. Fisher-F. Yates type of experimental design to buyer behavior under field conditions to inspire optimism. Specifically, these applications have been in retail stores with price, point-of-purchase advertising, type of display, and the like as the independent variables and volume of sales as the dependent variable.[11] There are currently some limitations, but, as so often happens, it may be possible to modify the techniques of experimental design and make them more effective in serving a particular need. Already, modifications have enabled us to detect the problem of carryover, which some thought would seriously limit the use of experimental design for the field study of consumer behavior. By carryover, I mean the tendency for the effect of the stimulus to carry over into future time periods in the experiment, such as when the consumer accumulates an inventory. It is possible to conclude that, at least for some food products, the existence of carryover may not preclude the use of the method.

Unfortunately, experimentation under field conditions has contributed little to a systematic body of knowledge about buyer behavior because in none of the works that has come to the writer's attention was there an attempt to relate either the design of the study or the findings to the existing knowledge of human behavior; the work has been noncumulative.

The drive-cue-response sequence is the barest description of the learning mechanism. Some additional details as to how change occurs will be added here, which give the learning model a greater flavor of relevance for marketing. First is the concept of *extinction*. When a learned response is repeated without reinforcement, the strength of the tendency to perform that response progressively decreases. Hence, extinction occurs when a response is practiced without reinforcement. Forgetting is the process that occurs during an interval in which the response is not practiced (Dollard and Miller, 1950, pp. 48–49).

The rate of extinction depends upon a number of conditions; for instance, the more effort that is involved in the response, the higher the rate of extinction is likely to be. A woman attempting to find a brand might be more likely to continue looking in a particular store if the store is more accessible, even though she did not find the brand there in previous attempts.

Generalization

In this discussion of learning, the problem of behavior with respect to new objects—objects with which the individual has had no previous experience—has not been examined. In the dynamic real world, where new products are continually appearing and where buyers are geographically and socially mobile, this constitutes one of the central problems of marketing. In terms of organization theory, I refer here to the buyer's search processes. Generalization is the mechanism by which this type of behavior, namely, learning about new objects, is incorporated into learning theory. Of specific interest to marketing is the use of the theory of generalization in investigating the relative effects of the audio and visual stimuli in television (*Research on the Communications Process,* 1960).

Generalization and *discrimination* are two important antithetical concepts. A reinforcement for making a specific response to a given pattern of cues strengthens not only the tendency for that pattern of cues to elicit that response, but also the tendency for *similar* patterns to elicit the same response. This could be, for instance, the process by which the buyer shifts his purchase response from one brand to a new one because it is similar. The shift to the new brand implies a reduced discrimination with respect to the old one. The individual, then, is generalizing his response to similar cues. The variation in the extent of this transfer to new brands is described by the term *gradient of generalization.*

In line with the principle of extinction, the tendency to respond is weakened if the new response is performed but not rewarded. If, however, the individual is rewarded in responding to one pattern of cues, but not to another, a *discrimination* for the first pattern of cues is gradually established. Discrimination increases the specificity of the cue-response connection. It would be hypothesized, for example, that if the buyer finds from his experience that the new brand seems to meet his needs better, he would confine his purchases to it. Put in marketing terms, discrimination is the process by which buyers strengthen their attachment to a particular brand or, in more general terms, the process by which the organism is restricted in its range of responses.

By presenting the generalization-discrimination principle graphically, a number of ideas can be related. First, the gradient of generalization mentioned above is shown in Figure 1. Brands are arranged on the horizontal axis in the order of decreasing similarity from the brand B_0, being studied. The particular order of similarity could be inferred empirically from an analysis of past purchases.[12] Thus, the B variable is a continuum of "similarity" as viewed by the buyer. D_1 indicates one level of drive, and D_2 a still higher level. K, the quantity of the product, is assumed constant. The slopes of the D lines are the generalization gradients. Response strength may be measured in various ways; "percentage of responses," which can be interpreted in terms of "probability of response," is used here.

Let us assume that the data in Figure 1 were obtained from six experiments, in each of which the housewife was offered a different brand. In the first experiment of twenty trials, she was offered B_0, with drive level D_1, and she took B_0 all the time; that is, 100%. In the second, she was offered only B_1, and she took it 80% of the time; when B_2 was offered alone, 60%; when B_3 was offered alone, 40%; etc. As the drive was increased, shown by D_2, the gradient was broadened. With the broader gradient, the housewife took B_5 about 20% of the time, whereas with D_1, she did not take B_5 at all when she was offered it alone.

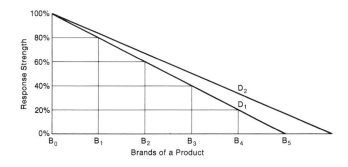

FIGURE 1.   An example of stimulus generalization.

It is well supported experimentally that the level of the drive determines the position, or height, of the gradient. Both the position and the slope of the generalization gradient are important; however, only position will be discussed.

The principle that increased drive causes increased generalization of response to similar cues suggests the difficult problem that the advertiser faces. Through his advertising, he may increase the learned drive of his buyers and create a tendency for them to purchase other brands instead of particularizing their responses to his brand. Thus, the advertiser walks the tightrope between increasing generalization and increasing discrimination. The generalization principle also argues that a company's product should be readily available. If it is not, the buyer is encouraged to settle for a similar brand, since he encounters both the delay in satisfaction and the effort of looking elsewhere.

In discussing Figure 1, we have assumed so far that the incentive potential is constant. K is any motivationally relevant attribute common to all B's. In experimental psychology, K has ordinarily been treated as variation in the magnitude of reward. Perhaps the concept could also be extended to other attributes of the incentive—taste and texture, for example. There is experimental evidence that K is subject to the same generalization principles as drive, for instance, that the generalization gradient increases with increased K, although it is not as well studied. If K were varied in Figure 1, there would be a generalization gradient for each combination of D and K values. The underlying principle here is that anything that affects response strength will necessarily influence breadth of generalization, since all responses generalize.

Let us examine more specifically the relevance of learning theory to some aspects of marketing strategy. From the Hullian model presented earlier, it will be recalled that drive (D), incentive potential (K), habit strength (H), and stimulus intensity (V) all influence response. In marketing, the incentive potential can be directly controlled. For instance, the value of B_0 could be changed, such as the quality, although a competitor's quality cannot be controlled. An orientation toward the relation between an incentive (the brand) and a particular drive (innate or learned) can be created in an individual, presumably, by using advertising to point out the relevance of the incentive for the drive. Hence, one of the advertiser's problems is to identify the relevant learned drive and, through his advertising, relate his product to that drive which was the rationale supporting the use of "motivation research" in marketing, as discussed earlier in the chapter.

The intensity of the cue (V) may also be controlled by advertising. Habit strength is subject to indirect control. If the brand functions as a reinforcement, that is, if acquiring and using the brand is satisfying, then the consumer's tendency to make the response of purchasing that brand when confronted by the cues associated with it increases. If quality should vary as a result of poor quality control in the factory, for example, habit strength would not continue to be increased, due to the lack of reinforcement.

Finally, a measure of the generalization gradient that is relevant to marketing could be an "index of brand restriction," which would quantify the tendency for a buyer to limit his choice among brands. The concept would be akin to "brand loyalty"—the tendency for buyers to repeat their purchases of a given brand bought by an individual as a proportion of the combined sales of all brands offered. The index would be a function of the respective values of D, K, and V, or of either separately, were the others held constant, which is easily accomplished in the case of K and V. . . .

Stochastic Learning Models

Psychologists have attempted to describe human and animal learning with mathematical models containing stochastic or probabilistic—rather than deterministic—elements, as illustrated by the Estes and the Bush-Mosteller learning models.[13] It is currently a flourishing area of research, and has been applied quite extensively to buying behavior, often under the title of brand-switching. The approach is to examine an individual's behavior over time, on the hypothesis that each of his acts is influenced by his earlier acts. Thus, in the framework of the Bush-Mosteller model, we generally consider all the past successes and failures of an individual, in a learning situation, as having some influence upon his subsequent response—recent events having a greater effect than older events. At one extreme, the parameters of the Bush-Mosteller model can be such that only the most recent event influences the outcome of future trials. At the other extreme, the parameters can be set so that success or failure on all past events will affect the probability of success on future trials. Hence, the model is highly flexible.

A stochastic (probabilistic) model can be applied to sequences of observed events; for instance, the brands of a product purchased by an individual or individuals over a period of time. The relative frequencies of such sequences are assumed to be generated by processes that can be described by mathematical relationships which determine the probabilities of a consumer's shifting from one brand to another. These are referred to as "transition probabilities." If such probabilities could be assumed constant over time with respect to consumer-brand-shifting, transient and equilibrium shares of market for individual brands could be computed for future time periods. However, the transition probabilities of an individual's repurchase of a brand may change as firms alter the merchandising efforts expended in behalf of individual brands. Kuehn (1958; 1961, Selection 1.8) and J. Mills (1959) have outlined simplified models of the mechanism by which advertising and such factors as product characteristics, price, and retail availability might affect these brand-shifting probabilities.

Several researchers have used stochastic models in empirical studies of consumer brand choice. Fourt (1960), Kuehn (1958, Selection 1.8), and Lipstein (1959) have reported results of attempts to describe brand-shifting as a first-order purchase-to-purchase Markov process. "First order" means a stochastic process in which it is assumed that only the consumer's single most recent purchase influences his next choice of a brand. Fourt and Kuehn report that purchases prior to the most recent purchase do, however, have predictive value with respect to the consumer's next choice. Kuehn's analysis of purchase sequences indicates that the importance of past brand choices as predictors of the next brand chosen declines, exponentially, the further the examination is extended back into the consumer's purchasing history. That is, each past purchase has an effect equivalent to a given fraction of the effect of the purchase following it chronologically.

Notes

1. For a splendid summary of the psychology of learning, see Hilgard (1956). Hilgard defines learning as follows: "Learning is the process by which an activity originates

or is changed through reacting to an encountered situation, provided that the characteristics of the change in activity cannot be explained on the basis of native response tendencies, maturation, or temporary states of the organism (e.g., fatigue, drugs, etc.)," p. 3.

2. Learning theory is attracting increasing interest among advertising people; see *Printers' Ink,* Jan. 29, 1960, pp. 31–34. For an application of Gestalt theory rather than stimulus-response reinforcement theory to advertising slogans, see Heller (1956).

3. For a fascinating and simple statement of some of this work, see Dollard and Miller (1950).

4. In order to maintain consistent terminology and point of view, Dollard and Miller (1950) will be the reference, except where otherwise indicated.

5. For an example of this point of view, see G. Katona (1960), especially p. 130: "On this basis . . . prosperous times in which very many people gratify many of their needs should bring forth reduction of motive strength or even saturation, and thereby business recession."

6. For a comparison, see F. H. Allport (1955) and Hilgard (1956).

7. "Reaction potential and response are not identical because reaction potential may be below threshold, hence not lead to response, or it may interact with competing tendencies and hence be incompletely revealed in response." (Hilgard, 1956, p. 132.) Professor R. A. Bauer has noted to me that the distinction between response and reaction potential is important in marketing, since some would argue that response alone is relevant, a point of view that is inconsistent with the theory here.

8. Whether the reinforced responses are interspersed with unreinforced responses does make a difference empirically. See Hilgard's (1956) discussion of patterning, pp. 90–94.

9. The alert reader may recall at this point that any cue or stimulus may have drive properties if it is intense enough; that is, if V is high enough. This would seem to indicate that at its upper values V overlaps with the concept D. What is stressed here, however, is the effect upon behavior of variations in stimulus intensity (V) which are not strong enough to motivate the individual.

10. J. N. Morgan has pointed out the parallelism between psychology and economics, but he does not state it in the terms of the Hullian model, since he approaches the problem essentially from the point of view of personality theory. See Morgan (1958), pp. 105–106; and also see his comments on "learning," p. 105.

11. For an example of a field experiment, see Henderson (1961).

12. In laboratory studies, determining similarity has not been difficult because different values of a single variable are used.

13. For a description of this area of psychological research, see Hilgard, 1956, pp. 388–401. Hilgard states, "The models of Estes, Estes and Burke, and of Bush and Mosteller have been quite successful in predicting the course of events within lever-pressing problems, simple runway problems, discrimination, and reactions to uncertainty. Data have been derived from both animal and human experimentation," *ibid.,* p. 398.

References

Allport, F. H. *Theories of Perception and the Concept of Structure.* Wiley, 1955.

Dollard, J., and N. E. Miller. *Personality and Psychotherapy.* McGraw-Hill, 1950.

Fourt, L. A., and J. W. Woodlock. "Early Prediction of Market Success for New Grocery Products." *J. Marketing,* Vol. 25 (Oct. 1960), 31–38.

Heller, N. "An Application of Psychological Learning Theory to Advertising." *J. Marketing,* Vol. 20 (Jan. 1956), 248–254.

Henderson, P. L., J. F. Hind, and S. E. Brown. "Sales Effects of Two Campaign Themes." *J. Advertising Research*, Vol. 1 (Dec. 1961), 2–11.

Hilgard, E. R. *Theories of Learning* (2nd ed.). Appleton-Century-Crofts, 1956.

Hull, C. L. *Principles of Behavior.* Appleton-Century-Crofts, 1943.

———. *Essentials of Behavior.* Yale Univ. Press, 1951.

———. *A Behavior System.* Yale Univ. Press, 1952.

Katona, G. *The Powerful Consumer.* McGraw-Hill, 1960.

Kuehn, A. A. "An Analysis of the Dynamics of Consumer Behavior and Its Implications for Marketing Management." Unpub. Ph.D. dissertation, Graduate School of Industrial Administration, Carnegie Institute of Technology, 1958.

———, "A Model for Budgeting Advertising." *Mathematical Models and Methods in Marketing,* ed. F. M. Bass, *et al.* Irwin (1961), 302–356.

Lipstein, B. "The Dynamics of Brand Loyalty and Brand Switching." *Proc. Advertising Research Foundation* (1959), 101–108.

Mills, J., E. Aronson, and H. Robinson. "Selectivity in Exposure to Information." *J. of Abnormal and Social Psychology,* Vol. 59 (Sept. 1959), 250–253.

Morgan, J. N. "A Review of Recent Research on Consumer Behavior." *Consumer Behavior: Research on Consumer Reactions,* Vol. III, ed. L. H. Clark. Harper & Row (1958), 93–262.

Research on the Communications Process. Division of Academic Research and Services, Penn. State Univ. (Oct. 1960), 6–15.

Spence, K. W. *Behavior Theory and Conditioning.* Yale Univ. Press, 1956.

1.8 Consumer Brand Choice as a Learning Process
ALFRED A. KUEHN

The phenomenon of consumer brand shifting is a central element underlying the dynamics of the marketplace. To understand and describe market trends adequately, we must first establish the nature of the influences on consumer choice with respect to products and brands. Research directed at establishing the conditions under which consumers will shift from one brand to another offers hope of providing a framework within which to evaluate the influence of price, advertising, distribution and shelf space, and various types of sales promotion.

What do we know about brand choice? What behavioral mechanisms appear to underlie this phenomenon? Is such behavior habitual? Is learning involved? Does repeated purchasing of a brand reinforce the brand choice response? What is the relationship between consumer purchase frequencies and brand shifting behavior? These questions will be discussed in the light of available empirical data and a model which appears to describe them.

A Model of Consumer Brand Shifting

A model equivalent to a generalized form of the Estes (1954) and Bush-Mosteller (1955) stochastic (probabilistic) learning models appears to describe consumer brand shifting quite well. To illustrate how this brand shifting model describes changes in the consumer's probability of purchasing any given brand as a result of his purchases of that brand (e.g., Brand A) and competing brands (e.g., Brand X), let us examine the effect of the four-purchase sequence XAAX on a consumer with initial probability $P_{A,1}$ (see Figure 1).

The model is described or defined in terms of four parameters, namely, the intercepts and slopes of the two lines referred to in Figure 1 as the "purchase operator" and the "rejection operator." If the brand in question is purchased by the consumer on a given buying occasion, the consumer's probability of again buying the same brand the next time that type of product is purchased is read from the purchaser operator. If the brand is rejected by the consumer on a given buying occasion, the consumer's probability of buying that brand when he next buys that type of product is read from the rejection operator. Thus in Figure 1 our hypothetical consumer begins on trial 1 with the probability $P_{A,1}$ of buying Brand A. The consumer chooses some other brand (X) on trial 1, however, and thus his probability of buying Brand A on trial 2 ($P_{A,2}$) is obtained from the rejection operator, resulting in a slight reduction in the probability of purchasing A on the next trial. On trial 2, however, the consumer does purchase

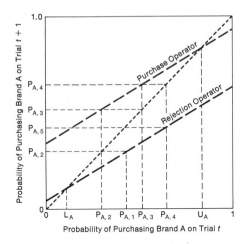

FIGURE 1.   Stochastic (probabilistic) brand-shifting model.

Brand A and thus increases the likelihood of his again buying the brand on the next occasion (trial 3) to $P_{A,3}$. Continuing in this fashion, the consumer again buys A on trial 3, thereby increasing his probability of purchasing Brand A on trial 4 to $P_{A,4}$. He again rejects A on trial 4, however, decreasing his probability of buying A on trial 5 to $P_{A,5}$.

    Two characteristics of the model should be noted: (1) the probability $P_{A,t}$ approaches but never exceeds the upper limit U_A with repeated purchasing of the brand, and (2) the probability $P_{A,t}$ approaches but never drops below the lower limit L_A with continued rejection of the brand. Using Bush and Mosteller's terminology, this would be referred to as an incomplete learning, incomplete extinction model insofar as U_A is less than one and L_A is greater than zero. This is equivalent to saying that consumers will generally not develop such strong brand loyalties (or buying habits) as to insure either the rejection or purchase of a given brand.

    It should also be pointed out that the purchase and rejection operators are functions of the time elapsed between the consumer's t^{th} and $t + 1^{st}$ purchases and of the merchandising activities of competitors. The time effect can be illustrated by the three sets of operators shown for high, medium, and very low frequency purchasers of a rapidly consumed, non-durable consumer product (see Figure 2). Note that the purchase and rejection operators decrease in slope and that the upper and lower limits approach each other as the time between purchases increases.

    At the one limit (time between purchases approaching zero) the purchase and rejection operators approach the diagonal, L approaches zero, and U approaches one. At the other limit (time between purchases approaching infinity), L and U approach each other and the purchase and rejection operators approach a slope equal to zero.

    The main problem that remains in making use of the model is then the estimation of the four parameters defining the purchase and rejection operators

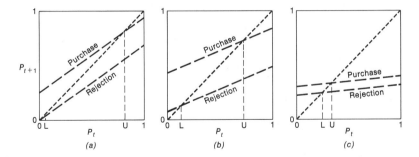

FIGURE 2. Effect of time between purchases upon purchases and rejection operators. (a) High frequency purchasers. (b) Medium frequency purchasers. (c) Very low frequency purchasers.

as a function of the time between purchases. If this could be done *a priori,* the model might be of value to marketing management for use in forecasting. At present, however, the model's primary use is in evaluating the effects of past and current competitive marketing activity. Thus the parameters of the model are estimated for short time periods and related to the actions of all competitors in the market. Since the path of aggregate consumer purchasing behavior could be established for any given set of parameter values, it follows that the parameter estimates obtained from fitting the model can provide a means for evaluating the influence of the market conditions prevailing during the period that the sequential purchase data were collected.

An efficient method has been developed to estimate these brand shifting parameters (maximum likelihood estimates) on the basis of sequences of two to four purchases. The method makes it feasible to relate this model to consumer purchasing behavior observed during relatively short periods of time. This is a must if the technique is to be useful, since merchandising conditions do not remain constant for long periods of time—products are modified, advertising themes and budgets are altered, special promotions are generally temporary in nature, and price levels may change from time to time. . . .

The Bush-Mosteller approach to estimating the parameters of their stochastic learning model, cannot, in its current state of development, be applied to the brand shifting model since (1) techniques have not been developed to estimate simultaneously the four basic parameters of the model, and (2) the methods outlined require a long history or record of trials (and, therefore, data collected over a long period of time during which there is stability in merchandising activity) from which to develop parameter estimates.

Empirical Brand Shifting Research

What evidence is there in support of the model? Three types of empirical studies have led to the formulation and continued development of the above model:

1. Analysis of three-, four-, five-, and six-purchase sequences of consumer brand purchases (Kuehn, 1958).
2. Analysis of effects of time between consumer purchases on a consumer's probability of purchasing individual brands of product (Kuehn, 1958).
3. Simulation of consumer brand choice behavior.

Each of these three studies is discussed briefly below.

Analysis of Brand Purchase Sequences

Sequential purchase data can provide some insight into consumer brand switching. The data analyzed below represent the frozen orange juice purchases of approximately 600 Chicago families in the three years 1950 to 1952, covering more than 15,000 individual purchases collected in monthly diaries by the Chicago Tribune Consumer Panel. The data were analyzed as sequences of five purchases by means of a factorial analysis to determine the influence of the consumer's first four sequential brand choices on his choice of a brand on the fifth buying occasion. The data and analysis prepared for Snow Crop brand are summarized in Table 1.

In column 1, the letter S is used to represent a purchase of the Snow Crop brand, the letter O to represent the purchase of any *other* brand of frozen orange juice. Thus SSSS indicates a sequence of four purchases of Snow Crop.

TABLE 1. Comparison of Observed and Predicted Probability of Purchasing Snow Crop Given the Four Previous Brand Purchases

Previous Purchase Pattern (1)	Sample Size (2)	Observed Probability of Purchase (3)	Predicted Probability of Purchase[a] (4)	Deviation of Predictions (5)
SSSS	1,047	.806	.832	+.026
OSSS	277	.690	.691	+.001
SOSS	206	.665	.705	+.040
SSOS	222	.595	.634	+.039
SSSO	296	.486	.511	+.025
OOSS	248	.552	.564	+.012
SOOS	138	.565	.507	−.058
OSOS	149	.497	.493	−.004
SOSO	163	.405	.384	−.021
OSSO	181	.414	.370	−.044
SSOO	256	.305	.313	+.008
OOOS	500	.330	.366	+.033
OOSO	404	.191	.243	+.052
OSOO	433	.129	.172	+.043
SOOO	557	.154	.186	+.032
OOOO	8,442	.048	.045	−.003

[a]To illustrate the computation of the values in column 4, the probability of a Snow Crop purchase given the history SOOO is .045 (the probability of purchase given OOOO) plus .141, or .186; the probability given SOOS is .045 + .141 + .321 = .507; and the predicted probability given OSSS is .045 + .127 + .198 + .321 = .691.

The sequence OSSS represents one purchase of some other brand followed by three purchases of Snow Crop.

Column 2 tabulates the sample sizes from which were calculated the observed and predicted probabilities of purchasing Snow Crop on the subsequent (fifth) purchase in the sequence.

Column 3 is computed on the basis of the observed frequencies of the five-purchase sequences. Thus, there were 296 sequences exhibiting the pattern SSSO in the first four positions of the sequence. Snow Crop was purchased on the fifth buying occasion in 144 of these sequences. The best estimate of the observed probability of buying Snow Crop given the past purchase record of SSSO is therefore 144/296 = .486.

The predicted column is based on the results of the factorial analysis of past purchase effects. Each of the four past brand purchases was examined with respect to its individual (primary) effect and the effect of its interactions with the other purchases. The individual effects of the past four purchase positions were highly significant but the interaction effects were not significantly different from zero at the 5% level of significance; that is, there was greater than 5% probability of results as extreme as those observed arising by chance if there were in fact no interaction effects.

There is close agreement between the observed and predicted probabilities, in view of the limited sample size. The predicted values, however, appear to deviate systematically on the high side when Snow Crop is purchased either one or three times on the last four buying occasions; also, predictions are generally low given two purchases. Subsequent analysis indicated that these systematic deviations were reduced or eliminated when a record of the fifth past brand purchase was included in the analysis.

Casual inspection of Table 1 suggests that the most recent purchase of the consumer is not the only one influencing his brand choice. This finding raises some question about the uses currently being made of purchase-to-purchase Markov chain analyses which assume that only the most recent purchase of the consumer is influential. The analysis of "primary" effects referred to above showed that the purchase of Snow Crop on the most recent buying occasion added .321 to the probability of the consumer's buying Snow Crop on his next purchase. Similarly, the second most recent purchase added .198, the third .127, and the fourth .141 (see footnote, Table 1).

Note that the first three purchase effects decline roughly exponentially. That is, the ratio of the importance of the first purchase to that of the second is approximately equal to the ratio of the second to the third. The fourth, however, increases rather than decreases! This reversal occurs because past purchases beyond the fourth most recent purchase were excluded from the analysis. The increased importance attached to the fourth most recent purchase for prediction purposes reflects its high correlation with the fifth and earlier past purchases not incorporated in the study. When these same data were reanalyzed using six-purchase sequences, the exponential relationship of declining primary purchase effects fits the first through fourth past purchases. As would be expected, however, the fifth past purchase effect was larger than the fourth because of its higher correlation with the consumer's sixth and even earlier past purchases.

Observations of the exponentially declining effects of past purchases led to the testing of the brand shifting model outlined in Figure 1, since that model has the characteristics of weighting the influence of past brand choices exponentially when the slopes of the purchase and rejection operators are identical. Subsequent research with products other than frozen orange juice has tended to confirm the predictive value of exponential weighting of past brand purchases by consumers. The exponential weights vary substantially, however, among product classes. Products such as toilet soaps, cereals, and toothpaste were found to have substantially lower rates of decline in weights as one goes back into the purchase history, as a result of the tendency of purchasing families to use some mix of brands on a routine basis so as to satisfy different uses, desires for variety, and differences in preference of individual family members. To be sure, this brand-mix effect is operative even in the case of frozen orange juice, but for quite a different reason. Many families use a mix of brands of frozen orange juice because of the unavailability of specific brands in all the stores among which the consumer shifts in the course of his week-to-week shopping trips.

Effect of Consumer Purchase Frequencies

Let us consider the effect of time between purchases on the consumer's probability of repurchasing the same brand. In Figure 3 we observe that the probability of a consumer's buying the same brand on two consecutive purchases of the product decreases to that brand's share of market as time between purchases increases. Whenever a great amount of time has elapsed since the consumer's last purchase of the product, the brand he last bought has little influence on his choice of a brand—the probability of his buying any given brand in this case is approximately equal to the share of market of that brand. Note that the probability of repurchase decreases at a constant rate with the passing of time; this characteristic, which we shall refer to as the "time rate of decay of purchase probability," provides a simple framework for incorporating the effects of time into a procedure for forecasting consumer purchase probabilities.

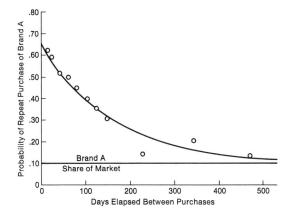

FIGURE 3.   The probability of a consumer's buying the same brand for two consecutive purchases.

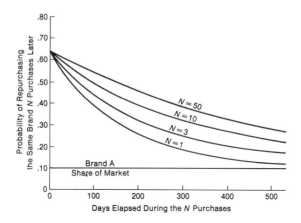

FIGURE 4.   Frequency of purchase related to probability of continued purchase of the same brand.

Let us now expand our view of the effects of time on repurchase probability in terms of the time period required for the consumer to make N individual purchases of frozen orange juice concentrate. Note that the curve in Figure 4 labeled $N = 1$ is the same curve as in Figure 3. Observe also that the probability of repurchasing the same brand at any given time in the future, without regard to the brands chosen in the interim, increases as we go up from $N = 1$ to $N = 3$, $N = 10$, and $N = 50$. Thus on the average a consumer who makes his fiftieth purchase of frozen orange juice 300 days after some arbitrary purchase of a given brand has a much higher probability of again choosing that brand than does the consumer who makes only one, three, or ten purchases in that interval of time.

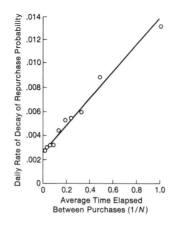

FIGURE 5.   Relationship of decay rates to time between purchases.

Figure 5 illustrates the relationship between the rates of decay of purchase probability associated with the curves in Figure 4 and the average time elapsed between purchases. The rate of decay of $N = 1$ in Figure 4 is .01298 per day. The rate of decay of $N = 50$ is .00282. Here again we find a relationship which, because of its simplicity, can after some manipulation be conveniently incorporated into a model forecasting consumer brand choice probabilities. The rate of decay increases linearly with an increase in the average time between purchases. The data points plotted in Figure 5 represent the rates of decay computed for ten values of N, four of which were illustrated by the curves in Figure 4.

Simulation of Consumer Brand Choice

The brand shifting model outlined in Figure 1 has been tested by computing the predicted purchase probabilities of consumers on each of approximately 13,000 occasions of purchase of frozen orange juice, and comparing aggregates of these predictions with recorded brand purchases. The procedure followed was first to divide the probability space, zero to one, into 76 probability ranges. Then, whenever the computer-programed model predicted a certain probability of a given family's buying a particular brand on a given buying occasion, the results of that purchase were recorded in the computer storage location representing the corresponding probability range. Thus it was possible within each of the 76 probability cells to compare the average predicted probability of purchasing individual brands with the observed proportion of trials on which the brand was in fact purchased. The predicted probabilities and observed proportions of purchases were then compared individually and simultaneously for all 76 cells with respect to the binomial and chi square distributions that would be expected if the model were perfect. The 76 normal deviates, referred to here by t, computed for the individual cells with respect to the Snow Crop predictions, were approximately normally distributed, 50 lying within one standard deviation, 71 lying within two standard deviations, and 76 falling within three standard deviations. The chi square value indicated no significant deviation at the 10% level. Similar results were obtained in an analysis of predictions for the Minute Maid brand, 53 t values lying within one standard deviation, 70 lying within two standard deviations, and all 76 cases falling within three standard deviations.

The above results suggest that the model offers promise for use in describing consumer behavior in probabilistic terms. The model was not tested with respect to individual families, the number of purchases made by most individual families providing too small a sample to yield a reasonably powerful test of the predictions from the model. In other words, since rejection is unlikely with a small sample size per family, acceptance does not carry much weight with respect to an evaluation of the model. In the aggregate, the model stood up surprisingly well, given the overall test sample size of approximately 13,000 purchase predictions. Of course, if the sample size were to be increased substantially, significant deviations would be obtained, since the model is not a perfect representation of the brand purchase sequences of consumers.

The predictions of the model were also used to obtain a frequency distribution of consumers throughout the three year time period according to their probability of buying specific brands of product. Figure 6 provides a comparison of the smoothed profiles for Libby and Minute Maid frozen orange juice. As might be expected, most consumers have a low probability of buying any specific brand. Those consumers who have a high probability of buying one brand must necessarily have a low probability of buying several other brands. Minute Maid was in the enviable position of having a small group of customers with a very high probability of buying the brand. Libby did not have such a following. Minute Maid developed frozen orange juice and was the first brand available to consumers; these facts probably helped develop the group of loyal (or habitual) customers, a sizable portion of whom were retained in the face of growing competition. As the innovator of frozen orange juice, Minute Maid also developed a pre-eminent market position in terms of retail availability, a factor which undoubtedly helped the firm maintain a sales advantage relative to competition.

FIGURE 6.   Probability of purchasing specific brands.

Adaptive Behavior or Spurious Results?

Ronald Frank (1962) reported that certain results concerning repeat purchase probabilities as a function of a brand's run length appear similar to what would be expected with associative learning under conditions of reward. He then observed in a footnote that my data (Kuehn, 1961) also seem to suggest this interpretation, a point on which there is agreement. The balance of Frank's article is then directed at demonstrating that (1) purchase sequence data generated by families for a given brand using a Monte Carlo approach, on the assumption that each family's probability of purchasing the brand remained constant throughout the time period, produced repeat purchase probabilities as a function of run length which closely approximated in the aggregate the actual observed probabilities, and (2) the number of runs observed for *most* families is consistent with what might be expected under the assumption that each family's probability of purchasing any given brand remained constant throughout the time period.

As a result of his success in generating a relationship that has the appearance of actual data, Frank states, "These results cast suspicion on the use of a 'learning' model to describe the observations." In view of this statement, which bears directly on the work outlined here, in my thesis, and elsewhere, some defense appears to be in order.

Frank's observations in no way invalidate the findings outlined earlier in this paper. He has shown that it is inappropriate to attribute to learning *all* the increase in repeat purchase probability associated with increases in run length, an error probably made by more than a few researchers. This, however, is not the approach outlined here or in my thesis. The approach used in my thesis could be applied to Frank's coffee data to test whether the probabilities are in fact constant and, if this is not the case, to estimate the appropriate weightings. If consumers were to have a constant probability of brand choice from trial to trial, the most recent purchase positions would not have a greater primary effect on the predicted purchase probabilities than would any other purchase position—all the primary effects would be identical except for sampling variations. Similarly, if the probabilities of brand choice were constant from trial to trial, the purchase and rejection operators in the adaptive brand shifting model would be superimposed on the diagonal (see Figure 1). In other words, the special case considered by Frank can be treated successfully by both of the analytic techniques used in my studies and discussed in this paper. Frank is correct when he states that much of what might appear to be a learning effect on the basis of repeat purchase probabilities as a function of run length is due to the aggregation of consumers with different probabilities (at the start of the run). But this is no problem when one takes into account the effect of all past purchases which have a significant impact on the consumer's purchase probability; such an approach does not disregard the information contained in purchases prior to the current run—an important consideration when the run is very short. Since past purchases will, except in highly unusual cases, have decreasing effects (as one goes back in time) on the consumer's subsequent purchase probability, taking into account all significant past purchases does not generally require the availability of an unduly long record of the consumer's purchase history.

The second point that Frank makes—namely, that most consumers behave as though they had constant purchase probabilities—would appear to represent a misinterpretation of statistical results. Frank sets up his hypothesis, tests it at some level of significance for each of a large number of cases (families), and then interprets the results as though all cases not shown to deviate statistically on an individual basis are consistent with the hypothesis. Actually, the hypothesis was that consumers have a constant probability of purchase, and the results indicated that a larger number of the individual cases tested lay outside the confidence limits than is consistent with the hypothesis, thereby rejecting the hypothesis *in toto!*

To be sure, the hypothesis of constant probability is, in effect, a straw man. It is generally recognized that consumers do change their buying behavior over time. Whether such behavior is called adjustment, adaptation, or learning is unimportant. It should be noted, however, that even though the overall market for coffee was quite stable in the period studied by Frank, and the sample sizes were limited to 14 months of purchase by each family, the hypothesis was in fact rejected on an overall basis, the only appropriate way in which to interpret the results of the test. Perhaps, as Frank suggests, some consumers do have constant probabilities of choosing individual brands during certain periods of time. Such a hypothesis cannot be tested, however, unless a procedure independent of the test is available for identifying these consumers and the relevant time periods.

Summary

A model describing brand shifting behavior as a probabilistic process and incorporating the effects of past purchases and time elapsed between purchases has been outlined. A defense of this approach to the study of mechanisms underlying consumer brand choice has also been presented. What has not been discussed is the way in which such merchandising factors as price, advertising, product characteristics, retail availability, and promotions (price off, coupons, merchandise packs, etc.) influence the parameters of the model and the extensions of the model that might be required to incorporate such effects. Some earlier results of research on the influence of these variables have been incorporated into an aggregate "expected value" form of the model presented here (Kuehn, 1961). Much work, however, remains to be done.

References

Bush, R. R., and F. Mosteller. *Stochastic Models for Learning*. Wiley, 1955.

Estes, W. K. "Individual Behavior in Uncertain Situations: An Interpretation in Terms of Statistical Association Theory." *Decision Processes,* ed. R. M. Thrall *et al.* Wiley, 1954.

Frank, R. E. "Brand Choice as a Probability Process." *J. Business,* Vol. 35 (Jan. 1962), 43–56.

Kuehn, A. A. "An Analysis of the Dynamics of Consumer Behavior and Its Implications for Marketing Management." Unpub. Ph.D. dissertation, Graduate School of Industrial Administration, Carnegie Institute of Technology, 1958.

———. "A Model for Budgeting Advertising." *Mathematical Models and Methods in Marketing*, ed. F. M. Bass *et al.* Irwin (1961), 302–356.

1.9 The Impact of Television Advertising: Learning Without Involvement

HERBERT E. KRUGMAN

Among the wonders of the twentieth century has been the ability of the mass media repeatedly to expose audiences numbered in millions to campaigns of coordinated messages. In the post–World War I years it was assumed that exposure equaled persuasion and that media content therefore was the all-important object of study or censure. Now we believe that the powers of the mass media are limited. No one has done more to bring about a counterbalancing perspective than ex-AAPOR president Joseph Klapper, with his well-known book *The Effects of Mass Media,*[1] and the new AAPOR president Raymond Bauer, with such articles as "The Limits of Persuasion."[2]

It has been acknowledged, however, that this more carefully delimited view of mass media influence is based upon analysis of largely noncommercial cases and data. We have all wondered how many of these limitations apply also to the world of commerce, specifically advertising. These limitations will be discussed here as they apply to television advertising only, since the other media include stimuli and responses of a different psychological nature, which play a perhaps different role in the steps leading to a purchasing decision.

The tendency is to say that the accepted limitations of mass media do apply, that advertising's use of the television medium has limited impact. We tend to feel this way, I think, because (1) we rarely feel converted or greatly persuaded by a particular TV campaign, and (2) so much of TV advertising content is trivial and sometimes even silly. Nevertheless, trivia have their own special qualities, and some of these may be important to our understanding of the commercial *or* the noncommercial use and impact of mass media.

To begin, let us go back to Neil Borden's classic Harvard Business School evaluation of the economic effects of advertising.[3] Published in 1942, it concluded that advertising (1) accelerates growing demand or retards falling demand, i.e. it quickens the pulse of the market, and (2) encourages price rigidity but increases quality and choice of products. The study warned, however, that companies had been led to overlook price strategies and the elasticity of consumer demand. This was borne out after World War II by the rise of the discounters!

The end of World War II also brought mass television and an increased barrage of advertising messages. How much could the public take? Not only were early TV commercials often irritating, but one wondered whether all the competition would not end in a great big buzzing confusion. Apparently not! Trend studies of advertising penetration have shown that the public is able to "hold in memory," as we would say of a computer, a very large number of TV campaign themes correctly related to brands. The fact that huge sums and energies were expended to achieve retention of these many little bits of information should not deter us from acknowledging the success of the over-all effort.

It is true that in some categories of products the sharpness of brand differentiation is slipping, as advertising themes and appeals grow more similar. Here the data look, as one colleague put it, "mushy." In such categories the product is well on its way toward becoming a commodity; even while brand advertising continues, the real competition is more and more one of price and distribution. But prices, too, are advertised, although in different media, and recalled.

What is lacking in the required "evaluation" of TV advertising is any significant body of research specifically relating advertising to attitudes, and these in turn to purchasing behavior or sales. That is, we have had in mind a model of the correct and effective influence process which has not yet been verified. This is the bugaboo that has been the hope and the despair of research people within the industry. Always there looms that famous pie in the sky: If the client will put up enough money, if he will be understanding enough to cooperate in blacking out certain cities or areas to permit a controlled experiment, if the cities or areas under study will be correctly matched, if the panels of consumers to be studied will not melt away in later not-at-homes, refusals, or changes of residence, if the sales data will be "clean" enough to serve as adequate criteria—*then surely* one can truly assess the impact of a particular ad campaign! Some advertisers, too, are learning to ask about this type of evaluation, while the advertising agencies are ambivalent and unsure of their strength.

This seems to be where we are today. The economic impact of TV advertising is substantial and documented. Its messages have been learned by the public. Only the lack of specific case histories relating advertising to attitudes to sales keeps researchers from concluding that the commercial use of the medium is a success. We are faced then with the odd situation of knowing that advertising works but being unable to say much about why.

Perhaps our model of the influence process is wrong. Perhaps it is incompletely understood. Back in 1959 Herbert Zielske, in "The Remembering and Forgetting of Advertising," demonstrated that advertising will be quickly forgotten if not continuously exposed.[4] Why such need for constant reinforcement? Why so easy-in and easy-out of short-term memory? One answer is that much of advertising content is learned as meaningless nonsense material. Therefore, let us ask about the nature of such learning.

An important distinction between the learning of sense and nonsense was laid down by Ebbinghaus in 1902 when he identified the greater effects of order of presentation of stimuli on the learning of nonsense material. He demonstrated a U curve of recall, with first and last items in a series best remembered, thus giving rise also to the principles of primacy and recency.[5]

In 1957, many years later, Carl Hovland reported that in studying persuasion he found the effects of primacy and recency greater when dealing with material of lesser ego-involvement. He wrote, "Order of presentation is a more significant factor in influencing opinions for subjects with relatively weak desires for understanding, than for those with high 'cognitive needs'."[6] It seems, therefore, that the nonsensical à la Ebbinghaus and the unimportant à la Hovland work alike.

At the 1962 AAPOR meetings I had the pleasure of reading a paper on some applications of learning theory to copy testing. Here it was reported that the spontaneous recall of TV commercials presented four in a row formed a distinct U curve. In the same paper a re-analysis of increment scores of fifty-seven commercials tested in a three-position series by the Schwerin television testing method also showed a distinct U curve, despite the earlier contentions of the Schwerin organization. That real advertising materials presented in so short a series could produce distinct U curves seemed to confirm that the learning of advertising was similar to the learning of the nonsensical or the unimportant.[7]

What is common to the learning of the nonsensical and the unimportant is lack of involvement. We seem to be saying, then, that much of the impact of television advertising is in the form of learning without involvement, or what Hartley calls "un-anchored learning."[8] If this is so, is it a source of weakness or of strength to the advertising industry? Is it good or bad for our society? What are the implications for research on advertising effectiveness?

Let us consider some qualities of sensory perception with and without involvement. Last October I participated along with Ray Bauer, Elihu Katz, and Nat Maccoby in a Gould House seminar sponsored by the Foundation for Research on Human Behavior. Nat reported some studies conducted with Leon Festinger in which fraternity members learned a TV message better when hearing the audio and watching unrelated video than when they watched the speaker giving them the message directly, i.e. video *and* audio together.[9] Apparently, the distraction of watching something unrelated to the audio message lowered whatever resistance there might have been to the message.

As Nat put it, "Comprehension equals persuasion": Any disagreement ("Oh no! That can't be true!") with any message must come after some real interval, however minute. Ray asked Nat if he would accept a statement of this point as "Perception precedes perceptual defense," and Nat agreed. The initial development of this view goes back before World War II to the psychologist W. E. Guthrie.[10] It receives more recent support from British research on perception and communication, specifically that of D. E. Broadbent, who has noted the usefulness of defining perception as "immediate memory."[11]

The historical importance of the Maccoby view, however, is that it takes us almost all the way back to our older view of the potent propaganda content of World War I, that exposure to mass media content is persuasive per se! What is implied here is that in cases of involvement with mass media content perceptual defense is very briefly postponed, while in cases of noninvolvement perceptual defense may be absent.

Does this suggest that if television bombards us with enough trivia about a product we may be persuaded to believe it? On the contrary, it suggests that persuasion as such, i.e. overcoming a resistant attitude, is not involved at all and that it is a mistake to look for it in our personal lives as a test of television's advertising impact. Instead, as trivia are repeatedly learned and repeatedly forgotten and then repeatedly learned a little more, it is probable that two things will happen: (1) more simply, that so-called "overlearning" will move some information out of short-term and into long-term memory systems, and (2) more complexly, that we will permit significant alterations in the *structure* of our perception of a brand or product, but in ways which may fall short of persuasion or of attitude change. One way we may do this is by shifting the relative salience of attributes suggested to us by advertising as we organize our perception of brands and products.

Thanks to Sherif we have long used the term "frame of reference," and Osgood in particular has impressed us with the fact that the meaning of an object may be perceived along many separate dimensions. Let us say that a number of frames of reference are available as the primary anchor for the percept in question. We may then alter the psychological salience of these frames or dimensions and shift a product seen primarily as "reliable" to one seen primarily as "modern."[12] The product is still seen as reliable and perhaps no *less* reliable than before, but this quality no longer provides the primary perceptual emphasis. Similarly, the product was perhaps previously seen as modern, and perhaps no *more* modern now—yet exposure to new or repeated messages may give modernity the primary role in the organization of the percept.

There is no reason to believe that such shifts are completely limited to trivia. In fact, when Hartley first introduced the concept of psychological salience, he illustrated it with a suggestion that Hitler did not so much increase anti-Semitic attitudes in Germany as bring already existing anti-Semitic attitudes into more prominent use for defining the everyday world (*ibid.*, p. 97). This, of course, increased the probability of anti-Semitic behavior. While the shift in salience does not tell the whole story, it seems to be one of the dynamics operating in response to massive repetition. Although a rather simple dynamic, it may be a major one when there is no cause for resistance, or when uninvolved consumers do not provide their own perceptual emphases or anchors.

It may be painful to reject as incomplete a model of the influence process of television advertising that requires changes in attitude *prior to* changes in behavior. It may be difficult to see how the viewer of television can go from perceptual impact directly to behavioral impact, unless *the full perceptual impact is delayed.* This would not mean going into unexplored areas. Sociologists have met "sleeper effects" before, and some psychologists have long asserted that the effects of "latent" learning are only or most noticeable at the point of reward. In this case, it would be at the behavioral level involved in product purchases rather than at some intervening point along the way. That is, the purchase situation is the catalyst that reassembles or brings out all the potentials for shifts in salience that have accumulated up to that point. The product or package is then suddenly seen in a new, "somehow different" light although nothing verbalizable may have changed *up to that point.* What we ordinarily call "change of attitude" may then occur after some real interval, however minute. Such change of attitude after product purchase is *not.* as has sometimes been said, in "rationalization" of the purchase but is an emergent response aspect of the previously changed perception. We would perhaps see it more often if products always lived up to expectations and did not sometimes create negative interference with the emerging response.

I have tried to say that the public lets down its guard to the repetitive commercial use of the television medium and that it easily changes its ways of perceiving products and brands and its purchasing behavior without thinking very much about it at the time of TV exposure or at any time prior to purchase, and without up to then changing verbalized attitudes. This adds up, I think, to an understandable success story for advertising's use of the television medium. Furthermore, this success seems to be based on a left-handed kind of public trust that sees no great importance in the matter.

But now I wonder about those so-called "limits of effectiveness" of the noncommercial use of the mass media. I wonder if we were not overusing attitudes and attitude changes as our primary criterion of effectiveness? In looking for behavioral changes, did we sometimes despair too soon simply because we did not find earlier attitude changes? I wonder if we projected our own attitudes and values too much onto the audiences studied and assumed that they, too, would treat information about such matters as the United Nations as serious and involving? I wonder also how many of those public-spirited campaigns ever asked their audiences to *do* something, *i.e.*, asked for the kind of concrete behavior that at some point triggers whatever real potentials may have developed for an attitude change to begin or perhaps to complete its work.

I would like to suggest, therefore, that the distinction between the commercial and the noncommercial use of the mass media, as well as the distinction between "commercial" and "academic" research, has blinded us to the existence of two entirely different ways of experiencing and being influenced by mass media. One way is characterized by lack of personal involvement, which, while perhaps more common in response to commercial subject matter, is by no means limited to it. The second is characterized by a high degree of personal involvement. By this we do *not* mean attention, interest, or excitement but the number of conscious "bridging experiences," connections, or personal references per minute that the viewer makes between his own life and the stimulus. This may vary from none to many.

The significance of conditions of low or high involvement is not that one is better than the other, but that the processes of communication impact are different. That is, there is a difference in the change processes that are at work. Thus, with low involvement one might look for gradual shifts in perceptual structure, aided by repetition, activated by behavioral-choice situations, and *followed* at some time by attitude change. With high involvement one would look for the classic, more dramatic, and more familiar conflict of ideas at the level of conscious opinion and attitude that precedes changes in overt behavior.

I think now we can appreciate again why Madison Avenue may be of little use in the Cold War or even in a medium-hot presidential campaign. The more common skills of Madison Avenue concern the change processes associated with low involvement, while the very different skills required for high-involvement campaigns are usually found elsewhere. However, although Madison Avenue generally seems to know its limitations, the advertising researchers tend to be less clear about theirs. For example, from New York to Los Angeles researchers in television advertising are daily exacting "attitude change" or "persuasion" scores from captive audiences, these scores based on questionnaires and methods which, though plausible, have no demonstrated predictive validity. The plausibility of these methods rests on the presence of a more or less explicit model of communication effectiveness. Unfortunately, the model in use is the familiar one that assumes high involvement. Perhaps it is the questionnaires and the research procedures themselves that are responsible for creating what high involvement is present, which would not otherwise exist. The wiser or more cautious researchers meanwhile retreat to the possibilities of impersonal exactness in controlled field experiments and behavioral criteria. What has been left out, unfortunately, is the development of a low-involvement model, and the pre-test measures based on such a model. The further development of this model is an important next step, not only for the perhaps trivial world of television advertising but for the better understanding of all those areas of public opinion and education which, socially important as they may be, may simply not be very involving to significant segments of the audience.

In time we may come to understand the effectiveness of mass media primarily in terms of the *consistency* with which a given campaign, commercial or noncommercial, employs talent and research sensitively attuned to the real level of audience involvement. In time, also, we may come to understand that behavior, that is, verbal behavior and overt behavior, is always consistent provided we do not impose premature and narrowly conceived rules as to which must precede, or where, when, and how it must be measured.[13]

Notes and References

1. Joseph Klapper, *The Effects of Mass Media*, Glencoe, Ill., Free Press, 1960.

2. Raymond Bauer, "The Limits of Persuasion," *Harvard Business Review*, September-October 1958, 105–110.

3. Neil Borden, *The Economic Effects of Advertising*, Chicago, Irwin, 1942.

4. H. A. Zielske, "The Remembering and Forgetting of Advertising," *Journal of Marketing*, January 1959, 239–243.

5. H. Ebbinghaus, *Grundzuge der Psychologie,* Leipzig, Germany, Veit, 1902.

6. C. T. Hovland *et al., The Order of Presentation in Persuasion,* New Haven, Yale University Press, 1957, 136.

7. H. E. Krugman, "An Application of Learning Theory to TV Copy Testing," *Public Opinion Quarterly*, Vol. 26, 1962, 626–634.

8. This is the title of a working manuscript distributed privately by E. L. Hartley in 1964, which concerns his experimentation with new methods of health education in the Philippine Islands.

9. L. Festinger and N. Maccoby, "On Resistance to Persuasive Communications," *Journal of Abnormal and Social Psychology,* Vol. 68, No. 4, 1964, 359–366.

10. E. R. Guthrie, *The Psychology of Learning*, New York, Harper, 1935, 26.

11. D. E. Broadbent, *Perception and Communication,* London, Pergamon Press, 1958, Chap. 9.

12. Psychological salience was first discussed in this manner by E. L. Hartley, *Problems in Prejudice*, New York, Kings Crown Press, 1946, 107–115.

13. The consistency of verbal and overt behavior has also been reasserted by Hovland, who attributes pseudo-differences to those *research designs* which carelessly compare results of laboratory experiments with results of field surveys (C. I. Hovland, "Reconciling Conflicting Results Derived from Experimental and Survey Studies of Attitude Change," *American Psychologist*, Vol. 14, 1959, 8–17); by Campbell, who attributes pseudo-differences to the fact that verbal and overt behaviors have different situational thresholds (D. T. Campbell, "Social Attitudes and Other Acquired Behavioral Dispositions," in S. Koch, ed., *Psychology: A Study of a Science*, Vol. 6, McGraw-Hill, 1963, 94–172); and by Rokeach, who attributes pseudo-differences to the fact that overt behavior is the result of interaction between *two* sets of attitudes, one toward the object and one toward the situation, and that most research leaves one of the two attitudes unstudied (M. Rokeach, "Attitude Changes and Behavior Change," paper presented at the annual conference of the World Association for Public Opinion Research, Dublin, Ireland, Sept. 9, 1965).

1.10 Consumer Behavior: A Field Theoretical Approach

HAROLD H. KASSARJIAN

In its short history, the field of consumer behavior has often reminded me of Diogenes who, somewhat near sighted, traveled down paths and through uncharted forests looking for the truth. So consumer behavior has been looking, under bushes, behind trees, in musty social science books, at economics and mathematics, searching but never quite finding a theory.

Steeped in the tradition of economics, buying behavior was first explained by the elegant, yet simple, utility theory of economics. At all times a rational consumer would work toward one goal—the maximization of utility. Further many economists considered behavior to be caused entirely by environmental stimuli in much the same way that a billiard ball responds to the impact of a cue. For example, unit sales were considered to respond to changes in price, and borrowing was considered to respond to changes in the rate of interest. The consumer was implicitly considered to be passive; his behavior was predictable and deterministic; he was assumed to react in a known way to a given stimulus.

Not unlike the traditional stimulus-response views in American psychology of the early 1900's, complex hypothetical constructs were not deemed necessary under utility theory. Intervening variables such as values, beliefs, aspirations, and group pressures need not be accounted for in its parsimonious elegance.

However, the constructs of drive, motivation, and values could not be long ignored or naively assumed in the social sciences. It was left to the psychoanalytically oriented motivation researchers to introduce and emphasize both conscious and unconscious motivation in marketing. Deep seated forces that may or may not lead to psychotic behavior, in the views of the Freudian and Neo-Freudian marketing theorists, also led to the choice of a car, the selection of Sunkist oranges over Florida oranges, and the consumption of Camel cigarettes over a filtered brand—still deterministic in view and Aristotelian in their approach to causality. The sociological and social-psychological theorists were soon to follow with their emphasis on interpersonal approaches, group pressures and behavioral norms, although they brought with them no theory of consumer behavior as such.

Finally, the concept of determinism was to be challenged by the mathematical model theorists. Again from psychology and the impetus of Hull, the stochastic learning models of Estes, Burke, and Bush and Mosteller were adapted to consumer behavior. Now the entelechy of simple causality was to be replaced either by a belief that all behavior at its core is probabilistic, or at best the use of probability concepts to represent a host of causal factors without attempt at explanation....

A common characteristic of many of these approaches to consumer behavior is their reliance to a greater or lesser extent upon Aristotelian logic and modes of thought rather than the Galileian and post-Galileian scientific logic that has served so well in the physical sciences.

Aristotelian Concepts

Aristotelian logic is distinguishable by several characteristics.[1] The first of these is its heavy dependence upon valuative and normative concepts. There exist ethical and unethical influences on behavior, rational and irrational consumers, good and bad decisions. Much of the justification and criticism of marketing and advertising relies on this form of anthropomorphism.

Secondly, when Galileian and post-Galileian physics extended the field of natural law, it was not due only to the exclusion of value concepts but also a changed interpretation of classification. "For Aristotelian physics the membership of an object in a given class was of critical importance, because for Aristotle the class defined the essence or essential nature of the object and thus determined its behavior in both positive and negative respects." The basic logic of market segmentation, the classification of goods and the attempts to derive distinct "laws of behavior" for the separate classifications, approach the Aristotelian conceptualizations of nature.

Aristotle's classification schema in turn determined lawfulness and chance. Those things are lawful which occur without exception. And, also, those things are lawful which occur frequently. "Excluded from the class of the conceptually intelligible as mere chance are those things which occur only once, individual events as such. Actually the behavior of a thing is determined by its essential nature, and this essential nature is exactly the abstractly defined class (*i.e.,* the sum total of the common characteristics of a whole group of objects), it follows that each event, as a particular event, is chance, undetermined."

Finally, in premedieval Aristotelian logic, regularity is to be understood entirely in historical terms. Behavior is determined by past events, not the immediate present. The purchase of a product, the decision process, is to be understood in terms of childhood frustrations and fixations for the motivation researcher, the personality development for the Neo-Freudians, and the number of trials for stimulus-response and mathematical theorists. Present behavior is either predetermined by past events or is to be explained by chance and not by law.

Galileian Concepts

Turning to the Galileian and post-Galileian concepts in physics and to their counterpart in psychology—Gestalt and Field Theory—one finds a new set of conceptualizations about nature, reality and lawfulness. First, there are no valuative or classificatory schema. The same laws govern the course of the stars, the falling of stones, and the flight of super-sonic jets. The behavior of the ghetto Negro can be explained in the same terms as that of a rural Peruvian peasant or a pretender to the throne on the Riviera. Such assumptions as rational and irrational behavior, logical or illogical decisions, or even normal or psychotic actions become meaningless. Classification can be made only according to the underlying genotypic laws rather than the observable phenotypic properties. Behavior cannot be explained or understood by resorting to a statistical or historical analysis. For example, the law of falling bodies, $s = \frac{1}{2} gt^2$, applies to stars, baseballs, and dead butterflies, irrespective of their observable phenotypic differences. The law does not state that the relationship holds regularly or frequently, 60% of the time or even at the .05 level of statistical confidence. And in fact, outside of theory, the relationship can never be observed on earth and can only be approximated under the most carefully constructed and artificially controlled conditions. The law is not determined historically, by historical actuary, or by counting and empirically measuring falling apples to see what percentage behave according to hypothesis and what percentage do not. In short, the falling of all bodies is determined by genotypic relationships—the fortuitousness of the individual case is not undetermined, random, chance or an exception to the data to be ignored.

Although some evidence exists that previous purchases of coffee, orange juice, or bread will allow for predictions of future behavior, the relationship does not hold for any given individual or even for an aggregate in the purchase of a new home, a fruit tree to be planted in the back yard, or the color and design of a new tie. To create a separate behavioral law for the purchase of an orange tree and for the purchase of orange juice appears most Aristotelian in logic. . . .

Concepts such as "perceived risk" and the literature on group dynamics in consumer behavior show the Lewinian influence. In psychology, literally hundreds and perhaps thousands of studies have been conducted by Lewin and his followers, such as Cartwright, Festinger, Zajonc, Bavelas, Likert, French, Kelley and dozens of others familiar to students of consumer behavior. Unfortunately the basic theoretical structure is not well known in marketing, although a few consumer studies have been conducted.[2] In fact, and more important, the theory has been seriously misunderstood. . . .

A Field Theoretical Approach

The Constructive Method

The classificatory approach, rampant in marketing and consumer behavior, has as a basic assumption that concepts can be derived from data that somehow capture the essential characteristics of that data, and that somehow by collecting data on the aggregate, we will understand the consumer and his actions. Hence generalizations from individual consumers lead to concepts about housewives in a given socio-economic class and to female consumers in general. However, using such a phenotypic approach, there is no logical way back from the concept "lower-class female consumer" to the individual.[3] Hence, one resorts to statistics and probability. Perhaps it was fortunate for the development of the physical sciences that modern statistics, representative samples and factor analysis were not available to Galileo and Newton. Seldom do the physical sciences resort to statistics, since it is not the purpose of laws to summarize the distribution of observed events. Once a law of consumer behavior is proposed, it must be tested against all conditions included under the law whether these occur frequently or not. Laws, then, cannot be developed by generalizing from molecular data. In other words, in studying some event or act, say purchase behavior, one cannot study the isolated parts such as price, personality, reference groups, frequency of purchase, or political conditions, separately in the expectation that it will eventually be possible to reconstruct the whole by adding together the parts. This is the familiar Gestalt dictum: the whole is different from, if not greater than, the sum of the isolated parts. To understand the entire event one must study the whole problem, then by continuous experimentation and logical manipulation the parts of the whole can be differentiated and placed in correct relationship with each other.

If one studies the effect of price of, say, early American style furniture, the influence of the retail outlet, pressures exerted by children in a family decision, and the personal influence of neighbors, and hence develops abstractions and generalizations, these individual parts cannot be put together to describe or predict why any individual made the purchase he did. What is lost is the interrelationship of the parts, the interactions and confounding of one influence with the other. Hence, a field theoretical approach, a level of analysis that attempts to transform the phenotypic language of data into a language of constructs or genotypes; a mode of analysis that starts with the entire behavior pattern and attempts to extract the relevant relationships rather than first studying the individual parts and from them futilely attempting to reconstruct the purchase act.

Ahistorical Approach

A second basic foundation of a field theoretical approach to consumer behavior is its emphasis on an ahistorical approach. Only facts that exist in the present can directly affect present events. Since consumer behavior depends upon the forces and influences acting upon the individual at a given moment in time, the moment the behavior itself occurs, past events and future events which do not exist now cannot effect his behavior. The relationship of the past to the present is so indirect that its explanatory value is slight. This is not to deny completely the effect of previous experiences in the behavior of the consumer, but rather to keep it in perspective. Only the directly relevant facts from previous behavior which exert an influence on the present are to be considered, rather than childhood experiences in general as used by the motivation researcher or number of previous trials for the learning theorist or Markov analyst. Further, future events, aspirations and expectations, as they are relevant and represented in the present are accounted for by field theory, concepts difficult to deal with in many of the theoretical approaches to consumer behavior. Consumer behavior, however, must be explained in terms of the properties which exist at the time the event occurs.

The Life Space

The most fundamental of the Lewinian concepts is that of the life space or psychological field. All behavior—consuming, purchasing, thinking, crying—is a function of the life space, which in turn consists of the total manifold of "facts" which psychologically exist, all of the influences, for an individual at a given moment in time. The life space is the totality of the individual's world as he himself perceives it; it is the individual's perception of "reality," the totality of possible events.

The life space, thus, includes the person and the environment. The person is represented by a differentiated region within the life space in a dynamic interrelationship with the environment. The environment, in turn, does not refer to the objective world of physical stimuli, but rather is the psychological world as it exists for the individual under study. It contains only those facts which exist for him at a given point in time, somewhat analogous to a phenomonological field, although unconscious determinants of behavior are not excluded. The term behavior has been employed by Lewin to refer to any change within the life space. For behavior to occur, some perceived change within the life space must exist. A change in the geographic world or "objective" environment, such as a change in package design, color of label, price or physical characteristics of a consumer product which is not represented by a change in the psychological field of the consumer, cannot lead to a behavior change.

The life space of the newborn child may be described as a field which has relatively few and only vaguely distinguishable areas, perhaps only greater or less comfort. No definite representations of objects or persons exist, future events or aspirations do not exist, nor is there even an area that can be called "my own body." The child is ruled by the situation immediately at hand; he has no conception of past experiences. As he grows there is an increased differentiation within this life space. Areas such as his own body, his mother, edible food, non-edible objects can be distinguished. Included also is a differentiation of the time dimension as plans extend further into the future, and activities of increasingly longer duration are cognitively organized as one unit. A mature adult can differentiate between brands of products, two models of an automobile or two candidates within the same political party.

The various differentiated regions, however, are not equally accessible to the person. The boundaries of the region may from time to time become more or less permeable, and in fact may act as a barrier to locomotion into the region. To the child the region representing his mother may be easily accessible at all times. Roller skating with much older children may be a less permeable region, while consuming a bottle of scotch may represent an impermeable area. Movement or locomotion from one region to another is usually carried out in a definite sequence of steps or a path that is perceived by the person as necessary to move from where he is to his goal.

Thus, the behavior of the consumer, either in a supermarket selecting among products or in the living room semi-consciously planning the purchase of a dishwasher or a new home, can be represented as a function of the psychological field or cognitive structure of the individual—a dynamic relationship in which change in any one region will lead to changes in the entire field.

Mathematization

A final foundation to consumer behavior from a field theory approach is an emphasis on the need to mathematize the theoretical structure. One of the most significant features of the work of Lewin and his followers has been the use of mathematics to quantify the theory. The first attempt was to apply non-Euclidean topological geometry modified somewhat by vector and scaler mathematics.[4] The contributions of J. F. Brown and the more recent introduction of graph theory by Harary and Norman[5] indicate the potential for the use of mathematics in a field theoretical approach both on a theoretical and applied plane. Unfortunately time does not allow for an elaboration of these approaches in this paper, but must await later attempts.

Dynamic Concepts

The life space, then, is a topological representation of the cognitive organization of the individual. However the topological or nonmetric concepts in and of themselves are not enough to account for behavior—why one purchases Standard Oil products rather than a private brand. To explain consumer behavior fully several dynamic concepts are needed.

Tension. The first of these concepts is that of tension, a state of the person within the life space. Just as the environment is differentiated into regions, so too the person can be considered a system of dynamically interdependent regions. These in turn consist of two sub-systems, the more central inner-personal or need-value system and the peripheral perceptual-motor system. A tension is a state of an inner-personal region relative to other inner-personal regions. The concept of tension can probably replace such undefinable and vague generalizations as needs, wants, motives, drive or urge. Physiological conditions such as hunger or sex, and social demands such as high fashion clothing, a new hat, a Corvette or a candy bar, are best conceptualized as tension or pressure against the boundaries of some region within the inner-personal system. A need or drive can be defined as a term trying to explain a syndrome of behavior which takes into account the tension within a person to achieve some goal. As soon as the goal is reached the region is no longer in tension; that is, the system achieves equilibrium.

A state of tension in a particular region will tend to equalize itself with the amount of tension in the surrounding regions. Hence a need for sexual gratification may lead to a need for sports cars, cosmetics, group membership, high fashion, clothing and an expensive apartment, or *vice versa*. The tension can be equalized by any process such as thinking, remembering, purchasing, consuming or even day dreaming to achieve equilibrium.

Energy. Further, the person can be seen as a complex energy system. This psychical energy is released as the person attempts to return to equilibrium, after it has been thrown into a state of disequilibrium by the arousal of a tension or need in one part of the system.

Valence.   The third dynamic property of a field theoretical approach is that of valence, a conceptual property of a region of the psychological environment representing its attractiveness or unattractiveness. A valence is obviously coordinated with a need; that is, whether a particular region of the environment has a positive or negative value depends directly upon a system in a state of tension. To a hungry person food will have a positive valence; to a satiated individual even the odor of food can be quite repelling or negative. Although food in general may well have a positive valence, a particular product that is sold by a disliked retailer, or manufactured by a producer that supports lunatic political causes, is responsible for obnoxious advertising or engages in disagreeable labor practices, may well take on a negative valence. Hence, even to a hungry person a particular food may be repelling. The strength of the "need" in combination with other prevailing factors determines the strength of the valence.

Force or Vector.   A valence plus energy creates a force—a property of the environment rather than of the person. The strength and direction of the force can be represented as a vector acting upon the person, causing locomotion, or in our terminology, behavior. Of course, more than one vector at any given moment is likely to exist—the decision between two brands of gasoline, both of which have a positive valence, the choice between being drafted or branded a coward, both with negative valence, or the purchase of a dishwasher with a positive valence related to its function and a negative vector created by its cost. In such cases the direction of locomotion will be the resultant of the various vectors. The net valence, if above threshold, will determine whether or not the dishwasher is purchased. Similarly the selection of a service station will depend upon the relative strength of the valences. Presuming both brands are perceived to be exactly identical within the life space of the individual— vacillation, indecision, greater tension, and a high non-pecuniary cost of consumption should result. Perhaps it is the need to reduce the non-pecuniary cost of consumption that leads to very fine discriminations among brands and manufacturers and to brand loyalty, when in fact the physical products are "known" to be identical.[6]

With the topological structure of the life space and the dynamic properties of tensions, need, valence, and vectors let us consider an example. On a midweek afternoon a housewife considers going downtown to see a motion picture. The need to "do something" and the desirability or positive valence of the goal—the motion picture—create a vector or force in the direction of the goal within her life space. Her life space is structured to contain two paths to the goal: one, walk to the corner, take the bus, buy a ticket and enter the goal region; and two, get the car keys, walk to garage, drive car, park car, buy ticket and enter goal region. Suddenly remembering that the garage is locked and her husband walked off with the key, the region of the life space encompassing "drive car" is inaccessible, the boundaries of her life space are impermeable. To overcome the barrier to her psychological movement requires a circuitous route. She decides to walk, and in preparation for the trip, passes by the refrigerator. A new stimulus has now entered her life space as she remembers she has no vegetables for dinner that evening and that she must go to the supermarket.

Suddenly, plans for the theater are discarded, her life space is restructured around her grocery shopping. The new regions of her life space consist of walking to the market, selecting the produce, paying for it, and entering the positive goal region to reduce the tension. Other possible paths or methods of obtaining vegetables such as planting seeds and raising carrots do not occur to her, are not part of her life space. Having selected the carrots at the market, her life space again is restructured as she contemplates a new path for entering the goal region. Rather than pay for the vegetables she can shoplift; however, the negative consequences of this behavior and the concomitant negative vector induce her to pass through the check-out stand to reach the goal, reduce the tension, and restore equilibrium.

Summary

In conclusion, it is maintained that consumer behavior can be and should be conceptualized from a field theoretical perspective. Causality is the resultant of co-existing forces and is not probabilistic. Analysis of the consumer's actions must begin with the entire situation as a whole, from which the relevant parts can be differentiated, rather than study of the isolated parts leading to reconstruction of the behavioral act. The behavior of the consumer is a function of the psychological field which exists at the time the behavior occurs. This field of life space consists of the person and environment interacting in a mutually interdependent relationship. And finally, the field can be represented mathematically by the use of non-Euclidian geometry and vector theory.

The purpose of this paper has been to reintroduce and summarize a few of the basic field theoretical concepts that relate to consumer behavior. Elaboration of the scientific method, the details of the theory, and its concomitant mathematics as well as quantitative research must be left for future discussions.

Notes and References

1. Portions of this and the following section have been taken from, "The Conflict Between Aristotelian and Galileian Modes of Thought in Contemporary Psychology," in Kurt Lewin, *A Dynamic Theory of Personality* (New York: McGraw-Hill, 1935), 1–42.

2. Warren J. Bilkey, "The Vector Hypothesis of Consumer Behavior," *Journal of Marketing*, Oct. 1951, 137–151; "A Psychological Approach to Consumer Behavior Analysis," *Journal of Marketing*, July 1953, 18–25; "Psychic Tensions and Purchasing Behavior," *Journal of Social Psychology*, 1955, 247–257; "Consistency Test of Psychic Tension Ratings Involved in Consumer Purchase Behavior," *Journal of Social Psychology*, 1957, 81–91; Kurt Lewin, "Forces Behind Food Habits and Methods of Change," *Bulletin of the National Research Council*, Vol. 108

(1943). Results of the studies are summarized in Kurt Lewin, "Group Decision and Social Change," in *Readings in Social Psychology,* 3rd ed., Eleanor E. Maccoby, *et al.* (eds.) New York: Holt, Rinehart and Winston, 1958).

3. Kurt Lewin, "Field Theory and Learning," in *Field Theory in Social Science* (New York: Harper & Row, 1951).

4. Kurt Lewin, "The Conceptual Representation and the Measurement of Psychological Forces," *Contributions to Psychological Theory,* Vol. 1, No. 4, Serial No. 4 (Durham, N.C.: Duke Univ. Press, 1938).

5. F. Harary and R. Z. Norman, *Graph Theory as a Mathematical Model in the Social Sciences* (Ann Arbor, Mich.: Institute for Social Research, 1953).

6. For a discussion of factors influencing brand choice, see William F. Brown, "The Determination of Factors Influencing Brand Choice," *Journal of Marketing*, Apr. 1950, 699–706.

2 Motivation and Personality

Overview

From Chapter 1 it is evident that many of the actions of the consumer depend on his perceptions of the world around him, his unique concepts of reality, and his learned reactions to the stimuli that impinge upon him. But why does he act at all? What is the driving force behind his behavior? Or, more simply, what are his motives? *Motivation* may be thought of as a driving force or a necessity to reduce a state of tension. Basically, the function of an individual's motives is to protect, satisfy, and enhance himself. The particular ways in which an individual goes about protecting and enhancing himself define his *personality*.

Motivation

Physiological Needs

One large set of motives stems from biological need systems. These are the tensions that must be reduced if the body is to survive—the need for oxygen, water, food, and waste elimination; relief from pain; protection from heat, cold, or fatigue; and so on.

Although biologically determined, the physiological drives are subject to social influence. Any digestible food containing fat, carbohydrates, or protein will reduce hunger, but not all foods are socially acceptable to any given culture. The typical American will not eat horse meat unless he is starving. On the other hand, he will consume corn, often right off the cob, to the disbelief of many Europeans, who consider corn fit only to feed livestock and eating it off the cob to be extremely boorish behavior.

Outside its theoretical contributions, the study of physiological drives has generally been of little concern in the field of consumer behavior. Typically most of our physiological needs are met, and although some people, especially the poor, may be short of vitamins, sufficient proteins, or milk, these drives seldom determine more complex decision making. A hungry person seeks food; there is little complexity to the process and little that cannot be easily understood. To us, what is far more fascinating is why one person will buy an automobile heavily laden with accessories and high profit margins, while another individual with the same discretionary income will select a small car with an inexpensive price tag.

However, we do not mean to underrate the basic physiological drives. For example, in the first selection in this chapter, Nisbett and Kanouse show the relationship between number of hours of food deprivation and the total amount of money spent in supermarkets. Their data clearly indicate that the longer it has been since a shopper has eaten, the higher his cash-register receipt total will be. Particularly fascinating is the fact that fat people seem to react quite differently than people of normal weight.

In addition to purely physiological needs, there are several motives that have a biological basis, but that are confounded with social and learned elements. Sexual activity, for example, is a hormonal drive, yet is guided by values, mores, attitudes, and expectations. In many ways emotions are similar. The biological correlates to fear, anxiety, joy, love, and so on are quite similar to one another. Yet the reaction to fear can be quite dissimilar from the reaction to love. This dissimilarity is most probably caused by learned mores, norms, and values of society.

In fact, fear has been one of the very few emotions thoroughly researched in the field of consumer behavior. Early studies (e.g., Janis and Feshbach, 1953) indicate that strong fear appeals were less effective than moderate or mild fear appeals in producing reported adherence to recommended dental hygiene practices. According to Ray and Wilkie (1970) some ninety follow-up studies have been conducted. Quite a few of these studies confirmed the original Janis and Feshbach findings that strong fear is less effective than mild fear. The assumption is that people tend to shy away from strong fear-arousing situations and to repress the appeals made. However, there have also been numerous studies that obtained exactly the reverse results, finding that high fear arousal was more effective than neutral or mild fear arousal. These latter findings, of course, tend to pose an ethical dilemma for the change agent. On the one hand, he is seeking attitude and behavior change; on the other hand, he must be concerned about what moral right he has to arouse the anxieties or fears of another person. The second article in this chapter, by Spence and Moinpour, reviews some of the literature on fear-arousing appeals and discusses the ethical problems in their use.

Psychological Needs

A second large set of motives stems from psychological needs related to social environment. These demands begin in childhood as the child discovers a need to interact with his parents. Later, surrounding social institutions demand his conformity to certain values and patterns of behavior. He is expected to go to school, marry, work at an occupation, and live in a manner appropriate to his place in society (Lazarus, 1963). Often he is expected to delay the immediate gratification of his wants. In order to complete his education, he must delay getting the job which would enable him to purchase a new car. In rare cases, social motives have become potent enough to overcome the biological survival needs. Religious and political martyrs will suffer great deprivation and even death for the sake of certain values and principles (ibid.). The hunger strikes of Ghandi or Cesar Chavez are clear examples.

As we attempt to extract, from the complex interdependencies of tissue demands, parental pressures, and societal expectations, a set of drives that can be neatly classified as psychological motivations, we can appreciate why researchers and scholars in this area do not agree. The particular philosophy or theory of personality a researcher adheres to will color his views. Some scholars focus on the biophysical nature of man, as did Sigmund Freud and Carl Jung. A number of Freud's followers (Alfred Adler, Karen Horney, Erich Fromm, and Harry Stack Sullivan) later refocused their efforts on the interaction between physical needs and societal demands. Still others turned their attention completely away from the physiological view (Kurt Lewin, Gordon Allport, Clark Hull, and Carl Rogers, for example). Some classified social needs into many categories (e.g., Henry A. Murray), and others into a few categories (e.g., Abraham Maslow).

A widely quoted view is that of Maslow (1943), who proposed five hierarchical categories of needs:

1. Physiological needs—hunger, thirst, etc.
2. Safety needs—security, protection, and order or routine.
3. Love needs—affection, as distinct from the biological need for sex, and belonging, the need for family and friends.
4. Esteem needs—self-respect, prestige, success, and achievement.
5. Self-actualization needs—the desire for self-fulfillment.

Maslow concluded that the lower order needs must be more or less fulfilled before the higher needs emerge. Only after tissue needs are met do safety needs become important, for example.

In middle-class America, most individuals seem to be attempting to satisfy their love or esteem needs, since their more basic needs generally are satisfied. If advertising at all reflects the American need structure, this becomes evident from a casual perusal of present-day ads. One seldom sees an ad message like "Crispy crackers fill your stomach fuller than other products"; more typically one sees "Serve Crispy crackers with exotic cheese and impress your friends." Again presuming Maslow's views to be correct, we may then also wonder if the security and safety themes of insurance companies are the most fruitful approaches for the particular market segment at which they are aimed.

Maslow further claimed (1954) that, even when the need for self-actualization if fulfilled in the small percentage of the population that has reached that stage, seldom is the self satisfied, for new and higher needs emerge: for example, the desires to *know* or to *understand* and the need for *aesthetic* satisfaction.

Henry A. Murray (1938), an early needs theorist, held a different view of motivation. He presented a long list of needs which must be satisfied to appease the organism. Although his list has been frequently modified and elaborated, a sampling of it (Hall and Lindzey, 1957) indicates his theory:

1. Abasement—the need to accept blame, criticism, error, inferiority.
2. Achievement—the need to master, manipulate, organize, surpass others.
3. Affiliation—the need to win affection.
4. Autonomy—the need to become free of restraint.
5. Defendence—the need to defend the self against criticism, blame, and assault.
6. Deference—the need to admire superiors, to yield to the influence of others.
7. Dominance—the need to control and direct the behavior of others.
8. Exhibition—the need to be seen and heard.
9. Play—the need to act for fun without other purpose.
10. Sex—the need for an erotic relationship.
11. Understanding—the need to ask or answer general questions.

Murray emphasized the importance of unconscious sources of motivation and throughout stressed the relation of motivation to brain processes. His conceptions have had a major influence in the field of psychology, particularly on investigators, including motivation researchers in advertising, who have used his Thematic Apperception Test, a research tool discussed in the next chapter.

It should be evident that it is nearly impossible to discuss motivation, except perhaps in relation to tissue needs, outside the context of a particular theory of behavior. Moreover, a discussion of motivation cannot be separated from theories of personality. Maslow's work, for example, although called a theory of motivation, is also clearly a theory of personality. However, other theories, often classified as personality theories, involve primarily motivations and drives.

Personality

The term *personality* is used by psychologists to denote a consistent pattern of responses to the world that impinges upon the individual internally and externally. Often, behavior is governed by an immediate stimulus in the perceptual field; for example, if an individual is approached by something or someone threatening, hostile, or dangerous, he may prepare to fight back, run, hide, or freeze in terror. Or he may faint, scream for help, or beg for mercy. The means of self-protection he initiates depends partly upon his perception and evaluation of the threatening object and partly upon his generalized mode of coping with his environment. Individuals react in a consistent, usually stable fashion to a variety of environmental circumstances. In fact, it is not consistency of behavior that is remarkable, but rather the occasional circumstance in which an individual behaves inconsistently with his usual pattern. It is this stability of reaction that allows us to type people and to talk of their personality.

Theories of Personality

Human behavior and its subset personality have been written about for centuries both by scholars and by playwrights, novelists, and poets. During the twentieth century, both the theoretical and empirical contributions to this topic have accelerated at a rapid pace. The third selection in this chapter, by Harold Kassarjian, briefly reviews the various theories and approaches to personality and discusses the dozens of empirical studies that have attempted to tie personality into purchasing behavior, media reading habits, innovativeness, opinion leadership, and other such topics. Kassarjian discusses the several basic thrusts that personality theory has taken, ranging from the biological theories of Freud and the psychoanalytic movement to the neo-Freudian theories of such scholars as Erich Fromm, Karen Horney, and Alfred Adler to the more quantitatively sophisticated views of the trait and factor theorists.

The Freudian movement is perhaps best represented in consumer behavior by the motivation researchers who enjoyed great popularity after World War II. In more recent years, the view of motivation researchers that much of consumption behavior could be accounted for by deep-seated unconscious drives and motives has been replaced by the more parsimonious views of trait and factor theorists. These theorists consider personality to be composed of a set of traits and motives. (Much of the work of Murray can be perceived as a set of traits that will describe an individual, although Murray himself was psychoanalytically oriented.) Hence, a person can be described by his scores on a variety of dimensions. As can be seen in the Kassarjian paper, many of these variables have been correlated with such topics as brand choice, automobile purchase, cigarette smoking, preferences for advertising, etc. However, the results have been mixed. In turn, Nakanishi (1972) has argued that situational or environmental factors are more important than trait approaches admit and that this has led to the mixed results.

The paper by Jacoby on the relationship between innovativeness and dogmatism is a good example of the trait and factor type of study. Jacoby found the individuals low on a dogmatic scale were more likely to be innovators than their more dogmatic counterparts.

Early studies often took a single personality variable and studied its relationship to a single behavioral variable, such as brand preference. In recent years the research has become considerably more sophisticated statistically. The Sparks and Tucker article is an example of this type of work using canonical correlations, a multivariate statistical technique, in the attempt to relate product to personality. (The usual statistical techniques used in personality studies are univariate, such as Pearsonian correlation coefficient or Chi Square, in which the relationship between a single dependent variable and single independent variable is measured. In some cases, multiple regression is employed, in which the correlation of a single dependent variable with several independent variables is measured. A canonical correlation is one in which the correlations of several dependent and several independent variables are examined.)

Another type of personality research has emerged, variously called *psychographic* or life-style research. According to its proponents, it offers the richness of motivation research combined with the statistical and methodological sophistication of trait and factor theory. Psychographic analysis attempts to segment groups of individuals on the basis of their interests, values, opinions, attitudes, and demographic characteristics. The purchasing behavior, media reading habits, retail store patronage, and other consumer variables are then compared among the various segments or life-style patterns.

Just how valuable the psychographic approach will become is yet to be seen. The last selection in this chapter, by Wells and Tigert, further explains the technique and presents some examples.

Conclusion

It must be assumed that personality and motivation are important variables in the consumer decision-making process. At this point in the development of the state of the art the evidence is somewhat ambiguous. Some studies show a tight relationship between personality and motivation and behavior in the marketplace. Others do not. The issue, however, is just what are the influences, how do they operate, and how important are they? Answers to these questions must be left for future theorizing and research.

References

Janis, I., and S. Feshbach. "Effects of Fear Arousing Communications." *Journal of Abnormal and Social Psychology*, Vol. 48 (Jan. 1953), 78–92.

Lazarus, R. S. *Personality and Adjustment*, Prentice-Hall, 1963.

Hall, C. S., and G. Lindzey. *Theories of Personality.* Wiley, 1957.

Maslow, A. H. "A Theory of Human Motivation." *Psychological Review,* Vol. 50 (1943), 370–396.

Murray, H. A., *et al. Explorations in Personality.* Oxford University Press, 1938.

Nakanishi, M. "Personality and Consumer Behavior: An Extension." *Proceedings of the Third Annual Conference,* ed. M. Venkatesan. Association for Consumer Research (1972), in press.

Ray, M. L., and W. L. Wilkie. "Fear: The Potential of an Appeal Neglected by Marketing." *Journal of Marketing Research,* Vol. 34 (Jan. 1970), 54–62.

2.1 Obesity, Hunger, and Supermarket Shopping Behavior
RICHARD E. NISBETT, DAVID E. KANOUSE

Several recent studies by Schachter and his colleagues have demonstrated that the types of stimuli which motivate eating for the obese individual differ from those which motivate eating for the individual of normal weight. For the most part, overweight individuals are quite responsive to a variety of environmental and food-related cues which have nothing to do with nutritional needs. The amount they eat is strongly affected by such factors as the amount of food immediately present (Nisbett, in press-a), the taste of food (Nisbett, in press-b) and whether they believe it is mealtime (Schachter & Gross, in press). Conversely, the obese are less responsive than normal individuals to stimuli which vary with nutritional state and which are presumed to signal hunger and satiety, such as the state of food deprivation and gastric motility (e.g., Schachter, Goldman, & Gordon, in press).

The proposition that the overweight are unresponsive to nutritional state is supported primarily by evidence about their actual eating behavior; the obese eat no more when deprived of food for a period of time than when recently fed. Intuitively it seems that behavior in the supermarket should reflect this same insensitivity. For most of us, when we shop on an empty stomach, supermarket aisles are lined with temptations. When we have recently eaten, however, we are quite capable of viewing the shelves with an efficient and dispassionate eye.

We anticipate, then, that individuals of normal weight will spend more time and money in the supermarket when deprived than when recently fed. For overweight individuals, who are presumably insensitive to nutritional state, we do not expect such a relationship.

Method

The data were collected in a New Haven supermarket from 9:00 A.M. to to 6:00 P.M. on a single day. Before the store opened for business, the shopping carts were tagged with identifying numbers. After customers had selected a cart, they were approached by an interviewer who explained that he was taking a survey and asked the following questions:

1. How many people do you shop for?
2. How many times a week do you ordinarily shop?
3. How much do you expect to spend in the store today?
4. When did you last have something to eat?

During the questioning, interviewers recorded the sex and race of S, made judgments about his weight and age and noted his shopping cart number and the time.

Observers stood at the check out lanes and recorded totals from the cash registers. Observers also recorded shopping cart numbers, a description of S, and the time when the total was rung on the register.

Due to the fact that not all Ss were interviewed or observed, some problems of matching "in" and "out" cases arose. These were resolved by discarding cases where interviewer and observer did not agree on the race or sex of S, or on age within 15 years, or where S's estimate of his bill and the bill on the cash register did not agree within $15.

The final sample included 283 Ss. The sample was 81% female and averaged about 45 years of age. It was predominantly upper-lower, lower-middle class, and heavily Italian-American.

Results

It was anticipated that there would be a positive relationship between deprivation and the amount of food purchased for normal Ss and no relationship for the obese.

Figure 1 presents the total on the cash register as a function of the number of hours Ss had been deprived of food at the time of the interview. It may be seen in Figure 1 that for normal Ss there is a decidedly positive relationship between amount purchased and hours of deprivation. The linear component of this curve is significant at the .05 level ($F = 4.30$, $df = 1/128$). The relationship for overweight Ss has precisely the opposite form—increased deprivation is associated with decreased purchase (linear $F = 8.66$, $df = 1/143$, $p < .01$).

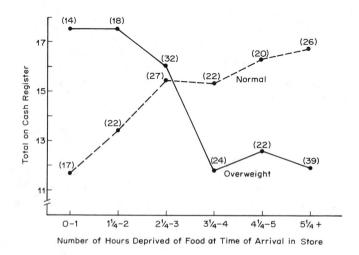

FIGURE 1.   Amount of groceries purchased by normal and overweight shoppers as a function of number of hours of food deprivation.

⸙ It appears then that deprivation has the predicted effect of increasing purchases for normal individuals. The significant *negative* relationship between deprivation and purchase for overweight Ss is puzzling, however, in that it suggests a kind of reverse sensitivity to deprivation for the overweight. Fortunately, further analysis of the data clarifies this finding. It is clear that the amount spent in the store is not a pure measure of the effects of the attractiveness of the food on display. Differences in amount spent may primarily reflect differences in objective shopping needs, such as family size. What is needed is a measure of unplanned spending, or impulse buying. Fotunately such a measure was available in the present study, since Ss estimated their bills when they entered the store. By examining the amount spent in relation to estimate, through covariance techniques, a sensitive measure of unplanned spending can be obtained. The analysis of covariance reveals that there is a significant increase in the amount of unplanned spending for normal individuals (linear $F = 9.55$, $df = 1/127$, $p < .001$) and no effect of deprivation on the unplanned spending of the overweight. To put the matter another way, the increased spending of deprived normal Ss is due to impulse buying rather than larger shopping lists, while the decreased purchasing of deprived obese Ss is exclusively a reflection of decreased buying intentions. We discuss below a possible interpretation of the negative relationship between buying intentions and deprivation for the overweight Ss.

We can expect that the evidence on time spent in the store will resemble the evidence on amount of money spent; that is, normal individuals should shop more slowly when deprived than when they have eaten recently, and this should be less true for overweight individuals. Of course, since shopping time is strongly related to amount purchased, it is necessary to covary amount purchased from shopping time in order to focus on differences in shopping *rates*. The resulting analysis of covariance provides clear support to the prediction.

The interaction between weight and deprivation is significant at the .05 level ($F = 4.85$, $df = 1/278$). Normal Ss shopped less rapidly when deprived while overweight Ss shopped more rapidly.

Discussion

The results are quite consistent with the hypothesis that the overweight are relatively unresponsive to variations in nutritional state. It was found that: (*a*) normal Ss increased their purchases as their deprivation state increased, while overweight Ss decreased their purchases; (*b*) the increase in purchase for normal Ss was due to increased impulse buying, while the decrease for overweight Ss was due to decreased buying intentions; (*c*) normal Ss shopped more slowly when deprived, while overweight Ss did not.

One aspect of the results was unanticipated and deserves some discussion. The overweight Ss intended to buy less when deprived than when they had recently eaten, a result which the "deprivation insensitivity" hypothesis does not require or even comfortably handle. It is possible however that, for the overweight individual, eating begets eating. On completing a meal, the overweight individual may in effect say "My, that was good. I think I'll go out and buy some more." This notion is consistent with the demonstrated responsiveness of the overweight to food- and environment-related cues. To the extent that the overweight individual is influenced by such cues, the act of eating may increase the attractiveness of food rather than diminish it.

References

Nisbett, R. E. Determinants of food intake in obesity. *Science*, Vol. 161 (Aug. 1968), 751–756.

Nisbett, R. E. Taste, deprivation and weight determinants of eating behavior. *Journal of Personality and Social Psychology,* Vol. 10 (Oct. 1968), 107–116.

Schachter, S., Goldman, R., and Gordon, A. The effects of fear, food deprivation and obesity on eating. *Journal of Personality and Social Psychology*, Vol. 10 (Oct. 1968), 91–97.

Schachter, S., and Gross, L. Manipulated time and eating behavior. *Journal of Personality and Social Psychology,* Vol. 10 (Oct. 1968), 98–106.

2.2 Fear Appeals in Marketing: A Social Perspective
HOMER E. SPENCE, REZA MOINPOUR

There has been considerable interest in the effectiveness of fear appeals in marketing communications. For example, Ray and Wilkie reviewed the relevant literature on the potential use of fear appeals in marketing, and Stuteville studied a special case of individual defenses against high fear appeals.[1] While neither of these articles explicitly defined fear appeal, both placed major emphasis on appeals that referred to potential *physiological* damage that might occur (e.g., cancer, accidents) if some behavior were not adopted or discontinued.

Stuteville acknowledged that there was "heavy and continuous reliance on fear appeals in the sale of personal products. . . ." He suggested that such appeals can most effectively be used in the following situations: (1) The feared condition is avoided through use of the sponsor's product. (2) There is no psychological investment in not using the product. (3) What is feared is damage to the *social image* of the self rather than to the *physical* self (*ibid.*, p. 41). Unfortunately, this third situation has received little research attention even though advertising which suggests a threat to one's social image or self-concept is more common than that which raises the possibility of physical harm.

This article raises some questions in hopes that additional thought and research into the use and subsequent effect of fear appeals will be stimulated. It focuses on the more controversial question of whether the use of fear appeals in marketing is desirable from a social welfare perspective. More specifically, the article considers the following issues: What is the nature of appeals concerned with damage to one's social image or self-concept? What are the effects on the audience of employing such appeals? Is it possible to determine whether their use is justified in an economic or social sense?

Fear Appeals and Stimulation of Anxiety

Communications using fear appeals are designed to stimulate anxiety in an audience with the expectation that the audience will attempt to reduce this anxiety by adopting, continuing, discontinuing, or avoiding a specified course of thought or action.

The critical difference between fear appeals and positive appeals is that the former contain a *deliberate* attempt to arouse anxiety. While a positive appeal may also arouse anxiety, it is usually incidental to the main thrust of the message which is a presentation of the product's want-satisfying attributes. For example, a tire manufacturer using appeal began his ad by portraying the plight of a woman stranded along a dark road with a flat tire. The message seemed to say, "Would you allow your wife to get into this situation through your failure to properly equip the family car?" On the other hand, a positive appeal for automobile tires may contain primarily a series of claims about the safety, reliability, and price of the company's product without attempting to stimulate anxiety over the potentially harmful consequences to one's family if tire failure occurs.

Learned Anxiety

Psychologists have shown that anxiety can be learned merely by observing another person produce such a response.[2] For example, many children learn the fears displayed by their parents. If the fears are displayed frequently enough, the children will avoid the situation in which the fear or anxiety occurred (e.g., a parent's fear of insects or snakes). While anxiety appears to be easily learned, several psychologists have hypothesized that "psychological needs" also result from anxiety.[3] Longstreth, for example, explained the role of anxiety as follows: "A child or adult will appear to have a 'need' for something (call it 'X') to ... the extent that the absence of X has been associated with anxiety, and ... to the extent that the presence of X has been associated with reduction in anxiety and/or increases in other pleasant emotional responses."[4]

This research has important implications for advertising using fear appeals directed at children or adults. First, since anxiety appears to be easily conditionable, the continued bombardment of consumers by fear appeals transmitted through mass media may be creating new fears and anxieties or exacerbating old ones. For example, the ad for dish soap which implies that mother's hands will be as soft as her daughter's, and therefore mother will "appear" as young as her daughter, is a play on the fear of looking and growing old. Second, given an increasing number of daily fear-arousing situations, what effect will these have on the average person's threshold of anxiety? The preceding research has shown that with an increased level of anxiety the individual usually responds in some fashion either to avoid the aversive situation or responds in a manner that is concurrent with the anxiety situation. In view of these findings, more concern should be given to the ethical aspects of the manner in which consumers are persuaded to buy products through anxiety-arousing advertisements.

Effects of Anxiety-Arousing Communications

Psychologists' attempts to arouse anxiety through the use of a single exposure to a fear-appeal message have been successful; a positive relationship has been established between the level of fear utilized in a communication and the level of anxiety produced in the receiver. Evans et al. in a study of fear appeals and dental hygiene behavior found that high-fear appeals created more anxiety than low-fear appeals, while low-fear appeals caused more anxiety than positive appeals.[5]

It has also been demonstrated that the level of anxiety can have both positive and negative effects on individuals.[6] Characterization of effects as "positive" or "negative," however, depends upon the frame of reference of the evaluator. Positive effects often mean that the individual is motivated to behave in some manner which is socially defined as "in his interest" or "in the interest of society." Negative effects would be the opposite; however, this delineation is quite arbitrary. Political propaganda campaigns designed to create anxieties and thus generate "war fever" illustrate this conflict. In a marketing context, Ray and Wilkie touch upon this subject:

The basic question here is whether the fear necessary for effective marketing communications may have deleterious consequences for those high-anxiety persons who happen to be in the message audience (*op. cit.*, p. 62).

If a *single* high-fear appeal message can have negative effects, it is perhaps a tenable hypothesis that *multiple* exposures to messages containing fear appeals of an intensity just below that sufficient for a single message to create negative effects may also, in the long run, have similar effects. Research is, therefore, necessary to determine: (1) whether continuous exposure to fear-appeal advertising creates high-anxiety persons in the message audience itself; and (2) whether the effect of fear appeal advertising on low-anxiety individuals is different than on high-anxiety individuals.

An issue which cannot satisfactorily be resolved in this short article concerns the effect of continually stimulating anxiety in a society which has been characterized as exhibiting signs of becoming *overly* anxious.[7] The complexity and pace of contemporary social life creates many situations which are potential sources of anxiety, such as a deteriorating physical environment, increasing incidence of violent crime, international confrontations, and the threat of nuclear war. An important question is whether the general level of an individual's anxiety may be further increased as a result of advertising that uses fear appeals.

Consequences: Fear Appeals and Product Performance

What are the consequences of a "successful" attempt at anxiety arousal? From the firm's viewpoint, anxiety arousal is a means to an end—the purchase of its product; however, this does not invariably occur. What happens to the consumer when a purchase or even repeated purchases do result? Is his anxiety reduced following the successful use of the product? An answer to these questions requires a more detailed investigation of the relationship between product performance and the implied promises in advertisements.

The most persistent ethical question involves the use of fear appeals when the proposed solution to the feared condition is a product which has at best an *indeterminant* effect on the actual causes of that condition. The typical mouthwash or deodorant ad first suggests the possibility of social disapproval and then strongly suggests that some odor is the cause of this feared condition. The sponsor's product is then offered as the *explicit* solution to the *cause* of the feared condition while the *implicit* claim is made that the feared condition will thus be avoided.

However, while deodorants do retard perspiration odor, and mouthwashes do perfume the breath, a consumer has no legal recourse against a firm if the improvement in his *social image* "promised" in an implicit claim does not materialize after using the product. This difficulty does not apply exclusively to fear appeal advertisements. Positive appeals promising enhanced status or improved social image if one wears a certain suit or drives the advertised automobile leave the consumer in a similar position. While the manufacturer can continually remind the consumer that he lives in a world in which social disapproval is a potential problem and offer trite or even unrelated "solutions," presently he may not be held responsible for not delivering the "implied promises" in his advertisements.

The FTC has become increasingly interested in this area as part of the "consumer protection" work of the Commission. In a press release, announcing the Commission's plan to hold a hearing on the impact of advertising on consumers, it stated:

> Some current advertising, and especially that appearing on television, has been challenged as calculated to appeal to nonrational concerns and considerations. These forms of advertising, which are essentially non-informational in character, may raise questions as to their fundamental fairness, their conformity with the traditional economic justifications for advertising as sources of information upon which a free and reasonably informed choice may be made and the extent to which such advertising is designed to exploit such fears or anxieties as social acceptance or personal well being, without fulfilling the desires raised (*FTC News,* May 12, 1971).

For those who point out that bad breath and body odor *are* causes of social disapproval it must be noted that advertisers have not played a totally passive role in the process that brought them to their present level of emphasis. Lambert's "discovery" of halitosis in the 1920s is the classic example; however, the recent introduction and heavy promotion of feminine hygiene deodorants further illustrates the power of this process. The same may be said about detergent advertisements which emphasize the social stigma attached to a "ring around the collar," and advertisements which emphasize the stigma of driving old cars and wearing out-of-style clothing.

While advertisers are not the *cause* of these odor and stigma problems, they do appear to play a role in establishing and perpetuating their existence as standards of social comparison and, thus, perhaps make them more persistent and important than they otherwise might be. Marketers do have an interest in the continuance of these social norms, and fear appeals are an important tool in accomplishing this objective.

Commissioner Jones has recognized the formative nature of marketing activities and the significant part that advertising plays in influencing consumer attitudes and behavior. She has called attention to the need for more information in the following areas:

> The social and cultural impact of advertising . . . and . . . the consumers' physical, emotional and psychological responses to advertising, as they may affect the standards by which advertising is judged.[8]

It is commonly argued that a product's failure to deliver on implied as well as explicit promises about product performance will lead to eventual failure in the marketplace. If a product does not perform on an *explicit* promise, the very real possibility of market failure is not accepted today as a sufficient remedy for the resulting damage to consumer welfare. Legal actions are taken to eliminate the deception, even though the defrauded or deceived consumer may never repurchase the product.

The case of failure to deliver on an *implied* promise is more complex due to the consumer's inability to clearly evaluate performance on the implied claim. The consumer's strong desire to eliminate the feared condition may have led him to initially purchase the product. If this promised performance fails to occur, the consumer may switch to another brand of the same product rather than give up the product category altogether, because he may have accepted the premise that the product has the potential to eliminate the feared conditions. Research into consumers' concepts of implied product claims is lacking and represents a critical need.

In markets where a dominant firm has several brands, such shifting around of demand may be a strong factor contributing to the proliferation of brands and the shortening of brand life-cycles. In such situations, the traditional concept of failure in the marketplace acquires a new meaning. Even if brands frequently fail, firms in oligopolistic markets will replace them with others. Such "new" products are usually launched with advertising containing the same implied promises.

The above hypotheses can be tested by combined efforts of researchers working in the areas of brand loyalty, market economics, and managerial marketing.

Is the Use of Fear Appeals in Marketing Justified?

The use of fear appeals in advertising is open to question because of the possible negative social effects of anxiety stimulation. In addition, there is but a tenuous relation between the fears aroused and solutions offered to remedy them. Therefore, one must examine possible justifications for their use in marketing.

The issue of justification has largely been sidestepped in the marketing literature, perhaps because most research and discussion of fear appeals have centered around campaigns in which the communicator's goal has been to discourage smoking or encourage adoption of better health or safety practices. It is typically easier to achieve a consensus of favorable evaluation of the communicators' *goals* in these cases than in those instances when a deodorant or cosmetic marketing application is being promoted.

A firm chooses a particular advertising theme because it appears to be the most effective alternative available. If the criterion for effectiveness in advertising is derived from the firm's profit-maximization goal it might be concluded that the widespread use of fear appeals is evidence that they are more effective than positive appeals. However, Evans and others *(op. cit.)* found that fear appeal messages *were* more effective in creating anxiety, but that they *were not* more successful in modifying attitudes or behavior than positive appeals.

Differences in effectiveness or profitability between positive and fear appeals can best be determined in a properly designed market study. One issue that might be considered in such a study is that one of these approaches may be more profitable than the other as intensity of exposure reaches either very high or very low levels. It might be hypothesized that for heavily advertised products, such as detergents and personal care products, fear appeals are more profitable which could explain their widespread use in these areas. In a broader sense, research needs to be conducted concerning the general use and the relative importance of fear advertising in various product categories, and the effect of fear appeals on the perceived importance of the purchase. In a recent study Wheatley supported the Ray-Wilkie hypothesis that anxiety-arousing advertising measures are more effective with nonowners of a product than with owners.[9] Further research is needed to provide explanation for the differences of results between these groups.

Summary and Conclusions

In developing this article the authors intended to point out several issues of the fear-appeal controversy which seem to have been neglected. The delineation of these issues will hopefully give some direction to future research on the use of fear appeals in marketing communications.

While anxiety is an acknowledged facet of human existence, its causes are complex, and its effects can be unfavorable to both the individual who becomes highly anxious and to the society in which the anxious individuals live. Anxiety can be stimulated using impersonal and mass media, and behavior modification can result. Advertising which utilizes fear appeals can contribute to individual, and hence social levels of anxiety, although it is not the only contributing factor or even likely the primary one. However, it does appear to be a factor that deserves attention as would be any other potentially harmful practice.

To date, marketers have primarily been concerned with improving the effectiveness of advertising's use of fear appeals. The authors suggest that concern for consumer welfare includes an obligation to critically evaluate all marketing techniques that have indeterminant psychological effects.

The following suggested research areas are important in order to more fully understand the impact of anxiety-arousing advertising:

(1) There is an urgent need for research regarding the impact of communication messages containing fear appeals on consumers. What is the extent of variation of this impact on various socioeconomic classes of consumers? Specific attention should be given to effects of such advertisements on children.

(2) To what extent is anxiety arousal in a consumer a function of his exposure to all fear-appeal advertising? Studies may be designed to measure the aggregate effects on level of anxiety resulting from single and multiple exposure to fear-appeal ads for a single product, several products, and social issues.

(3) What is the relationship between exposure to fear appeals and perception of product attributes and performance; and between alternative appeals and product or brand-loyalty patterns? A longitudinal design may be used to test the hypothesis that anxiety is reduced by product use and is further reflected in the development of brand or product loyalty. In addition, one must determine whether the consumer perceives the product as possessing the ability to reduce or eliminate the feared condition on which the fear appeal is based. The use of multidimensional scaling and unfolding techniques are appropriate for this type of research.

Recognizing the multivariate character of the communication message, buyer behavior models which incorporate fear as an intervening variable should be adopted as a frame of reference for the above investigations. Research findings can be integrated with the help of such models to clearly describe the relationship between anxiety-arousing appeals and perceived need and to provide meaningful explanations for behavior.

(4) Manufacturers and their advertising agencies must be encouraged to publish the results of research they may have conducted which demonstrate the purported effectiveness of fear appeals.

References

1. Michael L. Ray and William L. Wilkie, "Fear: The Potential of an Appeal Neglected by Marketing," *Journal of Marketing,* Vol. 34 (January 1970), 54–62; and John R. Stuteville, "Psychic Defenses Against High Fear Appeals: A Key Marketing Variable," *Journal of Marketing,* Vol. 34 (April 1970), 39–45.

2. A. Bandura and R. H. Walters, *Social Learning Theory and Personality Development* (New York: Holt, Rinehart and Winston, 1963); E. E. Maccoby, "Effects of the Mass Media," in *Review of Child Development Research,* M. L. Hoffman and L. W. Hoffman, eds. (New York: Russell Sage Foundation, 1964), 323–348; C. M. Berger, "Conditioning Through Vicarious Instigation," *Psychological Review,* Vol. 69 (1962), 450–466; and V. LiLollo and S. M. Berger, "Effects of Apparent Pain in Others on Observers' Reaction Time," *Journal of Personality and Social Psychology,* Vol. 2 (1965), 573–575.

3. J. S. Brown, "Problems Presented by the Concept of Acquired Drives," in *Current Theory and Research in Motivation* (Lincoln, Neb.: University of Nebraska Press, 1953), 1–21.

4. L. E. Longstreth, *Psychological Development of the Child* (New York: Ronald Press, 1968), 215.

5. Richard I. Evans, Richard M. Rozelle, Thomas M. Lasater, Theodore M. Dembroski, and Ben M. Allen, "Fear Arousal, Persuasion, and Actual Versus Implied Behavioral Change; New Perspective Utilizing a Real-Life Dental Hygiene Program," *Journal of Personality and Social Psychology,* Vol. 16 (1970), 220–227.

6. S. Schacter, *The Psychology of Affiliation: Experimental Studies of the Sources of Gregariousness* (Stanford: Stanford University Press, 1959); and Martin L. Hoffman, "Conformity as a Defense Mechanism and a Form of Resistance to Genuine Group Influence," *Journal of Personality,* Vol. 25 (1957), 412–424.

7. Orrin E. Klapp, *Collective Search for Identity* (New York: Holt, Rinehart and Winston, 1969), 4.

8. Mary Gardiner Jones, FTC Commissioner, "The FTC's Need for Social Science Research," address before the Second Annual Conference of the Association for Consumer Research, University of Maryland, September, 1971.

9. John J. Wheatley, "Marketing and the Use of Fear- or Anxiety-arousing Appeals," *Journal of Marketing,* Vol. 35 (April 1971), 62–64.

2.3 Personality and Consumer Behavior: A Review

HAROLD H. KASSARJIAN

The past two decades, especially the last five years, have been exciting times in the field of consumer behavior. New data, theories, relationships, and models have been received with such enthusiasm that, in fact, a new field of scientific inquiry has developed. Studies such as consumer economics, rural sociology, social and mathematical psychology, social anthropology, and political science have been so churned and milled that from their amorphous mass the study of consumer behavior has become a relatively well delineated scientific discipline.

One of the more engrossing concepts in the study of consumer behavior is that of personality. Purchasing behavior, media choice, innovation, segmentation, fear, social influence, product choice, opinion leadership, risk taking, attitude change, and almost anything else one can think of have been linked to personality. The purpose of this article is to review the literature of consumer behavior and organize its contributions around the theoretical stems from which it grows.

Unfortunately, analysts do not agree on any general definition of the term "personality,"[1] except to somehow tie it to the concept of consistent responses to the world of stimuli surrounding the individual. Man does tend to be consistent in coping with his environment. This consistency of response allows us to type politicians as charismatic or obnoxious, students as aggressive or submissive, and colleagues as charming or "blah." Since individuals do react fairly consistently in a variety of environmental situations, these generalized patterns of response or modes of coping with the world can be called personality.

Personality, or better yet, the inferred hypothetical constructs relating to certain persistent qualities in human behavior, have fascinated both laymen and scholars for many centuries. The study of the relationship between behavior and personality has a most impressive history, ranging back to the earliest writings of the Chinese and Egyptians, Hippocrates, and some of the great European philosophers. In the fields of marketing and consumer behavior, the work in personality dates from Sigmund Freud and his popularizers in the commercial world, and the motivation researchers of the post-World War II era, e.g. [25, 26, 66].

Psychoanalytic Theory

The psychoanalytic theories and philosophies of Freud have influenced not only psychology but also literature, social science, and medicine, as well as marketing. Freud stressed the unconscious nature of personality and motivation and said that much, if not all, behavior is related to the stresses within the personality system. The personality's three interacting sets of forces, the id, ego, and superego, interact to produce behavior.

According to Freudian theory, the id is the source of all driving psychic energy, but its unrestrained impulses cannot be expressed without running afoul of society's values. The superego is the internal representative of the traditional values and can be conceptualized as the moral arm of personality. The manner in which the ego guides the libidinal energies of the id and the moralistic demands of the superego accounts for the rich variety of personalities, interests, motives, attitudes, and behavior patterns of people. It accounts for the purchase of a four-door sedan rather than a racy sports car, the adoption of a miniskirt, and the use of Ultra-Brite toothpaste (with its promise of sex appeal) as a substitute for the rental of a motel room. The tools of the ego are defenses such as rationalization, projection, identification, and repression; its goals are integrated action.

Freud further believed that the child passes through various stages of development—the oral, anal, phallic, and genital periods—that determine the dynamics of his personality. The degree of tension, frustration, and love at these stages leads to his adult personality and behavior.

The influence of Freud and psychoanalytic theory cannot be overestimated. Most of the greatest names in psychiatry and psychology have been followers, disciples, or critics of Freud, much as many good marketing research studies have been criticisms of motivation researchers or experiments applying scientific procedures to motivation research. The work of Sidney Levy, Burleigh Gardner and Lee Rainwater, some of the projects of Martineau, and the proprietary studies of Social Research, Inc., are in the latter tradition. Although today the critics of psychoanalytic applications to consumer behavior far outweigh the adherents, Freud and his critics have contributed much to advances in marketing theory.

Social Theorists

In his lifetime, several members of Freud's inner ring became disillusioned with his insistence on the biological basis of personality and began to develop their own views and their own followers. Alfred Adler, for example, felt that the basic drive of man is not the channelization of the libido, but rather a striving for superiority. The basic aim of life, he reasoned, is to overcome feelings of inferiority imposed during childhood. Occupations and spouses are selected, homes purchased, and automobiles owned in the effort to perfect the self and feel less inferior to others.

Erich Fromm stressed man's loneliness in society and his seeking of love, brotherliness, and security. The search for satisfying human relationships is of central focus to behavior and motivations.

Karen Horney, also one of the neo-Freudian social theorists, reacted against theories of the biological libido, as did Adler, but felt that childhood insecurities stemming from parent-child relationships create basic anxieties and that the personality is developed as the individual learns to cope with his anxieties.

Although these and other neo-Freudians have influenced the work of motivation researchers, they have had minimal impact on research on consumer behavior. However, much of their theorizing can be seen in advertising today, which exploits the striving for superiority and the needs for love, security, and escape from loneliness to sell toothpaste, deodorants, cigarettes, and even detergents.

The only research in consumer behavior based directly on a neo-Freudian approach is Cohen's psychological test that purports to measure Horney's three basic orientations toward coping with anxiety—the compliant, aggressive, and detached types [22, 23]. Cohen found that compliant types prefer brand names and use more mouthwash and toilet soaps; aggressive types tend to use a razor rather than an electric shaver, use more cologne and after-shave lotion, and buy Old Spice deodorant and Van Heusen shirts; and detached types seem to be least aware of brands. Cohen, however, admitted to picking and choosing from his data, and although the published results are by no means conclusive, his work does indicate that the Horney typology may have some relevance to marketing. Several follow-up studies using his instruments are unpublished as of 1970.

Stimulus-Response Theories

The stimulus-response or learning theory approach to personality presents perhaps the most elegant view, with a respected history of research and laboratory experimentation supporting it. Its origins are in the work of Pavlov, Thorndike, Skinner, Spence, Hull, and the Institute of Human Relations at Yale University. Although the various theorists differ among themselves, there is agreement that the link between stimulus and response is persistent and relatively stable. Personality is seen as a conglomerate of habitual responses acquired over time to specific and generalized cues. The bulk of theorizing and empirical research has been concerned with specifying conditions under which habits are formed, changed, replaced, or broken.

A drive leads to a response to a particular stimulus, and if the response is reinforced or rewarded, a particular habit is learned. Unrewarded and inappropriate responses are extinguished or eliminated. Complex behavior such as consumer decision processes is learned in a similar manner.

According to Dollard and Miller, a drive is a stimulus strong enough to impel activity; it energizes behavior but, by itself, does not direct it. Any stimulus may become a drive if it reaches sufficient intensity [43]. Some stimuli are linked to the physiological processes necessary for the survival of the individual, others are secondary or acquired. With the concepts of cues, drives, responses, and reinforcement, complex motives such as the need for achievement or self-esteem are learned in the same manner as brand preference, racism, attitudes towards big business, purchasing habits, or dislike of canned spinach.

Marketing is replete with examples of the influence of learning theory, ranging from Krugman's work to the Yale studies on attitudes and attitude change, from lightweight discussions on the influence of repetition and reinforcement in advertising texts to Howard and Sheth's buyer behavior theory and the work in mathematical models. However, very few personality studies have used this theoretical orientation.

The reason for the lack of impact is probably that personality tests and measuring instruments using this theoretical base do not exist. Typically, clinical psychologists have developed measuring instruments, but until this past decade clinicians were not trained directly in learning theory. Recently, however, behavior modification based on the work of Skinner has become a psychotherapeutic technique. Many clinical psychologists are turning to learning theory for guidelines in the treatment of abnormality. Unfortunately, they do not seem to be predisposed to create psychological tests to measure personality in line with their definitions, but are more concerned with behavioral change. Until such instruments are developed there will be little use of these theories in relating consumer behavior to personality, irrespective of their completeness and extreme relevance.

Trait and Factor Theories

As learning theory approaches to personality have evolved from the tough-minded empirical experimentation of the animal laboratories, factor theories have evolved from the quantitative sophistication of statistical techniques and computer technology. The core of these theories is that personality is composed of a set of traits or factors, some general and others specific to a particular situation or test. In constructing a personality instrument, the theorist typically begins with a wide array of behavioral measures, mostly responses to test items, and with statistical techniques distills factors which are then defined as the personality variables.

For one large group of personality instruments the researcher begins with the intent to measure certain variables, for example, need for achievement or aggressiveness. Large samples of subjects predetermined as aggressive or not aggressive (say, by ratings from teachers and employers) are given the instrument. Each item is statistically analyzed to see if it discriminates aggressive from nonaggressive subjects. By a series of such distilling measures and additional validation and reliability studies, an instrument is produced which measures traits the researcher originally was attempting to gauge. Several of these variables are often embodied in, for example, a single 200-item instrument.

A second type of personality instrument is created not with theoretically predetermined variables in mind, but rather to identify a few items (by factor analysis) which account for a significant portion of the variance. Subjects are given questionnaires, ratings, or tests on a wide variety of topics, and test items are grouped in the factor analysis by how well they measure the same statistical factor. The meaning of a particular factor is thus empirically determined and a label arbitrarily attached to it that hopefully best describes what the researcher presumes the particular subset of items measures. Further reliability and validation measures lead to creation of a test instrument with several variables that supposedly account for the diversity and complexity of behavior. The theoretical structure is statistical and the variables are empirically determined and creatively named or labeled.

The concept of traits, factors, or variables that can be quantitatively measured has led to virtually hundreds of personality scales and dozens of studies in consumer behavior. Instruments of this type are discussed below.

Gordon Personal Profile

This instrument purports to measure ascendency, responsibility, emotional stability, and sociability. Tucker and Painter [86] found significant correlations between use of headache remedies, vitamins, mouthwash, alcoholic drinks, automobiles, chewing gum, and the acceptance of new fashions and one or more of these four personality variables. The correlations ranged from .27 to .46, accounting for perhaps 10% of the variance.

Kernan [57] used decision theory in an empirical test of the relationship between decision behavior and personality. He added the Gordon Personal Inventory to measure cautiousness, original thinking, personal relations, and vigor. Pearsonian and multiple correlations indicated few significant relationships, but canonical correlation between sets of personality variables and decision behavior gave a coefficient of association of .77, significant at the .10 level. Cluster analysis then showed that behavior is consistent with personality profiles within clusters. Kernan's results, like those of Tucker and Painter [86], show interesting relationships but are by no means startling.

Edwards Personal Preference Schedule

The EPPS has been used in about two dozen studies or rebuttals in consumer behavior from a trait and factor theory approach. The purpose of the instrument was to develop a factor-analyzed, paper-and-pencil, objective instrument to measure the psychoanalytically-oriented needs or themes developed by Henry Murray. Its popularity in consumer behavior can be traced to Evans' landmark study [30], in which he could find no differences between Ford and Chevrolet owners to an extent that would allow for prediction. He was, however, able to account for about 10% of the variance. Criticism of Evans' study and conclusions came from many fronts and on many grounds [49, 65, 67, 69, 83, 95]. Rejoinders were written [31, 32, 33, 36], and finally Evans replicated the study [34]. Using Evans' original data, Kuehn then concluded that predictive ability can be improved if one computes a discriminant function based on the two needs displaying the largest initial predictive ability [59]. Kuehn improved Evans' results by using dominance scores minus affiliation scores. However, the psychological significance of dominance minus affiliation has escaped me for five years. Nevertheless, the controversy over Evans' study is in the very finest tradition of the physical and social sciences, with argument and counterargument, rejoinder and replication, until the facts begin to emerge, something very seldom seen in marketing and consumer behavior research. The final conclusion that seems to trickle through is that personality does account for some variance but not enough to give much solace to personality researchers in marketing.

Along other lines, Koponen used the EPPS scale with data collected on 9,000 persons in the J. Walter Thompson panel [58]. His results indicate that cigarette smoking is positively related to sex dominance, aggression, and achievement needs among males and negatively related to order and compliance needs. Further, he found differences between filter and nonfilter smokers and found that these differences were made more pronounced by heavy smoking. In addition, there seemed to be a relationship between personality variables and readership of three unnamed magazines.

Massy, Frank, and Lodahl used the same data in a study of the purchase of coffee, tea, and beer [68]. Their conclusion was that personality accounted for a very small percentage of the variance. In fact, personality plus socioeconomic variables accounted for only 5% to 10% of the variance in purchases.

In a sophisticated study, Claycamp presented the EPPS to 174 subjects who held savings accounts in banks or savings and loan associations [21]. His results indicate that personality variables predict better than demographic variables whether an individual is a customer of a bank or a savings and loan association. These results contradict those of Evans, who concluded that socioeconomic variables are more effective than personality as measured by the same instrument. Using personality variables alone, Claycamp correctly classified 72% of the subjects.

Brody and Cunningham reanalyzed Koponen's data employing techniques like those of Claycamp and Massy, Frank, and Lodahl with similar results [16], accounting for about 3% of the variance. Further, these results are similar to those from the Advertising Research Foundation's study on toilet paper [1] in which 5% to 10% of the variance was accounted for by personality and other variables. Brody and Cunningham argued that the weak relationships may have been caused by an inadequate theoretical framework. Theirs consisted of three categories: perceived performance risk—the extent different brands perform differently in important ways; specific self-confidence—how certain the consumer is that a brand performs as he expects; and perceived social risk—the extent he thinks he will be judged on the basis of his brand decision. The authors concluded that, "when trying to discriminate the brand choice of people most likely to have perceived-high performance risk and to have high specific self-confidence, personality variables were very useful" [16, p. 56]. For people who were 100% brand loyal, 8 personality variables explained 32% of the variance. As the minimum purchase of the favorite brand dropped from 100% to 40%, the explained variance fell to 13%.

Thurstone Temperament Schedule

This is another factor-analyzed instrument. Westfall, in a well known study that is often interpreted as a replication of Evans' study, compared personalities of automobile owners and could find no differences between brands [92]. He further found no differences between compact and standard car owners on the Thurstone variables. However, personality characteristics did differ between owners of convertibles and standard models.

Using the same instrument, Kamen showed a relationship between the number of people who had no opinion on foods to be rated and the number of items they left unanswered on the Thurstone scale. Using a specially created questionnaire, he concluded that the dimension of "no opinion" is not related to food preference [52]. Proneness to have an opinion does not seem to be a general trait, but rather is dependent on the content area.

California Personality Inventory

This is the newest paper-and-pencil test to be used extensively. Robertson and Myers [77]—see also [78] and Bruce and Witt [17]—developed measures for innovativeness and opinion leadership in the areas of food, clothing, and appliances. A multiple stepwise regression with 18 traits on the CPI indicated poor R^2 's; the portion of variance accounted for was 4% for clothing,

5% for food, and 23% for appliances. The study tends to support the several dozen previous studies on innovation and opinion leadership that show a minimal relationship between personality variables and behavior toward new products. Several studies indicate that gregariousness and venturesomeness are relevant to opinion leadership. Two studies using personality inventories have found a relationship between innovation and personality, while three others could find none. Other traits, such as informal and formal social participation, cosmopolitanism, and perceived risk, are related to innovative behavior in about half a dozen studies, while an additional half a dozen studies show no differences. These studies are reviewed in [76].

A very recent study by Boone attempted to relate the variables on the California Personality Inventory to the consumer innovator on the topic of a community antenna television system [15]. His results indicate significant differences between innovators and followers on 10 of 18 scales. Unfortunately, the statistical techniques were quite different from those employed by Robertson and Myers, so it is not possible to determine whether or not the two studies are in basic agreement.

Finally, Vitz and Johnston, using the masculinity scale of both the CPI and the Minnesota Multiphasic Personality Inventory, hypothesized that the more masculine a smoker's personality, the more masculine the image of his regular brand of cigarettes [88]. The correlations were low but statistically significant, and the authors concluded that the results moderately support product preference as a predictable interaction between the consumer's personality and the product's image.

Theories of Self and Self-Concept

Relationships of product image and self-image have been studied quite thoroughly by the motivation researchers, and particularly Levy [63] and Gardner [38]. The theoretical base for this work, I presume, rests in the writings and philosophies of Carl Rogers, William James, and Abraham Maslow and the symbolic interactionism proposed by Susan Langer and others.

The core of these views is that the individual has a real- and an ideal-self. This *me* or *self* is "the sum total of all that a man can call his—his body, traits, and abilities; his material possessions; his family, friends, and enemies; his vocations and avocations and much else" [43, first edition, p. 467]. It includes evaluations and definitions of one's self and may be reflected in much of his actions, including his evaluations and purchase of products and services. The belief is that individuals perceive products that they own, would like to own, or do not want to own in terms of symbolic meaning to themselves and to others. Congruence between the symbolic image of a product (e.g., a .38 caliber is aggressive and masculine, a Lincoln automobile is extravagant and wealthy) and a consumer's self-image implies greater probability of positive evaluation, preference, or ownership of that product or brand. For example, Jacobson and Kossoff studied self-perception and attitudes toward small cars [48]. Individuals who perceived themselves as "cautious conservatives" were more likely to favor small cars as a practical and economic convenience. Another self-classified group of "confident explorers" preferred large cars, which they saw as a means of expressing their ability to control the environment.

Birdwell, using the semantic differential, tested the hypotheses that: (1) an automobile owner's perception of his car is essentially congruent with his perception of himself and (2) the average perception of a specific car type and brand is different for owners of different sorts of cars [12, 13, 14]; see also [35]. The hypotheses were confirmed with varying degrees of strength. However, this does not imply that products have personalities and that a consumer purchases those brands whose images are congruent with his self-concept; Birdwell's study did not test causality. It could very well be that only after a product is purchased does the owner begin to perceive it as an extension of his own personality.

Grubb [39] and Grubb and Grathwohl [40] found that consumers' different self-perceptions are associated with varying patterns of consumer behavior. They claimed that self-concept is a meaningful mode of market segmentation. Grubb found that beer drinkers perceived themselves as more confident, social, extroverted, forward, sophisticated, impulsive, and temperamental than their non-beer-drinking brethren. However, the comparison of self-concept and beer brand profiles revealed inconclusive results: drinkers and nondrinkers perceived brands similarly.

In a follow-up study of Pontiac and Volkswagen owners, Grubb and Hupp indicated that owners of one brand of automobile perceive themselves as similar to others who own the same brand and significantly different from owners of the other brand [41]. Sommers indicated by the use of a Q-sort of products that subjects are reliably able to describe themselves and others by products rather than adjectives, say on a semantic differential or adjective checklist [81, 82]. That is, individuals are able to answer the questions, "What kind of a person am I?" and "What kind of a person is he?" by Q-sorting products.

Dolich further tested the congruence relationship between self-images and product brands and concluded that there is a greater similarity between one's self-concept and images of his most preferred brands than images of least preferred brands [27]. Dolich claimed that favored brands are consistent with and reinforce self-concept.

Finally, Hamm [44] and Hamm and Cundiff [45] related product perception to what they call self-actualization, that is, the discrepancy between the self and ideal-self. Those with a small discrepancy were called low self-actualizers, a definition which does not seem consistent with Maslow's work on the hierarchy of needs. High self-actualizers describe themselves in terms of products differently from low self-actualizers, and in turn perceive products differently. For both groups, some products such as house, dress, automatic dishwasher, and art prints tend to represent an ideal-self, wife, or mother, while others such as cigarettes, TV dinners, or a mop do not.

Life Style

An integration of the richness of motivation research studies and the tough-mindedness and statistical sophistication of computer technology has led to another type of research involving personality, variously called psychographic or life-style research. The life-style concept is based on distinctive or characteristic modes of living of segments of a society [60]. The technique divides the total market into segments based on interests, values, opinions, personality characteristics, attitudes, and demographic variables using techniques of cluster analysis, factor analysis, and canonical correlation. Wells dubbed the methodology "backward segmentation" because it groups people by behavioral characteristics before seeking correlates [90]. Pessemier and Tigert reported that some preliminary relationships were found between the factor-analyzed clusters of people and market behavior [74]. Similar results were reported in [8, 62, 73, 85, 91, 93, 94].

Generally, the relationship of the attitude-interest-personality clusters, when correlated with actual buyer behavior, indicates once again that 10% or less of the variance is accounted for. Yet quite properly the proponents of the technique claim that very rich data are available in the analyses for the researcher and practitioner interested in consumer behavior.

Miscellaneous Other Approaches

The overall results of other studies with other points of view are quite similar. Some researchers interpret their results as insignificant while others interpret similarly minimal relationships as significant, depending on the degree of statistical sophistication and the statistical tools used. A hodgepodge of other studies indicates that heavy and light users of several product classes do not differ on the McClosky Personality Inventory or Dunnette Adjective Checklist [79]. Axelrod found a predictable relationship between the mood produced by viewing a movie—*The Nuremburg Trial*—and attitudes towards consumer products such as savings bonds, sewing machines, typewriters, and daiquiris [4]. Eysenck, Tarrant, Woolf, and England indicated that smoking is related to genotypic personality differences [37]. Summers found a minimal relationship between characteristics of opinion leaders and the Borgatta personality variables [84]. Pennington and Peterson have shown that product preferences are related to vocational interests as measured on the Strong Vocational Interest Blank [72, 75]. Finally, Jacoby has demonstrated that Rokeach's concepts of open and closed mindedness are relevant to consumer behavior and found that low dogmatics tend to be more prone to innovation [50, 51]. The correlation between innovation and dogmatism was $-.32$, the explained variance about 10%. Myers, in a study of private brand attitudes, found that Cattell's 16-Personality Factor Inventory explained about 5% of the variance [70, 71]. Once again, the results are in the same order—5% to 10% of the variance accounted for.

Social Character

In the usual pattern of applying psychological and sociological concepts to marketing and consumer behavior, several researchers have turned their attention to Riesman's theories, which group human beings into three types of social character: tradition-directed, inner-directed, and other-directed. A society manifests one type predominantly, according to its particular phase of development.

Riesman by no means intended his typology to be interpreted as a personality schema, yet in the consumer behavior literature social character has been grouped with personality, and hence the material is included in this review.

A society of tradition-directed people, seldom encountered in the United States today, is characterized by general slowness of change, a dependence on kin, low social mobility, and a tight web of values. Inner-directed people are most often found in a rapidly changing, industrialized society with division of labor, high social mobility, and less security; these persons must turn to inner values for guidance. In contrast, other-directed persons depend upon those around them to give direction to their actions. The other-directed society is industrialized to the point that its orientation shifts from production to consumption. Thus success in the other-directed society is not through production and hard work but rather through one's ability to be liked by others, develop charm or "personality," and manipulate other people. The contemporary United States is considered by Riesman to be almost exclusively populated by the latter two social character types and is rapidly moving towards an other-directed orientation.

Dornbusch and Hickman content analyzed consumer goods advertising over the past decades and noted a clear trend from inner- to other-direction [29]. Kassarjian [55] and Centers [19] have shown that youth is significantly more other-directed and that those foreign born or reared in small towns tend to be inner-directed.

Gruen found no relationship between preference for new or old products and inner-other-direction [42]. Arndt [2, 3] and Barban, Sandage, Kassarjian, and Kassarjian [7] could find little relationship between innovation and social character; Donnelly, however, has shown a relationship between housewives' acceptance of innovations and social character, with the inner-directed being slightly more innovative [28]. Linton and Graham indicated that inner-directed persons are less easily persuaded than other-directed persons [64]. Centers and Horowitz found that other-directed individuals were more susceptible to social influence in an experimental setting than were inner-directed subjects [20]. Kassarjian found that subjects expressed a preference for appeals based on their particular social character type. There was minimal evidence for differential exposure to various mass media between the two Riesman types [53].

In a similar study, Woodside found no relationship between consumer products and social character, although he did find a minimal relationship between advertising appeals and inner-other-direction [96].

Finally, Kassarjian and Kassarjian found a relationship between social character and Allport's scale of values as well as vocational interests but could find no relationship between inner-other-direction and personality variables as measured by the MMPI [54, 56]. Once again, the results follow the same pattern: a few studies find and a few do not find meaningful relationships between consumer behavior and other measures.

Personality and Persuasibility

To complete a review on the relationship between personality and consumer behavior, the wide body of research findings relating personality to persuasibility and attitude change must be included. In addition to the dozens of studies carried out under Carl Hovland, e.g., [47], there are many relating personality characteristics to conformity, attitude change, fear appeals, and opinions on various topics; see [61]. The consumer behavior literature studies by Cox and Bauer [24], Bell [10, 11], Carey [18], and Barach [5, 6] tied self-confidence to persuasibility in the purchase of goods. These studies indicated a curvilinear relationship between generalized self-confidence and persuasibility and between specific self-confidence and persuasibility. Venkatesan's results, however, throw some doubt on these findings [87]. In recent reanalysis and review of much of this literature, Shuchman and Perry found contradictory data and felt these were inconsequential. The authors claim that neither generalized nor specific self-confidence appears to be an important determinant of persuasibility in marketing [80]. Bauer, in turn, has found fault with the Shuchman and Perry reanalysis [9].

Summary and Conclusions

A review of these dozens of studies and papers can be summarized in the single word, *equivocal.* A few studies indicate a strong relationship between personality and aspects of consumer behavior, a few indicate no relationship, and the great majority indicate that if correlations do exist they are so weak as to be questionable or perhaps meaningless. Several reasons can be postulated to account for these discrepancies. Perhaps the major one is based on the validity of the particular personality measuring instruments used: a typically "good" instrument has a test-retest reliability of about .80 and a split-half reliability of about .90. Validity coefficients range at most from .40 to about .70; that is, when correlated against a criterion variable, the instrument typically accounts for about 20% to 40% of the variance. Too often the marketing researcher is just plain disinterested in reliability and validity criteria. *Tests validated for specific uses on specific populations, such as college students, or as part of mental hospital intake batteries are applied to available subjects in the general population.* The results may indicate that 10% of the variance is accounted for; this is then interpreted as a weak relationship and personality is rejected as a determinant of purchase. The consumer researcher too often expects more from an instrument than it was originally intended to furnish.

An additional problem for the marketing researcher is the conditions under which the test instrument is given. The instrument is often presented in the classroom or on the doorstep, rather than in the office of a psychometrician, psychotherapist, or vocational counselor. As Wells has pointed out [89, p. 188]:

> The measurements we take may come from some housewife sitting in a bathrobe at her kitchen table, trying to figure out what it is she is supposed to say in answering a questionnaire. Too often, she is not telling us about herself as she really is, but instead is telling us about herself as she thinks she is or wants us to think she is.

To compound the error, consumer researchers often forget that the strength of a correlation is limited by the reliability of the measures being correlated. Not only the personality test but also the criterion itself may be unreliable under these conditions, as Wells has pointed out. Often the criterion used in these studies is the consumer's own account of her purchasing behavior. More often than not, these data are far more unreliable than we may wish to admit.

Adaptation of Instruments

Much too often, in order to adjust test items to fit specific demands, changes are made in the instrument. Items are taken out of context of the total instrument, words are changed, items are arbitrarily discarded, and the test is often shortened drastically. This adjustment would undoubtedly horrify the original developer of the instrument, and the disregard for the validity of the modified instrument should horrify the rest of us. Just how much damage is done when a measure of self-confidence or extroversion is adapted, revised, and restructured is simply not known, but it would not be a serious exaggeration to claim it is considerable. And, most unfortunately, from time to time even the name of the variable is changed to fit the needs of the researcher. For example, Cohen has pointed out that in the Koponen study male smokers scored higher than average on self-depreciation and association, variables not included in the Edwards instrument. The researcher was apparently using the abasement and affiliation scales [23]. Such changes may or may not be proper, and although they may not necessarily violate scientific canons, they certainly do not help reduce the confusion in attempting to sort out what little we know about the relationships of personality to consumer behavior.

Psychological Instruments in Marketing Research

A second reason for discrepancies in the literature is that instruments originally intended to measure gross personality characteristics such as sociability, emotional stability, introversion, or neuroticism have been used to make predictions of the chosen brand of toothpaste or cigarettes. The variables that lead to the assassination of a president, confinement in a mental hospital, or suicide may not be identical to those that lead to the purchase of a washing machine, a pair of shoes, or chewing gum. *Clearly, if unequivocal results are to emerge, consumer behavior researchers must develop their own definitions and design their own instruments to measure the personality variables that go into the purchase decision rather than using tools designed as part of a medical model to measure schizophrenia or mental stability.*

Development of definitions and instruments can perhaps be handled in two ways. One will require some brilliant theorizing as to what variables do relate to the consumer decision process. If neuroticism and sociability are not the relevant personality variables, then perhaps new terms such as risk aversion, status seeking, and conspicuous consumption will emerge. Personality variables that in fact are relevant to the consumer model need to be theorized and tests developed and validated.

Another approach to developing such instruments might be that of the factor theorists. Dozens of items measuring behavior, opinions, purchases, feelings, or attitudes can be factor analyzed in the search for general and specific factors that in turn can be validated against the marketing behavior of the individual. The research group at Purdue, e.g., [73] and the recent work of

Wells [91] and Wilkie [93], have made refreshingly new attempts at personality measurement and come very close to the research techniques developed by the factor theorists. Whether or not these attempts will succeed in producing a new approach to personality research is yet to be proved; the studies to date are encouraging.

Only with marketing-oriented instruments will we be able to determine just what part personality variables play in the consumer decision process and, further, if they can be generalized across product and service classes or must be product-specific instruments. At that stage, questions of the relevancy of these criteria for market segmentation, shifting demand curves, or creating and sustaining promotional and advertising campaigns can be asked.

Hypotheses

A third reason for the lackluster results in the personality and consumer behavior literature is that *many studies have been conducted by a shotgun approach with no specific hypotheses or theoretical justification.* Typically a convenient, available, easily scored, and easy-to-administer personality inventory is selected and administered along with questionnaires on purchase data and preferences. The lack of proper scientific method and hypothesis generation is supposedly justified by the often-used disclaimer that the study is exploratory. As Jacoby has pointed out [51, p. 244]:

> Careful examination reveals that, in most cases, no a priori thought is directed to *how,* or especially *why,* personality should or should not be related to that aspect of consumer behavior being studied. Moreover, the few studies which do report statistically significant findings usually do so on the basis of post-hoc "picking and choosing" out of large data arrays.

Statistical techniques are applied and anything that turns up looking halfway interesting furnishes the basis for the discussion section [49].

An excellent example of the shotgun approach to science, albeit a more sophisticated one than most, is Evans' original study examining personality differences between Ford and Chevrolet owners. Jacoby, in an excellent and most thoughtful paper, noted that Evans began his study with specific hypotheses culled from the literature and folklore pertaining to personality differences to be expected between Ford and Chevrolet owners [49]. He then presented the EPPS to subjects, measuring 11 variables, 5 of which seemed to be measuring the variables in question; the remaining 6 were irrelevant to the hypotheses with no a priori basis for expecting differences. If predictions were to have been made on these six scales, Jacoby says, they should have been ones of *no* difference. Using one-tailed tests of significance, since the directions also should have been hypothesized, 3 of the 5 key variables were significant at the .05 level and none of the remaining 6 were significant. In short, Evans' data could have been interpreted such that 9 of the 11 scales were "significant" according to prediction. Jacoby's interpretation leads to a conclusion quite different from Evans', that there are no personality differences between Ford and Chevrolet owners. Also, with a priori predictions, Jacoby did not have to pick and choose from his data, as Kuehn was forced to do in showing a relationship between "dominance minus affiliation" scores and car ownership [59].

Finally, personality researchers and researchers in other aspects of marketing seem to need simple variables which can be somehow applied in the marketplace. We seem to feel that the only function of science and research is to predict rather than to understand, to persuade rather than to appreciate. Social scientists can fully accept that personality variables are related to suicide or crime, to assassinations, racial prejudice, attitudes towards the USSR, or the selection of a spouse. They do not get upset that personality is not the only relevant variable or that the portion of the explained variance is merely 20% or 10% or 5%. Yet personality researchers in consumer behavior much too often ignore the many interrelated influences on the consumer decision process, ranging from price and packaging to availability, advertising, group influences, learned responses, and preferences of family members, in addition to personality. *To expect the influence of personality variables to account for a large portion of the variance is most certainly asking too much.* What is amazing is not that there are many studies that show no correlation between consumer behavior and personality, but rather that there are any studies at all with positive results. That 5% or 10% or any portion of the variance can be accounted for by personality variables measured on ill-chosen and inadequate instruments is most remarkable, indeed!

Note

1. Hall and Lindzey, in attempting to deal with the dozens of approaches that exist in the literature, frustratingly submit that *personality is defined by the particular concepts which are part of the theory of personality employed by the observer.* Because this article reviews marketing literature rather than psychological literature, the various theories are not described in detail. For a very brief description of several theories and a bibliographic listing of primary sources and references, as well as examples of about a dozen well known volumes on the general topic, see [43, 46].

References

1. *Are There Consumer Types?* New York: Advertising Research Foundation, 1964.

2. Arndt, Johan. "Role of Product-Related Conversations in the Diffusion of a New Product," *Journal of Marketing Research,* Vol. 4 (August 1967), 291–295.

3. ———. "Profiling Consumer Innovators," in Johan Arndt, ed., *Insights Into Consumer Behavior.* Boston: Allyn and Bacon, 1968, 71–83.

4. Axelrod, Joel N. "Induced Moods and Attitudes Towards Products," *Journal of Advertising Research,* Vol. 3 (June 1963), 19–24.

5. Barach, Jeffrey A. "Self-Confidence and Reactions to Television Commercials," in Donald F. Cox, ed., *Risk Taking and Information Handling in Consumer Behavior.* Boston: Division of Research, Graduate School of Business, Harvard University, 1967, 428–441.

6. ———. "Advertising Effectiveness and Risk in the Consumer Decision Process," *Journal of Marketing Research,* Vol. 6 (August 1969), 314–320.

7. Barban, Arnold N., C. H. Sandage, Waltraud M. Kassarjian, and Harold H. Kassarjian. "A Study of Riesman's Inner-Other-Directedness Among Farmers," *Rural Sociology,* Vol. 35 (June 1970), 232–243.

8. Bass, Frank M., Douglas J. Tigert, and Ronald T. Lonsdale. "Market Segmentation: Group Versus Individual Behavior," *Journal of Marketing Research,* Vol. 5 (August 1968), 264–270.

9. Bauer, Raymond A. "Self-Confidence and Persuasibility: One More Time," *Journal of Marketing Research,* Vol. 7 (May 1970), 256–258.

10. Bell, Gerald D. "Persuasibility and Buyer Remorse Among Automobile Purchasers," in Montrose S. Sommers and Jerome B. Kernan, eds., *Consumer Behavior.* Austin: Bureau of Business Research, The University of Texas, 1968, 77–102.

11. ———. "Self-Confidence and Persuasion in Car Buying," *Journal of Marketing Research,* Vol. 4 (February 1967), 46–52.

12. Birdwell, Al E. "Influence of Image Congruence on Consumer Choice," *Proceedings.* Winter Conference, American Marketing Association, 1964, 290–303.

13. ———. "A Study of the Influence of Image Congruence on Consumer Choice," *Journal of Business,* Vol. 41 (January 1968), 76–88.

14. ———. "Automobiles and Self Imagery: Reply," *Journal of Business,* Vol. 41 (October 1968), 486–487.

15. Boone, Louis E. "The Search for the Consumer Innovator," *Journal of Business,* Vol. 48 (April 1970), 135–140.

16. Brody, Robert R. and Scott M. Cunningham. "Personality Variables and the Consumer Decision Process," *Journal of Marketing Research,* Vol. 5 (February 1968), 50–57.

17. Bruce, Grady D. and Robert E. Witt. "Personality Correlates of Innovative Buying Behavior," *Journal of Marketing Research,* Vol. 7 (May 1970), 259–260.

18. Carey, James W. "Personality Correlates of Persuasibility," *Proceedings,* Winter Conference, American Marketing Association, 1963, 30–43.

19. Centers, Richard. "An Examination of the Riesman Social Character Typology: A Metropolitan Survey," *Sociometry,* Vol. 25 (September 1962), 231–240.

20. ——— and Miriam Horowitz. "Social Character and Conformity," *Journal of Social Psychology,* Vol. 60 (August 1963), 343–349.

21. Claycamp, Henry J. "Characteristics of Owners of Thrift Deposits in Commercial Banks and Savings and Loan Associations," *Journal of Marketing Research,* Vol. 2 (May 1965), 163–170.

22. Cohen, Joel B. "An Interpersonal Orientation to the Study of Consumer Behavior," *Journal of Marketing Research,* Vol. 4 (August 1967), 270–278.

23. ———."Toward an Interpersonal Theory of Consumer Behavior," *California Management Review,* Vol. 10 (Spring 1968), 73–80.

24. Cox, Donald F. and Raymond A. Bauer. "Self-Confidence and Persuasibility in Women," *Public Opinion Quarterly,* Vol. 28 (Fall 1964), 453–466.

25. Dichter, Ernest. *The Strategy of Desire.* New York: Doubleday, 1960.

26. ———. *Handbook of Consumer Motivations.* New York: McGraw-Hill, 1964.

27. Dolich, Ira J. "Congruence Relationships Between Self Images and Product Brands," *Journal of Marketing Research,* Vol. 6 (February 1969), 80–84.

28. Donnelly, James H., Jr. "Social Character and Acceptance of New Products," *Journal of Marketing Research,* Vol. 7 (February 1970), 111–113.

29. Dornbusch, Sanford M. and Lauren C. Hickman. "Other-Directedness in Consumer Goods Advertising: A Test of Riesman's Historical Theory," *Social Forces,* Vol. 38 (December 1959), 99–102.

30. Evans, Franklin B. "Psychological and Objective Factors in the Prediction of Brand Choice," *Journal of Business,* Vol. 32 (October 1959), 340–369.

31. ———. "Reply: You Still Can't Tell a Ford Owner From a Chevrolet Owner," *Journal of Business,* Vol. 34 (January 1961), 67–73.

32. ———. "Correlates of Automobile Shopping Behavior," *Journal of Marketing,* Vol. 26 (October 1962), 74–77.

33. ———. "True Correlates of Automobile Shopping Behavior," *Journal of Marketing,* Vol. 28 (January 1964), 65–66.

34. ———. "Ford Versus Chevrolet: Park Forest Revisited," *Journal of Business,* Vol. 41 (October 1968), 445–459.

35. ———. "Automobiles and Self-Imagery: Comment," *Journal of Business,* Vol. 41 (October 1968), 484–485.

36. ——— and Harry V. Roberts. "Fords, Chevrolets, and the Problem of Discrimination," *Journal of Business,* Vol. 36 (April 1963), 242–249.

37. Eysenck, H. J., Mollie Tarrant, Myra Woolf, and L. England. "Smoking and Personality," *British Medical Journal,* Vol. 1 (May 1960), 1456–1460.

38. Gardner, Burleigh B. and Sidney J. Levy. "The Product and the Brand," *Harvard Business Review,* Vol. 33 (March-April 1955), 33–39.

39. Grubb, Edward L. "Consumer Perception of 'Self Concept' and Its Relationship to Brand Choice of Selected Product Types," *Proceedings.* Winter Conference, American Marketing Association, 1965, 419–422.

40. ——— and Harrison L. Grathwohl. "Consumer Self-Concept, Symbolism and Market Behavior: A Theoretical Approach," *Journal of Marketing,* Vol. 31 (October 1967), 22–27.

41. Grubb, Edward L. and Gregg Hupp. "Perception of Self, Generalized Stereotypes, and Brand Selection," *Journal of Marketing Research,* Vol. 5 (February 1968), 58–63.

42. Gruen, Walter. "Preference for New Products and Its Relationship to Different Measures of Conformity," *Journal of Applied Psychology,* Vol. 44 (December 1960), 361–366.

43. Hall, Calvin S. and Gardner Lindzey. *Theories of Personality.* New York: John Wiley & Sons, 1957 (first edition), 1969 (second edition).

44. Hamm, B. Curtis. "A Study of the Differences Between Self-Actualizing Scores and Product Perceptions Among Female Consumers," *Proceedings.* Winter Conference, American Marketing Association, (1967), 275–276.

45. ——— and Edward W. Cundiff. "Self-Actualization and Product Perception," *Journal of Marketing Research,* Vol. 6 (November 1969), 470–472.

46. Hilgard, Ernest R. and Gordon H. Bower. *Theories of Learning,* third edition. New York: Appleton-Century-Crofts, 1966.

47. Hovland, Carl I. and Irving L. Janis, eds. *Personality and Persuasibility.* New Haven, Conn.: Yale University Press, 1959.

48. Jacobson, Eugene and Jerome Kossoff. "Self-Percept and Consumer Attitudes Toward Small Cars," *Journal of Applied Psychology,* Vol. 47 (August 1963), 242–245.

49. Jacoby, Jacob. "Personality and Consumer Behavior: How Not to Find Relationships," Purdue Papers in Consumer Psychology, N. 102, Purdue University, 1969.

50. ———. "A Multiple Indicant Approach for Studying Innovators," Purdue Papers in Consumer Psychology, No. 108, Purdue University, 1970.

51. ———. "Personality and Innovation Proneness," *Journal of Marketing Research,* Vol. 8 (May 1971), 244–247.

52. Kamen, Joseph M. "Personality and Food Preferences," *Journal of Advertising Research,* Vol. 4 (September 1964), 29–32.

53. Kassarjian, Harold H. "Social Character and Differential Preference for Mass Communication," *Journal of Marketing Research,* Vol. 2 (May 1965), 146–153.

54. —— and Waltraud M. Kassarjian. "Personality Correlates of Inner- and Other-Direction," *Journal of Social Psychology,* Vol. 70 (June 1966), 281–285.

55. Kassarjian, Waltraud M. "A Study of Riesman's Theory of Social Character," *Sociometry,* Vol. 25 (September 1962), 213–230.

56. —— and Harold H. Kassarjian. "Occupational Interests, Social Values and Social Character," *Journal of Counseling Psychology,* Vol. 12 (January 1966), 48–54.

57. Kernan, Jerome. "Choice Criteria, Decision Behavior, and Personality," *Journal of Marketing Research,* Vol. 5 (May 1968), 155–164.

58. Koponen, Arthur. "Personality Characteristics of Purchasers," *Journal of Advertising Research,* Vol. 1 (September 1960), 6–12.

59. Kuehn, Alfred A. "Demonstration of a Relationship Between Psychological Factors and Brand Choice," *Journal of Business,* Vol. 36 (April 1963), 237–241.

60. Lazer, William. "Life Style Concepts and Marketing," *Proceedings.* Winter Conference, American Marketing Association, (1963), 130–139.

61. Lehmann, Stanley. "Personality and Compliance: A Study of Anxiety and Self-Esteem in Opinion and Behavior Change," *Journal of Personality and Social Psychology,* Vol. 15 (May 1970), 76–86.

62. Lessig, V. Parker and John O. Tollefson. "Market Segmentation Through Numerical Taxonomy," *Journal of Marketing Research,* Vol. 8 (November 1971), 480–487.

63. Levy, Sidney J. "Symbols for Sale," *Harvard Business Review,* Vol. 37 (July-August 1959), 117–124.

64. Linton, Harriet and Elaine Graham. "Personality Correlates of Persuasibility," in Carl I. Hovland and Irving L. Janis, eds., *Personality and Persuasibility.* New Haven: Yale University Press, (1959), 69–101.

65. Marcus, Alan S. "Obtaining Group Measures from Personality Test Scores: Auto Brand Choice Predicted from the Edwards Personal Preference Schedule," *Psychological Reports,* Vol. 17 (October 1965), 523–531.

66. Martineau, Pierre. *Motivation in Advertising.* New York: McGraw-Hill, 1957.

67. ——. "Letter to the Editor," *Advertising Age,* Vol. 30 (December 21, 1959), 76.

68. Massy, William F., Ronald E. Frank, and Thomas M. Lodahl. *Purchasing Behavior and Personal Attributes.* Philadelphia: University of Pennsylvania Press, 1968.

69. Murphy, Joseph R. "Questionable Correlates of Automobile Shopping Behavior," *Journal of Marketing,* Vol. 27 (October 1963), 71–72.

70. Myers, John G. "Determination of Private Brand Attitudes," *Journal of Marketing Research,* Vol. 4 (February 1967), 73–81.

71. ———. *Consumer Image and Attitude.* Berkeley: Institute of Business and Economic Research, University of California, 1968.

72. Pennington, Allan A. and Robert A. Peterson. "Interest Patterns and Product Preferences: An Exploratory Analysis," *Journal of Marketing Research,* Vol. 6 (August 1969), 284–290.

73. Pessemier, Edgar A. and Douglas J. Tigert. "Personality, Activity and Attitude Predictors of Consumer Behavior," *Proceedings.* World Congress, American Marketing Association (1966), 332–347.

74. ———. "Socio-Economic Status of the Family and Housewife Personality, Life Style and Opinion Factors," Paper No. 197, Institute For Research on the Behavioral, Economic and Management Sciences, Purdue University, 1967.

75. Peterson, Robert A. and Allan L. Pennington. "SVIB Interests and Product Preference," *Journal of Applied Psychology,* Vol. 53 (August 1969), 304–308.

76. Robertson, Thomas S. *Innovation and the Consumer.* New York: Holt, Rinehart and Winston, 1971.

77. ——— and James H. Myers. "Personality Correlates of Opinion Leadership and Innovative Buying Behavior," *Journal of Marketing Research,* Vol. 6 (May 1969), 164–168.

78. ———. "Personality Correlates of Innovative Buying Behavior: A Reply," *Journal of Marketing Research,* Vol. 7 (May 1970), 260–261.

79. Ruch, Dudley M. "Limitations of Current Approaches to Understanding Brand Buying Behavior," in Joseph W. Newman, ed., *On Knowing the Consumer.* New York: John Wiley & Sons, 1966, 173–186.

80. Shuchman, Abe and Michael Perry. "Self-Confidence and Persuasibility in Marketing: A Reappraisal," *Journal of Marketing Research,* Vol. 6 (May 1969), 146–154.

81. Sommers, Montrose S. "Product Symbolism and the Perception of Social Strata," *Proceedings.* Winter Conference, American Marketing Association, 1963, 200–216.

82. ———. "The Use of Product Symbolism to Differentiate Social Strata," *University of Houston Business Review,* Vol. 11 (Fall 1964), 1–102.

83. Steiner, Gary A. "Notes on Franklin B. Evans' 'Psychological and Objective Factors in the Prediction of Brand Choice,'" *Journal of Business,* Vol. 34 (January 1961), 57–60.

84. Summers, John O. "The Identity of Women's Clothing Fashion Opinion Leaders," *Journal of Marketing Research,* Vol. 7 (May 1970), 178–185.

85. Tigert, Douglas J. "A Psychological Profile of Magazine Audiences: An Investigation of a Media's Climate," paper presented at the American Marketing Association Consumer Behavior Workshop, 1969.

86. Tucker, William T. and John Painter. "Personality and Product Use," *Journal of Applied Psychology,* Vol. 45 (October 1961), 325–329.

87. Venkatesan, M. "Personality and Persuasibility in Consumer Decision Making," *Journal of Advertising Research,* Vol. 8 (March 1968), 39–45.

88. Vitz, Paul C. and Donald Johnston. "Masculinity of Smokers and the Masculinity of Cigarette Images," *Journal of Applied Psychology,* Vol. 49 (June 1965), 155–159.

89. Wells, William D. "General Personality Tests and Consumer Behavior," in Joseph Newman, ed., *On Knowing the Consumer.* New York: John Wiley & Sons, 1966, 187–189.

90. ———. "Backward Segmentation," in Johan Arndt, ed., *Insights into Consumer Behavior.* Boston: Allyn and Bacon, 1968, 85–100.

91. ——— and Douglas J. Tigert. "Activities, Interests and Opinions," *Journal of Advertising Research,* Vol. 11 (August 1971), 27–35.

92. Westfall, Ralph. "Psychological Factors in Predicting Product Choice," *Journal of Marketing,* Vol. 26 (April 1962), 34–40.

93. Wilkie, William. "Psychological Descriptors," paper presented at the Fall Conference, American Marketing Association, 1970.

94. Wilson, Clark L. "Homemaker Living Patterns and Marketplace Behavior—A Psychometric Approach," *Proceedings.* World Congress, American Marketing Association, 1966, 305–331.

95. Winick, Charles. "The Relationship Among Personality Needs, Objective Factors, and Brand Choice: A Re-examination," *Journal of Business,* Vol. 34 (January 1961), 61–66.

96. Woodside, Arch G. "Social Character, Product Use and Advertising Appeal," *Journal of Advertising Research,* Vol. 8 (December 1969), 31–35.

2.4 Personality and Innovation Proneness
JACOB JACOBY

Attempts at relating personality variables to consumer behavior have generally been disappointing [1, 2, 3, 4, 9, 10, 13, 14, 16, 17, 20, 29, 31]. Robertson and Myers [24, p. 167] concluded "that at best personality variables, as measured by a standardized, normative, self-designating personality inventory, have little, if any, relationship to innovative behavior." However, acceptance of the conclusion that personality variables have little, if any, explanatory value or predictive utility with respect to consumer behavior would be without justification. Investigators in the typical study of this relationship usually administer a broad-coverage personality inventory and attempt to correlate responses with statements of product use or preference. However, in most cases, no a priori thought is directed to *how*, or especially *why*, personality should or should not be related to given aspects of consumer behavior. Moreover, most of the studies which report statistically significant findings usually do so on the basis of post-hoc picking and choosing out of large data arrays [4, 17, 18, 29].

Many investigators naively and unreasonably assume that, given both the general hypothesis that behavior is determined to a certain extent by personality and the availability of an easy-to-administer personality inventory, differentiation among groups of consumers should be possible; if not, they assume that the general hypothesis fails. Usually, results obtained are inconclusive or at best mildly suggestive. However, if investigators selected specific personality traits based on theoretically derived hypotheses, made specific predictions on the interactions of these traits with specific aspects of consumer behavior, and utilized experimental rather than correlational paradigms, the likelihood of obtaining significant, meaningful, and usable findings would be enhanced.

The Study

For example, the personality variable of dogmatism [25, 30] provides a sound theoretical and empirical foundation for predicting new product acceptance. This study considered the relationship of dogmatism to anxiety, novelty, and creativity.

Highly dogmatic mental systems represent a cognitive-psychodynamic network of defenses against anxiety [25]. Dogmatism is functional: the more persistently anxious or threatened the individual, the more he manifests a closed mind [11, 12, 23, 25, 27, 28]. Recent research on consumer decision processes [5] indicates that brand-switching usually entails some perceived risk which increases when switching to a *new* brand or product is contemplated. Because perceived risk can induce anxiety, high dogmatics should be less likely than low dogmatics to try new products.

Studies on the relationship of dogmatism to novelty are similarly suggestive. Low dogmatics have been found to score significantly higher on acceptance of change in a variety of situations [7, 19, 22, 25, 32]. High dogmatics are, in general, more resistant to change [7]. Finally, it has been suggested that innovators and early adopters tend to be more creative than later adopters [34], and open-mindedness may be a necessary precondition for creativity [15, 26, 33].

The operational definition of innovation most often used by consumer researchers is any form of a product recently available in a market [7]. Thus, totally new products, new brands, modifications of old brands, and even brands previously not available in a given geographical area may be considered innovations. This definition has been adopted for this study. Based upon both theoretical rationale and the weight of related empirical evidence, it is predicted that low dogmatics will be more likely to make innovative selections than will high dogmatics.

Method

Subjects were 60 unmarried 18 to 26-year-old coeds attending Purdue University during the fall 1969 semester. All were volunteers.

To obtain an index of innovation proneness, 15 sets of photographs, with five pictures per set, were collected for 15 different product categories. One picture in each set was of an innovation (as operationally defined), while the other four were of more traditional varieties of the product, either in terms of brand, style, or function. For example, one product category contained pictures of four women's dress-length coats and one maxicoat, a fashion innovation. For cigarettes, Virginia Slims, a brand innovation, was pictured next to Kent, Marlboro, Viceroy, and Parliament. A third category exhibited four waist-high panty hose and one lower cut, a functional innovation.

The 15 products, classified according to category and type of innovation examined, are presented in Table 1. Across six cosmetic, four clothing, and five miscellaneous products, there were six new brands, five fashion innovations, and four functional innovations.

TABLE 1. Products and Type of Innovation Investigated

Product	Category	Type of Innovation
1. Hair Conditioner	Cosmetics	New brand
2. Lipstick	Cosmetics	New brand
3. Hair Lightener	Cosmetics	Functional[a]
4. Perfume	Cosmetics	New brand
5. Blush-on	Cosmetics	Functional[a]
6. Makeup Base	Cosmetics	Functional[a]
7. Men's Cologne	Miscellaneous	New brand
8. Diamond Ring	Miscellaneous	Fashion
9. Beer	Miscellaneous	New brand
10. Luggage	Miscellaneous	Fashion
11. Cigarettes	Miscellaneous	New brand
12. Shoes	Clothing	Fashion
13. Slack Outfit	Clothing	Fashion
14. Panty Hose	Clothing	Functional[a]
15. Coat	Clothing	Fashion

[a]New form of product or method of use.

All five pictures in each product set were randomly mounted so that all could be viewed at once. Pictures within each set were matched on such factors as size, color vs. black and white, branded vs. unbranded, photograph vs. sketch, and container type. The standard Form E of the Rokeach Dogmatism Scale [25], which has demonstrated validity and high test-retest reliability, was used to measure dogmatism.

Individual subjects selected one item in each set that they would buy if given the choice. The experimenter said, "Do not let the colors of the products or brands affect your decision. For example, do not choose a lipstick for the particular shade pictured. If you do not use a set of products, buy for someone else." Thus each subject received an innovation score ranging from zero to 15, depending upon the number of innovations selected. The 15 sets were presented in the same order, and each subject proceeded at her own pace. The dogmatism scale was administered upon completion, again with no time limit.

Results

Based upon their dogmatism scores, subjects were split into two groups at the median. Table 2 indicates that the between-group difference in dogmatism scores was significant beyond the .001 levels. As predicted, there was a significant overall difference ($p < .01$) in innovation scores between the two groups. Low dogmatic individuals made significantly more innovative responses.

Product-by-product analysis indicated that the low dogmatics gave more innovative responses to 11 sets. Four of these differences (Products 7, 9, 11, and 12 in Table 1) were significant beyond the .05 level. The remaining 11 tests yielded probability values in excess of .20.

TABLE 2.　Dogmatics' Mean Innovation Score Differences

	Low Dogmatics ($n = 30$)	High Dogmatics ($n = 30$)	t	p
Dogmatism	$\overline{X} = 118.40$	$\overline{X} = 161.13$	10.87^a	$<.001$
	$\sigma = 14.53$	$\sigma = 15.90$		
Innovation Index	$\overline{X} = 3.27$	$\overline{X} = 2.17$	2.53^a	$<.01^b$
	$\sigma = 2.03$	$\sigma = 1.23$		
Dogmatism $\times$ Innovation Index: $r = -.316$, $p < .01$				

[a]One-tailed tests.
[b]Given heterogeneity of variance and using d.f. $= 29$ [6, p. 108].

Table 3 analyzes innovative responses according to type of product and innovation. Low dogmatics were considerably more likely ($p < .001$) to select new brands, especially in the miscellaneous category ($p < .05$).

TABLE 3.   Frequency of Innovative Responses

	Low Dogmatics	High Dogmatics	Chi Square	p [a]
Type of Product				
Cosmetics (6)	31	23	1.185	n.s.
Clothing (4)	17	11	1.286	n.s.
Miscellaneous (5)	50	31	4.457	<.05
Type of Innovation				
New brand (6)	48	20	11.530	<.001
Fashion (5)	29	28	.690	n.s.
Function (4)	21	17	.421	n.s.

[a] One-tailed tests.

Discussion

As predicted, low dogmatic individuals tended to make significantly more innovative selections than did high dogmatic individuals. However, the relationship did not appear to be exceptionally strong. Only 10% of the variance was accounted for by the correlation between dogmatism and innovation proneness ($r = -.316$). Moreover, the mean low dogmatic innovation score of 3.27 is only .27 above—and the high dogmatic mean only .83 below—the 3.00 value to be expected on a chance basis ($\frac{1}{5}$ innovations × 15 product sets).

However, the notion of practical significance is more important for practitioners than statistical significance or even the size of the relationship. To the extent that marketers and advertisers can capitalize on the relationship between dogmatism and innovation proneness and can thereby increase the likelihood of gaining that all-important toehold, the relationship is important. How, then, might this information be applied?

It has been suggested that when introducing new products "advertisements should emphasize the prestige of owning the item—to appeal specifically to the early adopters" [34, p. 52]. Given that low dogmatics are more innovative and tend to adopt earlier than high dogmatics, then quite the opposite prediction should be made. Rokeach states that low dogmatics "act on relevant information from the outside on its own intrinsic merits, unencumbered by irrelevant factors in the situation arising from within the person or from the outside" [25, p. 57]. He cites irrational ego-motives and the need for self-aggrandizement as examples of irrelevant internal factors, while pressures arising from peers, reference groups, authority figures, social, institutional, and cultural norms are examples of irrelevant external factors. High dogmatics prefer to rely heavily on the pronouncements of authorities and tend to accept information primarily on the basis of its source, while low dogmatics tend to act upon their independent evaluation of message content [7, 21, 25, 30].

This suggests that the marketer-advertiser introducing a new product would be wise to focus on product attributes rather than emphasizing irrelevant ego or social factors. As a hypothetical example, advertisers of a cigarette with a new type of filter would do well to stress and describe the filter rather than emphasize enjoying the cigarette in social situations.

In conclusion, low dogmatic individuals were found to be significantly more likely to be innovators than high dogmatic individuals. To the extent that such innovators are also more likely to prefer objective information, advertisers seeking a market position for an innovation ought to focus on factual information rather than on irrelevancies.

References

1. Advertising Research Foundation. *Are There Consumer Types?* New York: Advertising Research Foundation, 1964.

2. Brody, Robert P. and Scott M. Cunningham. "Personality Variables and the Consumer Decision Process," *Journal of Marketing Research,* Vol. 5 (February 1968), 50–57.

3. Claycamp, Henry J. "Characteristics of Owners of Thrift Deposits in Commercial and Savings and Loan Associations," *Journal of Marketing Research,* Vol. 2 (May 1965), 163–170.

4. Cohen, Joel B. "The Role of Personality in Consumer Behavior," in Harold H. Kassarjian and Thomas S. Robertson, eds., *Perspectives in Consumer Behavior.* Glenview, Ill.: Scott, Foresman, 1968, 220–234.

5. Cox, Donald F., ed. *Risk Taking and Information Handling in Consumer Behavior.* Boston: Graduate School of Business Administration, Harvard University, 1967.

6. Edwards, Allen L. *Experimental Design in Psychological Research.* New York: Holt, Rinehart and Winston, 1960.

7. Ehrlich, Howard J. and Dorothy Lee. "Dogmatism, Learning, and Resistance to Change: A Review and a New Paradigm," *Psychological Bulletin,* 71 (April 1969), 249–260.

8. Engel, James F., David T. Kollat, and Roger D. Blackwell. *Consumer Behavior.* New York: Holt, Rinehart and Winston, 1968.

9. Evans, Franklin B. "Psychological and Objective Factors in the Prediction of Brand Choice: Ford versus Chevrolet," *Journal of Business,* Vol. 32 (October 1959), 340–369.

10. ———. "Ford versus Chevrolet: Park Forest Revisited," *Journal of Business,* Vol. 41 (October 1968), 445–459.

11. Fillenbaum, Samuel and Arnold Jackman. "Dogmatism and Anxiety in Relation to Problem Solving: An Extension of Rokeach's Results," *Journal of Abnormal and Social Psychology,* Vol. 63 (July 1961), 212–214.

12. Fruchter, Benjamin, Milton Rokeach, and Edwin G. Novak. "A Factorial Study of Dogmatism, Opinionation, and Related Scales," *Psychological Reports,* Vol. 4 (March 1958), 19–22.

13. Gottlieb, Morris J. "Segmentation by Personality Types," *Proceedings*. National Conference, American Marketing Association, 1958, 148–158.

14. Gruen, Walter. "Preference for New Products and Its Relationship to Different Measures of Conformity," *Journal of Applied Psychology*, Vol. 44 (Dec. 1960), 361–366.

15. Jacoby, Jacob. "Open-mindedness and Creativity," *Psychological Reports*, Vol. 20 (June 1967), 822.

16. Kamen, Joseph M. "Personality and Food Preference," *Journal of Advertising Research*, Vol. 4 (Sept. 1964), 29–32.

17. Koponen, Arthur. "Personality Characteristics of Purchasers," *Journal of Advertising Research*, Vol. 1 (Sept. 1960), 6–12.

18. Massy, William F., Ronald E. Frank, and Thomas Lodahl. *Purchasing Behavior and Personal Attributes*. Philadelphia: University of Pennsylvania Press, 1968.

19. Mikol, Bernard. "The Enjoyment of New Musical Systems," in Milton Rokeach. *The Open and Closed Mind*. New York: Basic Books, (1960), 270–284.

20. Myers, John G. "Determinants of Private Brand Attitude," *Journal of Marketing Research*, Vol. 4 (Feb. 1967), 73–81.

21. Powell, Fredric A. "Open- and Closed-mindedness and the Ability to Differentiate Source and Message," *Journal of Abnormal and Social Psychology*, Vol. 65 (July 1962), 61–64.

22. Pyron, Bernard. "Rejection of Avant-garde Art and the Need for Simple Order," *Journal of Psychology*, Vol. 63 (July 1966), 159–178.

23. Rebhun, Martin T. "Dogmatism and Test Anxiety," *Journal of Psychology*, Vol. 62 (Jan. 1966), 39–40.

24. Robertson, Thomas S. and James H. Myers. "Personality Correlates of Opinion Leadership and Innovative Buying Behavior," *Journal of Marketing Research*, Vol. 6 (May 1969), 164–168.

25. Rokeach, Milton. *The Open and Closed Mind*. New York: Basic Books, 1960.

26. ———. "In Pursuit of the Creative Process," in Gary A. Steiner, ed., *The Creative Organization*. Chicago: University of Chicago Press, 1965, 66–88.

27. ——— and Benjamin Fruchter. "A Factorial Study of Dogmatism and Related Concepts," *Journal of Abnormal and Social Psychology*, Vol. 53 (Nov. 1956), 356–360.

28. Sticht, Thomas G. and Wayne Fox. "Geographical Mobility and Dogmatism, Anxiety, and Age," *Journal of Social Psychology*, Vol. 68 (Feb. 1966), 171–174.

29. Tucker, W. T. and John J. Painter. "Personality and Product Use," *Journal of Applied Psychology,* Vol. 45 (Oct. 1961), 325–329.

30. Vacchiano, Ralph B., Paul S. Strauss, and Leonard Hochman. "The Open and Closed Mind: A Review of Dogmatism," *Psychological Bulletin,* Vol. 71 (April 1969), 261–273.

31. Westfall, Ralph. "Psychological Factors in Predicting Product Choice," *Journal of Marketing,* Vol. 36 (April 1962), 34–40.

32. Zagona, Salvatore V. and Merywell A. Kelly. "The Resistance of the Closed Mind to a Novel and Complex Audiovisual Experience," *Journal of Social Psychology,* Vol. 70 (Oct. 1966), 123–131.

33. Zagona, Salvatore V. and Louis A. Zurcher. "Participation, Interaction and Role Behavior in Groups Selected from the Extremes of the Open-closed Cognitive Continuum," *Journal of Psychology,* Vol. 60 (July 1965), 213–219.

34. Zaltman, Gerald. *Marketing: Contributions from the Behavioral Sciences.* New York: Harcourt, Brace, and World, 1965.

2.5 A Multivariate Analysis of Personality and Product Use

DAVID L. SPARKS, W. T. TUCKER

Despite the general failure of empirical studies over the past ten or more years to locate important relationships between personality and consumptive behavior, there remains among students of marketing this item of faith: behavior in the marketplace is critically reflective of individual personality. The corollary of that belief is that the measuring instruments or statistical techniques (or both) that have been commonly used in empirical work are incapable of giving more than glimpses of the structures and processes involved.

Statistical Techniques

Most of the work attempting to relate personality to consumer behavior has used bivariate inferential techniques or regression including multiple correlation. This implies the view (probably not held by any researcher) of personality as a bundle of discrete and independent traits which either do not interact or do so only in the simple sense that a number of diverse forces can be resolved into a *single* vector.

A recent study by Kernan notes that canonical analysis, alone or in conjunction with hierarchical grouping, can suggest the existence of molar personality types that are essentially synthesized out of the individual traits of a simple personality test [6]. Since Kernan's data delivered only one significant canonical root (at the .10 level), he could not use that technique to draw inferences about the complexity of personality trait interaction; but a hierarchical clustering of subjects based on choice strategies in a game playing situation posited four synthetic character types in which total personalities rather than specific traits seemed to be the operant variables.

The present study parallels the Kernan research with the intention of using hierarchical grouping in the same way, unless canonical analysis infers several significant roots.

In effect, the statistical techniques used in many previous studies relating personality to consumer behavior [2, 3, 7, 8, 9, 10] probably constitute a part of the "inadequate theoretical framework" referred to by Brody and Cunningham [1].

Measuring Instruments

Psychologists are no more elated than those in marketing with current personality theory or the attendant measuring instruments. There is no persuasive theoretical basis for preferring one sort of personality test to another, despite a great variety of tests. On one hand, instruments like the Edwards or the California Personality Inventory measure a host of individual traits; on the other, the I-O scale locates everyone at some point on a unidimensional continuum. (Clinical techniques requiring subjective judgments are disregarded here for operational reasons.)

Additionally, instruments may be roughly categorized into two subclasses, those asking largely for: (1) direct reports on thoughts and feelings, and (2) reports of activities, actual or preferred. Preferences for one or the other of these subclasses will in some measure depend upon the way the experimenter regards personality. It is legitimate to think of personality as an intimate aspect of the cognitive and affective organization of the central nervous system (or the total organism). It is equally legitimate to regard it as a verbal construct describing behavioral regularities. When someone is described as anti-intraceptive or rigid, it is the cognitive and affective organization that is the principal reference. To call someone sociable or kleptomaniac is to classify him behaviorally with little regard for central processes. This dichotomy is not rigorous; a number of personality tests, Cohen's CAD for instance [2], ask for cognitive evaluations of behavior or otherwise provide mixed cases.

Research Design

A sample of 190 college students (173 of whom accurately completed forms) chosen for their availability in introductory marketing classes were used to explore the relationship between consumer behavior and personality. The choice of such a sample (in this case all of the males present in particular classes on a particular day) seems appropriate when the effort is to locate the existence of relationships rather than to describe or define them for particular universes. Beyond this, the sample method was essentially that of Kernan [6] and Tucker and Painter [9]. Both previous studies showed that the frequency distributions on the Gordon Personal Profile [5] and Gordon Personal Inventory [4] for such a sample varied little from those of groups on which the test was normed.

The use of the Gordon tests was based on several considerations: (1) the bias of the authors toward the behaviorally-oriented rather than the cognitively-oriented test as relevant to consumer behavior, (2) the previous and partially successful use of that test [6, 9], and (3) the short time required for subjects to complete the tests. The fact that eight traits isolated by the test are not fully independent is of concern but seems of less consequence than the test's demonstrated ability to differentiate people with regard to the kinds of behavior under study.

The instrument to measure the subjects' product use had 17 multiple-choice questions. The products, considered to be typical for this subject group, were: headache remedies, mouthwash, men's cologne, hair spray, shampoo, antacid remedies, *Playboy,* alcoholic beverages, complexion aids, vitamins, cigarettes, coffee, chewing gum, and after-shave lotion. In addition, subjects were asked how often they brushed their teeth and had their hair cut. Another question asked about their adoption of new clothing fashions. Response categories were, generally: never, less than once a week, about once a week, more than once a week but less than once a day, and about once a day. For five of the products, dichotomous or specially worded response categories were required. While these products were not a complete inventory of typical products, they did represent a reasonable number and were considered sufficient for this investigation.

A pretest of the 17-item product-use questionnaire with 62 male undergraduates led to minor changes in the question wording and response categories. A varimax factor analysis of the pretest data showed the 17 questions to be almost completely independent, the last of the 17 factors extracting nearly as much variance as the first. While desirable in one sense, independence as extensive as this raises critical issues which will be discussed later.

Findings

A correlation analysis of the data (Table 1) shows essentially the same weak and spotty relationships between personality traits and particular product use reported previously. It may lead one to conclude that some two percent of the variance in the use of mouthwash may be accounted for by cautiousness or that some six percent of the variance in the use of men's cologne is associated with sociability. The total of 18 significant but low correlations in a matrix where seven would be expected to occur by chance may be persuasive that something is responsible, but the findings seem to be of minimal value.

Canonical analysis provides both a more persuasive case for the relationship under study and some hints concerning the kinds of personality structures involved. That is far from saying that canonical analysis illuminates the field; it is notoriously difficult to interpret beyond the significance levels of R's associated with particular roots.

TABLE 1. Correlation Matrix: Product Use and Personality Trait

Product	Ascendancy	Responsibility	Emotional Stability	Sociability	Cautiousness	Original Thinking	Personal Relations	Vigor
Headache Remedy	.0254	−.1391	−.2104[a]	.1490	−.0073	−.0649	−.0875	−.0907
Mouthwash	.0702	−.0983	−.1308	.1125	.1501[a]	−.0242	.0443	−.1238
Men's Cologne	.1473	−.1066	−.1222	.2599[a]	.1247	.0715	−.0459	.0008
Hair Spray	−.0580	−.1241	−.0725	.0388	−.0824	−.0668	−.0664	−.0159
Shampoo	.1735[a]	−.1420	.0729	.1459	−.0449	.0757	.0412	.0116
Antacid Remedy	.0217	−.1521[a]	−.2692[a]	.0393	−.1222	−.0974	−.1119	−.0886
Playboy	.1293	−.0218	.0787	.2621[a]	−.1038	.0650	.0169	.1185
Alcoholic Beverages	.2001[a]	−.1605[a]	.0159	.1973[a]	−.2861[a]	.0041	−.1436	.0261
Brush Teeth	−.1324	−.0418	.0196	−.0624	−.0663	−.1645[a]	.0329	−.1074
Fashion Adoption	.2892[a]	−.1647[a]	−.0628	.3858[a]	−.0919	.0924	.0838	.0557
Complexion Aids	.0065	.0591	−.0106	.0845	.1131	−.0826	−.0667	−.0902
Vitamin Capsules	.1384	−.1197	−.1759[a]	.1288	−.0855	.0963	−.0414	.0016
Haircut	−.0587	.0616	.0655	−.0774	−.0670	−.0247	−.0394	−.0311
Cigarettes	.0869	−.1465	−.1213	.0954	−.1313	.1408	−.0376	−.0305
Coffee	−.0413	−.0265	−.1478	−.0185	.0403	−.0781	−.0683	−.0734
Chewing Gum	.1645[a]	−.1035	−.1165	.2581[a]	−.1209	−.0447	.0433	−.0446
After-Shave Lotion	.0506	.1016	.0429	.0751	.0091	.1288	.0168	.0676

[a]Indicates correlation coefficient is significant at the .05 level.

TABLE 2.   Results of the Canonical Analysis

Variables	Canonical Coefficients		
	1	2	3
Criterion Set (Product Use)			
Headache Remedy	−.0081	−.4433	.1123
Mouthwash	−.1598	−.4538	.2809
Men's Cologne	.2231	−.1935	−.2121
Hair Spray	.0664	.0706	.0857
Shampoo	.3784	.1587	−.0063
Antacid Remedy	−.1421	−.1746	−.3226
Playboy	.1511	.1591	.5220
Alcoholic Beverages	.4639	.3098	−.1329
Brush Teeth	−.1879	−.0152	.2341
Fashion Adoption	.3226	−.3993	.0856
Complexion Aids	−.0243	.0925	.1799
Vitamin Capsules	.2870	−.0599	−.4975
Haircut	−.1698	.1855	−.0170
Cigarettes	.4065	.0551	−.2894
Coffee	−.2441	−.2453	.1330
Chewing Gum	.2051	−.1320	.1342
After-Shave Lotion	−.0270	.3022	.0108
Predictor Set (Personality Traits)			
Ascendancy	.0182	−.0517	−.4375
Responsibility	−.5125	.0777	−.1688
Emotional Stability	.4309	.6405	.4880
Sociability	.6072	−.3597	.6199
Cautiousness	−.2869	−.5959	.2438
Original Thinking	.2377	.1620	−.3076
Personal Relations	−.1245	−.0567	.0369
Vigor	.1681	.2592	.0481
Roots	.3671	.3000	.1711
Canonical R	.606	.548	.413
x^2	72.7419	56.7026	29.8417
d.f.	24	22	20
Probability	.0000	.0002	.0752

Table 2 shows the first three canonical roots with R's of .606, .548, and .413. These have significance levels of .0001, .0002, and .0752 respectively, leaving little doubt that there are significant relationships involved. More interesting, since the basic relationship involved has not really been in doubt, is the nature of the relationship suggested. The meanings of the roots can be crudely approximated by extracting the items with heavy loadings from the predictor and criterion sets, somewhat simplifying the picture. In this case, items with coefficients above .30 are used.

The first root is associated with the use of shampoo, alcoholic beverages, cigarettes, and early fashion adoption. Those involved are best described as sociable, emotionally stable, and irresponsible (minus responsibility). The relationships are intuitively acceptable, although they are certainly not the only ones that would be so. Nevertheless, it makes sense to think that early fashion adopters are those particular sociables who are also emotionally stable (not easily upset) and also somewhat irresponsible (responsibility has previously been associated with modal behavior [9]).

The second root is associated with (again converting signs verbally for ease of expression) the use of headache remedies and mouthwash, late fashion adoption, and infrequent use of after-shave lotion. The personality characteristics are sociability, cautiousness, and emotional instability. At this point there emerges a clear advantage to the methodology. Both early and late fashion adoption are related to sociability, but in different personality contexts.

This seems to be exactly the kind of relationship personality theory implies: not a simple connection between sociability and early fashion adoption, but a more complex one in which sociability combined with emotional stability and irresponsibility is oriented toward one sort of action while sociability combined with emotional instability and cautiousness is oriented toward its opposite.

In the third root (with the marginal significance level of .075) sociability again characterizes the individual, but in this context the relationship with fashion adoption is very low and there is an association with light or no use of cigarettes, again a reversal of the variate-to-variate relationship suggested by the first root.

The most obvious explanation for these findings lies in the notion that it is the person in some gestalt in which the entire personality and the entire situation form a particular configuration, who acts, not the individual personality trait. But this view includes the possibility that the most useful approach to the subject is to measure individual personality characteristics and synthesize the molar personality from such measures. The relationships of the above canonical analysis suggest that even a simple model based on trait interaction could prove more predictive than a trait-by-trait approach. Nevertheless, some of the relationships suggested could stem in large part from nonlinearity. Further, canonical analysis is a linear technique which can only indirectly suggest the presence of certain possible nonlinear associations while leaving others occult.

The present study parallels that of Kernan [6] closely enough that there is some interest in seeing whether a hierarchical clustering of subjects on the basis of their reported product-use behavior approximates the interesting personality profiles that related to particular game playing strategies. Table 3 shows the four clusters Kernan located and the six clusters that seem to best describe the present data. No persuasive case can be made for similarities in grouping, although the imaginative mind can perceive parallels. Nor does the cluster analysis, when compared with product use, add to the conclusions available through canonical analysis alone in this case. It seems possible that the near-fantasy situation of game playing in relative isolation may give freer play to personality expression than consumption patterns which operate under social, economic, and habitual constraints.

The annoying fragmentation of 17 questions into 17 factors of approximately equal magnitude is not readily explained. It is difficult to conceive that the frequency of use of mouthwash, men's cologne, hair spray, shampoo, and after-shave lotion are essentially independent behaviors not tied together. The problem may lie in the methodology, although it is difficult to understand how the response categories could mask associations when most were used by fairly large numbers of subjects. Yet on both pretest and test the same lack of structure appeared. The kind of post hoc explanations that come to mind do little to

TABLE 3. Results of Cluster Analysis

	Cluster					
	1	2	3	4	5	6
Personality Trait: Kernan's Study[a]						
Ascendancy	81.0	19.0	81.0	43.0		
Responsibility	43.0	11.0	19.0	80.0		
Emotional Stability	40.0	15.0	40.0	77.0		
Sociability	77.0	12.0	77.0	39.0		
Cautiousness	54.0	31.0	5.0	69.0		
Original Thinking	72.0	31.0	45.0	43.0		
Personal Relations	70.0	10.0	54.0	57.0		
Vigor	81.0	13.0	38.0	63.0		
Personality Trait: Present Study[a]						
Ascendancy	66.6	54.9	50.8	52.3	49.4	63.0
Responsibility	44.2	55.2	49.2	47.6	61.7	41.1
Emotional Stability	43.7	57.4	54.3	50.7	47.8	44.4
Sociability	63.6	49.1	42.9	37.9	36.4	59.8
Cautiousness	40.2	45.1	46.6	51.5	62.2	33.5
Original Thinking	52.2	54.5	53.1	48.3	43.9	51.0
Personal Relations	49.4	42.3	45.5	48.7	40.3	39.3
Vigor	49.4	61.2	61.5	54.1	44.3	52.3

[a] Mean percentile scores.

reassure one that there are not large areas of dissociated events in consumer behavior that will require explanatory models far more complex or far more numerous than one would wish.

Conclusions

The association of identical personality traits (within different sets of personality traits) with diverse consumer behavior suggests that trait inter-actions or nonlinear relationships may compose a significant portion of the personality-behavior relation. This may partially explain the difficulty in empirically demonstrating the commonly accepted hypothesis that personality influences consumer activities. Inferential techniques do not generally lend themselves to the location of the sorts of relationships implied by these findings.

The apparent lack of correlation among product-use patterns suggested by factor analyses of questionnaire responses leads to the conclusion that a general model applicable to all consumer behavior would prove extremely complex. The alternative of exploring personality in connection with particular behavior or particular products seems therefore the only current application to practical marketing problems.

The particular relationships among traits suggested by this study should be considered as merely representative of the sorts of interrelations that can occur. In all probability a study of other subjects, and other products, or other sorts of behavioral differences would show the relevance of different trait combinations.

References

1. Brody, Robert P. and Scott M. Cunningham. "Personality Variables and the Consumer Decision Process," *Journal of Marketing Research,* Vol. 5 (February 1968), 50–57.

2. Cohen, Joel B. "An Interpersonal Orientation to the Study of Consumer Behavior," *Journal of Marketing Research,* Vol. 4 (August 1967), 270–278.

3. Evans, Franklin B. "Psychological and Objective Factors in the Prediction of Brand Choice: Ford Versus Chevrolet," *Journal of Business,* Vol. 32 (October 1959), 340–369.

4. Gordon, Leonard V. *Gordon Personal Inventory.* New York: Harcourt, Brace, & World, 1963.

5. ———. *Gordon Personal Profile.* New York: Harcourt, Brace, & World, 1963.

6. Kernan, Jerome B. "Choice Criteria, Decision Behavior, and Personality," *Journal of Marketing Research,* Vol. 5 (May 1968), 155–164.

7. Koponen, Arthur. "Personality Characteristics of Purchasers," *Journal of Advertising Research,* Vol. 1 (September 1960), 6–12.

8. Pessemier, Edgar A., Philip C. Burger, and Douglas J. Tigert. "Can New Product Buyers Be Identified?" *Journal of Marketing Research,* Vol. 4 (November 1967), 349–355.

9. Tucker, W. T. and John J. Painter. "Personality and Product Use," *Journal of Applied Psychology,* Vol. 45 (October 1961), 325–329.

10. Westfall, Ralph. "Psychological Factors in Predicting Product Choice," *Journal of Marketing,* Vol. 26 (April 1962), 34–40.

2.6 Activities, Interests, and Opinions
WILLIAM D. WELLS, DOUGLAS J. TIGERT

In the early 1950s advertising and marketing were host to an extended and lively fad that came to be known as Motivation Research. Armed with "projective techniques" from clinical psychology and some exciting notions from psychoanalysis, MR practitioners penetrated deeply into the consumer's psyche, revealing for the first time to their astounded clients the "real" reasons people buy products.

The research establishment's reaction was predictable. Conventional researchers insisted that MR was unreliable, invalid, unobjective, too expensive, liable to be misleading, and altogether an instrument of the Devil—and whatever was good about motivation research had long been standard practice anyway. The motivation researchers replied that conventional research was sterile, dull, shallow, rigid, and superficial.

The controversy rolled on through the '50s until everything that could be said had been said too often. As the contestants and the audience wearied, the spotlight moved from MR and the couch to OR and the computer.

But MR left a legacy. Before MR, advertising and marketing research had in fact been a vast wasteland of percentages. The marketing manager who wanted to know why people ate the competitor's cornflakes was told "32% of the respondents said taste, 21% said flavor, 15% said texture, 10% said price, and 22% said don't know or no answer." The copywriter who wanted to know his audience was told: "32.4 years old, 12.62 years of schooling, 90% married with 2.1 children."

To this desert MR brought people. In addition to the exotic (and largely unworkable) projective tests, motivation researchers employed long, free-flowing narrative interviews, and through these interviews marched an array of mothers who worried about getting the kids to school on time, old ladies whose feet hurt, fretful young housewives who didn't know how to make a good pie crust, fathers who felt guilty about watching television when they should be painting the porch and skinny kids who secretly, but sincerely, believed that The Breakfast of Champions had something to do with their batting averages. For the first time, research brought the marketing manager and the copywriter face to face with an audience or a group of customers instead of a bunch of decimals. The marketing manager and the copywriter thought they were—and they probably were in fact—aided in their task of communication.

The rise of OR and the computer did nothing to change this need to have some sensible contact with believable humans. As the mathematical models proliferated, percentages and averages turned into dots, arrows, brackets, boxes, asterisks, and squiggles. The humans who used to show up in motivation research reports disappeared into the computer and emerged as regression coefficients and eigenvalues. The copywriter and the marketing manager, especially the copywriter, still needed some way to appreciate the consumer.

It begins to appear that this need will now be met at least in part by research that focuses on consumers' activities, interests, prejudices, and opinions. Variously called "psychographic" research, "life style" research and even (incorrectly) "attitude" research, it resembles motivation research in that a major aim is to draw recognizably human portraits of consumers. But it also resembles the tougher-minded, more conventional research in that it is amenable to quantification and respectable samples.

This paper is about this new and slightly more sanitary version of motivation research. It starts with a specific example. It mentions various uses. It describes some of the techniques of data gathering and analysis. It ends with a discussion of some criticisms and problems, and the usual rosy but cautious predictions about developments in the future.

Design

One thousand questionnaires were mailed to homemaker members of Market Facts' mail panel. In addition to the usual demographics and questions about a variety of products, the questionnaires contained 300 "activity, interest, and opinion" statements to which the respondent indicated degree of agreement on a six-point scale. For instance, the first statement was, "When I set my mind to do something I usually can do it," and the respondent answered on a scale that ran from 1 (definitely disagree) to 6 (definitely agree). The statements covered a wide variety of topics—including day-to-day activities; interests in media, the arts, clothes, cosmetics and homemaking; and opinions on many matters of general interest.

Swinging Eye Make-Up User

One of the products on the questionnaire was eye make-up. Respondents were asked how often they use it on a seven-step scale ranging from "never" to "more than once a day."

The demographic questions showed that eye make-up users tend to be young and well-educated, and tend to live in metropolitan areas. Usage rates were much higher for working wives than for full-time homemakers, and substantially higher in the West than in other parts of the country.

Cross-tabulation with other products showed the user of eye make-up to be a heavy user of other cosmetics—liquid face make-up base, lipstick, hair spray, perfume, and nail polish, for example. Perhaps less predictably, she also turned out to be an above-average cigarette smoker and an above-average user of gasoline and the long distance telephone.

On television, she liked the movies, the Tonight Show, and Run For Your Life; she didn't like panel programs or Westerns. She read fashion magazines, news magazines and *Life* and *Look;* she didn't read *True Confessions* or *Successful Farming.*

Thus, eye make-up is clearly not an isolated product. Instead, it is part of a behavior pattern, a pattern that suggests an organized set of tastes and values.

Cross-tabulation of eye make-up with the activity, interest, and opinion questions added significant detail to this emerging picture. Compared with the non-user of eye make-up, the user appeared to be much more interested in fashion. For instance, she was more apt to agree with statements like: "I often try the latest hairdo styles when they change"; "I usually have one or more outfits that are of the very latest style"; "An important part of my life and activities is dressing smartly"; and "I enjoy looking through fashion magazines."

Secondly, she said in a number of ways that being attractive to others, and especially to men, is an important aspect of her self image. (All the respondents in this study were homemakers. The large majority were married.) More than the non-user of eye make-up, the user said, "I like to feel attractive to all men"; "Looking attractive is important in keeping your husband"; "I want to look a little different from others"; and "I like what I see when I look in the mirror."

She indicated that she is very meticulous about her person: "I comb my hair and put on my lipstick first thing in the morning"; "I take good care of my skin"; "I do not feel clean without a daily bath"; and "Sloppy people feel terrible."

More than the non-user she said, "I would like to make a trip around the world"; "I would like to spend a year in London or Paris"; "I enjoy going through an art gallery"; and "I like ballet."

She said, "I like parties where there is lots of music and talk"; "I like things that are bright, gay and exciting"; and "I do more things socially than do most of my friends." Not surprisingly, she said "no" to "I am a homebody."

As far as household chores are concerned, she conceded that she is not a compulsive housekeeper. She said "yes" to "I would like to have a maid to do the housework" and "no" to: "I like to go grocery shopping" and "I enjoy most forms of housework."

Her reaction to her home was style-conscious rather than utilitarian: "I like to serve unusual dinners"; "I am interested in spices and seasonings"; "If I had to choose I would rather have a color television set than a new refrigerator." She said "no" to "I furnish my home for comfort, not for style"; "I try to arrange my home for my children's convenience"; and "It is more important to have good appliances in the home than good furniture."

Finally, she ascribed to a number of statements that suggest acceptance of the contemporary and rejection of traditional ideas. More than the non-user she tended to agree with, "I like to think I am a bit of a swinger"; "I like bright, splashy colors"; and "I really do believe that blondes have more fun." She rejected statements like, "Women should not smoke in public"; "There is too much emphasis on sex today"; "Spiritual values are more important than material things"; and "If it was good enough for my mother, it is good enough for me."

The Heavy User of Shortening

In the same study, another product—shortening—produced a vividly contrasting picture. Compared with the heavy user of eye make-up, the heavy user of shortening was not as young, had a larger family and was much less likely to have a job outside the home. She was also much more apt to be living outside a metropolitan area, and to be living in the South, especially the Southeast.

The clues continued in the product use pattern. Heavy users of shortening tended to be heavy users of flour, sugar, laundry detergent, canned lunch meat, canned vegetables, cooked pudding, mustard, and catsup—all products that go with large families. They were not heavy users of eye make-up or any of the cosmetics that go with it.

In the activity, interest, and opinion questions the contrast deepened. Almost none of the items that correlated with use of eye make-up also correlated with use of shortening. When the same question did correlate with both products, the correlations were usually in opposite directions.

Compared with the light user of shortening, the heavy user expressed a much stronger interest in cooking and baking. With much greater frequency she said "yes" to, "I love to bake and frequently do"; "I save recipes from newspapers and magazines"; "I always bake my cakes from scratch"; and "The kitchen is my favorite room." She also said, "I love to eat" and "I love candy."

Instead of disliking the job of keeping house, she said she likes it: "I enjoy most forms of housework"; "Usually I have regular days for washing, cleaning, etc. around the house"; "I am uncomfortable when my house is not completely clean." She *disagreed* with "I would like to have a maid to do the housework" and "My idea of housekeeping is 'once over lightly.'"

She said she sews: "I often make my own or my children's clothes" and "I like to sew and frequently do."

She indicated heavy involvement with her children and with the positive emotional tone of her family: "I try to arrange my home for my children's convenience," a statement that correlated *negatively* with eye make-up use. She also said, "Our family is a close-knit group"; "There is a lot of love in our family"; and "I spend a lot of time with my children talking about their activities, friends, and problems."

An unexpected and certainly nonobvious finding was that she is unusually health conscious, and this frame of mind extends to a personal interest in fresh air and exercise: "Everyone should take walks, bicycle, garden, or otherwise exercise several times a week"; "Clothes should be dried in the fresh air and sunshine"; "I love the fresh air and out-of-doors"; "It is very important for people to wash their hands before eating each meal"; and "You should have a medical checkup at least once a year."

Finally, she said she is not a partygoer, and she is definitely not cosmopolitan: "I would rather spend a quiet evening at home than go to a party" and "I would rather go to a sporting event than a dance." She said "No" to "Classical music is more interesting than popular music"; "I like ballet"; and "I'd like to spend a year in London or Paris."

These two sharply contrasting portraits—the eye make-up user and the shortening user—show how recognizable humans emerge from quantified activity, interest and opinion data.

Portraits of Target Groups

Perhaps the most obvious use of this kind of research is the one already mentioned—portraits of target groups in the advertising and marketing of products. If it is granted that all forms of advertising and marketing are in some sense communication, and if it is granted that a communicator can usually do a better job when he can visualize his audience than when he cannot, it seems obvious that this level of descriptive detail is a significant improvement over the rather sparse and sterile demographic profiles that have been traditional in marketing research.

The target group is often, but by no means always, the product's heavy user. The target group may be the light user or the non-user. It may be some special segment, such as smokers of mentholated cigarettes. It may be some demographic segment, such as young married men with a college education. If a target group can be specified and identified a useful portrait is at least a possibility.

Media Values Not in the Numbers

Media representatives insist that an audience's quality, as well as its size, should be considered. Activity, interest, and opinion questions provide some insight into audience quality by drawing a portrait of the medium's user. The

Playboy reader, for instance, turns out to be pretty much the male counterpart of the swinging eye make-up user, while the male *Reader's Digest* reader emerges as the soul of conservative middle class values—pro-business, anti-government welfare, anti-union power, interested in politics, interested in community projects and activities. The *Time*-only reader, compared with the *Newsweek*-only reader, emerges as less concerned about job security, less worried about government and union power, less worried about the peril of communism and more favorably disposed toward advertising (Tigert, 1969).

Media analysts know that, compared with magazines, television is a very "blunt" medium. Since magazine audiences select themselves in accordance with the magazine's specialized editorial content, while television program audiences are usually very large and very heterogeneous, it is usually much easier to find distinct demographic differences among the readers of different magazines than among the viewers of different television programs. But work with activity, interest, and opinion variables suggests that television program audiences may be more different than some suspect.

Before Brand Rating Index, Simmons, and other syndicated product-media services became widely available, it was customary to match media with products by demographic "profile": "Our product is used by young, upscale housewives, so we want to be in a book that appeals to young, upscale housewives." It has sometimes been suggested that the psychographic profile be substituted for the demographic profile as a link between product and media: "Our product is used by women with a certain activity, interest, and opinion pattern, so we want to be in books or on TV programs that appeal to people who match that description." But this intuitively appealing idea has the same drawbacks as demographic profile matching. The correlations that link products to media through psychographics are no stronger than the correlations that link products to media through demographics, so a product and a medium can have similar activity, interest, and opinion profiles without being much related to each other. It is always safer to use the direct product-medium link in selecting media than to try to infer this link through some third set of variables.

Where psychographics can be of help in media selection is in improving the analyst's understanding of the product-medium linkages that are found through direct cross-tabulation. For instance, if direct cross-tabulation shows that many heavy users of home permanents are devoted readers of *True Story,* the activities, interests, and opinions of the women who *both use the product and read the magazine* will help explain the reasons behind this relationship by showing what, exactly, home permanent users and *True Story* readers have in common. That sort of understanding is often of great help in making sensible decisions.

Other Variables

Questions about activities, interests, and opinions can shed light on topics other than products and media. They can give additional meaning to the standard demographic classifications by showing how the executive's wife differs from the homemaker in a blue-collar household. They can further define the generation gap. They can add to what is known about sex differences. They can further describe the opinion leader, the new product tryer, the television addict, the trading stamp saver, the discount shopper, the political activist, the lady who thinks there is too much advertising to children on television. For almost any identifiable type of behavior there is at least the possibility of new insight when the behavior is viewed in the context of opinions, interests, and activities. Topics studied in this way include age and social class (Tigert, 1970), opinion leadership and information seeking (Reynolds and Darden, 1971), fashion interest and leadership (Summers, 1970), reactions to new product concepts (Nelson, 1971), furniture store choice and preferences for furniture styles (Good and Suchland, 1970) and Stone's concept of "shopping orientations" (Darden and Reynolds, 1971).

Getting the Data

Since activity, interest, and opinion items are self-administering to literate respondents, data can be obtained through either personal contact or established mail panels. Personal contact permits probability samples. It can also, with enough effort, reach hard-to-find respondents like young single males, transients, hippies, and prisoners. For many purposes, however, established mail panels yield a satisfactory return at a good cost. Because activity, interest, and opinion questions are in general so very interesting to respondents, mail questionnaires as long as 25 pages have yielded usable returns from 75 to 80% of mail panel samples.

Good items come from intuition, hunches, conversations with friends, other research, reading, head scratching, day-dreaming, and group or individual narrative interviews. Appendix 1 is a list of items that came from these sources and from Wilson (1966), Pessemier and Tigert (1966), and a set of unpublished studies by Social Research, Inc. for MacFadden-Bartell Corporation. The items are grouped into "scales" through factor analysis.

Individual Items vs. Scales

The user of activity, interest, and opinion material has the option of employing a large, highly diversified collection of statements that cover as many different topics as possible, or of using a more limited number of multi-item scales. The multi-item scale approach is favored by psychometric tradition because properly constructed scales are invariably more reliable than individual items.

Unhappily, however, scales have four important disadvantages: (1) They limit coverage because they reduce the number of topics covered by any given number of items, and the longer the scales, the greater the reduction. (2) The shorthand of the scale name (e.g., "Credit User," "Fashion Conscious") encourages the analyst to think only in terms of the name rather than the richness of detail in the individual items. (3) Since scale items are never exact duplicates of each other, there are times when the scale as a whole correlates with some other variable but individual items do not, and there are times when individual items correlate with some other variable but the scale as a whole does not. Thus, the scale approach sometimes misses some potentially useful relationships. (4) Use of pre-established scales limits the findings to dimensions the analyst thought would be important, thereby precluding discovery of the unexpected.

The alternative is to throw a wide net and hope to catch something interesting, a practice sometimes disparagingly referred to as a fishing expedition. While this criticism should not be taken lightly, it should also be borne in mind that going on a fishing expedition is one of the best ways to catch fish. The items listed in Appendix 1, and the items cited in the examples, typify items that have worked well in past studies. An item library too large for reproduction here is available from the authors.

Forced Choice vs. Scalar Responses

As an alternative to having the respondent mark a scale position to indicate his answer, some analysts prefer to present two AIO statements and ask the respondent to indicate which he agrees with more. Others prefer to ask the respondent to rank a set of statements from most to least agreement. When carefully applied, these alternatives can help suppress the undesirable effects of "yeasaying," social desirability, and other troublesome response styles, and they force discrimination among items that might otherwise be marked at the same scale position. On the other hand, forced-choice and ranking questions are often difficult to administer and difficult for the respondent to handle, and analysis of the data presents certain sticky problems. Studies that used the forced choice approach successfully are described by Nelson (1969, 1971). The analysis problems are described by Hicks (1970).

Clinical vs. AIO Variables

Some of the earliest attempts to use this sort of material in advertising and marketing research employed standardized inventories designed to measure general personality traits, with results that were usually somewhat disappointing (Evans, 1959; Westfall, 1962). Much of the later work has tended to move away from general personality traits toward variables that are more closely related to the behavior under consideration—homemaking activities and interests for household products, sociability items for cosmetics, and so on. As a result, it has often been found that significant relationships emerged where none had been found before, and it has often been easier to visualize uses for the relationships that were uncovered.

Nevertheless, the use of general personality traits has not been abandoned. Their value, especially when combined with activity, interest, and opinion items, is clearly demonstrated in studies by Nelson (1969) and Ziff (1971).

Analyses

When the sample is large and responses are well scattered, the simplest way to look at AIO material is ordinary cross-tabulation. For instance if the AIO scale has six steps, and the product use scale has seven, the relationship between each AIO and the product would appear in an ordinary 6 × 7 table.

But when the sample is small, or when either AIO or product responses are highly skewed, a 6 × 7 table will have many empty or nearly empty cells. In these common situations, it is best to condense the data beforehand by grouping scale steps to embrace reasonable numbers of respondents. When using a six-step scale, a strategy that usually works satisfactorily is to group steps 1-2, 3-4, 5-6.

If many relationships must be considered, for instance 100 products × 300 AIO items, the analyst who orders a complete cross-tabulation will find 30,000 tables on his desk before he can shut off the computer. One alternative is to order a product's × AIO's correlation matrix, and to have only those product-AIO correlations that are statistically significant cross-tabulated. This strategy may throw away some significant and potentially interesting curvilinear relationships, but it avoids the stupefying effect of 30,000 tables. A more detailed description of this approach can be found in an article by Plummer (1971).

Once the significant relationships have been found, the problem is to organize and understand them. Here the analyst's skill, experience, and ingenuity come to work, just as they did in the analysis of motivation research interview data. Factor analysis is a great help. R factor analysis can help condense AIO data by putting related statements together into categories. Q factor analysis can further simplify the problem by grouping respondents into types with similar response patterns. Neither of these procedures is automatic or fool-proof, however, and there is little danger that the computer will replace the experienced and insightful analyst in the bridge between data gathering and application.

Applications

Here are three examples of the way relationships between products and AIO items have been turned into action. They are derived from real situations, but, for obvious reasons, they are heavily disguised.

A new car wax is a significant improvement over products now on the market. The plan is to present this new wax in the context of fantastic and futuristic space gadgetry, a product so much better than anything now available that it belongs in the twenty-first century. An examination of the AIO profile of the target group shows no special interest in the future, in fantasy, in science, or in space. Instead the potential customer appears to be preoccupied with the here and now, and to be most impressed by facts, by proof, by the testimony of others he trusts and by demonstration. The campaign is reoriented to take account of this disposition.

A product traditionally advertised in folksy, homey, small town settings is found to be most heavily used by young housewives with an AIO profile almost as swinging as that of the eye make-up user. This finding fosters consideration of new advertising, and produces recommendations for changes in promotion and packaging.

The advertising for a heavy duty floor cleaner has been emphasizing its ability to remove visible dirt such as mud, dog tracks, and spilled food. The AIO profile of the target group shows great concern about germs and odors, and unusual preoccupation with the appearance of surfaces. The recommendation is to place special emphasis on the product's germicidal qualities and to feature the shiny surface the product leaves when the job is finished.

Further examples of actual and potential uses of AIO material can be found in Husted and Pessemier (1971), Nelson (1971), Plummer (1971) and Tigert (1969, 1971).

Criticisms and Problems

It has been said that the relationships between AIOs and products or media are merely surface manifestations of the more familiar, more "basic" demographics. The psychographic profile of the *Playboy* reader, for instance, might be thought of as merely a sign that *Playboy*'s readers are young, relatively well-educated males. While this assertion is in part correct, two considerations suggest that it would be wrong to depend on demographics only. First, two products with very similar demographic profiles sometimes turn out to have usefully different psychographic profiles. Fresh oranges and fresh lemons are one example, as noted later in this paper.

Second, a demographic bracket in itself means little unless one has a clear picture of its life style implications. Everyone has some idea of what it means to be a young mother with a college education, or a middle-aged male with a blue-collar job, but such designations can be richly supplemented by information about the activities, interests, and opinions that go with them. Plummer's (1971) study of bank charge card users shows explicitly how AIO data can produce results that did not emerge when only demographic data were available.

Low Correlations

When expressed as product-moment correlations, the relationships between AIO items and products or media are low—often around .2, and seldom higher than .3 or .4. Thus, they do not "explain the variance" very well, even when put together in a prediction equation.

It should be remembered, however, that the variance "explained" is the variance in the behavior of individuals, not the variance in the average behavior of groups, so a product-moment correlation of .2 is deceptively small. Consider the following cross-tabulation table. The product-moment correlation is .2—4% of the variance "explained"—yet the relationship is obviously meaningful.

This point has been discussed in detail by Bass, Tigert, and Lonsdale (1968), so it will not be belabored here. Perhaps it is sufficient to say that anyone who refuses to look at the relationships between AIOs and products, or AIOs and media, must also—to be consistent—refuse to look at the relationships between products or media and demographics, because the correlations are the same size, or smaller. Further, anyone who rejects the relationships between AIOs and products, or AIOs and media, must also reject the use of media selection models that depend upon relationships between media use and product use. These relationships, too, when expressed as product-moment correlations, are rarely higher than .3.

TABLE 1. Cross-Tabulation of Shortening Use and Degree of Agreement with "I Save Recipes from Newspapers and Magazines"[a]

	Once a Week or Less (286)	Few Times a Week (296)	Once a Day or More (204)
Definitely Agree	42%	52%	63%
Generally Agree	24%	25%	19%
Moderately Agree	20%	12%	14%
Moderately, Generally or Definitely Disagree	14%	11%	4%

[a]To avoid small cell frequencies both variables are condensed by combining adjacent categories.

Overlapping Portraits

AIO portraits do not always differ as much as the portraits of the eye make-up user and the shortening user. Many cosmetics are much alike. The heavy user of sugar looks like the heavy user of shortening and heavy user of flour. These overlaps occur because products themselves overlap, forming families that denote life styles (Wells, 1968).

But even similar portraits sometimes show useful differences, like the differences between heavy users of fresh oranges and heavy users of fresh lemons. Both groups of respondents show a strong interest in cooking and baking, especially with unusual recipes. Both also show unusual interest in community activities. However, the heavy user of fresh oranges, but *not* the heavy user of fresh lemons is distinguished by a strong need for cleanliness: "A house should be dusted and polished at least three times a week." "It is very important for people to brush their teeth at least five times a day." "Odors in the house embarrass me." The heavy user of fresh lemons, but *not* the heavy user of fresh oranges, is distinguished by an unusual interest in fresh air and exercise: "I love the fresh air and out-of-doors." "I bowl, play tennis, golf or other active sports quite often." And the heavy user of fresh oranges, but *not* the heavy user of fresh lemons, indicates she is a bargain hunter: "I usually watch the advertisements for announcements of sales," and "I'm not a penny-pincher but I love to shop for bargains."

Thus, the two groups are much alike, but they also differ along interesting and actionable dimensions.

Are Heavy Users All Alike?

Certain products may be heavily used for two or more quite different purposes. For instance, mouthwash may be used as a precaution against colds, or as a cosmetic. Since the cold user and the cosmetic user have very different life styles (Nelson, 1969), the picture presented by "the heavy user" will be a jumble of the two. It is important to be aware of this possibility and to separate users into subgroups whenever there is reason to suspect that the product plays a variety of roles.

Thin Products

Not all products correlate significantly with a large number of activity, interest, and opinion items. In one typical study, of 127 products, 32 correlated significantly with fewer than ten of the 300 AIO items, 67 correlated significantly with more than 10 but fewer than 30, and 35 correlated significantly with more than 30. Since portraits provided by fewer than ten correlations are usually not very helpful, a general rule of thumb would be that the chances of drawing a blank are about one in four.

It is hard to know why some products are so "thin." It is not because "rich" products are used by small, way-out segments of the population, while "thin" products are used by people in general. Instant coffee, cat food, laxatives, and cold cereal have all shown few AIO associations; laundry detergent, stomach remedies, gasoline, and floor wax have shown many. The potential user should be aware that "rich" results are not automatic.

The Future

In a recent issue of this Journal, James Benson, chairman of Ogilvy and Mather, was quoted:

> There is more similarity between the consumer in New England and the consumer in Old England than there is between the consumer in New England and the consumer in New Orleans. Increasingly, markets will need to be segmented more on psychological, social and attitudinal criteria than on the traditional bases of geography and demography.

Partly as a result of such urging, the use of psychographics and related techniques is gaining considerable momentum. A substantial number of large scale proprietary studies have been conducted, with enough success that at least some of the sponsors have come back to ask for more. The approach has sparked interest among academic researchers, and papers on it or using it are beginning to appear.

The danger, of course, is that this somewhat novel way of sizing up consumers will be oversold, and that users will be disappointed when it does not turn out magic answers to all conceivable questions. Readers who respond "definitely agree" to the statement, "Most people have a lot of common sense," will hope that that won't happen.

References

Bass, Frank M., Douglas J. Tigert, and Richard T. Lonsdale. Market Segmentation: Group Versus Individual Behavior. *Journal of Marketing Research,* Vol. 5, No. 3, (August 1968), 264–270.

Darden, William R. and Fred D. Reynolds. Shopping Orientations and Product Usage Rates. *Journal of Marketing Research.* Vol. 8 (Nov. 1971), 505–508.

Evans, Franklin B. Psychological and Objective Factors in the Prediction of Brand Choice: Ford vs. Chevrolet. *Journal of Business*, Vol. 32, (October 1959), 340–369.

Good, Walter S. and Otto Suchland. Consumer Life Styles and Their Relationship to Market Behavior Regarding Household Furniture. Research Bulletin, No. 26, Michigan State University, 1970.

Hicks, Lou E. Some Properties of Ipsative, Normative, and Forced Choice Measures. *Psychological Bulletin,* Vol. 74, No. 3, 167–184.

Husted, Thomas P. and Edgar A. Pessemier. Segmenting Consumer Markets with Activity and Attitude Measures. Paper No. 298, Institute for Research in the Behavioral, Economic and Management Sciences, Krannert Graduate School of Industrial Administration, Purdue University, March, 1971.

Nelson, Alan R. A National Study of Psychographics. Paper presented at the 52nd International Marketing Congress, American Marketing Association, Atlanta, Georgia, June 1969.

Nelson, Alan R. New Psychographics: Action-Creating Ideas, Not Lifeless Statistics. *Advertising Age,* June 28, 1971, pp. 1, 34.

Pessemier, Edgar A. and Douglas J. Tigert. In J. S. Wright and J. L. Goldstucker (Eds.) *New Ideas for Successful Marketing,* Chicago, Ill.: American Marketing Association, 1966.

Plummer, Joseph T. Life Style and Advertising: Case Studies. Paper given at 54th Annual International Marketing Congress, American Marketing Association, San Francisco, California, April, 1971.

Plummer, Joseph T. Life Style Patterns and Commercial Bank Credit Card Usage. *Journal of Marketing,* Vol. 35, No. 2, 35–41.

Reynolds, Fred D. and William R. Darden. Mutually Adaptive Effects of Interpersonal Communication. *Journal of Marketing Research,* Vol. 8 (Nov. 1971), 449–454.

Summers, John O. The Identity of Women's Clothing Fashion Opinion Leaders. *Journal of Marketing Research,* Vol. 7, 1970, 178–185.

Tigert, Douglas J. Life Style Correlates of Age and Social Class. Paper presented at the first annual meeting of the Association for Consumer Research, Amherst, Mass., August, 1970.

Tigert, Douglas J. A Psychographic Profile of Magazine Audiences: An Investigation of a Media's Climate. Paper presented at the American Marketing Association Consumer Behavior Workshop, Ohio State University, Columbus, Ohio, 1969.

Wells, William D. In J. Arndt (Ed.). *Insights into Consumer Behavior.* New York: Allyn and Bacon, 1968.

Westfall, Ralph. Psychological Factors in Predicting Product Choice. *Journal of Marketing,* Vol. 26 (April 1962), 34–50.

Wilson, Clark C. Homemaker Living Patterns and Marketplace Behavior—A Psychometric Approach. In J. S. Wright and J. L. Goldstucker (Eds.). *New Ideas for Successful Marketing,* Chicago, Ill.: American Marketing Association, 1966, 305–331.

Ziff, Ruth. Psychographics for Market Segmentation. *Journal of Advertising Research,* Vol. 11, No. 2 (Feb. 1971), 3–9.

Appendix 1

PRICE CONSCIOUS

I shop a lot for "specials."

I find myself checking the prices in the grocery store even for small items.

I usually watch the advertisements for announcements of sales.

A person can save a lot of money by shopping around for bargains.

FASHION CONSCIOUS

I usually have one or more outfits that are of the very latest style.

When I must choose between the two I usually dress for fashion, not for comfort.

An important part of my life and activities is dressing smartly.

I often try the latest hairdo styles when they change.

CHILD ORIENTED

When my children are ill in bed I drop most everything else in order to see to their comfort.

My children are the most important thing in my life.

I try to arrange my home for my children's convenience.

I take a lot of time and effort to teach my children good habits.

COMPULSIVE HOUSEKEEPER

I don't like to see children's toys lying about.

I usually keep my house very neat and clean.

I am uncomfortable when my house is not completely clean.

Our days seem to follow a definite routine such as eating meals at a regular time, etc.

DISLIKES HOUSEKEEPING

I must admit I really don't like household chores.

I find cleaning my house an unpleasant task.

I enjoy most forms of housework. (Reverse scored)

My idea of housekeeping is "once over lightly."

SEWER

I like to sew and frequently do.

I often make my own or my children's clothes.

You can save a lot of money by making your own clothes.

I would like to know how to sew like an expert.

HOMEBODY

I would rather spend a quiet evening at home than go out to a party.

I like parties where there is lots of music and talk. (Reverse scored)

I would rather go to a sporting event than a dance.

I am a homebody.

COMMUNITY MINDED

I am an active member of more than one service organization.

I do volunteer work for a hospital or service organization on a fairly regular basis.

I like to work on community projects.

I have personally worked in a political campaign or for a candidate or an issue.

CREDIT USER

I buy many things with a credit card or a charge card.

I like to pay cash for everything I buy. (Reverse scored)

It is good to have charge accounts.

To buy anything, other than a house or a car, on credit is unwise. (Reverse scored)

SPORTS SPECTATOR

I like to watch or listen to baseball or football games.

I usually read the sports page in the daily paper.

I thoroughly enjoy conversations about sports.

I would rather go to a sporting event than a dance.

COOK

I love to cook.

I am a good cook.

I love to bake and frequently do.

I am interested in spices and seasonings.

SELF-CONFIDENT

I think I have more self-confidence than most people.

I am more independent than most people.

I think I have a lot of personal ability.

I like to be considered a leader.

SELF-DESIGNATED OPINION LEADER

My friends or neighbors often come to me for advice.

I sometimes influence what my friends buy.

People come to me more often than I go to them for information about brands.

INFORMATION SEEKER

I often seek out the advice of my friends regarding which brand to buy.

I spend a lot of time talking with my friends about products and brands.

My neighbors or friends usually give me good advice on what brands to buy in the grocery store.

NEW BRAND TRYER

When I see a new brand on the shelf I often buy it just to see what it's like.

I often try new brands before my friends and neighbors do.

I like to try new and different things.

SATISFIED WITH FINANCES

Our family income is high enough to satisfy nearly all our important desires.

No matter how fast our income goes up we never seem to get ahead. (Reverse scored)

I wish we had a lot more money. (Reverse scored)

CANNED FOOD USER

I depend on canned food for at least one meal a day.

I couldn't get along without canned foods.

Things just don't taste right if they come out of a can. (Reverse scored)

DIETER

During the warm weather I drink low calorie soft drinks several times a week.

I buy more low calorie foods than the average housewife.

I have used Metrecal or other diet foods at least one meal a day.

FINANCIAL OPTIMIST

I will probably have more money to spend next year than I have now.

Five years from now the family income will probably be a lot higher than it is now.

WRAPPER

Food should never be left in the refrigerator uncovered.

Leftovers should be wrapped before being put into the refrigerator.

WIDE HORIZONS

I'd like to spend a year in London or Paris.

I would like to take a trip around the world.

ARTS ENTHUSIAST

I enjoy going through an art gallery.

I enjoy going to concerts.

I like ballet.

3 Beliefs and Attitudes

Overview

A vast amount of human effort, by governments, churches, and marketing organizations, is devoted to the tasks of creating, reinforcing, or changing attitudes and beliefs. These efforts include the packaging and selling of presidential candidates, the conversion efforts of religious sects, attempts to change beliefs about chemical companies from munitions and napalm manufacturers to "better things for better living through chemistry," and the selling of "new and improved" detergents.

Beliefs and Values

Beliefs are an organized pattern of cognitions, the totality of the meanings of a thing. Krech and Crutchfield (1948) define a belief as *"an enduring organization of perceptions and cognitions about some aspect of the individual's world."* It is what a person "knows" about some aspect or object in the world. He holds his beliefs to be true and proper; he "knows" they are right. Obviously, there need not be a high or even any correlation between a belief and "objective facts." Even such established beliefs among scientists as gravitational theory change from time to time. But for any given moment in time, a belief is the totality of the cognitions and perceptions an individual holds about a given object.

Belief is further defined as a generic term encompassing *knowledge, opinion,* and *faith.* For example, we say we believe that man must eat to live when we mean that we have knowledge that man must eat. We may believe that the Mazda is a better constructed automobile than the Datsun. For most of us, who have limited knowledge of either car, what we mean is that we are of the opinion that the Mazda is better built. Finally when we believe that there is a higher being whom we call God, we have faith.

The attribute, according to Krech and Crutchfield, which differentiates these various sets of beliefs is *verifiability.* Those beliefs that the individual considers verified are defined as knowledge. For the individual, the proof is in. He believes (knows) that pure water freezes at 0° centigrade. On the other hand, for any of his opinions, the proof is not yet in. He feels that when the proof is complete, his opinion will be verified, but his opinion does not have the proven property of knowledge. Since the verification is not complete, reasonable men may conceivably hold opposing opinions.

Those beliefs which are intrinsically unverifiable are referred to as faith. Life after death cannot be proven. The "facts," the proof, do not exist and can never exist. A belief, however, can be all the stronger because the individual knows that it can never be disproven; hence, he can accept the belief unequivocally.

Whereas generic beliefs as well as attitudes generally tend to pertain to a specific object, the term *value* pertains to a much broader category or whole class of things. A value is a general orientation of beliefs, as well as attitudes, toward a system of abstract and concrete things—a system of attitudes and beliefs organized in a hierarchical structure. For example, a person holding altruistic values tends to have correlated beliefs and attitudes about social welfare, a national medical health program, equitable distribution of wealth, monopoly, war, fluoridation of water supplies, labor unions, and regressive taxes, among others.

Attitudes

Whereas a belief is the conglomerate of things a person "knows" about certain objects, an attitude is the motivational or emotional aspect of cognition. *Attitudes are enduring systems of positive or negative evaluations, emotional feelings, and pro or con action tendencies with respect to social objects* (Krech, Crutchfield, and Ballachey, 1962). Attitudes have an enduring emotionally charged character about them reflected in such statements as "I hate it," "I like it," "I am in favor," "I am vehemently opposed," and they often act as a triggering mechanism to behavior.

Although it is quite possible to hold a belief without an accompanying attitude, an attitude would naturally include and incorporate relevant beliefs. The positive or negative attitudinal feelings obviously must be an extension of an already held belief. That is, an evaluation, a pro or con attitude, must involve an object. One can be pro or con whiskey, women's lib, Republicans, war, and perhaps even pencil erasers, but an attitude object must exist, and beliefs about that object must also exist before there can be an attitude.

Naturally attitudes differ from each other. The charge or valence not only varies in the sign (positive or negative) but also can vary from quite mild to extremely strong. Further, they can vary in their relevance or *salience*. Seeing a black man shine shoes, tap dance, or eat watermelon on the curbside might not be highly salient to a bigot. Yet, that same black man running for vice-president, carrying a picket in front of city hall, or attempting to enter the exclusive college the bigot's daughter attends may lead to aggressive action. Under the right conditions and if enough pressure is applied, attitudes can lead to action, in the form of either behavior or a cognitive reorganization.

Further, attitudes can be simple or multiplex. An attitude can be simple, such as positive feelings and action tendencies toward an admired individual or product. On the other hand, the attitude can be multiplex, involving a number and variety of elements. For example, bigotry toward blacks may include not only attitudes toward black people themselves, but also toward "soul food," black-operated businesses, black-manufactured goods, welfare programs, school busing, and even politicians who favor civil rights.

Other Approaches to the Study of Attitudes

There exists a number of schools of thought on the subject of attitudes and attitude change. George Day, in the first selection in this chapter, critically reviews and describes many of these views.

Structural Approach

The structural view is perhaps best represented by Krech, Crutchfield, and Ballachey (1962). Rather than sharply discriminating between beliefs and attitudes, this school feels that attitudes can be conceptualized as having various components. The *cognitive component* refers to the beliefs which an individual holds about an object. Included in the cognitive component are evaluative beliefs and knowledge which attribute to an object a positive or negative valence, and provide the information upon which the consumer makes his judgments. The *affective component* deals with the person's overall feelings of liking or disliking about an object. It is the emotional, stirred-up aspect of the attitude. The *conative* component is that of *action tendency*. This refers to behavioral expectation: the readiness on the part of an individual to behave overtly toward the attitude object—he is very, somewhat, or not at all likely to buy a refrigerator, take a vacation on the Galapagos Islands, or picket in front of a schoolhouse.

A somewhat similar view is expressed by Martin Fishbein, whose ideas created a flurry of research in consumer behavior. Fishbein considers only the affective nature of attitudes, claiming that an individual's attitude toward any object can be predicted from a knowledge of his beliefs about what attributes an object possesses and his evaluation of those attributes. For example, it is claimed that brand preference can be predicted with a high degree of reliability if one measures the attributes of the brand (for example, price, taste, appearance, and decay prevention for brands of toothpaste) and the importance of these attributes to the buyer (Cohen and Ahtola, 1971).

The selection in this chapter by Fishbein describes and elaborates on this approach, and the papers by Flemming Hansen and Bither and Miller present some experimental data.

Functional Approach

Functional theorists look upon attitudes in the same manner as they look upon perception, thinking, reasoning, and other aspects of our cognitive organization. They want to know what functions attitudes serve for the individual holding them. If they serve no function at all, they would cease to exist. The crux of this view is that the same attitude may be held by different persons for different reasons or that the same stimuli and situational factors may lead to different attitudes in different individuals.

Day presents in some detail the functional conceptualizations of Daniel Katz (1960). In summary, Katz feels that attitudes can serve four basic functions within the individual. The *utilitarian function* is a recognition that attitudes can be instrumental in achieving desirable goals and avoiding undesirable alternatives.

The *knowledge function* helps the individual cope with a complex world that cannot be grasped in its entirety. It is these attitudes that aid the individual in his search for meaning and his attempt to structure what would otherwise be a chaotic universe.

The *expressive function* utilizes attitudes that express to the world the individual's central values and self-concept. For the conservative, provincial, buy-American individual, negative attitudes toward a Volkswagen, a Sony tape recorder, or Russian caviar are to be expected. His attitudes are an expression of his basic value system.

The *ego-defensive function* serves to help the individual deal with his inner conflicts. Such attitudes serve to build up defense mechanisms, rationalize problems, and generally serve to protect the self from what is perceived to be a hostile environment. These are attitudes that serve to enhance the individual or to protect him as a psychological entity.

Cognitive Consistency

In his paper Day discusses other approaches to attitudes, such as social judgment, information processing, and cognitive consistency. The first two do not need elaboration in this introduction, but the third, cognitive consistency, has had a great influence in marketing and consumer behavior. The basic assumption of the cognitive consistency theorists is that an individual strives to achieve consistency among his values, attitudes, and perceptions (the various cognitive elements) and his behavior.

In short, cognitions tend to exist in clusters, which are generally both internally consistent and consistent with behavior. Hence, a man who believes that a well-kept neighborhood adds value to his property will not fail to cut his grass regularly, nor will he welcome an industrial plant locating nearby. A woman who believes herself attractive will not wear drab clothes and no makeup. Many psychologists feel that individuals actively strive for cognitive consistency and that this need for consistency is a powerful motivating force.

The first researcher to discuss cognitive consistency (balance, congruity, or cognitive dissonance, as it is alternatively termed) was Fritz Heider. The Day paper elaborates on the work of Heider, and the selection by Bobby Calder extends this point of view further.

Cognitive Dissonance

As pointed out by Calder, man strives for consistency, but inconsistencies in behavior do exist. A person who knows that smoking cigarettes is clearly and unequivocally dangerous to his health may continue to smoke them. When inconsistencies are discovered, they are of interest primarily because of their dramatic contrast with consistency. We pay little attention to the World War II refugee who refuses to buy a Volkswagen because it is a German product. The person who is of interest is the one who purchases a VW in spite of negative attitudes toward Germany.

Such inconsistencies in cognitive systems are termed *cognitive dissonance* (post-decision conflict) (Leon Festinger, 1957). Festinger proposes that the existence of dissonance, being psychologically uncomfortable, will motivate the person to try to reduce the dissonance and achieve consonance. Although there are many dissonance reduction pathways, a few methods can be categorized.

Changing the Cognitive Elements. An individual can reduce dissonance by eliminating or revaluing either one of his cognitive elements or his responsibility or control over the act or decision. To reduce dissonance, he can sell his new car, or he can persuade himself that he had no choice: he had to buy the car he did because his wife insisted on it. Further, he can begin to believe that the product he owns is a superior product, clearly better than others. Brehm (1956) designed an experiment to test this alternative. Subjects were asked to rate products, all of them small electrical appliances, from extremely desirable to definitely undesirable. The subject was then informed that she would be given a gift for participating in the experiment and was offered a choice between two items she had rated. Her choice was then wrapped and handed to her. Next she was presented with research reports to read on the products, and then asked to rate each product once again. Between the first and second ratings, the selected product increased in desirability and the unselected product decreased in desirability. It would seem that "asking the man who owns one" is not really a good way of gathering unbiased information about a product.

Denying Information. Information can be denied, distorted, or forgotten in the service of dissonance reduction. Kassarjian and Cohen (1965) asked a sample of subjects if they felt the linkage between cigarette smoking and lung cancer and various other medical problems had been proven or disproven. Forty-one percent of the heavy smokers, twenty-one percent of light smokers, and eleven percent of nonsmokers felt the linkage had not been proven.

Minimizing the Issue. Dissonance can be effectively reduced by minimizing the importance of the issue or decision that led to the dissonant state. Although a buyer may have spent several hours deciding among several brands of a product, he later claims that he merely grabbed the first one on the shelf. Dissonance is reduced by the claimed lack of interest in an "unimportant" issue.

Adding New Elements. New cognitive elements can be added to support the decision. Once a new car is purchased, the buyer begins to read technical information, brochures, and ads to buttress his decision. He will begin to believe that a person with his station in life deserves such a car; smokers often assert that many doctors themselves smoke and that some scientists claim that smoking is not detrimental to health.

In summary, attitudes, values, and cognitions tend to be consistent with each other and with behavior. Inconsistencies which do exist are uncomfortable states which the individual attempts to change either by adding new cognitions, changing his behavior, distorting dissonant information, or by changing his attitudes and beliefs. The need for consistency is illustrated in the following conversation (Allport, 1954, as reported in Zajonc, 1960).

Mr. X: The trouble with Jews is that they only take care of their own group.

Mr. Y: But the record of the Community Chest shows that they give more generously than non-Jews.

Mr. X: That shows that they are always trying to buy favors and intrude into Christian affairs. They think of nothing but money, that is why there are so many Jewish bankers.

Mr. Y: But a recent study shows that the percent of Jews in banking is proportionally much smaller than the percent of non-Jews.

Mr. X: That's just it. They don't go in for respectable business. They would rather run night clubs.

The selection in this chapter by Knox and Inkster tests one of the first of the dissonance reduction pathways discussed by Day. They predicted that bettors at a racetrack would be less confident that their horse would win before making a bet than they would after the bet. That is, dissonance theory would suggest that once a decision is made, the individual begins to perceive it as a wise decision; hence, after the bet, the confidence in a horse should increase. The results of the study bear out the prediction.

One of the aspects of dissonance theory that has fascinated researchers is that under certain circumstances dissonance theory makes predictions opposed to common sense. For example, dissonance theory would predict that the more a person is punished in an act or a purchase the more favorable he will be toward the item.

The selection by Cohen and Goldberg tests this aspect of the theory. Subjects were offered their choice of either two ounces of a nationally known brand of instant coffee or six ounces of an unknown brand. No matter which alternative was chosen, some subjects should have experienced dissonance. Those who selected the national brand could have received six ounces of another brand. Those who chose an unknown brand could have received a known brand that had been tested and tried in the marketplace.

Dissonance theory would predict, as borne out in the Knox and Inkster study, that the chosen brand would be rated higher than the unchosen brand. What if the product was bad? In this case dissonance theory would predict that through selective perception and other dissonance reducing mechanisms, the owner of a bad product would selectively distort information to make his product appear less bad and, in fact, might choose it again. Learning theory would predict that if a product is bad, that is, if the individual is punished rather than rewarded, he would shy away from that brand.

To create a bad product, Cohen and Goldberg altered the taste of the unknown brand of coffee with chemical additives and served it to subjects with unaltered or good coffee representing the national brand. They then asked for quality ratings of the two coffees. The results did not bear out the dissonance theory prediction. Those served bad coffee rated it as bad. As a final test, subjects were then given the opportunity to switch the brand of coffee they had selected. Dissonance theory would predict there would be little switching. Again the results did not confirm the prediction.

In short, the results were quite the opposite of the prediction and quite the opposite of a great many other studies conducted in the field. In their paper, Cohen and Goldberg discuss the meaning of their findings.

Attitude Change

As one reads the various selections in this chapter, it can be seen that a considerable amount of attention has been given in the field of attitude and opinion research to the topic of attitude change. Without question, this is a most significant area of study in consumer behavior. However, very little attention has been paid to preventing attitude change, due to, say, the advertising of a competitor, the speeches of an opposing political party, or the propaganda of an enemy power. Hence, the selection by Bither, Dolich, and Nell presents a review of some of this literature and presents the results of an experiment in which they attempted to immunize subjects against attitude change from both high and medium prestige sources.

The Measurement of Attitudes and Opinions

Because of the importance and centrality of attitudes and opinions in consumer behavior research, it is relevant to discuss briefly some of the techniques that are currently used in measurement. A wide variety of tools is available to the researcher, with almost inexhaustible variations.

One of the basic problems, of course, is that attitudes cannot be measured directly in a manner similar to body temperature or blood pressure. Attitudes are so interwoven with affective feelings, motivations, and personality characteristics, in addition to experiences, that usually they cannot be verbally expressed and are often unconscious. Therefore, attitudes are typically inferred from expressed opinions and responses to the stimuli of measuring instruments.

Scales

Social psychologists and sociologists have given a great deal of attention to the construction of attitude and opinion scales. Although they differ in type and method of construction, their objectives are similar—to assign the subject's attitude a numerical score along a continuum or scale from highly favorable at one end to highly unfavorable at the other. The simpler types of scales ask dichotomous questions such as: In your opinion, are Sony radios well constructed or poorly constructed? Perhaps a dozen such questions can be asked, the responses totaled, and the individual assigned a score from which can be inferred consumer attitude toward Sony radios. Of course, one of the problems associated with totaling up the responses to several items is whether the scale is unidimensional and responses are of equal weight, or is the researcher trying to add up apples and oranges.

An additional problem is the neutral point or no opinion category. In most scales it is not clear what no opinion means. To some individuals it apparently implies that he has considered the issue (e.g., the construction of radios), weighed both alternatives, and just has not yet formed an opinion. To others, a no opinion response may mean, "Go away, I don't want to think about it." To still others, a neutral point implies a nonopinion or nonattitude. He does not know what a radio is, whether one shaves with it or eats it, and he does not care but responds anyhow.

A slightly more complex type of scale, that in addition to mere favor or disfavor attempts to measure the intensity of opinion, was originally developed by Rensis Likert (1932) and is today called a *Likert scale*. Here the subject is allowed responses on a scale with five or seven or more equal-appearing intervals, such as *strongly agree, agree, neutral, disagree,* and *strongly disagree.*

In marketing research, a comparison of brands, products, items, etc., is often measured by a *rank order* technique. The individual is presented with a list of brands, say of beer—Budweiser, Pabst, Schlitz, Miller's, Coors, and perhaps two or three others. He is asked to rank them into best liked, second-best liked, and so on, to least liked. The scores are summed across individuals in the attempt to rank order the public's opinions, images, or attitudes toward the various brands.

A similar technique often used is that of *paired comparisons.* Items, colors, brand logo, or products are presented in pairs to the subject, one pair at a time. The respondent is presented with all possible pairs and asked which of the two he or she prefers. The preferences for each item are then summed for a total score.

In recent years another technique that has become quite popular, almost to the point of a fad, is the *semantic differential* as developed by Osgood, Suci, and Tannenbaum (1957). Pairs of words or statements of opposite meaning which might describe a concept, product, or corporation (such as good–bad, reliable–unreliable, clean–dirty, strong–weak, active–passive) are presented to the respondent. He is asked to rate each concept on each dimension on a seven-point scale reflecting the intensity of his feeling—very reliable, moderately reliable, slightly reliable, neutral, slightly unreliable, moderately unreliable, very unreliable. The results, when summed across respondents, produce a profile of the concept that reflects its image—the meaning or the attitudes held toward it.

Open-Ended Questions and Depth Interviews

One alternative to elaborately constructed scales is the open-ended question. The subject is asked to respond to the question in his own words with the expectation that his attitudes can be inferred from his stated opinion. For example, the respondent may be asked, "What is your opinion of how well the President of the United States is doing his job?" The respondent's comments are written down verbatim and later analyzed.

A more complex attempt to get at the same variables is the depth interview. The respondents are interviewed singly or in small groups for several hours, typically on the same topic. Their comments are often tape-recorded, and the interviewer's task is to establish rapport with them, but not to guide the discussion excessively. The respondent is encouraged to talk about the subject in any manner he chooses. The protocols (responses) are then carefully studied in an attempt to infer his beliefs, attitudes, and values from the long conversations that have taken place. Obviously, this requires a great deal of skill on the part of the interviewer and the researcher in analyzing the data. In the better studies, only highly trained interviewers and psychologists are used.

Projective Techniques

The term *projection,* from which projective techniques derive their title, implies that the individual projects his own feelings, anxieties, needs, and values to the external world. This is not unlike the process of selective perception discussed in Chapter 1. What the individual perceives from the outer world is related to his needs, motivations, attitudes, and beliefs.

The philosophy of projective techniques is based on the idea that, if what a person perceives about the external world is related to his need-value system, we can present him with ambiguous stimuli and consider his responses to be a reflection of his personality, beliefs, and motivations (Kassarjian, 1973). Proponents of projective tests feel that these tests elicit responses that the subject will not or cannot give otherwise, and that direct questioning methods and public opinion surveys and scales have failed to meet all the demands placed upon them, despite their increasing sophistication.

The tests themselves consist of a variety of stimuli presented to the subject. Perhaps the one with the longest history both in psychology and marketing research is that of *word association.* A series of words is presented to the respondent; mixed among such neutral stimuli as water, house, table are critical words such as instant coffee, Betty Crocker cake mix, and premium beer. For example, George Smith (1954) reports a study in which just two stimulus words were used—Doeskin and Kleenex. The former drew a decidedly larger number of replies such as soft, softness, and downy, suggesting that the concept of softness is built into the Doeskin trade name.

Some years ago Mason Haire (1950) introduced to marketing a technique similar to word association in a study that is now considered a classic. He presented subjects with alternate shopping lists and asked them to describe the personality and character of the buyer of these groceries. The first list had the following items:

List 1.	*List 2.*
$1\frac{1}{2}$ lbs. of hamburger	$1\frac{1}{2}$ lbs. of hamburger
2 loaves of Wonder bread	2 loaves of Wonder bread
1 bunch of carrots	1 bunch of carrots
1 can of Rumford's baking powder	1 can of Rumford's baking powder
Nescafe instant coffee	Maxwell House coffee (drip grind)
2 cans of Del Monte peaches	2 cans of Del Monte peaches
5 lbs. of potatoes	5 lbs. of potatoes

The second list was identical except that Nescafe instant coffee was changed to one pound of Maxwell House coffee (drip grind). A brief summary of his results indicated that 48% of the subjects described the buyer of Nescafe as lazy, while only 4% described the purchaser of Maxwell House this way. Four percent described the Nescafe buyer as thrifty; 16% described the Maxwell House buyer as thrifty. Sixteen percent described the Nescafe purchaser as not a good housekeeper, while no one described the Maxwell House buyer this way, etc.

In short, a clear picture tends to emerge concerning the attitudes of subjects toward Nescafe instant coffee and the people who buy and serve instant coffee. The full protocols of the subjects present an even richer measure of attitudes and opinions than does our brief summary.

It is interesting to note that the Haire study has been replicated several times in the ensuing decades. For example, Hill (1968) and Webster and Von Pechmann (1970) could not get similar results. Both studies found no differences in the "personality and character" of those who purchased the two types of coffee. The follow-up studies suggest that attitudes toward instant coffee have changed significantly in twenty years. (An alternate interpretation may well be that Haire and the follow-up studies were measuring different variables, because of extraneous circumstances. However, this is not likely, and the explanation of attitude change over time seems reasonable.)

Many other projective methods are also available. In the *sentence completion* technique, the subject is given an incomplete and ambiguous sentence such as, "I get angry when ———," "I become disgusted with ———," "What I really enjoy after dinner is ———." An example of its use can be seen in a study conducted by Kassarjian and Cohen (1965). The researchers asked a sample of cigarette smokers who believed that smoking is a hazard to health why they continued to smoke. The majority gave responses such as "smoking is not much of a threat to me," and "pleasure is more important than health." However, to such sentence completion questions as "People who never smoke are ———," the responses were such comments as "better off," "happier," "smarter," "wiser," "more informed." Clearly, the impression one gets from these sentence completion tests is that smokers are anxious, uncomfortable, and dissatisfied with their habit—an impression quite different from the results of open-ended questions.

Still other projective techniques consist of presenting a photograph, a cartoon drawing, or a painting to the respondent and asking him to interpret the stimuli. The *Rosenzweig Picture Frustration Test* or balloon test consists of cartoon figures. For example, in one figure a waiter is serving food to a female patron with the comment, "I'm sorry, but the cook didn't prepare this the way you ordered it." The customer has a blank balloon pointing at her. The subject is to fill in the balloon in the cartoon. The *Thematic Apperception Test* consists of reproductions of ambiguous pictures. The person is asked to make up a story of what is happening, what has happened in the past, what will happen in the future, and what each person in the picture is thinking. The responses, it is claimed, reflect the attitudes, personality, and value system of the respondent. Because of its adaptability to many situations, this particular technique was widely used, by both psychologists and marketing researchers.

Many other techniques exist, ranging from the Rorschach *ink blot test,* to finger painting and graphology; most of them are not applicable to marketing, although some are, and many of them are used in attempts to gauge attitudes.

Reliability and Validity

The value of any instrument, whether it be a doorstep interview, a semantic differential, or a projective test, directly depends on the validity and reliability of the data gathered. *Reliability* refers to its stability. Attitudes and beliefs are enduring, relatively stable cognitions that do not change easily or quickly. If an instrument does not produce a similar score or give similar results from one time to another, that is, if it cannot be replicated, it is probably not reliable or useful. *Validity* refers to whether or not the instrument is measuring what it purports to measure. If the test or scale purports to measure attitudes toward various brands of gasoline, is it really measuring these attitudes or is it measuring something else, such as needs for companionship or attitudes toward newness of a retail establishment?

The techniques for establishing validity and reliability are too technical to discuss here; however, such problems occupy a great deal of time for the social scientist interested in attitude research. Unfortunately, in the field of consumer behavior and marketing research, too little concern is directed to validity and reliability. Often, if the question "looks good" and "sounds right," it is used without further concern.

References

Allport, G. W. *The Nature of Prejudice.* Addison-Wesley, 1954.

Brehm, J. W. "Post-decision Changes in the Desirability of Alternatives." *Journal of Abnormal and Social Psychology,* Vol. 52 (July 1956), 384–389.

Cohen, J. B., and O. T. Ahtola. "An Expectancy X Value Analysis of the Relationship Between Consumer Attitudes and Behavior." *Proceedings of the Second Annual Conference of the Association for Consumer Research,* ed. David M. Gardner. Association for Consumer Research, 1971.

Festinger, L. *A Theory of Cognitive Dissonance.* Harper and Row, 1957.

Haire, M. "Projective Techniques in Marketing Research." *Journal of Marketing,* Vol. 24 (April 1950), 649–656.

Hill, C. R. "Haire's Classic Instant Coffee Study—18 Years Later." *Journalism Quarterly*, Vol. 45 (August 1968), 466–472.

Kassarjian, H. H. "Projective Methods." *Handbook of Marketing Research,* ed. Robert Ferber. McGraw-Hill, 1973, in press.

——— and J. B. Cohen. "Cognitive Dissonance and Consumer Behavior: Reactions to the Surgeon General's Report on Smoking and Health." *California Management Review*, Vol. 8 (Fall 1965), 55–64.

Katz, D. "The Functional Approach to the Study of Attitudes." *Public Opinion Quarterly,* Vol. 24 (Summer 1960), 163–204.

Krech, D., and R. S. Crutchfield. *Theory and Problems of Social Psychology.* McGraw-Hill, 1948.

———, R. S. Crutchfield, and E. Ballachey. *Individual in Society.* McGraw-Hill, 1964.

Likert, R. A. "A Technique for the Measurement of Attitudes." *Archives of Psychology* (1932), No. 140.

Osgood, C. E., G. J. Suci, and P. H. Tannenbaum. *The Measurement of Meaning.* University of Illinois Press, 1957.

Smith, G. H. *Motivation Research in Advertising and Marketing.* McGraw-Hill, 1954.

Webster, F. E., and F. Von Pechmann. "A Replication of the Shopping List Study." *Journal of Marketing*, Vol. 34 (April 1970), 61–63.

Zajonc, R. B. "The Concepts of Balance, Congruity and Dissonance." *Public Opinion Quarterly*, Vol. 24 (Summer 1960), 280–296.

3.1 Attitudes and Attitude Change
GEORGE S. DAY

The study of attitudes is well-entrenched in marketing theory and practice. The acceptance by theorists is evident in the pivotal role that the concept of attitude plays in the major descriptive models of consumer behavior (Engel, Kollat, and Blackwell, 1968; Howard and Sheth, 1969; Nicosia, 1966). Practitioners have tended to take a more limited view of attitude as an easily measured construct they can use to understand their market, and perhaps to evaluate the effect of a persuasive communication. In reality, most practitioners are inveterate theorists, constantly invoking experimental theories of attitude change to predict changes in purchasing or usage behavior as a consequence of alternative strategies for changing attitudes.

The necessity for such theories can be illustrated by the following problems:

• A farm equipment manufacturer in a developing country wants prospective distributors to adopt a new scheme for financing inventories. First he has to change their presently negative attitudes toward investing in inventories; but how?
• Birth-control-pill manufacturers need to predict the response of pill users to negative information from a highly credible source, such as a U.S. Senate subcommittee. What proportion of the users are susceptible to change because of lack of conviction and ambivalent attitude?
• Consumers have a strong aversion to "reprocessed" forms of materials such as textiles and plastics. Can these attitudes be changed before the U.S. runs out of raw materials?

In these and literally thousands of other situations each year in the public and private sector, predictions and decisions are made on the basis of implicit or explicit theories of the conditions which lead to attitude change.

The basic premise of this article is that there are explicit theories of attitude change which can illuminate the problems of the decision maker and provide policy guidance. I will start with a definition of attitude, so that it will be clear what is being formed and changed. Since we are talking about consumer behavior, the emphasis will be on attitudes in choice situations where competing alternatives must be considered. The middle of this paper will describe and evaluate a number of complementary (although sometimes competing) theories of attitude change. I conclude by using the theories to compare the strategies of confirming existing attitudes, changing existing attitudes, or forming new attitudes.

The Nature of Attitudes

I will distinguish between the formal theories of "how attitudes work," and the pragmatic, measurement-oriented definitions of "what they are." The emphasis on measurement is important, for we are dealing with an underlying construct that can be only imperfectly observed. It is easy to make subtle theoretical distinctions that overtax both the measures and the respondents.

How Do Attitudes Work?

One answer to this question is that attitudes structure the way the consumer perceives his environment and guide the ways in which he responds to it (Lunn, 1970). A more precise definition, that effectively touches most of the interesting theoretical issues, was proposed by Allport (1935) and is still widely accepted. An attitude is: (1) a mental and neural state of readiness to respond, (2) organized (3) through experience (4) exerting a directive and/or dynamic influence on behavior. Following McGuire (1969), we shall describe the current thinking related to each of the four definite characteristics.

Mental and Neural State of Readiness to Respond. An attitude is viewed as a mediating (or intervening) construct that has two links with observable reality. One link is with the *antecedent* conditions which lead into it; these might be the stimulus of an advertisement, a move into a new house, and so forth. The second link is with the *consequents* that follow from the attitude, including search and purchase behavior. There is nothing in this definition that says we can directly observe the mediating construct, so researchers who adopt this definition generally feel anxious about the ability of their instruments to accurately infer the presence of an attitude.

The mental and neural distinction suggests that measures can be either verbal reports of introspection (of which I will say more later) or physiological measures of change in the person's autonomic activation level when he sees the object of the attitude. Early enthusiasm for such physiological indices as galvanic skin response (Cook and Selltiz, 1964) and pupil dilation (Hess, 1965) seems to have waned recently as evidence accumulates that these indices can say little about the favorable direction of the attitude.

Organized. In the next section, on the structure of attitudes, I will discuss the extent to which a single attitude is made up of separate components.

Through Experience. There is widespread agreement with this contention, although little longitudinal research has been done (some is reviewed by Smith, 1968) and a person can rarely explain how any of his attitudes were acquired. Among the various processes by which attitudes are thought to be formed are:

1. Integrating a number of similar experiences: direct experience through usage, observation of the outcomes of others' explorations, information about performance, and so forth.

2. Differentiating from general to specific situations. Most narrow, highly focused attitudes are partly derived from broad attitudes already held. This is the basis of consistency theory, which would, for example, predict that attitudes toward women drivers will be consistent with the basic underlying attitude toward the general competency of women.

3. Identification. Attitudes are often initially formed by imitating the attitudes of admired individuals. An individual who can engender imitation in this sense is an effective source in a persuasive communication. If this is so, the three components of source effect, credibility, attractiveness, and power, are useful predictors of the degree of identification. (These concepts are most fully developed by Kelman, 1961.) *Credibility* is the extent to which a source is perceived as knowing the right answer and being willing to communicate it. *Attractiveness* is determined by the receiver's similarity to, familiarity with, or liking of the source. Similarity of economic backgrounds, physical characteristics, and political and other attitudes are important determinants of a successful relationship between a salesman and a customer (Evans, 1963). The last component, *power*, depends on the ability of the source to apply positive and negative sanctions to the recipient and stay around to observe whether a desired attitude or behavior is achieved.

As we will see later, the above processes by which attitudes are formed by experience are similar to the ways that existing attitudes are changed.

Exerting a Directive and/or Dynamic Influence on Behavior. There is wide agreement that attitudes have at least a directive or preferential influence; they determine the choice of one among a set of alternatives. According to McGuire (1968), it appears that an attitude imposes this preferential influence by determining the *perception* of the various alternatives, rather than by determining which possible *response* will dominate the others. This distinction may not appear too meaningful in the abstract, but it is at the heart of the differences between response-oriented (learning) and perceptual theories of attitude change, as we will see shortly.

There is less agreement among psychologists as to whether attitudes also have a dynamic—or more accurately, energizing—influence. This would imply that they affect the absolute level of an activity, as well as determine the directions in which the activity is channeled. There seems to be no easy answer to this matter, although it is relevant to many issues, including whether the increased favor toward some products as objects of consumption will influence the overall need to consume.

Summary. So far I have established that an attitude is a readiness to respond in a preferential manner.[1] In a marketing context, this usually means the consumer's preference for, and readiness to buy, a brand or product, rather than the available alternatives (Maloney, 1966, p. 3). But these attitudes are not simple likes or dislikes. They are the complex outcome of many separate judgments about the various attributes of the object, such as styling, convenience, economic value, and so forth. Much of the diagnostic value of attitudes comes from the information about these attributes. In the next section I will look at one attempt to divide attitudes into component parts.

Attitude Structure: Cognitive-Affective-Conative Analysis

The notion that the intervening state between stimulus and behavior is richer than affect (or liking) is widely supported, and for good reason. By having three components to explain and interrelate, we have a richer and more flexible construct. Secondly, there is impressive empirical support from the measurement-of-meaning tradition (Osgood, Suci, and Tannenbaum, 1957) for the validity of this view.

The cognitive or perceptual component represents a person's information about an object. Each piece of information can be broadly classified as either beliefs in the existence of the object, or (evaluative) beliefs *about* the object (Fishbein and Raven, 1962). In the former category of beliefs are the familiar awareness measures, such as aided and unaided recall of brand names and advertising copy claims or awareness of services offered.

Evaluative beliefs provide information about the judgments the consumer makes. In marketing we are usually interested in various comparative judgments of one brand or product versus the alternatives. These may be *attribute judgments* (which one is bigger? which one tastes better? which one is more durable?)[2] or *similarity judgments* (which ask the individual whether he perceives the objects as being similar or different). Similarity judgments are highly generalized and respondents are not told the basis they are to use to make the judgments.

The affective or feeling component deals with the person's overall feelings of liking or disliking a situation, object, person, or concept. It is usually measured on a unidimensional scale. Most theorists regard affect as the core of the attitude concept and derived from the more specific cognitive components. However, there is some controversy over the nature of the cognitive-affective relationship, hinging largely on the distinction between affect (like-dislike) and evaluation (the object is good-bad, disagreeable-agreeable, harmful-beneficial, and so forth).

One group treats affect and evaluation as synonymous. The overall attitude is measured by a scale (or scales) involving general evaluative criteria (such as good-bad; see Osgood et al., 1957). The major implication of the affective-evaluative congruity notion is that overall attitude judgments can be predicted from the various evaluative beliefs.

A competing view holds that the affective component is only partially determined by the evaluative belief components. For example, Bem (1970, p. 15) offers the following "non-syllogism":

> Cigarettes taste terrible, cause cancer, make me cough, and offend others (evaluative beliefs). I dislike terrible tastes, cancer, coughing and offending others. But I still like cigarettes.

Bem argued that, "emotional, behavioral and social influences can also play important roles, and cognitive 'reasoning' of the type represented in the syllogism may be absent altogether." Greenberg (1968) brought the evaluative-affective distinction to a marketing context. He contrasted *attribute judgments*, which contain evaluative information, and *preference* (or affective) judgments, which combine information about product evaluation and the respondent's ideal point. The evaluative judgment is "which is sweeter? or bigger?" while the preference judgment indicates "which sweetness is preferred, or which is the better size." In many instances one prefers that which is highly evaluated, but evaluation and affect are not necessarily synonymous.

The conative or intentions component refers to the person's gross behavioral expectations regarding the object; is he "very, somewhat, or not at all likely" to buy a refrigerator, a foreign car if he buys any kind of car, or vacation on the Galapagos Islands? Usually, intentions are limited to a finite time period that depends on the prospective buyer's repurchase cycle or planning horizon. There is a widespread feeling within marketing that intentions differ from attitudes (as measured of affect) by "combining a consumer's regard for the item with an assessment of its purchase probability" (Wells, 1961, p. 82). A more appropriate position is that intentions are correlated or congruent with attitudes under certain conditions, such as (a) when the alternatives are reasonably close substitutes, as when auto market boundaries are defined by a class of cars (compacts, intermediate station-wagons, or Gran Prix touring cars), but not by all cars; and (b) the market is in equilibrium with respect to the number of brands. It appears that attitudes are less sensitive than intentions to short-run perturbations of demand created by a new entry into an established market (Day, 1970b).

Attitude Specificity

The discussion to this point has presumed that the attitudes are toward specific attributes, objects, or issues. These attitudes do not exist independently but are linked in complex ways to a hierarchy of increasingly fundamental beliefs and attitudes.

Most fundamental are *values,* which are attitudes toward end-states of existence (such as equality and self-fulfillment) or modes of conduct (like honesty and friendship) (Rokeach, 1968). Values are ends, and one controversial view holds that marketing deals with the means of achieving these ends (Bauer and Greyser, 1967). Motivation researchers have traditionally taken the point of view that this is the most productive level in the hierarchy to obtain insights into buying and consumption behavior. Unfortunately, these deep-seated values and attitudes are often unconsciously held and thus are difficult to unambiguously identify with the usual projective and related clinical techniques. Their remoteness from the specific attitudes and behaviors of interest to marketers has further reduced their usefulness for diagnostic purposes.

The relative failure of motivation research has focused research attention on middle-level beliefs and attitudes about buying, consumption patterns, and product requirements. The goal of this research (frequently called psychographics) is to find descriptive classifications, such as bargain seeking, economic orientation, experimentalism, style consciousness, home centeredness, and traditionalism (Lunn, 1966; Heller, 1968), that provide more insights and more clearly delineated market segments than those based on demographic variables. Although this area of research holds a great deal of promise for marketing, the realization of the promise will hinge on (a) improvements in the measuring instruments that will reduce the present cumbersome batteries of questions, (b) more effective utilization of data reduction techniques, and (c) a more precise specification of the scope of the research. This latter step will help reduce the confusion resulting from including explorations at the very general level of life cycle and life style with the very specific and product-related search for benefit segments within the same classification.

Attitude Change Theories

The focus of the remainder of this article is toward the questions of *how* people's attitudes are changed, *who* changes, and *why* they change. These questions pervade all programs that have the goal of modifying attitudes in a desired direction. Characteristically, the relevant theories have emphasized the *why* question, because the theorists are mainly interested in psychological processes, and because it is logically prior. In this review I will give extra emphasis to the more operational question of specifying the circumstances under which attitude change is most likely to occur.

The study of attitude change was launched into a mature stage of synthesis and reconciliation in the mid 1960's.[3] Out of this work has come a consensus that there are four basic theoretical approaches, which are more complementary than competitive. The information-processing approach is the most general, and the most widely adopted in marketing. It differs from the consistency, social judgment, and functional approaches by assuming a rational decision maker who tries to process and deal with new information as logically as possible. The emphasis is almost exclusively on the stimulus characteristics of the communication situation (i.e., order of arguments, source credibility, and characteristics of the audience). The other approaches "tend to view the person as more contentious or self-centered, depicting his behavior in a persuasive communication situation as attempting actively to resist it or to utilize it for needs of his own that have very little to do with the context of the communication" (McGuire, 1971).

The Information-Processing Approach

This approach explains the response to a persuasive communication in terms of (a) the receiver's initial position, (b) a series of behavioral steps through which he must proceed, and (c) his motivation for accepting the proposed position. These three elements act together so that a person's probability of proceeding from one step to another depends on both initial position and acceptance motivation. (Figure 1.)

Before an individual can be persuaded by a communication he must first have the message *presented* to him via informal or formal media; then the message must get and hold his attention. Attention-getting properties such as

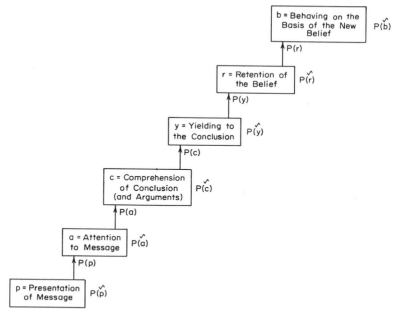

Probability of Desired Behavior = P(p) · P(a) · P(c) · P(y) · P(r) · P(b)

FIGURE 1.   Steps in the response to a communication.

novelty, opening rhetoric, and nature of competing stimuli will not necessarily hold attention. The ability of a message to hold attention depends on
whether the receiver can *comprehend* the arguments and conclusions. Comprehension is influenced by the complexity and clarity of the message, and "the
receiver's intelligence, relevant experience, openmindedness, and 'cognitive
tuning set' (readiness to pass the information on, to be entertained, etc.)"
(Zimbardo and Ebbesen, 1969, p. 21).

The likelihood of acceptance, or *yielding* to the comprehended message,
is theorized to depend on the extent of incentives. The incentives in the message
may be in the form of arguments or reasons why the advocated point of view
should be accepted in favor of the old attitude, or the arousal of expectations
that have reinforcing value. An important expectation, which is enhanced by
a highly credible source, is of being right or wrong. Suspicion of someone's
manipulative intent is another expectation that will nullify the prospects of
acceptance because it is seen as a threat to one's freedom to decide for oneself (see Brehm, 1966). Finally, a communication can lead to the expectation
of social approval or disapproval. Social approval is seen as rewarding; thus,
anything in the communication that credibly indicates that acceptance will be
socially rewarding will increase acceptability.

If the recipient has taken the fourth step of *yielding* or accepting the
message, there is the further question of whether he will *retain* the new position

until he has an opportunity to *behave* accordingly. As a rule, the retention of an opinion over time depends on the informational content of the message and the incentives for acceptance.

Each step in the chain is taken with only a certain probability, and its occurrence depends on the probabilities associated with the earlier steps in the chain. The model suggests that the probabilities are multiplicative; so if there were a probability of 0.5 at each step there would be a less than 0.02 probability that purchase behavior would be influenced by the persuasive message. If this were the true situation, it would go far toward explaining the ineffectiveness of most advertising campaigns. However, this analysis is largely speculative in the absence of knowledge about the various probabilities, and uncertainty as to whether a step such as attention is a prerequisite for subsequent yielding. Perhaps, as Krugman (1965) suggests, some attitudes are acquired by a process of incidental learning, without the aid of explicit attention.

Process Models of Behavior

The information-processing approach shares a number of characteristics with other process models of buying behavior. The most familiar of these related models are the "hierarchy of communication effects"—awareness–knowledge–liking–preferences–conviction–purchase (Lavidge and Steiner, 1962)—and the adoption-process model borrowed from rural sociology.

All these models share a view that consumers follow a rational problem-solving approach and base their decisions on the persuasive information provided. Furthermore, as Robertson (1971) notes, these models also share the same shortcomings: (a) The consumer may make decisions in a "non-rational" manner. That is, he may not secure, process, nor carefully evaluate all the available information; "he may make adoption decisions on impulse or to ingratiate himself with other people"; or he may be playing a psychosocial game (Bauer, 1964) rather than solving a problem. (b) There is not a specified *sequence* of stages which must occur. Any such model must make allowances for consumers to "skip" stages. (c) The model must also provide *feedback* loops, since such a process will not necessarily be linear and unidimensional.

Cognitive Consistency Theories

Consistency theories share the basic assumption that an individual strives to achieve consistency within his cognitive system and between his cognitive system and overt behavior. These theories usually make the further assumption that inconsistency produces a "psychological tension," which is uncomfortable or disturbing. The resulting tension is the motive force for the efforts to modify or change the cognitive system. The amount of the tension can be considerable. Consider the awkward position of a conservationist when Nader attacks Muskie on his efforts to control pollution; and if he is an avowed anticommunist how did he feel when Canada and Italy recognized Communist China? Appreciable tension is also a consequence of everyday problems, such as when a favorite brand is out of stock and only a previously disdained private brand is available, or the performance of a new appliance or toy does not match the high expectations formed by advertising.

The specific mode of resolution of these latter inconsistencies is obviously of concern to the manufacturer and retailers who are involved. A number of similar theories deal with the sources and resolution of inconsistency. I will limit my examination to cognitive consistency theory, which is the most popular and provocative of the family of theories. To put it in perspective, I will also show how a behaviorist would explain the same phenomenon.

Origins of Inconsistency. McGuire (1966) has noted the paradox of positing "a strong tendency towards consistency and yet always managing to find sufficient inconsistency within the system to allow predictions to be made and tested." He has listed a number of ways in which inconsistency can be created within an individual. Much inconsistency is a result of a person simultaneously occupying two or more conflicting social roles. Careful shopping, with considerable time devoted to the collection of information and comparison of alternatives, may complement one's social role as a well-informed individual and careful decision-maker. However, those time demands increasingly conflict with the need to spend more time on the job, at leisure, and attending to the social needs of the family. Linder (1970) predicts that the process of allocating decreasing personal time will lead to increasing tension in society. Second, McGuire suggests that a person's environment may change, leaving him "encumbered with a conceptual baggage that no longer accords with reality." Third, a person may be pressured into behaving in ways inconsistent with his attitudes. These "forced compliance" situations have been extensively studied by dissonance theorists. Fourth, a person may be persuaded to change his attitude via new information, interpersonal interactions, or direct experience, only to find that the cognitions associated with this attitude are inconsistent with other cognitions. Fifth, there are human logical shortcomings which may produce logical fallacies, although inconsistency theory is usually based on "psycho-logic" rather than formal logic (Abelson and Rosenberg, 1958). Finally, there is the possibility that the individual seeks inconsistency, either because of a desire for change or novelty (Fiske and Maddi, 1961; Fowler, 1965) or to mask more deep-seated conflicts that cannot be resolved through action (Pepitone, 1966).

The various theories based on the consistency principle generally emphasize different sources of inconsistency. The most notable differences occur between the dissonance and balance theories described below.

Cognitive Dissonance Theory. This theory has had a particular fascination for both marketers and social psychologists. The latter have been motivated by both theoretical fertility and controversy to produce over 300 studies in ten years (Zimbardo, 1970). Marketers are attracted by the unique insights the theory offers into post-decision behavior.

According to the theory (Festinger, 1957; Brehm and Cohen, 1962; and Aronson, 1968) any two cognitive elements—beliefs or bits of knowledge—may be consonant, dissonant, or irrelevant to one another. It is frequently difficult to specify which beliefs or attributes are relevant. But assuming they are, dissonance or inconsistency occurs when one cognitive element follows psychologically from the contrary of the other. Thus a buyer finds himself in a dissonant state by agreeing to a series of large credit payments on a new appliance, despite an overextended personal budget that leaves no room for such expenditures. It is emphasized that dissonance is a post-decision state of mind; when the buyer is in the process of making a choice decision, he is in a state of conflict.

The amount of the dissonance created depends on the situation. In purchase decision-making situations, for example, dissonance is likely to be high when:

1. the decision is important in terms of the financial outlays or the psychological significance to the individual. Furthermore, by making the commitment in public, the decision-maker has lost his flexibility in adjusting to new dissonant cognitions, i.e., when *Consumer Reports* issues a critical evaluation of the newly purchased brand (Brehm and Cohen, 1962).
2. a number of desirable alternatives are available (Brehm and Cohen, 1959; Anderson, Taylor, and Holloway, 1966).
3. the alternatives are dissimilar, and there is little "cognitive overlap," or sharing of features. Thus a choice between a car and a boat creates more dissonance than a choice between a Volkswagen and a Ford Pinto.
4. the choice decision is the result of free will, with little or no outside applied pressure. If pressure is applied, the individual complies without letting his cognitions be challenged (Festinger and Carlsmith, 1959).

Of course, dissonance is aroused in many other circumstances than those following a decision. The theory has also been applied to the topics of selective avoidance of information, defensive projection, and discrepancy between the positions of the source and the receiver.

Modes of Resolving Inconsistency. It is worthwhile to pay special attention to this issue because of valuable insights into the sometimes paradoxical feedback effects of choice behavior in attitudes. At least seven different modes have been identified. However, it should be understood that these are more likely to be complementary rather than mutually exclusive. First, one can attempt to *revoke the decision.* Retail stores with liberal return policies encourage this mode. They assume that the other modes may reduce future patronage.

A second basic mode involves a *change in the attitude* toward the product or situation by increasing cognitive overlap (searching for or misperceiving aspects of functional equivalence), or seeking out consonant elements. The latter mode does not remove the inconsistency but submerges it among a larger body of beliefs that are consistent with the conflicting one (Abelson, 1959). A related attitude-change mode for post-decision dissonance is to increase the attractiveness of the chosen alternative and/or decrease the attractiveness of the unchosen alternative. The net effect is that attitude change *follows,* and gives meaning to a prior behavior change. This is the basis for the frequent suggestion that a forced change in behavior is one of the most effective ways of changing behavior.

A third basic mode of resolution is *downrating* the importance of the area in which the inconsistency occurs. An implicit decision is made against investing emotional resources on the grounds that the issue is petty. This perhaps accounts for consumers' apparent tolerance of petty abuses or unconfirmed expectations about low-cost consumer products.

However, we should note that there are considerable individual differences in tolerance of inconsistency, which seem to depend on both personality and situational variables (Glass, 1967). Thus a further mode is to simply *accept* the inconsistency, which is relatively easy for some people.

McGuire (1966, p. 11) suggests that inconsistency may also be reduced by changing the perception of the object, rather than the attitude toward the object. Thus, a college student will increase the status of "politician" after being told his peers ranked the profession much higher than he, by reinterpreting "politicians" as statesmen rather than ward heelers (Asch, 1948).

One specific implication of the various modes of inconsistency resolution, and of cognitive dissonance theory in particular, is that a buyer experiencing dissonance will *seek* information that confirms his choice and *avoid* discrepant information. The former postulate has been consistently supported in field and experimental studies, while evidence for a selective avoidance tendency is equivocal at best (Freedman and Sears, 1965). In response, dissonance theorists have posited an interaction effect, wherein the selective avoidance tendency is accentuated as the person's confidence in his choice weakens (Canon, 1964). So long as the buyer is confident of his decision or of his original belief, he perceives himself to be capable of utilizing relevant information from any source. He may also have a "set" to notice any information that is pertinent, regardless of source. This would explain why those who have recently purchased new cars tend to notice advertisements about all brands.

Behavioristic Alternative to Dissonance Theory.   Considerable controversy has recently been stirred by Bem's (1967; 1968) development of "self-perception" theory as an alternative interpretation of cognitive dissonance phenomena. He argues that "an individual's attitudes and the attitudes that an outside observer would attribute to him may be functionally similar, in that both are partial 'inferences' from the same evidence: the public behaviors and accompanying cues upon which the socializing community has relied in training him to make such self-descriptive statements in the first place" (1968, pp. 201–202). That is, an individual infers his own attitude by observing his own overt behavior.

This seemingly simple concept has been employed to explain consistency phenomena as learning of the appropriate responses to inconsistency; with the motivational basis for the learning residing in the needs satisfied by the rewards originally used to reinforce the responses. This is quite different from dissonance theory, which postulates that inconsistency has a distinct motivating property, and that the rewards come from reduction of the inconsistency. These two competing formulations usually make the same predictions, which has made it difficult to devise comparative tests.

One approach is to put people in the role of observers of a subject in a dissonance experiment and ask them to infer the subject's attitude. The justification is that observers will take account of the behavior of the subject as well as the circumstances surrounding the behavior. As an illustration (Bem, 1970), we attribute the enthusiasm of a celebrity for a product he is endorsing to cash rather than conviction. Bem observes that, in the face of such skepticism, advertisers have moved to "candid camera" interviews with "homey folks." The advertisers hope that, because the endorsers are not paid, viewers will infer that they really must prefer the product when they say so. In a similar fashion, observers have been able to successfully estimate the attitudes of subjects in a number of well-known forced-compliance and free-choice dissonance experiments.

Social Judgment Theory

Although this theory has long been overshadowed by cognitive dissonance theory, it may in the long run prove more relevant in the marketing context. Its virtues are explicit hypotheses about the joint effects of discrepant communications and differential ego-involvement on the extent of changes in comparative judgments of objects or concepts. The theory itself is based on empirical generalizations about judgment processes that are largely derived from the psychophysical literature (see Sherif and Hovland, 1961; and Sherif, Sherif, and Nebergall, 1965; for a summary of these generalizations).

Attitude Organization. In social judgment theory, an individual's attitude toward an object or a social issue is treated as a range of acceptable positions (an acceptance region) rather than a single point. Operationally, this region is usually defined by the Thurstone-type statements that are considered acceptable or tolerable, including the single most acceptable statement. The rest of the attitude dimension is divided into a rejection region and a noncommitment region. The latter category is generally the residue after the acceptable and objectionable positions have been determined. For people with moderate positions on an issue, there may be two rejection regions—one at each extreme. This accommodates those who cannot tolerate the far left or the far right wing of the political spectrum, for example. This view of attitude structure resembles the familiar brand-attitude scale, which identifies a "consideration" class, a "buying" class, and a "non-consideration" class of brands (Smith, 1965; Day, 1970b). The consideration of acceptable class is also akin to the theoretical notion of an "evoked set" of brands which are within the buyer's reach and are adequate for his needs (Howard and Sheth, 1969).

Contrast and Assimilation. Attitude change in response to a persuasive communication is seen in social judgment theory as a two-step process. First, the recipient makes a judgment that positions the message on a subjective scale of favorability with respect to the issue or object. The amount of attitude change then depends on the judged discrepancy between the message and the

recipient's own position. When the message falls within the recipient's acceptance or neutral region, it will be seen as more nearly similar to the recipient's
position than it actually is (*assimilation* effect). A persuasive message will be
maximally effective when the position advocated by the message falls close to
the boundary of the rejection region. However, if the message advocates a
position that is *within* the rejection region, a *contrast* effect will occur. Then
the judged discrepancy is likely to be exaggerated, the communication will
be unfavorably evaluated, and the recipient will resist persuasion. Worse, a
very discrepant message is likely to reinforce the recipient's initial attitude and
perhaps produce a boomerang effect.

This simple judgment displacement process is highly subject to distortion from the following sources: (a) ambiguity as to the position of the communication (Sherif and Sherif, 1967); (b) limited past experience; (c) situational factors which do not require the respondent to discriminate between
attitude positions; and (d) deep involvement in one's position on an issue
(Kiesler, Collins, and Miller, 1969, p. 246). Most of the research, however, has
focused on the effect of involvement.

Role of Involvement.   According to social-judgment theory, the attitude
of a person highly involved in his position will be hard to change because that
position is strongly anchored within the total belief system. The consequence
of increasing involvement is that discrepant communications pose greater
threats to one's position and are more likely to fall in the rejection region.
This is the reason that involvement is defined operationally by the size of the
rejection region. In the early formulations of the theory, it was hypothesized
that increasing involvement would lead to a shrinking of the range of acceptable
positions. However, the empirical findings have been ambiguous on this matter
(Sherif, Sherif, and Nebergall, 1965), and it is now assumed that the acceptance
region remains constant for a given stimulus situation.

The involvement level also influences the degree of perceptual distortion of a discrepant message, as well as whether an assimilation or contrast
effect will occur. For a communication within the acceptance region, the
involved respondent will assimilate the message much more than an uninvolved
respondent and consequently will perceive the message as advocating less
change. Analogously, when the message is in the rejection region, the involved
respondent will displace it further from his own position and find it less credible
and less persuasive. Thus, regardless of the level of discrepancy, an involved
subject will always be more difficult to persuade.

Involvement-Discrepancy Controversy

When two theories make competing predictions about important
phenomena, the ensuing attempts at explanation or reconciliation can effectively illuminate the strengths and weaknesses of the theories. In this
controversy, we find that social-judgment theory predicts a curvilinear relationship between discrepancy and attitude change, and decreased persuasion
as involvement with a stand becomes more intense. In opposition is cognitive
dissonance theory: greater discrepancy is predicted to generate more dissonance, which would lead to increasing attitude change, if this were the mode

of reducing dissonance. Dissonance theory also predicts that the more important the initial attitude becomes, the more dissonance is created by a discrepant communication, and the greater the pressure to reduce dissonance (and change the initial attitude). As might be expected, considerable ingenuity has been expended to specify alternate modes of resolution of the discomfort occasioned by these seemingly incompatible predictions.

The preferred resolution of the *discrepancy* controversy has been to introduce communicator credibility characteristics into the analysis. This is a recognition that there are other differences between a communicator and his audience than simply a discrepancy in the positions advocated. First, it has been noted that a nonmonotonic relationship is more likely to occur with low-credibility sources (Aronson, Turner, and Carlsmith, 1963) when the issues are unambiguous (Insko, Murashima, and Saiyadain, 1966). This is a convenient finding for dissonance theory, for it suggests that as communicator credibility decreases, derogation replaces attitude change as the mode of dissonance reduction when discrepancy is great.

This phenomenon is largely ignored by social-judgment theory. However, Kiesler, Collins, and Miller (1969) suggest that as the communicator becomes more credible, the respondent's latitude of acceptance broadens: "This simply implies that the inflection point in the function relating attitude change to discrepancy is shifted to higher levels of discrepancy as positive attributes of the source are increased" (p. 295). With one exception (Freedman, 1964), the relevant research supports these hypotheses about the interactive effect of credibility. To the extent that advertisers are seen as low in credibility, the implication is clearly that discrepant messages will be counter-productive.

The controversy over the role of *involvement* has been confused by difficulties in defining and measuring involvement. Both dissonance and social-judgment theory define involvement in terms of the original position. That is, will mention of the issue itself be sufficient to generate concern and interest? However, most experiments which find that involvement increases attitude change have looked only at involvement in the response (Zimbardo, 1960; Freedman, 1964). This concerns the importance of the results of a new response to the individual. In effect, he is given an incentive to change toward the new position, such as a friend's approval or the opportunity to appear intelligent. Naturally he will change toward this new position. If only studies dealing with issue involvement are considered, the attitude change results are generally consistent with social-judgment theory. Once again, inconsistent results do not disconfirm dissonance theory, for attitude change is only one avenue for dissonance reduction. Apparently, as involvement increases, attitude change becomes a less preferred mode, while the probability of disparaging the source or distorting the position of the source is increased (Eagly and Manis, 1966).

Functional Theories

The theoretical approaches I have just considered put their stress on the relationship of a person's attitude toward an object and his information, perception, and behavior toward that object. Little attention is given to the motivational underpinnings of this attitude. The crux of the various functional approaches to attitudes (Smith, Bruner, and White, 1958; Katz and Stotland,

1959; Katz, 1960) is that the same attitude may be held by different persons for different reasons and require the employment of different techniques for change.

Utilitarian (Adaptive) Functions.   Positive attitudes are developed toward objects or paths that have been instrumental in achieving desirable goals, or avoiding undesirable goals. Similarly, negative attitudes are developed toward objects that thwart desirable goals. These are learned responses that depend on one's past reinforcing experiences with the object (Katz, 1960). Hence this function strongly resembles the behavioristic information-processing approach.

Because utilitarian attitudes toward objects are formed through experience, they are posited to be fairly difficult to change through direct verbal appeals. Also, "the area of freedom for changing utilitarian attitudes is, of course, much greater in dealing with methods of satisfying needs than with the needs themselves. Needs change more slowly than the means for gratifying them, even though one role of the advertiser is to create new needs" (Katz, 1960, p. 178). By a process of exclusion, the most effective means for changing such attitudes are changing the buyer's perception of the ability of the product or brand to satisfy the needs or emphasizing need and better ways of need satisfaction.

Knowledge Functions.   Attitudes also function to help the individual cope with a complex world that cannot be grasped in its entirety. Accordingly, people seek stereotypes and broad frames of reference or categories that will provide "a simplified and practical manual of appropriate behavior toward specific objects" (McGuire, 1969, p. 158). Thus, when a new object is placed in an existing category, it becomes the focus of the existing repertory of behaviors which are appropriate to that overall category. This spares the individual the time-consuming and sometimes painful effort of deciding how to relate to the new object. New-product marketers are acutely conscious of this fact and generally avoid positioning a new product where it defies easy categorization. A better strategy is to demonstrate that the new product fits into several existing categories at the same time and thus delivers additional benefits.

Expressive (Self-Realizing) Functions.   Attitudes also function as part of the total belief system to give positive expression to the individual's central values and his self-concept. As such, they reflect and confirm his notion of the kind of person he is. But, conversely, the expression of an attitude can also help the individual define his self-concept. This self-realization function appears to be very similar to the dissonance notion that a person adopts attitudes to bolster or justify his behavior—especially in the face of a difficult decision.

According to Katz (1960, p. 189) "people are much less likely to find their values uncongenial than they are to find some of the attitudes inappropriate to their values." Thus one way to change a specific value-expressive attitude is to show that it is inconsistent with a more basic value. Marketers are more likely to take advantage of existing attitudes by portraying their brand as a means of expressing the values and self-concepts of particular market segments. This is particularly true in hard-to-evaluate products such as cosmetics and cigarettes. However, the available research on self-concept as a determinant of brand or product choice has not been particularly successful; either because of poor implementation of the strategy, inadequate methodology, or an inapplicable theory. The worth of this approach is still open to question.

Ego-Defensive (Externalization) Function.   Some attitudes toward objects or social situations serve primarily to help an individual deal with his inner conflicts and have only the most limited relationship to that object. They may protect him from internal anxieties or from facing up to potential danger, through building defense mechanisms or rationalizing the problem. Of greater interest is the tendency noted by Smith, Bruner, and White (1958) for people to see events or objects in terms of their own concerns, "covert strivings," or "preferred adjustive strategies." Internal problems, which may be unconscious, may well color or bias a person's perception of a social problem. Thus a person who has suffered from a series of problems with product quality or service is especially sensitive to revelations that others are suffering from the same problems. Furthermore, such a person is likely to propose solutions that resemble a successful strategy for dealing with a personal problem. Because ego-defensive attitudes are often irrelevant to the object and may be unconscious, they are probably impervious to conventional informational approaches. Indeed, knowledge of such attitudes may only be useful to marketers insofar as it is possible to avoid communications which elicit them.

Overview.   So little research has been devoted to functional theories that their ultimate usefulness cannot be appraised. While their scope is appealing, it appears that many aspects have been subject to more detailed interpretation within the other theories reviewed in this article. The major contribution, and the greatest value for marketing, should come from insights into individual differences. Other theories (such as social-judgment theory) also incorporate individual differences, but predict the main effects of persuasive messages. With functional theories no such prediction can be made without knowing the function the attitude serves for the individual. At present this cannot be determined, for there is virtually no technology for assessing the function of attitudes. Such a development would be very useful for the design and evaluation of marketing communications.

Summary

The research on attitude change reviewed here is provocative; it speaks directly to the immediate problems of communicators. But at the same time it is difficult to utilize directly for developing promotional strategy. For example, it is characteristic of laboratory experiments to obtain large changes in attitude, while the direct attitudinal effects of mass media are sometimes indiscernible in the field. Too few field studies of attitude exist for one to be confident of the generality of the many specific findings from the laboratory that have been reviewed in this article. One area where there is increasing agreement (see Hovland, 1959; Klapper, 1960; Bauer, 1964) is that an audience exerts considerable initiative in interpreting and using incoming persuasive messages for its own purposes. This initiative may be so large outside the laboratory as to suppress the desired effects, unless other environmental conditions are supportive (LeFleur, 1970). It is more probable that the environment of competing brands has an overall cancelling effect.

A further limitation of the existing research is a cavalier disregard of the subtleties of attitude structure (Smith, 1968), or the interaction of mass media and word-of-mouth communications (Katz and Lazarsfeld, 1955). There is growing evidence (summarized in Day, 1971) that marketing communications can better achieve objectives other than attitude change, including (1) increasing awareness, (2) forming attitudes, (3) triggering favorable word of mouth (Arndt, 1967), (4) changing the perception of product-category membership to include the product being advertised, (5) changing the saliency of individual product attributes (perhaps even making consumers aware of an attribute of a product which was not previously considered salient), (6) denigrating the competition, and (7) reinforcing existing attitudes. In fact, a recent review of the related voting literature (Weiss, 1969) concluded that "the preponderance of total media effects is contributed by the reinforcement or substantiation of vote decisions brought about by other factors, such as habitual patterns of voting or social and personal influences." What is clearly needed is more research on the effects of persuasive communications on all aspects of attitude structures to tease out these subtle but important effects. This is not an unreasonable hope in view of recent improvements in our understanding of attitude structures.

Notes

1. This implies that there is a predictive relationship with purchase or choice behavior. For insights into this complex issue, see Day (1970a) and Wicker (1969).

2. I assume that you are familiar with the semantic-differential and Likert ratings, which are usually employed to measure these judgments. If not, see Green and Tull (1970) and Upshaw (1968).

3. The outcome of this process of synthesis was a series of comprehensive and valuable reviews of research published between 1967 and 1969. (Insko, 1967; Smith, 1968; Abelson et al., 1969; Kiesler, Collins, and Miller, 1969; and McGuire, 1969.) These have been extensively employed in the preparation of this paper. The guiding and clarifying role of these reviews at each point in the discussion may not always be appropriately acknowledged, but was substantial indeed.

References

Abelson, R. P. "Modes of Resolution of Belief Dilemmas." *Journal of Conflict Resolution,* Vol. 3 (1959), 343–352.

Abelson, R. P., E. Aronson, W. J. McGuire, T. N. Newcomb, M. J. Rosenberg, and P. Tannenbaum (eds.). *Theories of Cognitive Consistency: A Sourcebook.* Rand McNally, 1969.

———, and M. J. Rosenberg. "Symbolic Psycho-Logic: a Model of Attitudinal Cognition." *Behavioral Science,* Vol. 3 (1958), 1–13.

Allport, G. W. "Attitudes." In *Handbook of Social Psychology,* ed. C. Murchison. Clark Univ. Press (1935), 798–884.

Anderson, L. K., J. R. Taylor, and R. J. Holloway. "The Consumer and His Alternatives: An Experimental Approach." *Journal of Marketing Research,* Vol. 3 (February 1966), 62–67.

Arndt, J. *Word of Mouth Advertising.* Advertising Research Foundation, 1967.

Aronson, E. "Dissonance Theory: Progress and Problems." In Abelson et al., 1969.

———, J. A. Turner, and J. M. Carlsmith. "Communicator Credibility and Communicator Discrepancy as Determinants of Opinion Change." *Journal of Abnormal and Social Psychology,* Vol. 67 (1963), 31–37.

Asch, S. E. "The Doctrine of Suggestion, Prestige, and Imitation in Social Psychology." *Psychological Review,* Vol. 55 (1948), 250–276.

Bauer, R. A. "The Obstinate Audience: The Influence Process from the Point of View of Social Communication." *American Psychologist,* Vol. 19 (1964), 319–328.

———. "Consumer Behavior as Risk-Taking." In *Dynamic Marketing for a Changing World,* ed. R. S. Hancock. American Marketing Association (1960), 389–398.

———, and S. A. Greyser. "The Dialogue That Never Happens." *Harvard Business Review,* Vol. 45, November–December 1967.

———. "Self-Perception: An Alternative Interpretation of Cognitive Dissonance Phenomena." *Psychological Review,* Vol. 74 (1967), 183–200.

Bem, D. J. "Attitudes as Self-Descriptions: Another Look at the Attitude-Behavior Links." In *Psychological Foundations of Attitudes,* ed. A. G. Greenwald, T. C. Brock, and T. M. Ostrom. Academic Press (1968), 197–215.

———. *Beliefs, Attitudes and Human Affairs.* Wadsworth, 1970.

Brehm, J. W. *A Theory of Psychological Reactance.* Academic Press, 1966.

———, and A. R. Cohen. *Explorations in Cognitive Dissonance.* Wiley, 1962.

———, and ———. "Re-evaluation of Choice Alternatives as a Function of Their Number and Qualitative Similarity." *Journal of Abnormal and Social Psychology,* Vol. 58 (1959), 373–378.

Campbell, D. T. "Social Attitudes and Other Acquired Behavioral Dispositions." In Volume 6 of *Psychology: A Study of a Science,* ed. S. Koch. McGraw-Hill, 1963.

Canon, L. K. "Self-Confidence and Selective Exposure to Information." In *Conflict, Decision and Dissonance*, ed. L. Festinger. Stanford University Press, 1964, 83–95.

Claycamp, H. J., and L. E. Liddy. "Prediction of New Product Performance: An Analytical Approach." *Journal of Marketing Research,* Vol. 6 (November 1969), 414–420.

Cook, S. W., and C. Selltiz. "A Multiple-Indicator Approach to Attitude Measurement." *Psychological Bulletin,* Vol. 62 (1964), 36–55.

Coombs, C. H. *A Theory of Data.* Wiley, 1964.

Day, G. S. "Attitude Change and the Relative Influence of Media and Word of Mouth Sources." *Journal of Advertising Research,* 1971.

———. *Buyer Attitudes and Brand Choice Behavior.* The Free Press, 1970a.

———. "Using Attitude Change Measures to Evaluate New Product Introductions." *Journal of Marketing Research,* Vol. 7 (November 1970b), 474–482.

Eagly, A. H., and M. Manis. "Evaluation of Message and Communication as a Function of Involvement." *Journal of Personality and Social Psychology,* Vol. 3 (1966), 483–485.

Engel, J. F., D. T. Kollat, and R. D. Blackwell. *Consumer Behavior.* Holt, Rinehart and Winston, 1968.

Evans, F. B. "Psychological and Objective Factors in the Prediction of Brand Choice: Ford versus Chevrolet." *Journal of Business,* Vol. 32 (1959), 340–369.

Festinger, L. *A Theory of Cognitive Dissonance.* Stanford University Press, 1957.

———, and J. Merrill Carlsmith. "Cognitive Consequences of Forced Compliance." *Journal of Abnormal and Social Psychology,* Vol. 58 (1959), 203–210.

Fishbein, M. "The Relationships between Beliefs, Attitudes and Behavior." In *Cognitive Consistency: Motivational Antecedents and Behavioral Consequents,* ed. S. Feldman. Academic Press, 1966.

———, and B. H. Raven. "The A-B-Scales: An Operational Definition of Belief and Attitude." *Human Relations,* Vol. 15 (1962), 35–44.

Fiske, D. W., and S. R. Maddi. *Functions of Varied Experience.* Irwin-Dorsey, 1961.

Fothergill, J. "Do Attitudes Change Before Behavior?" In *Papers: Esomer Congress 1968.* Opatigo (September 1968), 875–900.

Fowler, H. *Curiosity and Exploratory Behavior.* Macmillan, 1965.

Freedman, J. L. "Involvement, Discrepancy and Change." *Journal of Abnormal and Social Psychology,* Vol. 69 (1964), 290–295.

———, and D. Sears. "Selective Exposure." In *Advances in Experimental Social Psychology,* Vol. 2, ed. L. Berkowitz. Academic Press (1965), 57–97.

Glass, D. "Theories of Consistency and the Study of Personality." In *Handbook of Personality Theory and Research,* ed. E. F. Borgatta and W. W. Lambert. Rand-McNally, 1967.

Green, P. E., and D. S. Tull. *Research Design for Marketing Decisions,* second edition. Prentice-Hall, 1970.

Greenberg, M. "The Analysis of Preference and Attribute Judgment Data." Unpublished working paper, November 1968.

Heller, H. E. "Defining Target Markets by Their Attitude Profiles." In *Attitude Research on the Rocks,* ed. L. Adler and I. Crespi. American Marketing Association, 1968.

Hess, E. H. "Attitude and Pupil Size." *Scientific American,* Vol. 212 (1965), 46–54.

Hovland, C. I. "Reconciling Conflicting Results Derived from Experimental and Survey Studies of Attitude Change." *American Psychologist,* Vol. 14 (1959), 8–17.

Howard, J. A., and J. N. Sheth. *Theory of Buyer Behavior.* Wiley, 1969.

Hustad, T. P., and E. A. Pessemier. "Segmenting Consumer Markets with Activity and Attitude Measures." Unpublished working paper, Purdue University, March 1971.

Insko, C. A. *Theories of Attitude Change.* Appleton-Century-Crofts, 1967.

———, F. Murashima, and M. Saiyadain. "Communicator Discrepancy, Stimulus Ambiguity and Influence." *Journal of Personality,* Vol. 34 (1966), 262–274.

Katz, D. "The Functional Approach to the Study of Attitudes." *Public Opinion Quarterly,* Vol. 24 (1960), 163–204.

———, and E. Stotland. "A Preliminary Statement to a Theory of Attitude Structure and Change." In *Psychology: A Study of a Science,* Vol. 3, ed. S. Koch. McGraw-Hill, 1959, 423–475.

Katz, E., and P. F. Lazarsfeld. *Personal Influence.* The Free Press, 1955.

Kelman, H. C. "Processes of Opinion Change." *Public Opinion Quarterly,* Vol. 25 (1961), 57–78.

Kiesler, C. A., B. E. Collins, and N. Miller. *Attitude Change: A Critical Analysis of Theoretical Approaches.* Wiley, 1969.

Klapper, J. T. *Effects of Mass Communication.* The Free Press, 1960.

Krugman, H. E. "The Impact of Television Advertising: Learning without Involvement." *Public Opinion Quarterly,* Vol. 29 (Fall 1965), 349–356.

Lavidge, R. C., and G. A. Steiner. "A Model for Predictive Measurements of Advertising Effectiveness." *Journal of Marketing,* Vol. 25 (October 1961), 59–62.

LeFleur, M. *Theories of Mass Communication.* 2nd ed. David McKay, 1970.

Linder, S. B. *The Harried Leisure Class.* Columbia University Press, 1970.

Lunn, J. A. "Attitudes and Behavior in Consumer Behavior—A Reappraisal." Unpublished paper, Research Bureau Limited, 1970.

McGuire, W. J. "An Information-Processing Model of Advertising Effectiveness." In *Behavioral and Management Science in Marketing,* ed. H. Davis and A. Silk. Ronald Press, in press.

———. "The Nature of Attitudes and Attitude Change." In *The Handbook of Social Psychology,* 2nd ed., Vol. 3, ed. G. Lindsay and E. Aronson. Addison-Wesley, 1969, 136–314.

———. "The Current Status of Cognitive Consistency Theories." In *Cognitive Consistency: Motivational Antecedents and Behavioral Consequents*, ed. S. Feldman. Academic Press, 1966.

Maloney, J. C. "Attitude Measurement and Prediction." Paper presented at the Test Market Design and Measurement Workshop, American Marketing Association, Chicago, April 1966.

Nicosia, F. M. *Consumer Decision Processes: Marketing and Advertising Implications.* Prentice-Hall, 1966.

Osgood, C. E., G. I. Suci, and P. H. Tannenbaum. *The Measurement of Meaning.* University of Illinois Press, 1957.

Pepitone, A. "Some Conceptual and Empirical Problems of Consistency Models." In S. Feldman *op. cit.,* 1966.

Robertson, T. S. *Innovative Behavior and Communication.* Holt, Rinehart and Winston, 1971.

Rokeach, M. "Attitude Change and Behavior Change." *Public Opinion Quarterly,* Vol. 30 (Winter 1966–67), 529–550.

Sherif, C. W., M. Sherif, and R. E. Nebergall. *Attitude and Attitude Change: The Social Judgment-Involvement Approach.* W. B. Saunders, 1965.

Sherif, M., and C. W. Sherif. "Attitude as the Individual's Own Categories: The Social Judgment-Involvement Approach to Attitude and Attitude Change." In *Attitude, Ego-Involvement and Change,* ed. C. W. Sherif and M. Sherif. Wiley (1967), 105–139.

————, and C. I. Hovland. *Social Judgment: Assimilation and Contrast Effects in Communication and Attitude Change.* Yale University Press, 1961.

Smith, G. "How GM Measures Ad Effectiveness." *Printer's Ink,* May 14, 1965.

Smith, M. B. "Attitude Change." In *Encyclopedia of the Social Sciences,* Vol. I, ed. D. L. Sills. Crowell-Collier and Macmillan (1968), 458–467.

————, J. S. Bruner, and R. W. White. *Opinions and Personality.* Wiley, 1958.

Tannenbaum, P. H. "The Congruity Principle Revisited: Studies in the Reduction, Induction and Generalization of Persuasion." In *Advances in Experimental Social Psychology,* ed. L. Berkowitz. Academic Press, 1967.

Turner, J. S. *The Chemical Feast.* Grossman, 1970.

Upshaw, H. S. "Attitude Measurement." In *Methodology in Social Research,* ed. H. M. and A. B. Blalock. McGraw-Hill, 1968.

Weiss, W. "Effects of the Mass Media of Communication." In *Handbook of Social Psychology,* 2nd ed., Vol. 5, ed. G. Lindzey and E. Aronson. Addison-Wesley (1969), 77–195.

Wells, W. D. "Measuring Readiness to Buy." *Harvard Business Review,* Vol. 39 (July–August 1961), 81–87.

Wicker, A. W. "Attitudes versus Actions: The Relationship of Verbal and Overt Behavioral Responses to Attitude Objects." *The Journal of Social Issues,* Vol. 25 (Autumn 1969), 41–78.

Zimbardo, P., and E. B. Ebbesen. *Influencing Attitudes and Changing Behavior.* Addison-Wesley, 1969.

Zimbardo, P. G. "Involvement and Communication Discrepancy as Determinants of Opinion Conformity." *Journal of Abnormal and Social Psychology,* Vol. 60 (1960), 86–94.

3.2 The Search for Attitudinal-Behavioral Consistency
MARTIN FISHBEIN

After more than seventy-five years of attitude research, there is still little, if any, consistent evidence supporting the hypothesis that knowledge of an individual's attitude toward some object will allow one to predict the way he will behave with respect to the object. Indeed, what little evidence there is to support any relationship between attitude and behavior comes from studies showing that a person tends to bring his attitude into line with his behavior rather than from studies demonstrating that behavior is a function of attitude (e.g., Cohen, 1960; Gerard, 1965; Landy, 1966).

It is my contention that we psychologists have been rather naive in our attempts to understand and to investigate the relationships between attitude and behavior. More often than not, we have attempted to predict some behavior from some measure of attitude and found little or no relationship between these variables. Yet, rather than questioning our basic assumption that there is a strong relationship between attitude and behavior, we have tended to blame our failures on our measuring instruments, on our definition of attitude, or on both.[1] Thus, from its relatively simple beginning as a uni-dimensional concept that referred to the amount of affect for or against some psychological object, the concept of attitude has grown into a complex, multi-dimensional concept consisting of affective, cognitive, and conative components.

While this latter view has done a great deal to stimulate new types of research, it, unfortunately, has contributed relatively little to an understanding of the specific relationships between attitude and behavior. In some respects, however, the multicomponent view of attitude can be seen as a precursor of a growing awareness that the understanding and prediction of behavior will necessitate the simultaneous consideration of many variables.[2] That is, to a certain extent at least, the multicomponent view of attitude implicitly recognizes that an individual's behavior with respect to a given object *cannot* be predicted solely from a consideration of the individual's feelings of favorableness or unfavorableness toward that object. Indeed, what this view suggests is that if we wish to predict behavior, vis-à-vis some object, not only must we consider an individual's affective feelings toward that object (i.e., his attitude) but we must also take other variables into account. That is to say, this approach points out how we might predict behavior in those situations where traditional measures of attitude appear unrelated to the behavior. While the suggestion that we might be able to predict behavior by considering other variables is obviously reasonable, it seems unfortunate that the two variables most commonly suggested (namely, cognitions and conations) have been arrived at through a consideration of the attitude concept, rather than through a consideration of behavior itself. More specifically, if we are going to look for other variables that influence behavior, it seems inappropriate to consider variables that correlate with the predictor rather than to look for variables that should be correlated with the behavior. For example, there is a considerable amount of evidence that behavior is influenced by normative, motivational, situational, and personality variables. Although many investigators have recognized the importance of these "other" variables as determinants of behavior, most treatments of attitude have not dealt with these factors explicitly. Rather, they have usually been viewed as sources of "error" variance. Clearly, however, if behavioral prediction is to be possible, this larger constellation of behavioral determinants will have to be taken into account. The purpose of the present paper is to present a theory that attempts to integrate these other determinants into a single attitudinal formulation and to discuss some of the research that has been generated by the theory. It is hoped that, among other things, this approach will lead to a clearer understanding of the relationships between traditional measures of attitude and overt behavior by identifying some of the ways in which other variables interact with attitudes as determinants of behavior. Further, an attempt will be made to show that the theory provides a clear and straightforward explanation for the lack of any systematic relationship between traditional measures of attitudes and overt behavior.

The theory to be presented can best be seen as an adaptation of Dulany's (1967) theory of propositional control. Although Dulany's theory has largely been developed within the context of studies of verbal conditioning and concept attainment, it is essentially a theory that leads to the prediction of overt behavior. More specifically, Dulany has been concerned with predicting the probability with which an individual will make a particular verbal response or class of verbal responses. The central equation of the theory can be expressed as follows:

$$B \approx BI = [(RHd)(RSv)]_{w_0} + [(BH)(Mc)]_{w_1}$$

where B = behavior
BI = the subject's intention to make a particular response or class of responses
RHd = a "hypothesis of the distribution of reinforcement," i.e., the subject's hypothesis that the occurrence of the particular response will lead to a certain event or class of events
RSv = the affective value of the reinforcement, i.e., the subject's evaluations of those events
BH = the subject's "behavioral hypothesis," i.e., his belief as to what he is *expected* to do, or what he *should* do in the situation
Mc = the subject's "motivation to comply," i.e., how much the subject *wants* to do what he believes is expected of him
w_0 and w_1 = beta weights which may take any value.

Two additional points about the theory should be mentioned:

1. According to the theory, behavioral intention is the immediate antecedent of overt behavior. Unlike the general types of behavioral intentions that most attitude researchers (e.g., Triandis, 1964; Triandis et al., 1968) have been concerned with (e.g., intentions to marry, to show social distance, to subordinate, to accept as a friend), Dulany has been concerned with a more precise and specific type of behavioral intention—namely, an individual's intention to perform a given action in a given situation. That is, the intention refers directly to the particular overt response one wishes to predict. Because of this close correspondence between the measure of the behavioral intention and the actual

behavior, the correlation between the measure of behavioral intention and the actual overt behavior is exceptionally strong (i.e., the correlations are always in the high .80s and mid .90s). Thus if one can predict the specific behavioral intention, one may, with only slightly attenuated accuracy, predict the overt behavior. It must be emphasized, however, that these near-perfect correlations between behavioral intentions and behavior are only obtained, *and are only expected*, when one considers an individual's intention to perform a specific act in a specific situation. The more abstract or generalized the intention becomes, the lower will be its correlation with a specific behavior.[3]

2. As can be seen above, the algebraic expression of the theory takes the form of a linear multiple regression equation. That is, $[(RHd)(RSv)]$ is viewed as one component influencing behavioral intentions and $[(BH)(Mc)]$ is seen as a second component. The precise weights to be given these two components as determinants of behavioral intentions within a given situation must be determined by standard multiple regression procedures.

In a recent paper, Fishbein (1967c) has provided an interpretation of this theory as applied to social behavior. More specifically, according to Fishbein, an individual's intention to perform a specific act, with respect to a given stimulus object, in a given situation, is a function of:

$RHd \approx B_i$ = his beliefs about the consequences of performing a particular behavior (in a given situation), i.e., the probability or
improbability that the performance of behavior x will lead
to some consequences y_i

$RSv \approx a_i$ = the evaluative aspect of B_i, i.e., the S's evaluation of
(attitude toward) y_i

$BH \approx NB$ = a normative belief, i.e., the S's belief about what "others"
expect him to do or say he *should* do in this situation

Mc = his motivation to comply with the norm, i.e., his desire, or
lack of desire, to do what he thinks he should do

Thus in this adaptation of Dulany's theory, *RHd* (the hypothesis of the distribution of a reinforcer) is conceptualized as being analogous to an individual's beliefs about the consequences of performing a specific behavior, and *RSv* (the affective value of the reinforcer) is conceptualized as being equivalent to the evaluative aspects of those beliefs. It is interesting to note that this conceptualization redefines the first component of Dulany's theory $[(RHd)(RSv)]$ as a measure of attitude. That is, the work of Rosenberg (1956, 1965), Zajonc (1954), Fishbein (1963, 1965, 1967a, 1967b), and others has provided strong evidence that an individual's attitude toward any object can be predicted from a knowledge of the individual's beliefs about the object and the evaluative aspects of those beliefs. Algebraically, this may be expressed as follows:

$$A_o = \sum_{i=1}^{n} B_i a_i$$

where A_o = the attitude toward some object "o"
B_i = belief i about o, i.e., the probability that o is related to some other object x_i
a_i = the evaluative aspect of B_i, i.e., the respondent's attitude toward x_i
n = the number of beliefs

It must be emphasized, however, that the attitude under consideration is an attitude toward performing a given behavioral act and is *not* an attitude toward a given object, person, or situation. That is, the algebraic formula presented above leads to the hypothesis that an individual's attitude toward any object is a function of the individual's beliefs about *that* object. In the present analysis, we are concerned with an individual's beliefs about the performance of a given behavioral act, and thus the attitude being assessed is the individual's attitude toward the performance of that act. More specifically, from the point of view of the theory, we should be assessing the individual's beliefs about what will happen if he performs behavior X with respect to stimulus Y in situation Z, and the evaluative aspects of those beliefs. Thus, the attitude being assessed is also very specific—it's an attitude toward performing a given action, with respect to a given object, in a given situation. Clearly, this attitude may vary considerably as a function of either the stimulus the act is directed toward (i.e., an individual may have different beliefs about the consequences of performing a given act with respect to Person A as opposed to Person B) or the situation in which the act is to occur (i.e., an individual may have different beliefs about the consequences of performing a given act in public than he would have about performing the same act in private). The main point, however, is that the attitude under consideration is an attitude toward the performance of a given act, and not an attitude toward a given object or situation. We shall return to this distinction shortly.

Turning to the second component of Dulany's theory [$(BH)(Mc)$], it can be seen that BH (the behavioral hypothesis) has been conceptualized as a normative belief, i.e., a belief about what others expect or say *should* be done in the situation. Of course, the potential reference groups or individuals whose expectations are perceived to be relevant will vary with the behavioral situation. Thus, while in some instances the expectations of a person's friends or family may be most relevant, in others it may be the expectations of his supervisors or even the society at large which are most influential.[4]

The final element in the equation (Mc—an individual's motivation to comply) is self-explanatory. Here we are concerned with the degree to which the individual "wants" to comply with the norm. Clearly, if two or more norms are considered (i.e., if the "expectation" of more than one "other" is considered), it will be necessary to measure the individual's motivation to comply with each of them.

To summarize briefly then, it can be seen that in its adapted form, the theory essentially leads to the prediction that an individual's intention to perform any behavior in a given situation (and thus his actual performance of the behavior) is a function of (1) his attitude toward performing the behavior in the situation, (2) his perception of the norms governing that behavior in that situation, and (3) his motivation to comply with those norms. Algebraically, this can be expressed as follows:

$$B \approx BI = [A_{\text{act}}]_{w_0} + [(NB)(Mc)]_{w_1}$$

Thus as mentioned previously, the present approach suggests a radical change in investigating and understanding the attitude-behavior relationship. Instead of assuming some underlying relationship between an individual's attitude toward a given object and his behavior with respect to the object, the proposed theory recognizes the importance of situational variables, norms, and motivation, as factors influencing behavior. Rather than viewing attitude toward a stimulus object as a major determinant of behavior with respect to that object, the theory identifies three kinds of variables that function as the basic determinants of behavioral intentions (and thus behavior): (1) attitudes toward the behavior, (2) normative beliefs, and (3) motivation to comply with the norms. Further, although the theory suggests that other variables can also influence behavior, it indicates that these other variables operate *indirectly,* i.e., by influencing either of the two components or their relative weights.

Thus, it can be seen that according to the theory, there are two major factors influencing behavior: first, there is a personal or attitudinal influence; and, second, there is a social or normative influence. However, it must again be emphasized that the attitudinal component is very different from traditional considerations of attitude since we are here concerned with an attitude toward performing a specific behavior in a given situation, rather than with an attitude toward a given person, object, value, or institution. Further, it should be recalled that the relative weight put on these two components should be empirically determined. That is, we would expect that the relative importance of the two components will vary systematically across types of behavior *and* across different individuals. More specifically, it seems quite reasonable to assume that certain types of behavior will be more under the influence of attitudinal considerations than normative ones, while the opposite should be true of other types of behaviors. Similarly, we would expect some types of people to be more under the influence of normative considerations than others. We shall return to these points shortly. First, however, let us consider traditional attitude measures and their relationship to overt behaviors.

If you recall, according to the theory, any variable external to the model can only influence behavior indirectly by influencing either of the two components or their relative weights. Thus, it can be seen that an individual's feelings of favorableness or unfavorableness toward some person (i.e., his attitude toward the person—or any of his cognitions about that person) will only be related to some specific behavior toward that person if:

1. His attitude toward the person is correlated with his attitude toward performing that specific behavior *and* the attitudinal component carries a significant amount of weight in determining his behavioral intention.

and/or

2. His attitude toward the person is correlated with the normative component *and* the normative component carries a significant amount of weight in determining his behavioral intention.

That is, even though a traditional measure of attitude may be correlated with one of the two components, it will still be unrelated to behavior if that component carries little or no weight in the determination of behavioral intentions and thus behavior per se.

Further, it should be fairly clear that there is no necessary relation between traditional attitude measures and any of the variables in the model. For example, while it is true that in some situations the consequences of performing a certain behavior vis-à-vis a liked person may be very different than the consequences of performing the same behavior vis-à-vis a disliked person, it is equally true that in other situations the behavior will lead to the same consequences irrespective of who the stimulus person is. In the former case, some correlation between the traditional measure of attitude and behavior might be obtained, while this is quite unlikely in the latter case. A similar argument can be made for the second component. Clearly, there are some situations in which one is expected to behave very differently toward a liked person than toward a disliked one, yet in other situations one is expected to behave the same way irrespective of his affective feeling toward the person. Once again, some attitudinal-behavioral relationship might be obtained in the former case, but it is quite unlikely in the latter case.

Along these same lines, it can also be seen that variations in the situation may also influence one or more of the primary determinants of behavior. Clearly, an individual *may* have quite different beliefs about the consequences of performing a given behavior in a public situation than in a private situation. Similarly, the individual may also have different normative beliefs for different situations. Here too, however, it must be noted that if the situational variables that are being considered do *not* influence the individual's attitude toward the act, or his normative beliefs, or his motivation to comply with these norms, then, according to the theory, they will not influence his behavior. Thus, it can be seen that the theory provides an explanation for a large number of results that may initially appear inconsistent. That is, from the point of view presented here, one would expect a considerable amount of variation in the relationship between any given variable and behavior.

Clearly then, if this theory is valid, there seems to be little basis for continuing the search for attitudinal-behavioral consistency, at least when traditional attitude scores are considered. Thus, let us now turn to the question of the validity of the theory. As was mentioned earlier, the theory was originally developed by Dulany in the context of studies of verbal conditioning and concept attainment. Dulany (1961, 1964, 1967) and his students (Dulany & O'Connell, 1963; Schwartz, 1966) have conducted several studies, all of which have amply demonstrated the theory's validity. Generally speaking, they have found multiple correlations in the high .80s and .90s between the model's predictors and behavioral intentions. Since his *BI*'s correlate in the high .80s and .90s with overt behavior, he has also obtained multiple correlations in the .80s between the model's predictors and overt behavior. Of more relevance to the present discussion, however, are several studies by Fishbein and his associates (e.g., Fishbein, 1966; Ajzen, 1969; Ajzen & Fishbein, 1969, 1970; Carlson, 1968; Fishbein et al., 1970; Devries & Ajzen, 1971) that are based directly on the extension of the theory presented above. In these studies, attempts have been made to predict behaviors ranging from the percent of a subject's cooperative responses in a two-person Prisoner's Dilemma Game to the likelihood that undergraduates will engage in premarital sexual intercourse.

Altogether nine studies have now been run, three of which have overt behaviors as the ultimate criterion, three of which have self-reports of behavior as the criterion, and three of which only attempt to predict behavioral intentions. Overall, the average multiple correlation between the model's two components and behavioral intentions is about .85. In those studies with either self-reports of behavior or an actual behavioral criterion, the *BI-B* correlations have ranged from .30 to .97, with an average at approximately .70. Interestingly, both extreme *BI-B* correlations were obtained in the same study. While a male's intention to engage in premarital sexual intercourse is only minimally related to his actual behavior, the correlation is almost perfect for females. The reason for this is fairly obvious—an intention is just that, and it seems clear that if a different behavioral criterion had been used for men (e.g., some measure of trying behavior) the *BI-B* correlation would have been much better. One other interesting finding from this study is worth reporting. If you will recall, it was pointed out above that the relative weights of the two components should vary systematically across different types of behavior and different types of individuals. Consistent with this, we have found that a male's intention to engage in premarital sexual intercourse is primarily determined by normative considerations while a female's intentions to engage in premarital sexual intercourse is primarily determined by attitudinal considerations (Fishbein, 1966).

In a more direct test of the hypothesis that the relative weights of the two components vary systematically with different behaviors and different individuals Carlson (1968) asked subjects to indicate their intentions to engage in 30 different behaviors with respect to a given stimulus person. Each subject also indicated their attitudes toward performing each of these behaviors, their beliefs about whether "most other people" would expect him to engage or not to engage in each behavior, and their motivation to comply with these expectations. Thus, it was possible to compute separate beta weights for each behavior (over the *S*s) and for each subject (over the 30 behaviors). In support of the theory, the multiple-correlations between the model's predictors and the 30 behavioral intentions ranged from .71 to .99, and the average $R = .93$. Even more importantly, a factor-analysis of the 30 behavioral intentions yielded five dimensions, *and* significant correlations between the beta weights and the factor loadings were obtained. Thus, for example, the higher a given intention loaded on the Formal Social Acceptance Factor, the more that intention was under attitudinal control (i.e., the higher was the beta weight of the attitudinal component). In contrast to this, the higher an intention loaded on the Marital Acceptance Factor the higher was the beta weight of the normative component. Further, the consideration of the beta weights for individuals also supported the theory. Carlson obtained a measure of authoritarianism for each subject, and consistent with expectations, the more authoritarian the *S*, the higher was the obtained beta weight placed on the normative component in determining his intentions.

Finally, let us consider two studies in which there were overt behavioral criteria. The first study (Ajzen & Fishbein, 1970) was an attempt to predict cooperative behavior in the context of a Prisoner's Dilemma Game. The main experimental manipulation involved Deutsch's (1960) instructions for inducing motivational orientations: one group of *S*s received a competitive orientation, one group an individualistic orientation, and one a cooperative orientation. Over all three conditions, the *BI-B* correlation = .847 ($N = 96$), and the multiple R between the model's predictors and $BI = .888$. Thus, the multiple correlation with S's actual behavior on the last 10 trials $= .732$. One of the main purposes of the study, however, was to test the hypothesis that behavior in these different conditions would be under the control of different factors. More specifically, we felt that while people with cooperative sets would be primarily under normative influence, (i.e., would place considerable weight on their partner's expectations) people under competitive sets would be primarily under attitudinal influence (i.e., would place considerable weight on the probability of obtaining valued outcomes). Consistent with this hypothesis the obtained beta weights in the cooperative condition were .223 (n.s.) and .438 ($p < .01$) for the attitudinal and normative components, respectively. In the competitive condition, these weights were reversed: the beta weight for the attitudinal component was .664 ($p < .01$), while that for the normative component was .186 (n.s.).

In the next study (Ajzen, 1969), an attempt was made to manipulate the S's behavior in the Prisoner's Dilemma Game. On the basis of the findings reported above it was hypothesized that messages designed to change the attitudinal component would produce behavioral change in the competitive condition but *not* in the cooperative condition. Similarly, messages designed to change the normative component should produce behavioral change in the cooperative condition but *not* in the competitive condition. The obtained results were entirely consistent with this hypothesis. The attitudinal message produced behavioral change only in the competitive condition, while the normative message was only effective (i.e., only produced behavioral change) in the cooperative condition. The importance of these findings should be apparent, for they clearly indicate that even when appropriate attitudes are considered (i.e., attitudes toward the performance of a behavior rather than attitudes toward an object or person) a change in that attitude may not produce behavioral change and thus even under these conditions (i.e., where appropriate attitudes are considered) there is little reason to expect attitudinal-behavioral consistency. Thus, in conclusion, it appears that although the notion of consistency may be very useful in contributing to our understanding of some psychological phenomena, the continued search for attitudinal-behavioral consistency will only serve to delay our attempts to understand and predict overt behavior of the non-pencil and paper variety. Clearly, the time has come to stop worrying about consistency and to start worrying about those factors that control behavior.

Notes

1. In the past few years, the assumption of a strong relationship between attitude and behavior has been questioned by an increasing number of investigators (Festinger, 1964; McGuire, 1969; Warner and DeFleur, 1969; Wicker, 1970; etc.).

2. Of particular relevance to the attitude-behavior question are the papers of Ehrlich (1969), Warner and DeFleur (1969), and Wicker (1970).

3. Several other factors will also influence the size of the obtained correlation between behavioral intention and behavior. For example, the longer the time interval between the measure of intention and the observation of behavior, the lower the

obtained correlation will tend to be. Similarly, the more the carrying out of the intention is dependent upon other people or events the lower will the obtained correlation tend to be. For a more complete discussion of the factors influencing the *BI-B* correlation, see Fishbein et al., 1970.

4. In the original adaptation of the theory (Fishbein, 1967c), it was suggested that the normative component also included the individual's personal normative beliefs, i.e., his own beliefs as to what he should do in a given situation. It appears however, that in many situations the subject's report of his personal normative belief (i.e., I personally feel I should perform behavior X) serves mainly as an alternative measure of his behavioral intention, and thus including this measure serves to confound, rather than clarify, the problem of understanding the determinants of behavioral intentions. For this reason, personal normative beliefs have been deleted from the present version of the theory.

References

Ajzen, I. Prediction and change of behavior in the Prisoner's Dilemma. Unpublished doctoral dissertation, University of Illinois, 1969.

Ajzen, I., & Fishbein, M. The prediction of behavioral intentions in a choice situation. *Journal of Experimental Social Psychology,* Vol. 5 (1969), 400–416.

Ajzen, I., & Fishbein, M. The prediction of behavior from attitudinal and normative variables. *Journal of Experimental Social Psychology,* (1970), in press.

Carlson, A. R. The relationship between a behavioral intention, attitude toward the behavior, and normative beliefs about the behavior. Unpublished doctoral dissertation, University of Illinois, 1968.

Cohen, A. R. Attitudinal consequences of induced discrepancies between cognitions and behavior. *Public Opinion Quarterly,* Vol. 24 (1960), 297–318.

Deutsch, M. The effects of motivational orientation upon threat and suspicion. *Human Relations,* Vol. 13 (1960), 123–139.

DeVries, D. L., & Ajzen, I. The relationship of attitudes and normative beliefs to cheating in college. *Journal of Social Psychology,* 1971.

Dulany, D. E. Hypotheses and habits in verbal operant conditioning. *Journal of Abnormal and Social Psychology,* Vol. 63 (1961), 251–263.

Dulany, D. E. The separable effects of the information and affect conveyed by a reinforcer. Paper presented at the meeting of the Psychonomic Society, 1964.

Dulany, D. E. Awareness, rules, and propositional control: A confrontation with S-R behavior theory. In D. Horton and T. Dixon (Eds.), *Verbal behavioral and S-R behavior theory.* New York: Prentice Hall, 1967.

Dulany, D. E., & O'Connell, D. C. Does partial reinforcement dissociate verbal rules and the behavior they might be presumed to control? *Journal of Verbal Learning and Verbal Behavior,* Vol. 2 (1963), 361–372.

Ehrlich, H. J. Attitudes, behavior, and the intervening variables. *The American Sociologist,* Vol. 4 (1969), 29–34.

Festinger, L. Behavioral support for opinion change. *Public Opinion Quarterly,* Vol. 24 (1964), 404–417.

Fishbein, M. An investigation of the relationships between beliefs about an object and the attitude toward that object. *Human Relations,* Vol. 16 (1963), 233–240.

Fishbein, M. The prediction of interpersonal preferences and group member satisfaction from estimated attitudes. *Journal of Personality and Social Psychology,* Vol. 1 (1965), 663–667.

Fishbein, M. Sexual behavior and propositional control. Paper presented at the meeting of the Psychonomic Society, 1966.

Fishbein, M. A consideration of beliefs, and their role in attitude measurement. In M. Fishbein (Ed.), *Readings in attitude theory and measurement.* New York: Wiley, 1967 (a).

Fishbein, M. A behavior theory approach to the relations between beliefs about an object and the attitude toward that object. In M. Fishbein (Ed.), *Readings in attitude theory and measurement.* New York: Wiley, 1967 (b).

Fishbein, M. Attitude and the prediction of behavior. In M. Fishbein (Ed.), *Readings in attitude theory and measurement.* New York: Wiley, 1967 (c).

Fishbein, M., Ajzen, I., Landy, E., & Anderson, L. R. Attitudinal variables and behavior: Three empirical studies and a theoretical reanalysis. Tech. Rep. No. 70–71. University of Washington, 1970.

Gerard, H. B. Deviation, conformity, and commitment. In I. D. Steiner and M. Fishbein (Eds.), *Current studies in social psychology.* New York: Holt, 1965.

Landy, E. An investigation of the relationships between attitude and two classes of overt behavior. Unpublished master's thesis, University of Illinois, 1966.

McGuire, W. J. The nature of attitudes and attitude change. In G. Lindzey and E. Aronson (Eds.), *The handbook of social psychology.* (2nd ed.) Reading, Mass.: Addison-Wesley, 1969.

Rosenberg, M. J. Cognitive structure and attitudinal affect. *Journal of Abnormal and Social Psychology,* Vol. 53 (1956), 367–372.

Rosenberg, M. J. Inconsistency arousal and reduction in attitude change. In I. D.

Steiner and M. Fishbein (Eds.), *Current studies in social psychology.* New York: Holt, 1965.

Schwartz, S. Trial-by-trial analysis of processes in simple and disjunctive concept attainment tasks. *Journal of Experimental Psychology,* Vol. 72 (1966), 456–465.

Triandis, H. C. Exploratory factor analysis of the behavioral component of social attitudes. *Journal of Abnormal and Social Psychology,* Vol. 68 (1964), 420–430.

Triandis, H. C., Fishbein, M., Hall, E., Shanmugam, A. V., & Tanaka, Y. Affect and behavioral intentions. In A. K. P. Sinha, H. K. Misra, A. K. Kanth, and K. S. Rao (Eds.), *Contributions to Psychology.* New Delhi: Institute for Social and Psychological Research, 1968.

Warner, L. G., & DeFleur, M. L. Attitudes as an interactional concept: Social constraint and social distance as intervening variables between attitudes and action. *American Sociological Review,* Vol. 34 (1969), 153–169.

Wicker, A. W. Attitudes versus action: The relationship of verbal and overt behavioral responses to attitude objects. *Journal of Social Issues,* Vol. 25 (1970), 41–78.

Zajonc, R. B. Structure of the cognitive field. Unpublished doctoral dissertation, University of Michigan, 1954.

3.3 A Cognitive Theory View of Brand Preference
STEWART W. BITHER, STEPHEN J. MILLER

Introduction

Over the last century, American business has gradually moved from production-oriented toward consumer-oriented planning. This orientation toward consumer wants and needs has evolved as supply of standard goods and services has exceeded demand. Firms have found it necessary to seek out new market opportunities by adjusting product output to fit customer needs more closely. In order to adjust product offerings properly, it has been necessary to focus specific attention upon the behavior of consumers.

This paper explores in more detail one critical area of consumer behavior—attitude formation and change. Attitudes have long been accepted as critical to consumer behavior. Following the lead of the marketing theorists who show the development of product attitudes in levels from brand unawareness to brand preference,[1] marketers have focused upon consumer knowledge of and feelings about a brand.[2] These two factors are viewed as the consumer's predisposition about the product. It is generally assumed that the creation of favorable consumer predispositions toward a product will lead to an increased probability of brand preference.

Armed with the assumption that positive predispositions increase the likelihood of brand preference, marketing men have devised numerous means of exposing the consumer to favorable information about their products. Simultaneously, instruments have been employed to measure the marketer's success in developing these predispositions. Techniques for measuring ad recall and brand awareness are employed to determine how much information the consumer has perceived and remembered. Image studies and so called "standard" attitude scales are used to determine whether the perceived or remembered information has been interpreted in a favorable light by the consumer. Given this data about the consumer's product knowledge and his tendency to evaluate this knowledge either favorably or not, the critical concern is to relate this information to active product preference.

In marketing as well as in other disciplines, success has not always been achieved in relating predispositions to behavior or purchase activity.[3] The simplified view has often been taken that favorable predispositions result directly in preference. Often, however, consumer's product knowledge and feelings do not correlate highly with an increased probability of purchase. This suggests that processes intervening between the individual's reception of positive information about a brand and his subsequent behavior regarding that brand should be subjected to more study. With few exceptions—perhaps Andreasen,[4] Howard,[5] and Nicosia[6]—only rudimentary attention in marketing has been focused upon processes intervening between initial stimulus and ultimate response tendencies in research concerning product attitudes.

This paper will first indicate some of the parameters of an attitude. Next exploratory research within the framework of a tentative attitude model will be reported. In later sections of the paper, the results of the research will be related to several theoretical controversies in the area of attitude research. Finally, the importance of these theoretical controversies and the practical implications of this research to marketers will be cited.

The Emphasis of This Research

The authors have focused attention on the study of processes intervening between initial stimulus and ultimate response tendencies. In reviewing the work of psychologists who have studied these intervening processes, it appears to these writers that primary emphasis has been placed on the encoding process. Study of the encoding process has accounted for such behavioral phenomena as stereotypes, prejudice and habit. However, theory in this area has shed little light on the equally important processes of attitude formation and attitude change. An elaboration of constructs designed to relate encoding to decoding might be a useful contribution to theory. Although much attention has been focused upon the intervening variables under consideration, [note theoretical developments in cognitive structure[7] and the work on cognitive consistency[8]] little has been reported in the area of linking these intervening variables to behavior through an explicit consideration of the encoding and decoding processes. Nothing of this nature has been reported in the marketing literature.[9]

The Multidimensional Nature of Attitudes

It is commonly noted in the psychological literature that attitudes are multidimensional. Three interrelated but separate dimensions are often cited. Recently popularized by Krech, et al.,[10] the three components, cognitive, affective, and conative, date back to the Greek classical period in philosophy. This classical trichotomy of knowing, feeling and acting continues to focus attitude research. Although agreement exists among many psychologists[11] active in attitude research that these three constructs are presently necessary to describe the phenomenon, less agreement exists about the way the three components are interrelated. Research generated by those who have studied affective and cognitive components suggests their belief that theories relating these components (in conjunction with stimulus objects) have the capacity to become powerful predictors of the conative or response tendency part of attitude.

Until the present decade, the majority of attitude research effort was directed toward an exploration of the affective component (note the undimensional rating procedures of Guttman[12] and Likert[13]). The emphasis in this decade has focused jointly upon affective and cognitive components with increasing attention paid to the cognitive component.[14]

The Cognitive Dimension

The literature of this decade indicates that the structure of the intervening cognitive variable is complex. Katz and Stotland[15] believe that at least three parameters in the cognitive component of attitude may exist. These three parameters are (1) the number of elements, (2) the degree of structure of interrelationship among these elements, and (3) the extensiveness of the objects to which the cognitive component applies. This isolation of cognitive parameters suggests numerous interesting hypotheses about the nature of attitude formation, stability, and change. Examples of the more interesting questions raised by this isolation of components are the following. To what degree is information differentiated into the storage of cognitive elements? Can the intensity of an individual's attitude be defined by the number, kind or affective loading of these elements? Can the scope of an attitude be defined by the structure of the elements or by the number of attitude objects to which these elements are relevant? It is quite obvious that these questions raised by the research of the last decade are unlikely to be answered completely even during the next decade. It is also clear that global theories of consumer decision processes and even theories of the middle range in comprehensiveness are most difficult to construct in light of present knowledge about and the complexity of attitude issues. Clearly, an incremental approach to exploring these phenomena is warranted. When using such an approach, assumptions must be made about the nature of a part of attitude structure while other parts are subjected to experimental study. This involves developing at least a skeleton of theoretical constructs defining interrelationships among attitude components.

Theoretical Constructs About Attitudes

In developing constructs about attitude components, one assumption is that attributes of attitude objects (in this case, products) may be represented as elements in the cognitive structure. A further assumption is that values or needs may be represented as a part of the cognitive structure and as a formative or energizing influence on the cognitive structure. The influence of value-need systems takes at least two forms. First, they may direct the structuring of the cognitions. Second, and more important in the context of the present research, values operate in the cognitive structures to determine the affect portion of attitude. Affect is determined by relating the perceived attributes of the attitude object to the value-need structure. The attributes are related through the perceived instrumentality of the attribute to either enhance or block the value structure.[16] One additional assumption is made for the purposes of this research. It is assumed that the instrumentality of attitude object attributes for blocking or enhancing the value system can be approximated by the perceived instrumentality of the attitude object itself for blocking or enhancing the system. This sets the stage for a kind of analysis known as *instrumentality-value analysis.*

Instrumentality-Value Analysis

Instrumentality-value analysis is most closely associated with the work of the Michigan school.[17] The work reported in this paper is a direct extension of earlier research reported by Rosenberg.[18] Rosenberg, believing that values and needs are pervasive in cognitive structuring, attempted to link univariate measures of attitudes to a multiple index of attitude components. He used a Likert-type scale to obtain a univariate attitude scale score toward an attitude object. He then constructed an index of value system components measuring both the importance of value items and the perceived instrumentality of the attitude object in enhancing or blocking the value system. Rosenberg successfully demonstrated that attitude predisposition (as measured on a univariate scale) related across subjects to the multidimensional indexes of value system components and the perceived instrumentality of the attitude object in enhancing or blocking the value system. Rosenberg's research dealt with the highly controversial and heavily value-laden topic, communism. The current research is designed to investigate two major extensions of Rosenberg's findings. The two extensions are (1) that an index similar to Rosenberg's will relate to univariate *product* ratings and that his results are not unique to highly controversial political issues and (2) that the index can be used to differentiate among univariate ratings of different competitive products. The two hypotheses tested in this study are stated below in their null form.

Research Hypotheses

The research in this study is designed to test two basic hypotheses. Each hypothesis interrelates univariate ratings of product appeal, value importance, and attitude object instrumentality. They are as follows:

1. Across subjects, the univariate rating of product appeal is independent of an index comprised of the individual's value system ratings and the perceived instrumentality of the attitude object in enhancing or blocking the value system.
2. Across products for each subject, differences in univariate ratings of product appeal are independent of value-instrumentality index differences.

Empirical Evaluation of Hypotheses

A research design was developed and executed in order to test the hypotheses. Survey methodology was selected for data collection in this exploratory phase of research. The study was conducted at The Pennsylvania State University during the Spring of 1969. From an initial sample of 107 undergraduate students, 98 completed questionnaires were obtained from two sessions. Nine subjects were eliminated due to absence from one of the sessions or for incomplete questionnaires.

Product Selection

Three brands of domestic automobiles were selected for the study. Two were automobiles of competitive intermediate price range (B and C) while the third was a lower priced sport-type (A). Automobile brands were chosen because of the extensive product knowledge students were believed to possess about them. The attitude object, automobile, is also of such importance to the individual that an extensive set of values may be involved. Many studies of automobile purchase behavior have been conducted.[19] This study is not intended as a definitive work on attitudes toward automobiles. This study is concerned with attitude structure. Automobile brands were chosen as a convenient product class.

Data Collection

Each subject was administered a questionnaire which asked him to rate the appeal of a number of products, including the selected brands. Appeal was measured on a seven point bi-polar scale with poles labeled "extremely high appeal" and "extremely low appeal."

Following an interval of several days, the subjects completed a second questionnaire consisting of 27 value items. The value questionnaire was constructed in light of Rosenberg's earlier value questionnaire and previous market research into values relating to automobile purchase.[20] The value items employed in this study are given in Table 1.

The second questionnaire consisted of four parts. The first part measured the importance to the subject of each of the 27 value items. The value importance measures were recorded on an eleven point bi-polar Likert-type scale with extremes labeled "provides me maximum satisfaction" and "provides me maximum dissatisfaction." The next three parts measured the subject's evaluation of the instrumentality of the three automobile brands in achieving or blocking attainment of the value item. An eleven point bi-polar

TABLE 1.   Value Items Used in the Value-Instrumentality Index

1. living a conservative life	15. socializing with other people
2. protecting against physical harm	16. projecting a young dynamic image
3. projecting a carefree image	17. being considered cautious by others
4. participating in risky situations	18. being admired by the opposite sex
5. displaying expensive material goods	19. being like others
6. being looked up to by others	20. being out of doors
7. experiencing change and variety	21. being good looking
8. achieving superiority over others	22. having new experiences
9. projecting a masculine image	23. being the center of attention
10. being thrifty	24. having power and authority over others
11. projecting an adventurous image	25. projecting a feminine image
12. possessing high quality goods	26. living a sensible life
13. projecting a mature image	27. having family approval of my views
14. associating with the opposite sex	

scale was again used with extremes of "strongly agree" and "strongly disagree." The response measured agreement with the statement that the purchase of a given automobile brand would enhance attainment of the relevant value item.

The data collection method above yielded three types of information for each individual over the three brands. First, brand appeal was obtained. Second, the importance of a set of value items to the individual was obtained. Third, the perceived role that the individual brands could play in the enhancing or blocking of each value item was measured.

Results

The null hypotheses in the study state that subject position on a univariate rating of brand appeal is not associated with value importance or attitude object instrumentality. For each subject, brand indices were computed that jointly reflected value-item importance and attitude object instrumentality. These indices reflected the summated product of value item importance and instrumentality measures across the 27 value items. The maximum and minimum possible index values were 675 and -675, respectively ($27 \times (\pm)$ $5 \times (\pm)$ 5). Observed index levels were considerably smaller in magnitude.

Initial tests of the hypotheses were statistically evaluated through Contingency Table analysis using two-by-two tables. Subjects were cross-classified by relative position on the appeal scale and relative value index scores. Split halves were determined for appeal and value index scores. The null hypothesis in each instance was that the dimensions were independent of one another.

Inter-Subject Brand Appeal and Value Index

The first major hypothesis test evaluated the association between brand appeal position and value index levels. Table 2 shows this Chi Square test of independence for Brands A, B, and C. The hypothesis of independence can be rejected at a high level of significance in each brand instance.

TABLE 2.   Brand Appeal and Value Index[a]

Brand	Index	Appeal	
		Low %	High %
A	Low	28	22
	High	17	31
	$P(X^2 > 4.178) = 0.041$		
B	Low	28	21
	High	19	30
	$P(X^2 > 3.312) = 0.069$		
C	Low	29	22
	High	18	29
	$P(X^2 > 3.378) = 0.066$		

[a]N = 98

The direction of association is also as expected. Greater appeal is associated with larger index levels. Therefore, value importance and attitude-object instrumentality do relate to brand appeal.

Brand Appeal and Instrumentality

A part of the value index, instrumentality, has been postulated to be the frequently measured affect component of attitude. Thus, given a large number of positive values, a relationship might be anticipated between appeal and affect. This condition holds in the present value index as it did in Rosenberg's. In order to compare appeal and affect, a brand instrumentality score was computed for each subject by simply summing this component over the 27 items. The statistical test for independence between brand appeal and instrumentality is indicated in Table 3 for the three brands.

TABLE 3.   Brand Appeal and Instrumentality[a]

Brand	Instrumentality	Appeal	
		Low %	High %
A	Low	27	21
	High	18	32
	$P(X^2 > 4.044) = 0.044$		
B	Low	30	18
	High	17	33
	$P(X^2 > 7.970) = 0.005$		
C	Low	27	24
	High	20	27
	$P(X^2 > 1.058) = 0.304$		

[a]N = 98

Independence is rejected at low risk levels in two of the three cases as might be expected. In addition, the directional association between the variables is positive as would be expected. However, in the Brand C analysis, independence would be accepted even at very high risk levels. Apparently, instrumentality by itself is not as consistent a predictor of the univariate appeal measure as is the value index. Instrumentality by itself does show a surprisingly strong association with appeal for Brand A and Brand B. As noted earlier, the large number of positive values in the index may account for the strength of the association. All subjects were undergraduate college students with relatively homogeneous value systems. More diversity existed among subjects regarding instrumentality than was the case with value importance. As the value systems of individuals converge, it would be expected that the value ratings should act as a constant in the index and contribute little to the explanation of brand appeal. As the value system heterogeneity increases through broadening the sample representation of the general population, the value importance measure should increase appeal predictability greatly.

Intra-Subject Brand Appeal and Value Index

The second major hypothesis of this study concerned comparative appeal measures across brands for each subject. It was predicted that each subject's differences in brand appeal as measured on the univariate scale could be explained by differences in the value indices of the respective brands.

The brand indices for a subject will contain a common value importance with different instrumentality measures. This evaluation is perhaps of more significance to the theory development presented earlier than was the analysis in Table 2 or Table 3. In any analysis across subjects using Likert-type scales, diversity exists among subject interpretation of polar extremes. However, each subject would be expected to interpret scale positions consistently from one brand to another.

The appeal and value index differences across brands can be evaluated with three different pairings (A-B, A-C, B-C). For each of the three pairs, differences in appeal and in value indices were obtained for the 98 subjects. It was predicted that divergence in brand appeal for two brands should be reflected in divergence in value indices for the respective brands. The test for independence between these two dimensions for the brand pairs, is given in Table 4.

TABLE 4. Relative Brand Appeal and Value Indices[a]

Brand Pair	Indices	Appeal	
		Low %	High %
A-B	Low	26	23
	High	14	35
	$P(X^2 > 6.083) = 0.014$		
A-C	Low	23	24
	High	13	38
	$P(X^2 > 5.785) = 0.016$		
B-C	Low	40	9
	High	25	24
	$P(X^2 > 10.280) = 0.001$		

[a]N = 98

The tests for independence are rejected at the .05 level of significance for all three brand pairs. As we anticipated, intra-subject comparisons yield a stronger link than was found in the inter-subject comparisons. The directional movements are also positive as would be postulated.

Discussion

In the first section of this paper major theoretical positions in the area of attitude research were outlined. Following this, a multidimensional view of attitude was presented and a framework of constructs for the research presented in this paper was developed. Instrumentality-value analysis was introduced as a means of relating values to attitude objects through a decoding process in the intervening cognitive set. This analysis bears upon important controversies in the area of attitude research.

Psychologists have studied attitudes for more than half a century. During this period, no commonly accepted definition has arisen. Two points of some agreement exist, however. One is that attitudes are learned through experience and the other is that they are related to behavior.[21] Only surface agreement exists on these two points.

Attitudes and Learning

Controversy exists about the process of learning. A range of positions regarding the process may be defined. At one extreme, the radical positivists such as Bain[22] and Horowitz,[23] define attitude as a direct response tendency with no variables intervening between the stimulus and the response tendency. At the other extreme are the Hullians and cognitive theorists who posit various kinds of constructs and feedback learning processes intervening between initial stimulus and response tendencies.[24] Although Hullians and cognitive theorists may be classed together on this particular spectrum, it should be noted they have little else in common and approach the process of intervening processes from very different perspectives.

Attitudes and Behavior

Agreement on the second major point, that attitudes are related to behavior is also limited. Most theorists agree that attitudes are at least directive in the determination of behavior. Controversy exists as to whether attitudes direct through an encoding or a decoding process.[25] McGuire[26] interprets Cantril and Sherif's "frame of reference," Campbell's "pattern of meaning," Miller and Dollard's "acquired distinctiveness of cue" and Lippman's "stereotype" to imply that encoding is a major determinant of behavior. However, theorists such as Allport and Doob[27] see attitudes as having energizing properties as well as directive properties. This dynamic view suggests that interaction properties may also direct behavior through intervening variables relating to the decoding process. Dissonance and other balance theories may be viewed as operating in a manner analogous to this.

Relevance to Marketers

The above two areas of surface agreement and underlying controversy about attitudes are of more than passing interest to the marketer. If one assumes the radical positivist stance in regard to the relationship between learning and attitudes, then serious questions are raised about the usefulness of any brand recall or brand attitude research in the traditional scale response manner. If a stance is taken which leaves open the possibility of intervening variables of a feedback or interactionist kind, then questions about the nature of these processes become of serious import.

Marketers regularly measure consumer brand knowledge and feelings toward their brand. It is important to know whether or not these measures actually correspond to any of the intervening variables. If they do, and enough evidence exists to make this a reasonable working hypothesis, then the next question focuses upon the possible existence of other intervening variables. Certainly, knowledge and feelings not directly related to the brand must also exist. In addition, it seems likely that needs and values comprise part of the intervening set.

Given the existence of variables such as those posited above, it becomes critical to determine the structure and processes involved in the intervening variable set. Two different theoretical positions selected from a range of possible positions, will suffice to indicate the importance of this inquiry to marketers. First, the structure of the intervening variables may be determined largely through an encoding of perceptual stimuli into certain patterns which lead directly to deterministic response sets. If this is the case, marketers should concentrate research efforts on perceptual processes. Individual differences, both socio-economic and psychological, may be accounted for in terms of stimulus reception variations. A second position might posit encoding of stimuli, then interaction through various secondary stimulus processes leading to the choice of response sets. This latter position indicates that for the marketer, the emphasis of inquiry must turn from exhaustive classification of stimulus input and response set outcome to a concentration of interest on intervening processes.

The present research has concentrated upon these intervening processes. The research provides a formal link among some of the components that may give rise to attitudes and attitude itself. The importance of values and the instrumentality of certain attitude objects for blocking or enhancing these values were measured and combined into an index. This index was used to predict univariate attitude object ratings. The index successfully differentiated attitude levels across subjects for a single attitude object. The index also successfully delineated across attitude objects for individual subjects.

Implications for Marketing Decision-Making

The implications for marketing decision-making are significant. Given that the index successfully delineates between those with favorable and those with unfavorable attitudes toward a marketer's product, an analysis of the index itself may provide strategic decision information. First, it can be determined through item analysis whether or not the two groups hold similar or dissimilar values. If it is found that those with unfavorable attitudes have different value systems, then a product change designed to enhance this value set might be in order. If on the other hand no significant differences in value sets can be determined, then the perceived instrumentality of the product should be subjected to scrutiny. All potential customers may hold prestige, for example, as an important value, but those with unfavorable attitudes may not perceive that ownership of the product supplies prestige. In this case, either a change in product or in the product's promotion might be warranted. The implication here is that value systems are likely to be relatively stable and not susceptible to change in the short run. The perceived instrumentality of the attitude object is probably more susceptible to change.

Notes and References

1. Robert J. Lavidge and Gary A. Steiner, "A Model for Predictive Measurements of Advertising Effectiveness," *Journal of Marketing.* Vol. XXV (October 1961), 59–62.

2. Note the criticisms of Lavidge & Steiner by Kristian S. Palda, "The Hypothesis of a Hierarchy of Effects: A Partial Evaluation," *Journal of Marketing Research,* Vol. III (February 1966), 13–24.

3. L. Festinger, "Behavioral Support for Opinion Change," *Public Opinion Quarterly,* Vol. XXVII (Fall 1965), 404–417.

4. Alan R. Andreasen, "Attitudes and Customer Behavior: A Decision Model," Lee E. Preston, Editor, *New Research in Marketing* (Berkeley, California: University of California Institute of Business and Economic Research, 1965), 1–16.

5. John A. Howard, *Marketing Managements: Analysis and Planning* (Homewood. Illinois: Richard D. Irwin, Inc., 1963) and John A. Howard and J. N. Sheth, "Theory of Buyer Behavior," in Reed Moyer, Editor, *Changing Marketing Systems: Consumer, Corporate and Government Interfaces* (Chicago, Illinois: American Marketing Association, Winter 1967), 253–262.

6. F. M. Nicosia, "Toward a Model of Consumer Decision-Making," *Proceedings AMA* (December 1962), 422–437; F. M. Nicosia, *Consumer Decision Processes* (Englewood Cliffs, New Jersey: Prentice-Hall, 1966).

7. R. B. Zajonc, "The Concepts of Balance, Congruity, and Dissonance," *Public Opinion Quarterly,* Vol. 24 (1960), 280–286.

8. L. Festinger, *A Theory of Cognitive Dissonance* (Stanford, Calif.: Stanford University Press, 1957); R. P. Abelson and M. J. Rosenberg, "Symbolic Psychologic: A Model of Attitudinal Cognition," *Behavioral Science,* Vol. 3 (1958), 1–13; C. E. Osgood, G. J. Suci, and P. H. Tannenbaum, *The Measurement of Meaning* (Urbana, Ill.: University of Illinois Press, 1957).

9. Palda, *loc. cit.*

10. D. Krech and R. S. Crutchfield, *Individual in Society* (New York, McGraw-Hill, 1962.

11. M. Sherif and H. Cantril, "The Psychology of Attitudes: I," *Psychological Review,* Vol. 52 (1945), 295–319; D. T. Campbell, The Generality of Social Attitudes, Doctoral Dissertation (University of California, Berkeley, 1947); D. Kretch, R. S. Crutchfield, and E. L. Ballachey, *Individual in Society* (New York: McGraw-Hill, 1962); R. Brown, *Social Psychology* (New York: Free Press, 1965).

12. L. Guttmen, "A Basis for Scaling Qualitative Data," *American Sociological Review,* Vol. 9 (1944), 139–150.

13. R. Likert, "A Technique for the Measurement of Attitudes," *Arch. Psychol.,* New York (1932), No. 140.

14. See references cited in footnote 8.

15. D. Katz and E. Stotland, "A Preliminary Statement of a Theory of Attitude Structure and Change," in S. Koch, Editor, *Psychology: Study of a Science,* Vol. 3 (New York: McGraw-Hill, 1959), 423–475.

16. For a more detailed explanation of this process, see Stewart W. Bither and Stephen J. Miller, "An Experimental Evaluation of Advertising Influence on Attitude Change," A Working Paper.

17. E. R. Carlson, "Attitude Change Through Modification of Attitude Structure," *Journal of Abnormal and Social Psychology,* Vol. 52 (1956), 256–261: Helen Peak, "Attitude and Motivation," in *Nebraska Symposium on Motivation,* Mr. R. Jones, Editor (Lincoln: University of Nebraska Press, 1955), 149–188; Helen Peak, "Psychological Structure and Psychological Activity," *Psychological Review,* Vol. 65 (1958), 325–347; M. J. Rosenberg, "Cognitive Structure and Attitudinal Effect," *Journal of Abnormal and Social Psychology,* Vol. 53 (1956), 367–372; M. J. Rosenberg, "Cognitive Reorganization in Response to the Hypnotic Reversal of Attitudinal Affect," *Journal of Personality,* Vol. 28 (1960), 39–63; M. J. Rosenberg, "An Analysis of Affective-Cognitive Consistency," in *Attitude Organization and Change,* C. I. Hovland and M. J. Rosenberg, Editors (New Haven: Yale University Press, 1960), 15–64; R. B. Zajonc, "The Process of Cognitive Turning in Communication," *Journal of Abnormal and Social Psychology,* Vol. 61 (1960), 159–167.

18. Milton J. Rosenberg, "Inconsistency Arousal and Reduction in Attitude Change," *The Public Opinion Quarterly,* Vol. 24 (1960), 319–340.

19. Franklin B. Evans, "You Still Can't Tell a Ford Owner from a Chevrolet Owner," *Journal of Business* (January 1961), 67–73; Charles Wineck, "The Relationship Among Personality Needs, Objective Factors and Brand Choice: A Re-examination," *Journal of Business* (January 1961), 61–66; Franklin B. Evans and Harry V.

Roberts, "Fords, Chevrolets, and the Problem of Discrimination," *Journal of Business* (April 1963), 242–249.

20. Rikuma Ito, "Differential Attitudes of New Car Buyers," *Journal of Advertising Research,* Vol. 7 (March 1967), 38–42; Nelson Foote, Editor, *Household Decision-Making,* Vol. IV (New York University Press, 1961).

21. William J. McGuire, "The Nature of Attitudes and Attude Change," in *The Handbook of Social Psychology,* Second Edition, Gardner Lindzey and Elliot Aronson, Editors (Reading, Mass.: Addison-Wesley Publishing Company, 1968), Vol. 3, 136–314.

22. R. Bain, "An Attitude on Attitude Research," *American Journal of Sociology,* Vol. 33 (1928), 940–957.

23. E. L. Horowitz, "Race Attitudes," in *Characteristics of the American Negro*, O. Klineberg, Editor (New York: Harper, 1944), 139–247.

24. L. W. Doob, "Some Factors Determining Change in Attitude," *Journal of Abnormal and Social Psychology,* Vol. 35 (1940), 549–565; C. E. Osgood, *Method and Theory in Experimental Psychology* (New York: Oxford University Press, 1953); L. Berkowitz, *Aggression: A Social Psychological Analysis* (New York: McGraw-Hill, 1962).

25. Zajonc, *loc. cit.*

26. McGuire, *loc. cit.*

27. G. W. Allport, "Attitudes," in *Handbook of Social Psychology,* C. Murchison, Editor (Worcester, Mass.: Clark University Press, 1935), 798–884; L. W. Doob, "The Behavior of Attitudes," *Psychological Review,* Vol. 54 (1947), 135–156.

3.4 Consumer Choice Behavior: An Experimental Approach
FLEMMING HANSEN

Many variables have been proposed as intervening between the communication consumers receive and the choices they make. Palda [21] lists attitudes, preferences, and images as common variables. Generally more is known about how communication influences these variables [6, 14, 16] than about how the variables influence consumer choices. This article presents some theoretical considerations and experimental results pertinent to the latter question.

What happens when a consumer is faced with several alternatives among brands, products, etc.? Sometimes the consumer simply repeats a response that proved satisfactory in previous similar situations. No real choice is made, no conflict is experienced, and no intervening variables are at work. In other instances, however, the consumer finds a conflict among alternative responses and releases energy to reduce conflict and make the choice.

Consumer choices are made in several ways, ranging from complicated, conscious decision-making processes to quick judgments. However, consumers usually make choices that fall between these two extremes. Commonly, two sets of factors are at work: (1) values, goals, or motives by which alternatives are evaluated and (2) attitudes about the alternatives that relate them to the values [11].

Several researchers have described the individual's total value structure [2, 19, 23]. However, only a few of these values are salient in any given decision situation because the individual can only handle a few factors [18] and the amount of energy released for the decision is limited [4]. Which values will be salient depends on the total decision-making situation. Such factors as the novelty and complexity of the situation have been shown to be important [4], as well as the extent to which the situation involves the consumer.

Given the salient values, the choice will depend on two independent factors: (1) the importance of these values and (2) the extent to which the alternatives favor the values. In this article these two factors will be called "value importance" and "perceived instrumentality" [23].

Value importance is how concepts affect decisions. For example, in a choice between two restaurants the concept of "intimacy" may (consciously or unconsciously) be salient. Intimacy of restaurants can be evaluated positively or negatively and mainly depends on past experiences. If the consumer has had pleasant experiences associated with intimate restaurants, the effect will be positive, and unpleasant experiences will have a negative effect. More generally the effect (or the value's importance) depends on the amount of positive or negative reward previously associated with the value.

Perceived instrumentality reflects the extent to which an alternative favors the consumer's salient values. The more intimate a restaurant is regarded, the more instrumental it is for the value "intimacy." The alternatives are evaluated along as many dimensions as there are salient values. It will be seen that the total perceived instrumentality resembles the image of the alternative (product or brand) [21], except that all aspects to which no salient values correspond are disregarded. Thus the perceived instrumentality may vary among decision situations because of changes in the salient values.

If, in a given decision situation, one knows the importance of the salient values and the perceived instrumentality of the alternatives, the outcome of the decision can be predicted. Given the perceived instrumentality of the alternatives with regard to a salient value, the greater the importance of the value, the more likely the alternative most instrumental to that value will be chosen. On the other hand, the more instrumental one alternative is to a salient value, the more likely it will be chosen. This principle can be formulated as:

(1)
$$A_1 = \sum_{j=1}^{m} V_j I_{j_1}$$

where

A_1 is overall attractiveness of Alternative 1
V_j is value importance of the jth value
I_{j_1} is perceived instrumentality of Alternative 1 with regard to value j
m is number of salient values.

The sign of $V_j I_{j1}$ depends on the signs of V_j and I_{j1}. If they are both positive or both negative, the combined expression is positive, but if V_j and I_{j1} have opposite signs, the combined expression is negative. The larger the A-measure, the more attractive is the alternative in question. If A-measures are computed for all the alternatives, the one with the highest A-measure will be chosen.

If only two alternatives are considered, the difference between the two attractiveness scores may be rewritten as:

$$(2) \qquad A_{1-2} = A_1 - A_2 = \sum_{j=1}^{m} V_j (I_{j1} - I_{j2})$$

This formulation makes it possible to deal with the differences in perceived instrumentality instead of the absolute instrumentality of each alternative. This will often make applications easier.

Application of the Model

In summary, it has been proposed that consumer choices are influenced by values salient in the decision situation and the way the alternatives are perceived. Compared with traditional attitude models (see, for example, [15]), this article suggests a more complex picture of the consumer decision process. One main advantage of traditional attitude models is the ease with which measurements can be obtained. A major disadvantage is the model's only moderate success in predicting consumer choices [1, 3, 10]. The present model is expected to give considerably better predictions, but at the expense of increased complexity.

The importance of salient values raises several questions which will be discussed:

1. Can value importance (effect) be measured?
2. Can salient values in a given decision situation be predicted?
3. Can more easily measured values at one level in the individual's value structure be substituted for values which are less easily quantified?

Value importance or effect can be measured. Most techniques used in attitude studies are ultimately aimed at measuring the affective aspects associated with the attitude object. Perhaps this is most evident in the evaluative dimension of the semantic differential [20], but other techniques give essentially the same information.

It is difficult to predict which values will be salient in a given situation. This problem is common to all research, but there are no procedures that give direct answers to this kind of open question. Less important values can be eliminated to concentrate on the significant ones only to the extent that relevant consumer decision situations can be specified and hypotheses formulated as to salient values.

The question of substituting easily measured values is closely related to the previous one. It also deals with the selection of values to be incorporated in consumer choice studies. The problem is illustrated by the following example. In some situations consumers may ascribe high importance to durability.

However, closer analysis reveals that in itself durability is not rewarding. Durability gains importance only to the extent that it implies reduced repair expenses and postponed repurchase. Consequently, the question is whether to measure the value importance of durability itself or of values at other levels in the consumer's value structure. The question becomes more complicated when one realizes that most values can be measured at several different levels. To the extent that the relationship between values at different levels is fixed and predictable, one may substitute values at one level for values at another level. However, as long as we do not know more about the relationship among such values,[1] it seems advisable to attempt to operate with the values the consumer applies to the decision process.

Measuring perceived instrumentality is less complicated. When values are defined, the dimensions for measuring perceived instrumentality are also defined. Besides, what is measured in much advertising and marketing research closely resembles perceived instrumentality. As pointed out, image studies deal essentially with perceived instrumentality of products and brands, and many techniques are available for measuring images. Usually it is also possible to have respondents rate perceived instrumentality directly along the relevant dimensions.

With value importance and perceived instrumentality measured, it is possible to predict choices based on either (1) or (2). The experiments to be presented here sought primarily to verify this, but for the procedure to be useful two further requirements must be met. First, the procedure should lead to better predictions than those based on traditional attitude scales. Second, both value importance and perceived instrumentality should add significantly to the prediction, and the combined expression should make better predictions than either of the components taken separately.

It would have been ideal to have two sets of measures, one that explains the situational influence on the choice, and one that explains the influence of the consumer's salient values. If such measures were obtainable, the first would vary from situation to situation to show small differences among individuals. However, the second set of variables would vary among consumers, but for the same consumer it should remain stable across situations.

Value importance and perceived instrumentality do not have these ideal properties. Both are influenced by the situation, and both depend on the consumer's past experiences. However, it is expected that value importance is more stable and less influenced by communication than perceived instrumentality, since it is part of the individual's total value structure.

On the other hand, perceived instrumentality is mainly a function of product experiences, advertising, communication in the store, package and word of mouth advertising. This is not to say the marketer cannot influence value importance, but this would be more expensive and time-consuming than any attempt to influence perceived instrumentality. Although the marketer does not have complete control over the consumer's perceived instrumentality either, he controls relatively more factors determining this variable. In an attempt to confirm this view, interest has been focused on whether advertising mainly influences value importance or perceived instrumentality, whether value importance can be measured independently of the decision situation and still add to choice prediction, and whether the same measure of value importance can add significantly to the prediction of choices in different situations and among different products.

Earlier it was assumed that in any decision situation the number of salient values is small, since it is difficult to work with the model otherwise. Consequently, in this experimental work the number of values entering into different decision situations has also been studied.

Hypotheses

In this article a model of consumer choice behavior is presented with several requirements. Six experiments tested the extent to which these requirements are met. These are reflected in the following six hypotheses:

1. Perceived instrumentality and value importance can be measured and based on these measures; predictions of consumer choices can be made using equations (1) and (2).
2. The model will make predictions superior to those made from a traditional attitude measurement.
3. Value importance and instrumentality are highly independent and are determined by different factors.
4. Both value importance and perceived instrumentality add significantly to the prediction of consumer choices.
5. Value importance is more stable than perceived instrumentality.
6. For a single consumer the number of salient values in a given decision situation is small.

Experimental Procedure

It would be preferable to study consumer decisions in real-life situations. However, the information that can be obtained from such studies is incomplete. Here perceived instrumentality and value importance are of special interest, since they occur in the decision situation. These variables cannot be measured in real-life decision situations, since it is not known exactly when the decision is made.

To obtain measures that relate to the choice in a known way, it is necessary to manipulate the choice. Faced with problems of this kind, experimenters have often turned to simulated choices [5, 9, 22, 25]. The same approach is used here. In all six experiments subjects were asked to simulate consumer decisions for different situational descriptions with various alternatives.

Experiment 1 (First Hairdryer Choice)

In this experiment 80 male junior students at the Whittemore School of Business and Economics were asked to choose between two hairdryers to be used as a gift. The hairdryer was used since it was desirable to have a product with which subjects probably had no previous experiences. Thereby subjects could be expected to rely heavily on the material presented.

The descriptions of the hairdryers centered on their durability, efficiency, and price. Since it was desirable to have a certain number of choices of each hairdryer (named Schnell and Varig), the prices were varied so that some subjects would choose the Varig and others would choose the Schnell. This also made it possible to study the influence of price variations on value importance and perceived instrumentality.

Four different price combinations were applied. Half the subjects made their choice after rating perceived instrumentality and value importance, and the other half made their choice before rating. Hence, 8 (2 × 4) experimental conditions were applied. The rating-before-choice and choice-before-rating variation were used to compare post- and pre-decision processes.[2] This article considers results of the rating-before-choice conditions.

In this experiment value importance was measured before and after the situation was described. Subjects were presented with 11-point scales ranging from zero to one and were asked to rate the importance of price, efficiency, and durability. Perceived instrumentality was only measured after the situational description since the alternatives were not known before. These variables were rated on similar 11-point scales where "1" was attached to "Varig (Schnell) extremely more durable, (expensive, efficient)" and "0" to "no difference at all." Based on these measures the attractiveness score (A) can be computed with (2).

Experiment 2 (Second Hairdryer Choice)

This experiment used another group of 34 male students in a basic marketing class at the University of New Hampshire. The experiment used an almost identical procedure, but with the following main differences:

1. The situational description contained a detailed account of a fictional person, "Mr. Blomberg," and the choice was to be made on his behalf. Subjects were told that Mr. Blomberg wanted to buy a hairdryer for his wife.
2. The description of the two hairdryers differed in that the Varig alternative was described more favorably than in the first experiment.
3. The experimental design was different. A 2 × 2 factorial design was used with rating-before-choice and choice-before-rating conditions as in the first experiment, but with no price differences. Instead, the situational description was varied. Half the subjects were told the wife favored an efficient hairdryer, but the other subjects did not have this information.

Experiment 3 (Restaurant Choice)

Part of this experiment and the following two tested the hypothesis that different choices can be predicted from the same value measures. Consequently, in these experiments the same subjects were used—89 undergraduate male and female students at the University of New Hampshire. The situational description told subjects that during a stay in a large city they were to choose between two restaurants. Since the same subjects made several decisions, the order of the choices was reversed. Also, choice-before-rating and rating-before-choice conditions were applied.

Compared with the first two experiments, this one applied considerably more values. The two restaurants were described along as many as ten dimensions (expensiveness, intimacy, kind of food served, etc.). Consequently, both value importance and perceived instrumentality were rated on ten different scales.

Value importance was measured in much the same way as in the first two experiments, but the measurement of perceived instrumentality differed somewhat. In the first two experiments subjects were asked to rate the relative advantage of one alternative; in this experiment subjects rated the absolute instrumentality of both alternatives. That is, for each value measures were obtained on two 11-point scales, ranging from "extremely expensive (intimate, etc.)" to "not expensive (intimate, etc.) at all." Based on these measures, overall attractiveness (A) was computed using (1).

Here, as in the first two experiments, the values were closely related to the specific choice situation. Except for a few values, such as "price," the same values could not be applied to different decisions. Instead, more general values had to be applied. For this experiment general values were selected by first making a list of approximately 200 value statements taken from [2, 7, 19, 24]. Then 24 values were selected from the basic list. These values, such as independence, socializing and strict moral standards, were applicable to the three choices but not closely interrelated.[3]

Before the situations were described, subjects were asked to rate the importance of the 24 values on 21-point scales ranging from "the attainment of this value gives me maximum satisfaction" to "the attainment of this value gives me maximum dissatisfaction" with the zero point as "gives me neither satisfaction nor dissatisfaction." After introduction of the situational description and several filler items in between, the values were restated and subjects were asked how instrumental to the values they considered the alternatives to be. This again was done on 21-point scales ranging from "this value is completely attained by going to (name of restaurant)" to "this value is completely blocked by going to (name of restaurant)" with the zero point labeled "completely irrelevant." Based on these measures a second set of attractiveness scores were computed using (1).

Experiment 4 (Book Choice)

For this experiment subjects were the same as in the previous one. A 2×2 factorial design was used with conditions of choice-before-rating and rating-before-choice. Also, an experimental variation was introduced by telling half the subjects they could keep the book they chose, an offer the other subjects were not given. This variation was to reveal differences, if any, between the simulated choice and a real choice.[4]

The situational description presented subjects with a choice between two books, both of which were handed out for inspection. None of the subjects were familiar with the alternatives before the experiment.[5] Both books were selected as likely to appeal to college students without being too similar. Value importance and instrumentality were only measured for the 24 values described earlier.

Experiment 5 (Travel Choice)

In this experiment subjects were told that for a vacation in Europe they could choose to go by boat or plane. Since subjects were assumed to be familiar with both alternatives, preference for boat versus plane, value importance and perceived instrumentality could be measured before the situation was described.

In a 2 × 2 factorial design subjects were assigned to four conditions, choice-before-rating, rating-before-choice, and two different situational descriptions. The first of these described the situation and gave the alternatives. The second introduced copy from two ads for a major ocean line. The ads were from recent issues of the *Boston Herald Traveller* and *Time* and described the boat trip as pleasant and fashionable. This experimental variation was introduced to study whether this kind of material would mainly influence value importance, perceived instrumentality, or both.

Rating was conducted as in the third experiment, the only difference being that perceived instrumentality was measured both before and after the situation was described.

Experiment 6 (Menu Choice)

This experiment tested whether the model can predict choices among several alternatives. Again subjects were (90) male and female students at the University of New Hampshire. Subjects were told that they were to imagine themselves seated in a specific restaurant; half in a popular steak house, and half in an intimate French restaurant.

All rating was done before introduction of the situational description. First, 16 menu items were rated for liking on 21-point scales ranging from "like extremely well," to "dislike extremely." Then nine fixed menus were rated for overall liking, expensiveness, and heaviness. Finally, value importance was rated in connection with liking, expensiveness and heaviness. Based on these measures overall attractiveness was computed for each of the nine menus offered for choice using Equation 1.

Results

Hypothesis 1: Prediction of Choice

In all but one experiment either relative attractiveness or attractiveness of each alternative could be predicted. How well these scores predicted the choices can be tested by comparing the evaluations of chosen and rejected alternatives (see Table 1).

In all but one case the attractiveness scores varied significantly between chosen and rejected alternatives. Since all but one of the results were based on measurements before the choice (in the second experiment perceived instrumentality was measured after the choice), it can be concluded that the attractiveness score predicts the outcome of the decisions.

Hypothesis 2: Predictions Based on Attitude Measures

It may be argued that results like those presented in Table 1 could have been obtained using a simple attitude rating scale. To test this, preference ratings were obtained in the travel choice experiment from two 11-point scales.

TABLE 1.   Attractiveness Scores for Chosen Alternatives
(Measured after situation)

Choice	Chosen Alternative	Rejected Alternative
First Hairdryer (n = 41)[c]		
First Alternative	0.456[a]	N.A.
Second Alternative	0.287[a]	N.A.
Second Hairdryer (n = 34)[c]		
First Alternative	0.860[a]	N.A.
Second Alternative	−0.153[a]	N.A.
Restaurant (n = 43)		
First Alternative[d]	1.110	0.326
Second Alternative[e]	1.204	0.976
Travel (n = 41)[c]		
First Alternative	0.380[a]	N.A.
Second Alternative	−0.554[a]	N.A.
Menu (n = 90)[c]	0.386	−0.091[b]

[a]Relative advantage of first alternative compared with second alternative.
[b]Average for eight rejected alternatives.
[c]Difference significant at $p \leq 0.001$ (t-test).
[d]Difference significant at $p \leq 0.01$ (t-test).
[e]Difference significant at $p \leq 0.15$ (t-test).
[f]N.A. is not available.

As discussed earlier, it was possible to obtain these ratings before the situation was described.

The plane trip was the most positively evaluated alternative. Despite this, the boat trip was preferred by a majority of the subjects. This was reflected in the rating of alternatives. The chosen alternative received an average rating of .769 as opposed to a rating of .685 for the rejected alternative, a difference that is not significant.

However, these ratings are not directly comparable with the results in Table 1, which are based on ratings completed after the situational description was introduced. Consequently, the comparison should be made with the measures of perceived instrumentality and value measure obtained before the situation was described. Computed from these measures the average attractiveness score for the chosen alternative becomes .414 as opposed to an attractiveness score for the rejected alternative of .238. The difference is significant at the .05 level.

Hypothesis 3: Relationship Between Value Importance and Perceived Instrumentality

From the six experiments it is possible to analyze 175 different correlations between corresponding measures of value importance and perceived instrumentality. From a listing of these a random sample of approximately 10 percent was drawn, or 18 correlation coefficients. Since none of these were significant, it can be concluded that value importance and perceived instrumentality are highly independent.

Hypothesis 4: Choices Predicted Based on Value Importance and Instrumentality Separately

The fourth hypothesis stated that both value importance and perceived instrumentality add significantly to the quality of the overall predictions. This was tested with data from the two hairdryer experiments, the restaurant choice experiment, and the travel choice experiment.

To test this hypothesis it was necessary to compute the total value importance and the total perceived instrumentality for each alternative. Table 2 gives a typical summary for a single subject in one of the hairdryer experiments. In computing the total relative perceived instrumentality for this subject the figures in the third column were added to give five. Whether perceived instrumentality predicts the choice made was tested by computing similar perceived instrumentality for all subjects and comparing the averages among subjects choosing either of the two alternatives (see Table 3).

Table 3 shows that perceived instrumentality added to the overall prediction. Furthermore, a comparison of the significance levels in Table 1 with those in Table 3 shows that the overall attractiveness score was a better predictor than perceived instrumentality alone.

Value importance was treated similarly. However, in totaling it was necessary to apply the sign on the value determined by the measure of perceived instrumentality (see Table 2). Results from these computations are also presented in Table 3. It can be seen also that value importance added to the overall prediction. By comparing this with Table 1, it can be concluded that value importance taken alone is a poorer predictor than the overall attractiveness score.

In conclusion, both value importance and perceived instrumentality added to the predictive value of the overall attractiveness score, but neither of them taken separately was as good a predictor as the overall score.

Hypothesis 5: Stability of Value Importance and Perceived Instrumentality

To what extent are value importance and perceived instrumentality influenced by environmental and other factors? To study this question several approaches were tried.

TABLE 2. Sample Computational Sheet from First Hairdryer Experiment

Subject	Value Importance (1)	Perceived Instrumentality (2)	Attractiveness (1) × (2)
Efficiency	.3	−.3	−.09
Durability	.4	.2	.08
Price	.5	.6	.30
Total Advantage of Varig Over Schnell	.6[a]	.5	.29

[a]Sign applied from Column 2.

TABLE 3.   Perceived Instrumentality and Value Importance for Chosen Alternatives

Choice	Average Perceived Instrumentality Among Subjects Choosing		Average Value Importance Among Subjects Choosing	
	First Alternative	Second Alternative	First Alternative	Second Alternative
Restaurant (n = 43)	1.755[c]	1.685[c]	0.348[c]	1.081[c]
Travel (n = 41)	0.093[c]	−0.323[c]	12.266[b]	0.323[b]
First Hairdryer (n = 41)	0.756[b]	0.496[b]	0.830[b]	0.393[b]
Second Hairdryer (n = 34)	1.041[a]	0.043[a]	0.646[b]	0.480[b]

[a] Difference significant at $p \leq 0.001$ (t-test).
[b] Difference significant at $p \leq 0.01$ (t-test).
[c] Difference not significant.

In Experiments 1, 2, and 5, 22 comparisons were made between identical values measured before and after introduction of the situational description. Of these, ten changed significantly (at the .05 level).

The relative stability of values was tested further with data from Experiments 3, 4, and 5 in which the 24 basic values were applied. In all three experiments the same 24 values could be used for predictions. The more stable the values, the better these predictions. Based on the 24 values and corresponding perceived instrumentalities, attractiveness scores were computed (Table 4).

In all three experiments the attractiveness score was higher for the chosen than for the rejected alternative. However, these predictions were poorer than those presented in Table 1. This may be ascribable to the values chosen for study or situational influence on value importance. In any event, the results do not support the view that values are completely independent of the situations.

To test the stability of value importance and perceived instrumentality, advertising copy was introduced in the travel experiment, price was varied in Experiment 1, and the situational description was varied in Experiment 2. In these experiments comparisons were made among nine pairs of value measures

TABLE 4.   Attractiveness Scores Based on 24 Values

Choice	Chosen Alternative	Rejected Alternative
Restaurant[a] (n = 41)	2.450[b]	1.726[b]
Travel[a] (n = 39)	3.305[b]	2.465[b]
Book (n = 48)	3.548[c]	3.040[c]

[a] Two subjects deleted since all questions were not completed.
[b] Difference significant at $p \leq 0.10$ (t-test).
[c] Difference significant at $p \leq 0.15$ (t-test).

TABLE 5.   Attractiveness Scores of Travel Choice Based on Measures Before and
After Situation

Time of Measurement	Boat Choosers	Plane Choosers	Difference in Attractiveness Score
Value importance and perceived instrumentality measured after situation	−0.554	0.380	.934[a]
Value importance measured before and perceived instrumentality measured after situation	0.024	0.492	.468[b]
Value importance and perceived instrumentality measured before situation	0.285	0.439	.154[c]

[a]Difference significant at $p \leq 0.001$ (t-test).
[b]Difference significant at $p \leq 0.10$.
[c]Difference not significant.

and among nine pairs of instrumentality measures. Of the value importance
measures, two differed significantly between subjects exposed to different
situational descriptions. So again we find some indication of situational influence on value importance. One measure of perceived instrumentality also
differed significantly.

In the travel choice experiment values and perceived instrumentality
were measured before and after the situation was described. Thus, it is possible
to compare predictions based on (a) value importance and perceived instrumentality measured after the situation is described, (b) value importance
measured before and perceived instrumentality measured after the situation,
and (c) both variables measured before the situation is described.

Table 5 presents the three sets of attractiveness scores. It can be seen
that introducing value importance measures obtained independently of the
situation decreased the difference between the attractiveness scores, and that
the difference decreased further when perceived instrumentality was also
measured before the situation.

In conclusion, value importance depends on the actual situation. However, measures of value importance obtained in other situations add to choice
prediction. It is more doubtful to so conclude with regard to perceived instrumentality, since few relevant data are available.

Hypothesis 6: Number of Salient Values

In most of the experiments the number of important aspects was limited
to the extent that the situational descriptions only presented information pertinent to a limited number of values. However, it is possible for subjects to
reduce further the number of aspects considered. If either value importance or
perceived instrumentality is rated zero, it implies that this aspect does not
influence the attractiveness score. Table 6 shows the number of aspects that

entered into the attractiveness scores in the six experiments together with the maximum possible number. It can be seen that in the experiments with more experimentally introduced values the tendency to reduce the number of salient values is more evident.

This problem can also be approached differently. In Experiments 3, 4, and 5 measures were obtained on 24 value dimensions. Table 6 shows that a considerable reduction in the number of values occurred, though the number is still large. However, from the raw data it is clear that a limited number of values accounted for most of the difference in the attractiveness scores. To pursue this further, the three most important values were taken for each subject, and attractiveness scores were computed. These predictions were as good as those based on the total number of values. This further emphasizes that the number of values actually influencing the choice is limited. How many values one should consider deserves further testing, but the number of salient values seems not so large as to make it impossible to apply the model in practical marketing research.

TABLE 6.   Number of Salient Values in Choices

Choice	Based on limited number of values		Based on 24 Values
	Maximum	Actual	
Restaurant	10	8.39	12.14
Book		N.A.[a]	17.58
Menu	3	2.82	N.A.[a]
Travel	6	4.54	12.91
First Hairdryer	3	2.95	N.A.[a]
Second Hairdryer	3	2.94	N.A.

[a]N.A. is not available.

Conclusion

It has been suggested that predictions of consumer choices can be based on the values the consumer consciously or unconsciously applies in decision situations, and the way in which he relates the alternatives to these values. This article showed it is possible and worthwhile to distinguish between these two sets of variables. It has also been suggested that value importance can be measured more or less independently of the choice situation, but perceived instrumentality and the selection of values applied depend largely on the decision situation. Therefore it becomes important to study the kinds of situations in which consumers make decisions, a problem rarely considered in marketing contexts. This together with studies of consumer decision processes are promising areas for future research.

Notes

1. Most studies dealing with the relationship between values emphasize their close interconnection. See [8, 17, 20, 24].

2. Results pertinent to this question are discussed in [13].

3. A few of the values were actually significantly correlated. However, since the correlation coefficients were small, all 24 values were retained in the subsequent tabulations.

4. No significant differences were found in choice, decision time and uncertainty about the choice. Ratings in the rating-before-choice conditions were similar, but those in the choice-before-rating conditions differed indicating that real choice mainly differs from simulated choice in post-decisional processes.

5. The alternatives were recently published books retailing at approximately $5.00 (*Les Belles Images,* Simone de Beauvoir, Ronald Press, 1967; and *Queen Victoria's Bomb,* Ronald Clark, William Morrow and Co., Inc., 1968).

References

1. Lee Adler, "Can Attitudes Predict Behavior?" in John S. Wright and Jac L. Goldstucker, eds., *New Ideas for Successful Marketing, Proceedings*, 1966 World Congress, Chicago: American Marketing Association (1966), 348–352.

2. Gordon W. Allport, Philip E. Vernon and Gardner Lindzey, *Study of Values,* 3rd ed., Boston: Houghton Mifflin Company, 1960.

3. Valentine Apple, "Attitude Change: Another Dubious Method for Measuring Advertising Effectiveness," in Lee Adler and Irving Crespi, eds., *Attitude Research at Sea,* Chicago: American Marketing Association (1966), 141–152.

4. Daniel E. Berlyne, *Conflict, Arousal and Curiosity,* New York: McGraw-Hill Book Co., 1960.

5. Jack W. Brehm and Arthur R. Cohen, *Explorations in Cognitive Dissonance,* New York: McGraw-Hill Book Co., 1962.

6. Edgar Crane, *Marketing Communication,* New York: John Wiley & Sons, Inc., 1965.

7. Allen L. Edwards, *Edwards Personal Preference Schedule,* New York: The Psychological Corporation, 1953.

8. Leon Festinger, *A Theory of Cognitive Dissonance,* Stanford, Calif.: Stanford University Press, 1957.

9. ———, *Conflict, Decision and Dissonance,* Stanford, Calif.: Stanford University Press, 1964.

10. ———, "Behavioral Support for Opinion Change," *Public Opinion Quarterly,* Vol. 28 (Fall 1964), 404–417.

11. Martin Fishbein, "Attitudes and Prediction of Behavior," in Martin Fishbein, ed., *Readings in Attitude Theory and Measurement,* New York: John Wiley & Sons, Inc., (1967), 477–492.

12. Flemming Hansen, "An Attitude Model for Analyzing Consumer Behavior," in Lee Adler and Irving Crespi, eds., *Attitude Research on the Rocks,* Chicago: American Marketing Association, 1968.

13. ———, "An Experimental Test of a Consumer Choice Model," in *Marketing and the New Science of Planning, Proceedings,* Fall Conference. Chicago: American Marketing Association, 1968.

14. Carl J. Hovland, Irving L. Janis and Harold H. Kelley, *Communication and Persuasion,* New Haven, Conn.: Yale University Press, 1953.

15. George Katona, *The Powerful Consumer,* New York: McGraw-Hill Book Co., 1960.

16. Joseph T. Klapper, *The Effects of Mass Communication,* Glencoe, Ill.: The Free Press, 1960.

17. William J. McGuire, "Cognitive Consistency and Attitude Change," *Journal of Abnormal and Social Psychology,* Vol. 60 (May 1960), 345–353.

18. George A. Miller, "The Magic Number Seven, Plus and Minus Two: Some Limits on Our Capacity for Processing Information," *Psychological Review,* Vol. 63 (March 1956), 81–97.

19. Henry A. Murray, *Explorations in Personality,* New York: Science Editions, Inc., 1962.

20. Charles E. Osgood, George J. Suci and Percy H. Tannenbaum, *The Measurement of Meaning,* Urbana, Ill.: University of Illinois Press, 1957.

21. Kristian S. Palda, "The Hypothesis of a Hierarchy of Effects: A Partial Evaluation," *Journal of Marketing Research,* Vol. 3 (Feb. 1966), 13–25.

22. Edgar A. Pessemier and Richard D. Teach, "Pricing Experiments, Scaling Consumer Preferences, and Predicting Purchase Behavior": in Raymond M. Hass, ed., *Science Technology & Marketing, Proceedings,* Fall Conference, Chicago: American Marketing Association, 1966.

23. Milton Rokeach, *The Open and Closed Mind,* New York: Basic Books, 1960.

24. Milton J. Rosenberg, "Cognitive Structure and Attitudinal Effect," *Journal of Abnormal and Social Psychology,* Vol. 53 (Fall 1956), 367–372.

25. ———, and Robert P. Abelson, "An Analysis of Cognitive Balancing," in Milton J. Rosenberg, *et al.,* eds., *Attitude Organization and Change,* New Haven, Conn.: Yale University Press (1960), 112–163.

3.5 Cognitive Consistency and Consumer Behavior

BOBBY J. CALDER

In developing psychological models of consumer behavior, a family of concepts called cognitive consistency theories may prove very powerful. These theories postulate, not logical, but psychological operations. In this sense they may provide a valuable supplement to the more rationalistic treatments of consumer behavior. Although consistency theories have received *some* attention with regard to consumer processes, their potential has not been generally recognized. This discussion briefly reviews three of the major consistency approaches and notes some of the more promising relevant research evidence from the social psychology, communication, and marketing literatures. The goal is to establish the relevance of cognitive consistency to consumer behavior and to point out some directions for further research.

Cognitive consistency is perhaps most relevant to consumer behavior in terms of attitude theory. The basic notion behind all of the consistency concepts is that people are motivated to maintain a state of psychological harmony within the system of beliefs and attitudes about a given issue or situation. The various approaches to cognitive consistency differ mostly in the manner in which they attempt to characterize the psychological processes involved in attaining this equilibrium.

Balance Theory

One line of research dealing with cognitive consistency is closely associated with the pioneering work of Fritz Heider. Heider (1946, 1958) was concerned mainly with our perception of the social world. Various perceptual constancies received considerable attention from the early Gestalt psychologists. For instance, most people see the lines below not as a series of eight vertical lines but as a set of four pairs of vertical lines:

It seems that we are biased toward creating such perceptual unity or harmony. Heider's contribution was to extend this thinking to the way people perceive social events.

The social events of principal interest to Heider consisted of three elements in a given person's experience, the person himself (symbolized P), some other person (symbolized 0), and some event, idea, or object (symbolized X). (See Figure 1.) Two types of beliefs relating these cognitive elements in the P-O-X system were postulated. Each type may be positive or negative. Sentiment relations refer to beliefs that two elements are connected by liking (+) or disliking (−), favorable feelings (+) or unfavorable (−) feelings, or some other evaluative relation. Unit relations refer to beliefs that two elements belong together (+) or do not belong together (−) in some sense, e.g., P buys X or O owns X. It was Heider's purpose to explore any systematic tendencies people possess in cognitively organizing a P-O-X system. He proposed that people attempt to maintain a psychological state called balance in which there is no strain or stress in a system. A system is balanced if all three of the signs of the relations between P, O, and X are positive or if any two signs are negative and one is positive. If only one sign is negative and the other two are positive or if all three are negative, a system is imbalanced. Thus, the system P buys X, P admires O, and O buys X is balanced whereas P buys X, P admires O, but O never buys X is imbalanced. Heider postulated that people attempt to restore balance in an imbalanced system by changing the signs of the relations. In the imbalanced system just mentioned, balance could be obtained by changing the perceived relation between P and X so that P never buys X, P admires O, and O never buys X.

Heider's formulation of balance theory has proven valuable in stimulating research. Cartwright and Harary (1956) formalized the theory using mathematical graph theory and extended it to relations between N elements. This work gives a general principle for determining balance: Balance exists if the product of all the signs is positive, imbalance if the product is negative.

Empirical support for the notion of balance has been obtained from

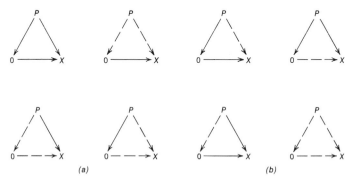

FIGURE 1.   Examples of balanced and unbalanced states according to Heider's definition of balance. Solid lines represent positive, and broken lines negative, relations. (a) Balanced states. (b) Unbalanced states. Source: R. B. Zajonc, "The concepts of balance, congruity, and dissonance," *The Public Opinion Quarterly*, Vol. 24 (Summer 1960), 280–296.

two types of studies. The first simply presents a subject with hypothetical relationships and asks him to rate the pleasantness of each one. It is predicted that balanced relationships will be more pleasant. Jordan (1953) gave subjects 64 hypothetical P-O-X situations, half of which were balanced and half unbalanced. In general, balanced relationships were in fact judged more pleasant than imbalanced ones.

The second type of study conducted to test balance theory gives the subject a set of situations and then asks him questions about the relations or requires him to reproduce them. Burnstein (1967) administered a questionnaire to students immediately before the 1964 presidential election containing a series of situations involving hypothetical relations among two people and their feelings about a candidate. Students were then asked which situations were likely to change and how. The results indicated that initially balanced situations were seen as less likely to change. As to what changes would occur, increases in positive relations in excess of the number needed for balance were predicted by the subjects. These predictions also favored changes in interpersonal relations as opposed to feelings about a candidate. Subjects evidently expect balance, positivity, and a preference for interpersonal changes.

Zajonc and Burnstein (1965) tested the ability of subjects to learn balanced versus imbalanced situations. If imbalanced relationships are stressful, they should be harder to learn. The relations involved two people and their feelings about either integration (important issue) or *Newsweek* (unimportant issue). For instance, Dick approves of *Newsweek*, Don approves of *Newsweek*, and Dick dislikes Don, or Tom approves of integration, Ted disapproves of integration, and Tom likes Ted. Subjects were presented each relation one at a time and had to remember whether it was positive or negative. Zajonc and Burnstein found that unbalanced situations were more difficult to learn but only when the issue was important (integration). In addition, negative relations were more difficult to learn, another positivity finding. Other studies (e.g., Gerard and Fleischer, 1967) indicate the effects of balance may be more complicated still. It seems that perhaps balanced situations may be remembered more easily with long-term memory and imbalanced situations with short-term memory, or even that some situations are intrinsically more interesting and easier to remember because of their imbalance.

Taken together these studies demonstrate that balance does seem to be an important force in social perception, though the principle is not in itself a theory of social perception. The relevance of the basic notion of balance for consumer behavior lies in focusing attention on how the particular sentiment or unit relation linking the consumer and the product fits in with his entire system of beliefs arising in connection with the product. The emphasis of the theory on interpersonal relations might also be fruitful in exploring the effects of social context on product evaluations.

For work in consumer behavior, however, it may be desirable to have a more explicit formulation of balance possessing a greater predictive power. Fortunately Heider's work has directly stimulated research along these lines. Rosenberg (1956, 1960a, 1960b) defines attitudes as pro or con feelings toward objects of affective significance. Attitudes possess a structure composed of an affective component and a cognitive (belief) component. According to Rosenberg there exists a homeostatic tendency to maintain consistency

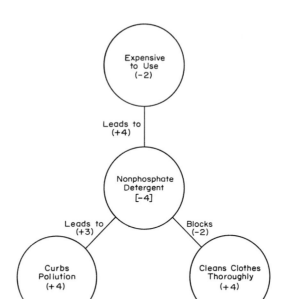

FIGURE 2.   A hypothetical attitude structure for a product.

between these components. Because of this tendency, a mathematical index can be calculated for predicting attitudes. Two variables are involved, the importance of the attitude object in leading to or blocking valued states (instrumental relations or beliefs) and the affect felt toward a given value. Figure 2 shows a hypothetical attitude structure concerning "nonphosphate detergents." To compute Rosenberg's index, it is necessary to obtain ratings of the affect associated with each value and the strength of the instrumental relation linking the value and the attitude object. Each value rating is then multiplied by its instrumentality and these products are summed to form the index of attitude. In our example (see Figure 2), the person's overall attitude, based on the hypothetical ratings given in parentheses, is predicted to be −4.

The affective-cognitive consistency side of this approach was later elaborated more extensively by Rosenberg and Abelson (Abelson, 1959; Abelson and Rosenberg, 1958; Rosenberg and Abelson, 1960). The later version of the theory deals with cognitive elements, the objects of human thought, and the cognitive relations between these elements. Both cognitive elements and relations can be either positive, negative, or null (neutral). No distinction is made between affective or instrumental relations, both are allowed. The conceptual arena refers to the set of all cognitive elements which are relevant to a given attitude object. It may be thought of as a network of cognitive bands, where a band is two cognitive elements connected by a relation. Figure 2 may be interpreted in these terms since each instrumental relation forms a band with an element and the attitude object. Conceptual arenas have the property of being balanced or imbalanced. Balance is achieved when all of the cognitive bands involve either elements of the same sign linked with a positive relation or elements of unlike sign linked with a negative relation. Notice that balance is defined in terms of signs, without reference to any numerical values. As before, balance is associated with a positive product and imbalance a negative product. Note that our example in Figure 2 is imbalanced. Abelson and Rosenberg further posit explicit "psycho-logical" rules which govern how a person thinks about elements in his conceptual arena. One rule states, for instance, that if A is positively related to B and B is negatively related to C, then A is negatively related to C. A conceptual arena is balanced if no application of these rules leads to the discovery of a negative cognitive band.

A unique feature of Rosenberg and Abelson's theory is that imbalance is predicted to create a pressure toward change only if the individual thinks about the imbalance. Imbalance may be resolved in one of three general ways. A person may change the sign of one or more cognitive elements, change the sign of one or more cognitive relations, or stop thinking about the imbalance. Abelson (1959) specifies four means by which changing the sign of an element or relation may be accomplished: denial, bolstering, transcendence, and differentiation. The affective sign may be simply denied or changed to its opposite. The imbalance in the structure shown in Figure 2 may be resolved by denying that non-phosphate detergent really leads to less pollution. An element in an imbalanced cognitive band may be bolstered by relating it to other elements in a balanced way. If curbing pollution is linked to political fads, increased government spending, etc., imbalance should decrease. Imbalance may be transcended by placing both elements in some superordinate classification. Curbing pollution (+) and nonphosphate detergent (−) may be combined into the larger element "popular gimmick" (−) or "social responsibility" (+), of which only the former would resolve the imbalance in our example. Finally, a very common method of imbalance reduction is to differentiate an element into two different elements which are balanced. Thus our hypothetical person may decide that only air pollution needs curbing (+) while water pollution does not (−) and that nonphosphate detergent (−) leads to (+) the latter, a −, +, − band, but not the former, a −, −, + band.

Attitude change to accomplish imbalance reduction follows one of two sequences: affective change followed by cognitive change or cognitive change followed by affective change. Using posthypnotic suggestions, Rosenberg (1960a) instructed subjects to feel differently about an attitude object. He found that this affective change also produced changes in cognitive instrumental linkages. If, for example, a subject's feeling about blacks living in white neighborhoods was changed, the relations between integrating blacks and various values changed too. Carlson (1956) demonstrated the reverse sequence by convincing students that allowing blacks to move into white neighborhoods leads to values such as equal opportunity, and showing that this cognitive change led to affective change regarding integration.

Another contribution of the Rosenberg and Abelson theory is to hypothesize that imbalance reduction follows the easiest possible path. That is, balance tends to be restored with the fewest number of operations. Support for this contention was gained (Rosenberg and Abelson, 1960) by having subjects play the role of a department store manager where the role was defined by various cognitive bands, e.g., high sales is a positive cognitive element. The total structure represented by these bands was imbalanced in different ways for different subjects. When subjects were asked to evaluate three research reports which had the effect of restoring balance, they favored the report which resolved their particular imbalance in the fewest number of changes. However, these particular experiments also revealed the operation of other factors, a positivity effect and a tendency toward maximizing gain and minimizing loss (subjects did not reduce imbalance in a way that would reduce sales). This latter factor led Rosenberg and Abelson (1960) to postulate a "dual force conception" which is extremely important for consumer behavior. Balance represents one force on a cognitive band and hedonic satisfaction another. In some cognitive bands these forces may conflict. Rosenberg (1965) provides a valuable discussion of this problem. He argues that imbalance will be less likely to result in change for a hedonic cognitive band than an antihedonic one. For example, the imbalance in "My mother-in-law ($-$) supports ($+$) my plan to buy a new car ($+$)" is less stressful than in "The distinguished firm of Schlag and Sons ($+$) have put on the market ($+$) a completely worthless sphygmomanometer (Rosenberg, 1965, p. 133)." Rosenberg (1965) also presents experimental data supporting the prediction that hedonic imbalance is less stressful than antihedonic imbalance. It may be possible, however, to account for this hedonic force within balance theory by employing the self as a separate cognitive element. When the self ($+$) is associated with ($+$) a motive-frustrating state of affairs ($-$), imbalance is greater than when it is associated with a rewarding state ($+$), because another imbalanced band has been added to the structure in the former case (Rosenberg and Abelson, 1960, p. 146). The above example then becomes "My mother-in-law ($-$) supports ($+$) my plan to buy a new car ($+$)" and "I ($+$) am associated ($+$) with this benefit ($+$)," an imbalanced and a balanced band. The worthless sphygmomanometer band, however, is coupled with an unbeneficial self-association, which creates two imbalances instead of one. It is perhaps worth noting that these authors attribute much of the interest in dissonance theory to the fact that it usually analyzes these doubly stressful antihedonic imbalances involving the self. This entire problem is worth considerable attention from consumer behavior researchers, for many of the important imbalances in this area are of the conflicting hedonic variety. Is "nonphosphate detergent ($-$) leads to ($+$) curbing pollution ($+$)" really imbalanced?

To suggest the potential of this research, a study by Insko, Blake, Cialdini, and Mulaik (1970) provides a good example. A survey was administered in which cognitive elements and statements relating these elements to some aspects of birth control were rated, the former on a good-bad scale, the latter on a true-false scale. Respondents were women in a public housing project. The data were analyzed by means of factor analyses to determine differences between users and nonusers of contraceptives. Cognitive consistency seemed to be greater for users than nonusers. The data indicated several requirements for both control campaigns including educating the husband as well as the wife and creating cognitive links between birth control and family goals.

While attitudes are certainly a crucial aspect of consumer behavior, the nature of the relationship between attitudes and behavior is an open question (see Calder and Ross, in press; Fishbein and Ajzen, 1972). Thus, before leaving balance theory, we should describe an extension of Rosenberg and Abelson's theory explicitly incorporating behavior as a variable. Insko and Schopler

(1967) present a model treating behavior, an actual goal directed activity, as well as cognitive elements and relations. All three are classified as either positive or negative. Insko and Schopler contend that people try to maintain not only affective-cognitive consistency but triadic consistency too. Consider a person who enjoys smoking (affect) and who smokes two packs of cigarettes a day (behavior). Now suppose he believes (cognition) that he should not be smoking for reasons of health. This triad is composed of a positively evaluated cognitive element, a negative cognitive relation, and a positive behavior. The product of the signs is negative, indicating triadic imbalance. Insko and Schopler predict some change in the triad to restore balance. It follows from this theory that behavior change can produce attitude change as well as that attitude change can cause behavior change. As we shall see, it is important in consumer behavior research for a model to allow for both sequences.

Congruity Theory

The congruity model of cognitive consistency developed independently of balance theory, though it is certainly similar in spirit. Whereas Heider had been interested in social perception, congruity theory stemmed from Osgood, Suci, and Tannenbaum's (1957) work on the semantic differential as a measure of meaning. One result of this research was to find a general evaluative dimension of meaning which could be equated with attitude. From its inception, the model was oriented toward the changes in attitude produced by source effects (Tannenbaum, 1968, p. 54). Source effects involve a situation where a person has an attitude about a communication source and about an issue. The source then makes an assertion about the issue. How does this assertion affect both the attitude toward the source and the attitude toward the issue?

The theory (Osgood and Tannenbaum, 1955; Osgood, 1960; Tannenbaum, 1967) is stated in terms of communication sources and objects of judgment which are connected by either an associative assertion (e.g., likes, buys, praises) or a dissociative assertion (e.g., dislikes, refuses to buy, criticizes). While assertions have only two values, associative or dissociative, sources and objects can take on values ranging from $+3$ to -3 according to their semantic differential ratings. An example of the type of attitude structure we have in mind is diagramed in Figure 3 in a manner introduced by Brown (1962). In this example (see Figure 3a) the source is the magazine *Consumer Reports,* which has been previously evaluated positively $(+2)$ by our respondent, and the object of judgment is a certain automobile make previously evaluated as slightly negative (-1). *Consumer Reports* publishes a story recommending that people buy this automobile, an associative assertion.

According to the theory, a state of congruity exists whenever a source and an object with the same numerical evaluation are associated and whenever a source and an object with opposite evaluations (e.g., $+2$ and -2) are dissociated. The lack of congruity, or incongruity, creates a pressure to change both the source and object attitudes to a congruent state. This pressure, P, is postulated to be different for the source and the object. It equals the amount each one would have to change alone to bring about congruity. In our example (see Figure 3a), the pressure on *Consumer Reports* is -3, a change of three units

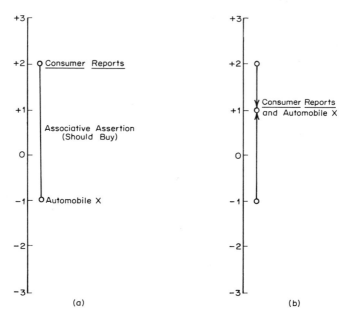

FIGURE 3.   Attitude change produced by an associative assertion.

in the minus direction would produce congruity. Similarly, the pressure on the automobile attitude is $+3$. (If the assertion were dissociative, the pressures would be -1 and -1 respectively.) When incongruity exists, both the source (S) and object (O) undergo pressure to change. The theory assumes, however, that the actual change depends on how extreme the attitude value is, a more extreme attitude changes proportionately less. The following equation gives the change for the attitude object:

$$AC_O = \frac{|S|}{|O| + |S|} P_O \pm i \pm A$$

where AC is the attitude change of the object, S is the absolute numerical value of the source attitude, O is the absolute numerical value of the object attitude, P_O is the pressure toward congruity on the object, and i and A are constants. Similarly, attitude change for the source is given by:

$$AC_S = \frac{|O|}{|O| + |S|} P_S \pm i$$

In short, attitudes change a certain proportion of the total distance required to create congruity, this proportion being determined by the relative extremity of the attitude. The two constants are corrections to the equations: i corrects for incredulity, the tendency to disbelieve a highly incongruent assertion (e.g., "the United States government has advocated that people buy Soviet-made automobiles"). The incredulity constant takes the opposite sign as P, thereby reducing the amount of change necessary. The assertion constant builds in the assumption that the object of an assertion should change more than the source. It is positive for an associative assertion and negative for a dissociative assertion; it is determined empirically. Without bothering with the correction constants, we may calculate that in our example (see Figure 3b), attitude toward *Consumer Reports* should change − 1 units and attitude toward the automobile should change + 2 units. These changes would achieve congruity, a similarly evaluated source and object associated by an assertion.

We should note that incongruity need not necessarily lead to attitude change. Tannenbaum, Macaulay, and Norris (1966) have described several alternatives to attitude change as a means of reducing incongruity. A person can deny or distort the association between the source and object (e.g., "a prestige figure was *paid* to endorse a product"). Alternatively a person can bolster his attitude toward the concept by seeking new information or he can alter his attitude toward the source alone and maintain the same attitude toward the concept. Unlike balance theory, these alternatives have not been emphasized.

Although congruity theory focuses on source effects, it can clearly be extended to the same situations as balance by treating more than one object and relation at a time. In fact it appears that balance theory is a subcase of congruity theory in that any situation which is imbalanced is also incongruent, though the converse is not necessary. It should be clear that even with its formalization congruity theory is probably of more narrow interest than balance theory. Notice also that the congruity approach calls for averaging the elements of a cognitive unit whereas Rosenberg's index employs a summation.

Research on congruity theory has yielded mixed results. Osgood and Tannenbaum (1955) found that the equations predicted the direction of attitude change better than the amount of change. Even more troublesome is Kerrick's (1959) finding that like sign attitudes when associated may change to become more extreme than either were separately. Recent research on congruity has tended to discard the mathematics of the theory, concentrating instead on its general implications. Tannenbaum (1966) demonstrated that attitude change toward an object does generalize to a source and to other objects connected to the source as well. In a review of this work, Tannenbaum (1968) explicitly recommends keeping the attitude change through communication aspect of the model separate from its status as a "general model of cognitive interaction." In view of the obvious importance of the source effect situation for consumer behavior, congruity theory could provide a valuable supplement to balance theory in just this connection.

Dissonance Theory

The origins of dissonance theory probably lie in Gestalt psychology via the field theory approach of Kurt Lewin which postulated that changes in a person's life space could occur as a result of psychological tension. Like balance and congruity, dissonance is stated in terms of cognitive elements and relations (Festinger, 1957). Cognitive elements are defined much more loosely though. They may include any knowledge a person has about himself, his behavior, or his world. Cognitive elements may be perceived as related in one of two ways. If the existence of one element x does not follow from another element y (i.e., x implies not-y), the relation is dissonant; otherwise it is consonant. The cognition, "I purchase nonphosphate detergent," is dissonant with the cognition, "nonphosphate detergent does not get clothes clean"; the one does not follow from the other.

Cognitive dissonance is supposed to create a noxious state of psychological tension in the individual. A person is thus motivated to reduce dissonance and to avoid events that would produce dissonance. The intensity of this motivation increases with the relative number of dissonant cognitions and their importance. Dissonance may be reduced by adding new cognitive elements favoring consonance or changing existing cognitions toward consonance. In our example, dissonance may be reduced by adding new cognitions such as "nonphosphate detergents curb pollution" and "nonphosphate detergent makes clothes smell fresh." Alternatively, the person may change his behavior ("I no longer purchase nonphosphate detergent") or his belief about cleaning power ("nonphosphate detergent actually does get clothes clean").

Dissonance theory has not remained static since its introduction. A number of researchers have attempted to modify the theory, usually by specifying the conditions under which dissonance will or will not be aroused. Brehm and Cohen (1962) emphasized the role of commitment and volition in producing dissonance. More recently, Aronson (1968, 1969), Bramel (1968), and Collins (1969) have argued that dissonance is connected with violations of a person's self-concept. Aronson states perhaps the most general form of this argument. He characterizes dissonance as arising most clearly from a violation of strong expectancies. One of the strongest expectancies most people have is that their self-concept will remain positive.

> Thus, at the very heart of dissonance theory, where it makes its clearest and neatest predictions, we are not dealing with any two cognitions; rather, we are usually dealing with the self-concept and predictions about some behavior. If dissonance exists it is because the individual's behavior is inconsistent with his self-concept (Aronson, 1969, p. 27).

Aronson goes on to cite as an example a study by Erlich, Guttman, Schonbach, and Mills (1957) showing that new car owners selectively expose themselves to ads for their car. To have bought a lemon would certainly violate most people's self-concepts.

Recall now our earlier discussion of a similar point in connection with Rosenberg and Abelson's theory: antihedonic imbalance was supposed to be greater than hedonic imbalance. Clearly Aronson is identifying dissonance with antihedonic imbalance. If one considers when either of these cases is likely to arise, it would seem that hedonic imbalance is more prevalent before a behavior is performed and antihedonic imbalance afterward. One does not often intend to do antihedonic things beforehand but may well be trapped by them later. You do not intend to buy a lemon, but you may well find yourself with one. For this reason, it is not surprising that dissonance theory has proven especially powerful in analyzing the effects of having already performed a behavior. It is here that the greatest opportunity for antihedonic violations of self-expectancies exist.

In considering the relationship between attitudes and behavior, there are two possible causal sequences, attitudes may affect behavior or behavior may affect attitudes. It was argued in the above discussion that dissonance theory is more relevant to the effects of behavior on attitudes because of the greater likelihood of antihedonic imbalance. Moreover, dissonance may well produce changes in a person's future behavior (e.g., a person can't deny having smoked for twenty years). For both of these reasons, research has concentrated on how dissonance connected with having performed a behavior affects one's private attitudes.

In this vein Engel and Light have correctly commented on the significance of dissonance theory for consumer behavior:

> Do consumers ever become so committed (for instance, to a brand, a product, or a store) that they will become dissonant if their preference is challenged? The authors are of the opinion that such commitment indeed *does occur* for two different reasons: (1) loyalty to a product or a store can develop because one alternative becomes ego-involved and is, in effect, an extension of the consumer's self-concept; and (2) consumers establish buying routines or habits for the purpose of greater shopping efficiency. Loyalty from this latter source can represent genuine commitment (1968, p. 189).

In terms of the more recent versions of dissonance theory, we might add that loyalty through involvement of the self-concept should be most likely to create the possibility of dissonance.

Although many consumer behaviors might be examined by dissonance theory, perhaps the most salient is the purchase decision. In many cases the act of purchase may be closely identified with consumption itself. One line of dissonance research which is particularly relevant to the effects of purchasing deals with free choice situations. Consider a person wishing to buy a new car who cannot decide between a Pinto and a Vega. Finally he makes a decision, buying, say, the Vega. Dissonance theory predicts that, unless one considers himself a "schnook" (Aronson, 1969, p. 27), once the decision is made the person's evaluation of the Pinto will decrease and the evaluation of the Vega will increase. This revaluation occurs because the positive aspects of the rejected alternative (the Pinto) are now dissonant with the purchase behavior, as are the negative aspects of the chosen alternative (the Vega). Several studies have tested this prediction. Brehm (1956) asked female subjects to evaluate several products such as small appliances. Subjects then chose one of two similarly evaluated products as a gift and were asked to evaluate all the products again. The results indicate that subjects increased their evaluation of the chosen product and decreased their evaluation of the rejected product. This revaluation does not seem to be due to the mere possession of the product. Control subjects who were simply given a product did not change their evaluations. Later studies have improved on the methodology of Brehm's study and have generally supported this finding (e.g., Brock, 1963; Walster, 1964; Deutsch, Krauss, and Rosenau, 1962).

Cohen and Goldberg (1970) conducted an elaborate experimental test of the dissonance account of postdecision product revaluation. They distinguished between the decision and the actual consumption of a product. As a gift one group of subjects was allowed to choose between a national brand of coffee (prior information) and a larger container of a test brand (no prior information). They were then allowed to inspect but not consume samples of the two brands which, unknown to them, were the same. The results indicated a marginally significant tendency for subjects choosing the national brand to evaluate it more highly than a second group of subjects who had not received either brand as a gift; there was no such tendency for the test brand. As predicted by dissonance, choosing the national brand led to an increased evaluation whereas merely inspecting it did not. The authors tentatively conclude that prior information may affect product revaluation.

Subjects next were allowed to taste the two brands. By mixing an unpleasant additive in a cup of coffee, it was possible to have about half the subjects' choices confirmed (their choice tasted better) and the other subjects' choices disconfirmed. The brands were evaluated again and subjects indicated which they would probably buy. The results revealed that subjects positively revalued their choice if it were confirmed and devalued their choice if it were disconfirmed. The dissonance effect obtained for the first, nonconsumption measure of revaluation approached significance only for the measure of purchase intention. These findings are valuable in that they demonstrate the interactive nature of dissonance effects within a consumer behavior context. Without prior information in the form of brand familiarity, subjects' decisions probably carried little commitment and thus should not have aroused dissonance leading to the revaluation of the test brand. (There is an alternative, methodological interpretation: Subjects who chose the test brand may not have cared about its evaluation—a self-selection problem.) In any event, the weakness of the dissonance effects, especially after the powerful confirmation-disconfirmation manipulation, should not be surprising, for as the authors note the product choice was not ego-involving. Future research along these lines would add considerably to our knowledge of how purchase decisions affect behavior.

In addition to revaluation a purchase decision may lead to other behaviors because of dissonance. Ehrlich et al. (1957), as noted earlier, found that after the purchase of a new car consumers read more ads for the chosen car than for other cars. This study also found, contrary to dissonance theory, that readership of ads for rejected cars was slightly greater than readership of ads for cars not considered in the purchasing decision. The new owners should have found these rejected car ads dissonance provoking. Mills (1965) showed, however, that ratings of product desirability are highly correlated with interest in ads. He argued therefore that the new car owners may have read the rejected car ads because the rejected cars were still more desirable than the other cars. Alternatively the owners may have been seeking faults in the rejected cars. Although Oshikawa (1969) does not find either of these explanations compelling, they do illustrate the myriad possible effects of dissonance. Other investigators have explored reactions to possibly dissonant new product information (e.g.,

Carter, Pyszka, and Gerrero, 1969; Straits, 1964). Freedman and Sears (1965), Mills (1965), and Donohew and Palmgreen (1971) provide recent reviews of how people tend to seek consistent information.

An excellent example of how intriguing a dissonance analysis of the effects of purchase behavior can be is presented by Doob, Carlsmith, Freedman, Landauer, and Tom (1969). The "introductory low-price offer" is a standard marketing technique. Conventional wisdom has it that the low price will attract buyers who will continue to purchase the product after the price is raised. Doob et al. advance a dissonance account disputing this conclusion. The higher the price a consumer can be induced to pay for a product, the greater will be his tendency to reduce any possible dissonance by convincing himself of the value of the product. By buying a product at an introductory low price, the consumer is less likely to convince himself it is a good product. To test this hypothesis, Doob et al. conducted several experiments with groups of stores matched on sales and randomly assigned to one of two conditions. One group of stores introduced a product such as mouthwash at a lower price for two weeks and then switched to the regular price while the other group sold the product at the regular price all along. During the first two weeks sales at the lower priced stores were understandably higher. However, after the price was raised, sales fell in these stores to an amount below that of the stores which had the higher price all along. Although other interpretations of the data are possible, these results still support the dissonance prediction that the lower price purchase decisions did not engender as much loyalty as the higher priced ones. Nor is this to say the exposure gained by introductory offers would not raise sales for some products. Even so, in this study a 50% increase in sales from the lower price was insufficient to overcome later the loyalty produced by the higher price.

Research on dissonance theory is voluminous. Our comments have been intended to point out the relevance of the theory to consumer behavior. Although much of the research on dissonance is complex and frequently conflicting, it should be remembered that the theory is intended to function less as a formal model than as a heuristic and language for deriving interesting empirical hypotheses. In fact, an entire style of research has grown up around the theory. While to some "much of the research on dissonance theory has studied behavior in artificial and often trivial situations (Cohen and Goldberg, 1970, p. 316)," in fact much of this research has been ingenious in providing a context for behavior in which dissonance theory predictions could be tested experimentally. The real problem has been in tying down the theory. The very looseness which invites creative derivations renders the theory all but impossible to disprove. As Calder, Ross, and Insko (in press) put it, "At present cognitive dissonance theory is neither very cognitive nor very theoretical." In the face of all its ambiguities, however, dissonance theory remains a novel and creative framework for explaining the effects of behavior.

Conclusion

All three of the approaches to cognitive consistency have a place in current consumer behavior research. Balance theory is perhaps most relevant for understanding cognitive structure and predicting behavior where a more formal model is desired. Congruity theory is especially suited for analyzing the effects of communication sources such as the media on consumer product evaluations. Dissonance theory provides a rich framework for predicting the effects of behavior on other consumer processes. Taken together, cognitive consistency theories add a valuable dimension to consumer research.

References

Abelson, R. "Modes of Resolution of Belief Dilemmas." *Journal of Conflict Resolution,* Vol. 3 (1959), 343–352.

Abelson, R., and M. Rosenberg. "Symbolic psycho-logic: A Model of Attitudinal Cognition." *Behavioral Science*, Vol. 3 (1958), 1–13.

Aronson, E. "The Theory of Cognitive Dissonance: A Current Perspective." In L. Berkowitz (Ed.), *Advances in experimental social psychology,* Vol. 4. New York: Academic Press, 1969.

Aronson, E. "Dissonance Theory: Progress and Problems." In R. Abelson, E. Aronson, W. McGuire, T. Newcomb, M. Rosenberg, and P. Tannenbaum (Eds.), *Theories of Cognitive Consistency: A Sourcebook*. Chicago: Rand McNally, 1968.

Bramel, D. "Dissonance, Expectation, and the Self." In R. Abelson, E. Aronson, W. McGuire, T. Newcomb, M. Rosenberg, and P. Tannenbaum (Eds.), *Theories of Cognitive Consistency: A Sourcebook*. Chicago: Rand McNally, 1968.

Brehm, J. "Post-Decision Changes in the Desirability of Alternatives." *Journal of Abnormal and Social Psychology,* Vol. 52 (1956), 384–389.

Brehm, J., and A. Cohen, *Explorations in Cognitive Dissonance*. New York: Wiley, 1962.

Brock, T. "Effects of Prior Dishonesty on Postdecision Dissonance." *Journal of Abnormal and Social Psychology,* Vol. 66 (1963), 325–331.

Brown, R. "Models of Attitude Change." In R. Brown, E. Galanter, E. Hess, and G. Mandler (Contributors), *New Directions in Psychology*. New York: Holt, Rinehart, and Winston, 1962.

Burstein, E. "Sources of Cognitive Bias in the Representation of Simple Social Structures." *Journal of Personality and Social Psychology,* Vol. 7 (1967), 36–48.

Calder, B., and M. Ross. *Attitudes and Behavior*. New York: General Learning Press, in press.

Calder, B., M. Ross, and C. Insko. "Attitude Change and Attitude Attribution." *Journal of Personality and Social Psychology,* in press.

Carlson, E. "Attitude Change through Modification of Attitude Structure." *Journal of Abnormal and Social Psychology,* Vol. 52 (1956), 256–261.

Carter, R., R. Pyszka, and J. Guerrero. "Dissonance and Exposure to Aversive Information." *Journalism Quarterly,* Vol. 46 (1969), 37–42.

Cartwright, D., and F. Harary. "Structural Balance: A Generalization of Heider's Theory." *Psychological Review,* Vol. 63 (1956), 277–293.

Cohen, J., and M. Goldberg. "The Dissonance Model in Post-Decision Product Evaluation." *Journal of Marketing Research,* Vol. 7 (1970), 315–321.

Cohen, J., M. Fishbein, and O. Ahtola. "The Nature and Uses of Expectancy × Value Models in Consumer Attitude Research." *Journal of Marketing Research,* Vol. 9 (Nov. 1972), 456–460.

Collins, B. E. "Financial Inducements and Attitude Changes Produced by Role Players." In A. C. Elms (Ed.), *Role Playing, Reward, and Attitude Change.* New York: Van Nostrand, 1969.

Deutsch, M., R. Krauss, and N. Rosenau. "Dissonance or Defensiveness?" *Journal of Personality,* Vol. 30 (1962), 16–28.

Donohew, L., and P. Palmgreen. "A Reappraisal of Dissonance and the Selective Exposure Hypothesis." *Journalism Quarterly,* Vol. 48 (1971), 412–420.

Doob, A., J. Carlsmith, J. Freedman, T. Landauer, and S. Tom. "Effect of Initial Selling Price on Subsequent Sales." *Journal of Personality and Social Psychology,* Vol. 11 (1969), 345–350.

Mills, J. "Interest in Supporting and Discrepant Information." In R. Abelson, E. Aronson, M. Rosenberg, and P. Tannenbaum (Eds.), *Theories of Cognitive Consistency: A Sourcebook.* Chicago: Rand McNally, 1968.

Ehrlich, D., I. Guttman, P. Schonbach, and J. Mills. "Postdecision Exposure to Relevant Information." *Journal of Abnormal and Social Psychology*, Vol. 54 (1957), 98–102.

Engel, J., and L. Light. "The Role of Psychological Commitment in Consumer Behavior: An Evaluation of the Theory of Cognitive Dissonance." In F. Bass, C. King, and E. Pessemier (Eds.), *Applications of the Sciences in Marketing Management.* New York: Wiley, 1968.

Festinger, L. *A Theory of Cognitive Dissonance.* Stanford: Stanford University Press, 1957.

Fishbein, M., and I. Ajzen. "Attitudes and Opinions." *Annual Review of Psychology,* Vol. 23 (1972), 487–544.

Freedman, J., and D. Sears. "Selective Exposure." In L. Berkowitz (Ed.), *Advances in Social Psychology,* Vol. 2. New York: Academic Press, 1965.

Gerard, H., and L. Fleischer. "Recall and Pleasantness of Balanced and Unbalanced Cognitive Structures." *Journal of Personality and Social Psychology,* Vol. 7 (1967), 332–337.

Heider, F. *The Psychology of Interpersonal Relations.* New York: Wiley, 1958.

————. "Attitudes and Cognitive Organization." *Journal of Psychology,* Vol. 21 (1946), 107–112.

Insko, C., and J. Schopler. "Triadic Consistency: A Statement of Affective-Cognitive-Conative Consistency." *Psychological Review,* Vol. 72 (1967), 361–376.

————, R. Blake, R. Cialdini, and S. Mulaik. "Attitude Toward Birth Control and Cognitive Consistency: Theoretical and Practical Implications of Survey Data." *Journal of Personality and Social Psychology,* Vol. 16 (1970), 228–237.

Jordan, N. "Behavioral Forces that are a Function of Attitudes and of Cognitive Organization." *Human Relations,* Vol. 6 (1953), 273–287.

Kerrick, J. "News Pictures, Captions and the Point of Resolution." *Journalism Quarterly,* Vol. 36 (1959), 183–188.

Lambert, R. "An Examination of the Consistency Characteristics of Abelson and Rosenberg's 'Symbolic Psycho-logic.'" *Behavioral Science*, Vol. 11 (1966), 126–130.

Mills, J. "Avoidance of Dissonant Information." *Journal of Personality and Social Psychology,* Vol. 2 (1965), 589–593.

Osgood, C. "Cognitive Dynamics in the Conduct of Human Affairs," *Public Opinion Quarterly,* Vol. 24 (1960), 341–365.

————, and P. Tannenbaum. "The Principle of Congruity in the Prediction of Attitude Change." *Psychological Review,* Vol. 62 (1955), 42–55.

————, G. Suci, and P. Tannenbaum. *The Measurement of Meaning.* Urbana: University of Illinois Press, 1957.

Oshikawa, S. "Can Cognitive Dissonance Theory explain Consumer Behavior?" *Journal of Marketing,* Vol. 33 (1969), 44–49.

Price, K., E. Harburg, and T. Newcomb. "Psychological Balance in Situations of Negative Interpersonal Attitudes." *Journal of Personality and Social Psychology,* Vol. 3 (1966), 265–270.

Rodrigues, A. "Effects of Balance, Positivity, and Agreement in Triadic Social Relations." *Journal of Personality and Social Psychology,* Vol. 5 (1967), 472–476.

Rosenberg, M. "Some Content Determinants of Intolerance for Attitudinal Inconsistency." In S. Tompkins and C. Izard (Eds.), *Effect, Cognition, and Personality.* New York: Springer, 1965.

————. "An Analysis of Affective-Cognitive Consistency." In C. Hovland and M. Rosenberg (Eds.), *Attitude Organization and Change*. New Haven: Yale University Press, 1960a.

————. "A Structural Theory of Attitude Dynamics." *Public Opinion Quarterly*, Vol. 24 (1960b), 319–340.

————."Cognitive Structure and Attitudinal Affect." *Journal of Abnormal and Social Psychology*, Vol. 53 (1956), 367–372.

————, and R. Abelson. "An Analysis of Cognitive Balancing." In C. Hovland and M. Rosenberg (Eds.), *Attitude Organization and Change*. New Haven: Yale University Press, 1960.

Runkel, P., and D. Peizer, "The Two-Valued Orientation of Current Equilibrium Theory." *Behavioral Science*, Vol. 13 (1968), 56–65.

Sheth, J., and W. Talarzyk. "Perceived Instrumentality and Value Importance as Determinants of Attitudes." *Journal of Marketing Research*, Vol. 9 (1972), 6–9.

Straits, B. "The Pursuit of the Dissonant Consumer." *Journal of Marketing*, Vol. 28 (1964), 62–66.

Stroebe, W., V. Thompson, C. Insko, and S. Reisman. "Balance and Differentiation in the Evaluation of Linked Attitude Objects." *Journal of Personality and Social Psychology*, Vol. 16 (1970), 38–47.

Tannenbaum, P. "The Congruity Principle: Retrospective Reflections and Recent Research." In R. Abelson, E. Aronson, W. McGuire, T. Newcomb, M. Rosenberg, and P. Tannenbaum (Eds.), *Theories of Cognitive Consistency: A Sourcebook*. Chicago: Rand McNally, 1968.

————. "The Congruity Principle Revisited: Studies in the Reduction, Induction, and Generalization of Persuasion." In L. Berkowitz (Ed.), *Advances in Experimental Social Psychology*, Vol. 3. New York: Academic Press, 1967.

————. "Mediated Generalization of Attitude Change via the Principle of Congruity." *Journal of Personality and Social Psychology*, Vol. 3 (1966), 493–499.

————, J. Macaulay, and E. Norris. "Principle of Congruity and Reduction of Persuasion." *Journal of Personality and Social Psychology*, Vol. 3 (1966), 233–238.

Walster, E. "The Temporal Sequence of Post-decision Processes." In L. Festinger (Ed.), *Conflict, Decision, and Dissonance*. Stanford: University Press, 1964.

Zajonc, R., and E. Burnstein. "The Learning of Balanced and Unbalanced Social Structures." *Journal of Personality*, Vol. 33 (1965), 153–163.

3.6 Postdecision Dissonance at Post Time
ROBERT E. KNOX, JAMES A. INKSTER

In the last decade there have been numerous laboratory experiments conducted to test various implications of Festinger's (1957) theory of cognitive dissonance. In spite of sometimes serious methodological faults (cf. Chapanis & Chapanis, 1964), the laboratory evidence as a whole has tended to support Festinger's notions. Confidence in the theory, as Brehm and Cohen (1962) have previously suggested, can now be further strengthened by extending empirical tests from lifelike to real life situations. The present study investigates the effects of post-decision dissonance on bettors in their natural habitat, the race track.

Festinger (1957) had originally contended that due to the lingering cognitions about the favorable characteristics of the rejected alternative(s), dissonance was an inevitable consequence of a decision. Subsequently, however, Festinger (1964) accepted the qualification that in order for dissonance to occur, the decision must also have the effect of committing the person. A favorite technique for reducing postdecisional dissonance, according to the theory, is to change cognitions in such a manner as to increase the attractiveness of the chosen alternative relative to the unchosen alternative(s). At the race track a bettor becomes financially committed to his decision when he purchases a parimutuel ticket on a particular horse. Once this occurs, postdecisional processes should operate to reduce dissonance by increasing the attractiveness of the chosen horse relative to the unchosen horses in the race. These processes would be reflected by the bettor's expression of greater confidence in his having picked a winner after his bet had been made than before.

In order to test this notion, one need only go to a race track, acquire a prebet and postbet sample, and ask members of each how confident they are that they have selected the winning horse in the forthcoming race. The two samples should be independent since the same subjects in a before-after design could contravene the observed effects of dissonance reduction by carrying over consistent responses in the brief interval between pre- and postmeasurements. In essence, this was the approach employed in the two natural experiments reported here. More formally, the experimental hypothesis in both experiments was that bettors would be more confident of their selected horse just after betting $2 than just before betting.

Experiment I

Subjects

Subjects were 141 bettors at the Exhibition Park Race Track in Vancouver, British Columbia. Sixty-nine of these subjects, the prebet group, were interviewed less than 30 seconds *before* making a $2 Win bet. Seventy-two subjects, the postbet group, were interviewed a few seconds after making a $2 Win bet. Fifty-one subjects, interviewed before the fourth and fifth races, were obtained in the exclusive Clubhouse section. Data from the remaining 90 bettors were collected prior to the second, third, sixth, and seventh races at various betting locations in the General Admission or grandstand area.

No formal rituals were performed to guarantee random sampling, but instead, every person approaching or leaving a $2 Win window at a time when the experimenters were not already engaged in an interview was contacted. Of those contacted, approximately 15% refused to cooperate further because they could not speak English, refused to talk to "race touts," never discussed their racing information with strangers, or because of some unexpressed other reason. The final sample consisted of white, Negro, and Oriental men and women ranging in estimated age from the early twenties to late sixties and ranging in style from ladies in fur to shabby old men. The final sample was felt to be reasonably representative of the Vancouver race-track crowd.

Procedure

The two experimenters were stationed in the immediate vicinity of the "Sellers" window during the 25-minute betting interval between races. For any given race, one experimenter intercepted bettors as they approached a $2 Win window and the other experimenter intercepted different bettors as they left these windows. Prebet and postbet interview roles were alternated with each race between the two experimenters.

The introductory appeal to subjects and instructions for their ratings were as follows:

> I beg your pardon. I am a member of a University of British Colum-
> bia research team studying risk-taking behavior. Are you about to
> place a $2 Win bet? [Have you just made a $2 Win bet?] Have we
> already talked to you today? I wonder if you would mind looking at
> this card and telling me what chance you think the horse you are
> going to bet on [have just bet on] has of winning this race. The scale
> goes from 1, a slight chance, to 7, an excellent chance. Just tell me
> the number from 1 to 7 that best describes the chance that you think
> your horse has of winning. Never mind now what the tote board or
> professional handicappers say; what chance do *you* think your horse
> has?

It was, of course, sometimes necessary to give some of the subjects further explanation of the task or to elaborate further on the cover story for the study.

The scale, reproduced here in Figure 1, was prepared on $8\frac{1}{2} \times 11$-inch posterboard. The subjects responded verbally with a number or, in some cases, with the corresponding descriptive word from the scale.

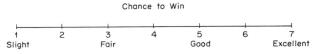

Chance to Win

| 1 | 2 | 3 | 4 | 5 | 6 | 7 |
| Slight | | Fair | | Good | | Excellent |

FIGURE 1. The rating scale shown to subjects in the study.

After each prebet rating the experimenter visually confirmed that his subject proceeded directly to a $2 Win window. In the few instances that subjects did wander elsewhere, their data were discarded. No effort was made to collect data in the 3 frantic minutes of betting just prior to post time.

Results

Since no stronger than ordinal properties may be safely assumed for the rating scale, nonparametric statistics were employed in the analysis. Several χ^2 approximations of the Kolmogorov–Smirnov test (Siegel, 1956) were first performed to test for distributional differences between the ratings collected by the two experiments. For prebet ratings ($\chi^2 = .274$, $df = 2$, $p > .80$) and for the combined pre- and postbet ratings ($\chi^2 = 2.16$, $df = 2$, $p > .30$) the differences in the two distributions may be considered negligible according to these tests. Distributional differences on postbet ratings ($\chi^2 = 3.14$, $df = 2$, $p > .20$) were greater but still did not meet even the .20 probability level.[1] On the basis of these tests the two experimenters were assumed to have collected sufficiently comparable ratings to justify pooling of their data for the subsequent test of the major hypothesis of the study.

The median for the 69 subjects in the prebet group was 3.48. In qualitative terms they gave their horse little better than a "fair" chance of winning its race. The median for the 72 subjects in the postbet group, on the other hand, was 4.81. They gave their horse close to a "good" chance in the race. The median test for the data summarized in Table 1 produced a χ^2 of 8.70, ($df = 1$), significant beyond the .01 level.

These results, in accord with our predictions from dissonance theory, might also have arisen, however, had a substantial number of bettors simply made last-minute switches from relative long shots to favorites in these races. Although this possibility was not pursued with the above sample of subjects, two follow-up inquiries on another day at the same race track indicated that the "switch to favorites" explanation was unlikely. The first of these inquiries involved 38 $2 bettors who were contacted prior to the first race and merely asked if they ever changed their mind about which horse to bet on in the last minute or so before actually reaching a Sellers window. Nine of the 38 indicated that they sometimes changed, but among the 9 occasional changers a clear tendency to switch to long shots rather than to favorites was reported. Additional evidence against a "switch to favorites" explanation was obtained from a sample of 46 bettors for whom the prebet procedure of Experiment I was repeated. Each of these bettors was then contacted by a second interviewer just as he was leaving the $2 Win window and asked if he had changed to a

TABLE 1.   Division of Subjects with Respect to the Overall Median for the Prebet and Postbet Groups: Experiment 1

	Prebet Group	Postbet Group
Above the *Mdn*	25	45
Below the *Mdn*	44	27

different horse since talking to the first interviewer. All 46 responded that they had not changed horses in midinterviews.

In order to investigate the robustness of the findings in Experiment I a second study was undertaken which was like the first study in its essentials but employed different experimenters, a different response scale, and a different population of subjects. It also provided for a test of the "switch to favorites" explanation among subjects in a postbet group.

Experiment II

Subjects and Procedure

Ninety-four subjects were interviewed at the Patterson Park Harness Raceway in Ladner, British Columbia. Forty-eight of these subjects, the prebet group, were interviewed prior to the first six races as they approached one of the track's four $2 Win windows. This contact was usually completed just a few seconds before the subject actually reached the window to make his bet, but occasionally, when the betting lines were long, up to $\frac{3}{4}$ minute elapsed between interview and bet. Forty-six subjects, the postbet group, were interviewed a few seconds after leaving one of the $2 Win windows. As in Experiment I, all persons approaching or leaving a $2 Win window at a time when the experimenters were not already engaged were contacted. Of those contacted, fewer than 10% refused to cooperate, thus producing a heterogeneous and, presumably, representative sample of $2 Win bettors.

The overall design was the same in the first study. Two experimenters, different from those who interviewed bettors in Experiment I, were located in the immediate area of the Sellers windows. One of these experimenters would intercept bettors as they approached a $2 Win window and the other intercepted different bettors as they left a $2 Win window. The prebet and postbet interview roles were alternated between the two experimenters as in the first study.

After a brief introductory preamble, the experimenter established whether a bettor was about to make a $2 Win bet (or had just made such a bet) and whether he had been previously interviewed. The experimenters proceeded only with those $2 bettors who had not already provided data. These subjects were then asked to indicate on a 23-centimeter scale how confident they felt that they had picked the winning horse. The mimeographed response scales were labeled with the words "No confidence" at the extreme left and "Complete confidence" at the extreme right. Although no other labels were printed on the scale, the experimenters made explicit that mild confidence would fall in the middle of the scale and ". . . the more confident that a person felt, the further along he should put his mark on the scale." When subjects indicated understanding, they were handed a pencil and a mimeographed scale and directed to ". . . just draw a line across the point in the scale that best corresponds to your own confidence." All bettors in the postbet sample were also asked if they changed their mind about which horse to bet on while waiting in line or while on the way to the window.

Within the limits permitted by extremely crowded conditions, the prebet experimenter visually confirmed that subjects in his sample proceeded to a

$2 Win window. Data collection was suspended during the last minute before post time.

Confidence scores for each subject were determined by laying a ruler along the 23-centimeter scale and measuring his response to the nearest millimeter.

TABLE 2. Division of Subjects with Respect to the Overall Median for the Prebet and Postbet Groups: Experiment II

	Prebet Group	Postbet Group
Above the *Mdn*	19	28
Below the *Mdn*	29	18

Results

On the strength of insignificant Kolmogorov-Smirnov tests for distributional differences between ratings collected by the two experimenters, data from the two experimenters were combined to test the major hypothesis of the study. The median rating for the 48 subjects in the prebet groups was 14.60, and for the postbet group it was 19.30. The median test for these data, summarized in Table 2, produced a X^2 of 4.26 ($df = 1$), significant at less than the .05 level.

Since data in Experiment II might reasonably be assumed to satisfy interval scale assumptions, a t test between pre- and postbet means was also performed. The difference between the prebet mean of 14.73 and the postbet mean of 17.47 was also significant ($t = 2.31$, $p < .05$).

No subject in the postbet sample indicated that he had changed horses while waiting in line or, if there were no line, just before reaching the window.

Discussion

These studies have examined the effects of real life postdecisional dissonance in the uncontrived setting of a race track. The data furnished by two relatively heterogeneous samples of bettors strongly support our hypothesis derived from Festinger's theory. The reaction of one bettor in Experiment I well illustrates the overall effect observed in the data. This particular bettor had been a subject in the prebet sample and had then proceeded to the parimutuel window to place his bet. Following that transaction, he approached the postbet experimenter and volunteered the following:

> Are you working with that other fellow there? [indicating the prebet experimenter who was by then engaged in another interview] Well, I just told him that my horse had a fair chance of winning. Will you have him change that to a good chance? No, by God, make that an excellent chance.

It might reasonably be conjectured, that, at least until the finish of the race, this bettor felt more comfortable about his decision to wager on a horse with an excellent chance than he could have felt about a decision to wager on a horse with only a fair chance. In the human race, dissonance had won again.

The results also bear upon the issue of rapidity of onset of dissonance-reducing processes discussed by Festinger (1964). On the basis of an experiment by Davidson described in that work, Festinger argued that predecisional cognitive familiarity with the characteristics of alternatives facilitated the onset of dissonance reduction. It is reasonable to assume that most bettors in the present studies were informed, to some extent, about the virtues and liabilities of all the horses in a race before making a $2 commitment on one. Since never more than 30 seconds elapsed between the time of commitment at the window and confrontation with the rating task, the present results are consistent with the notion that the effects of dissonance reduction can, indeed, be observed very soon after a commitment is made to one alternative, providing that some information about the unchosen alternatives is already possessed. Furthermore, the exceedingly short time span here suggests that the cognitive reevaluation process could hardly have been very explicit or as deliberate as conscious rationalization.

Finally, these studies, like the earlier Ehrlich, Guttman, Schonbach, and Mills (1957) study which showed that recent new car buyers preferred to read automobile advertisements that were consonant with their purchase, demonstrate that meaningful tests of dissonance theory can be made in the context of real life situations. Insofar as real life studies are unaffected by contrived circumstances, improbable events, and credibility gaps, they may offer stronger and less contentious support for dissonance theory than their laboratory counterparts. It is also clear that such studies will help to define the range of applicability of the theory in natural settings.

Note

1. The X^2 approximation for Kolmogorov-Smirnov is designed for one-tailed tests, whereas the hypothesis tested here is nondirectional. However, since the differences were insignificant by a one-tailed test, they would necessarily be insignificant by the two-tailed test.

References

Brehm, J. W., & Cohen, A. R. *Explorations in cognitive dissonance.* New York: Wiley, 1962.

Chapanis, N. P., & Chapanis, A. Cognitive dissonance: Five years later. *Psychological Bulletin* (1964), Vol. 61, 1–22.

Ehrlich, D., Guttman, I., Schonbach, P., & Mills, J. Postdecision exposure to relevant information. *Journal of Abnormal and Social Psychology* (1957), Vol. 54, 98–102.

Festinger, L. *A theory of cognitive dissonance.* Evanston, Ill.: Row, Peterson, 1957.

Festinger, L. *Conflict, decision, and dissonance.* Stanford, Calif.: Stanford University Press, 1964.

Siegel, S. *Nonparametric statistics for the behavioral sciences.* New York: McGraw-Hill, 1956.

3.7 The Dissonance Model in Post-Decision Product Evaluation
JOEL B. COHEN, MARVIN E. GOLDBERG

One of the most fundamental states of conflict in human behavior which can be heightened by decision making is that between the need for openness and flexibility, on the one hand, and structure and consistency on the other. To what extent does one approach a situation less than openly, guided by experience and expectations and recognizing, identifying, and evaluating stimuli according to what one "knows" is there?

Coping with the environment demands a balance between accuracy and economy. Precise perception and categorization, for all their value, are costly in time and effort since the time needed to make any one response may not only be crucial for its associated rewards and punishments but also for coming to terms with all other salient stimuli. Cognitive structures facilitate perception and categorization of stimuli, but they may distort or modify certain aspects of the situation. Ease of recognition and identification plus the fact that specific interpretations of many stimuli are socially learned and shared add to the utility of a compromise between unbounded flexibility and consistency.

As one becomes personally involved in an issue or sees a direct relationship between his self concept and an object or person, the exact nature of this compromise may change. He may wish to interpret such objects, issues, and events in a manner consistent with important beliefs, especially following decisions in which psychological commitment and observable behavior combine to increase personal involvement. In such cases the balance may turn more toward consistency than openness. One's general preference for consonant (rather than dissonant) cognitions to give order, stability, and consistency to his perception may thus assume more of the qualities of a drive.

A vast amount of evidence testifies to the pervasiveness of attempts to avoid and reduce cognitive dissonance. Critics argue that the evidence has been gathered largely in situations in which the value of openness and flexibility (relative to consistency) is often quite low. The controversy surrounding dissonance theory and the increasing amount of contradictory evidence accumulated over the past few years (for recent reviews see [5, 8, 9]) have led to some disaffection with the theory [2, 5, 10].

Dissonance theory may not fit the role of a general theory within which all consumer decision making can be subsumed. The great enthusiasm, creativity, and sheer productivity of dissonance researchers have helped to oversell the theory to all too willing buyers. In part, this is because of the relative frustration of cognitively-oriented researchers to an absence of a general predictive model in any way comparable, for example, to that of reinforcement-oriented stimulus-response theorists. It has become increasingly clear that the dissonance model will not serve this function.

On the other hand, a hostile over-reaction by those who expected too much from the theory may be equally unwise and nonobjective. Despite discrepant findings and severe critics, dissonance theory does offer a parsimonious explanation for many otherwise disconnected observations. If it can account for important aspects of purchasing behavior, students of consumer behavior should identify those factors which increase its relevancy. An even more imposing task would be to combine dissonance theory with competing formulations (such as stimulus-response learning theory) in a more inclusive theory of the middle range.

Much of the research on dissonance theory has studied behavior in artificial and often trivial situations. For example, subjects have been paid to participate in boring or tedious tasks, to lie to others, or to write essays counter to commonly held positions, e.g., [1, 4, 11, 14]. In much of this research, the individual's prior experience, the relevance to him of the experimental task, and what he does after the experiment are irrelevant to the experimenter. For students of consumer behavior, however, these omissions are often of direct concern. Consumers' prior experience, perceived importance of decisions, and anticipation of product performance are all factors which influence not only whether there will be a cognitive reevaluation following a purchase, but, perhaps more importantly, what form it will take: decision justification or outcome-based learning.

One criticism levelled against the theory of cognitive dissonance is that the individual, rather than learning from his mistakes, increases the likelihood of making them again through justification and rationalization. This study attempts to define and examine two factors in consumer decision processes which should, in part, determine the form of cognitive reevaluation (learning vs. justification) expected: (1) prior information resulting from brand familiarity; and (2) the nature and quality of the post-purchase evidence.

Methodology

One hundred and twenty-eight subjects of both sexes were allocated by quiz sections to the various experimental conditions. They were students in an introductory marketing course at the University of Illinois who had signed up in 21 groups of up to 10 for a "new product research study" as part of the course requirement that they participate in a marketing research study that semester. They were told that the study was conducted jointly by the marketing department and "one of the country's outstanding marketing research firms."

The experiment was grouped into four stages: decision, immediate post-decision, nonconsumption, and post-consumption, described below. The figure summarizes the measures taken at each stage. Specific questions used are reported in the respective tables.

Measures Taken at Each Stage

Decision	Immediate Post-Decision	Non-Consumption	Post-Consumption
1. Importance of Decision (Table 1)	1. Expressed Dissonance (Table 1)	1. Brand Preference (Table 4)	1. Brand Preference (Table 7)
2. Brand Choice	2. Purchase Intention (Table 3)	2. Purchase Intention (Table 5)	2. Purchase Intention (Table 8)
			3. Distortion of Product Attributes (Table 9)
			4. Gift Selection (Table 10)

Decision Stage

Two-ounce jars of the four leading national brands of instant coffee and 6-ounce jars of the unmarked test brand were displayed. It was explained that the test brand was presently available only in the 6-ounce size and that we had been sent the 2-ounce size of the other brands. Subjects were asked to select one jar as a gift. This technique was used to generate a reasonable distribution between choices of the test brand and national brands and to pose a dilemma likely to generate a workable amount of dissonance. Faced with such a decision, the uncertain quality of the larger gift made some dissonance inevitable no matter which brand was selected. Subjects were then told to carry their chosen brand with them through the rest of the experiment, since they would not be coming back to the room they were in.

Forty-eight subjects chose the test brand and 30 chose one of the national brands. Prior information about the chosen brand could not provide a filter through which the former group could interpret subsequent information about their chosen brand. However, national brands may have more stable and favorable initial evaluations and hence be much more immune [6, 7] to isolated and discrepant bits of information, especially extremely discrepant information. Inconsistent information may be seen as less believable, sources as less trustworthy.

The study design also called for a manipulation of ego-involvement in the process of decision making (distinct from involvement in the product, per se). Although the data presented include involvement as one of the sources of variation, a discussion of this variable may be found elsewhere [3] and is not relevant to the focus of this paper.

Subjects assigned to the no dissonance and control conditions were not told about their selection of a gift until the end of the experiment. It was not until all of the experimental manipulations were carried out that these groups selected a gift.

Immediate Post-Decision Stage

Subjects were assigned to high and low dissonance groups to determine if the amount of dissonance led to differences in post-decision brand evaluation. Ideally this assignment might be made on the basis of the conflict among

TABLE 1.   Importance of Purchase Decision[a] and Expressed Dissonance[b]

	Percentage	
	High Dissonance	Low Dissonance
High Importance	60	17
Low Importance	40	83
Total	100	100
N	43	35

$\chi^2 = 7.11\ p < .01.$

[a]*Pre-selection measure of importance:* "Some people feel that in buying instant coffee getting a certain brand is important. Others feel that it doesn't make a great deal of difference which brand one buys. How do you feel about this?"

High importance: "Getting the brand I want is:
        very important/
        reasonably important.

Low importance: "Getting the brand I want is:
        neither too important nor too unimportant/
        reasonably unimportant/
        very unimportant."

[b]*Measure of dissonance:* "When you compared your favorite national brand with the test brand, were there features of the gift you did *not* choose which (considering these by themselves) might have led you to choose *that* gift?"

High dissonance: "Definitely, some aspects of the other brand had a very positive appeal for me."
"Possibly, some aspects of the other brand had a small, but positive, appeal for me."

Low dissonance: "Neither alternative had more than a neutral appeal for me."
"Probably not, hardly any aspects of the other brand had even a small positive appeal for me."
"Definitely not, no aspect of the other brand had any positive appeal for me."

alternatives at the moment of decision. It was felt, however, that forcing a person to report his perceived conflict during the decision-making process would not only create a highly artificial setting, but would probably directly influence his effort, commitment, and subsequent dissonance.

The assignment was made on the basis of a post-decision reconstruction of each person's prior state of conflict.[1] Table 1 presents the question used to generate subjects' expressed level of dissonance and a comparison with a pre-decision measure of perceived product importance. As expected from prior studies, there is a significant relationship between importance and dissonance, providing some evidence that the expressed dissonance question is valid.

Of the 78 subjects asked to select a brand as a gift, 43 expressed a high amount of dissonance following their choice; 35 expressed a low amount. Both groups were then asked to indicate the probability that they would buy either their favorite national brand or the test brand.

Non-Consumption Stage

A comparative evaluation of the non-taste attributes of the brands was undertaken by the high, low, and no dissonance groups. This was described as an "inspection test," a usual initial evaluation by the marketing research firm of the non-taste attributes of a food product. Those selecting a national brand as a gift compared it with the test brand. Those selecting the test brand as a gift were asked to compare it with their favorite national brand; the no dissonance group performed this same comparison.

Subjects were instructed to evaluate the appearance and aroma of the two coffees in labelled beakers. The intent, of course, was to provide a set of ambiguous stimuli to determine to what extent the process of choosing a gift influenced perception and evaluation of the chosen and unchosen alternatives. For this reason, the coffee in each of the beakers was *exactly the same.* Questions regarding brand preference and purchase intentions were then administered to each of the subjects in the three dissonance conditions.

Post-Consumption Stage

Subjects were next served a cup of each of the two brands compared earlier. At this point, roughly half the subjects had their choice of coffee confirmed or disconfirmed by altering the taste of the test coffee with a poor tasting additive.[2]

Table 2 provides a check on the adequacy of the disconfirmation procedure. The 50 subjects not selecting a gift (no dissonance and control groups) rated this specially prepared coffee as somewhat more bitter and reasonably

TABLE 2.   Control Groups' Ratings of Test Coffee by 7-Point Semantic Differential

	Percentage	
	Tasted Bad Test Coffee (N = 26)	Tasted Good Test Coffee (N = 24)
Bitter (1, 2)	42	17
Neutral (3–5)	27	58
Not Bitter (6, 7)	31	25
Total	100	100
Worthless (1, 2)	35	8
Neutral (3–5)	61	92
Valuable (6, 7)	4	0
Total	100	100
Sick (1, 2)	23	13
Neutral (3–5)	77	70
Healthy (6, 7)	0	17
Total	100	100
Bad (1, 2)	65	21
Neutral (3–5)	31	58
Good (6, 7	4	21
Total	100	100
Poor Quality (1, 2)	31	21
Neutral (3–5)	69	62
High Quality (6, 7)	0	17
Total	100	100

lower in quality and general evaluation than the good test coffee. Thus the manipulation seems to have succeeded in producing a believably bad coffee around which to structure disconfirmation experiences.

All subjects were then given a final questionnaire. Just before leaving the experiment subjects were told to leave the jars they had been carrying with them and take a fresh jar as a gift. The experimenter explained that they might as well take home a new-looking gift. As they filed by a table near the exit which contained a large number of jars of each brand, their choice was recorded by an assistant stationed at a distance behind the group.

Results and Discussion

Immediate Post-Decision Stage

Table 3 reveals that, in the absence of any discrepant information or opportunity to selectively compare and evaluate the brands, only the brand selected (national or test) produced a significantly different comparative rating. Those selecting a national brand rated their choice higher than those selecting the test brand. Since control subjects also rated national brands higher than the test brand without tasting either one (Table 6) it seems reasonable to assume that this belief existed prior to the experiment and was not materially altered by the choice process. Apparently prior information about national brands enabled those choosing one to rate it more highly relative to a new and unknown brand than those choosing the test brand could rate their choice relative to a national brand.

Neither the main effect of dissonance or situational involvement nor any of the interactions proved to be significant. Since this rating was made immediately after the self-report of expressed dissonance, it is possible that the effect of stating that "aspects of the unchosen alternative had a positive appeal" constrained immediate changes in the relative ratings of the two alternatives.

TABLE 3.   Immediate Post-Selection Rating[a]

Source of Variation	df	MS	F
Involvement (A)	1	1.44	1.85
Brand Selected (B)	1	27.59	35.51[b]
Dissonance (C)	1	.89	1.14
A × B	1	1.18	1.52
A × C	1	.51	.66
B × C	1	1.11	1.43
A × B × C	1	.02	.03
Residual	70	.78	

Group	N	$\overline{X}$
Selected a National Brand	30	3.93
Selected the Test Brand	48	2.64

[a] "If your favorite national brand and the test brand were priced the same for the 6 oz. size, which of these do you think you would buy?" (Would buy other brand 1——5 Would buy selected brand)
[b] $p < .001$.

Non-Consumption Stage

Subjects went to a second room, where a different experimenter conducted non-consumption evaluations of the coffees. Preference ratings are shown in Table 4. The dissonance-brand selected interaction approached significance ($p < .10$). No other significant relationships were found. The interaction indicated that the dissonance model correctly predicted the direction of preference ratings for the national brands but not for the test brand.

No support can be given for the dissonance model on the question of purchase intention (Table 5). When Dunnett's test [13, p. 89] comparing all means with a control was run (Table 6) there was a consistent tendency of high dissonance national brand subjects to be stronger in praise of their own selection (columns 1 and 2) and more critical in their evaluation of the test brand (columns 3, 4, and 5) than low dissonance national brand subjects. Looking

TABLE 4.   Non-Consumption Preference[a]

Source of Variation	df	MS	F
Involvement (A)	1	.13	.05
Brand Selected (B)	1	.34	.14
Dissonance (C)	1	2.01	.80
A × B	1	.00	.00
A × C	1	.98	.39
B × C	1	8.22	3.28[b]
A × B × C	1	2.66	1.06
Residual	70	2.51	

Selected a National Brand		Selected Test Brand	
High Dissonance	Low Dissonance	High Dissonance	Low Dissonance
$N = 20$ $\bar{X} = 6.18$	$N = 10$ $\bar{X} = 5.13$	$N = 23$ $\bar{X} = 5.33$	$N = 25$ $\bar{X} = 5.69$

[a]"On an overall basis which of the two brands you compared do you prefer?" (Prefer other brand 1——9 Prefer selected brand)

[b]$p < .10$.

TABLE 5.   Non-Consumption Purchase Intention[a]

Source of Variation	df	MS	F
Involvement (A)	1	4.73	1.41
Brand Selected (B)	1	.29	.09
Dissonance (C)	1	2.97	.88
A × B	1	4.05	1.21
A × C	1	3.19	.95
B × C	1	2.59	.77
A × B × C	1	.99	.30
Residual	70	3.35	

[a]"If both brands were sold at the same price for a 6 oz. size, which brand would you probably buy?" (Would buy other brand 1——9 Would buy selected brand)

TABLE 6.   Comparison of Treatment Means with Control: Non-Consumption Ratings

Treatment	N	Preference Test (1) National (9)	Purchase Intention Test (1) National (9)	Evaluation of Test Brand		
				Inferior (1) Superior (7)	Bad (1) Good (7)	Worthless (1) Valuable (7)
Test Brand-High Dissonance	23	4.70	5.22	3.78	4.74[b]	4.30
Test Brand-Low Dissonance	25	4.32	4.36	4.32	4.60[b]	4.44
Control	36	5.22	5.81	3.75	3.83	4.19
National Brand-Low Dissonance	10	5.20	5.50	4.60[a]	4.60[b]	4.40
National Brand-High Dissonance	20	6.15	6.15	4.20	4.15	4.25

[a](Dunnett t) $p < .05$.
[b](Dunnett t) $p < .01$.

at the same comparison for the test brand subjects, in four of the five post-decision evaluations there was a tendency for the low dissonance subjects to be more favorably disposed towards the test brand than the high dissonance subjects.

The evidence suggests that the dissonance model can account, to some extent, for differential behavior in the case of national brand subjects but not for those selecting the test brand. Prior information on the well established national brands would seem to be an important interactive variable determining the form of cognitive reevaluation. Caution is needed in interpreting these results since, for the most part, the experimental groups do not differ significantly in their evaluations from the control group.

The data presented thus far illustrate the effects of the first variable, prior information resulting from brand familiarity. In the post-consumption stage, the second variable (nature and quality of post-purchase evidence) is no longer ambiguous, but provides a definite confirmation or disconfirmation experience. The first stage of the experiment may be roughly compared to a typical post-decision first stage in which the consumer has little definitive feedback from his decision. This kind of situation is not conducive to learning or objective validation of behavior. It should be difficult to really evaluate the merits of the two products without meaningful performance information. Prior to the actual use of the product, the simplest and most gratifying course of action may be a positive reappraisal of one's decision. The post-consumption stage of the experiment provided an opportunity to measure behavior with respect to information clearly confirmational or disconfirmational in nature.

Post-Consumption Stage

Would high dissonance subjects be motivated enough to perceptually distort a clear disconfirmation of their selection, or would this be interactive with prior information based on brand familiarity? Tables 7 and 8 provide evidence that significantly different evaluations of the selected brand were a function of the confirmation-disconfirmation experience. If prior information regarding brands is a significant source of influence on the form of dissonance reduction, then there should be a significant interaction between brand selected

TABLE 7.   Post-Consumption Preference[a]

Source of Variation	df	MS	F
Confirmation-Disconfirmation (A)	1	117.22	26.15[b]
Brand Selected (B)	1	67.11	14.97
Dissonance (C)	1	.00	.00
A × B	1	.35	.08
A × C	1	.29	.06
B × C	1	9.55	2.13
A × B × C	1	.92	.20
Residual	70	4.48	

Group	N	$\overline{X}$
Selection Was Confirmed	40	6.54
Selection Was Disconfirmed	38	3.81

[a] "Now that you have completed the brand comparison, which of the two brands do you prefer?" (Prefer other brand 1——9 Prefer selected brand)
[b] $p < .001$.

TABLE 8.   Post-Consumption Purchase Intention[a]

Source of variation	df	MS	F
Confirmation-Disconfirmation (A)	1	110.52	27.95[c]
Brand Selected (B)	1	87.04	22.01
Dissonance (C)	1	.33	.08
A × B	1	.45	.11
A × C	1	1.48	.37
B × C	1	14.00	3.54[b]
A × B × C	1	1.50	.38
Residual	70	3.95	

Group	N	$\overline{X}$
Selection Was Confirmed	40	6.41
Selection Was Disconfirmed	38	3.76
Selected a National Brand × High Dissonance	20	6.80
Selected a National Brand × Low Dissonance	10	5.71
Selected the Test Brand × High Dissonance	23	3.51
Selected the Test Brand × Low Dissonance	25	4.31

[a] "Which would you probably buy if the national brand and the test brand were sold at the same price for each size jar?" (Would buy other brand 1——9 Would buy selected brand)
[b] $p < .10$.
[c] $p < .001$.

and dissonance.[3] This was not the case for preference ratings (Table 7). However, the hypothesized factor did approach significance ($p < .10$) for purchase intention (Table 8). In neither table, however, was there a significant main effect due to dissonance.

Results coded for an open-ended brand comparison question (Table 9) give further evidence regarding subjects' treatment of brand attribute information. High dissonance subjects, contrary to dissonance theory, did

TABLE 9.   Distortion of Product Attributes[a]

	High Dissonance		Low Dissonance	
	N	Percent	N	Percent
Comparison Consonant with Brand Selected	13	30	17	50
Comparison Dissonant with Brand Selected	11	26	7	21
Lack of Distortion	19	44	10	29
Total	43	100	34	100

[a] "In your own words compare the two brands you tasted in this study."
$x^2 = 3.20$, n.s.

not highlight positive attributes of the chosen brand and negative attributes of the unchosen brand to a significantly greater·degree than low dissonance subjects. In fact, the direction of the results is opposite to the theory.

Perhaps the most telling data in support of the learning model are reported in Table 10. With the invitation to take fresh jars on the way out, subjects had an opportunity to take any brand, and could not see their new choices being recorded. Eighty percent of those whose choices were confirmed reselected the same brand as compared to 32% of those whose choices were disconfirmed. Of the 25 high dissonance subjects who reselected the same brand, only 32% did so following disconfirmation. Chi-square analysis demonstrated the significant relationship between brand switching and disconfirmation. There was no significant relationship between level of dissonance and brand switching.

Conclusions

The presence of a confirmation-disconfirmation experience appears to be the overwhelming factor in the cognitive reevaluation process. Subjects reevaluated positively when their choice was confirmed by the evidence and negatively when their choice was disconfirmed, a result suggested by learning theory.

It would be useful to categorize at least two post-purchase stages in a consumer decision model in terms of the potential for learning at each stage.

TABLE 10.   Post-Consumption Gift Selection

	Choice Confirmed[a]				Choice Disconfirmed			
	High Dissonance[b]		Low Dissonance		High Dissonance		Low Dissonance	
	N	Percent	N	Percent	N	Percent	N	Percent
Reselected Original Choice	4	24	17	77	8	38	15	83
Switched	13	76	5	23	13	62	3	17

[a] Confirmation-disconfirmation $x^2 = 18.58$, $p < .001$.
[b] High dissonance-low dissonance $x^2 = 1.17$, n.s.

If there is a reasonable time interval between purchase and product use, the potential for outcome-based learning is likely to be initially low. The probability of consistency-based justification would be greatest in this interval. The extent of cognitive justification at this point, especially if accompanied by increasing commitment (e.g., telling others about the purchase), may interfere with more objective appraisal following product use. A more conclusive disconfirmation may then be required before the buyer is willing to admit that the choice was not a good one, and there may be a greater probability that the mistake will be repeated.

It might be a good idea to be skeptical of product evaluations taken during the pre-consumption stage (e.g., in supermarkets), especially pertaining to brands or products the consumer has not previously used. With little opportunity for the consumer's choice to be disconfirmed, one may be recording the full effect of cognitive justification. Follow-up studies with these same people might also be biased by the increased commitment generated by the earlier response.

The amount of dissonance was an important source of influence only as it interacted with brand selected, leading to the belief that differential prior information about brands must be taken into account in predicting the kind of cognitive reevaluation that will take place. This interaction seems reasonable since the impact of the new information should be less in the presence of considerable prior information. Viewed in this light, one function of advertising and other pre-decision sources of product information is probably to create a standard for judging product attributes and performance. This standard or baseline enables consumers to more easily discard isolated, discrepant information about a product obtained either through its direct use or from indirect sources.

These results were obtained for a product of probably minor importance for most people. Instant coffee may well be representative in this respect of a broad category of frequently purchased consumer non-durables. It should be noted, however, that the desire to positively reappraise one's product choice is likely to be an increasing function of ego-related product importance. For this reason one should be careful in generalizing the results of this study to products believed to be highly ego-involving.

References

1. Timothy C. Brock and James E. Blackwood, "Dissonance Reduction, Social Comparison and Modification of Others' Opinions," *Journal of Abnormal and Social Psychology,* Vol. 65 (November 1962), 319–324.

2. Natalia P. Chapanis and Alphonse Chapanis, "Cognitive Dissonance: Five Years Later," *Psychological Bulletin,* Vol. 61 (January 1964), 1–22.

3. Joel B. Cohen, "Product Choice and Consumer Response: Post-Decision Processes," paper presented at the American Association for Public Opinion Research Annual Meetings, May 1969.

4. Leon Festinger and James M. Carlsmith, "Cognitive Consequences of Forced Compliance," *Journal of Abnormal and Social Psychology,* Vol. 58 (March 1959), 203–210.

5. Chester A. Insko, *Theories of Attitude Change,* New York: Appleton-Century-Crofts, 1967.

6. William J. McGuire, "Persistence of the Resistance to Persuasion Induced by Various Types of Prior Belief Defenses," *Journal of Abnormal and Social Psychology,* Vol. 64 (April 1962), 241–248.

7. ———, "Inducing Resistance to Persuasion," in Leonard Berkowitz, ed., *Advances in Experimental Social Psychology,* New York: Academic Press (1964), 192–231.

8. ———, "Attitudes and Opinions," in Paul R. Farnsworth, Olga McNemar, and Quinn McNemar, eds., *Annual Review of Psychology,* Vol. 17, Palo Alto: Annual Reviews, Inc. (1966), 475–514.

9. ———, "The Current Status of Cognitive Consistency Theories," in Shel Feldman, ed., *Cognitive Consistency: Motivational Antecedents and Behavioral Consequences,* New York: Academic Press (1966), 1–46.

10. Milton J. Rosenberg, "When Dissonance Fails: On Eliminating Evaluation Apprehension from Attitude Measurement," *Journal of Personality and Social Psychology,* Vol. 1 (January 1965), 28–42.

11. Ewert E. Smith. "The Power of Dissonance Techniques to Change Attitudes," *Public Opinion Quarterly,* Vol. 25 (Winter 1961), 626–639.

12. Elaine Walster, "The Temporal Sequence of Post-Decision Processes," in Leon Festinger, ed., *Conflict, Decision, and Dissonance,* Stanford: Stanford University Press (1964), 112–117.

13. B. J. Winer, *Statistical Principles in Experimental Design,* New York: McGraw-Hill Book Company, 1962.

14. Ruby B. Yaryan and Leon Festinger, "Preparatory Action and Belief in the Probable Occurrence of Future Events," *Journal of Abnormal and Social Psychology,* Vol. 63 (November 1961), 603–606.

Notes

1. This measure was made immediately after subjects announced their selections. Following a choice between alternatives, one tends to come to terms with post-decision regret inherent in giving up benefits associated with unchosen alternatives. Opposing forces operating to produce regret, on the one hand, and decision-justification (dissonance reduction) on the other should roughly equalize shortly after the decision. Less biased recall of one's pre-decision brand evaluation should be possible at this point. Walster [12] who varied the time interval between choice and second rating

of alternatives, provides supporting evidence. She found little spreading apart of chosen and unchosen alternatives immediately after army recruits chose occupational specialty assignments. Regret predominated with a four-minute delay, and dissonance reduction thereafter. Regret might very well be less a factor with a decision having fewer personal implications, such as in the present study.

2. The fact that the confirmation-disconfirmation experience was manipulated by altering the taste only of the test brand is important in that much greater variance in post-consumption evaluation of the test brand is expected. Approximately half of those choosing a test brand experienced much stronger disconfirmation than those choosing a national brand. Altering the taste of the national brand might well have produced disbelief.

3. A significant main effect for brand selected is an artifact of the previously discussed disconfirmation manipulation.

3.8 The Application of Attitude Immunization Techniques in Marketing

STEWART W. BITHER, IRA J. DOLICH, ELAINE B. NELL

With accelerating rates of new product development, growth, and obsolescence, a major problem is to extend the most profitable portion of the product life cycle as long as possible, usually the maturity stage [11]. A consumer-oriented analogy to the product life cycle may be drawn in terms of attitude changes over time. During the introduction, growth, and maturity stages, consumers develop favorable attitudes toward the product. The phase in which the function decreases is characterized by consumers changing their attitudes and buying competing products. Often the products to which these consumers change are neither significantly different from nor better than the product left behind. Thus, the marketer must investigate methods to make consumers' favorable attitudes more resistant to change.

Attitude researchers have attempted to account for attitude change as a function of many factors, e.g., order of presentation [3] and personality [4]. In a review of the concepts investigated in attitude change research, Cohen warned that an investigation of *resistance to change* studied in the context of *what makes for more change* is little more than a tacit assumption that the two processes are mirror images [2]. Soon after the initial era of attitude change research, McGuire and Papageorgis began to investigate effective methods for inducing resistance to persuasion [8]. This research was conducted using cultural truisms, attitudes so prevalent and strongly held in society that one is rarely if ever subjected to counterarguments. They found that exposure to strong counterarguments caused a significant decrease in belief. However, exposure to weakened versions of refuted arguments before the strong attack resulted in less decrease in belief.

The current research is an extension of that of McGuire and Papageorgis. This study is a step toward marketing applications because it uses beliefs which are *not* universally held in this society. Since consumers' opinions about products vary from extremely favorable to extremely unfavorable and almost never reach the level of a culturally held truism, research conducted with cultural truisms requires modification and additional testing for marketing applications.

The hypotheses tested by McGuire and Papageorgis were suggested by the biological analogy of a person being reared in a relatively germ-free environment [8, p. 327]. There are two ways to build up the disease resistance of such a person: (1) to give supportive therapy, or (2) by inoculation therapy, to stimulate without overcoming the person's defenses. McGuire and Papageorgis used this analogy in reasoning that beliefs could be made more defensible by stimulating the person to defend them in the face of weakened conterarguments. They hypothesized that this procedure would have more immunizing effectiveness than supportive therapy, which exposes the person to favorable arguments [8, p. 328]. Their studies indicated an inoculation treatment preceding a strong attack conferred significantly greater immunizing effectiveness than supportive treatment [8, p. 330].

Generality of Immunization

Papageorgis and McGuire next explored the generality of the immunity produced [10]. Previous research included only arguments in the strong attack which had been weakened and refuted in the preceding immunization message. Would immunization be effective against arguments in the attack which had not been mentioned in the immunization? Two factors made this generalization of immunity to different counterarguments seem logical: (1) the experience of being exposed to an effective refutation of some arguments against a belief may reduce the impressiveness of other counterarguments, and (2) by exposure to counterarguments, the subject may be shocked into realizing the vulnerability of his belief and as a result be stimulated to develop appropriate defenses [10, p. 475]. They were able to demonstrate that the immunization messages produced significant resistance to subsequent strong forms of different as well as of same counterarguments [10, p. 479]. This finding is most critical if the results of immunization research are to be generalized to a marketing context.

Theoretical Framework and Research Hypothesis

The theoretical framework of the present research had its basis in the postulate of selective exposure, which contains two predictions: (1) a selective seeking of belief-supportive information and (2) a selective avoidance of contrary information [1]. The first prediction received a good deal of support; the second has created more controversy.

Experimental evidence supporting both has been presented. From a review of the literature, it appears that situational influences have an important bearing upon the kind of information selected or avoided. For example, some studies indicating a preference for supporting information may be explained by noting that people have a tendency to choose to read about or listen to people like, rather than different from, themselves [9]. Other studies to determine whether people prefer supporting or discrepant information have been conducted within the academic environment. When subjects are faced with a choice between supporting or discrepant information, the academic environment has encouraged them to choose that which is discrepant [12].

Still other studies have suggested utility as a basis of selectivity [7]. As an example, if one is expecting a subsequent attack on his belief, he is likely to prefer discrepant information in order to prepare a defense. Mills' review of the literature found a number of studies which support the hypothesis that people prefer supporting to discrepant information, but found no studies which provide substantial evidence against the hypothesis [9, p. 272]. Rather than pursue the controversy toward a definitive conclusion, Sears suggests another approach [12, p. 783]:

> Implicitly, the question of a general preference for supportive information pits man's defensiveness against his curiosity. Which one has won out in his nature is of little interest, because both are obviously strong. This conclusion seems likely not to be altered no matter how many subsequent studies are done. The more important question is what determines which tendency will be dominant under any given set of conditions.

In terms of the current research, when a culturally controversial belief is strongly held, the person might protect this belief by selective exposure. However, if discrepant information were received, then prior immunization treatment should afford the best protection against a lowering of that belief level.

Research Hypothesis

From a population of individuals, a subpopulation in strong agreement with a stated belief is defined. The belief is not strongly held outside that population, and the subpopulation should not have been called upon to defend the belief openly. The central research hypothesis of the current research is:

> A portion of the subpopulation exposed to an immunization message designed to induce resistance to persuasion will show less change in belief level following an attack on the belief than will those subjects who were not exposed to the immunization message prior to the attack.

Experimental Design

The Belief and the Criteria for Its Selection

The belief chosen was that there should be little or no censorship of movies. It is not likely that students would have been called on to refute pointed counterarguments against the belief. The pretest conducted with two introductory marketing management classes indicated the belief was relatively strongly held (mode $= 14$ on a 20-point scale, where 20 indicated strongest degree of acceptance).

Research done with health-oriented cultural truisms generally indicated stronger degrees of acceptance (mode $= 15$ on a 15-point scale, where 15 indicated strongest degree of acceptance). However, since the current research is a step toward marketing applications, the belief manipulated should not be as high on the scale as a cultural truism. A belief of that intensity in the marketing environment would be uncommon except possibly in the case of extremely brand loyal consumers.

Data Collection Procedures

The current research design was longitudinal, since the issue concerned attitude changes over a period of time during which subjects were exposed to experimental treatments. There were four data collection stages. First, the belief level was measured before any experimental treatments were administered. Second, subjects were exposed to the immunization message designed to induce resistance to persuasion. Third, they were exposed to the attack message intended to argue strongly against the initial attitude. Fourth, the belief level was measured again. The difference between the initial and the final raw scores of the attitude measure was the dependent variable and provided the input data for the factorial model.

Subjects were led to believe they were involved in two separate research projects. The instructions for the first session stated a graduate student in the department needed an indication of student belief levels on some current issues. Each student completed a ten-item questionnaire which included the question on censorship. The second experimental session was administered under the guise of a reading comprehension test. Students were told the research was intended to test timed reading comprehension and was to be conducted in high schools, colleges, and graduate schools. Each subject read four messages disguised as newspaper editorials on current topics of interest. Six different combinations of messages were used (see Table 1). The four messages within each group were randomly ordered, except for Groups 4a and 4b. These received

TABLE 1. Experimental Groups and Treatments Received

Group	Messages Received		
Group 1 $(X_{111}$ and $X_{121})$	No Immunization	No Attack	4 Dummy Messages
Group 2 $(X_{112}$ and $X_{122})$	No Immunization	Attack	3 Dummy Messages
Group 3a (X_{211})	High Prestige Source Immunization	No Attack	3 Dummy Messages
Group 3b (X_{221})	Medium Prestige Source Immunization	No Attack	3 Dummy Messages
Group 4a (X_{212})	High Prestige Source Immunization	Attack	2 Dummy Messages
Group 4b (X_{222})	Medium Prestige Source Immunization	Attack	2 Dummy Messages

randomly ordered messages with the stipulation that the immunization message precede the attack message. Subjects were given seven minutes to complete each passage and to underline those phrases which they considered to be most important.

The third session was conducted in a manner similar to the first. Subjects were told the same graduate student would like information from students on additional current topics of interest. The second questionnaire contained ten items. Nine were different from the first questionnaire, and the tenth item was the same censorship item of the first questionnaire.

Another group of subjects completed *only* the second questionnaire, at the same time the experimental groups were completing it. This after-only group, although not a part of the factorial analysis of variance, was used as a control group for additional comparisons. At the completion of the experiment, subjects were given a debriefing message.

The data analysis was accomplished by a 2 × 2 × 2 factorial analysis of variance fixed-effects model (see Table 2). The three independent variables were: (1) level of immunization (immunization or no immunization), (2) source of immunization (high-prestige source or medium-prestige source), and (3) level of attack (strong argument or no strong argument).

The top half of Table 2 includes all subjects who did not receive the immunization message. Since they were not exposed to an immunization source, the source difference for those not receiving the immunization message was an artificial dichotomy. Although subjects were randomly assigned to no immunization-no attack (X_{1j1}) and to no immunization-attack (X_{1j2}) groups, assignment to sources was made to provide intragroup equality of means [13]. In effect, this tends to attenuate the source treatment factor in the overall design and makes it more difficult to reject the null hypothesis of no difference between sources. Sources of high and medium prestige were chosen on the basis of a pretest, where subjects ranked 14 newspapers according to source credibility. Their choices showed the *New York Times* as the highest (first choice) prestige source and the *Philadelphia Inquirer* (fifth choice) as a medium-prestige source.

Additional Control Group

In order to determine whether external events (such as a powerful newspaper editorial) might have influenced the results and whether or not complet-

TABLE 2.   Experimental Model: Summary of Mean Changes (Questionnaire 2 Minus Questionnaire 1)[a]

No Immunization	No Attack	Attack
High Prestige Source (Source 1)	$\overline{X}_{111} = -0.571$	$\overline{X}_{112} = -3.00$
Medium Prestige Source (Source 2)	$\overline{X}_{121} = -0.533$	$\overline{X}_{122} = -3.00$
Immunization		
High Prestige Source (Source 1)	$\overline{X}_{211} = 4.929$	$\overline{X}_{212} = 1.188$
Medium Prestige Source (Source 2)	$\overline{X}_{221} = 1.071$	$\overline{X}_{222} = -0.385$

[a]$\overline{X}_{ijk}$ = Mean difference score for subjects receiving the *i*th level of immunization, the *j*th level of source prestige and the *k*th level of attack.

ing the first questionnaire had an effect on completing the second, one group of subjects was administered the questionnaire at the conclusion of the experiment. Effects of possible external influences were assessed by comparing the raw scores on the initial questionnaire of the after-only group to those of a randomly selected group (X_{1j1}) which received subsequent experimental treatments.

Results

A $2 \times 2 \times 2$ factorial analysis of variance fixed-effects model was computed. Analysis was based on the difference score for each subject for the question of interest (scale value on Questionnaire 2 minus that on Questionnaire 1). The results are given in Table 3. Table 2 shows the mean changes in each cell of the design.

Main Effect 1: Immunization

Tables 2 and 3 show that immunization produced large mean difference changes significant at the .001 level, because immunization appears to have increased the positive attitude level. McGuire, Papageorgis, and other psychologists who pioneered in this area were concerned that the presentation of weakened counterarguments to a person's opinion, even when these counterarguments were refuted, would lower his belief level. This lowering, termed the "boomerang effect," has not occurred in any of the studies. The opposite of the "boomerang effect," an increase in belief level, has been detected in earlier studies, and although beliefs were moved as much as 60% of the remaining upper scale distance, the movement was not significant due to the extremely high original belief levels [10, p. 748]. Thus, the opposite of the "boomerang effect" seems to have occurred here. The attitude may have been made less susceptible to change, but the attitude level was substantially increased by the immunization message, which argued against the belief and then refuted these arguments.

TABLE 3. Summary of Fractional Analysis of Variance Results

Source	Sum of Squares	d.f.	Mean Square	F-Ratio
Attack	143.686	1	143.686	6.873[a]
Immunization	313.695	1	313.695	15.004[b]
Source	55.070	1	55.070	2.634
Attack × Immunization	25.296	1	25.296	1.210
Attack × Source	12.479	1	12.479	0.597
Immunization × Source	38.328	1	38.328	1.833
Attack × Immunization × Source	16.004	1	16.004	0.765
Error	2,132.533	102	20.907	
Total	2,737.091	109		

[a]$P[F] \leq 0.01$.
[b]$P[F] \leq 0.001$.

Main Effect 2: Attack

Again, referring to Tables 2 and 3, the attack message produced large mean difference changes, significant at the .01 level, resulting from significant lowering of beliefs *following attack* in both the immunized and non-immunized subjects. As with the immunization effect, the amount of change following attack was not predicted.

Main Effect 3: Source

With only about half the subjects in the overall design subjected to different source effects, this variable proved not significant at the .05 level, although some changes were observed. The higher prestige source led to larger increases in belief levels in the immunized but no attack cells. In the immunization-attack cells, the higher prestige source subjects showed a higher post-attack belief level than those exposed to lower prestige source immunization messages. Presumably, this resulted from the greater increase in pre-attack belief level noted in the high-prestige immunized subjects.

Although not significant at the .05 level, the direction of change seems to support the selective exposure rationale developed for the present study. With a high-prestige source, the subject is less likely to read critically and more likely to selectively expose himself to supportive information—in this case the refutation of the counterarguments. This would be less likely to occur with a lower prestige source, where the individual might read more critically and consider the arguments upon their merit.

Interaction Effect: Immunization—Attack

Tables 2 and 3 indicate that there is no significant main interaction effect between levels of immunization and levels of attack. As noted, the two main effects alone account for the majority of variance. This indicates the null hypothesis of this study must be accepted when the two source effects are considered together. More will be said about this in the discussion section which follows.

Attack Effect for High-Prestige Source Among Immunized Subjects

As previously noted, the attack versus no attack main effect was significant. The attack treatments at the no immunization level are essentially for control purposes, with the major interest on the attack effects at the immu-

TABLE 4. Analysis of Variance Summary: Attack with Immunization

Source	Sum of Squares	d.f.	Mean Square	F-Ratio
Attack (High Source)	104.501	1	104.501	4.998[a]
Attack (Medium Source)	14.291	1	14.291	0.684
Error	2,132.533	102	20.907	

[a]$P[F] \leq 0.05$.

nization level. Table 4 presents the analysis of attack effects for subjects immunized by high and medium-prestige sources. There is significant difference between post-attack belief levels for immunized subjects by source, lending tentative support to the immunization hypothesis. With a high-prestige source offering counterarguments against a strongly held belief, and then refuting these counterarguments, the subject may reinforce his previously held belief and be more able to withstand subsequent attack.

External Control

A control group was administered the final questionnaire only. In order to determine if external influences had intervened between the first and second questionnaires the control group's raw scores were compared to those for the first questionnaire of a randomly selected cell. Table 5 indicates that no significant differences were found between the two groups.

One additional control was examined. An analysis of the effect of completing the questionnaire twice was run using a single classification analysis of variance. The raw scores of the after-only group were compared to those on the final questionnaire of the no immunization–no attack group. The latter had been exposed to none of the experimental messages. The differences between the raw scores of these two groups were not significant (see Table 6). The analysis indicated that completing the questionnaire twice did not result in a confounding variable.

Discussion

Controls in the research design indicated that an unpredicted phenomenon occurred: the immunization message itself increased the initial belief level. Previous work with immunization techniques was concerned about

TABLE 5. Summary Table of One-Way Analysis of Variance: Control Group on External Influences

Source	Sum of Squares	d.f.	Mean Square	F-Ratio
Treatment	25.6390	1	25.6390	1.0700[a]
Error	1,461.6308	61	23.9612	
Total	1,487.2698	62		

[a] $F_{.95}$ (1,61) = 4.00.

TABLE 6. Summary of One-Way Analysis of Variance: Control Group on Questionnaire Bias

Source	Sum of Squares	d.f.	Mean Square	F-Ratio
Treatment	48.6275	1	48.6275	2.1068[a]
Error	1,407.9757	61	23.0816	
Total	1,456.6032	62		

[a] $F_{.95}$ (1,61) = 4.00.

lowering beliefs with the immunization message. A review of this work indicates that movement in an upward direction has occurred. This effect has not been obvious, because in studies with culturally held truisms the belief selected has approached the upper limits of the measuring instrument.

The initial belief level of the subjects in the current research had a mode of 14 on a 20-point scale. Subjects below ten were initially opposed to the belief being attacked with weakened arguments in the immunization message. It is interesting to note that the attacks (which in this case would support the subjects' opinion) did not reinforce their belief level. This might indicate that the refutation of the counterarguments in the message was so effective that the immunizing power of the counterargument was lost and the interaction between immunization and attack did not prove to be significant.

Although the immunization question is still unresolved, the present experiment indicates the extent to which counterarguments to the communicator's position may be included in the message, even when part of the audience is opposed to the communicator's position.

The two-sided immunization appeals seem to be effective in strengthening and reinforcing belief levels. This supports previous research showing that two-sided appeals are effective for increasing an initially negative belief level [6]. In addition, this type of presentation is effective in maintaining the belief level when a counterattack is likely to follow, such as when a competitive industry makes heavy use of the mass media [5].

The results of this research have implications for advertising to different market segments and for personal selling communications. For example, marketers often attempt to segment their audience by differentiating users from nonusers. Two-sided immunization type messages may make it possible to address both groups effectively. For consumers who use the product, the messages would strengthen and reinforce against competitor's claims. The messages could change nonusers' attitudes from negative to positive and immunize against competitors' attacks.

The current research deals with a rather unique product, movies. Further research will be necessary to determine whether these results may be generalized to other products. Until that has been accomplished, the preceding conclusions must be labeled as tentative.

References

1. Abelson, Robert P., *et al. Theories of Cognitive Consistency: A Sourcebook*. Chicago: Rand McNally, 1968, 769.

2. Cohen, Arthur R. *Attitude Change and Social Influence*. London: Basic Books, 1964, 121.

3. Hovland, Carl I., ed. *The Order of Presentation in Persuasion*. New Haven: Yale University Press, 1957.

4. ———, and Irving L. Janis, eds. *Personality and Persuasibility*. New Haven: Yale University Press, 1959.

5. ——, and Harold H. Kelly. *Communication and Persuasion*. New Haven: Yale University Press, 1953.

6. Hovland, Carl I., Arthur Lumsdaine, *et al*. *Experiments on Mass Communications*. Princeton: Princeton University Press, 1949.

7. Katz, Elihu. "On Reopening the Question of Selectivity in Exposure to Mass Communications," in Abelson, *op. cit.*, 792.

8. McGuire, William, and Demetrios Papageorgis. "The Relative Efficacy of Various Types of Prior Belief-Defenses in Producing Immunity Against Persuasion," *Journal of Abnormal and Social Psychology,* Vol. 62 (May 1961), 327–337.

9. Mills, Judson. "Interest in Supporting and Discrepant Information," in Abelson, *op. cit.*, 772.

0. Papageorgis, Demetrios, and William J. McGuire. "The Generality of Immunity to Persuasion Produced by Preexposure to Weakened Counterarguments," *Journal of Abnormal and Social Psychology,* 62 (August 1961), 475–481.

11. Patton, Arch. "Top Management's Stake in the Product Life Cycle," *The Management Review,* Vol. 48 (June 1959), 9–14, 67–71, 76–79.

12. Sears, David O. "The Paradox of De Facto Selective Exposure Without Preferences for Supportive Information," in Abelson, *op. cit.*, 780.

13. Winer, B. J. *Statistical Principles in Experimental Design*. New York: McGraw-Hill, 1962, 267.

4 Social Processes

Overview

Up to this point, the consumer has been viewed as a psychological unit; however, he does not function as an independent entity in society. He interacts with other people, and they influence his responses to the world around him. These interactions can range from the fairly simple—a casual conversation with a friend—to the very complex—the social interrelationships found in formal groups or large organizations. The purpose of this chapter is to examine these social influences and their role in consumption.

Concept of Groups

What distinguishes, from any random collection of people, a group that exercises significant and continuing influence on an individual? The people riding a public bus are not a group. However, if that busload of people were to be stranded in a snowstorm, they might rapidly become a group, since they would suddenly have common needs and goals, and might begin to interact in the pursuit of these needs and goals. Thus, one definitive feature of a group is membership *interaction* over time, that is, an interlocking set of social relationships such that the members are interdependent, every member perceiving every other member as part of the group.

In contemporary U.S. society, the individual belongs to a great variety of groups and usually aspires to belong to many others. These groups include family, school, church, job, neighborhood, and labor unions. Each group has certain beliefs, values, and norms and expects its members to conform to these belief systems by behaving in appropriate ways. Sharing an *ideology*—a set of beliefs, values, attitudes, and norms—is a necessary feature of a group (Krech, 1962).

Reference Groups

As might be expected, not all groups to which an individual belongs exert the same amount of influence or have the same relevance for him. A *refer-*

ence group is that group which the individual uses most often as a point of reference in determining his judgments, beliefs, and behavior.

The individual may have multiple reference groups, and he may use reference groups to which he does not belong. An example is the upwardly striving family that uses certain key members of the "social set" for attitudinal and behavioral guidance. A person may also have one or more negative reference groups; that is, groups whose behavioral guides he avoids following.

This chapter's first selection, by Tomatsu Shibutani, is one of the most widely quoted discussions of reference groups and represents a definitive formulation of the concept. Obviously, reference groups can influence purchasing decisions. Consumers are often influenced by what others buy, especially those persons with whom they compare themselves or who belong to groups the consumer uses as reference groups. The impact of socially distant and negative reference groups is demonstrated in the selection by Cocanougher and Bruce.

Formal and Informal Groups

In a *formal* group, the organizational structure and the functions for which it exists are specified. Examples include union, university, and legislative units. Often the organizational structure is rigidly defined by charts and manuals that outline the duties of each position. Conformity may be enforced by an explicit system of sanctions.

A circle of friends, an office clique, a teen-age gang, and a neighborhood collection of housewives who meet for coffee are typical *informal* groups. The structure of an informal group is less evident than that of a formal group, and the functions an informal group performs are also usually less explicit, although nonetheless real and important.

Role Theory

Each position in a group has attached to it an expected pattern of behavior or *role*. The person occupying a particular position is expected to act in a certain way and to be cognizant of the roles of others. Role performance amounts to a division of labor, and assures that the group's functions are fulfilled. Roles also reduce ambiguity and lessen tension, since the group member occupying a particular position knows what is expected of him in his interactions with other members. Ralph Turner (1967) provides an insightful and important definition of role:

It provides a comprehensive *pattern* for behavior and attitudes; it constitutes a *strategy* for coping with a recurrent type of situation; it is *socially identified,* more or less clearly, as an entity; it is subject to being played recognizably by *different individuals;* and it supplies a major basis for *identifying* and *placing* persons in society (p. 552).

Opinion Leader Role

One of the most researched roles in the marketing literature is that of the *opinion leader,* i.e., the individual within a group to whom others turn for information and advice. The opinion leader concept is rooted in research by Katz and Lazarsfeld (1955), who tested the "two-step hypothesis" that information often flows from mass media to opinion leaders and *then* to the less active segments of the population. The "two-step flow" is discussed in the selection by Johan Arndt.

Katz and Lazarsfeld analyzed the flow of influence in four areas of interest—marketing, which in this case meant food shopping; fashion; public affairs; and movies. Differing opinion leader profiles were obtained. The *food opinion leader* tended to be a married woman with a comparatively large family and with a gregarious or outgoing nature. She could be identified on all status levels, and her influence was limited to the status level on which she was found. The *fashion leader* was more likely to be young and highly gregarious. She was also somewhat more likely to be of higher status. The *public affairs leader* was a woman of high status and considerable gregariousness. In public affairs, influence did cross status boundaries, the direction being from high to low status. Finally, in the case of *moviegoing,* the leader was most often a young woman, often unmarried.

Rogers and Shoemaker (1971) have offered a general summary of the opinion leader's profile in terms of the following characteristics:

1. Opinion leaders have more social participation than their followers.
2. They have higher social status than followers, "but not too much higher."
3. They are more cosmopolitan than followers, that is, more oriented beyond their communities.
4. They are more innovative, that is, they buy more new products—a finding confirmed by Arndt.
5. They have greater exposure to mass media than do followers.
6. They are more norm-abiding. Klapper (1960) states that opinion leaders "are usually supernormative [group] members" and are "especially familiar with and loyal to group standards and values" (p. 460).

The Arndt and Robertson selections in this chapter examine the operation of opinion leadership regarding consumption. The Arndt study focuses specifically on the "two-step flow" hypothesis, whereas the Robertson study traces patterns of interaction in small groups via sociograms and examines the influence process.

Roles Within the Family

A familiar distinction made, for example, by Kenkel (1961), is that two underlying kinds of behavior are exhibited in small groups: task or goal-oriented behavior and social-emotional or expressive behavior. It has been traditional in U.S. society to think of men usually engaging in task-oriented behavior and women engaging in social-emotional behavior.

This specialization, according to Kenkel, has implications for family decision making. It might be expected, for example, that the male would be more concerned with functional product attributes and would have more influence in actually deciding to buy and concluding the sale, since these are task-oriented behaviors. The female, in contrast, would be more concerned with aesthetic product attributes and suggesting purchase, since these are expressive behaviors. In fact, these expectations are fairly well confirmed in the selection by Davis, on automobile and furniture decisions within families.

Another interesting distinction with implications for marketing is the degree of *role integration* (shared role taking) versus *role segregation* within a family. This seems to vary as a function of several factors. Role integration and an accompanying joint involvement in decision making seems to be most pronounced at middle-class levels, whereas role segregation is most pronounced at upper and lower social class levels (Komarovsky, 1961). Upward mobility in social class seems to be associated with greater role integration. Research across subcultures by Dalrymple et al. (included as a selection in Chapter 5) suggests that joint decision making is most pronounced among white couples, whereas husband dominance in consumption decisions is more frequent among Japanese-American couples, and wife dominance is more pronounced among black couples. Finally, role integration is found to increase at later stages of the life cycle.

Some attention has also been devoted to the roles played by children in the family consumption system. The selection by Ward and Wackman in this chapter analyzes the frequency and correlates of parental yielding to children's purchase requests. It appears that mothers are more likely to yield to such requests if they themselves watch a lot of television and have positive attitudes toward advertising.

Female Role: "Women's Lib"

Within U.S. society as a whole, roles may also be said to exist. The social roles of women are the focus of the women's lib movement. Two articles on this topic (by Bem and Bem and by Courtney and Lockeretz) are included in this chapter. Courtney and Lockeretz find that magazine advertising tends not to depict women in working roles but rather as sexual or decorative objects dependent on males. Courtney and Lockeretz also conclude that advertisements sanction the ideas that "a woman's place is in the home" and "women do not make important decisions or do important things."

The roles of women, as depicted in advertising, appear this way to another observer of the current media scene:

There are, to begin with, only four stages of womanhood in TV product pitches. There is the teen-age sexpot, flashing hair and gleaming teeth, swinging with her mod swain. There is the young mother murmuring into her little girl's ear how to grow up with soft skin like Mommy's by buying you-know-what-brand. There is the housewife with a voice like a saw, seen only at sink, stove, or toilet-bowl. And finally, there is the elderly lady (presumably a widow) who needs a laxative or has iron-poor blood. All of these women are blissfully free of intellect, skill, or talent. . . . The female is either man-bait (and nothing else), or full-time housewife (and nothing else) (Mannes, 1970, p. 55).

A question which deserves extended thought is the potential of advertising to restrict social change. Does twenty billion dollars of annual advertising expenditure reinforcing an image of women as dependent sex objects retard the social change movement which seeks to broaden the scope of the woman's role in U.S. society?

Socialization Processes

Socialization is the process by which someone learns the ways of a group or the society so that he can function within it. In terms of role theory, we can think of socialization as the process by which someone learns to perform his various roles adequately (Brim, 1968, p. 186).

Processes of socialization are of course most intense for children, but continue throughout life as individuals join new groups and take on new roles. We can also speak of *anticipatory socialization,* in the sense that an individual might practice or begin to live a role to which he aspires; for example, the medical student quickly dons his white coat and carries his stethoscope conspicuously hanging out of his pocket.

It is in the socialization process that little girls learn the female role. Much of this involves the transmission of a nonconscious ideology; parents frequently are unaware of the cues they give their children to define sex roles. Bem and Bem, in their selection in this chapter, trace the impact of boys being encouraged to be aggressive, competitive, and independent while girls are being encouraged to be passive and dependent.

The *consumption role* refers to the acquisition of values and skills for the performance of the role of consumer. The child learns this role from parents, peers, media, and to some extent the school system. A very important issue in U.S. society today, however, is the impact of mass media on the child's con-

TABLE 1.   **Views of the Effect of Advertising on Children**

	Critic's View	Marketer's View
Persuasive processes	Advertising can unduly persuade and manipulate the unsophisticated child.	Advertising mainly reinforces existing opinions. Parents have the key role in what a child believes.
Intrafamily influence processes	Advertising encourages the child to pressure his parents to buy. This can be damaging to the parent-child relationship.	Advertising may result in a positive interaction between parent and child and may be an occasion for learning about consumption.
Socialization processes	Advertising may imbue undesirable values, such as materialism and the need to consume. It also encourages irrational consumer decision making.	Advertising only reflects the value system of a society and prepares the child for his role as a consumer.

Source: Robertson (1972).

sumption desires. The allegations by consumer advocates against advertising to children, and the typical marketing management responses, are summarized in Table 1. This debate will probably intensify, given recent proposals to ban advertising directed at children. The levels of advertising to which the child is now exposed on children's programming make mass media a powerful agent in the consumer socialization process.

Group Conformity

Every group exerts pressure on the individual to conform to its particular ideology—its belief systems, values, and norms. In the case of beliefs and values, this pressure is not usually coercive. In most cases, the individual joins a group because his beliefs and values are similar to those of the group, and he is free to leave it if his own ideology differs significantly. In addition, beliefs and values tend to be self-reinforcing, since group members are exposed to each other and to similar experiences, thus strengthening their adherence to the values and beliefs of the group.

On the other hand, group *norms* flow from beliefs and values and do tend to be coercive. In the words of sociologist George Homans (1950):

A norm is an idea in the minds of the members of a group, an idea that can be put in the form of a statement specifying what the members or other men should do, ought to do, are expected to do, under given circumstances . . . . A statement of the kind described is a norm only if any departure of real behavior from the norm is followed by some punishment.

A classic study by Asch, presented in this chapter, clearly demonstrates the power of a group to extract from its members conformity to its norms. Under the group pressure of majority opinion, a lone minority member often conformed to obviously misleading majority decisions. Similarly, Venkatesan in another selection in this chapter demonstrates the power of group persuasion in consumption decisions involving ambiguous stimuli.

Other researchers before and after Asch have found similar results. For example, in another classic study, conducted by Sherif (1936), subjects in small groups were asked to judge the distance and direction a point of light appeared to move in a dark room. In actuality the light was stationary, but because of a physiological process called the autokinetic effect, the light should have appeared to be moving in a random manner to all members in the group. In the autokinetic effect, any dim visual stimulus which lacks a spatial frame of reference will appear to move in a random manner. The apparent movement may be due to minor tremors that exist in the eye. The results indicated that the members of the group tended to structure the situation by converging toward a common norm in their judgments. Conformity to these norms was sufficiently powerful that when the group was dispersed and individual judgments were obtained, the subjects continued to maintain the norms established by the group.

Normative versus Informational Social Influence

We do not mean to suggest that group influence is always based on normative pressure. In fact, most often it is not. Deutsch and Gerard (1955) have proposed the interesting distinction of *normative* social influence—an influence to conform to the expectations of others—versus *informational* social influence—an influence to accept information contributed by others as evidence of reality. The Asch experiment, whereby subjects yield to group pressure and deny the objective reality, is an example of normative social influence. The Sherif experiment, whereby subjects use each other to establish a reality base in an ambiguous situation, is an example of informational social influence.

Personal Influence

The marketing literature has been largely concerned with informational social influence. *Personal influence* refers to the attitudinal or behavioral change occurring as a result of an encounter between two or more people. Hearing a neighbor talk about his new automobile, discussing a new cake recipe over coffee, or admiring a friend's new outfit are not uncommon occurrences. The individual who has just bought a new home, new car, or a new dress may experience a need to talk about the purchase, possibly to help alleviate post-purchase dissonance.

On the other side of the influence process, the recipient may be looking for new ideas or more objective information than is available through such marketer-controlled communication channels as advertising, point-of-purchase displays, or sales talks. Festinger's (1954) theory of social comparison processes seems to account for such behavior. He argues that the individual has a need to evaluate his opinions and abilities, and when objective, nonsocial means are not available to him, he will evaluate them by comparison with the opinions and abilities of others.

Thus, as individuals interact with each other in both formal and informal groups, they transmit information and attitudes. Through this interaction and participation, major as well as minor purchasing decisions are often made. The operation of such influence is not usually deliberate; often, the influencer might be surprised to discover that his casual friendliness had led to a change in attitude or behavior. Yet this type of personal communication is of crucial importance in the purchase-decision process.

References

Brim, O. G., Jr. "Adult Socialization." In *Socialization and Society*, ed. J. A. Clausen. Little, Brown, 1968.

Deutsch, M., and H. B. Gerard. "A Study of Normative and Informational Social Influences Upon Individual Judgment." *Journal of Abnormal and Social Psychology,* Vol. 51 (1955), 629–636.

Festinger, L. "A Theory of Social Comparison Processes." *Human Relations,* Vol. 7 (May 1954), 117–140.

Homans, G. C. *The Human Group.* Harcourt Brace Jovanovich, 1950.

Katz, E., and P. F. Lazarsfeld. *Personal Influence.* The Free Press, 1955.

Kenkel, W. "Family Interaction in Decision-Making on Spending." In *Household Decision-Making,* ed. N. N. Foote. New York University Press (1961), 140–164.

Klapper, J. T. *The Effects of Mass Communication.* The Free Press, 1960.

Komarovsky, M. "Class Differences in Family Decision-Making." In *Household Decision-Making,* ed. N. N. Foote. New York University Press (1961), 255–265.

Krech, D., R. Crutchfield, and E. Ballachey. *Individual in Society.* McGraw-Hill, 1962.

Mannes, M. "The Female of the Species." *Boston Magazine,* September 1970.

Robertson, T. S. "The Impact of Television Advertising on Children." *Wharton Quarterly,* Fall 1972.

Rogers, E. M., and F. F. Shoemaker. *Communication of Innovations.* The Free Press, 1971.

Sherif, M. *The Psychology of Social Norms.* Harper & Row, 1936.

Turner, R. "Sociological Aspects." In *International Encyclopedia of the Social Sciences* (1967), 552–556.

4.1 Reference Groups as Perspectives
TAMOTSU SHIBUTANI

[During the years since Herbert Hyman coined the term], the concept of reference group has become one of the central analytic tools in social psychology, being used in the construction of hypotheses concerning a variety of social phenomena. The inconsistency in behavior as a person moves from one social context to another is accounted for in terms of a change in reference groups; the exploits of juvenile delinquents, especially in interstitial areas, are being explained by the expectations of peer-group gangs; modifications in social attitudes are found to be related to changes in associations. The concept has been particularly useful in accounting for the choices made among apparent alternatives, particularly where the selections seem to be contrary to the "best interests" of the actor. Status problems—aspirations of social climbers, conflicts in group loyalty, the dilemmas of marginal men—have also been analyzed in terms of reference groups, as have the differential sensitivity and reaction of various segments of an audience to mass communication. It is recognized that the same generic processes are involved in these phenomenally diverse events, and the increasing popularity of the concept attests to its utility in analysis.

As might be expected during the exploratory phases in any field of inquiry, however, there is some confusion involved in the use of this concept, arising largely from vagueness of signification. The available formal definitions are inconsistent, and sometimes formal definitions are contradicted in usage. The fact that social psychologists can understand one another in spite of these ambiguities, however, implies an intuitive recognition of some central meaning, and an explicit statement of this will enhance the utility of the concept as an analytic tool. The literature reveals that all discussions of reference groups involve some identifiable grouping to which an actor is related in some manner and the norms and values shared in that group. However, the relationship between these three terms is not always clear. Our initial task, then is to examine the conceptions of reference group implicit in actual usage, irrespective of formal definitions.

One common usage of the concept is in the designation of that group which serves as the point of reference in making comparisons or contrasts, especially in forming judgments about one's self. In the original use of the concept Hyman (1942) spoke of reference groups as points of comparison in evaluating one's own status, and he found that the estimates varied according to the group with which the respondent compared himself. Merton and Kitt (1950), in their reformulation of Stouffer's theory of relative deprivation, also use the concept in this manner; the judgments of rear-echelon soldiers overseas concerning their fate varied, depending upon whether they compared themselves to soldiers who were still at home or men in combat. They also propose concrete research operations in which respondents are to be asked to compare themselves with various groups. The study of aspiration levels by Chapman and Volkmann (1939), frequently cited in discussions of reference-group theory, also involves variations in judgment arising from a comparison of one's own group with others. In this mode of application, then, a reference group is a standard or check point which an actor uses in forming his estimate of the situation, particularly his own position within it. Logically, then, *any* group with which an actor is familiar may become a reference group.

A second referent of the concept is that group in which the actor aspires to gain or maintain acceptance: hence, a group whose claims are paramount in situations requiring choice. The reference group of the socially ambitious is said to consist of people of higher strata whose status symbols are imitated. Merton and Kitt interpret the expressions of willingness and felt readiness for combat on the part of inexperienced troops, as opposed to the humility of battle-hardened veterans, as the efforts of newcomers to identify themselves with veterans to whom they had mistakenly imputed certain values. Thus, the concept is used to point to an association of human beings among whom one seeks to gain, maintain, or enhance his status; a reference group is that group in which one desires to participate.

In a third usage the concept signifies that group whose perspective constitutes the frame of reference of the actor. Thus, Sherif (1953) speaks of reference groups as groups whose norms are used as anchoring points in structuring the perceptual field, and Merton and Kitt speak of a "social frame of reference" for interpretations. Through direct or vicarious participation in a group one comes to perceive the world from its standpoint. Yet this group need not be one in which he aspires for acceptance; a member of some minority group may despise it but still see the world largely through its eyes. When used in this manner, the concept of reference group points more to a psychological phenomenon than to an objectively existing group of men; it refers to an organization of the actor's experience. That is to say, it is a structuring of his perceptual field. In this usage a reference group becomes any collectivity, real or imagined, envied or despised, whose perspective is assumed by the actor.

Thus, an examination of current usage discloses three distinct referents for a single concept: (1) groups which serve as comparison points; (2) groups to which men aspire; and (3) groups whose perspectives are assumed by the actor. Although these terms may be related, treating together what should be clearly delineated as generically different can lead only to further confusion. It is the contention of this paper that the restriction of the concept of reference group to the third alternative—that group whose perspective constitutes the frame of reference of the actor—will increase its usefulness in research. Any group or object may be used for comparisons, and one need not assume the role of those with whom he compares his fate; hence, the first usage serves a quite different purpose and may be eliminated from further consideration. Under some circumstances, however, group loyalties and aspirations are related to perspectives assumed, and the character of this relationship calls for further exploration. Such a discussion necessitates a restatement of the familiar, but, in view of the difficulties in some of the work on reference groups, repetition may not be entirely out of order. In spite of the enthusiasm of some proponents there is actually nothing new in reference-group theory.

Culture and Personal Controls

Thomas pointed out many years ago that what a man does depends largely upon his definition of the situation. One may add that the manner in which one consistently defines a succession of situations depends upon his organized perspective. A perspective is an ordered view of one's world—what is taken for granted about the attributes of various objects, events, and human nature. It is an order of things remembered and expected as well as things actually perceived, an organized conception of what is plausible and what is possible; it constitutes the matrix through which one perceives his environment. The fact that men have such ordered perspectives enables them to conceive of their ever changing world as relatively stable, orderly, and predictable. As Riezler puts it, one's perspective is an outline scheme which, running ahead of experience, defines and guides it.

There is abundant experimental evidence to show that perception is selective; that the organization of perceptual experience depends in part upon what is anticipated and what is taken for granted. Judgments rest upon perspectives, and people with different outlooks define identical situations differently, responding selectively to the environment. Thus, a prostitute and a social worker walking through a slum area notice different things; a sociologist should perceive relationships that others fail to observe. Any change of perspectives—becoming a parent for the first time, learning that one will die in a few months, or suffering the failure of well-laid plans—leads one to notice things previously overlooked and to see the familiar world in a different light. As Goethe contended, history is continually rewritten, not so much because of the discovery of new documentary evidence, but because the changing perspectives of historians lead to new selections from the data.

Culture, as the concept is used by Redfield (1941) refers to a perspective that is shared by those in a particular group; it consists of those "conventional understandings, manifest in act and artifact, that characterize societies." (For a more explicit presentation of a behavioristic theory of culture, see Sapir, 1949.) Since these conventional understandings are the premises of action, those who share a common culture engage in common modes of action. Culture is not a static entity but a continuing process; norms are creatively reaffirmed from day to day in social interaction. Those taking part in collective transactions approach one another with set expectations, and the realization of what is anticipated successively confirms and reinforces their perspectives. In this way, people in each cultural group are continuously supporting one another's perspectives, each by responding to the others in expected ways. In this sense culture is a product of communication.

In his discussion of endopsychic social control, Mead (1925, 1934) spoke of men "taking the role of the generalized other," meaning by that that each person approaches his world from the standpoint of the culture of his group. Each perceives, thinks, forms judgments, and controls himself according to the frame of reference of the group in which he is participating. Since he defines objects, other people, the world, and himself from the perspective that he shares with others, he can visualize his proposed line of action from this generalized standpoint, anticipate the reactions of others, inhibit undesirable impulses, and thus guide his conduct. The socialized person is a society in miniature; he sets the same standards of conduct for himself as he sets for others, and he judges himself in the same terms. He can define situations properly and meet his obligations, even in the absence of other people, because, as already noted, his perspective always takes into account the expectations of others. Thus, it is the ability to define situations from the same standpoint as others that makes personal controls possible (Mead, 1925, 1934; cf. Parsons, 1952). When Mead spoke of assuming the role of the generalized other, he was not referring to people but to perspectives shared with others in a transaction.

The consistency in the behavior of a man in a wide variety of social contexts is to be accounted for, then, in terms of his organized perspective. Once one has incorporated a particular outlook from his group, it becomes his orientation toward the world, and he brings this frame of reference to bear on all new situations. Thus, immigrants and tourists often misinterpret the strange things they see, and a disciplined Communist would define each situation differently from the non-Communist. Although reference-group behavior is generally studied in situations where choices seem possible, the actor himself is often unaware that there are alternatives.

The proposition that men think, feel, and see things from a standpoint peculiar to the group in which they participate is an old one, repeatedly emphasized by students of anthropology and of the sociology of knowledge. Why, then, the sudden [fairly recent] concern with reference-group theory?

The concept of reference group actually introduces a minor refinement in the long familiar theory, made necessary by the special characteristics of modern mass societies. First of all, in modern societies special problems arise from the fact that men sometimes use the standards of groups in which they are *not* recognized members, sometimes of groups in which they have never participated directly, and sometimes of groups that do not exist at all. Second, in our mass society, characterized as it is by cultural pluralism, each person internalizes several perspectives, and this occasionally gives rise to embarrassing dilemmas which call for systematic study. Finally, the development of reference-group theory has been facilitated by the increasing interest in social psychology and the subjective aspects of group life, a shift from a predominant concern with objective social structures to an interest in the experiences of the participants whose regularized activities make such structures discernible.

A reference group, then, is that group whose outlook is used by the actor as the frame of reference in the organization of his perceptual field. All kinds of groupings, with great variations in size, composition, and structure, may become reference groups. Of greatest importance for most people are those groups in which they participate directly—what have been called membership groups—especially those containing a number of persons with whom one stands in a primary relationship. But in some transactions one may assume the perspective attributed to some social category—a social class, an ethnic group, those in a given community, or those concerned with some special interest. On the other hand, reference groups may be imaginary, as in the case of artists who are "born ahead of their times," scientists who work for "humanity," or philanthropists who give for "posterity." Such persons estimate their endeavors from a postulated perspective imputed to people who have not yet been born. There are others who live for a distant past, idealizing some period in history and longing for "the good old days," criticizing current events from a standpoint imputed to people long since dead. Reference groups, then, arise through the internalization of norms; they constitute the structure of expectations imputed to some audience for whom one organizes his conduct.

The Construction of Social Worlds

As Dewey emphasized, society exists in and through communication; common perspectives—common cultures—emerge through participation in common communication channels. It is through social participation that perspectives shared in a group are internalized. Despite the frequent recitation of this proposition, its full implications, especially for the analysis of mass societies, are not often appreciated. Variations in outlook arise through differential contact and association; the maintenance of social distance—through segregation, conflict, or simply the reading of different literature—leads to the formation of distinct cultures. Thus, people in different social classes develop different modes of life and outlook, not because of anything inherent in economic position, but because similarity of occupation and limitations set by income level dispose them to certain restricted communication channels. Those in different ethnic groups form their own distinctive cultures because their identifications incline them to interact intimately with each other and to maintain reserve before outsiders. Different intellectual traditions within social psychology—psychoanalysis, scale analysis, *Gestalt*, pragmatism—will remain separated as long as those in each tradition restrict their sympathetic attention to works of their own school and view others with contempt or hostility. Some social scientists are out of touch with the masses of the American people because they eschew the mass media, especially television, or expose themselves only condescendingly. Even the outlook that the *avantgarde* regards as "cosmopolitan" is culturebound, for it also is a product of participation in restricted communication channels—books, magazines, meetings, exhibits, and taverns which are out of bounds for most people in the middle classes. Social participation may even be vicarious, as it is in the case of a medievalist who acquires his perspective solely through books.

Even casual observation reveals the amazing variety of standards by which Americans live. The inconsistencies and contradictions which characterize modern mass societies are products of the multitude of communication channels and the ease of participation in them. Studying relatively isolated societies, anthropologists can speak meaningfully of "culture areas" in geographical terms; in such societies common cultures have a territorial base, for only those who live together can interact. In modern industrial societies, however, because of the development of rapid transportation and the media of mass communication, people who are geographically dispersed can communicate effectively. Culture areas are coterminous with communication channels; since communication networks are no longer coterminous with territorial boundaries, culture areas overlap and have lost their territorial bases. Thus, next-door neighbors may be complete strangers; even in common parlance there is an intuitive recognition of the diversity of perspectives, and we speak meaningfully of people living in different social worlds—the academic world, the world of children, the world of fashion.

Modern mass societies, indeed, are made up of a bewildering variety of social worlds. Each is an organized outlook, built up by people in their interaction with one another; hence, each communication channel gives rise to a separate world. Probably the greatest sense of identification and solidarity is to be found in the various communal structures—the underworld, ethnic minorities, the social elite. Such communities are frequently spatially segregated, which isolates them further from the outer world, while the "grapevine" and foreign-language presses provide internal contacts. Another common type of social world consists of the associational structures—the world of medicine, of organized labor, of the theater, of café society. These are held together not only by various voluntary associations within each locality but also by periodicals like *Variety*, specialized journals, and feature sections in newspapers. Finally, there are the loosely connected universes of special interest—the world of sports, of the stamp collector, of the daytime serial—serviced by mass media programs and magazines like *Field and Stream*. Each of these worlds is a unity of order, a universe of regularized mutual response. Each is an area in which there is some structure which permits reasonable anticipation of the behavior of others, hence, an area in which one may act with a sense of security and confidence (cf. Landgrebe, 1940; Riezler, 1950; Schuetz, 1944). Each social world, then, is a culture area, the boundaries of which are set neither by territory nor by formal group membership but by the limits of effective communication.

Since there is a variety of communication channels, differing in stability and extent, social worlds differ in composition, size, and the territorial distribution of the participants. Some, like local cults, are small and concentrated; others, like the intellectual world, are vast and the participants dispersed. Worlds differ in the extent and clarity of their boundaries; each is confined by some kind of horizon, but this may be wide or narrow, clear or vague. The fact that social worlds are not coterminous with the universe of men is recognized; those in the underworld are well aware of the fact that outsiders do not share their values. Worlds differ in exclusiveness and in the extent to which they demand the loyalty of their participants. Most important of all, social worlds are not static entities; shared perspectives are continually being reconstituted. Worlds come into existence with the establishment of communication channels; when life conditions change, social relationships may also change, and these worlds may disappear.

Every social world has some kind of communication system—often nothing more than differential association—in which there develops a special universe of discourse, sometimes an argot. Special meanings and symbols further accentuate differences and increase social distance from outsiders. In each world there are special norms of conduct, a set of values, a special prestige ladder, characteristic career lines, and a common outlook toward life—a Weltanschauung. In the case of elites there may even arise a code of honor which holds only for those who belong, while others are dismissed as beings somewhat less than human from whom bad manners may be expected. A social world, then, is an order conceived which serves as the stage on which each participant seeks to carve out his career and to maintain and enhance his status.

One of the characteristics of life in modern mass societies is simultaneous participation in a variety of social worlds. Because of the ease with which the individual may expose himself to a number of communication channels, he may lead a segmentalized life, participating successively in a number of unrelated activities. Furthermore, the particular combination of social worlds differs from person to person; this is what led Simmel to declare that each stands at that point at which a unique combination of social circles intersects. The geometric analogy is a happy one, for it enables us to conceive the numerous possibilities of combinations and the different degrees of participation in each circle. To understand what a man does, we must get at his unique perspective—what he takes for granted and how he defines the situation—but in mass societies we must learn in addition the social world in which he is participating in a given act.

Loyalty and Selective Responsiveness

In a mass society where each person internalizes numerous perspectives there are bound to be some incongruities and conflicts. The overlapping of group affiliation and participation, however, need not lead to difficulties and is usually unnoticed. The reference groups of most persons are mutually sustaining. Thus, the soldier who volunteers for hazardous duty on the battle-field may provoke anxiety in his family but is not acting contrary to their values; both his family and his comrades admire courage and disdain coward-ice. Behavior may be inconsistent, as in the case of the proverbial office tyrant who is meek before his wife, but it is not noticed if the transactions occur in dissociated contexts. Most people live more or less compartmentalized lives, shifting from one social world to another as they participate in a succession of transactions. In each world their roles are different, their relations to other participants are different, and they reveal a different facet of their personalities. Men have become so accustomed to this mode of life that they manage to con-ceive of themselves as reasonably consistent human beings in spite of this segmentalization and are generally not aware of the fact that their acts do not fit into a coherent pattern.

People become acutely aware of the existence of different outlooks only when they are successively caught in situations in which conflicting demands are made upon them, all of which cannot possibly be satisfied. While men generally avoid making difficult decisions, these dilemmas and con-tradictions of status may force a choice between two social worlds. These con-flicts are essentially alternative ways of defining the same situation, arising from several possible perspectives. In the words of William James, "As a man I pity you, but as an official I must show you no mercy; as a politician I regard him as an ally, but as a moralist I loathe him." In playing roles in different social worlds, one imputes different expectations to others whose differences cannot always be compromised. The problem is that of selecting the per-spective for defining the situation. In Mead's terminology, which generalized other's role is to be taken? It is only in situations where alternative definitions are possible that problems of loyalty arise.

Generally such conflicts are ephemeral; in critical situations contra-dictions otherwise unnoticed are brought into the open, and painful choices are forced. In poorly integrated societies, however, some people find them-selves continually beset with such conflicts. The Negro intellectual, children of mixed marriages or of immigrants, the foreman in a factory, the profes-sional woman, the military chaplain—all live in the interstices of well-organized structures and are marginal men [sic] (cf. Hughes, 1945; Stonequist, 1937). In most instances they manage to make their way through their compartmental-ized lives, although personal maladjustments are apparently frequent. In ex-treme cases amnesia and dissociation of personality can occur.

Much of the interest in reference groups arises out of concern with situations in which a person is confronted with the necessity of choosing between two or more organized perspectives. The hypothesis has been ad-vanced that the choice of reference groups—conformity to the norms of the group whose perspective is assumed—is a function of one's interpersonal relations; to what extent the culture of a group serves as the matrix for the organization of perceptual experience depends upon one's relationship and personal loyalty to others who share that outlook. Thus, when personal rela-tions to others in the group deteriorate, as sometimes happens in a military unit after continued defeat, the norms become less binding, and the unit may disintegrate in panic. Similarly, with the transformation of personal relationships between parent and child in late adolescence, the desires and standards of the parents often become less obligatory.

It has been suggested further that choice of reference groups rests upon personal loyalty to significant others of that social world. "Significant others," for Sullivan (1947), are those persons directly responsible for the internalization of norms. Socialization is a product of a gradual accumulation of experiences with certain people, particularly those with whom we stand in primary relations, and significant others are those who are actually involved in the cultivation of abilities, values, and outlook. Crucial, apparently, is the character of one's emotional ties with them. Those who think the significant others have treated them with affection and consideration have a sense of personal obligation that is binding under all circumstances, and they will be loyal even at great personal sacrifice. Since primary relations are not necessarily satisfactory, however, the reactions may be negative. A person who is well aware of the expectations of significant others may go out of his way to reject them. This may account for the bifurcation of orientation in minority groups, where some remain loyal to the parental culture while others seek desperately to become assimilated in the larger world. Some who withdraw from the uncertainties of real life may establish loyalties to perspectives acquired through vicarious relationships with characters encountered in books (Grinker and Spiegel, 1945; Shils and Janowitz, 1948).

Perspectives are continually subjected to the test of reality. All perception is hypothetical. Because of what is taken for granted from each standpoint, each situation is approached with a set of expectations; if transactions actually take place as anticipated, the perspective itself is reinforced. It is thus the confirming responses of other people that provide support for perspectives (cf. G. H. Mead, 1938; Postman, 1951). But in mass societies the responses of others vary, and in the study of reference groups the problem is that of ascertaining *whose* confirming responses will sustain a given point of view.

The Study of Mass Societies

Because of the differentiated character of modern mass societies, the concept of reference group, or some suitable substitute, will always have a central place in any realistic conceptual scheme for its analysis. As is pointed out above, it will be most useful if it is used to designate that group whose perspective is assumed by the actor as the frame of reference for the organization of his perceptual experience. Organized perspectives arise in and become shared through participation in common communication channels, and the diversity of mass societies arises from the multiplicity of channels and the ease with which one may participate in them.

Mass societies are not only diversified and pluralistic but also continually changing. The successive modification of life-conditions compels changes in social relationships, and any adequate analysis requires a study of these transformational processes themselves. Here the concept of reference group can be of crucial importance. For example, all forms of social mobility, from sudden conversions to gradual assimilation, may be regarded essentially as displacements of reference groups, for they involve a loss of responsiveness to the demands of one social world and the adoption of the perspective of another. It may be hypothesized that the disaffection occurs first on the level of personal relations, followed by a weakening sense of obligation, a rejection of old claims, and the establishment of new loyalties and incorporation of a new perspective. The conflicts that characterize all persons in marginal roles are of special interest in that they provide opportunities for cross-sectional analyses of the processes of social change.

In the analysis of the behavior of men in mass societies the crucial problem is that of ascertaining how a person defines the situation, which perspective he uses in arriving at such a definition, and who constitutes the audience whose responses provide the necessary confirmation and support for his position. This calls for focusing attention upon the expectations the actor imputes to others, the communication channels in which he participates, and his relations with those with whom he identifies himself. In the study of conflict, imagery provides a fertile source of data. At moments of indecision, when in doubt and confusion, who appears in imagery? In this manner the significant other can be identified.

An adequate analysis of modern mass societies requires the development of concepts and operations for the description of the manner in which each actor's orientation toward his world is successively reconstituted. Since perception is selective and perspectives differ, different items are noticed and a progressively diverse set of images arises, even among those exposed to the same media of mass communication. The concept of reference group summarizes differential associations and loyalties and thus facilitates the study of selective perception. It becomes, therefore, an indispensable tool for comprehending the diversity and dynamic character of the kind of society in which we live.

References

Chapman, D. W., and J. Volkmann. "A Social Determinant of the Level of Aspiration." *J. Abnormal & Social Psychology*, Vol. 34 (1939), 225–238.

Grinker, R. R., and J. P. Spiegel. *Men Under Stress*. Blakiston, 1945.

Hughes, E. C. "Dilemmas and Contradictions of Status." *Amer. J. Sociology*, Vol. 50 (1945), 353–359.

Hyman, H. H. "The Psychology of Status." *Archives of Psychology*, Vol. 38 (1942), 15.

Landgrebe, L. "The World as a Phenomenological Problem." *Philosophy & Phenomenological Research*, Vol. 1 (1940), 38–58.

Mead, G. H. "The Genesis of the Self and Social Control." *International J. Ethics*, Vol. 35 (1925), 251–277.

———. *Mind, Self and Society*, ed. C. W. Morris. Univ. Chicago Press, 1934.

———. *The Philosophy of the Act.* Univ. Chicago Press, 1938.

Merton, R. K., and A. Kitt. "Contributions to the Theory of Reference Group Behavior." *Studies in the Scope and Method of "The American Soldier,"* ed. R. K. Merton and P. F. Lazarsfeld. The Free Press, 1950.

Parsons, T. "The Superego and the Theory of Social Systems." *Psychiatry*, Vol. 15 (1952), 15–25.

Postman, L. "Toward a General Theory of Cognition." *Social Psychology at the Crossroads,* ed. J. H. Rohrer and M. Sherif. Harper & Row (1951), 242–272.

Redfield, R. *The Folk Culture of Yucatan,* Univ. Chicago Press, 1941.

Riezler, K. *Man: Mutable and Immutable.* Regnery, 1950.

Sapir, E. *The Selected Writings of Edward Sapir in Language, Culture, and Personality,* ed. D. G. Mandelbaum. Univ. of California Press, 1949.

Schuetz, A. "The Stranger: An Essay in Social Psychology." *Amer. J. of Sociology,* Vol. 49 (May 1944), 499–507.

Sherif, M. "The Concept of Reference Groups in Human Relations." *Group Relations at the Crossroads,* ed. M. Sherif and M. O. Wilson. Harper & Row (1953), 203–231.

Shils, E. A., and M. Janowitz. "Cohesion and Disintegration in the Wehrmacht in World War II." *Public Opinion Quarterly,* Vol. 12 (Summer 1948), 280–315.

Stonequist, E. V. *The Marginal Man.* Scribner's, 1937.

Sullivan, H. S. *Conceptions of Modern Psychiatry.* White Psychiatric Foundation, 1947.

4.2 Socially Distant Reference Groups and Consumer Aspirations
A. BENTON COCANOUGHER, GRADY D. BRUCE

Several specific effects of various social groups on consumer behavior have been studied. Venkatesan demonstrated experimentally that individuals' product choices may be affected by conformity and reactance in small face-to-face groups [10]. Stafford [9] and Witt [11] found that small primary groups influence certain brand choice decisions, and Bourne suggested that the purchase of certain types and brands of products may be influenced by a person's reference group [1]. However, there is a significant gap in knowledge about the effects on consumer behavior of the socially distant reference group.[1]

Conceptual Framework

Theorists disagree about the functions reference groups perform in influencing individual attitudes, values, and behavior. However, Kelley identified two primary functions which incorporate most reference group theorists' viewpoints: the normative and comparative functions [5]. The normative function is the setting and enforcing of standards for the individual, and most previous research has explored the efficacy of small groups in enforcing such group norms on interacting individuals.

The comparative function is the group's capacity to serve as a point of comparison against which an individual can evaluate himself and others. That is, a group can influence an individual to the extent that the attitudes, values, and behavior of its members represent standards which he voluntarily uses in making judgments and evaluations. Unlike the normative influence, which requires at least enough interaction to enable the group to evaluate the extent of the individual's conformity to group norms, comparative influence depends only upon the influence recipient being attracted to group members or activities [3].

This research was designed to investigate the relationship between an individual's choice of a socially distant aspiration group and the development of his aspirations as a consumer. Thus it is concerned with the comparative function: the influence on purchase aspirations of the individual's perceptions of the behavior of a group to which he is attracted, but with which he has little or no interaction. Since, as previously stated, attraction may exist along two dimensions, a two-part proposition was tested: the amount of influence exerted by the aspiration reference group will be related to the individual's expressed attitudes toward: (1) group members and (2) their activities.

Methodology

Subjects for the study were 114 male undergraduate students at The University of Texas at Austin, and the socially distant reference group used was business executives. This reference group was deemed especially appropriate with student subjects since it represents a potential career and since most students have some perception of the behavior and activities of this group. Student subjects were from business and nonbusiness classes in order to get a wide range of expressed attraction to the business executive group.

The working hypotheses were:

1. The amount of influence exerted by the business executive group will be related to subjects' expressed attitudes toward a career in business, with those subjects having the most favorable attitudes being the most influenced.
2. The amount of influence exerted by the business executive group will be related to subjects' attitudes toward business executives, with those subjects having the most favorable attitudes being the most influenced.

The Remmers short-form adaptation of the Miller Attitude Toward Any Occupation Test was employed to evaluate the subjects' attitudes toward business careers [6]. This is a Thurstone equal-appearing interval scale test with 17 statements; reliabilities ranging from .71 to .92 have been reported.

A semantic differential test was used to measure subjects' attitudes toward business executives. Pretesting and subsequent revisions helped identify those adjectives offering the most appropriate and discriminating choices to the subjects in this study. The eight adjective pairs finally used in a seven-point scale were: interesting-uninteresting, honest-hypocritical, skillful-unskillful, selfish-unselfish, fair-biased, cruel-kind, sincere-insincere, and ethical-unethical. Eight other pairs of adjectives were used as buffer items. The test score for each subject was derived by summing the scale values for the appropriate eight items.

Operationalizing the dependent variable (reference group influence as measured in terms of consumer product aspirations) presented a problem. However, since a number of recent marketing studies have demonstrated the adaptability of Q-methodology to problems of this nature, that technique was used in this study [7, 8]. Basically, Q-methodology involves the use of a forced choice method whereby a subject is provided with a number of items and asked to use them to describe his actual-self, ideal-self, or some defined "other." When two or more such sorts are made under different sets of instructions, such as one sort for self and one sort for other, the resulting arrays can be correlated to determine the effect of different conditions of instruction on the test items [7].

In this application of the technique, every subject was given two decks of 38 cards each, each card with the name of a consumer product imprinted on the front. The two decks were identical, except for color: one was blue, the other green. The different colors were used to help respondents distinguish between the different frames of reference called for in the sorting instructions.

The subjects were first instructed to sort the blue deck according to whether or not the product shown on a card was representative of what he would ideally like to have five years after graduation. All 38 cards were rank ordered from most to least descriptive of a futuristic ideal-self. Then subjects were instructed to perform the same task with the green deck, except that with this deck the products should be used to describe their perception of the products used by a typical business executive, again from the most to least descriptive.

The two independent sorts performed by each subject were then subjected to correlation analysis to determine the degree of congruency between his ideal-self and his perception of a typical business executive. These r-values were calculated by correlating sets of Q-sorts [2]. The r-values thus derived were operationally defined as indicating the degree of influence which the business executive reference group exerted on the subject's development of ideal-self.

A pretest was conducted to select products to be used by subjects to describe their future ideal-self and a typical business executive. One hundred and six male students in an introductory marketing course were given a list of 76 relatively common consumer products and asked to indicate those which they felt were most characteristic of the following individuals: (1) self, (2) best friend, (3) father, (4) male social worker, (5) attorney, (6) truck driver, (7) male "hippie," and (8) male business executive. These rankings were tabulated and analyzed to select products highly descriptive of either self or a business executive.

In addition, an effort was made to select the products with strong business executive identification so that the same products were not equally descriptive of other occupational types or significant others. This step was taken to reduce the likelihood of a subject's displaying a high degree of congruency between ideal-self and his perception of business executives which is, in reality, merely a reflection of influence exerted by a reference group other than business executives. The 38 products listed in Table 1 were those chosen as best meeting this criterion.

Analysis and Findings

Since the basic premise upon which the working hypotheses were analyzed is that the degree of congruency between the two Q-sort rankings is a measure of the reference group's influence on the subject, correlation coefficients were calculated for each subject's Q-rankings. These were transformed to z-values, which were the criterion variables used in correlation and covariance analysis with the predictors: attitudes toward a career in business and attitudes toward business executives.[2]

The variable of attraction to group activities, or the measure of attitudes toward a career in business, correlated with group influence at $r = .53$, significant at $p < .0001$. Attitudes toward business executives, the measure of attraction to group members, correlated with group influence at $r = .45$, also significant at $p < .0001$ (see Table 2). Thus, both working hypotheses were clearly supported.

In order to evaluate the predictive power of total attraction to the reference group, multiple correlation analysis was performed using both independent variables. Covariance analysis revealed that the resulting multiple R of .57 was significantly greater than the correlation obtained when using only attitudes toward a career in business or attitudes toward business executives at $p = .0075$ and $p = .0001$, respectively. This suggests the advisability of using both predictors (or *total* attraction to reference group) to explain variations in an individual's choice of a socially distant reference group.

TABLE 1.   Q-Sort Products

Lincoln Continental	*Sports Illustrated*	Buick Riviera
Stereo Equipment	Electric Shoe Polisher	*Newsweek*
Mercedes Sports Car	Camping Equipment	Corvette
Cardigan Sweater	*Playboy*	Lawn Furniture
Theatre Tickets	Portable Radio	Tennis Racquet
Reclining Chair	Sport Coat	Bar B-Q Grill
King-size Bed	Hair Spray	*Time*
Fireplace	Loafer Shoes	Golf Clubs
Attache Case	Manicure Set	Tuxedo
Cadillac	Swim Suit	Dress Shoes
Hair Brush	Rifle	Fishing Rod
Camera	Pipe (Smoking)	Mustang
Speedboat	Dark Suit	

Implications

The use of "distant others"—for example, cultural heroes, such as movie stars, athletes, and the like—in all forms of advertising is a clear illustration of the basic assumption in marketing that there is a relationship between an individual's attraction to a socially distant reference group and the amount of influence the group exerts. Indeed, any marketing communication which urges consumers to act in terms of the behavior of a referent individual or group with whom the consumer has no regular personal interaction would appear to be based on the assumption that such distant referents can influence the consumer's product aspirations or formulation of his ideal-self-image. Yet despite the prevailing acceptance of such an influence, little empirical support has been generated, because most previous reference group research has concentrated on small face-to-face groups where interaction is on a regular, routine basis or where it has been experimentally induced.

Although exploratory in nature, the findings of this study may be suggestive in a number of contexts. First, since market segments represent relatively homogeneous groupings of individuals, it may be possible to identify similarities among individuals within a segment with regard to the distant referents they find most attractive. Along this same line, it may even prove useful to formulate new classifications of market segments based on potentially influential distant referents. Such a segmentation would be useful in advertising and, perhaps, product development.

Second, individuals do have negative reference groups whose norms they seek to avoid adopting as their own [4]. Therefore, it may be necessary to recognize that the use of any referent group in advertising necessarily repels some individuals who may be potential consumers.

Notes

1. "Socially distant" is used in this context to describe that relationship between the potential influence recipient and the reference group characterized by the absence of regular interaction.

2. One additional evaluation of the subjects' Q-sorts consisted of correlating the average business executive ranking for those subjects in the upper quartile of both attraction variables with the average business executive ranking for those subjects in the lower quartile of both attraction variables. The resulting r of .80 indicates

TABLE 2.   Correlation Models

Model Number	Independent Variable	Correlation Coefficient	Coefficient of Determination
I	Attitudes Toward Career	.53[a]	.28
II	Attitudes Toward Executives	.45[a]	.20
III	Both Attraction Variables	.57[a]	.32

[a] $p < .0001$.

that even those subjects feeling widely divergent attraction to the group had similar perceptions of group norms.

References

1. Bourne, Francis S. "Group Influence in Marketing and Public Relations," in James U. McNeal, ed., *Dimensions of Consumer Behavior.* New York: Appleton-Century-Crofts (1965), 137–146.

2. Hilden, Arnold H. "Manual for Q-Sort and Random Sets of Personal Concepts," unpublished paper, Washington University, 1954.

3. Hollander, Edwin P. "Conformity, Status, and Idiosyncrasy Credit," in Edwin P. Hollander and Raymond G. Hunt, eds., *Current Perspectives in Social Psychology.* New York: Oxford Press (1967), 465–475.

4. Kassarjian, Harold H., and Thomas S. Robertson, eds. *Perspectives in Consumer Behavior.* Glenview, Ill.: Scott, Foresman (1968), 274–275.

5. Kelley, Harold H. "Two Functions of Reference Groups," in Harold Proshansky and Bernard Siedenberg, eds., *Basic Studies in Social Psychology.* New York: Holt, Rinehart and Winston (1965), 210–214.

6. Shaw, Marvin E., and Jack M. Wright, eds. *Scales for the Measurement of Attitudes.* New York: McGraw-Hill (1967), 129–131.

7. Sommers, Montrose S. "The Use of Product Symbolism to Differentiate Social Strata," *University of Houston Business Review,* Vol. 11 (Fall 1964), 28–29.

8. ———, and Grady D. Bruce. "Blacks, Whites, and Products: Relative Deprivation and Reference Group Behavior," *Social Science Quarterly,* Vol. 49 (December 1968), 631–642.

9. Stafford, James E. "Effects of Group Influence on Consumer Brand Preferences," *Journal of Marketing Research,* Vol. 3 (February 1966), 68–74.

10. Venkatesan, M. "Consumer Behavior: Conformity and Independence," in [4], 306–312.

11. Witt, Robert E. "Informal Social Group Influence on Consumer Brand Choice," *Journal of Marketing Research,* Vol. 6 (November 1969), 473–476.

4.3 Effects of Group Pressure Upon the Modification and Distortion of Judgments

SOLOMON E. ASCH

We shall here describe in summary form the conception and first findings of a program of investigation into the conditions of independence and submission to group pressure.[1]

Our immediate object was to study the social and personal conditions that induce individuals to resist or to yield to group pressures when the latter are perceived to be *contrary to fact*. The issues which this problem raises are of obvious consequence for society; it can be of decisive importance whether or not a group will, under certain conditions, submit to existing pressures. Equally direct are the consequences for individuals and our understanding of them, since it is a decisive fact about a person whether he possesses the freedom to act independently, or whether he characteristically submits to group pressures.

The problem under investigation requires the direct observation of certain basic processes in the interaction between individuals, and between individuals and groups. To clarify these seems necessary if we are to make fundamental advances in the understanding of the formation and reorganization of attitudes, of the functioning of public opinion, and of the operation of propaganda. Today we do not possess an adequate theory of these central psycho-social processes. Empirical investigation has been predominantly controlled by general propositions concerning group influence which have as a rule been assumed but not tested. With few exceptions investigation has relied upon descriptive formulations concerning the operation of suggestion and prestige, the inadequacy of which is becoming increasingly obvious, and upon schematic applications of stimulus-response theory.

Basic to the current approach has been the axiom that group pressures characteristically induce psychological changes *arbitrarily,* in far-reaching disregard of the material properties of the given conditions. This mode of thinking has almost exclusively stressed the slavish submission of individuals to group forces, has neglected to inquire into their possibilities for independence and for productive relations with the human environment, and has virtually denied the capacity of men under certain conditions to rise above group passion and prejudice. It was our aim to contribute to a clarification of these questions, important both for theory and for their human implications, by means of direct observation of the effects of groups upon the decisions and evaluations of individuals.

The Experiment and First Results

To this end we developed an experimental technique which has served as the basis for the present series of studies. We employed the procedure of placing an individual in a relation of radical conflict with all the other members of a group, of measuring its effect upon him in quantitative terms, and of describing its psychological consequences. A group of eight individuals was instructed to judge a series of simple, clearly structured perceptual relations—

to match the length of a given line with one of three unequal lines. Each member of the group announced his judgments publicly. In the midst of this monotonous "test" one individual found himself suddenly contradicted by the entire group, and this contradiction was repeated again and again in the course of the experiment. The group in question had, with the exception of one member, previously met with the experimenter and received instructions to respond at certain points with wrong—and unanimous—judgments. The errors of the majority were large (ranging between $\frac{1}{2}$ in. and $1\frac{3}{4}$ in.) and of an order not encountered under control conditions. The outstanding person—the critical subject—whom we had placed in the position of a *minority of one* in the midst of a *unanimous majority*—was the object of investigation. He faced, possibly for the first time in his life, a situation in which a group unanimously contradicted the evidence of his senses.

This procedure was the starting point of the investigation and the point of departure for the study of further problems. Its main features were the following: (1) The critical subject was submitted to two contradictory and irreconcilable forces—the evidence of his own experience of a clearly perceived relation, and the unanimous evidence of a group of equals. (2) Both forces were part of the immediate situation; the majority was concretely present, surrounding the subject physically. (3) The critical subject, who was requested together with all others to state his judgments publicly, was obliged to declare himself and to take a definite stand *vis-à-vis* the group. (4) The situation possessed a self-contained character. The critical subject could not avoid or evade the dilemma by reference to conditions external to the experimental situation. (It may be mentioned at this point that the forces generated by the given conditions acted so quickly upon the critical subjects that instances of suspicion were infrequent.)

The technique employed permitted a simple quantitative measure of the "majority effect" in terms of the frequency of errors in the direction of the distorted estimates of the majority. At the same time we were concerned to obtain evidence of the ways in which the subjects perceived the group, to establish whether they became doubtful, whether they were tempted to join the majority. Most important, it was our object to establish the grounds of the subject's independence or yielding—whether, for example, the yielding subject was aware of the effect of the majority upon him, whether he abandoned his judgment deliberately or compulsively. To this end we constructed a comprehensive set of questions which served as the basis of an individual interview immediately following the experimental period. Toward the conclusion of the interview each subject was informed fully of the purpose of the experiment, of his role and of that of the majority. The reactions to the disclosure of the purpose of the experiment became in fact an integral part of the procedure. The information derived from the interview became an indispensable source of evidence and insight into the psychological structure of the experimental situation, and in particular, of the nature of the individual differences. It should be added that it is not justified or advisable to allow the subject to leave without giving him a full explanation of the experimental conditions. The experimenter has a responsibility to the subject to clarify his doubts and to state the reasons for placing him in the experimental situation. When this is done most subjects react with interest, and some express gratification at having lived through a striking situation which has some bearing on them personally and on wider human issues.

Both the members of the majority and the critical subjects were male college students. We shall report the results for a total of 50 critical subjects in this experiment. In Table 1 we summarize the successive comparison trials and the majority estimates. The reader will note that on certain trials the majority responded correctly; these were the "neutral" trials. There were 12 critical trials on which the majority responded incorrectly.

The quantitative results are clear and unambiguous.

1. There was a marked movement toward the majority. One third of all the estimates in the critical group were errors identical with or in the direction of the distorted estimates of the majority. The significance of this finding becomes clear in the light of the virtual absence of errors in the control group, the members of which recorded their estimates in writing. The relevant data of the critical and control groups are summarized in Table 2.

2. At the same time the effect of the majority was far from complete. The preponderance of estimates in the critical group (68%) was correct despite the pressure of the majority.

3. We found evidence of extreme individual differences. There were in the critical group subjects who remained independent without exception, and there were those who went nearly all the time with the majority. (The maximum possible number of errors was 12, while the actual range of errors was 0–11.) One fourth of the critical subjects was completely independent; at the other extreme, one third of the group displaced the estimates toward the majority in one half or more of the trials.

The differences between the critical subjects in their reactions to the given conditions were equally striking. There were subjects who remained completely confident throughout. At the other extreme were those who became disoriented, doubt-ridden, and experienced a powerful impulse not to appear different from the majority.

For purposes of illustration we include a brief description of one independent and one yielding subject.

Independent

After a few trials he appeared puzzled, hesitant. He announced all disagreeing answers in the form of "Three, sir; two, sir"; not so with the unanimous answers on the neutral trials. At Trial 4 he answered immediately after the first member of the group, shook his head, blinked, and whispered to his neighbor: "Can't help it, that's one." His later answers came in a whispered voice, accompanied by a deprecating smile. At one point he grinned embarrassedly, and whispered explosively to his neighbor: "I always disagree—darn it!" During the questioning, this subject's constant refrain was: "I called them as I saw them, sir." He insisted that his estimates were right without, however, committing himself as to whether the others were wrong, remarking that "that's the way I see them and that's the way they see them." If he had to make a practical decision under similar circumstances, he declared, "I would follow my own view, though part of my reason would tell me that I might be wrong." Immediately following the experiment the majority engaged this subject in a brief

TABLE 1.   Lengths of Standard and Comparison Lines

Trial	Length of Standard Line (in Inches)	Comparison Lines (in Inches) 1	2	3	Correct Response	Group Response	Majority Error (in Inches)
1	10	$8\frac{3}{4}$	10	8	2	2	—
2	2	2	1	$1\frac{1}{2}$	1	1	—
3	3	$3\frac{3}{4}$	$4\frac{1}{4}$	3	3	1*	$+\frac{3}{4}$
4	5	5	4	$6\frac{1}{2}$	1	2*	-1.0
5	4	3	5	4	3	3	—
6	3	$3\frac{3}{4}$	$4\frac{1}{4}$	3	3	2*	$+1\frac{1}{4}$
7	8	$6\frac{1}{4}$	8	$6\frac{3}{4}$	2	3*	$-1\frac{1}{4}$
8	5	5	4	$6\frac{1}{2}$	1	3*	$+1\frac{1}{2}$
9	8	$6\frac{1}{4}$	8	$6\frac{3}{4}$	2	1*	$-1\frac{3}{4}$
10	10	$8\frac{3}{4}$	10	8	2	2	—
11	2	2	1	$1\frac{1}{2}$	1	1	—
12	3	$3\frac{3}{4}$	$4\frac{1}{4}$	3	3	1*	$+\frac{3}{4}$
13	5	5	4	$6\frac{1}{2}$	1	2*	-1.0
14	4	3	5	4	3	3	—
15	3	$3\frac{3}{4}$	$4\frac{1}{4}$	3	3	2*	$+1\frac{1}{4}$
16	8	$6\frac{1}{4}$	8	$6\frac{3}{4}$	2	3*	$-1\frac{1}{4}$
17	5	5	4	$6\frac{1}{2}$	1	3*	$+1\frac{1}{2}$
18	8	$6\frac{1}{4}$	8	$6\frac{3}{4}$	2	1*	$-1\frac{3}{4}$

*Starred figures designate the erroneous estimates by the majority.

TABLE 2.   Distribution of Errors in Experimental and Control Groups

Number of Critical Errors	Critical Group[a] (N = 50) F	Control Group (N = 37) F
0	13	35
1	4	1
2	5	1
3	6	
4	3	
5	4	
6	1	
7	2	
8	5	
9	3	
10	3	
11	1	
12	0	
Total	50	37
Mean	3.84	0.08

[a]All errors in the critical group were in the direction of the majority estimates.

discussion. When they pressed him to say whether the entire group was wrong and he alone right, he turned upon them defiantly, exclaiming: "You're *probably* right, but you *may* be wrong!" To the disclosure of the experiment this subject reacted with the statement that he felt "exultant and relieved," adding, "I do not deny that at times I had the feeling: 'to heck with it, I'll go along with the rest.'"

Yielding

This subject went with the majority in 11 out of 12 trials. He appeared nervous and somewhat confused, but he did not attempt to evade discussion; on the contrary, he was helpful and tried to answer to the best of his ability. He opened the discussion with the statement: "If I'd been first I probably would have responded differently"; this was his way of stating that he had adopted the majority estimates. The primary factor in his case was loss of confidence. He perceived the majority as a decided group, acting without hesitation: "If they had been doubtful I probably would have changed, but they answered with such confidence." Certain of his errors, he explained, were due to the doubtful nature of the comparisons; in such instances he went with the majority. When the object of the experiment was explained, the subject volunteered: "I suspected about the middle—but tried to push it out of my mind." It is of interest that his suspicion did not restore his confidence or diminish the power of the majority. Equally striking is his report that he assumed the experiment to involve an "illusion" to which the others, but not he, were subject. This assumption too did not help to free him; on the contrary, he acted as if his divergence from the majority was a sign of defect. The principal impression this subject produced was of one so caught up by immediate difficulties that he lost clear reasons for his actions, and could make no reasonable decisions.

A First Analysis of Individual Differences

On the basis of the interview data described earlier, we undertook to differentiate and describe the major forms of reaction to the experimental situation, which we shall now briefly summarize.

Among the *independent* subjects we distinguished the following main categories:

1. Independence based on *confidence* in one's perception and experience. The most striking characteristic of these subjects is the vigor with which they withstand the group opposition. Though they are sensitive to the group, and experience the conflict, they show a resilience in coping with it, which is expressed in their continuing reliance on their perception and the effectiveness with which they shake off the oppressive group opposition.

2. Quite different are those subjects who are independent and *withdrawn*. These do not react in a spontaneously emotional way, but rather on the basis of explicit principles concerning the necessity of being an individual.

3. A third group of independent subjects manifests considerable tension and doubt, but adhere to their judgment on the basis of a felt necessity to deal adequately with the task.

The following were the main categories of reaction among the *yielding* subjects, or those who went with the majority during one half or more of the trials.

1. *Distortion of perception* under the stress of group pressure. In this category belong a very few subjects who yield completely, but are not aware that their estimates have been displaced or distorted by the majority. These subjects report that they came to perceive the majority estimates as correct.

2. *Distortion of judgment.* Most submitting subjects belong to this category. The factor of greatest importance in this group is a decision the subjects reach that their perceptions are inaccurate, and that those of the majority are correct. These subjects suffer from primary doubt and lack of confidence; on this basis they feel a strong tendency to join the majority.

3. *Distortion of action.* The subjects in this group do not suffer a modification of perception nor do they conclude that they are wrong. They yield because of an overmastering need not to appear different from or inferior to others, because of an inability to tolerate the appearance of defectiveness in the eyes of the group. These subjects suppress their observations and voice the majority position with awareness of what they are doing.

The results are sufficient to establish that independence and yielding are not psychologically homogeneous, that submission to group pressure and freedom from pressure can be the result of different psychological conditions. It should also be noted that the categories described above, being based exclusively on the subjects' reactions to the experimental conditions, are descriptive, not presuming to explain why a given individual responded in one way rather than another. The further exploration of the basis for the individual differences is a separate task.

Experimental Variations

The results described are clearly a joint function of two broadly different sets of conditions. They are determined first by the specific external conditions, by the particular character of the relation between social evidence and one's own experience. Second, the presence of pronounced individual differences points to the important role of personal factors, or factors connected with the individual's character structure. We reasoned that there are group conditions which would produce independence in all subjects, and that there probably are group conditions which would induce intensified yielding in many, though not in all. Secondly, we deemed it reasonable to assume that behavior under the experimental social pressure is significantly related to certain characteristics of the individual. The present account will be limited to the effect of the surrounding conditions upon independence and submission. To this end we followed the procedure of experimental variation, systematically altering the quality of social evidence by means of systematic variation of the group conditions and of the task.

The Effect of Nonunanimous Majorities

Evidence obtained from the basic experiment suggested that the condition of being exposed *alone* to the opposition of a "compact majority" may have played a decisive role in determining the course and strength of the effects observed. Accordingly we undertook to investigate in a series of successive variations the effects of *nonunanimous* majorities. The technical problem of altering the uniformity of a majority is, in terms of our procedure, relatively simple. In most instances we merely directed one or more members of the instructed group to deviate from the majority in prescribed ways. It is obvious that we cannot hope to compare the performance of the same individual in two situations on the assumption that they remain independent of one another; at best we can investigate the effect of an earlier upon a later experimental condition. The comparison of different experimental situations therefore requires the use of different but comparable groups of critical subjects. This is the procedure we have followed. In the variations to be described we have maintained the conditions of the basic experiment (e.g., the sex of the subjects, the size of the majority, the content of the task, and so on) save for the specific factor that was varied. The following were some of the variations studied:

1. *The presence of a "true partner."* (a) In the midst of the majority were *two* naïve, critical subjects. The subjects were separated spatially, being seated in the fourth and eighth positions, respectively. Each therefore heard his judgments confirmed by one other person (provided the other person remained independent), one prior to, the other after announcing his own judgment. In addition, each experienced a break in the unanimity of the majority. There were six pairs of critical subjects. (b) In a further variation the "partner" to the critical subject was a member of the group who had been instructed to respond correctly throughout. This procedure permits the exact control of the partner's responses. The partner was always seated in the fourth position; he therefore announced his estimates in each case before the critical subject.

The results clearly demonstrate that a disturbance of the unanimity of the majority markedly increased the independence of the critical subjects. The frequency of promajority errors dropped to 10.4% of the total number of estimates in variation (a), and to 5.5% in variation (b). These results are to be compared with the frequency of yielding to the unanimous majorities in the basic experiment, which was 32% of the total number of estimates. It is clear that the presence in the field of *one other* individual who responded correctly was sufficient to deplete the power of the majority, and in some cases to destroy it. This finding is all the more striking in the light of other variations which demonstrate the effect of even small minorities provided they are unanimous. Indeed, we have been able to show that a unanimous majority of three is, under the given conditions, far more effective than a majority of eight containing one dissenter. That critical subjects will under these conditions free themselves of a majority of seven and join forces with one other person in the minority is, we believe, a result significant for theory. It points to a fundamental psychological difference between the condition of being alone and having a minimum of human support. It further demonstrates that the effects obtained are not the result of a summation of influences proceeding from each member of the group; it is necessary to conceive [of] the results as being relationally determined.

2. *Withdrawal of a "true partner."* What will be the effect of providing

the critical subject with a partner who responds correctly and then withdrawing him? The critical subject started with a partner who responded correctly. The partner was a member of the majority who had been instructed to respond correctly and to "desert" to the majority in the middle of the experiment. This procedure permits the observation of the same subject in the course of the transition from one condition to another. The withdrawal of the partner produced a powerful and unexpected result. We had assumed that the critical subject, having gone through the experience of opposing the majority with a minimum of support, would maintain his independence when alone. Contrary to this expectation, we found that the experience of having had and then lost a partner restored the majority effect to its full force, the proportion of errors rising to 28.5% of all judgments, in contrast to the preceding level of 5.5%. Further experimentation is needed to establish whether the critical subjects were responding to the sheer fact of being alone, or to the fact that the partner abandoned them.

3. *Late arrival of a "true partner."* The critical subject started as a minority of one in the midst of a unanimous majority. Toward the conclusion of the experiment one member of the majority "broke" away and began announcing correct estimates. This procedure, which reverses the order of conditions of the preceding experiment, permits the observation of the transition from being alone to being a member of a pair against a majority. It is obvious that those critical subjects who were independent when alone would continue to be so when joined by a partner. The variation is therefore of significance primarily for those subjects who yielded during the first phase of the experiment. The appearance of the late partner exerts a freeing effect, reducing the level of yielding to 8.7%. Those who had previously yielded also became markedly more independent, but not completely so, continuing to yield more than previously independent subjects. The reports of the subjects do not cast much light on the factors responsible for the result. It is our impression that some subjects, having once committed themselves to yielding, find it difficult to change their direction completely. To do so is tantamount to a public admission that they had not acted rightly. They therefore follow to an extent the precarious course they had chosen in order to maintain an outward semblance of consistency and conviction.

4. *The presence of a "compromise partner."* The majority was consistently extremist, always matching the standard with the most unequal line. One instructed subject (who, as in the other variations, preceded the critical subject) also responded incorrectly, but his estimates were always intermediate between the truth and the majority position. The critical subject therefore faced an extremist majority whose unanimity was broken by one more moderately erring person. Under these conditions the frequency of errors was reduced but not significantly. However, the lack of unanimity determined in a strikingly consistent way the *direction* of the errors. The preponderance of the errors, 75.7% of the total, was moderate, whereas in a parallel experiment in which the majority was unanimously extremist (i.e., with the "compromise" partner excluded), the incidence of moderate errors was 42% of the total. As might be expected, in a unanimously moderate majority, the errors of the critical subjects were without exception moderate.

The Role of Majority Size

To gain further understanding of the majority effect, we varied the size of the majority in several different variations. The majorities, which were in each case unanimous, consisted of 2, 3, 4, 8, and 10–15 persons, respectively. In addition, we studied the limiting case in which the critical subject was opposed by one instructed subject. Table 3 contains the mean and the range of errors under each condition.

TABLE 3.   Errors of Critical Subjects with Unanimous Majorities of Different Size

Size of Majority	Control	1	2	3	4	8	10–15
N	37	10	15	10	10	50	12
Mean Number of Errors	0.08	0.33	1.53	4.0	4.20	3.84	3.75
Range of Errors	0–2	0–1	0–5	1–12	0–11	0–11	0–10

With the opposition reduced to one, the majority effect all but disappeared. When the opposition proceeded from a group of two, it produced a measurable though small distortion, the errors being 12.8% of the total number of estimates. The effect appeared in full force with a majority of three. Larger majorities did not produce effects greater than a majority of three.

The effect of a majority is often silent, revealing little of its operation to the subject, and often hiding it from the experimenter. To examine the range of effects it is capable of inducing, decisive variations of conditions are necessary. An indication of one effect is furnished by the following variation in which the conditions of the basic experiment were simply reversed. Here the majority, consisting of a group of 16, was naïve; in the midst of it we placed a single individual who responded wrongly according to instructions. Under these conditions the members of the naïve majority reacted to the lone dissenter with amusement. Contagious laughter spread through the group at the droll minority of one. Of significance is the fact that the members lacked awareness that they drew their strength from the majority, and that their reactions would change radically if they faced the dissenter individually. These observations demonstrate the role of social support as a source of power and stability, in contrast to the preceding investigations which stressed the effects of social opposition. Both aspects must be explicitly considered in a unified formulation of the effects of group conditions on the formation and change of judgments.

The Role of the Stimulus Situation

It is obviously not possible to divorce the quality and course of the group forces which act upon the individual from the specific stimulus conditions. Of necessity the structure of the situation molds the group forces and determines their direction as well as their strength. Indeed, this was the reason that we took pains in the investigations described above to center the issue between the individual and the group around an elementary matter of fact. And there can be no doubt that the resulting reactions were directly a function of the contradiction between the observed relations and the majority position. These general considerations are sufficient to establish the need to vary the stimulus conditions and to observe their effect on the resulting group forces.

Accordingly we have studied the effect of increasing and decreasing the discrepancy between the correct relation and the position of the majority, going beyond the basic experiment which contained discrepancies of a relatively moderate order. Our technique permits the easy variation of this factor, since we can vary at will the deviation of the majority from the correct relation. At this point we can only summarize the trend of the results which is entirely clear. The degree of independence increases with the distance of the majority from correctness. However, even glaring discrepancies (of the order of 3 to 6 in.) did not produce independence in all. While independence increases with the magnitude of contradiction, a certain proportion of individuals continues to yield under extreme conditions.

We have also varied systematically the structural clarity of the task, employing judgments based on mental standards. In agreement with other investigators, we find that the majority effect grows stronger as the situation diminishes in clarity. Concurrently, however, the disturbance of the subjects and the conflict quality of the situation decrease markedly. We consider it of significance that the majority achieves its most pronounced effect when it acts most painlessly.

Summary

We have investigated the effects upon individuals of majority opinions when the latter were seen to be in a direction contrary to fact. By means of a simple technique we produced a radical divergence between a majority and a minority, and observed the ways in which individuals coped with the resulting difficulty. Despite the stress of the given conditions, a substantial proportion of individuals retained their independence throughout. At the same time a substantial minority yielded, modifying their judgments in accordance with the majority. Independence and yielding are a joint function of the following major factors:

1. *The character of the stimulus situation.* Variations in structural clarity have a decisive effect: with diminishing clarity of the stimulus conditions the majority effect increases.

2. *The character of the group forces.* Individuals are highly sensitive to the structural qualities of group opposition. In particular, we demonstrated the great importance of the factor of unanimity. Also, the majority effect is a function of the size of group opposition.

3. *The character of the individual.* There were wide and, indeed, striking differences among individuals within the same experimental situation.

Note

1. The earlier experiments out of which the present work developed and the theoretical issues which prompted it are discussed in Asch, S. E., *Social Psychology,* Prentice-Hall, 1952, Ch. 16.

4.4 Consumer Behavior: Conformity and Independence

M. VENKATESAN

Although group influence is one of the important factors in the attention-directing stage of the purchase process, "very little empirical work has been carried out" on this stage of the decision process (Ferber, 1962[b]). Attempts have been made to relate the findings on group influence from small group studies to consumer behavior (Bourne, 1957). While the investigations of group influence in consumer behavior are relatively recent, social psychology has long focused on the small group and its influence on the perceptions, opinions, and attitudes of its members.

Now there is a sizable body of social psychology literature on the experimental study of social influence. A number of experiments have demonstrated that with sufficient group pressure it is possible to influence what the individual believes he perceives. Other experiments suggested that in the absence of objective standards, an individual turns to other people for judgment and evaluation.

The conformity studies of Asch (1953) and the social judgment experiments of Sherif (1936) are best known and most representative. In the Asch experiment the task was to state which of the three lines on a card was equal in length to a comparison line. The critical subjects were exposed to the contrary-to-fact opinion of a unanimous majority (three or more confederates). The confederates had been instructed to give the same incorrect answer. Asch found that 37% of the critical subjects also gave the same incorrect response despite the fact that the majority response was obviously incorrect. In the autokinetic experiment of Sherif the subjects individually and in groups estimated the range of movement of a light which, in fact, was stationary. He demonstrated that in an unstructured situation the subjects, in making their decisions, were entirely dependent on the group for the norm and range.

Generally, laboratory studies of social influence demonstrated that individuals are highly susceptible to group pressure. A majority of the individuals conform to a *group norm.*[1] When objective standards were absent, more individuals tended to conform to a group norm than when the objective standards were present. The small-group studies were not concerned with group influence in buying situations. Assessing their relevance to buyer behavior after an exhaustive search of the social psychological literature, Howard (1963) concluded:

> Other people seem to be an important influence on the individual's perception. There are two hypotheses in this connection. *First,* a number of experiments suggest that, in the presence of a sufficient amount of group pressure, it is possible to influence what the individual believes he perceives. The *second* hypothesis is that, in the absence of objective standards or accepted authority, an individual will turn to

other people for judgments and evaluations. To whom he turns depends upon the circumstances (p. 136).

From these hypotheses he speculated about marketing situations.

Although knowledge about conformity to group norms in the marketplace is slight, common sense would lead us to conclude that consumer decision making takes place in an environment where conformity is a major force. However, the operation of group norms in many buying situations needs to be empirically established, and the social influence of groups on consumer behavior needs to be investigated systematically.

Although group influence in the consumer decision-making process is recognized, generally the attempts to influence are thought of as "pressures toward conformity." This view probably results from lack of attention to the phenomenon of independence in the social psychological literature. Little attention has been given to conditions under which independence occurs. Jahoda (1959) pointed out that "there is ample evidence for the existence of independence not only in common-sense observations but also in every single experiment which rejects the null-hypotheses of independence on statistically impressive levels of confidence" (p. 99).

Many buying actions come from a desire to identify with a membership or reference group. The influence exerted by given groups, such as neighborhood groups, bridge clubs, on its members is informal and subtle. Moreover, group norms establish a range of tolerable behavior or a frame of reference. Ferber (1962[a], p. 49) divided the consumer decision-making process into three distinct stages: (1) attention-directing stage; (2) deliberation among alternative forms of action; and (3) the actual choice. Awareness, therefore, of a group norm and any tendency to conform to that norm relate to the attention-directing stage of consumer decision making.

Few individuals would care to be complete conformists in their consumption patterns. In many buying situations, an acceptable range of alternatives is available within a given norm. We all know cases where individuals conformed to the group norm by buying a product, but each individual purchased a different color, brand, etc., thus maintaining a feeling of independence. Any attempt to force compliance[2] in a buying situation would tend to restrict the consumer's choices and consequently his independence. Therefore, to study the phenomenon of independence in consumer decision making, one would have to study the effect of restriction or usurpation of choices by group pressure on the consumer decision-making process.

In a recent theoretical paper by Brehm (1965), the motivational state which impels an individual to establish his freedom has been called "reactance."[3] Reactance is viewed as dissonant with compliance. According to this theory, any attempt by the inducing agent, in our case the group influence, which threatens the freedom of the individual would lead to a tendency for the individual to avoid compliance. Brehm, in an exploratory experiment, found that in a dyadic situation the attempted influence by the confederate tended to make the subject do the opposite of what was suggested. Generally, other exploratory studies in this area support the view that if an inducing force threatens the individual's freedom, the individual tends to oppose the inducement.

The Study

The two main objectives of this study were: (1) to gain insight into this phenomenon—conformity to group pressure in the consumer decision-making process; and (2) to study the effects of choice restriction by group pressure in the consumer decision-making process. Based on the theoretical discussion so far, the following two hypotheses were derived:

1. In a consumer decision-making situation where no objective standards are present, individuals who are exposed to a group norm will tend to conform to that group norm.
2. In a consumer decision-making situation where no objective standards are present, individuals who are exposed to a group norm, and are induced to comply, will show less tendency to conform to the group judgment.

Research Plan

Since this study is exploratory, what we learn in the laboratory can help in understanding the effect of group pressure on the consumer decision-making process. Therefore, a controlled laboratory experiment was used to evaluate the above hypotheses.

In most instances the laboratory studies of group influence created artificial situations unlike those found in everyday buying. For this study, a laboratory situation was devised in which the consumer decision-making process would come close to an actual buying situation. Since the subjects for this study were male college students, a buying situation was chosen that would reflect their familiarity with the buying process for that product.

Procedure

Subjects were 144 college juniors and seniors who were drawn from a pool of the basic students in the School of Business Administration, University of Minnesota.

The task required the subjects to evaluate and choose the *best* suit among three identical men's suits labeled A, B, and C. The three suits were of the same style, color, and size. All other means of identification were removed from the suits. The positional arrangements were varied in Latin square design so that each suit was displayed in each position with equal frequency. The subjects were told (1) that the three suits were from three different manufacturers, (2) that there were quality differences, (3) that the previous studies conducted at the Center for Experimental Studies in Business had indicated that experienced clothiers and tailors were able to pick the *best* one, and (4) that the present study was to find out whether consumers would be able to pick the *best* one.

Three experimental conditions were created for the experiment: Condition I was a control condition; in Conditions II and III, which will be called conformity condition and reactance condition, respectively, group pressure (independent variable) was manipulated.

The task remained the same for all three conditions. In each condition, the subjects were allowed two minutes each to physically examine the suits to help them arrive at their choices. In the control condition, after the subject had been seated, the experimenter read aloud the instructions. After examining the suits for two minutes, the subject returned to his seat and indicated his choice on a form provided for this purpose. Thus, in the control condition the subjects evaluated the suits individually in the absence of any group influence.

In Conditions II and III the suits were evaluated and the choices were made in a face-to-face group consisting of four individuals, three confederates of the experimenter, and one subject. The confederates had been told to choose B as the *best* suit. In addition, the confederates had been instructed earlier about seating arrangements. In these two conditions, after the subjects were seated around a table, the experimenter read instructions explaining the task. They were told that after they each examined the suits, they were to publicly announce their choices of the best suit. After examination of the suits, the subjects returned to their seats. Then the experimenter asked each person to announce his choice. Because of the seating and the prior instructions to the confederates, the first confederate was the first to be asked and to respond; then it was the turn of the second and the third confederates respectively. The naïve subject was always last to respond.

In the conformity condition the unanimous majority judgment of suit B was communicated by each confederate enunciating his choice clearly and unmistakably. The naïve subject was faced with a unanimous majority opinion (group norm).

The manipulation of group pressure in the reactance condition was similar to that in the conformity condition. The task, the instructions, and the procedures were the same, but the response pattern of the confederates was changed. The responses were as follows:

Confederate 1: I am not sure if there is a difference—it is not great; but if I have to choose, then B is the *best* suit.

Confederate 2: (Looking at Confederate 1) You say B. . . . Well, I cannot see any difference either—I will *"go along with you"*—B is the *best* suit for me.

Confederate 3: Well, you guys chose B. Although I am not sure, I am *just going along* to be a good guy. I choose B too.

Then it was subject's turn to announce his choice. As in the above condition, group pressure was aimed at restricting the individual's choice.

Forty-eight subjects were run in the control condition and 48 subjects in each of the other conditions. Confederates came from the "subjects pool" and from the subjects who had been through the control condition.

The situation permitted a quantitative measure of yielding. The proportion of choices for B was taken to be the measure of yielding, and the proportion of choices for A or C was taken to be the measure of nonyielding. The experimenter casually recorded the choices while the subjects were filling out a questionnaire in phase 2. The responses had not been recorded during the public announcements of the choices, to avoid creating suspicion about the sequence used in the interrogation.

After the post-experimental interview, the subject was debriefed and requested not to disclose the nature and method of the experiment to any other student until results were officially announced in class by his instructor.

Results and Discussion

The distribution of choices obtained for the three conditions are shown in Table 1.[4]

The choices made in the control condition provided the base rate for evaluating the effectiveness of group influence in the experimental conditions. The results of the control condition indicated that in the absence of any social influence, the distribution of choices did not deviate significantly from a chance distribution ($x^2 = 3.4$, $df = 2$). Thus, in the absence of any group influence, each suit was equally likely to have been selected as the *best* suit.

Analysis of the proportion of choices obtained for choice B in the conformity condition indicated that it was significantly greater than one-third. ($Z = 2.5$, $p < .01$). Therefore, by rejecting the null-hypothesis, it was concluded that group pressure was effective and that individuals tended to conform to the group norm. The results supported Hypothesis 1.

Hypothesis 2 was also supported by the results obtained for the reactance condition. Analysis of the proportion of choices for choice B in this condition indicated that it was not significantly different than one-third. The null-hypothesis cannot be rejected for this condition ($Z = -0.63$, *NS*). Therefore, it was concluded that in this condition, where acceptance of group pressure would have restricted the choices available, the subjects tended either to be indifferent or to deliberately make a choice that would negate the effect of group pressure.

TABLE 1.   Distribution of Choices of Best Suit

Condition	Choice			
	A	*B*	*C*	*N*
Control	17	10	20	47
Conformity	11	22	9	42
Reactance	14	14	19	47

Implications for Marketing

Implications from this study for consumer decision-making processes are limited because study was exploratory and was set in the laboratory. However, the findings support other small group studies on conformity to group pressure and the preliminary findings of the studies based on the theory of reactance.

The acceptance of social influence, as shown in the conformity condition, implies that consumers accept information provided by their peer groups on the quality of a product, of a style, etc., which is hard to evaluate objectively. More generally, the group norm or the prevailing group standard directs attention of its members to a new style or a product. It provides a frame of reference which is the first stage in the consumer decision-making process. In many buying situations there exists no objective standard independent of others' opinions. For those situations the implications are clear. The findings also imply that peer groups, friends, and acquaintances may be a major source of influence and information in the attention-directing stage of the buying process for major items.

The findings that group pressure for compliant behavior is ineffective implies that any attempt to restrict independent choice behavior in the consumer decision-making process may be resisted *under certain conditions*. In the marketplace we can observe that individuals purchase a product or adopt a new style, but reserve the right to choose different brands or variations. In this way, it seems, the feeling of independence in the consumer decision-making process is maintained. The theory of reactance is undergoing extensive empirical testing. However, our findings are supported by Whyte's (1954) study of the effectiveness of personal interaction in influencing the purchase of air conditioners. His analysis indicated that an "individual may sell his neighbor on the *idea* of an (air) conditioner; *he does not necessarily sell him on a particular brand or a particular store;* where you see a row of adjacent (air) conditioners, only a few of them will be of the same make, and only a few from the same store" (p. 117).

Notes

1. A norm has been defined in two ways: (1) as role expectations, and (2) as modal patterns of behavior. Thus, in the experimental studies, group norm has been defined as the modal patterns of behavior or modal response of the group. For purposes of this study the unanimous majority judgment of an *ad hoc* group will be taken to be the norm of this group.

2. Many authors have made it clear that distinctions between the processes of social influence are necessary for understanding the different meanings of conformity behavior. Kelman (1961, p. 62) distinguishes three processes of social influences, all of which have generally been termed as "conformity" by others: compliance, identification, and internalization. "Compliance can be said to occur when an individual accepts influence from another person or from a group because he hopes to achieve a favorable reaction from the other. He may be interested in attaining certain specific rewards or in avoiding certain specific punishments that the influencing agent controls."

3. "Reactance is a motivational state which impels the individual to resist further reduction in his set of free behaviors, and which also impels him to restore the potential behaviors lost, or eliminate any jeopardy to them" (Brehm, 1965, p. 2).

4. The results are based on the *N* shown in the table. The data for the remaining were discarded because of the subjects' familiarity with the experimental procedure.

References

Asch, S. E. "Effects of Group Pressure upon the Modification and Distortion of Judgments." *Group Dynamics*, ed. D. Cartwright and A. Zander, Harper & Row, 1953.

Bourne, F. S. "Group Influence in Marketing." *Some Applications of Behavioural Research*, ed. R. Likert and S. P. Hayes, Jr. Paris: UNESCO (1957), 208–224.

Brehm, J. W. "A Theory of Psychological Reactance." Unpub. paper, Duke Univ., 1965.

Ferber, R. "Brand Choice and Social Stratification." *Quarterly Review of Economics & Business,* Vol. 2 (Feb. 1962[a]), 71–78.

———. "Research on Household Behavior." *Amer. Economic Review,* Vol. 52 (March 1962[b]), 19–63.

Howard, J. A. *Marketing: Executive and Buyer Behavior.* Columbia Univ. Press, 1963.

Jahoda, M. "Conformity and Independence: A Psychological Analysis." *Human Relations,* Vol. 12 (1959), 99–120.

Kelman, H. C. "Processes of Opinion Change." *Public Opinion Quarterly,* Vol. 25 (Spring 1961), 57–78.

Sherif, M. *The Psychology of Social Norms.* Harper & Row, 1936.

Whyte, W. H., Jr. "The Web of the Word of Mouth." *Fortune,* Vol. 50 (Nov. 1954), 140ff.

4.5 A Test of the Two-Step Flow in Diffusion of a New Product
JOHAN ARNDT

One of the most frequently quoted but least well documented findings from the 1940 Erie County voting study was the hypothesis of the "two-step flow of communication." Finding that opinion leaders were more exposed to the mass media than nonleaders and that word-of-mouth appeared to be the most important source of information for the voters, Lazarsfeld, Berelson and Gaudet hypothesized that:

> . . . ideas often flow *from* radio and print *to* the opinion leaders and *from* them to the less active sections of the population.[1]

In its original formulation, the two-step flow hypothesis may be restated as follows.

1. Messages (information) flow from impersonal sources (mass media) to the opinion leaders—the first step.

2. The opinion leaders influence the nonleaders (who are less affected by the impersonal sources) by means of word-of-mouth—the second step.

This conceptualization linked the formal channels of communication—the mass media—with the informal channels, placing the opinion leaders between the media and the mass. It may be that few formulations in the behavioral sciences have had more impact than the two-step flow model. First, this conceptualization contributed to the "rediscovery of people" in social research and led to the rejection of the concept of the atomized audience.[2] Second, the theoretical framework contained in the hypothesis appears to have guided most of the later research on the flow of mass communications and diffusion of innovations.[3] It is therefore surprising to find that the hypothesis *as a whole* has never really been subjected to the test of empirical verification. As will be shown in the next section, existing published research has been concerned with individual parts of the hypothesis and not with the hypothesis in its entirety.

Review of Research Evidence

The role of interpersonal relations was not anticipated in the Erie County study of voting behavior.[4] Thus the design called for a cross-sectional study of randomly selected individuals and not for a mapping of social networks which would seem to be a necessary requirement for an adequate investigation of the second step. Moreover, the first step was only partially investigated in that the study only reported the general mass media exposure of leaders and nonleaders, instead of examining how specific messages in the mass media reached the leaders.

The design of the 1948 Elmira voting study, also conducted by Lazarsfeld and his associates, had the same methodological shortcomings as the Erie County study.[5] Though each respondent was questioned about voting intentions of friends and election-oriented discussion, no attempt was made to map the interpersonal flow of influence.

In the Decatur study of decision-making in marketing, fashions, movie going and public affairs, Katz and Lazarsfeld endeavored to reach both parties of the discussion dyads with mixed success.[6] By comparing transmitters and receivers in terms of age, social status and gregariousness, the study threw some light on the second step. Unfortunately, the specific content of the conversations was not reported. And, like the previous studies, measures were obtained of exposure to certain groups of mass media rather than reception of specific, relevant messages featured in the media. Hence, the Decatur study was not able to provide the missing link between the formal and informal channels.

The Columbia University drug studies introduced two methodological advances.[7] First, the studies, introducing "survey sociometry," involved a complete mapping of relevant social networks of physicians. Second, tracing the diffusion of one specific item, the gammanym drug, the drug studies used prescription records to obtain an objective measure of time of adoption. However, the word-of-mouth activity was not measured directly but was inferred from the relationship between degree of social integration and early adoption of gammanym.

Hence, while the drug studies reaffirmed the importance of personal influence in new product adoption, little information was collected regarding the nature of the word-of-mouth interaction among leaders and nonleaders in the second step. In addition, like the other Columbia studies, the drug studies failed to examine the flow of specific messages from the mass media to the leaders.

An ambitious field of study is reported by Troldahl.[8] In contrast to previous research, Troldahl attempted to test the two-step flow hypothesis by means of an experimental design. An experimental group of suburban subscribers to a horticultural bulletin received an issue containing six "planted" messages concerning topics like care of lawns, shrubs, etc. These messages were not included in the version sent to a control group. The dependent variables were changes in awareness, comprehension and belief. The study did not aim at accounting for specific decisions or for changes in behavior. Yet, the design of this study would seem to provide for an adequate test of the first step flow.

Unfortunately, the messages failed to arouse much interest so the findings cannot be considered conclusive.[9] However, it is interesting to note that some of the findings were contrary to the theoretical expectations. For instance, the opinion leaders did not report awareness more often than the nonleaders. Nor did media exposure induce more comprehension change or belief change among the leaders. In regard to the second-step flow, the Troldahl study suffered from the same methodological limitations as most of the previous research using the random sample approach.

In conclusion, with the exception of the Troldahl study, the cumulative research evidence has tended to support individual assertions derived from the two-step flow model. However, the studies suffer from methodological shortcomings and the evidence is far from definitive. So far no published study has addressed itself to the hypothesis as a whole in a rigorous manner.

In a way, this brief review of the empirical findings on the two-step model reveals how little evidence really is required for an hypothesis to be accepted. But why is it that no study has produced conclusive support for the two-step flow hypothesis? The reason may be that it is most difficult to design a field study which would provide a rigorous test of the hypothesis as a whole. Such a test would have to fulfill at least the following requirements:

1) It should be possible to measure the differential impact of the messages from impersonal sources on opinion leaders and nonleaders.
2) It should be possible to trace the flow of personal influence among leaders and nonleaders.
3) It should be possible to compare the content of the messages from the impersonal sources with the content of the word-of-mouth communication at the second step.
4) It should be possible to isolate the effect of word-of-mouth messages on the receivers of those messages.

Hypotheses

The set of specific hypotheses tested in this study was derived from the two-step flow model, modified to fit a new product diffusion situation. The following predictions were made:

1) Opinion leaders are more affected than nonleaders by impersonal communication sources.
2) Word-of-mouth communications are more likely to flow from leaders to nonleaders than in the opposite direction.
3) In the second step, the informal communicators interpret and add to the messages received from the impersonal sources.
4) Compared with those not exposed to word-of-mouth, receivers of favorable word-of-mouth communications are more likely to buy the new product and receivers of unfavorable word-of-mouth are less likely to buy.
5) Compared with early buyers of the new product, later buyers are more likely to receive word of mouth.

Method

A new brand of a frequently purchased food product was displayed in a commissary catering solely to the residents of a 495-unit apartment complex for married Harvard students. Each wife in the complex was sent a cover letter (from the manufacturer) and a coupon allowing her to buy the product at one-third of the retail price. After the expiration of a 16-day test period, personal interviews were completed with 91% (449) of the wives. The measures of the key variables (adopter category, opinion leadership and word-of-mouth behavior) are presented below.

Adopter Category.   The primary source of information regarding time of purchase was the coupon redemptions. In addition, to detect cases in which persons other than the original receiver redeemed the coupon, the respondents were asked in the interview whether—and, if so, when—they had purchased the product.[10] At closing time every day, the coupons redeemed were collected. In all, 42% of the wives in the sample bought at least one unit of new product. On the basis of relative time of purchase, the respondents were classified into four adopter categories as shown in Table 1.

Opinion Leadership.   Opinion leadership was measured by the sociometric method. Each respondent was asked the following question: "When you want information about new food products you have not tried yet, are there any persons you would be particularly likely to discuss the new products with?" Three names were requested and a person's opinion leadership status was determined by the number of choices received. Those receiving at least one choice were classified as opinion leaders.

TABLE 1.   Classification of Adopters of the New Product

Adopter Category	N	%	Time of Adoption
Pioneers	53	12	First Two Days
Early Adopters	80	18	3rd to 9th Day
Late Adopters	54	12	10th to 16th Day
Nonadopters	262	58	
Total	449	100%	

Word-of-Mouth Behavior. A distinction was made between product-related comments *received* and comments *given* to others. In all, 332 comments were reported as received, excluding comments from the husband of the respondent. For each comment received, the respondent was questioned about its content, when it occurred, whether it preceded or followed purchase and the name of the word-of-mouth transmitter. Eighty per cent of the comments were received from other wives in the complex identified by name. In the remaining 20% of the cases, the transmitters were unidentified wives in the complex, husbands of other respondents, or people not living in the complex.

Since each respondent was questioned about both comments received and comments given, the comments reported as received from other wives in the complex could be cross-checked by comparing the questionnaires of both parties in the discussion dyads. In this way, 90% of the comments were confirmed, which suggests that respondent recall of comments was accurate enough for the purposes of the study.

Findings

The presentation of the findings is organized as follows: 1) The opinion leaders and the impact of impersonal sources; 2) The flow of word-of-mouth; 3) The content of word-of-mouth; 4) The impact of word-of-mouth; 5) Word-of-mouth and adopter category.

The Opinion Leaders and the Impact of Impersonal Sources

The impact of the direct mailing may be inferred from whether or not the receiver purchased the new product. The Columbia drug studies found that opinion leaders were quicker than non-leaders to adopt the new gammanym drug.[11] Thus it was expected that the leaders in the apartment complex would be more likely to purchase the new product. As seen in Table 2, columns 5 and 6, the results are in the direction of the hypothesis, though the magnitude of the differences (50% vs. 42%) did not reach statistical significance.

As will be shown later, content of word-of-mouth communications received was an important determinant of whether or not the respondent purchased the product. Therefore, the above measure of impersonal source impact is not "pure" in that it reflects the combined impact of the direct mailing and word-of-mouth. To isolate the effect of the mailing, it is necessary to control for word-of-mouth. Referring again to Table 2, the picture emerging is somewhat more complex than expected. Among the receivers of word-of-mouth communications, the leaders were *not* more likely to buy the new product (columns 1 and 2). On the other hand, among those not exposed to word-of-mouth, the leaders were more likely to buy by 14 percentage points (columns 3 and 4). Reading the results in a different way, among the leaders, exposure to word-of-mouth actually *decreased* the probability of purchase. But the nonleaders exposed to word-of-mouth were *more* likely to purchase the new product than were the unexposed nonleaders. This would suggest that the leaders were more affected by the direct mailing, while the nonleaders appeared to be more affected by word-of-mouth.

The results suggest that though the leaders are more exposed to word-of-

TABLE 2.   Adopter Category, Word-of-Mouth Behavior, and Opinion Leadership Status (Users of the generic product category only)[a]

	Received Word-of-Mouth		Did not Receive Word-of-Mouth		Total	
	Opinion Leaders Col. 1	Nonleaders 2	Opinion Leaders 3	Nonleaders 4	Opinion Leaders 5	Nonleaders 6
Adopters:	47%	49%	53%	39%	50%	42%
Pioneers[b]	16	8	19	10	17	10
Early Adopters[b]	14	24	22	18	18	20
Late Adopters[b]	17	17	12	11	15	12
Nonadopters	53%	51%	47%	61%	50%	58%
Total	100%	100%	100%	100%	100%	100%
Base	(70)	(72)	(68)	(206)	(138)	(278)

[a] In the table, post-purchase comments are excluded.
[b] Grouped for Chi Square.

Cols. 5 vs. 6	$X^2 = 2.57$	$p < .20$	(1 d.f.)
Cols. 1 vs. 2	$X^2 = .03.$	$p < .90$	(1 d.f.)
Cols. 3 vs. 4	$X^2 = 3.87$	$p < .05$	(1 d.f.)
Cols. 1 vs. 3	$X^2 = .47$	$p < .50$	(1 d.f.)
Cols. 2 vs. 4	$X^2 = 1.88$	$p < .20$	(1 d.f.)

mouth, personal influence is not "needed" to clinch a buying decision. The leaders, being more influenced by impersonal sources, tend to buy new products with or without exposure to word-of-mouth.

It may be that the earlier adoption among the leaders can be partly explained in terms of role expectations relating to opinion leadership. The leaders may feel that they are expected by their followers to gain first-hand experience with new brands. After all, their leadership position rests on their ability to offer useful advice about new products. Thus early purchase of new products may mean enactment of their subjective leadership role.[12]

In conclusion, the findings support the notion of a first-step flow of influence from impersonal sources to opinion leaders. The remainder of the findings are concerned with the second step, the flow of word-of-mouth.

The Flow of Word-of-Mouth

A consistent finding in previous research is that leaders not only transmit more word-of-mouth communications than nonleaders, but that they are also more likely to *receive* word-of-mouth.[13] This suggests a multistep rather than a two-step flow, since the leaders appear to be influenced by other leaders.

However, one of the limitations of previous research is that the unit of analysis has been the individual participant in the communication process and not the discussion *dyad*. The cross-sectional technique does not permit satisfactory analysis of who talks to whom, because both members of the discussion dyads are unlikely to be included in the sample. Therefore, the results are somewhat ambiguous. As Katz appropriately observed, the cross-sectional data do not necessarily show that leaders influence nonleaders. Another, perhaps equally plausible, interpretation is that the leaders only influence each other, while the nonleaders stand outside the influence market altogether.[14]

What is needed is an investigation of the flow of word-of-mouth messages among leaders and nonleaders. The present study was designed to ensure that most of the conversation pairs were interviewed. This made it possible to identify the opinion leadership status of each participant in a given conversation, using each comment as the unit of analysis. In Table 3, the comments are classified by the leadership status of the transmitter and the receiver of the comment. The data in Table 3 support the findings in other studies that the leaders are more active participants in the word-of-mouth process, both as transmitters and receivers of word-of-mouth. It was predicted in the second hypothesis that word-of-mouth would be more likely to flow from leaders to nonleaders than in the opposite direction. As seen in Table 3, the data only weakly support the hypothesis, for 23% of the messages went from leaders to nonleaders and as much as 19% of the comments went from the nonleaders to the leaders.

What is the reason? A closer analysis of the data revealed that in many of the cases in which leaders talked to nonleaders, the nonleaders voiced their opinions too. In other words, when discussing the new product, the leaders and nonleaders often exchanged transmitter and receiver roles. The data in the present study are consistent with the findings of Troldahl and Van Dam, who reported that face-to-face communication (on major news topics) was more characterized by opinion sharing than opinion seeking.[15]

The Content of Word-of-Mouth

Two aspects of word-of-mouth content will be treated here. First, what aspects of the product or the direct mailing were discussed? Second, to what extent was the information from the impersonal sources passed on in the discussions?

Analysis of the content of the comments revealed that 72% of the messages were concerned with the coupon and the worthiness of buying the product. Twenty per cent of the comments mentioned the taste and the flavor of the product, while 8% of the comments related to the direct mailing or the in-store display. Over time, the share of comments concerning coupon and

TABLE 3. The Flow of Word-of-Mouth Messages Among Opinion Leaders and Nonleaders (Base numbers in parentheses)[a]

| | | Receiver of Word-of-Mouth | | |
		Opinion Leader	Nonleader	Total
Transmitter of Word-of-Mouth	Opinion Leader	39% (99)[b]	23% (57)	62% (156)
	Nonleader	19% (47)	19% (49)	38% (96)
Total		58% (146)	42% (106)	100% (252)

[a]Comments received from unidentified wives in the complex, husbands of other respondents and people not living in the complex are not included.

[b]Of a total of 252 comments, 99 (39%) went from opinion leaders to other leaders.

buying decreased, while the share of evaluative comments about the product increased.

A reasonable explanation for this is that there were two main sets of word-of-mouth stimuli at work: first, the letter and the coupon, and, second, experience with the product itself. The stimuli provided by the direct mailing appeared to have triggered a large number of early comments, but seemed to lose their potency over time, as suggested by the rapidly shrinking number of coupon-related comments. On the other hand, the stimuli provided by product itself became probably stronger over time as more and more people bought and tasted the product.

The second point to be explored is the relationship between impersonal source content and word-of-mouth content. An implicit assumption in the two-step flow hypothesis is that the opinion leaders pass on the mass media messages to the nonleaders. To the extent that this implies that the leaders passively parrot the messages to their followers, the term "opinion *leader*" seems inappropriate. However, common sense would indicate that informal communicators are selective in what they transmit and that they often shade the messages with their own evaluations. Cox is quite explicit on this point, arguing that opinion leaders play an active role by either adding to or filtering mass media information in order to provide "new" information to their audiences.[16]

The data in the present study supports Cox's position. Analysis of the comments suggested that the word-of-mouth transmitters processed and evaluated the information received from sources external to the social system. Though the letter and the coupon appeared to have started much word of mouth, the appeals and the selling points of the letter, the in-store display material and the package of the product were passed on only in two of the 332 comments reported. Instead, the message transmitters voiced their own opinions of the product and the coupon offer.

In conclusion, the data are consistent with the third hypothesis, which predicted that the leaders would be more than relayers of information from impersonal sources. The leaders appeared to play an active part in the communications process by transmitting their personal evaluations of the product.

The Impact of Word-of-Mouth

This section relates exposure to word-of-mouth communications to the probability of purchasing the new product.

In order to develop an index of word-of-mouth exposure, the receivers of word of mouth were requested to rate each comment received as favorable (to buying the product), neutral, or unfavorable. A value of 1 was assigned for each favorable comment, a value of zero for each neutral comment, and a value of − 1 for each unfavorable comment. Comments received after the respondent had purchased the product were excluded, as they could not be considered a cause of that purchase. A total score of 1 or more was classified as "favorable pressure," and a score of − 1 or less, "unfavorable pressure." A score of zero was classified as "no pressure" if the respondent was exposed to word-of-mouth. Nonexposure or postpurchase exposure only was indicated by "no comments received".

As seen in Table 4, the comments exchanged tended to be favorable to the new product. The respondents were 8 times as likely to report favorable as unfavorable pressure. The data show that what the respondents heard about the new product influenced their buying decision, as predicted in the fourth hypothesis. Of the respondents exposed to favorable word-of-mouth, 54% purchased the product, compared with 42% of the nonexposed group. Only 18% of those receiving unfavorable word-of-mouth bought the product. Those reporting no pressure were as likely to buy as the nonexposed respondents.

Word-of-Mouth and Adopter Category

On the basis of findings reported by rural sociologists, it was hypothesized that later buyers would be more likely than earlier buyers to report prepurchase exposure to word-of-mouth communications.[17] One reason for this is that there would be little word-of-mouth in circulation at the time before the earlier buyers purchased the product. Another reason would be that the later buyers, being less venturesome, would be expected to need more personal influence to "legitimate" the buying decision.

As shown in Table 5, the differences between earlier and later adopters

TABLE 4. The Relationship Between Word-of-Mouth Pressure and Purchase of the New Product

| | Word-of-Mouth Pressure | | | | |
	Favorable Pressure	No Pressure[a]	Unfavorable Pressure	No Comments Received	Total
Adopters	54%	42%	18%	42%	44%
Pioneers [b]	11	14	9	12	12
Early Adopters [b]	26	7	9	19	19
Late Adopters [b]	17	21	0	11	13
Non-Adopters	46%	58%	82%	58%	56%
Total	100%	100%	100%	100%	100%
Base	(88)	(43)	(11)	(274)	(416)

[a] Not included in Chi Square analysis.
[b] Combined for Chi Square. $X^2 = 6.01$ $p < .05$ (2 d.f.)

TABLE 5. Adopter Category and Probability of Receiving Prepurchase Word-of-Mouth Communications

Adopter Category	Received Word-of-Mouth	Word-of-Mouth Did Not Receive	Total	Base
Pioneers[a]	33%	67%	100%	(51)
Early Adopters[a]	34%	66%	100%	(80)
Late Adopters	44%	56%	100%	(54)
Nonadopters[b]	32%	68%	100%	(231)
Total	34%	66%	100%	(416)

[a] Combined for Chi Square.
[b] Not included in Chi Square analysis.
$X^2 = 1.94$ $p < .20$ (1 d.f.)

are in the direction of the theoretical expectations, though the results were not statistically significant. Table 5 also shows that the nonadopters were less likely than the adopters to receive word-of-mouth. A plausible explanation is that persons not favorably predisposed to buy new products also exhibit a lower probability of participating in the word-of-mouth process. Indifferent persons are less likely to engage in product-related discussions and are less likely to buy.

Summary

The two-step flow of communication hypothesis was tested in a field experiment involving diffusion of a new brand of a familiar food product in a university-operated apartment complex. The opinion leaders seemed to be more influenced by the impersonal source (the direct mail letter) than were the nonleaders. Hence, the data supported the notion of a first-step flow of influence. In regard to the second step, the leaders were found to be more active communicators, both as transmitters and receivers of word-of-mouth communicators.

An unexpected finding was the relatively large amount of word-of-mouth flowing from nonleaders to leaders. This finding was explained in terms of the opinion-sharing nature of the communication situation. The word-of-mouth transmitters did not simply pass on the messages received from impersonal sources, but shaded the messages with their own evaluations. The content of word-of-mouth messages influenced the buying decisions of the receivers. Those receiving favorable word-of-mouth communications were three times as likely to buy the new product as were those receiving unfavorable word-of-mouth. Later buyers were somewhat more likely than earlier buyers to receive word-of-mouth.

In conclusion, the findings of the present study generally conformed to the predictions derived from the two-step flow model.

Notes and References

1. Paul F. Lazarsfeld, Bernard Berelson and Hazel Gaudet, *The People's Choice,* 2nd ed. (New York: Columbia University Press, 1948), 151.

2. For a discussion of the atomized audience concept and the "rediscovery of people" in several social science fields, see Elihu Katz and Paul F. Lazarsfeld, *Personal Influence: The Part Played by People in the Flow of Mass Communications* (Glencoe, Ill.: The Free Press, 1955), 15–42.

3. Everett M. Rogers, *Diffusion of Innovations* (New York: The Free Press of Glencoe, 1962), 211–214.

4. Comprehensive reviews of key studies conducted by Lazarsfeld and his associates at Columbia University's Bureau of Applied Social Research may be found in Elihu Katz, "The Two-Step Flow of Communication: An up-to-Date Report on Hypothesis," *Public Opinion Quarterly*, Vol. 21, (1957) 61–78, and Paul F. Lazars-

feld and Herbert Menzel, "Mass Media and Personal Influence," in Wilbur Schramm, ed., *The Science of Human Communication* (New York: Basic Books, 1963), 94–115.

5. Bernard R. Berelson, Paul F. Lazarsfeld and William N. McPhee, *Voting: A Study of Opinion Formation in a Presidential Campaign* (Chicago: University of Chicago Press, 1954).

6. Of a total of 1,549 cases, Katz and Lazarsfeld (*op. cit.*, p. 151) managed to reach only 634 (41%) of the persons designated as discussion partners by respondents in the original sample.

7. A report on the pilot phase of the drug studies may be found in Herbert Menzel and Elihu Katz, "Social Relations and Innovation in the Medical Profession: The Epidemiology of a New Drug," *Public Opinion Quarterly*, Vol. 19 (1955), 337–352. Findings in the main project are reported in James Coleman, Elihu Katz and Herbert Menzel, "The Diffusion of an Innovation Among Physicians," *Sociometry*, Vol. 20 (1957), 253–270, and James Coleman, Herbert Menzel and Elihu Katz, "Social Processes in Physicians' Adoption of a New Drug," *Journal of Chronic Diseases*, Vol. 9 (1959), 1–19.

8. Verling C. Troldahl, "A Field Test of a Modified 'Two-Step Flow of Communication' Model," *Public Opinion Quarterly*, Vol. 30 (1966), 609–623. A more detailed report on this study may be found in Verling C. Troldahl, *The Communication of Horticultural Information and Influence in a Suburban Community,* Boston University Communications Research Center Report No. 10, 1963.

9. For instance, while the experimental group reported more awareness of the experimental content than the control group, there were no significant differences for comprehension and belief change.

10. Four nonusers of the product were found to have given their coupons to other residents, who redeemed them. For various reasons, three respondents bought the product without coupons.

11. Coleman, Katz and Menzel, *op. cit.;* Coleman, Menzel and Katz, *op. cit.*

12. For a discussion of role expectations in interpersonal behavior, see Morton Deutsch and Robert M. Krauss, *Theories in Social Psychology* (New York: Basic Books, Inc., 1965), 173–211.

13. See Lazarsfeld, Berelson and Gaudet. *op. cit.*, p. 51, and Berelson, Lazarsfeld and McPhee, *op. cit.*, p. 110.

14. Katz, *op. cit.*

15. Verling C. Troldahl and Robert Van Dam, "Face-to-Face Communication About Major Topics in the News," *Public Opinion Quarterly,* Vol. 29 (Winter 1965), 626–634.

16. Donald F. Cox, "The Audience as Communicators," in Stephen A. Greyser, ed., *Toward Scientific Marketing, Proceedings,* Winter Conference, December, 1963, Chicago: American Marketing Association, 1964, p. 65.

17. For a summary see Rogers, *op. cit.,* p. 179.

4.6 The Effect of the Informal Group Upon Member Innovative Behavior
THOMAS S. ROBERTSON

Innovative behavior is an *activity* engaged in by individuals. Within the confines of a social system, such as a neighborhood, individuals meet, see, and talk with one another—*interaction* occurs. If such interaction among a set of people is on a continuing basis, *sentiment* may exist within the group in terms of differential liking among group members and the formation of group ideology and norms governing expected activity patterns.

The research objective of this study can be formulated in terms of this conceptual scheme, developed by Homans,[1] so as to assess the effect of interaction and sentiment variables upon the activity of new product adoption, both on a group and individual basis.

Relevant Concepts

Interaction Affects Activity

Homans postulates that: "Persons who interact with one another frequently are more like one another in their activities than they are like other persons with whom they interact less frequently." Myers has found that the exercise of opinion leadership in the interaction process is reflected in likeness of innovative activity patterns among group members.[2] Other research evidence is that the innovator is generally higher on opinion leadership than the average group member.

Sentiment Affects Activity

It is basic to sociological theory that group norms affect member behavior. Rogers has used the ideal types of "modern" and "traditional" norms to account for high and low innovativeness in social systems. Festinger proposed that there will be high reliance upon social reality and normative influence when the physical reality is ambiguous or unstructured,[3] as perhaps in the case of new products.

Research by Festinger and Back has found that the greater the attractiveness of the group to its members, the greater the amount of influence successfully exerted upon the members, and the greater the behavioral conformity resulting. Coleman, Katz, and Menzel have documented the "interaction" or "snowball" effect in new product diffusion, that the socially more integrated members of a social system adopt sooner than the socially less integrated members.[4] Literature exploring the perceived risk concept has found that if the individual is experiencing risk, he will seek to reduce it. Arndt has documented that avoiding new products is a risk-handling tactic used by high-risk perceivers.[5]

These concepts are drawn from a variety of contexts and research traditions. The basic question is whether the hypotheses will be confirmed for consumer innovative behavior across product categories. If such activity is not of sufficient relevance to the groups studied, lack of positive relationships may well occur.

Hypotheses

Group Analysis

Interaction (I).

I-1. Communication about innovation among group members will be positively related to: a) group similarity of, and b) extent of innovativeness.

I-2. Exercise of opinion leadership within the group will be positively related to: a) group similarity of, and b) extent of innovativeness.

Sentiment (S)

S-1. Favorability of the group norm on innovation will be positively related to extent of innovativeness.

S-2. Group cohesiveness will be positively related to similarity of innovativeness.

S-3. Perceived risk will be negatively related to extent of innovativeness.

Individual Analysis

Interaction (I).

I-3. Communication about innovation with other group members will be positively related to the individual's innovativeness.

I-4. Exercise of opinion leadership within the group will be positively related to innovativeness.

Sentiment (S).

S-4. Favorability of the norm on innovation which the individual reflects will be positively related to innovativeness.

S-5. Social integration will be positively related to innovativeness.

S-6. Perceived risk will be negatively related to innovativeness.

Research Design

Research was conducted in the spring of 1967 in the Los Angeles suburb of Encino. The neighborhood selected was middle class in profile with almost all heads of households holding white collar or semiprofessional positions. Most households were composed of families with children living at home.

The design of the research involved identification of small, informal neighborhood groups. These groups were preferred—for purposes of investigating buying behavior—to formal groups, such as PTA or church groups, which carry out explicit functions and possess a specified organizational structure. It was felt that the formal group is not the relevant reference group for most consumption-related activities. Consumer information may be transferred within the formal group, but it is more incidental to the ongoing group purpose. It is realized that the informal neighborhood group need not be the relevant reference point for buying activities either.

Another possible approach would have been to identify a defined social system in terms of some common attribute, such as residing in the same apartment complex, which would have again simplified the research design. A pilot venture along these lines in the Los Angeles area, however, revealed that too little interaction occurred among residents to identify groups meaningfully. A married students' housing project, where interaction is considerable, could have again been used, as in other research by Arndt and Myers, but the range of consumption of concern to student wives is limited.

Sampling

Identification of informal neighborhood groups proceeded as follows:

1. One woman was randomly selected from each block within the 32 block area. She was interviewed and asked: "Could you name some women within the neighborhood—say within a mile—that you see most often and with whom you are most friendly?" A minimum of three names was sought and these mentions constituted the preliminary definition of the group.

2. The actual existence of groups was then tested by subsequently interviewing each person mentioned and measuring the level of interaction among group members. A sociogram depicting the flow of interaction for one of the groups obtained is given in Figure 1.

3. The operational definition employed for the existence of a group was that it must include at least three people, all of whom interacted with one another.

Under these conditions, nonresponse could not be tolerated since the existence of a group could not be determined, nor could group characteristics be completely assessed. An elaborate procedure to insure response was used, consisting of an advance letter requesting cooperation, follow-up telephone calls to arrange appointments, and further letters and calls where necessary. The final sample included 20 groups consisting of 85 members.

Data Collection and Analysis

In-home personal interviews were conducted with the 85 group members. Interviews took approximately 90 minutes to complete.

The group characteristics of concern and their forms of measurement are noted in Table 1. These characteristics were measured for each individual and then over-all group means and standard deviations were computed. Basically, three types of measures were involved:

1. reported behavior measures—innovativeness and new product communication;
2. peer evaluations—opinion leadership and group cohesion;
3. attitudinal measures—norms on innovation, social integration and perceived risk.

    While the measure of innovativeness used in the presentation of these results is self-report of number of innovations purchased, other measures were also obtained. One such measure was self-perceived innovativeness (Q: "Are you generally among the first to buy new products or do you prefer to wait?"). A zero-order correlation coefficient of .34, significant beyond a .01 level, was obtained between this measure and total number of innovations reported purchased. This is a higher correlation than that reported by Summers[6] between self-perceived innovativeness and fashion ownership, but is considerably lower than might be expected.

    Another measure was peer evaluation of each group member's innovativeness (Q: "Indicate for each person mentioned how willing you feel she is to buy new products"). The zero-order correlation coefficient obtained between this measure and actual purchases was .23, significant beyond the .05 level. It appears, therefore, that while these measures are significantly correlated, different results could be forthcoming depending on the measure used.

    Data were secured, where appropriate, for three product categories—

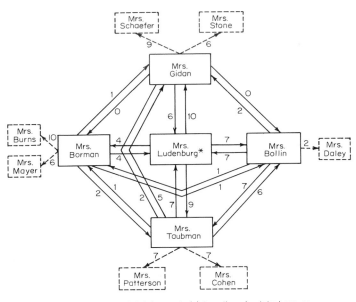

Note: 1. Numbers represent total reported interactions by telephone or in-person per week

2. ▢ represents specified group

⌐ ⌐ represents subsidiary friendship mentions

*Initial respondent who identified group

FIGURE 1.   Reported interaction, group #6.

TABLE 1. Measurement

Characteristic	Measure	Questionnaire Component
Activity		
Innovativeness: Food, Clothing, Appliances, Total	Number of new products purchased from a list of 42	"Which of the following items have you purchased?"
Interaction		
New Product Communication: Food, Clothing, Appliances, Total	Discussion with group members about new products	"How often do you talk with the women mentioned above about new (food/clothing/appliance) items on the market?" Often O o . . o O Seldom
Opinion Leadership: Food, Clothing, Appliances, Total	Peer evaluation of member influence	"Mark an *F* next to the woman's name who would be your best source of information about foods." (Repeats for clothing, appliances, and total)
Sentiment		
Norm on Innovation: Food, Clothing, Appliances, Total	Attitude toward new products	"How do you feel about buying *new* food items?" (Repeats)
Group Cohesion	Liking of group members for one another	"Indicate how much you like to get together with each person mentioned." Very much O o . . o O Very much like to dislike to
Social Integration	Participation in neighborhood activities	"How do you feel about socializing with the other women in the neighborhood?" "List the organizations, if any, to which you belong."
Perceived Risk: Food, Clothing, Appliances, Total	Scale ranking how "dangerous" or "safe"	"We all know that not all products work as well as others. Please indicate how dangerous or safe you feel it is to buy new products instead of established products." Dangerous O o . . o O Safe

TABLE 2.   Overall Means and Standard Deviations of Characteristics

Characteristic	Mean/Maximum	Standard Deviation
Activity		
Innovativeness:		
Food	8.7/14.0	2.6
Clothing	3.2/14.0	2.0
Appliances	4.2/14.0	1.8
Total	16.0/42.0	4.5
Interaction		
New Product Communication:		
Food	4.0/6.0	1.7
Clothing	4.2/6.0	1.5
Appliances	3.2/6.0	1.4
Total	3.8/6.0	1.3
Opinion Leadership:		
Food	0.5[a]	0.6
Clothing	0.4[a]	0.6
Appliances	0.5[a]	0.7
Total	1.5[a]	1.1
Sentiment		
Norm on Innovation:		
Food	3.9/6.0	1.7
Clothing	3.1/6.0	1.4
Appliances	3.2/6.0	1.5
Total	4.1/6.0	0.9
Group Cohesion	4.8/6.0	0.9
Social Integration	3.4/6.0	1.7
Perceived Risk:		
Food	2.4/6.0	1.2
Clothing	2.6/6.0	1.3
Appliances	2.7/6.0	1.3
Total	2.5/6.0	1.1

[a] Mean score is based on frequency of mentions without a specified range.

food, clothing, and appliances—and a "total" score was generally based on these three component scores. It is thus possible to identify differences in findings depending upon the product category under consideration. Such differences can be noted initially in Table 2, which shows the total sample mean and standard deviation scores for each characteristic under investigation.

Hypothesis testing for the group analysis uses nonparametric techniques, basically the Spearman (r_s) rank correlation coefficient. Hypothesis testing for the individual analysis is in terms of zero-order correlation.

Findings: Group Analysis

Interaction

Rank correlation coefficients for each hypothesis are presented in Table 3. Extent of new product communication in and of itself apparently does not lead to high group innovativeness (the summation of member innovativeness) nor to similarity in innovative behavior patterns (in terms of the standard deviation for the innovativeness variable within the group) (I-l). This may be due to the facts that both positive and negative information is transferred and that group agreement does not exist on the topic of new product adoption. Arndt has found that women who were exposed to positive word-of-mouth information about a new product were more likely to buy, and women who were exposed to negative information were less likely to buy. To the extent that a mixture of positive and negative information is relayed, a high level of innovative behavior would not be expected.

Festinger has found that group pressure to communicate concerning an "item x" increases with perceived discrepancy in opinion among members of the group concerning that item. Thus, higher communication about new products may not relate to consistency of innovative behavior as much as to perceived inconsistency. This may reflect the fact that members of a group do not have the same probability of buying new products—no matter how much communication occurs. Innovative behavior is very much related to certain predispositions on the part of the person. The innovator has, in fact, been found to be "different" from the later adopter. Within a group are found individuals who may represent several adopter categories, from innovators to early adopters, early majority, late majority, to laggards.

The remaining interaction hypothesis, concerning a posited relationship between opinion leadership and consistency and extent of innovative behavior is not supported (I-2).[7] Again, it would appear that both positive and negative influence transfer can occur; that the exercise of opinion leadership

TABLE 3.   Hypothesis Testing: Rank Correlations for Group Analysis

Hypothesis	r_s
Interaction (I)	
I-1. a) > communication, > likeness	−.06
b) > communication, > innovativeness	
total	−.19
food	−.10
clothing	.31
appliances	.00
I-2. a) > opinion leadership, > likeness	−.03
b) > opinion leadership, > innovativeness	−.07
Sentiment (S)	
S-1. > norm, > innovativeness	
total	.49[a]
food	.20
clothing	.53[b]
appliances	.34
S-2. > Cohesiveness, > likeness	−.16
S-3. < perceived risk, > innovativeness	
total	.56[b]
food	.53[b]
clothing	.00
appliances	.23

[a]r_s significant at or beyond .05 level.
[b]r_s significant at or beyond .01 level.

need not change the person's propensity to innovate; and that various underlying needs, which may not relate to consistency and extent of innovativeness, may prompt influence transfer.

In the framing of this hypothesis, opinion leadership was not viewed as a discrete trait which either does or does not exist within the individual. Instead, opinion leadership is a matter of degree. All persons can exercise a certain amount of influence. Also, opinion leadership was not viewed as a one-way occurrence, *i.e.*, a dominant opinion leader influencing others, but as most often a two-way occurrence, whereby in the process of interaction, group members influence and are influenced.

The "opinion leadership" concept is misleading in many ways. The tendency is to think in terms of a dominant influential seeking out influences who never influence the influential. Yet, both source-initiated and recipient-initiated influence occurs; influence is often two-way; and influence is a matter of degree—no one person is exclusively influential. The idea of opinion transfer or *influence transfer* may more accurately reflect the underlying process.

Sentiment

Group innovativeness is significantly correlated with favorability of the group norm on innovation (S-1, $r_s = .49$, $< .05$ level). The extent of this relationship, however, varies for the three product categories. Food ($r_s = .20$) and appliance ($r_s = .34$) innovativeness scores, while positively related to group norms, are not significantly so. Clothing innovativeness, on the other hand, is highly related to group norm ($r_s = .53$, $< .01$ level).

It would be expected that a greater relationship would exist between an activity (such as innovativeness) and the group norm on that activity to the degree that one or both of the following conditions are met: 1) the more important the activity to the group, the more binding the norm and the more severe the sanction for norm violation; 2) the more likely the observation of norm violation, the greater the risk in deviate behavior. In the present case, the more significant norm-innovativeness correlation for clothing may be due to clothing activity being more meaningful than food and appliance activity and therefore a more rigidly defined norm being present. It may also be due to the greater visibility of clothing leading to greater norm adherence since deviance is readily observable and punishable. The latter explanation appears more likely.

Results for hypothesis S-2 are not supported and, in fact, a somewhat negative (although non-significant) relationship exists between group consistency on innovativeness and group cohesiveness. Greater attractiveness of the members for one another apparently does not mean that they will behave more alike in the purchase of new products. Again, the group seems to provide enough latitude for the performance of numerous innovativeness roles from innovator to laggard.

Innovativeness is found to be associated with lower levels of perceived risk (S-3, $r_s = .56$, $< .01$ level). Despite the high association on a total basis, food is the only product category for which innovativeness is significantly correlated with perceived risk (food: $r_s = .53$, $< .01$, level; clothing: $r_s = .00$; appliances: $r_s = .23$). Yet, slightly less risk is perceived for food than clothing or appliances, although the difference is not statistically meaningful (see Table

3). It has been found previously that innovators are more willing to take risks. The clothing realm may be where women exhibit their capacity for daring activity. If this is so, then a certain amount of risk may be desirable and yield the present finding. The appliance finding may, in part, be due to the fact that appliance purchases are most often joint husband-wife decisions, which spreads the risk and neutralizes the relationship with innovativeness.

Findings: Individual Analysis

Innovative Behavior Overlap

A question of initial interest is whether innovative behavior is specific to each product category or whether a general innovator exists. Innovators for each product category were therefore defined as the top 10 percent in number of new items purchased, and a test for overlap of innovators by product category was made. While 25 respondents were innovators in one product category, only 4 were innovators in two product categories, and there were no three-product category innovators. Using the Marcus and Bauer method to test significance of overlap, it was concluded that innovative behavior is bound to specific product categories.[8]

Analysis of the zero-order correlation coefficients reveals that appliance and food innovativeness are significantly related ($r = .28$, $< .01$ level), as are appliance and clothing innovativeness ($r = .28$, $< .01$ level). Clothing and food innovativeness are not significantly related ($r = .18$). These coefficients, while statistically significant, are pragmatically low, and seriously dispute much of the discussion in marketing circles of "innovators" and "innovator characteristics" which implicitly assumes that the innovator is a general innovator. If innovativeness is specific to a given product category, then varying innovator characteristics can be the case, necessitating varying marketing strategies.

Interaction

Communications about innovation and innovativeness are significantly related in the case of clothing (I-3, $r = .31$, $< .01$ level), but not in the case of food or appliances (Table 4). These findings bear some resemblance to group analysis findings in that clothing is again the area where communication and innovativeness are most related and, on the whole, the same general lack of relationship between the two variables is shown.

Opinion leadership and innovativeness correlate for two of the product categories (I-4, appliances: $r = .31$, $< .01$ level; clothing: $r = .29$, $< .01$ level). These results attest that while a statistically significant overlap of innovativeness and opinion leadership is the case, the overlap is minimal in terms of equating innovators with opinion leaders.

Prior research by Summers and Rossiter and Robertson[9] has also assessed the association between innovativeness and opinion leadership. Both studies focused on women's clothing fashions, a product category under analysis in the present research, and obtained very similar correlation coefficients of .33 and .35, respectively, as compared to the .29 value obtained in the present case.

TABLE 4. Zero-Order Correlations of Interaction and Sentiment Variables with Innovativeness: Individual Analysis

Independent Variables	Innovativeness			
	Total	Food	Clothing	Appliances
Interaction				
I-3 Communication about Innovation				
Total	.22[a]			
Food		.14		
Clothing			.31[b]	
Appliances				.11
I-4 Opinion Leadership				
Total	.12			
Food		.02		
Clothing			.29[b]	
Appliances				.31[b]
Sentiment				
S-4 Norm on Innovation				
Total	.43[b]			
Food		.40[b]		
Clothing			.41[b]	
Appliances				.22
S-5 Social Integration	.08	−.04	.13	.09[a]
S-6 Perceived Risk				
Total	.35[b]			
Food		.31[b]		
Clothing			.06	
Appliances				.18

[a]correlation significant at or beyond .05 level.
[b]correlation significant at or beyond .01 level.
Note: For purposes of individual analysis, N = 91 since data for three two-person groups, excluded in the group analysis, were included.

Sentiment

As was true in the group analysis, reflection of a favorable norm on innovativeness is associated with higher levels of new product purchases (S-4). This is especially true for the clothing (r = .41, < .01 level) and food (r = .40, < .01 level) product categories, and not so much so for the appliance (r = .22, < .05 level) product category.

Social integration and innovativeness are not much related, reflecting a fairly comparable lack of relationship as in the group cohesion-innovativeness analysis, although for the individual analysis no negative trend is reported (S-5). Acceptance by the group and participation within the group, therefore, do not seem to relate to the individual's innovative willingness.

The final relationship for analysis is that between perceived risk and innovativeness (S-6). Significant correlations are found on a total basis (r = .35, < .01 level) and for food (r = .31, < .01 level), but not for appliances, and almost no relationship is found for clothing. Thus, earlier findings that perceived risk varied by product may be extendable to product categories. It may be that the perceived risk variable is most meaningful for new food purchases, less meaningful for appliances, and of no meaning for clothing purchases, at least as suggested in this study.

Conclusion

Examination of small, informal neighborhood groups has revealed that certain group variables are correlated with aggregate innovative behavior, and that certain characteristics specifying the individual's relationship to the group are correlated with individual member innovative behavior. Generally, "sentiment" characteristics are more important than "interaction" characteristics in determining innovative "activity," especially in the group analysis.

Variables correlating most highly with innovativeness are group norms on innovation and level of perceived risk. Variables are found to have differential effect depending upon the product category, *e.g.*, food, clothing or appliances. The group has been found to be a meaningful unit of analysis which could lead to improved predictions of an individual's probability of new product adoption for a given product category.

Notes and References

1. George C. Homans, *The Human Group* (New York: Harcourt, Brace & World, Inc., 1950).

2. John G. Myers, "Patterns of Interpersonal Influence in the Adoption of New Products." In *Proceedings of the American Marketing Association*, ed. Raymond M. Haas, Chicago, 1966, pp. 750–757.

3. Leon Festinger, "Informal Social Communication," *Psychological Review*, Vol. 57, September, 1950, pp. 271–281.

4. James S. Coleman, Elihu Katz, and Herbert Menzel, *Medical Innovation: A Diffusion Study* (Indianapolis: The Bobbs-Merrill Company, 1966), chapter 7.

5. Johan Arndt, "Perceived Risk and Word of Mouth Advertising." In *Perspectives in Consumer Behavior*, 1st ed., eds. Harold H. Kassarjian and Thomas S. Robertson (Glenview: Scott, Foresman and Company, 1968), pp. 330–337.

6. John O. Summers, "The Identity of the Women's Clothing Fashion Transmitter," unpublished doctoral dissertation, Purdue University, 1967.

7. One of the few researchers to report a similar lack of relationship between these variables is Charles W. King, "Fashion Adoption: A Rebuttal to the 'Trickle Down' Theory." In *Proceedings of the American Marketing Association*, ed. Stephen A. Greyser, Chicago, 1963, pp. 108–125.

8. Alan S. Marcus and Raymond A. Bauer, "Yes: There are Generalized Opinion Leaders," *Public Opinion Quarterly*, Vol. 28, Winter, 1964, 628–632.

9. John R. Rossiter and Thomas S. Robertson, "A Conceptual Examination of Innovativeness and Opinion Leadership in the College Fashion Context." Working paper, Graduate School of Business Administration, UCLA, 1968.

4.7 Dimensions of Marital Roles in Consumer Decision Making

HARRY L. DAVIS

The literature on family role structure is characterized by diverse theories about the structure of marital roles in decision making. At one extreme are those researchers who assume unidimensionality, and whose studies describe families as "matriarchal," "patriarchal," and "companionship," e.g., Burgess and Locke [2], or who use "global influence questions," e.g., Heer [6] and "overall power scores," e.g., Blood and Wolfe [1]. Other sociologists recognize at least two power hierarchies within the family—e.g., the distinction between "instrumental" and "expressive" roles [15] or Farber's [3] dichotomy between "policy" and "routine household" decisions. Herbst [8] suggests four bases for role differentiation: (1) household duties; (2) child control and care; (3) social activities; and (4) economic activities. At the other extreme is the even more highly differentiated role structure implicit in the marketing literature. For example, Sharp and Mott [17] report that husbands exert more influence than wives in the purchase of automobiles, less influence than wives in deciding how much to spend on food, and equal influence in deciding about vacations and housing. Other studies [11, 19] suggest a further factoring of decisions for single purchases into numerous components.

These alternative views of family role structure undoubtedly reflect the different orientations of sociological and marketing research. Measurement of family authority is usually a first step in many sociological studies, and it is used as the independent or dependent variable in subsequent analyses. This may explain why the dimensionality of roles itself has been the subject of such little *empirical* research. While the sociological literature is strong on theory and somewhat weak on data, the literature in marketing is just the reverse. Measurement of purchase influence for specific products is often the only objective of such research.

Both of these approaches leave important questions unanswered. Sociologists, for example, often establish typologies on an *a priori* basis and then "force" data into these classifications. Whether Herbst's economic activities do, in fact, represent a unidimensional area of family structure has not been subject to adequate empirical testing. The absence of any explicit theory in the marketing literature, on the other hand, seriously limits generalizations. The roles of husband, wife, or children are discussed only on a product-by-product basis. Researchers have not questioned whether decision making influence within the family could be described in terms of a fewer number of dimensions that would subsume several products or several steps in the decision process for a single product. The answer to this question has implications for market research in suggesting what kinds of questions need to be asked, to whom, and with what degree of specificity.

Contributing to these alternative conceptualizations is the use of widely differing sources of information about purchase influence. A sampling of research shows that data have been collected from wives only, husbands only, a matched group of husbands and wives, husbands and wives within the same family, and children.

The extent to which wives can accurately report purchase influence is subject to considerable confusion in the literature. Some researchers stress the similarity between husbands' and wives' responses. Wolgast found a high level of agreement in husbands' and wives' reports about relative influence in four economic decisions. She concludes that "husbands and wives reflect one another's judgments almost perfectly" [21, p. 153]. Blood and Wolfe justify the use of wives as sole respondent by the fact that "other studies show that husbands and wives usually agree sufficiently to make it possible to rely on one partner's responses" [1, p. 273]. Heer also concludes that the agreement between husband and wife is "substantial though not unanimous" [6, p. 66]. Others emphasize the inconvenience and cost associated with interviewing more than one respondent per family. Scanzoni [16], for example, reasons that the decision to obtain data from both spouses often necessitates a smaller sample size, which, in turn, will lower the generalizability of results.

At the same time, the literature also contains studies that point to the considerable disagreement between husband and wife in their reporting of purchase influence. Ferber obtained independent assessments of relative influence in eight consumer decisions from the adult members of 237 families. Finding little correspondence between husbands' and wives' answers (R^2 ranging from .02 to .29) he concluded that "the reliability of ratings of relative influence of different family members, or different sexes, on purchases obtained by direct questioning of one member of the family is highly limited" [4, p. 232]. Several other studies [5, 12, 16] have found that the percentage of couples whose responses agree averages only slightly more than 50%. And more recently, Morgan [14] has observed that couples are likely to agree more about each other's personality than they do in reporting who decided about specific purchase decisions.

There is clearly a need to resolve the apparent confusion about the sufficiency of wives' responses. An answer is important for research on family decision making since role consensus itself may be related to the balance of power between husband and wife. An answer is equally important to market researchers who must decide whether to interview both spouses or only the wife.

This article is a response to these difficult problems surrounding the description and measurement of family role structure. Specifically, this article will consider these questions:

1. What are the dimensions of husband-wife roles in two consumer purchase decisions?
2. To what extent do husbands and wives agree in their perception of roles?

Method

The data reported are drawn from a questionnaire administered to 100 families living in four Chicago suburbs. A small convenience sample was obtained by contacting families through three churches (two Protestant and one Catholic) and a grade school P.T.A. Couples were solicited by means of a letter asking their cooperation in a research project on "family living" and "decision making." Both husband and wife were requested to come to the church or school at the same time in order to participate. Each spouse was directed to a separate room in order to fill out the questionnaire, making collaboration impossible.

Couples were asked a series of questions about the relative influence of husband and wife in two durable goods purchases—an automobile and living room furniture. Several interrelated decisions were included for each product. For the last automobile purchased, husband and wife were asked to report who decided: (1) when to purchase; (2) how much money to spend; (3) make; (4) model; (5) color; and (6) where to purchase. Similar decisions were investigated for the furniture purchase—who usually decides: (1) what furniture to purchase; (2) how much to spend; (3) where to purchase; (4) when to purchase; (5) style; and (6) color and fabric. The questions were rated on a 5-point scale (husband decided = 1; husband more influence than wife = 2; equal influence = 3; wife more influence than husband = 4; wife decided = 5). Since these five categories refer only to the roles of husband and wife, the response to any given question represents a respondent's perception of *relative* influence in the decision.

The selection of these two products and the techniques used to measure marital roles can be justified because both purchases represent important family decisions. Also, they usually involve substantial financial outlay, extended period of ownership, social importance, and joint use by several family members. In terms of other consumer research, both would undoubtedly be classified as "policy" or "major economic" decisions. Moreover, it is meaningful to speak of *marital* roles in reference to both decisions. Other studies [11, 19] have found that husbands and wives are the major participants in these purchases. This finding also supports the use of a simple rating scale limited to a measure of husband-wife influence.

The data presented in this paper differ in several ways from other studies. Whereas existing research has investigated marital roles across several economic decisions or for a single product purchase, these data can be analyzed both across and within product purchase decisions because of the use of the same question for each of the two product purchases and the same measure of influence for all 12 decisions. There are also responses to the same questions from both husband and wife, permitting comparison of husbands' responses as a group with wives', as well as between husband and wife within the same family. The extent of agreement can also be calculated for each of 12 decisions to determine whether the nature of the decision significantly affects the level of consensus.

Reliance on this small sample seems warranted in light of the exploratory nature of this study. No attempt is made to generalize the particular distribution of relative influence for any decision to all families. The interest is to consider the relationship between hushands' and wives' responses and between decisions within the same families. At the same time, the small sample size and the use of volunteer subjects urge caution in generalizing the findings.

Findings

Relative Influence in Purchase Decisions

Tables 1 and 2 show the distribution of husbands' and wives' responses to questions about relative influence in 12 automobile and furniture purchase decisions.[1] The individual questions are listed in order of increasing wife influence based on the average score for each decision. Data from husbands are reported in Table 1; the wives' responses are shown in Table 2.

The tables reveal considerable variability in husband-wife roles in these decisions, and it would be misleading to generalize about husband and wife roles in any absolute sense. For example, conclusions about which spouse makes "the furniture purchase decision" would necessarily depend on which

TABLE 1.   Marital Roles in Selected Automobile and Furniture Purchase Decisions As Perceived by Husbands (N = 97)

	Patterns of Influence (%)		
Who Decided:	Husband has more influence than wife	Husband and wife have equal influence	Wife has more influence than husband
When to buy the automobile?	68	29	3
Where to buy the automobile?	62	35	3
How much to spend for the automobile?	62	37	1
What make of automobile to buy?	60	32	8
What model of automobile to buy?	41	50	9
What color of automobile to buy?	25	50	25
How much to spend for furniture?	22	47	31
When to buy furniture?	16	45	39
Where to buy the furniture?	7	53	40
What furniture to buy?	3	33	64
What style of furniture to buy?	2	26	72
What color and fabric to select?	2	16	82

TABLE 2.   Marital Roles in Selected Automobile and Furniture Purchase Decisions as Perceived by Wives (N = 97)

	Patterns of Influence (%)		
Who Decided:	Husband has more influence than wife	Husband and wife have equal influence	Wife has more influence than husband
When to buy the automobile?	68	30	2
Where to buy the automobile?	59	39	2
How much to spend for the automobile?	62	34	4
What make of automobile to buy?	50	50	—
What model of automobile to buy?	47	52	1
What color of automobile to buy?	25	63	12
How much to spend for furniture?	17	63	20
When to buy the furniture?	18	52	30
Where to buy the furniture?	6	61	33
What furniture to buy?	4	52	44
What style of furniture to buy?	2	45	53
What color and fabric to select?	2	24	74

particular decision was being made. Marked differences in the wife's influence can be seen by comparing decisions about how much to spend and when to buy with those concerning style, color and fabric. The same thing can be seen for the automobile purchase decisions. The percentage of husband-dominant families decreases from 60% in the decision about what make of automobile to buy to 25% in the decision about what color to select.

Also, one cannot generalize about roles in a particular decision without reference to the product being purchased. For example, compare the percentage of husband-dominant families in two decisions—where to buy the automobile and where to buy furniture. The former is characterized by a large proportion of husband-dominant families while in the latter, less than 10% of the families are husband-dominant. The same is true when comparing the decision about how much to spend for the automobile and furniture. The modal response is husband-dominant for automobiles but joint for furniture.

Finally, note the substantial variability in roles for individual decisions. Only three decisions have more than 65% of the families in any one of the three influence types. For the other decisions there is a considerable spread over two (and in some cases, three) categories. Reliance on the modal response in such cases to classify *decisions* as either husband-dominant, joint, or wife-dominant would actually conceal the considerable amount of variability in roles that exists between families.

Patterns of Relative Influence

The discussion in the previous section has been limited to the distribution of relative influence for each decision. In this section consider the distribution of relative influence across all six automobile and furniture decisions simultaneously. The emphasis here is upon the *pattern* of husband-wife influence across several decisions. Under the assumption of unidimensionality, all families should fall into one of three different patterns—husband-dominant, wife-dominant or joint—across all decisions. Alternatively, a pattern might reflect a division of labor between husband and wife (e.g., some decisions shared while others the responsibility of one spouse) common to a large number of families.[2] The number of patterns and their frequency will tell more about the variability in marital roles across decisions and may suggest a way of classifying families into various influence or decision "types."

For the purpose of this analysis, the 5-point scale of relative influence was again collapsed into 3 points by combining "husband decided" with "husband more than wife" (scale positions 1 and 2) and "wife decided" with "wife more than husband" (scale positions 4 and 5). In addition, automobile and furniture decisions were considered separately, so that each pattern included only 6 decisions. Both of these actions should make any regularities in the data more apparent.

Even with these modifications, the data show considerable variability in the number of unique patterns. Husbands' and wives' responses to the 6 automobile decisions yielded 52 and 38 patterns respectively. Similar results were found for furniture decisions—50 patterns (husbands' responses) and 46 patterns (wives' responses). Since the total number of respondents was 97 for the automobile purchase and 98 for the furniture purchase, a different pattern of relative influence is found for about every two respondents.

A few patterns do account for considerably more than two respondents each. Three patterns account for 32% of all families in the case of the automobile purchase (husbands' responses). Two of these—all joint ($N = 6$) and all husband-dominant ($N = 13$)—indicate unidimensionality. The other pattern ($N = 12$) is husband-dominant with the exception of one joint decision ("What color of automobile to buy"). These same three patterns account for 45% of all families when the wives' responses are analyzed. The furniture purchase reveals somewhat more variability on this same criterion although four patterns continue to account for a large percentage of all families—31% (husbands' responses) and 41% (wives' responses). The most frequent pattern as reported by both husbands and wives is wife dominance for all six decisions ($N = 14$ and $N = 12$ respectively). Six other unique patterns (with frequencies of five or more) occur only once.

This analysis provides little basis for developing family "types" based upon patterns of relative influence since one would have to overlook more than 50% of the sample. The variability described in the previous section when roles were examined by decision across families is also apparent when families are studied across decisions.

Dimensions of Decision Roles

The discussion to this point has emphasized the variability of marital roles in two consumer purchases. In this section consider the interrelationship of roles between these decisions and then group decisions together on the basis of their similarities. The objective is to identify and delineate "dimensions" of decision roles.

Tables 3 (husbands' responses) and 4 (wives' responses) show the association between roles in 12 automobile and furniture purchase decisions. Gamma coefficients were computed from 5×5 contingency tables showing the distribution of relative influence for every pair of decisions.

Tables 3 and 4 reveal the same patterns for husbands and wives. The triangle in the upper left-hand corner of the two matrices shows the association between relative influence in six automobile purchase decisions. Relative influence in all of these decisions is positively associated. Moreover, the degree of association is generally high. Data from husbands yield gammas ranging from .21 to .74. The degree of association reported by wives is even stronger, ranging from .42 to .92. The same pattern characterizes the association between relative influence in furniture purchase decisions (see the triangle in the lower right-hand corner of each matrix). Although there is some variability in the size of these gammas, one would conclude that decision roles within these product purchases are strongly and positively related.

The relationship between relative influence in automobile and furniture decisions can be seen in the square or lower left-hand portion of the matrices in Tables 3 and 4. In contrast to the association among decision roles *within* each of the two product categories, there is little relationship *across* product categories. The majority of signs are negative, indicating an inverse relationship between influence in automobile purchase decisions and influence in the purchase of furniture. Moreover, the magnitude of gammas is low. The degree of association ranges from .00 to .26 for wives and from .01 to $-.38$

TABLE 3. Association (Gamma) Between Relative Influence in Selected Automobile and Furniture Purchase Decisions—Husbands' Responses (*N* = 97)

Decisions	Automobile Decisions						Furniture Decisions					
	1	2	3	4	5	6	7	8	9	10	11	12
Automobile Decisions:												
1. When to buy?												
2. Where to buy?	.44											
3. How much to spend?	.69	.44										
4. What make to buy?	.36	.74	.49									
5. What model to buy?	.21	.63	.57	.74								
6. What color to buy?	.24	.52	.37	.54	.59							
Furniture Decisions:												
7. How much to spend?	.15	−.34	−.05	−.38	−.34	−.14						
8. When to buy?	.30	−.12	.25	−.14	−.09	−.06	.53					
9. Where to buy?	−.06	−.17	−.10	−.20	−.06	.13	.62	.59				
10. What to buy?	.17	−.14	−.10	−.17	−.11	.01	.61	.47	.64			
11. What style to buy?	.01	−.17	−.23	−.23	−.27	−.01	.48	.20	.59	.80		
12. What color and fabric to select?	.01	.09	.05	−.09	−.04	.33	.33	.23	.54	.71	.81	

TABLE 4. Association (Gamma) Between Relative Influence in Selected Automobile and Furniture Purchase Decisions—Wives' Responses (*N* = 97)

Decisions	Automobile Decisions						Furniture Decisions					
	1	2	3	4	5	6	7	8	9	10	11	12
Automobile Decisions:												
1. When to buy?												
2. Where to buy?	.78											
3. How much to spend?	.79	.69										
4. What make to buy?	.73	.78	.51									
5. What model to buy?	.70	.71	.55	.92								
6. What color to buy?	.52	.65	.42	.72	.66							
Furniture Decisions:												
7. How much to spend?	.13	−.01	.14	.10	.08	.13						
8. When to buy?	.02	−.11	.26	−.18	.01	−.10	.77					
9. Where to buy?	.12	−.12	−.04	−.03	.01	.05	.67	.56				
10. What to buy?	.01	−.14	−.07	−.07	.03	−.09	.75	.60	.77			
11. What style to buy?	.00	−.10	−.17	−.14	−.09	−.10	.46	.26	.65	.75		
12. What color and fabric to select?	.03	−.07	.01	.05	.08	.04	.55	.40	.67	.71	.85	

for husbands, showing that purchase influence for automobiles is not related to purchase influence for furniture.

In an effort to more adequately delineate dimensions of decision roles, both matrices were analyzed using a clustering technique developed by Mc-Quitty [13]. This technique groups decisions into clusters so that the associations between pairs of decisions within a given cluster are high, while the associations between decisions in different clusters are low. First the two decisions in the matrix having the highest association are combined, and then the association between this "new" two-decision cluster and each of the remaining decisions is determined.[3] The matrix is thus reduced by one row and one column. The same procedure is applied as many times as there are columns in the original matrix, each time beginning with the two decisions (or two clusters) having the highest association. The association between the final two clusters is by definition the lowest gamma in the original matrix.

The results of this analysis can be seen in Figures 1 and 2, which give a graphic representation of how various decisions join together to form clusters. In addition, the height at which decisions or clusters merge represents the degree of association between them. Decisions were ordered along the x-axis to avoid intersecting lines as they were brought together.

Looking first at the wives' responses (Figure 1), four clusters of decisions are evident,[4] two of which represent product-related decisions in the purchase of automobiles and furniture. One cluster includes four automobile decisions—what make and model of automobile to buy, where to buy it, and what color to select. Similar subdecisions also cluster together for the furniture purchase—what style and what color and fabric to select, what furniture to buy, and where to buy it. Decisions about the timing and expense of

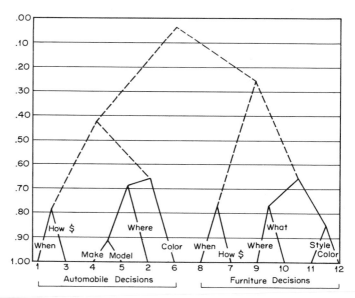

FIGURE 1. A classification of roles in selected automobile and furniture purchase decisions (wives' responses) (N = 97).

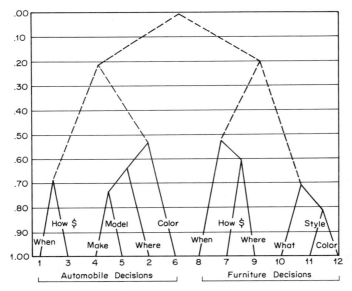

FIGURE 2. A classification of roles in selected automobile and furniture purchase decisions (husbands' responses) (N = 97).

each purchase form the remaining two clusters. With one exception, the same dimensions of decision roles are present in the analysis of husbands' responses (Figure 2).[5]

Thus, two bases for role differentiation can be seen in these two product purchases—one basis being the product itself. Decision roles in the purchase of automobiles are not related to decision roles in the purchase of furniture. Within each of these product categories, roles are further differentiated by the nature of the decision. Roles in "product-selection" decisions (e.g., model, make, color) differ from roles in "allocation" or "scheduling" decisions (e.g., how much to spend and when to buy).

Role Consensus

The discussion to this point has considered the responses to questions about purchase influence separately for husbands and for wives. In this section turn to the question of whether or not husbands and wives considered as groups and as individual families agree in their perception of roles.

Table 5 is a summary of Tables 1 and 2 and shows the average relative influence in the 12 purchase decisions as reported by husbands and wives. As before, the individual decisions are listed in order of increasing wife influence.

This table reveals a high level of agreement in husband-wife perception when viewed in these aggregate terms. Note first that the rank ordering of decisions in terms of increasing wife influence is identical for husbands and wives. Moreover, the differences between husbands' and wives' responses are not statistically significant on the basis of a multivariate test which considers all 12 decisions simultaneously ($F = .9041; df = 12, 187; p < .54$). It is not likely that the conclusions reached by advertisers would differ at all depending on whether they had examined the husbands' responses or the wives'.

Two noteworthy patterns can be detected in these data. First, the direction of differences between the mean response of husbands and wives is consistent across all 12 decisions. Either one or both spouses seem to be modest in the assessment of their own influence. That is, husbands attribute more influence to their wives than wives attribute to themselves, and/or vice-versa. Secondly, the largest disagreements between husbands and wives occur for decisions that involve what might be termed "aesthetic" considerations (e.g., what model and color of automobile to buy, what furniture, what style and what color of furniture to buy). One reason may be, for example, that a husband's assessment of his wife's importance in decisions requiring aesthetic skills tends to be biased upward as a result of cultural expectations about the "appropriate" role for women. Alternatively, a wife might bias downward her husband's participation in such decisions for the same reason.

The data contained in Table 5, of course, do not provide any evidence of the extent to which husbands and wives *within the same family* agree in their role perception. In an extreme case, husbands and wives could exhibit perfect agreement as groups but perfect disagreement on an intrafamily comparison.[6] What can be said about the extent of role consensus within families? Is there the same high level of agreement that was characteristic of the aggregate comparisons?

Table 6 shows the extent of agreement between husbands and wives in the 6 automobile and 6 furniture decisions. The determination of whether or not a couple agrees was based upon a comparison of a 3-point (as opposed to the 5-point) scale. Disagreements, therefore, indicate a significant difference in perception. At the extreme, a difference of two scale points means that one spouse perceived a decision as husband-dominant while the other per-

TABLE 5. Average Relative Influence in Selected Automobile and Furniture Purchase Decisions as Perceived by Husbands and Wives

	Mean Response From:		
Who Decided:	Husbands ($N = 97$)	Wives ($N = 97$)	Difference in Means
When to buy the automobile?	1.95	1.83	+.12
Where to buy the automobile?	1.97	1.95	+.02
How much to spend for the automobile?	2.05	1.98	+.07
What make of automobile to buy?	2.13	2.11	+.02
What model of automobile to buy?	2.41	2.17	+.24
What color of automobile to buy?	2.95	2.73	+.22
How much to spend for furniture?	3.17	3.04	+.13
When to buy the furniture?	3.27	3.18	+.09
Where to buy the furniture?	3.45	3.35	+.10
What furniture to buy?	3.80	3.55	+.25
What style of furniture to buy?	3.91	3.68	+.23
What color and fabric to select?	4.17	3.92	+.25

TABLE 6. Extent of Husband-Wife Agreement in Selected Automobile and Furniture Purchase Decisions (N = 97)

	Husband attributes *less* influence to wife than she attributes to herself		Husband and wife agree	Husband attributes *more* influence to wife than she attributes to herself	
	−2	−1		+1	+2
Who Decided:	%	%	%	%	%
When to buy the automobile?	2	14	66	16	2
How much to spend for the automobile?	1	22	63	12	2
What make of automobile to buy?	—	20	64	15	1
What model of automobile?	—	14	59	25	2
What color of automobile?	—	14	59	26	1
Where to buy the automobile?	—	18	68	13	1
What furniture to buy?	—	10	59	30	1
How much to spend for furniture?	1	18	57	21	3
Where to buy the furniture?	—	16	63	19	2
When to buy the furniture?	1	21	48	25	5
What style of furniture to buy?	—	10	62	28	—
What color and fabric to select?	—	9	75	16	—

ceived it as wife-dominant. A disagreement between whether a decision was husband-dominant or joint (and wife-dominant or joint) is represented by a difference of one scale point.

The percentage of couples who agree about their roles in decision making averages 63% for the 6 automobile purchase decisions and 61% for the 6 furniture purchase decisions. The range of agreement is somewhat greater for the furniture decisions. Although these percentages are higher than the 33% expected by chance, these results raise considerable doubt about the validity of assuming that wives' responses are sufficient. In a large number of cases— ranging from 25% to 52% of the families—one would obtain a *different* assessment of relative influence by asking the husband. To rely only on wives' responses would be both incomplete and possibly misleading. Hence, the similarity between husbands' and wives' responses when viewed in aggregate terms is clearly not present on a within-family comparison.

What can be said about the nature of the disagreements? Perhaps role consensus varies in some predictable ways by families, decisions, or relative influence. It is also possible that the disagreements are more or less random, reflecting an inherent ambiguity in questions about purchase influence.

The nature of the distribution of disagreements for each decision provides some evidence for this latter explanation. Notice that the great majority of disagreements are only one scale point. Moreover, the shape of the distributions tends to be symmetrical. Only in the case of three or four furniture purchase decisions is there any tendency for the disagreeing couples to overrepresent those in which husbands attribute *more* influence to the wife than the wife attributes to herself. If there were a consistent bias in the way couples responded to these questions, it is likely that these distributions would have been more highly skewed.

Another possible explanation for disagreement is the presence of real conflict surrounding the decision. If a husband and wife disagreed about what make of car to buy and had reached a compromise, an assessment of "who decided" might be difficult since it would be subject to different interpretations. One might, therefore, anticipate a positive relationship between reported conflict and the extent of disagreement about who actually made the decision. The data do not conform to this expectation, however. While the six automobile decisions tend to be seen as relatively conflict-free, each furniture decision involves "some disagreement" in about 40% of the families on the average.[7] If different perceptions of roles really do arise from such conflicts, one should find lower consensus for furniture decisions than for automobile decisions. As seen in Table 6, this is not apparent. In fact, it is the similarity in the magnitude of role consensus across these decisions rather than any difference that is noteworthy.

A third possibility is that relative influence is itself related to the magnitude of role consensus. It might be, for example, that disagreeing couples share decisions more equally. Couples with highly specialized roles (i.e., husband-dominant or wife-dominant), on the other hand, might display high consensus given less ambiguity about "who decides." In order to examine this possible relationship a comparison was made of average relative influence in each decision for three groups: (1) couples who agreed; (2) wives who disagreed with their husbands; and (3) husbands who disagreed with their wives. Differences in the mean values among these groups were not large. The only noteworthy pattern was the tendency for "disagreeing husbands" to attribute consistently more influence to wives than do their wives or the couples who agree. This finding suggests that the bias described earlier is due primarily to husbands rather than wives. It also suggests that relative influence has no relationship to the degree of consensus in the light of the husbands' consistent upward bias over both product categories.

Finally, is there any evidence that families tend to agree or disagree across several decisions? One simple test is merely to plot the number of disagreements (from 0 to 6) for each product. A bimodal distribution would be found if one group of families consistently agreed and another group consistently disagreed about their roles in these decisions. Regularity could also be represented by a relatively flat distribution in which couples formed a scale from high to low consensus. Rather than finding either of these two distributions, however, the data showed unimodal distributions for both automobile and furniture decisions with the mode in each case at two disagreements. Knowing that a couple disagreed about their roles in one decision does not increase the ability to predict whether they will agree or disagree about others.

The search for systematic differences in families, decisions, or relative influence as a basis for explaining the disagreement in spouses' perception of relative influence has produced largely negative results. It seems much more likely that disagreement reflects measurement error.

Discussion

The multidimensional role structure evident in these two purchase decisions contrasts with the unidimensional or bidimensional authority structures posited in much of the existing sociological literature. Instrumental decisions, in Parson's [15] terminology, or economic decisions, as defined by Herbst [8], of which the automobile and furniture decisions would seem to be a part, can be differentiated much further.[8] This finding also raises doubts about the common practice of summing over individual decisions in order to construct an "overall" power score for a family. There should be prior evidence that the decisions are, in fact, unidimensional. From a marketing point of view, the analysis suggests a *less* differentiated structure than that which is often implicit in the literature. It is possible to subsume several decisions under a more general category and hence begin to generalize about roles in consumer decisions. Of interest in future research is whether the same two clusters of product-related and allocation-related decisions are found for other product categories and whether these dimensions are sensitive to the demographic and social characteristics of families.

These results regarding role consensus have one direct implication for research. If the purpose of a study is merely to describe the relative influence of husbands and wives in various purchase decisions, then interview only one spouse. The conclusions reached by an advertiser in determining the appropriate audience for his message would not differ depending upon whether he had collected data from husbands or wives. If, on the other hand, a study uses purchase influence as a basis for classifying families for the purpose of further investigation, then the extent of within-family agreement becomes critical. The responses of one spouse may consistently provide better predictions of other aspects of a family's consumption behavior. Moreover, independent reports from husband and wife provide a basis for estimating the validity of measures used in a study.

How can the level of role consensus be increased? The findings of this study suggest that the use of specific, as opposed to global, measures of purchase influence is not the answer. It would appear that disagreement reflects each spouse's differing interpretations about the meaning of influence rather than any systematic bias inherent in these questions, whether general or specific. Attempts to increase consensus about roles will require more attention to the dynamics of the decision process. Information about the nature and frequency of discussion prior to each decision, length of the planning period, importance of each decision, and details about search activities may permit construction of meaningful classifications. Even with improved methodological procedures, however, one should consider that each spouse may have different but *equally legitimate* perceptions of relative influence. If this is true, the now common search for one "objective reality" or for the spouse who is "right" is misguided.

Notes

1. To simplify presentation, the original 5-point scale was collapsed by combining the categories "husband decided" with "husband more than wife," and "wife

decided" with "wife more than husband." The distribution of responses between the two "extreme" response categories (1 and 2; 4 and 5) provides no additional insights for the purpose of the first analysis.

2. The analysis of these patterns across three or more decisions does not lend itself to the usual factor analytic or clustering techniques which begin with a matrix of intercorrelations between pairs of variables. Such techniques could conceal the presence of meaningful regularity in relative influence across decisions.

3. An example illustrating this procedure may be useful. In Table 4 decisions about make and model of automobile are the most highly associated (.92). The association between this cluster and the remaining ten decisions is in each case determined by the pair with the lowest association. For example, the association between make of automobile and when to buy is .73; the association between model of automobile and when to buy is .70. To satisfy the classification assumption as specified by McQuitty—i.e., the three automobile decisions about make, model and when to buy must have as many common characteristics as the pair with the fewest—.70 is selected.

4. The stopping criteria for forming clusters of decisions is based upon the degree of association between decisions and/or clusters. The interrelationship of decisions through the formation of four clusters is high—greater than .60 for wives and .50 for husbands. Beyond this point, however, the association is markedly lower. In Figure 2, for example, the relationship between the two clusters of automobile decisions is only .21; the association between the two clusters of furniture decisions is also low—.20. It seems reasonable, therefore, to describe roles in these twelve purchase decisions in terms of four major dimensions.

5. The one exception is seen in the furniture decision clusters. Three decisions—what furniture to buy, what style and what color to select—form one cluster. The remaining three decisions (i.e., when to buy furniture, how much to spend and where to buy) group together into another. In contrast to the wives' perception of similarity between what furniture to buy and where to buy it, husbands perceive roles in deciding where to buy furniture as being more similar to the decision of how much to spend.

6. The distinction between these two definitions of agreement is sometimes confused in the literature. For example, Hill bases a decision to utilize the wife as respondent on Wolgast's study of economic decision making. She found, according to Hill, "the wife equally well informed, and more accurate in predicting plans than the husband" [9, p. 73]. This is hardly accurate, however, since Wolgast's findings were based upon a comparison of husbands as a group with wives as a group—who, incidentally, were rarely from the same family.

7. Using husbands' responses, the percentage of families who report disagreement in automobile decisions ranges from 3% to 13%. Disagreement is even less according to wives—from 2% to 8%. The percentage of families who report disagreement in furniture decisions ranges from 40% to 61% (husbands' responses) and from 25% to 51% (wives' responses).

8. This conclusion is consistent with several sociological studies that have found considerable role specialization within the family (Levinger [10]; Tharp [18]; and Wilkening and Bharadwaj [20]).

References

1. Robert O. Blood and Donald M. Wolfe, *Husbands and Wives: The Dynamics of Married Living,* Glencoe, Illinois: The Free Press, 1960.

2. Ernest W. Burgess and Harvey J. Locke, *The Family,* New York: American Book Company, 1960.

3. Bernard Farber, "A Study of Dependence and Decision-Making in Marriage," unpublished Doctoral dissertation, University of Chicago, September 1949.

4. Robert Ferber, "On the Reliability of Purchase Influence Studies," *Journal of Marketing,* Vol. 19 (January 1955), 225–232.

5. Paul W. Haberman and Jack Elinson, "Family Income Reported in Surveys: Husbands Versus Wives," *Journal of Marketing Research,* Vol. 4 (May 1967), 191–194.

6. David M. Heer, "Husband and Wife Perceptions of Family Power Structure," *Marriage and Family Living,* Vol. 36 (February 1962), 65–67.

7. ———, "Dominance and the Working Wife," *Social Forces,* Vol. 36 (May 1958), 341–347.

8. P. G. Herbst, "The Measurement of Family Relationships," *Human Relations,* Vol. 5 (February 1952), 3–35.

9. Reuben Hill, "Patterns of Decision-Making and the Accumulation of Family Assets," in Nelson Foote, ed., *Household Decision-Making,* New York: New York University Press, 1961, 57–80.

10. George Levinger, "Task and Social Behavior in Marriage," *Sociometry,* Vol. 27 (December 1964), 433–448.

11. *Male vs. Female Influence on the Purchase of Selected Products as Revealed by an Exploratory Depth Interview Study with Husbands and Wives,* New York: Fawcett Publications, 1958.

12. Glen C. McCann, "Consumer Decisions in the Rural Family in the South," paper presented at the annual meeting of the American Sociological Association, New York, August, 1960 (mimeographed).

13. Louis L. McQuitty, "Hierarchical Syndrome Analysis," *Educational and Psychological Measurement,* Vol. 20 (Summer 1960), 293–304.

14. James T. Morgan, "Some Pilot Studies of Communication and Consensus in the Family," *Public Opinion Quarterly,* Vol. 32 (Spring 1968), 113–121.

15. Talcott Parsons and Robert F. Bales, *Family, Socialization, and Interaction Process,* Glencoe, Illinois: The Free Press, 1955.

16. John Scanzoni, "A Note on the Sufficiency of Wife Responses in Family Research," *Pacific Sociological Review,* Vol. 8 (Fall 1965), 109–115.

17. Harry Sharp and Paul Mott, "Consumer Decisions in the Metropolitan Family," *Journal of Marketing,* Vol. 21 (October 1956), 149–156.

18. Roland C. Tharp, "Dimensions of Marriage Roles," *Marriage and Family Living,* Vol. 25 (November 1963), 389–404.

19. *Time Magazine,* "Family Decision-Making," Research Report 1428, 1967.

20. Eugene A. Wilkening and Lakschmi Bharadwaj, "Dimensions of Aspirations, Work Roles, and Decision-Making of Farm Husbands and Wives in Wisconsin," *Journal of Marriage and the Family,* Vol. 29 (November 1967), 703–711.

21. Elizabeth H. Wolgast, "Do Husbands or Wives Make the Purchasing Decisions?" *Journal of Marketing,* Vol. 23 (October 1958), 151–158.

4.8 Children's Purchase Influence Attempts and Parental Yielding
SCOTT WARD, DANIEL B. WACKMAN

Mass communication research has traditionally been concerned with relatively immediate consequences of mass media use, such as attitude change. Considerably less attention has been devoted to second-order consequences of mass communication exposure, such as interpersonal communication.

This research examined such second-order consequences, focusing on the impact of television advertising on mother-child interaction. Specifically, we studied children's attempts to influence mothers' purchases of various products and mothers' yielding to these attempts.

Some previous research has examined relationships between mass media use, parent-child interaction, and subsequent effects. For example, adolescents' mass media use has been related to parent-child interaction and political socialization processes [2, 6]. Halloran and his associates examined exposure to television and intrafamily communication among samples of delinquent and nondelinquent British adolescents [5].

Little empirical evidence has been found on the extent of television advertising's influence on intrafamily interaction and behavior. For example, while much commercial research attempts to relate mass media exposure to aspects of consumer behavior, little effort has been devoted to explicit examination of parent-child interaction intervening between media exposure and behavior [3]. Research on consumers' family decision making usually focuses on husband-wife interaction and is not concerned with the influence of children [4].

Some qualitative data indicate that mothers feel television commercials influence their children [8], citing the apparent formation of desires for various products. Parents resent the encouragement of overt attempts to influence their purchases, although many mothers are said to accept television advertising as a necessary evil. Such qualitative research, of course, does not explicitly link media exposure to specific family processes.

Berey and Pollay examined such processes in mothers' purchases of children's breakfast cereals [1]. While not concerned with mass media influences, the investigators found highly child-centered mothers purchased their children's favorite cereals less frequently than less child-centered mothers. The child's assertiveness was not correlated with purchase perhaps because the assertiveness measure was based on teachers' ratings, which are probably based more on peer interaction than parent-child interaction.

The present study examined the influence of three variables on children's purchase influence attempts and parental yielding: demographics, parent-child interaction, and mothers' mass communication behavior.

Methodology

Self-administered questionnaires were sent to 132 mothers of 5- to 12-year-old children in the Boston metropolitan area. The mothers had been recruited from area service clubs for participation in another study. While attempts were made to sample different socioeconomic areas of Boston, the sample was skewed toward the upper and upper-middle classes.

The questionnaire took about one hour to complete; women were paid a small amount for their participation. Some items asked the women to report on the behavior of one of their children, identified on the questionnaire. Completed questionnaires were received from 109 mothers (83%). Various scales were recoded by summing items.

Two kinds of analysis were used. First, age group differences were compared by means and percentages for three age groups.[1] Here we were simply looking for trends; no overall statistical test was used because no single test was appropriate, and a series of statistical tests of differences on items might be misleading.[2]

Second, zero-order and partial correlations were computed to examine relationships between various independent variables and the dependent variables. Multiple regression techniques were not used because we expected that there would be a number of interactions among the independent variables; the additive regression model tends to obscure these interactions and also some zero-order relationships, depending on the specific type of interactions which occur. On the other hand, the small number of cases prevented us from examining many variables at one time to look for second- and third-order interactions. Our analysis examined trends and variables which might prove to be useful predictors in subsequent research.

Findings

Purchase Influence Attempts

Mothers were asked to indicate the frequency of their child's purchase influence attempts for 22 products (Table 1). All were heavily advertised, but

TABLE 1.   Frequency of Children's Attempts to Influence Purchases and Percentage of Mothers' "Usually" Yielding

Products	Frequency of Requests[a]				Percentage of Yielding			
	5–7 Years	8–10 Years	11–12 Years	Total[b]	5–7 Years	8–10 Years	11–12 Years	Total[b]
Relevant Foods								
Breakfast Cereal	1.26	1.59	1.97	1.59	88	91	83	87
Snack Foods	1.71	2.00	1.71	1.80	52	62	77	63
Candy	1.60	2.09	2.17	1.93	40	28	57	42
Soft Drinks	2.00	2.03	2.00	2.01	38	47	54	46
Jell-o	2.54	2.94	2.97	2.80	40	41	26	36
Overall Mean	1.82	2.13	2.16	2.03				
Overall Percentage					51.6	53.8	59.4	54.8
Less Relevant Foods								
Bread	3.12	2.91	3.43	3.16	14	28	17	19
Coffee	3.93	3.91	3.97	3.94	2	0	0	1
Pet Food	3.29	3.59	3.24	3.36	7	3	11	7
Overall Mean	3.45	3.47	3.49	3.49				
Overall Percentage					7.6	10.3	9.3	9.0
Durables, for Child's Use								
Game, Toy	1.24	1.63	2.17	1.65	57	59	46	54
Clothing	2.76	2.47	2.29	2.52	21	34	57	37
Bicycle	2.48	2.59	2.77	2.61	7	9	9	8
Hot Wheels	2.43	2.41	3.20	2.67	29	19	17	22
Record Album	3.36	2.63	2.23	2.78	12	16	46	24
Camera	3.91	3.75	3.71	3.80	2	3	0	2
Overall Mean	2.70	2.58	2.73	2.67				
Overall Percentage					25.6	28.0	35.0	29.4
Notions, Toiletries								
Toothpaste	2.29	2.31	2.60	2.39	36	44	40	39
Bath Soap	3.10	2.97	3.46	3.17	9	9	9	9
Shampoo	3.48	3.31	3.03	3.28	17	6	23	16
Aspirin	3.64	3.78	3.97	3.79	5	6	0	4
Overall Mean	3.13	3.09	3.26	3.16				
Overall Percentage					16.8	16.3	18.0	17.0
Other Products								
Automobile	3.55	3.66	3.51	3.57	2	0	0	12
Gasoline Brand	3.64	3.63	3.83	3.70	2	0	3	2
Laundry Soap	3.69	3.75	3.71	3.72	2	0	3	2
Household Cleaner	3.71	3.84	3.74	3.76	2	3	0	2
Overall Mean	3.65	3.72	3.70	3.69				
Overall Percentage					2.0	.75	1.50	1.75

[a]On a scale from 1 = often to 4 = never.
[b]5–7 years, $n = 43$; 8–10 years, $n = 32$; 11–12 years, $n = 34$; $N = 109$.

varied in price, frequency of purchase, and relevance to the child (direct consumption or use by the child vs. consumption or use by other family members). Analysis of marginal data indicated that children frequently attempted to influence purchases for food products, but these attempts decreased with age.

Durables which the child uses directly were the second most requested product category. Mothers of younger children (5 to 7 years old) indicated frequent influence attempts for game and toy purchases, while mothers of older children (11 to 12 years old) indicated frequent purchase influence attempts for clothing and record albums. Across four product categories, purchase influence attempts appear to decrease with age.

Parental Yielding

Data in Table 1 indicate that across most product categories the older the child, the more likely mothers are to yield to influence attempts, perhaps because older children generally asked for less. It may also result from mothers' attributing greater competence in making judgments about products to older children. Mothers were most likely to yield to purchase influence attempts for food products—the same products children most often asked for.

Correlates of Influence Attempts and Yielding

The correlation between children's purchase influence attempts and mothers' yielding was positive and statistically significant ($r = .35$). Clearly, children who ask for products more often receive them more often. However, since the correlation was not high, it is likely that some of the independent variables were differentially related to these two dependent variables.

Table 2 shows relationships between the three kinds of independent variables and the two dependent variables. The various independent variables were relatively independent of each other, since correlations among them were rather low.

TABLE 2. Correlations Between Child's Purchase Influence Attempts, Parental Yielding, and the Independent Variables

	Child's Purchase Influence Attempts	Parental Yielding
Demographics		
Child's Age	−.13	.20[a]
Number of Children	−.00	−.00
Social Class	−.01	.00
Interpersonal Variables		
Parent-Child Conflict	.18[b]	−.00
Restrictions on Viewing	−.01	−.24[a]
Communication Variables		
Mother's Time Spent with Television	.18[b]	.23[a]
Recall of Commercials	.26[a]	.04
Attitudes Toward Advertising	−.00	.16[b]

[a] $p < .01$.
[b] $p < .05$.

Examining demographic predictors, essentially no relationships were found between the dependent variables and number of children in the family and social class. The relationship between age and influence attempts approached significance ($r = -.13$) and was negative. On the other hand, as revealed in previous analyses of means, a positive correlation obtained between age and parental yielding to purchase influence attempts. Thus, while parents may receive more purchase influence attempts from young children, they are more likely to act on them as the child grows older.

While many other parent-child variables may be important predictors of the dependent variables, conflict and restrictions on television viewing are presumably related to control parents may attempt to exert over children. The data indicate a significant positive relationship between conflict and influence attempts ($r = .18$), suggesting that purchase influence attempts may be part of a general pattern of disagreement and conflict between parents and children— perhaps even a cause of them. No relationship was observed between conflict and yielding. It seems that few parents "punish" their child by failing to yield to purchase influence attempts.

Restrictions on viewing and yielding were negatively related. Thus the more restrictions parents place on a child's television viewing, the less they yield to his purchase influence attempts. Interestingly, however, no relationship obtained between restrictions and influence attempts. Apparently, this form of parental control is not effective in reducing a child's purchase influence attempts.

For the final set of independent variables, the data indicated positive relationships between mothers' time spent watching television and influence attempts and yielding. This result may simply reflect the greater availability to children of mothers who watch a great deal of television. Moreover, perhaps influence attempts and promises of yielding occur when mothers and children watch television together.

Mothers' recall of commercial content, measured by a series of fill-in-the-blank advertising identification items, was positively related to purchase influence attempts, but not to yielding. Some previous research has suggested that recall of commercials is mainly a function of intelligence [7]. Thus the relationship between recall and the two dependent variables may indicate that although children of more intelligent mothers ask for more products, these mothers are less likely to yield to these influence attempts.

Finally, a weak positive relationship obtained between attitudes toward advertising and yielding. Mothers with more positive attitudes toward advertising were more likely to yield to purchase influence attempts than mothers with less favorable attitudes; their children were no more likely to ask for products than other children, however.

Partial correlation coefficients were also computed for all these relationships, with age of the child controlled. Data indicated only slight changes in the patterns of relationships reported above.

Summary

Children's purchase influence attempts may decrease somewhat with age, depending on the type of product, but mothers' yielding to requests increases with age, probably reflecting a perceived increased competence of older children in making judgments about purchase decisions.

Aspects of parent-child conflict are related to influence attempts and yielding. The data suggest that influence attempts may be part of a more general parent-child conflict; furthermore, mothers who restrict viewing are likely not to yield to purchase influence attempts. Finally, mothers' time spent watching television is positively related to influence attempts and yielding, while recall of commercials is positively related only to influence attempts. Mothers with positive attitudes toward advertising are more likely than mothers with negative attitudes to yield to influence attempts.

In future research, other aspects of parent-child interaction and their influence on the dependent variables will be examined. Moreover, characteristics of the viewing situation should be considered. It may be that joint parent-child or family viewing increases the incidence of purchase influence attempts and further, several children "ganging up" on parents may increase their yielding to purchase influence attempts. Finally, characteristics of children should be examined.

Notes

1. Analysis of variance to test for statistical significance of age group differences was not used because subjects were not randomly assigned to experimental groups.

2. Multivariate analysis of variance was not appropriate. First, we did not have random experimental groups. Second, we did not expect that all the items in a scale would have the same age group pattern—as indeed they did not; however, multivariate analysis of variance assumes that the pattern of differences across experimental groups is essentially the same for all items.

References

1. Berey, L. A. and R. W. Pollay. "The Influencing Role of the Child in Family Decision-Making," *Journal of Marketing Research,* Vol. 5 (Feb. 1968), 70–72.

2. Chaffee, Steven, Scott Ward, and Leonard Tipton. "Mass Communication and Political Socialization," *Journalism Quarterly*, Vol. 47 (Winter 1970), 647–659.

3. *The Dynamics of Household Brand Decision-Making.* New York: Time/Life, Inc., 1967.

4. Granbois, D. H. "The Role of Communication in the Family Decision-Making Process," unpublished paper, Indiana University, 1967.

5. Halloran, James D., Roger L. Brown, and David C. Chaney. *Television and Delinquency.* Leicester, Eng.: Leicester University Press, 1970.

6. McLeod, Jack, Garrett O'Keefe, and Daniel B. Wackman. "Communication and Political Socialization During the Adolescent Years," paper presented at meetings of the Association for Education in Journalism, 1969.

7. Ward, Scott, and Daniel B. Wackman. "Family and Media Influences on Adolescent Consumer Behavior," *American Behavioral Scientist*, Vol. 14 (Jan.–Feb. 1971), 415–427.

8. Yankelovich, Daniel, Inc. "Mothers' Attitudes Toward Children's Programs and Commercials," unpublished paper, Action for Children's Television, 1970.

4.9 Training the Woman to Know Her Place: The Power of a Nonconscious Ideology

SANDRA L. BEM, DARYL J. BEM

In the beginning God created the heaven and the earth. . . . And God said, Let us make man in our image, after our likeness; and let them have dominion over the fish of the sea, and over the fowl of the air, and over the cattle, and over all the earth. . . . And the rib, which the Lord God had taken from man, made he a woman and brought her unto the man. . . . And the Lord God said unto the woman, What is this that thou has done? And the woman said, The serpent beguiled me, and I did eat. . . . Unto the woman He said, I will greatly multiply thy sorrow and thy conception; in sorrow thou shalt bring forth children; and thy desire shall be to thy husband, and he shall rule over thee. (Gen. 1, 2, 3)

And lest anyone fail to grasp the moral of this story, Saint Paul provides further clarification:

For a man . . . is the image and glory of God; but the woman is the glory of the man. For the man is not of the woman, but the woman of the man. Neither was the man created for the woman, but the woman for the man. (1 Cor. 11)

Let the woman learn in silence with all subjection. But I suffer not a woman to teach, nor to usurp authority over the man, but to be in silence. For Adam was first formed, then Eve. And Adam was not deceived, but the woman, being deceived, was in the transgression. Notwithstanding, she shall be saved in childbearing, if they continue in faith and charity and holiness with sobriety. (1 Tim. 2)

And lest it be thought that only Christians have this rich heritage of ideology about women, consider the morning prayer of the Orthodox Jew:

Blessed art Thou, oh Lord our God, King of the Universe, that I was not born a gentile.

Blessed art Thou, oh Lord our God, King of the Universe, that I was not born a slave.

Blessed art Thou, oh Lord our God, King of the Universe, that I was not born a woman.

Or the Koran, the sacred text of Islam:

Men are superior to women on account of the qualities in which God has given them pre-eminence.

Because they think they sense a decline in feminine "faith, charity, and holiness with sobriety," many people today jump to the conclusion that the ideology expressed in these passages is a relic of the past. Not so. It has simply been obscured by an equalitarian veneer, and the ideology has now become nonconscious. That is, we remain unaware of it because alternative beliefs and attitudes about women go unimagined. We are like the fish who is unaware that his environment is wet. After all, what else could it be? Such is the nature of all nonconscious ideologies. Such is the nature of America's ideology about women. For even those Americans who agree that a black skin should not uniquely qualify its owner for janitorial or domestic service continue to act as if the possession of a uterus uniquely qualifies *its* owner for precisely that.

Consider, for example, the 1968 student rebellion at Columbia University. Students from the radical left took over some administration buildings in the name of equalitarian principles which they accused the university of flouting. Here were the most militant spokesmen one could hope to find in the cause of equalitarian ideals. But no sooner had they occupied the buildings than the male militants blandly turned to their sisters-in-arms and assigned them the task of preparing the food, while they—the menfolk—would presumably plan further strategy. The reply these males received was the reply they deserved, and the fact that domestic tasks behind the barricades were desegregated across the sex line that day is an everlasting tribute to the class consciousness of the ladies of the left.

But these conscious coeds are not typical, for the nonconscious assumptions about a woman's "natural" talents (or lack of them) are at least as prevalent among women as they are among men. A psychologist named Philip Goldberg (1968) demonstrated this by asking female college students to rate a number of professional articles from each of six fields. The articles were collated into two equal sets of booklets, and the names of the authors were changed so that the identical article was attributed to a male author (e.g., John T. McKay) in one set of booklets and to a female author (e.g., Joan T. McKay) in the other set. Each student was asked to read the articles in her booklet and to rate them for value, competence, persuasiveness, writing style, and so forth.

As he had anticipated, Goldberg found that the identical article received significantly lower ratings when it was attributed to a female author than when it was attributed to a male author. He had predicted this result for articles from professional fields generally considered the province of men, like law and city planning, but to his surprise, these coeds also downgraded articles from the fields of dietetics and elementary school education when they were attributed to female authors. In other words, these students rated the male authors as better at everything, agreeing with Aristotle that "we should regard the female nature as afflicted with a natural defectiveness." We repeated this experiment informally in our own classrooms and discovered that male students show the same implicit prejudice against female authors that Goldberg's female students showed. Such is the nature of a nonconscious ideology!

It is significant that examples like these can be drawn from the college world, for today's students have challenged the established ways of looking at almost every other issue, and they have been quick to reject those practices of our society which conflict explicitly with their major values. But as the above examples suggest, they will find it far more difficult to shed the more subtle aspects of a sex-role ideology which—as we shall now attempt to demonstrate— conflicts just as surely with their existential values as any of the other societal practices to which they have so effectively raised objection. And as we shall see, there is no better way to appreciate the power of a society's nonconscious ideology than to examine it within the framework of values held by that society's avant-garde.

Individuality and Self-Fulfillment

The dominant values of today's students concern personal growth on the one hand, and interpersonal relationships on the other. The first of these emphasizes individuality and self-fulfillment; the second stresses openness, honesty, and equality in all human relationships.

The values of individuality and self-fulfillment imply that each human being, male or female, is to be encouraged to "do his own thing." Men and women are no longer to be stereotyped by society's definitions. If sensitivity, emotionality, and warmth are desirable human characteristics, then they are desirable for men as well as for women. (John Wayne is no longer an idol of the young, but their pop-art satire.) If independence, assertiveness, and serious intellectual commitment are desirable human characteristics, then they are desirable for women as well as for men. The major prescription of this college generation is that each individual should be encouraged to discover and fulfill his own unique potential and identity, unfettered by society's presumptions.

But society's presumptions enter the scene much earlier than most people suspect, for parents begin to raise their children in accord with the popular stereotypes from the very first. Boys are encouraged to be aggressive, competitive, and independent, whereas girls are rewarded for being passive and dependent (Barry, Bacon, & Child, 1957; Sears, Maccoby, & Levin, 1957). In one study, six-month-old infant girls were already being touched and spoken to more by their mothers while they were playing than were infant boys. When they were thirteen months old, these same girls were more reluctant than the boys to leave their mothers; they returned more quickly and more frequently to them; and they remained closer to them throughout the entire play period. When a physical barrier was placed between mother and child, the girls tended to cry and motion for help; the boys made more active attempts to get around the barrier (Goldberg & Lewis, 1969). No one knows to what extent these sex differences at the age of thirteen months can be attributed to the mothers' behavior at the age of six months, but it is hard to believe that the two are unconnected.

As children grow older, more explicit sex-role training is introduced. Boys are encouraged to take more of an interest in mathematics and science.

Boys, not girls, are given chemistry sets and microscopes for Christmas. Moreover, all children quickly learn that mommy is proud to be a moron when it comes to mathematics and science, whereas daddy knows all about these things. When a young boy returns from school all excited about biology, he is almost certain to be encouraged to think of becoming a physician. A girl with similar enthusiasm is told that she might want to consider nurse's training later so she can have "an interesting job to fall back upon in case—God forbid—she ever needs to support herself." A very different kind of encouragement. And any girl who doggedly persists in her enthusiasm for science is likely to find her parents as horrified by the prospect of a permanent love affair with physics as they would be by the prospect of an interracial marriage.

These socialization practices quickly take their toll. By nursery school age, for example, boys are already asking more questions about how and why things work (Smith, 1933). In first and second grade, when asked to suggest ways of improving various toys, boys do better on the fire truck and girls do better on the nurse's kit, but by the third grade, boys do better regardless of the toy presented (Torrance, 1962). By the ninth grade, 25% of the boys, but only 3% of the girls, are considering careers in science or engineering (Flanagan, unpublished; cited by Kagan, 1964). When they apply for college, boys and girls are about equal on verbal aptitude tests, but boys score significantly higher on mathematical aptitude tests—about 60 points higher on the College Board examinations, for example (Brown, 1965, p. 162). Moreover, girls improve their mathematical performance if problems are reworded so that they deal with cooking and gardening, even though the abstract reasoning required for their solutions remains the same (Milton, 1958). Clearly, not just ability, but motivation too, has been affected.

But these effects in mathematics and science are only part of the story. A girl's long training in passivity and dependence appears to exact an even higher toll from her overall motivation to achieve, to search for new and independent ways of doing things, and to welcome the challenge of new and unsolved problems. In one study, for example, elementary school girls were more likely to try solving a puzzle by imitating an adult, whereas the boys were more likely to search for a novel solution not provided by the adult (McDavid, 1959). In another puzzle-solving study, young girls asked for help and approval from adults more frequently than the boys; and, when given the opportunity to return to the puzzles a second time, the girls were more likely to rework those they had already solved, whereas the boys were more likely to try puzzles they had been unable to solve previously (Crandall & Rabson, 1960). A girl's sigh of relief is almost audible when she marries and retires from the outside world of novel and unsolved problems. This, of course, is the most conspicuous outcome of all: the majority of American women become full-time homemakers. Such are the consequences of a nonconscious ideology.

But why does this process violate the values of individuality and self-fulfillment? It is *not* because some people may regard the role of homemaker as inferior to other roles. That is not the point. Rather, the point is that our society is managing to consign a large segment of its population to the role of homemaker solely on the basis of sex just as inexorably as it has in the past consigned the individual with a black skin to the role of janitor or domestic. It is not the quality of the role itself which is at issue here, but the fact that in spite of their unique identities, the majority of America's women end up in the *same* role.

Even so, however, several arguments are typically advanced to counter the claim that America's homogenization of its women subverts individuality and self-fulfillment. The three most common arguments invoke, respectively, (1) free will, (2) biology, and (3) complementarity.

1. The free will argument proposes that a 21-year-old woman is perfectly free to choose some other role if she cares to do so; no one is standing in her way. But this argument conveniently overlooks the fact that the society which has spent twenty years carefully marking the woman's ballot for her has nothing to lose in that twenty-first year by pretending to let her cast it for the alternative of her choice. Society has controlled not her alternatives, but her motivation to choose any but one of those alternatives. The so-called freedom to choose is illusory and cannot be invoked to justify the society which controls the motivation to choose.

2. The biological argument suggests that there may really be inborn differences between men and women in, say, independence or mathematical ability. Or that there may be biological factors beyond the fact that women can become pregnant and nurse children which uniquely dictate that they, but not men, should stay home all day and shun serious outside commitment. Maybe female hormones really are responsible somehow. One difficulty with this argument, of course, is that female hormones would have to be different in the Soviet Union, where one-third of the engineers and 75% of the physicians are women. In America, women constitute less than 1% of the engineers and only 7% of the physicians (Dodge, 1966). Female physiology *is* different, and it may account for some of the psychological differences between the sexes, but America's sex-role ideology still seems primarily responsible for the fact that so few women emerge from childhood with the motivation to seek out any role beyond the one that our society dictates.

But even if there really were biological differences between the sexes along these lines, the biological argument would still be irrelevant. The reason can best be illustrated with an analogy.

Suppose that every black American boy were to be socialized to become a jazz musician on the assumption that he has a "natural" talent in that direction, or suppose that his parents should subtly discourage him from other pursuits because it is considered "inappropriate" for black men to become physicians or physicists. Most liberal Americans, we submit, would disapprove. But suppose that it *could* be demonstrated that black Americans, *on the average*, did possess an inborn better sense of rhythm than white Americans. Would *that* justify ignoring the unique characteristics of a *particular* black youngster from the very beginning and specifically socializing him to become a musician? We don't think so. Similarly, as long as a woman's socialization does not nurture her uniqueness, but treats her only as a member of a group on the basis of some assumed *average* characteristic, she will not be prepared to realize her own potential in the way that the values of individuality and self-fulfillment imply she should.

The irony of the biological argument is that it does not take biological differences seriously enough. That is, it fails to recognize the range of biological differences between individuals within the same sex. Thus, recent research has revealed that biological factors help determine many personality traits. Dominance and submissiveness, for example, have been found to have large inheritable components; in other words, biological factors *do* have the potential for partially determining how dominant or submissive an individual, male or female, will turn out to be. But the effects of this biological potential could be detected only in males (Gottesman, 1963). This implies that only the males in our culture are raised with sufficient flexibility, with sufficient latitude given to their biological differences, for their "natural" or biologically determined potential to shine through. Females, on the other hand, are subjected to a socialization which so ignores their unique attributes that even the effects of biology seem to be swamped. In sum, the biological argument for continuing America's homogenization of its women gets hoist with its own petard.

3. Many people recognize that most women do end up as full-time homemakers because of their socialization and that these women do exemplify the failure of our society to raise girls as unique individuals. But, they point out, the role of the homemaker is not inferior to the role of the professional man: it is complementary but equal.

This argument is usually bolstered by pointing to the joys and importance of taking care of small children. Indeed, mothers *and* fathers find child-rearing rewarding, and it is certainly important. But this argument becomes insufficient when one considers that the average American woman now lives to age 74 and has her *last* child at about age 26; thus, by the time the woman is 33 or so, her children all have more important things to do with their daytime hours than to spend them entertaining an adult woman who has nothing to do during the second half of her life span. As for the other "joys" of homemaking, many writers (e.g., Friedan, 1963) have persuasively argued that the role of the homemaker has been glamorized far beyond its intrinsic worth. This charge becomes plausible when one considers that the average American homemaker spends the equivalent of a man's working day, 7.1 hours, in preparing meals, cleaning house, laundering, mending, shopping, and doing other household tasks. In other words, 43% of her waking time is spent in activity that would command an hourly wage on the open market well below the federally-set minimum for menial industrial work.

The point is not how little she would earn if she did these things in someone else's home, but that this use of time is virtually the same for home-makers with college degrees and for those with less than a grade school education, for women married to professional men and for women married to blue-collar workers. Talent, education, ability, interests, motivations: all are irrelevant. In our society, being female uniquely qualifies an individual for domestic work.

It is true, of course, that the American homemaker has, on the average, 5.1 hours of leisure time per day, and it is here, we are told, that each woman can express her unique identity. Thus, politically interested women can join the League of Women Voters; women with humane interests can become part-time Gray Ladies; women who love music can raise money for the symphony. Protestant women play Canasta; Jewish women play Mah-Jongg; brighter women of all denominations and faculty wives play bridge; and so forth.

But politically interested *men* serve in legislatures; *men* with humane interests become physicians or clinical psychologists; *men* who love music play in the symphony; and so forth. In other words, why should a woman's unique identity determine only the periphery of her life rather than its central core?

Again, the important point is not that the role of homemaker is necessarily inferior, but that the woman's unique identity has been rendered irrelevant. Consider the following "predictability test." When a boy is born, it is difficult to predict what he will be doing 25 years later. We cannot say whether he will be an artist, a doctor, or a college professor because he will be permitted to develop and to fulfill his own unique potential, particularly if he is white and middle-class. But if the newborn child is a girl, we can usually predict with confidence how she will be spending her time 25 years later. Her individuality doesn't have to be considered; it is irrelevant.

The socialization of the American male has closed off certain options for him too. Men are discouraged from developing certain desirable traits such as tenderness and sensitivity just as surely as women are discouraged from being assertive and, alas, "too bright." Young boys are encouraged to be incompetent at cooking and child care just as surely as young girls are urged to be incompetent at mathematics and science.

Indeed, one of the errors of the early feminist movement in this country was that it assumed that men had all the goodies and that women could attain self-fulfillment merely by being like men. But that is hardly the utopia implied by the values of individuality and self-fulfillment. Rather, these values would require society to raise its children so flexibly and with sufficient respect for the integrity of individual uniqueness that some men might emerge with the motivation, the ability, and the opportunity to stay home and raise children without bearing the stigma of being peculiar. If homemaking is as glamorous as the women's magazines and television commercials portray it, then men, too, should have that option. Even if homemaking isn't all that glamorous, it would probably still be more fulfilling for some men than the jobs in which they now find themselves.

And if biological differences really do exist between men and women in "nurturance," in their inborn motivations to care for children, then this will show up automatically in the final distribution of men and women across the various roles: relatively fewer men will choose to stay at home. The values of individuality and self-fulfillment do not imply that there must be equality of outcome, an equal number of men and women in each role, but that there should be the widest possible variation in outcome consistent with the range of individual differences among people, regardless of sex. At the very least, these values imply that society should raise its males so that they could freely engage in activities that might pay less than those being pursued by their wives without feeling that they were "living off their wives." One rarely hears it said of a woman that she is "living off her husband."

Thus, it is true that a man's options are limited by our society's sex-role ideology, but as the "predictability test" reveals, it is still the woman in our society whose identity is rendered irrelevant by America's socialization practices. In 1954, the United States Supreme Court declared that a fraud and hoax lay behind the slogan "separate but equal." It is unlikely that any court will ever do the same for the more subtle motto that successfully keeps the woman in her place: "complementary but equal."

Interpersonal Equality

Wives, submit yourselves unto your own husbands, as unto the Lord. For the husband is the head of the wife, even as Christ is the head of the church; and he is the savior of the body. Therefore, as the church is subject unto Christ, so let the wives be to their own husbands in everything. (Eph. 5).

As this passage reveals, the ideological rationalization that men and women hold complementary but equal positions is a recent invention of our modern "liberal" society, part of the equalitarian veneer which helps to keep today's version of the ideology nonconscious. Certainly those Americans who value open, honest, and equalitarian relationships generally are quick to reject this traditional view of the male-female relationship; and, an increasing number of young people even plan to enter "utopian" marriages very much like the following hypothetical example:

Both my wife and I earned Ph.D. degrees in our respective disciplines. I turned down a superior academic post in Oregon and accepted a slightly less desirable position in New York where my wife could obtain a part-time teaching job and do research at one of the several other colleges in the area. Although I would have preferred to live in a suburb, we purchased a home near my wife's college so that she could have an office at home where she would be when the children returned from school. Because my wife earns a good salary, she can easily afford to pay a maid to do her major household chores. My wife and I share all other tasks around the house equally. For example, she cooks the meals, but I do the laundry for her and help her with many of her other household tasks.

Without questioning the basic happiness of such a marriage or its appropriateness for many couples, we can legitimately ask if such a marriage is, in fact, an instance of interpersonal equality. Have all the hidden assumptions about the woman's "natural" role really been eliminated? Has the traditional ideology really been exorcised? There is a very simple test. If the marriage is truly equalitarian, then its description should retain the same flavor and tone even if the roles of the husband and wife were to be reversed:

Both my husband and I earned Ph.D. degrees in our respective disciplines. I turned down a superior academic post in Oregon and accepted a slightly less desirable position in New York where my husband could obtain a part-time teaching job and do research at one of the several other colleges in the area. Although I would have preferred to live in a suburb, we purchased a home near my husband's college so that he could have an office at home where he would be when the children returned from school. Because my husband earns a good salary, he can easily afford to pay a maid to do his major household chores. My husband and I share all other tasks around the house equally. For example, he cooks the meals, but I do the laundry for him and help him with many of his other household tasks.

It seems unlikely that many men or women in our society would mistake the marriage *just* described as either equalitarian or desirable, and thus it becomes apparent that the ideology about the woman's "natural" role non-consciously permeates the entire fabric of such "utopian" marriages. It is true that the wife gains some measure of equality when her career can influence the final place of residence, but why is it the unquestioned assumption that the husband's career solely determines the initial set of alternatives that are to be considered? Why is it the wife who automatically seeks the part-time position? Why is it *her* maid instead of *their* maid? Why *her* laundry? Why *her* household tasks? And so forth throughout the entire relationship.

The important point here is not that such marriages are bad or that their basic assumptions of inequality produce unhappy, frustrated women. Quite the contrary. It is the very happiness of the wives in such marriages that reveals society's smashing success in socializing its women. It is a measure of the distance our society must yet traverse toward the goals of self-fulfillment and interpersonal equality that such marriages are widely characterized as utopian and fully equalitarian. It is a mark of how well the woman has been kept in her place that the husband in such a marriage is often idolized by women, including his wife, for "permitting" her to squeeze a career into the interstices of their marriage as long as his own career is not unduly inconvenienced. Thus is the white man blessed for exercising his power benignly while his "natural" right to that power forever remains unquestioned.

Such is the subtlety of a nonconscious ideology!

A truly equalitarian marriage would permit both partners to pursue careers or outside commitments which carry equal weight when all important decisions are to be made. It is here, of course, that the "problem" of children arises. People often assume that the woman who seeks a role beyond home and family would not care to have children. They assume that if she wants a career or serious outside commitment, then children must be unimportant to her. But of course no one makes this assumption about her husband. No one assumes that a father's interest in his career necessarily precludes a deep and abiding affection for his children or a vital interest in their development. Once again America applies a double standard of judgment. Suppose that a father of small children suddenly lost his wife. No matter how much he loved his children, no one would expect him to sacrifice his career in order to stay home with them on a full-time basis—*even if he had an independent source of income.* No one would charge him with selfishness or lack of parental feeling if he sought professional care for his children during the day. An equalitarian marriage simply abolishes this double standard and extends the same freedom to the mother, while also providing the framework for the father to enter more fully into the pleasures and responsibilities of child rearing. In fact, it is the equalitarian marriage which has the most potential for giving children the love and concern of two parents rather than one.

But few women are prepared to make use of this freedom. Even those women who have managed to finesse society's attempt to rob them of their career motivations are likely to find themselves blocked by society's trump card: the feeling that the raising of the children is their unique responsibility and—in time of crisis—ultimately theirs alone. Such is the emotional power of a nonconscious ideology.

In addition to providing this potential for equalized child care, a truly equalitarian marriage embraces a more general division of labor which satisfies what might be called "the roommate test." That is, the labor is divided just as it is when two men or two women room together in college or set up a bachelor apartment together. Errands and domestic chores are assigned by preference, agreement, flipping a coin, given to hired help, or—as is sometimes the case—left undone.

It is significant that today's young people, many of whom live this way prior to marriage, find this kind of arrangement within marriage so foreign to their thinking. Consider an analogy. Suppose that a white male college student decided to room or set up a bachelor apartment with a black male friend. Surely the typical white student would not blithely assume that his black roommate was to handle all the domestic chores. Nor would his conscience allow him to do so even in the unlikely event that his roommate would say: "No, that's okay. I like doing housework. I'd be happy to do it." We suspect that the typical white student would still not be comfortable if he took advantage of this offer, if he took advantage of the fact that his roommate had been socialized to be "happy" with such an arrangement. But change this hypothetical black roommate to a female marriage partner, and somehow the student's conscience goes to sleep. At most it is quickly tranquilized by the thought that "she is happiest when she is ironing for her loved one." Such is the power of a nonconscious ideology.

Of course, it may well be that she *is* happiest when she is ironing for her loved one.

Such, indeed, is the power of a nonconscious ideology!

References

Barry, H., III, M. K. Bacon, and I. L. Child. A cross-cultural survey of some sex differences in socialization. *Journal of Abnormal and Social Psychology,* Vol. 55 (1957), 327–332.

Brown, R. *Social Psychology*. New York: Free Press, 1965.

Crandall, V. J., and A. Rabson. Children's repetition choices in an intellectual achievement situation following success and failure. *Journal of Genetic Psychology*, Vol. 97 (1960), 161–168.

Dodge, N. D. *Women in the Soviet Economy*. Baltimore: The Johns Hopkins Press, 1966.

Flanagan, J. C. Project talent. Unpublished manuscript.

Friedan, B. *The Feminine Mystique*. New York: Norton, 1963.

Goldberg, P. Are women prejudiced against women? *Transaction*, Vol. 5 (April 1968), 28–30.

Goldberg, S. and M. Lewis. Play behavior in the year-old infant: early sex differences. *Child Development*, Vol. 40 (1969), 21–31.

Gottesman, I. I. Heritability of personality: a demonstration. *Psychological Monographs*, Vol. 77 (1963), (Whole No. 572).

Kagan, J. Acquisition and significance of sex typing and sex role identity. In M. L. Hoffman and L. W. Hoffman (Eds.) *Review of Child Development Research*, Vol. 1. New York: Russell Sage Foundation (1964), 137–167.

McDavid, J. W. Imitative behavior in preschool children. *Psychological Monographs*, Vol. 73 (1959), (Whole No. 486).

Milton, G. A. Five studies of the relation between sex role identification and achievement in problem solving. Technical Report No. 3, Department of Industrial Administration, Department of Psychology, Yale University, (Dec. 1958).

Sears, R. R., E. E. Maccoby, and H. Levin. *Patterns of Child Rearing*. Evanston, Ill.: Row, Peterson, 1957.

Smith, M. E. The influence of age, sex, and situation on the frequency of form and functions of questions asked by preschool children. *Child Development*, Vol. 3 (1933), 201–213.

Torrance, E. P. *Guiding Creative Talent*. Englewood Cliffs, N.J.: Prentice-Hall, 1962.

4.10   A Woman's Place: An Analysis of the Roles Portrayed by Women in Magazine Advertisements

ALICE E. COURTNEY, SARAH W. LOCKERETZ

Some members of the female liberation movement have criticized the very limited and negative stereotypes of women in advertising [1, 2, 3, 4]. This article reports on an exploratory study that examined print advertisements to see if such stereotypes could be identified. Particular attention was concentrated on comparing the occupational and nonworking roles of men and women as portrayed in advertisements.

Methods

Magazines directed toward both male and female readers were analyzed for stereotypes. Seven magazines, published the week of April 18, 1970, were selected: *Life, Look, Newsweek, The New Yorker, Saturday Review, Time,* and *U.S. News and World Report.* The April 1970 issue of *Readers' Digest* was also included. These publications appeal to general audiences and presumably are more likely than specialized magazines to show women in a wide variety of roles. Women's magazines were not included because they are directed primarily toward women as housewives, whatever their other roles.

A record was made of each of a total of 729 advertisements in the magazines sampled. Each was coded by one or more content categories, including product type, the number and sexes of all adults, and their occupations or activities. Children and teenagers were not included. In addition, two ads showing crowd scenes were excluded since it was not possible to count or identify individuals' roles. The analysis was concerned with those 312 ads showing one or more adults.[1] More men (397) than women (278) were pictured in these ads.

Findings

The print advertisements examined very rarely showed women in working roles. About 33% of the full-time workers in the United States are women: however, only 12% of the workers shown in the ads were female. Moreover, if professional entertainers of both sexes are excluded, the proportion of women workers pictured drops to just seven percent. Almost half of the men (45%) were shown in working roles: in contrast, less than one-tenth of the women (9%) were shown in working roles.

Table 1 shows a breakdown of the occupations of the working men and women seen in the ads. Of 24 working women, 14 (58%) were entertainers. Not a single woman was shown as a professional or high-level business executive. Aside from entertainers, the working women were: clerks (3), stewardess (1), assembly line worker (1), airline employees engaged in food preparation (3), schoolteacher (1), and one woman identified only as a "working woman."[2]

Three nonworking roles for men and women portrayed in the advertisements were classed as family, recreational, and decorative (that is, nonactive). Table 2 summarizes the relationship between the sex composition of the ads and the nonworking roles shown. Men alone were usually pictured in working roles, and only 37% of the men shown alone or with other men were in non-

TABLE 1.   Occupations of Working Men and Women Shown in Advertisements[a]

	Percentage of Males	Percentage of Females
Proportion Shown as Workers	45	9
Occupational Categories		
High-Level Business Executives	10	0
Professional	9	0
Entertainers, Professional Sports	20	58
Sales, Middle-Level Business, Semi-Professional	7	8
Nonprofessional White Collar	2	17
Blue Collar	40	17
Soldiers, Police	12	0
	100	100
Number of Workers Shown	176	24

[a] Based on number of adults shown.

TABLE 2.   Nonworking Activities of Men and Women Shown in Advertisements[a]

	Percent of Males			Percent of Females		
	Alone or with Males	With Females	Total	Alone or with Females	With Males	Total
Proportion Portrayed as Nonworkers	37	71	55	90	92	91
Roles of nonworkers						
Family	18	24	22	21	25	23
Recreational	35	65	56	9	64	46
Decorative	47	11	22	70	11	31
	100	100	100	100	100	100
Number of Non-workers Shown	68	153	221	86	168	254

[a]Based on number of adults shown. Note that some ads showed mixed groups containing unequal numbers of males and females.

working roles. However, when women were shown alone or with other women, 90% were in nonworking roles. Of these, 70% were in the nonactive, decorative role.

When men appeared in ads with women, they were far less likely to be working than when alone or with other men. Of men depicted alone or with other men, 63% were working, compared to only 29% of the men shown with women. When men and women were pictured together, about half the time they were in recreational roles.

Differences in male and female roles portrayed were also evident in the number of males and females and the type of product advertised. Table 3 shows a division of the male and female "worlds" by product category.

These 16 product categories represent a broad segment of American life, in which women were shown operating independently in only a limited way; they took care of themselves and their homes. For major household buying decisions—appliances, furniture—advertisements showed the woman joined by the man.

In the advertisements studied, women rarely ventured far from the home by themselves or with other women. Women did smoke, drink, travel, drive in cars, and use banks, but primarily in the company of men. In about half of the exceptional ads that did show women without men in the male world, the women were portrayed as decorations, as in one ad where an attractive and elaborately dressed woman was used to display an automobile.

Male-female interaction in advertisements was also examined. Ads were classified into three categories: male(s) only, female(s) only, and both sexes shown. Men only were shown in 40% of the ads, 26% showed women only, and 34% showed the two sexes together. Thus women were more likely than men to be shown in the company of the other sex.

Women were rarely shown interacting with other women. Of the ads showing just women, only 11% showed more than one. Of these nine ads, eight

TABLE 3.   Product Categories and Sex Roles

Product Category	Sex Portrayed Most Often[a]	Ratio of Ads Showing Males/ Ads Showing Females[b]
Cleaning Products	Female	.00
Food Products	Female	.45
Beauty Products	Female	.60
Drugs	Female	.66
Furniture	Male	.71
Clothing	Female	.76
Home Appliances	Female	.86
Charity	—	1.00
Travel	Male	1.30
Cars	Male	1.37
Alcoholic Beverages	Male	1.63
Cigarettes	Male	1.90
Banks	Male	2.11
Industrial Products	Male	2.17
Entertainment, Media	Male	2.33
Institutional Ads	Male	2.50

[a] Based on number of adults shown.
[b] Based on number of advertisements.

showed women as illustrations for clothing or beauty products; the other showed women in a family setting. Thirty ads showed mixed groups with more than one woman. In two-thirds of these, the women were shown interacting only with male partners. No women were shown as co-workers unless men were also present. Men were more than twice as likely to be shown interacting with members of their own sex. Of ads with men only, 19% showed more than one man. Most of these ads portrayed co-workers.

Of the ads showing men *and* women, 67% showed only one man and one woman. Of these, only one showed co-workers—these were musicians who had interrupted a duet to embrace! In the ads showing working men with women, the women seldom appeared in working roles. For example, a male doctor was shown examining a baby with the mother nearby. There were some exceptions: male and female entertainers were often shown together, and there were two additional ads that portrayed men and women as co-workers. One ad showed a female secretary, a male clerk, and their male boss; the other contained a group photograph of airline workers engaged in food preparation.

Discussion

In the magazines surveyed, there were few individual advertisements that could be considered depreciatory of women. These advertisements seemed to reflect the world as it is—for example, the average executive *is* a male. However, the picture as a whole does fail to show the true range of women's roles within our society. The ads reflected a number of stereotypes, discussed below.

"A woman's place is in the home."   The ads studied here underrepresented the 29 million working American women. Feminists point out that while the vast majority of American women are wives and mothers, many of them have other roles.

"Women do not make important decisions or do important things."   The distribution of occupational and nonworking roles in the ads reinforces the feminists' impression that women are rarely shown engaged in important activities outside the home. In fact, in the advertisements examined, women were limited even in household decision making. They appeared to operate independently only for relatively inexpensive purchases—food, cosmetics, and cleaning products. For more expensive household purchases, men were brought into the ads, presumably because they share in buying decisions. Important business and societal institutions—banks, industrial firms, and the mass media—apparently did not consider women sufficiently significant to their businesses to feature them often in advertisements.

"Women are dependent and need men's protection."   The advertisements suggest that there are certain business and social activities which are still inappropriate for women to perform on their own. Although some cigarette brands are promoted primarily for women, in the study there was not one cigarette ad that showed a woman smoking unless a male was present.

The isolation of women from their own sex within the ads augments the impression of dependence. Moreover, the traditional family roles in which women are often depicted in ads are roles in which they are dependent on men.

"Men regard women primarily as sexual objects; they are not interested in women as people."   Some limited reflection of this stereotype is found in the decorative roles more often assigned to women than to men in the ads. The effect is heightened by showing women in relatively few working roles. Although ads showed men and women sharing recreational activities, women were rarely included in men's working lives.

Conclusion

There were few individual ads that could be considered offensive to women. In this study, only general magazines were selected on the assumption that they would be most likely to show women in meaningful occupational roles. Yet the total picture presented did reflect some clichés about women's roles that are considered by feminists to be highly unflattering.

The data suggest that feminists are at least partially justified in saying that advertisements do not present a full view of the variety of roles women actually play in American society. Consequently, advertisers as a group should be alert to the growing desire of many women that they be portrayed in their varied life roles. Those advertisers who choose to take the lead in portraying women in this way may benefit from favorable public reactions.

The data also suggest the need for more complete analysis of women's roles as shown in advertisements. Analysis of other categories of magazines and other media would be useful. In addition, images of women's intelligence and personality reflected in advertising should be analyzed more thoroughly. Finally, further research should attempt to discover what kinds of portraits of themselves women perceive as offensive.

Notes

1. The numbers of advertisements showing adults in each of the sampled magazines were: *Life,* 38; *Look,* 30; *Newsweek,* 45; *The New Yorker,* 89; *Readers' Digest,* 51; *Saturday Review,* 14; *Time,* 26; *U.S. News and World Report,* 19. Ten ads appeared twice, two appeared three times, and one appeared four times. Thus repeated ads account for 10% of the total.

2. In this last case, only a profile of the woman wearing earrings with a company's trademark was shown. Although she was coded as a semi-professional worker, it might have been equally appropriate to consider her role as decorative.

References

1. Grant, Don. "Women's Libs Fume at 'Insulting Ads': Ad Gals Unruffled," *Advertising Age,* Vol. 44 (June 27, 1970), 1.

2. Mannes, Marya. "Female of the Specious," *Boston,* Vol. 62 (September 1970), 54.

3. Smith, Janet. "Business and the Radicals, The Women—They Want Action," *Dun's,* Vol. 95 (June 1970), 46.

4. Wensberg, Peter. "Dubious Battlements," *Boston,* Vol. 62 (September 1970), 46.

5 Social Class

Overview

The existence of social classes reflects an unequal division of social prestige within a society. This may be on the basis of *ascribed* (inherited) status or on the basis of *achieved* status. Ascribed social prestige comes with birth and is based on inherited wealth and position. Achieved social prestige is earned by the individual and is based on the society's evaluation of his accomplishments. The architect, because of the society's assessment of his social contribution, is accorded higher status than the contractor who is accorded higher status than the skilled worker who, in turn, is accorded higher status than the laborer. Table 5-1 presents the prestige rankings for a set of occupations within the United States.

Social Class in the United States

In the United States we have been generally reluctant to admit the existence of a class order. It has been part of the U.S. heritage to dismiss visible symbols of ascribed status, such as titles of nobility, and to minimize belief in class distinctions. Yet a class hierarchy or *social stratification system* seems to be characteristic of all societies.

The relevant issue is really not whether a class order exists in the United States but rather the form that order takes. In examining a particular social stratification system, a paramount concern is the level of fluidity or rigidity within that system. This is usually measured in terms of the degree of *social mobility* which a system allows, that is, movement upward or downward in social class. A further measure is the extent to which social class placement is based on ascribed or achieved status. The United States compares favorably on these dimensions with other highly industrialized societies, although imperfections exist due to an unequal distribution of opportunities.

TABLE 5-1. Selected Occupational Prestige Ratings

Occupation	Score	Occupation	Score
U.S. Supreme Court justice	94	Welfare worker for a city	
Physician	93	government	74
Nuclear physicist	92	Policeman	72
State governor	91		
College professor	90	Average	71
Lawyer	89	Reporter on daily newspaper	71
Architect	88	Bookkeeper	70
Dentist	88	Insurance agent	69
Mayor of a large city	87	Local official of a labor union	67
Member of the board of directors		Manager of a small store in a city	67
of a large corporation	87	Traveling salesman for a	
Minister	87	wholesale concern	66
Psychologist	87	Plumber	65
Airline pilot	86	Barber	63
Civil engineer	86	Machine operator in a factory	63
Banker	85	Playground director	63
Biologist	85	Garage mechanic	62
Sociologist	83	Truck driver	59
Accountant for a large business	81	Clerk in a store	56
Public schoolteacher	81	Singer in a nightclub	54
Building contractor	80	Filling station attendant	51
Owner of a factory that employs		Dock worker	50
about 100 people	80	Night watchman	50
Author of novels	78	Restaurant waiter	49
Economist	78	Taxi driver	49
Official of an international		Bartender	48
labor union	77	Janitor	48
Electrician	76	Soda fountain clerk	44
Trained machinist	75	Garbage collector	39
Undertaker	74	Shoe shiner	34

Source: Hodge et al. (1964).

Social Stratification

One of the most commonly used systems of social stratification, in both the sociology and marketing literatures, is that of W. Lloyd Warner and his associates. His methodology and a summary of his most salient findings are presented in the first selection in this chapter. Essentially, Warner's definition of social class is based on how members of a community regard each other; he emphasizes the idea of reputation or participation in the community as the key to social class placement. This "evaluated-participation" method relies on intensive interviews with informants in the community under examination in order to assign individuals to a particular social class.

As a practical matter, measuring social class by the evaluated-participation method is difficult, costly, and time consuming. An alternative method, used by Warner and many other researchers, is to derive an index of social class based on more "objective" criteria. Some composite of such factors as income, education, and occupation is commonly used. Warner's objective classification scheme is based on four indicators—occupation, source of income, residential area, and type of dwelling.

It has been most common, based largely on the work of Warner, to utilize a social stratification system which divides the United States into six social classes (see Table 5-2). These may be described as follows:

1. The *upper-upper class* is the aristocracy of birth and wealth, the social register in a community. These are the locally prominent families with at least second or third generation wealth.
2. The *lower-upper class* is composed of families with new wealth, the *nouveau riche,* who are wealthy but not fully accepted socially. These families are headed by top executives, high-salaried professionals, or owners of businesses.
3. The *upper-middle class* consists of professionals and managers and frequently provides the community leadership.
4. The *lower-middle class* is comprised of white-collar office workers, small-business proprietors, and some highly skilled blue-collar workers.
5. The *upper-lower class* is the working class of blue-collar workers, including some skilled tradesmen, the semiskilled trades, and the composite of workers who essentially earn a living with their hands.
6. The *lower-lower class* consists of the disreputables in the society, particularly those not holding a job and whose existence is frequently at a slum level.

A somewhat different approach to the measurement of social class is the self-designation method, whereby members of the community locate themselves on the status hierarchy. Richard Centers (1952), who did the original work in support of this approach, argues that *class consciousness* as indicated by the self-designation method is a more powerful predictor of behavior than class placement by the sociologist on the basis of participation or objective measures.

A more recent study of self-perceived class awareness is that of Morris and Jeffries (1970). The findings of Centers and of Morris and Jeffries are presented in synopsis form in Table 5-3. It is worth noting the decrease in working class identification from 1945, when Centers conducted his research, to 1965, when Morris and Jeffries conducted their research.

TABLE 5-2.   **The Warner Social Class System**

Social Class	Membership	Population Percentage[a]
Upper-upper	Aristocracy	0.5
Lower-upper	New rich	1.5
Upper-middle	Professionals and managers	10.0
Lower-middle	White-collar workers	33.0
Upper-lower	Blue-collar workers	40.0
Lower-lower	Unskilled laborers	15.0

[a]Population percentages are approximations only and vary by the city under study. These estimates are based upon information reported in Warner (1960) and Hollingshead (1949).

TABLE 5-3.   Self-Perceived Social Class Placement

Social Class	Centers[a] (1952)	Morris and Jeffries[b] (1970)
Upper class	3%	3%
Upper-middle class		22
Middle class	43	50
Lower-middle class		5
Working class	51	16
Lower class	1	2
Other responses	2	2

[a] Centers (1952) asked the question: "If you were to use one of these four names for your social class, which would you say you belonged in: the middle class, lower class, working class, or upper class?"

[b] Morris and Jeffries (1970) asked the question: "If you were to use one of these names for your social group, to which one would you belong?" (The authors included the entire list of classifications in this table.)

Consequences of Class Placement

The underlying assumption of social class analysis is that placement within a social class leads to consistencies in values, life style, and behavior, including consumption behavior. Centers (1952), for example, concludes that social classes may be described as "psycho-social groupings of the population of persons whose socioeconomic positions are objectively similar, in the main, and whose politico-economic interests tend to coincide."

The consequences of social-class placement are demonstrated in Table 5-4, based mainly on census data. Lower class people have higher mortality rates, earn less income, are more subject to marital instability and female obesity, visit the dentist less often, and their children are less likely to attend college. In fact, the percentage of parents recommending college for their children falls precipitously from upper and middle to lower class levels, and this is a significant factor retarding upward social mobility among the lower classes.

Social class is also associated with religious affiliation, as shown in Table 5-5. The prestige religions appear to be Christian Scientist and Episcopal, whereas the Baptist and Mormon religions appear to appeal to lower class levels. Atheists and agnostics are particularly likely to come from higher social class levels. Nor is political behavior immune from social influence. In one recent study (Form and Huber, 1971), rich whites were almost four times more likely to be Republicans than poor whites, and a positive linear relationship was found between income and identification with the Republican party.

A final example of social class consequences can be taken from research on parent-child relationships. A key article in the literature of sociology is Kohn (1963), who demonstrates that: ". . . middle-class parental values differ from those of working-class parents; that these differences are rooted in basic differences between middle-class and working-class conditions of life; and that the differences [in] values have important consequences for their relationships with their children (p. 480)." In general, these differences in child-rearing practices can be summarized as follows:

TABLE 5-4. Stratification Correlates: Life Chances and Privileges, United States

Related Factors	Strata		
	Lower	Middle	Upper
Standardized mortality ratios[a]	Unskilled workers: 120	Skilled workers: 96	Professionals: 82
Lifetime income[b]	Less than 8 years of school— $131,000	High school graduates—$246,000	College graduates— $386,000
Annual mean income[c]	Less than 8 years of school—$3,641	High school graduates—$6,693	College graduates— $10,062
Attend college[d]	Children from families with incomes under $5,000—9%	Children from families with incomes $5,000–$7,500—17%	Children from families with incomes of $10,000 or more—44%
Index of marital instability[e]	Low income—23	Middle income— 10	High income—6
Dental visits per year per person[f]	Family income under $2,000— 0.8	Family income $4,000–$7,000 —1.4	Family income $7,000 or more —2.3
Obesity of women[g]	Low income—52%	Medium income— 43%	High income—9%

[a]L. Guralnick, "The Study of Mortality by Occupation in the United States," (Washington, D.C.: National Office of Vital Statistics, September, 1959). (Ratio between the number of deaths and the number of deaths expected, adult white males, 1950.)

[b]*Statistical Abstract of the United States, 1966,* Table 158. (Males only)

[c]*Statistical Abstract of the United States, 1966,* Table 158. (Males only)

[d]Herman P. Miller, *Rich Man, Poor Man* (New York: Crowell, 1964), p. 171.

[e]J. Richard Udry, "Marital Instability by Race and Income Based on 1960 Census Data," *American Journal of Sociology,* Vol. 72 (1967), 673. [The index is an estimate of the percentage of white males 25 through 34 years of age who have had one or more broken marriages. The index is higher for nonwhites at all income levels.]

[f]*Statistical Abstract of the United States, 1966,* Table 82.

[g]Robert G. Burnight and Parker G. Marden, "Social Correlates of Weight in an Aging Population," *The Milbank Memorial Fund Quarterly,* Vol. 45 (1967), 75–92.

Source: Broom and Selznick (1968).

TABLE 5-5. Social Class Profiles of American Religious Groups

Denomination	Upper Class	Middle Class	Lower Class	N
Christian Scientist	24.8%	36.5%	38.7%	(137)
Episcopal	24.1	33.7	42.2	(590)
Congregational	23.9	42.6	33.5	(376)
Presbyterian	21.9	40.0	38.1	(961)
Jewish	21.8	32.0	46.2	(537)
Reformed	19.1	31.3	49.6	(131)
Methodist	12.7	35.6	51.7	(2100)
Lutheran	10.9	36.1	53.0	(723)
Christian	10.0	35.4	54.6	(370)
Protestant (small bodies)	10.0	27.3	62.7	(888)
Roman Catholic	8.7	24.7	66.6	(2390)
Baptist	8.0	24.0	68.0	(1381)
Mormon	5.1	28.6	66.3	(175)
No preference	13.3	26.0	60.7	(466)
Protestant (undesignated)	12.4	24.1	63.5	(460)
Atheist, Agnostic	33.3	46.7	20.0	(15)
No answer or Don't know	11.0	29.5	59.5	(319)

Source: Schneider (1952), 228.

Goals for Children:
   Middle class—to be happy, sharing, cooperative, curious, eager to learn, loving, and self-controlled
   Working class—to be neat, clean, obedient, respectful, and to please adults
Method of Control:
   Middle class—self-direction and punishment based on the intent of the act
   Working class—external proscriptions and punishment based on the consequences of the act

Social Class and Market Segmentation

If, in fact, social classes exhibit consistencies in values, life style, and other aspects of behavior, we might then expect certain consistencies in consumption behavior. This is by no means to suggest that social class will discriminate between Instant Maxwell House and Nescafe buyers, or Ford and Chevrolet buyers, but it may well discriminate between buyers of Instant Maxwell House and imported Colombian coffee beans, or between buyers of Fords and Cadillacs.

In the words of Kahl (1957), "If a large group of families are approximately equal to each other and clearly differentiated from other families, we call them a *social class.*" If this is the case, then social class may allow meaningful segmentation, permitting differential product, pricing, channel, and promotional appeals in line with the specific characteristics, need-value systems, and media patterns of each social class.

Such *sociographic segmentation* (on the basis of social class) may actually be superior to income or demographic segmentation. The model posed is

social class $\longrightarrow$ values $\longrightarrow$ life style $\longrightarrow$ consumption patterns.

In contrast, there is less reason to expect any consistency in values or life style on the basis of income alone, since there is no identification or consciousness attached to income level. In fact, the point deserves emphasis: social class is not based on income, despite the fact that a significant relationship exists. For example, a college professor may earn $15,000 a year, as might an airplane mechanic, or an interstate truck driver working some overtime. Yet, society does not accord these individuals equal social prestige, and they would belong to different social classes.

For purposes of illustration let us consider an example provided by Coleman (1960) of three families with comparable incomes but aligned with different social classes and the resulting differences in consumption patterns. He suggests that an upper-middle-class family, consisting of a young lawyer and his wife, is apt to be found spending a relatively large share of its resources on housing in a prestige neighborhood, expensive furniture, and quality clothing chosen according to carefully prescribed standards of appropriateness.

A lower-middle-class family—a diesel engineer and his wife—probably has a nice house in a less than fancy neighborhood and furniture that is pretty in a way that suits the wife and hopefully might win praise from friends and neighbors, but none of it done by name designers. This family is apt to have a full, but not expensive, wardrobe and money in a savings account rather than in club memberships.

In comparison, an upper-lower-class family headed by a truck driver is apt to have a lesser house in a lesser neighborhood than the other two families but may well have a bigger and later model car, more expensive appliances in the kitchen, and a bigger television set in the living room. This family will spend less on clothing but more on sports equipment and sporting events.

A closer scrutiny of the relationships between social class, income, and consumption patterns reveals finer distinctions. Within each social class there are families whose incomes are above average relative to fellow social class members. The lower-middle-class salesman, for example, who earns more than his social class peers may be considered overprivileged, and the lower-middle-class high-school teacher who earns less than his peers may be designated underprivileged.

According to Coleman (1960), these overprivileged and underprivileged families tend to consume differently than typical members of their social class. For example, the color television market at first seemed to be concentrated among overprivileged members of each social class. This may also be the market for expensive recreational appliances and deluxe home appliances. In contrast, the diffusion of small cars may be concentrated among the under-privileged members of each social class. Thus, the concept of relative financial privilege allows more sophisticated analysis of the relationships between social class and consumption.

Social Class and Marketing Strategies

The consumption of some products is closely related to social class, but this is the exception rather than the rule. Manufacturers of china and silver, for example, can quite specifically define their market as upper-middle class and above. Most Americans can afford to indulge in alcoholic beverages, but beer finds its largest market at an upper-lower social class level, whereas imported wines find their largest market at upper-middle and upper social class levels.

Research by Hodge and Trieman (1968) has found that the holding of stocks, bonds, and real estate correlates significantly with higher social class levels. Mathews and Slocum, in a selection in this chapter, have found that the use of bank credit cards differs by social class level. These cards are used for installment buying at lower social class levels and for convenience at higher social class levels.

If a product is consumed across all social class levels, a manufacturer may still pursue a segmentation strategy based on social class by promoting different models at different prices or by appealing to different motivations for each social class. Bank credit cards may, for example, be differentially marketed on the basis of convenience or installment-buying motivation. Automobiles are designed, differentiated, priced, and promoted with different social classes in mind. Multiple branding of beer by a company allows it to cover a broader social class continuum than any single brand could reach.

Social class may also affect retail shopping patterns. Pierre Martineau (1958) has argued that shoppers select department stores by matching the social status of the store to their own social class level: "The shopper is not going to take a chance [of] feeling out of place by going to a store where she might not [feel comfortable]."

Research on another type of retail outlet by sociologist David Gottlieb (1957) contrasted the neighborhood tavern and the cocktail lounge. The lounge was found to cater to a transient clientele which could not be considered to be a cohesive group. The tavern, however, was a neighborhood phenomenon. It was "the center of a voluntary association, enforcing group norms and organizing group action." Gottlieb further found that the use of these two establishments varied by social class. The lounge was frequented more by the upper-middle class; the tavern appealed primarily to the upper-lower class.

Differential response to advertising media can also be documented by social class level. In a general sense, print media and especially magazines tend to have higher social class profiles than broadcast media, but this generalization must be qualified by content or programming and time of day. The time factor is shown, for example, in analysis of television audiences, where the early evening audience has a heavier working-class composition and the late evening audience has a heavier middle-class composition. The content factor is demonstrated by the fact that newsweekly, travel, and literary magazines are more often found in middle-class homes, whereas sports, outdoor, and romance magazines are more often found in working-class homes. The programming factor was addressed in research by Glick and Levy (1962) on television audiences, who found that the working class characteristically embraced television, the lower-middle class accommodated it, and the upper-middle class protested it. Analysis of program selection by social class revealed that the working class preferred known performers and plots without much subtlety or psychological complications. The lower-middle class sought lively and absorbing programs, such as adventures and westerns. The upper-middle class criticized television programming in general and exercised discrimination in viewing.

The Ghetto Consumer (The Subculture of Poverty)

Given the emerging social concern within marketing, a recent body of literature has developed concerning the consumption behavior of the poor. Key publications in this area are by David Caplovitz (1963) and Frederick Sturdivant (1969).

Despite an initial rush to dismiss the early findings, it does appear that the poor do pay more, although this is not uniformly true. Chain grocery stores in a number of cities now maintain uniform pricing books for the entire metropolitan area. Therefore, if a ghetto neighborhood has chain store outlets, its residents may not pay more than people living in other areas for food items.

The reasons that the poor pay more are tied to three central factors: (1) the captive market represented by the ghetto resident, and a certain level of retailer exploitation; (2) the lack of a modern retail structure; and (3) the consumer behavior of the poor.

Captive Market and Exploitation

The poor are typically a relatively captive market, lacking mobility and hemmed in by discrimination and language barriers. The ghetto retailer thus may have some degree of monopoly power and may take advantage of it by charging higher prices. Also, felt exploitation may be part of the "vengeance pattern" noted by Sturdivant (1968) after the Watts riots: "The possibility that the rioters were striking back at unethical merchants was reinforced by the fact that one store would be looted and burned while a competing unit across the street survived without so much as a cracked window" (p. 131).

The evidence for exploitation is not conclusive, however. The only available data is an economic report of the Federal Trade Commission (1968) for Washington, D.C., which compares profitability on furniture and appliances for ghetto retailers and general market retailers. "Despite their substantially higher prices, net profit on sales for low-income market retailers was only slightly higher and net profit return on net worth was considerably lower when compared to general market retailers." These findings have not been considered conclusive, since the sample may not have included the more transient ghetto retailers who are often the most flagrant price abusers.

The fact also remains that it simply costs more to do business in ghetto areas because of a whole string of factors, including insurance costs, theft, real estate costs, bad debt losses, and a less profitable sales mix due to the consumption of lower-margin products. Thus, in a very harsh sense, the poor pay more because it costs more to sell to the poor.

Lack of a Modern Retail Structure

As Sturdivant (1968) notes, "One of the cruelest ironies of our economic system is that the disadvantaged are generally served by the least efficient segments of the business community" (p. 132). In fact, in many poverty areas, "Ma and Pa" stores proliferate, and help raise the cost of distribution by management inefficiencies and the lack of economies of scale. Given an investment decision, most mass distribution retailers find a greater return on investment by locating in more affluent suburban areas.

Consumer Behavior of the Poor

Poverty seems to coincide with a lack of education, a lack of mobility, and sometimes the need for cultural reinforcement. Richards (1968) notes that shopping patterns are affected by familiarity and acceptance of American ways. "The Puerto Ricans are an example of a newly arrived group that prefers traditional, personal stores rather than more bureaucratic, price-competitive outlets, and so do Negro migrants from the rural South." Grocery shopping patterns are such that consumption is more on a hand-to-mouth basis; thus shopping is more frequent, and children are more involved in purchasing.

The life style of the poor is developed on a conceptual basis in the selection by Irelan and Besner in this chapter. It is particularly important to understand the consumption behavior of ghetto residents in its own terms and not from the point of view of a middle-class social analyst. What may seem as irrational consumption behavior, such as the inability to delay gratification, may simply be a response to the deprivation and feeling of anomie which pervades the subculture of poverty. Perceived relative deprivation would be particularly acute in our "global village" connected by television in over 95 percent of U.S. homes.

References

Broom, L., and P. Selznick, *Sociology*. Harper & Row, 1968.

Caplovitz, D. *The Poor Pay More*. The Free Press, 1963.

Centers, R. "The American Class Structure: A Psychological Analysis." *Readings in Social Psychology* (rev. ed.), ed. C. E. Swanson, et al. Holt, Rinehart & Winston (1952), 299–311.

Coleman, R. P. "The Significance of Social Stratification in Selling." *Proceedings AMA* (Dec. 1960), 171–184.

Federal Trade Commission. *Economic Report on Installment Credit and Retail Sales Practices of District of Columbia Retailers*. Superintendent of Documents.

Form, W. H., and J. Huber. "Income, Race, and the Ideology of Political Efficacy." *Journal of Politics*, Vol. 33 (August 1971), 659–688.

Glick, I. O., and S. J. Levy. *Living with Television*. Aldine, 1962.

Gottlieb, D. "The Neighborhood Tavern and the Cocktail Lounge: A Study of Class Differences." *American Journal of Sociology*, Vol. 62 (May 1957), 559–562.

Hodge, R. W., and D. J. Treiman. "Class Identification in the United States." *American Journal of Sociology*, Vol. 73 (March 1968), 535–547.

————, P. M. Seigel, and P. H. Rossi. "Occupational Prestige in the United States, 1925–1963." *American Journal of Sociology*, Vol. 70 (Nov. 1964), 286–302.

Hollingshead, A. B. *Elmtown's Youth*. Wiley, 1949.

Kahl, J. A. *The American Class Structure*. Holt, Rinehart & Winston, 1957.

Kohn, M. L. "Social Class and Parent-Child Relationships: An Interpretation." *American Journal of Sociology*, Vol. 68 (Jan. 1963), 471–480.

Martineau, P. D. "Social Classes and Spending Behavior." *Journal of Marketing*, Vol. 23 (Oct. 1958), 121–130.

Morris, R. T., and V. Jeffries. "Class Conflict: Forget It!" *Sociology and Social Research*, Vol. 54 (April 1970), 306–320.

Richards, L. G. "Consumer Practices of the Poor." In *Low Income Life Styles*, ed. L. M. Irelan, U.S. Department of Health, Education and Welfare, Publication No. 14 (1968), 67–86.

Schneider, H. *Religion in 20th Century America.* Harvard University Press, 1952.

Sturdivant, F. D. "Better Deal for Ghetto Shoppers." *Harvard Business Review*, Vol. 46 (March–April 1968), 130–139.

————, ed. *The Ghetto Marketplace.* The Free Press, 1969.

————. "Distribution in American Society: Some Questions of Efficiency and Relevance." *Vertical Marketing Systems*, ed. L. P. Bucklin. Scott, Foresman (1970), 94–113.

Warner, W. L., with M. Meeker and K. Eells. *Social Class in America.* Harper & Row, 1960.

5.1 Social Class in America
W. LLOYD WARNER

Recent scientific studies of social class in the several regions of the United States demonstrate that it is a major determinant of individual decisions and social actions; that every major area of American life is directly and indirectly influenced by our class order; and that the major decisions of most individuals are partly controlled by it. To act intelligently and know consciously how this basic factor in American life affects us and our society, it is essential and necessary that we have an explicit understanding of what our class order is, how it works, and what it does to the lives and personalities who live in it. Our most democratic institutions, including our schools, churches, business organizations, government, and even our family life, are molded by its all-pervading and exceedingly subtle but powerful influence. . . .

The Structural Imperative—Why We Have a Class System

The recognition of social class and other status hierarchies in this country comes as no surprise to students of society. Research on the social life of the tribes and civilizations of the world clearly demonstrates that some form of rank is always present and a necessity for our kind of society.

Just as students of comparative biology have demonstrated that the physical structure of the higher animals must have certain organs to survive, so students of social anthropology have shown that the social structures of the "higher," the more complex, societies must have rank orders to perform certain functions necessary for group survival.

When societies are complex and service large populations, they always possess some kind of status system which, by its own values, places people in higher or lower positions. Only the very simple hunting and gathering tribes, with very small populations and very simple social problems, are without systems of rank; but when a society is complex, when there are large numbers of individuals in it pursuing diverse and complex activities and functioning in a multiplicity of ways, individual positions and behaviors are evaluated and ranked (Hobhouse, 1915). This happens primarily because, to maintain itself, the society must co-ordinate the efforts of all its members into common enterprises necessary for the preservation of the group, and it must solidify and integrate all these enterprises into a working whole. In other words, as the division of labor increases and the social units become more numerous and diverse, the need for co-ordination and integration also increases and, when satisfied, enables the larger group to survive and develop. . . .

The studies of other societies have demonstrated one other basic point: the more complex the technological and economic structure, the more complex the social structure; so that some argue (the Marxians and many classical economists) that technological advancement is the cause of social complexity and all class and status systems. It cannot be denied that economic and technological factors are important in the determination of class and status orders. We must not lose sight of the fact, however, that the social system, with its beliefs, values, and rules, which governs human behavior may well determine what kind of technology and what kind of economic institutions will survive or thrive in any given tribe or nation. In any case, social complexity is necessary for economic advancement. Furthermore, social complexity is a basic factor determining the presence or absence of class. . . .

Class Among the New England Yankees

Studies of communities in New England clearly demonstrate the presence of a well-defined social-class system.[1] At the top is an aristocracy of birth and wealth. This is the so-called "old family" class. The people of Yankee City say the families who belong to it have been in the community for a long time—for at least three generations and preferably many generations more than three. "Old family" means not only old to the community but old to the class. Present members of the class were born into it; the families into which they were born can trace their lineage through many generations participating in a way of life characteristic of the upper class back to a generation marking the lowly beginnings out of which their family came. Although the men of this level are occupied gainfully, usually as large merchants, financiers, or in the higher professions, the wealth of the family, inherited from the husband's or the wife's side, and often from both, has been in the family for a long time. Ideally, it should stem from the sea trade when Yankee City's merchants and sea captains made large fortunes, built great Georgian houses on elm-lined Hill Street, and filled their houses and gardens with the proper symbols of their high position. They became the 400, the Brahmins, the Hill Streeters to whom others looked up; and they, well-mannered or not, looked down on the rest. They counted themselves, and were so counted, equals of similar levels in Salem, Boston, Providence, and other New England cities. Their sons and daughters married into the old families from these towns and at times, when family fortune was low or love was great, they married wealthy sons and daughters from the newly rich who occupied the class level below them. This was a happy event for the fathers and mothers of such fortunate young people in the lower half of the upper class, an event well publicized and sometimes not too discreetly bragged about by the parents of the lower-upper-class children, an occasion to be explained by the mothers from the old families in terms of the spiritual demands of romantic love and by their friends as "a good deal and a fair exchange all the way around for everyone concerned."

The new families, the lower level of the upper class, came up through the new industries—shoes, textiles, silverware—and finance. Their fathers were some of the men who established New England's trading and financial dominance throughout America. When New York's Wall Street rose to power, many of them transferred their activities to this new center of dominance. Except that they aspire to old-family status, if not for themselves then for their children, these men and their families have a design for living similar to the old-family group. But they are consciously aware that their money is too new and too recently earned to have the sacrosanct quality of wealth inherited from a long line of ancestors. They know, as do those about them, that, while a certain amount of wealth is necessary, birth and old family are what really matter. Each of them can cite critical cases to prove that particular individuals have no money at all, yet belong to the top class because they have the right lineage and right name. While they recognize the worth and importance of birth, they feel that somehow their family's achievements should be better rewarded than by a mere second place in relation to those who need do little more than be born and stay alive.

The presence of an old-family class in a community forces the newly rich to wait their turn if they aspire to "higher things." Meanwhile, they must learn how to act, fill their lives with good deeds, spend their money on approved philanthropy, and reduce their arrogance to manageable proportions.

The families of the upper and lower strata of the upper classes are organized into social cliques and exclusive clubs. The men gather fortnightly in dining clubs where they discuss matters that concern them. The women belong to small clubs or to the Garden Club and give their interest to subjects which symbolize their high status and evoke those sentiments necessary in each individual if the class is to maintain itself. Both sexes join philanthropic organizations whose good deeds are an asset to the community and an expression of the dominance and importance of the top class to those socially beneath them. They are the members of the Episcopalian and Unitarian and, occasionally, the Congregational and Presbyterian churches.

Below them are the members of the solid, highly respectable upper-middle class, the people who get things done and provide the active front in civic affairs for the classes above them. They aspire to the classes above and hope their good deeds, civic activities, and high moral principles will somehow be recognized far beyond the usual pat on the back and that they will be invited by those above them into the intimacies of upper-class cliques and exclusive clubs. Such recognition might increase their status and would be likely to make them members of the lower-upper group. The fact that this rarely happens seldom stops members of this level, once activated, from continuing to try. The men tend to be owners of stores and belong to the large proprietor and professional levels. Their incomes average less than those of the lower-upper class, this latter group having a larger income than any other group, including the old-family level.

These three strata, the two upper classes and the upper-middle, constitute the levels above the Common Man. There is a considerable distance socially between them and the mass of the people immediately below them. They comprise three of the six classes present in the community. Although in number of levels they constitute half the community, in population they have no more than a sixth, and sometimes less, of the Common Man's population. The three levels combined include approximately 13% of the total population.

The lower-middle class, the top of the Common Man level, is composed of clerks and other white-collar workers, small tradesmen, and a fraction of skilled workers. Their small houses fill "the side streets" down from Hill Street, where the upper classes and some of the upper-middle live, and are noticeably absent from the better suburbs where the upper-middle concentrate. "Side Streeter" is a term often used by those above them to imply an inferior way of life and an inconsequential status. They have accumulated little property but are frequently home owners. Some of the more successful members of ethnic groups, such as the Italians, Irish, French-Canadians, have reached this level. Only a few members of these cultural minorities have gone beyond it; none of them has reached the old-family level.

The old-family class (upper-upper) is smaller in size than the new-family class (lower-upper) below them. It has 1.4%, while the lower-upper class has 1.6%, of the total population. Ten per cent of the population belongs to the upper-middle class, and 28% to the lower-middle level. The upper-lower is the most populous class, with 34%, and the lower-lower has 25% of all the people in the town.

The prospects of the upper-middle-class children for higher education are not as good as those of the classes above. One hundred per cent of the children of the two upper classes take courses in the local high school that prepare them for college, and 88% of the upper-middle do; but only 44% of the lower-middle take these courses, 28% of the upper-lower, and 26% of the lower-lower. These percentages provide a good index of the position of the lower-middle class, ranking it well below the three upper classes, but placing it well above the upper-lower and the lower-lower (Warner and Lunt, 1941).

The upper-lower class, least differentiated from the adjacent levels and hardest to distinguish in the hierarchy, but clearly present, is composed of the "poor but honest workers" who more often than not are only semi-skilled or unskilled. Their relative place in the hierarchy of class is well portrayed by comparing them with the classes superior to them and with the lower-lower class beneath them in the category of how they spend their money. . . . Their feelings about doing the right thing, of being respectable and rearing their children to do better than they have, coupled with the limitations of their income, are well reflected in how they select and reject what can be purchased on the American market.[2]

The lower-lower class, referred to as "Riverbrookers" or the "low-down Yankees who live in the clam flats," have a "bad reputation" among those who are socially above them. This evaluation includes beliefs that they are lazy, shiftless, and won't work, all opposites of the good middle-class virtues belonging to the essence of the Protestant ethic. They are thought to be improvident and unwilling or unable to save their money for a rainy day and, therefore, often dependent on the philanthropy of the private or public agency and on poor relief. They are sometimes said to "live like animals" because it is believed that their sexual mores are not too exacting and that pre-marital intercourse, post-marital infidelity, and high rates of illegitimacy, sometimes too publicly mixed with incest, characterize their personal and family lives. It is certain that they deserve only part of this reputation. Research shows many of them guilty of no more than being poor and lacking in the desire to get ahead, this latter trait being common among those above them. For these reasons and others, this class is ranked in Yankee City below the level of the Common Man (lower-middle and upper-lower). For most of the indexes of status it ranks sixth and last. . . .

Class in the Deep South

Studies in the Deep South demonstrate that, in the older regions where social changes until recently have been less rapid and less disturbing to the status order, most of the towns above a few thousand population have a six-class system in which an old-family elite is socially dominant.

For example, in a study of a Mississippi community, a market town for a cotton-growing region around it, Davis and the Gardners (1941) found a six-class system.[3] Perhaps the southern status order is best described by Chart 1, which gives the names used by the people of the community for each class and succinctly tells how the members of each class regard themselves and the rest of the class order.

The people of the two upper classes make a clear distinction between an old aristocracy and an aristocracy which is not old. There is no doubt that the first is above the other; the upper-middle class views the two upper ones much as the upper classes do themselves but groups them in one level with two divisions, the older level above the other; the lower-middle class separates them but considers them co-ordinate; the bottom two classes, at a greater social distance than the others, group all the levels above the Common Man as "society" and one class. An examination of the terms used by the several classes for the other classes shows that similar principles are operating. . . .

The Generalities of American Class

It is now time to ask what are the basic characteristics of social status common to the communities of all regions in the United States and, once we have answered this question, to inquire what the variations are among the several systems. Economic factors are significant and important in determining the class position of any family or person, influencing the kind of behavior we find in any class, and contributing their share to the present form of our status system. But, while significant and necessary, the economic factors are not sufficient to predict where a particular family or individual will be or to explain completely the phenomena of social class. Something more than a large income is necessary for high social position. Money must be translated into socially approved behavior and possessions, and they in turn must be translated into intimate participation with, and acceptance by, members of a superior class. . . .

To belong to a particular level in the social-class system of America

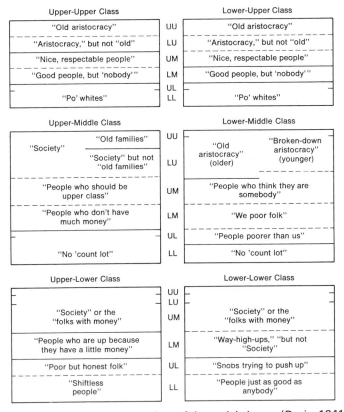

Upper-Upper Class

"Old aristocracy"	UU
"Aristocracy," but not "old"	LU
"Nice, respectable people"	UM
"Good people, but 'nobody'"	LM
	UL
"Po' whites"	LL

Lower-Upper Class

"Old aristocracy"	UU
"Aristocracy," but not "old"	LU
"Nice, respectable people"	UM
"Good people, but 'nobody'"	LM
	UL
"Po' whites"	LL

Upper-Middle Class

"Society"	"Old families"	UU
	"Society" but not "old families"	LU
"People who should be upper class"		UM
"People who don't have much money"		LM
		UL
"No 'count lot"		LL

Lower-Middle Class

"Old aristocracy" (older)	"Broken-down aristocracy" (younger)	UU / LU
"People who think they are somebody"		UM
"We poor folk"		LM
"People poorer than us"		UL
"No 'count lot"		LL

Upper-Lower Class

	UU / LU
"Society" or the "folks with money"	UM
"People who are up because they have a little money"	LM
"Poor but honest folk"	UL
"Shiftless people"	LL

Lower-Lower Class

	UU / LU
"Society" or the "folks with money"	UM
"Way-high-ups," "but not "Society"	LM
"Snobs trying to push up"	UL
"People just as good as anybody"	LL

CHART 1.   The social perspectives of the social classes (Davis, 1941).

means that a family or individual has gained acceptance as an equal by those who belong in the class. The behavior in this class and the participation of those in it must be rated by the rest of the community as being at a particular place in the social scale.

Although our democratic heritage makes us disapprove, our class order helps control a number of important functions. It unequally divides the highly and lowly valued things of our society among the several classes according to their rank. Our marriage rules conform to the rules of class, for the majority of marriages are between people of the same class. No class system, however, is so rigid that it completely prohibits marriages above and below one's own class. Furthermore, an open class system such as ours permits a person during his lifetime to move up or down from the level into which he was born. Vertical social mobility for individuals or families is characteristic of all class systems. The principal forms of mobility in this country are through the use of money, education, occupation, talent, skill, philanthropy, sex, and marriage. Although economic mobility is still important, it seems likely now that more people move to higher positions by education than by any other route. We have indicated before this that the mere possession of money is insufficient for gaining and keeping a higher social position. This is equally true of all other forms of mobility. In every case there must be social acceptance.

Class varies from community to community. The new city is less likely than an old one to have a well-organized class order; this is also true for cities whose growth has been rapid as compared with those which have not been disturbed by huge increases in population from other regions or countries or by the rapid displacement of old industries by new ones. The mill town's status hierarchy is more likely to follow the occupational hierarchy of the mill than the levels of evaluated participation found in market towns or those with diversified industries. Suburbs of large metropolises tend to respond to selective factors which reduce the number of classes to one or a very few. They do not represent or express all the cultural factors which make up the social pattern of an ordinary city.

Yet systematic studies from coast to coast, in cities large and small and of many economic types, indicate that, despite the variations and diversity, class levels do exist and that they conform to a particular pattern of organization.

How Class Operates in Our Daily Lives

Because social class permeates all parts of our existence, it is impossible to do more than indicate how it enters consciously or unconsciously into the success and failure of business, professional, and other occupations or to show how knowledge of its effects is necessary for increasing the predictive qualities of much of the research done by psychologists and social scientists. Class is vitally significant in marriage and training children as well as in most social activities of a community. Status plays a decisive role in the formation of personality at the various stages of development, for if young people are to learn to live adaptively as mature people in our society they must be trained by the informal controls of our society to fit into their places.

Education is now competing with economic mobility as the principal route to success. Today fewer men rise from the bottom to the top places in industry and business than did a generation ago. More and more, the sons of executives are replacing their fathers in such positions, leaving fewer positions into which the sons of those farther down can climb from the ranks. Captains of industry educate their sons to take their places or to occupy similar places in other industries. Also, more and more top jobs in industry are being filled by men coming from the technical and engineering schools or from the universities. The route up for them is no longer through a hierarchy of increasing skill to management and ownership as it was two generations ago. The prudent mobile man today must prepare himself by education if he wishes to fill an important job and provide his family with the money and prestige necessary to get "the better things of life." . . .

Studies of the relations of workers and managers in business and industry demonstrate how class operates selectively. Management is bringing college-trained men into the lower ranks of supervisors and promoting fewer from the ranks because it finds that the workers, while good men technically, do not have the necessary knowledge about handling men and relating themselves effectively to the higher reaches of management. Their education is often insufficient to make them good prospects for continuing advancement. The hiring of formally educated men effectively puts a ceiling over the legitimate aspirations of workers expecting to rise in the ranks. The blocking of the worker's mobility and the encouragement of college-trained men is the ultimate payoff of what began in the grade schools. Mobility for workers is becoming more difficult; this means for the United States generally that the American Dream is becoming less real.[4]

In another area, studies of magazine subscriptions show that the class factor is of real importance in the selection of magazines. Readers from different class levels prefer various magazines on the basis of the different symbolic appeal of the stories and pictures. The Yankee City research showed that class entered not only into the purchase of magazines but into newspaper reading (Warner and Lunt, 1941; Warner and Henry, 1948). Later research indicates it has a decided effect on radio listening.

A casual examination of the advertising displayed in various magazines demonstrates that advertising agencies and their clients often waste their money because they are ignorant of the operation of class values in their business. This is not surprising since so many status factors have to be considered. The class distribution of readers of the periodicals published in America varies enormously. The readers of certain magazines are confined to the narrow limits of the classes above the Common Man, others to the lower classes, still others to the Common Man level, but there are some who are not confined to any one segment, being well distributed throughout all class levels. The editors of the magazines last designated, intuitively, by trial and error, or some better means, have chosen reading matter which appeals to all levels. The others, not knowing how to extend their readership or appealing deliberately to a narrow range, have a status-limited range of readers.

The readers to whom the advertiser is appealing may or may not be the potential purchasers of his product. The product may be of such a nature that it appeals to only a narrow segment of the total society; to advertise in those media which have readers largely from other strata or to pay for advertising in journals which appeal to every level is a waste of money.

Although advertising agencies often spend their money foolishly when judged by class criteria, the fault is not always theirs, for frequently the manufacturer or retailer does not know how his product appeals to the different classes. Sometimes the product will appeal to but one level, but often a product might appeal to, and be used by, all class levels, were the producer aware of how his product is valued at different social levels. It is certain that the use and meaning of most objects sold on the American market shift from class to class.

The soap opera is a product of radio [and television]. The average upper-middle-class listener [or viewer] has little interest in soap operas; in fact, most of this group [is] actively hostile to these curious little dramas that fill the daytime air waves. Yet, millions and millions of American women daily listen to [or watch] their favorite soap operas, and advertisers of certain commodities have found them invaluable in selling their products.

Research has shown that the soap opera appeals particularly to the level of the Common Man. The problems raised in these folk dramas, their characters, plot, and values have a strong positive appeal to women of this class level, whereas they have little appeal to women above the Common Man level (Warner and Henry, 1948).

Other researches demonstrate that furniture, including drapes, floor coverings, chairs and other seating facilities, is class-typed.

Another phenomenon of class, social mobility, is enormously important in the daily lives of Americans and, to a very great degree, determines how they will act on the job or at home. Recent studies of executives in large business enterprises clearly demonstrate that the success or failure of all of them is partly determined by the presence or absence of a "mobility drive." Our research shows that when a family loses its desire to achieve and advance itself, this very often is reflected in the executive's "slowing down" or being unwilling to make the effort necessary for success as a manager. On the other hand, some men are too aggressively mobile and stir up trouble by their overly ambitious desires and their ruthless competition.

Tests combining knowledge of social class and personality demonstrate the necessity of knowing not only what the man's status level is, what it has been, and what he wants it to be, but how the class values and beliefs of his early training have become integral parts of his personality, and ever-present guides for what he thinks, what he feels, and how he acts. Those concerned with selecting executives need a personality inventory and a man's I.Q. to predict how a man will function in a given job; but they also need to find out what his experiences in our status order have done to his individuality and character structure.

Every aspect of American thought and action is powerfully influenced by social class; to think realistically and act effectively, we must know and understand our status system.

Notes

1. New and poorly organized towns sometimes have class systems which have no old-family (upper-upper) class.

2. The evidence for the statements in this paragraph can be found in Warner and Lunt, 1941, 287–300.

3. See also Dollard (1937), M. Hill (1936), and Walker (1945).

4. See Warner and Low (1947) for a discussion of how many of the strikes and conflicts with management are determined by the factor of workers' blocked opportunity.

References

Davis, A., B. B. Gardner, and M. R. Gardner. *Deep South.* University of Chicago Press, 1941.

Dollard, J. *Caste and Class in a Southern Town.* Yale University Press, 1937.

Hill, M. "The All-Negro Society in Oklahoma." Unpub. Ph.D. dissertation, University of Chicago, 1936.

Hobhouse, L. T., G. C. Wheeler, and E. Ginsberg. *The Material Culture and Social Institutions of the Simpler Peoples.* London: Chapman & Hall, 1915.

Walker, H. J. "Changes in Race Accommodation in a Southern Community." Unpub. Ph.D. dissertation, University of Chicago, 1945.

Warner, W. L., and P. S. Lunt. *The Social Life of a Modern Community.* Vol. 1, Yankee City Series. Yale University Press, 1941.

————, ————, and J. O. Low. *The Social System of the Modern Factory,* Vol. 4, Yankee City Series. Yale University Press, 1947.

————, and W. E. Henry, "Radio Daytime Serial: A Symbolic Analysis." *Genetic Psychology Monographs,* Vol. 37 (1948), 3–71.

5.2 Social Class and Consumer Behavior
SIDNEY J. LEVY

The study of market segmentation is a troublesome one. It raises many questions not easily answered. Numerous studies have sought to determine relationships between particular consumer variables and specific purchasing behavior. All too often these studies are frustrating because they mainly demonstrate that the variables most highly related to the behavior are those that are so close to the behavior as to be redundant in explaining it—or do not explain much at all. Diversity—almost a perversity of diversity—is the easiest generalization to fall back on. When we examine user groups, we find varieties of people, scores, and dimensions; when we examine sociological categories or groups, we find varieties of user behaviors. Either the person high in score on innovation does not show initiative in the area we want to study, or a dramatic example of high status values and philosophy in our sample turns out to be sociologically a lower status consumer. Although these may be exceptional cases, there are surely enough of them to muddy the waters and reduce correlations sharply; and science has the task of explaining exceptional cases in lawful terms also.

Thus, in trying to classify people as kinds of buyers we encounter the problem of the refusal of so many people to be consistent buyers, or at least consistent in the ways we seek to order their behavior.

But all this is to say that the study of market segmentation is certainly in no better condition than much of the behavioral sciences in trying to "explain" any human actions. And indeed the latter are worse off, because so few people are working to develop the multitudinous series of limited studies designed to test variable against variable which are tirelessly presented in social science journals. Nor are there enough workers governing basic investigations, building the intellectual edifice whose bricks are the little studies. . . .

In attempting to do this in the area of social class, I will start by saying, arrogant as the admission of my hope may be, that I did not find a Rosetta Stone of Social Class, or Newtonian Laws of Consumer Action and Reaction. I did not think it would be useful, either, to accumulate findings that show that people of one status or another are more or less apt to buy various classes of products, as facts in and of themselves. We would not be much furthered in our study simply by learning that lower status people buy relatively more hardware store items or Ann Page products, or that higher status people buy relatively more books or Crosse and Blackwell products. There are some such differences; and I would like to point out something of their general character and coherence.

Social class variations are variations in life style. Although social class groups are not sharply distinguished by their behavior in most studies, they do show behaviors that can be viewed as ranging along a continuum or as different patternings using common elements drawn from the core American culture. Differences are often subtle differences so that it is not easy to find truly marked and easily demonstrated contrasts even in such basic aspects as child rearing. This means that to many marketers such differences are not very important or useful, whereas other people do find them helpful in their thinking. Those who do not find these differences useful tend to be impressed by mass society and its increasingly homogeneous aspects, stressing the similarity between a prosperous lower class and an upper middle class kitchen, when both are well furnished with modern appliances, often of the same brands. However, even these "same kitchens" may have important differences in them, and have been arrived at through rather different marketing processes based on different values, thought processes, and purchasing actions.

Consumer actions are complexly interwoven with attitudes and feelings. The influence of social class on consumers may perhaps be interpreted by putting together a series of ideas which, taken together, show something of this complex; thus we gain by accumulation a sense of the importance of social class as pervasive—even if less meaningful in some areas than in others. Some generalizations are offered here that sum up findings from various specific studies carried out at Social Research over the past fifteen years. The emphasis is on differences, since there is a common tendency to gloss them over.

Values

Underlying the many other differences among social classes as consumer groups is the fact of differences in values. Lower status people value education less than middle class people do. This has repercussions in the market in various ways, since many products are consumed as part of gaining an education, as well as depending on having education. There is a sharper relative emphasis on morality, respectability, doing things right, among middle class people; they believe they can control their destinies and fortunes and achieve success by implementing these values. Lower status people are more apt to seek immediate gratifications, to rely on luck, and are less willing to risk their security. These are well-known sociological findings (Hyman, 1953). They are mentioned here to remind that such broad points of view as these have been repeatedly noted as characteristically varying among social classes. They suggest that social stratification produces different ways of seeing the world—and of consuming, since consuming is ultimately one of the ways in which people implement their values.

One study of femininity (SRI, 1960[d]) indicated that the lower class woman, who feels doomed to the lower end of the economic scale, is not likely to feel proud of what she does. There is little to value because life seems dull and unrewarding.

> I lead a dog's life ... work ... I get up in the morning ... cook all day ... pick up after four children and a husband ... sew ... what would you call that—peaches and cream?
> I consider my life very dull.
> Dull and boring ... I spend most of my time working and have nothing much to show for it.

Those who have achieved more economically show greater content and a more vigorous sense of acquisition; they feel they have gotten somewhere and do have something to show for it.

> I'm contented ... more contented than I was 15 or 20 years ago. I collect ... milk glass and copper things.
> I feel I lead a really happy life, I never had it so good. I collect salt and pepper shakers with a story behind them.

The higher one is in the social scale, the more comprehensive are one's values; there is a greater sense of one's participation in the community, as well as an increase in self-expressive activities. Self-fulfillment is more valued and more pursued as a real possibility.

> I sculpt, sail and love to dance. I like to read ... I'm very active from dawn 'til dusk.

Interpersonal Attitudes

Another broad factor influencing consumption is the nature of people's interpersonal attitudes. These are, of course, individually ramified in many ways, but some consistencies are visible. Attitudinal differences are seen at the most intimate levels, affecting sexual relations, the use of contraceptives, and conjugal roles. There are consequences in effectiveness of family planning and preferences in family size. For example, lower status women are much less likely to use diaphragms, since its use requires more interpersonal support from the husband than lower class men tend to give their wives (Rainwater, 1965).

More generally, upper middle class women tend to regard their husbands as companions, to feel like a peer in money matters. They are likely to demand much of themselves for achievement: to be a good wife, mother, an intellectually stimulating being, home economist, child therapist, organization woman, etc., and also to be a person of composure and competence. As parents, upper middles need their children to be bright, active, strong, lively, and precocious, and are given to characterizing their babies as active and alert. They look for products that will add to their success, competence, and proficiency as mothers and fathers.

By comparison, lower middle class parents are more apt to stress control and conformity, the meeting of values and requirements that relate to cleanliness, politeness, neatness, and order. These parents are most troubled by dirty diapers and the idea of things being messy. Most parents want "good" babies, but lower middles are particularly prone to want them well-behaved, well-scheduled, and manageable.

Working class fathers are relatively distant from their babies.

> I take little care of him, but help when I can. He laughs, and moves around, and seems to know me (at five months).

Working class mothers strongly need to enjoy their babies, to get pleasure from them. They will tolerate difficulties with their babies, finding in them self-justification and interpersonal responsiveness. In sum, to simplify, the upper middle wants her child bright and alert; the lower middle wants him properly behaved; and the working class woman wants a gratifying possession (SRI, 1960[a]).

In terms of more general relationships, lower class women tend to say they dress to please themselves, possibly to excuse their bold dress-up urges; lower middle class women give some emphasis to other women and much less to pleasing themselves. Upper middle class women have a broader sense of display and think of their audiences as spread among themselves, husbands, other women and men (SRI, 1960[b]).

The narrower interpersonal circles of working class people show themselves in many ways. They make less use of long distance (SRI, 1955[b]). They have a tendency to relate socially more to relatives than middle class people do; in spending vacations, working class people are distinctly more prone to visit relatives, to stay home, or have the husband go alone, than to follow the middle class custom of going away from home as a family group (SRI, 1961[e]).

Self-Perceptions

Consumer behavior may reflect the varied self-perceptions, or self-images held by individuals, as such; and, to some degree, as they are characteristic of members of social class groups.

These views of oneself provide a source of consumer action, since they are the expressions of needs, of aims, and of the individual's internal logic, all of which find their objects in the market place. To the extent that people seek products and services that are congruent with their self-perceptions (as they are and as they would like to be), their self-perceptions are a guide to understanding their marketing behavior. Certainly, individual personality is diverse, more so than the general values held characteristically within a group; relating consumer behavior meaningfully to personality is, therefore, one of marketing research's more challenging tasks. However, that there are some systematic differences among classes is suggested from various directions. For example, in a study of sanitary protection, it was indicated that women of lower social status tend to have more sense of taboo about their bodies and less understanding of them (SRI, 1957). They were prone to think of themselves as having menstrual problems. They were less receptive to the use of tampons, an instance of their lesser receptivity to important changes in behavior, their lesser scientific information, their more traditional ideas and feelings about sexual matters and interpersonal relations, etc. (SRI, 1958[d]).

Compare the ideas and tone of these two women, the first a lower class, ethnic girl.

> I am Spanish, you see, and Spanish girls are not made like American girls and are not brought up the same. We would not be able to use anything like that ... You see, we are closed up. American girls are opened up at birth, but Spanish girls are not and we are not opened until we are married and then we go to our husbands and he is the one who opens us.

The second is an upper middle class woman who commented on her use of tampons:

> I figured if I could accommodate one thing I could accommodate another.

Higher status people have more pride in their organisms. They think of themselves as fastidious people; upper middle class women express themselves less urgently when it comes to "needing a deodorant," not believing they smell so bad in the first place. The self-oriented aspects of grooming, of personal pride and self-esteem are prominent in the reactions of higher status women, less to the fore among lower middle status women where general social motives and self-consciousness tend to seem more pressing; lower class women respond more to immediate needs, thinking in terms of tonight's date and special occasions (SRI, 1951[b], 1955[a]).

Definitions of men, what a "real man" should be to fit the goals, norms, and values of his social class reflect many variables, especially those relating to his physical being, and his effectiveness in vocational and familial relations. Some relative emphases are discernible among the social classes. Upper middle class people tolerate a much more "feminine" conception of a real man. They do not think that a real man has to be crudely tough to be effective. They think that being clean, fastidious, and well-groomed, is part of being a successful person, and demonstrates the kind of narcissism one expects in a higher status person. They think of hygiene, grooming, and dress as especially related to one's career and how it is being lived up to. A higher status man may have distinctive specialized hobbies; some tendency to think of women as pals— and they think he should be a friend; and the idea that masculine know-how finds expression in knowing one's way about the world—in jet planes, restaurants, modern business.

Lower middle class people think a good man is particularly a good father, a responsible husband, a man who builds a solid home life. He is serious, earnest, somewhat depressed, eager for his children to do well in school so that they might become well-established, and fearful that they might be trespassed against by lower class people. He is the most conventional, generally, in dress, resistant to Ivy League and Continental influences, and hopeful that the double-breasted suit will come back to cover up his bulging middle.

Working class people think that a real man is a sturdy guy who can make a decent living. Lower class men like to have body know-how, physical adeptness and manual skills, to understand how things work. They want to get along, to get some fun out of life. They expect to work fairly hard and to relax as hard as they can, because they feel life uses them up faster than it does higher status people (SRI, 1951[a], 1958[e], 1960[c], 1961[d], 1963[a]; Levy, 1963). A study of age grading showed a trend for lower status people to think of themselves as mature and as old at younger ages than do higher status people (Neugarten and Peterson, 1957).

Daily Life

According to differences of occupations and activities (as well as income differences, socially evaluated differences, etc.), the manner in which the whole day is lived includes both subtle and gross differences. Lower status women are apt to get up earlier in the morning and to feel they can make do with less sleep; in general, working class people are especially faced with the problem of needing to get to bed early and wanting to watch late movies on television. Middle class housewives are more likely than lower class women to plan things with some care, to enjoy trying out some new things, to feel a sense of mastery over household chores; lower class women are more prone to agree that "a woman's job is never done."

In general, with increasing status there is more activity outside the home and in the time spent in expressive activities—reading, art, and music, and helping the children do various things. The distribution and use of time shows class trends; for example, the time for the dinner hour varies systematically from class to class. About a fourth of the lower lowers in one sample were likely to be at dinner before five o'clock, and very few after seven o'clock, while more than half the upper middles were still at dinner after seven o'clock. Also, more time is spent at the meal as status rises. The television set is also much more likely to be on during dinner in lower class homes than in middle class homes (SRI, 1949[a], 1949[c], 1964).

These four areas of values, interpersonal relations, self-perceptions, and daily life are broad in character. They reflect the basic facts that groups in our society do different kinds of work, have different types and amounts of financial reward, are evaluated differently along various dimensions of social esteem and importance to the community. As consequences, they think of themselves differently, behave differently, and want differently. In relation to some more specific marketing areas, these differences find further expression.

Shopping

Social status appears to affect how people feel about where they should shop. The tendencies here are for lower status people to prefer local, face-to-face places where they feel they will get a friendly reception, easy credit if needed, etc. As a consequence, the same products (and brands) may be purchased in different channels of distribution by members of different social classes. In the purchase of cosmetics, upper middle class women are more apt to shop in department stores than are lower status women who are, in turn, relatively more apt to shop in variety stores. Drug stores seem equally attractive or suitable to all. Studies of department stores also show that among the stores available, there are sharp differences in status reputation, and that consumers tend to sort themselves out in terms of where it is appropriate for themselves to shop. This is not a gross, either/or phenomenon. Most establishments will have customers of more than one social class. But their loadings will differ, and their purchasing patterns may differ. Upper middles characteristically go to Sears for certain kinds of goods, proportionately different from the array bought by lower status customers; and lower status people often go to Marshall Field's only to buy gifts, or even to acquire a gift wrapping. Food chains are similarly selected as varying in status suitability.

The upper middle class woman organizes shopping more purposefully and efficiently than women of lower status. She is more knowledgeable about what she wants, where she will go for it, when she will get it; her shopping is both selective and wide-ranging.

> I shop in Wanamakers, Lord and Taylor, Bonwit's, and Snellenberg, depending on what I want at the time I'm shopping. I go shopping with a specific thing in mind. I usually group my shopping for the coming season's needs for clothing for myself and the children. I shop for food regularly once a week at Penn Fruit.

Lower middle class women "work" more at their shopping, showing more anxiety about it, finding nonfood purchases especially demanding and tedious, and fraught with uncertainties. Their clothing purchases tend to be more piecemeal than upper middles' are, and there is more orientation to seeking out the best buy for the money.

> I'm always buying clothing for the family. I look around and buy the best I can for as little as I can. With supermarkets, I watch for ads on Thursdays. . . . For example, I just bought a blanket and I went to three stores to look. As it happened, we bought at Lits; they had the nicest blanket for the best price.

Lower class women are the most impulsive about shopping, the least organized. They often like to go out just to have a reason to get out of the house.

> My shopping is very broad and vague. I don't go anywhere in particular but for food and that I get at Best Market. For clothing, I usually go to one of the department stores or when they have an advertisement to show what is on sale and what is different than the usual run of things. I just shop wherever I find what I want.

The implications of these remarks overlap among women, but the continuum is discernible, and finds its most specific expression in the local, social orientation of the lower lower class shopper.

> Some people like to run around from store to store and buy in them large grocery chains. I sometimes buy can goods there, but the best

place, the one I like best, is Greene's (a small grocery store in the block). They'll save things for me and I can always get what I want.

Thus, the goals, methods, and places of shopping form patterns that distinguish members of the different social classes in various ways (SRI, 1956, 1958[a], 1958[c], 1961[c], 1962[a]).

Media

The fact that media are approached and used in contrasting (as well as similar) ways among social class groups is important for marketing understanding. At a rather simple level there are variations; for example, lower status people are less apt to *subscribe* to newspapers than are middle class people, and more likely to read and subscribe to *True Story,* for example; they are more likely to enjoy the comics freely, to embrace television, and to watch late movies. Upper middle class tastes on television are likely to run more actively to current events and drama; moving down the social scale, one finds a relative rise of interest in soap opera, quiz shows, situation comedy, and variety. Middle class people worry more about the effect of television on their children than do lower class people.

The different meanings of media have been explored in many studies. The media function in varied ways, and each also fits differentially into the lives of the social classes. There are (sometimes sharp) class preferences among the newspapers available in a community, in evaluating magazines, in selecting television shows, in listening to the radio, in how newspapers are read, in receipt and meaning of direct mail; and, in general, in the total volume of materials to which people are exposed and to which they attend in one or another of the media. Higher status people see more magazines, read more of the newspaper, and buy more newspapers. Lower class people tend to prefer the afternoon paper; middle class people tend to prefer the morning paper. Studies in the past three years of television in fifteen major cities show that upper middle class people consistently prefer the NBC channel, while lower middles prefer the CBS; and these preferences are in keeping with the images of the networks, and the characteristics of the social classes (SRI, 1954[a,b,c], 1962[b,c], 1963[b]; Glick and Levy, 1962).

Advertising

Attitudes toward advertising are diverse, and reflect much individual variety. However, the many background factors already noted lead to social class differences in this sphere also. The expressly symbolic nature of advertising is particularly meaningful in aiming it toward the differentiated understandings of members of different groups. Broadly speaking, upper middle class people are more critical of advertising, suspicious of its emotional appeals, and questioning of its claims. They are trained in pursuing subtle meanings and usually display an attitude of sophisticated superiority to advertising compared to the more straightforward, literal-minded, and pragmatic approach of lower middle and upper lower class people.

This does not mean that upper middle class people are unresponsive to advertising; although they insist on expressing detachment, they are more strongly appealed to by sheer difference, by approaches that seem somewhat individual in tone, that show some wit, that convey elements of sophistication, stylishness, that seem to appeal to good judgment, discriminating taste, that offer the kinds of objects and symbols that are significant of their status and self-expressive aims. Lower status people are relatively more receptive to advertising that is strongly visual in character, that shows activity, ongoing work and life, impressions of energy, and solutions to practical problems in daily requirements and social relationships (SRI, 1949[b], 1952[a], 1961[f]).

Some specific illustrations can be found in women's reactions to promotional advertising, offering coupons and special inducements. Upper lower class women are most receptive when the activity does not seem too difficult. They feel intrigued, economical, shrewd, that they would be fools not to take advantage of many offers that come their way, to cut costs, to get something a little extra.

> I think they are real nice. I like those coupons. I'm not rich enough to throw away 15 cents. I know some people think it is silly to save them, but I don't. Boy, they add up, you know.

Lower middle class women often feel the same attraction, but are more reserved in their reaction, feeling the need to question the utility of offers. They like to feel that they are sensible about their use of offers and promotions, that what they get is important or interesting enough to be worth the effort. They enjoy some sense of complexity, an enrichment of shopping in this kind of participation, but they can also be quite aloof.

> Another one of those. Not very interesting. Too much money to gamble on. If I wanted one of those I could go out and buy one. This doesn't interest me one little bit, I just wouldn't bother with it.

Upper middle class women feel the most remote, sensing lower class economic implications and looking down their noses at the quality of premiums, the size of savings, etc. Their interest vies with their sense of apartness.

> I have never used an offer. I see the coupons in all the papers. They are good for people with large families, they can save a lot if they use the coupons. I find them attractive but I never seem to use them.
>   Sometimes they offer knives in a set, Cannon towels, dolls, jewelry, blouses. They might interest some people, not me.

In general, values, level and quality of education, the different social aims, and socioeconomic variations produce such differences in characteristic reactions, although much of this is obscured by the volume of advertising learning that goes on, and the projective interpretation that can make the same advertisement mean different things to different people to suit their needs (SRI, 1960[e], 1963[c]; Levy, 1959, 1960).

The kinds of products people want to consume differ, and the reasons for which they consume the same products differ. Going up the social scale, one finds that gum chewing decreases and the reasons given for chewing gum tend to change; more services are used—hotels, motels, airplanes, telephones, dry cleaning, delivery, insurance, investments, etc.; taking of laxatives tends to decline.

There are general differences in whole areas of consumption. The use of food is a good example. Going up the social scale, one finds that food tends to be regarded and used in increasingly symbolic fashion, and going down the scale, one discovers that it is consumed more and more pragmatically. Also, it is apt to be used more self-indulgently at upper middle and lower class levels than at the lower middle, as is also true of drinking. Interest in furniture tends to take different forms. Upper middle class people prefer to search out furniture that is stylish and in keeping with some specified personal or family esthetic; lower class people are more apt to emphasize sturdiness, comfort, and maintenance; lower middles have the characteristic "middle" anxiety about doing what is "right," respectable, neat, pretty, etc. (SRI, 1952[b], 1958[b], 1961[a,b]).

Although the points and summary statements offered above would (when elaborated) have interest in themselves, and did so to various study sponsors in specific instances, they also gain interest for their contribution to a cumulative understanding. They imply a coherence in the marketplace that functions with a consistency that is at least potentially available for continued study. There is suggested a social class structure that may start (or end) with variations in income, but which operates more meaningfully then in terms of amount of money available for spending. However, it has come about that the individual person (or family) exists in and is a manifestation of a milieu that has certain limitations and certain opportunities. The results have recognizable and usually quite logical consequences.

Upper lower class people tend to be defined in their total patterning of personality and ways of living by the fact that society allots them, so to speak, a manual, physical, body-focused assignment. Being the doers, the handlers, they are expected to *act* or *behave* overtly, to accomplish in ways that emphasize locomotor activity. In law they are its concrete, physical expression, found driving cars, pounding on doors, laying on sticks and handcuffs. In commerce they sell, serve, retail, handle things, make change, wrap packages. In physical production, they are the mechanics and manipulators, using their hands and muscles with or without skill to produce concrete objects. Such workers, trained to their world, become generally restricted in ego functions. Their orientation is local, concrete, face-to-face, relatively deprived of long-range considerations or larger horizons. Immediate gratifications and readiness to express impulses tend to be observed in these people, since they do not usually perceive meaningful incentives to do otherwise.

Lower middle class people characteristically have "the cultural assignment" of applying known principles to defined problems in an accurate manner. Ideally speaking, they are expected to implement laws, regulations, systems, etc., to be caretakers, and intermediary supervisors. As such, in law they deal with its principles as lawyers and clerks; in commerce they may be bookkeepers, accountants, seeing to it that financial methods are systematically and precisely applied. In production, they are supervisors and engineers, again implementing and using known systems and generalizations about physical processes and structures. Such workers, trained to their world, become oriented to a functional and pragmatic view, coupled with anxiety about achieving respectability and success through virtuous performance. This gives them a larger perspective than that found in the lower class, reinforces the importance of education and of deferring gratifications in favor of long range goals.

Upper middle class people have the cultural assignment of initiating knowledge, establishing policy, of exerting judgment, and deciding on the methods and procedures to be used. They embody the intellectual, professional, and managerial point of view. In law they are judges and legislators; in commerce they are managers, controllers, determining the content of the procedures and actions to be carried out by workers of lower status. In a production hierarchy, they may be chiefs, physicists, and scientists. Such workers, trained to their world, emphasize ego processes, an awareness of more distant horizons, large social events and concern with individuality and achievement. They use more integrated and varied means of satisfying their aims, feeling free to satisfy impulses frowned on by lower middle class people, and are able to organize their lives from a point of view beyond the power of lower class people.

The differences listed in the earlier series of points that relate more or less closely to marketing have their roots in the differences suggested in these brief descriptions of three main social classes. These differences seem "real" differences, in that they are not simply the result of variations in income, but are expressions of the profoundly varied forms of experience that become available to members of each social class. They may be obscured by the commonalities in human aims and in American experience, and by the superficial significance of much consumption, but they seem consistent and persistent in governing, where relevant, the consumers' approaches to the market.

References

Glick, I. O., and S. J. Levy. *Living with Television.* Aldine, 1962.

Hyman, H. H. "The Value Systems of Different Classes: A Social Psychological Contribution to the Analysis of Stratification." In *Class, Status and Power,* ed. R. Bendix and S. M. Lipset. The Free Press (1953), 426–442.

Levy, S. J. "Symbols for Sale." *Harvard Business Review,* Vol. 37 (July–August 1959), 117–124.

———. "Symbols of Source, Substance, and Sorcery." *Art Direction Magazine,* 1960.

———. "The Meanings of Work." *Notes and Essays on Education for Adults,* No. 39. The Center for the Study of Liberal Education for Adults, May 1963.

Neugarten, B., and W. Peterson. "A Study of the American Age-Graded System." *Proceedings 4th Congress International Association of Gerontology,* Vol. 3 (1957), 497–502.

Rainwater, L. *Family Design: Marital Sexuality, Family Size and Contraception.* Aldine, 1965.

SRI: Social Research, Inc., reports
  A Day in the Life of Mrs. Middle Majority, 1949[a].
  The General Nature of Advertising Symbols, 1949[b].
  Life Patterns of Mrs. Middle Majority, 1949[c].
  Hair Product Preferences, 1951[a].
  Toothpaste: A Socio-Psychological Study, 1951[b].
  Attitudes toward Toilet Tissues and Their Advertising, 1952[a].
  The Laxative and Antacid Market, 1952[b].
  The Differing Meanings of Women's Magazines and Television, 1954[a].
  The Meaning of Newspapers, 1954[b].
  The Sunday Comics, 1954[c].
  Cleanliness and Personal Attraction, 1955[a].
  A Socio-Psychological Study of Telephone Users, 1955[b].
  Images of Seven Chicago Department Stores, 1956.
  Attitudes toward Feminine Hygiene, 1957.
  The American Drug Store: Image, Use and Function, 1958[a].
  The Kroehler Report, 1958[b].
  Major Retailers in the Philadelphia Market, 1958[c].
  Meanings and Motives in the Tampon Market, 1958[d].
  Men's Clothing and Tailoring, 1958[e].
  Babies and Baby Care Products, 1960[a].
  Chicagoland Women and Their Clothing, 1960[b].
  German Men, 1960[c].
  Images of Femininity, 1960[d].
  The Meanings and Influence of Promotional Advertising, 1960[e].
  Chewing Gum and the Consumer, 1961[a].
  Contemporary Patterns of Food Logic and Consumption, 1961[b].
  Credit Buying and Its Motivations, 1961[c].
  Images of Masculinity, 1961[d].
  Status of the Working Class in Changing American Society, 1961[e].
  A Study of Thematic Coherence in Advertising Approaches, 1961[f].
  Hair Products and Cosmetics, 1962[a].
  Magazine Readership as Related to Social Class, Age, and Sex, 1962[b].
  Patterns of Radio Listening in the New York Metropolitan Region, 1962[c].
  Marketing to Men, 1963[a].
  Newspapers in the Social World of Chicagoans, 1963[b].
  A Study of Stamps, 1963[c].
  Attitudes toward Television, 1964.

5.3 Social Class and Commercial Bank Credit Card Usage
H. LEE MATHEWS, JOHN W. SLOCUM, JR.

Consumer behavior models virtually always emphasize social class and income as variables affecting purchases.[1] Pierre Martineau suggested that social class is often more important than income in influencing purchasing behavior:

> While income has generally been the most widely used behavioral indicator in marketing, social class membership provides a richer dimension of meaning. The individual's consumption pattern actually symbolizes his class position, a more significant determinant of his buying behavior than just income.[2]

Recently, the concept of consumer credit has been expanded.[3] As the consumer has become a more sophisticated shopper, credit has played an increasing role in facilitating the acquisition of goods and services. Similarly, a greater number of retail and financial institutions are realizing that providing credit service is a means of reaching new market segments. Yet, social class membership has not been the subject of detailed analysis in understanding consumer credit. This study examines how a consumer's social class membership affects his use of one type of credit instrument—the commercial bank credit card. Implications of the study may go beyond credit cards to other applications of the marketing of credit service. For example, promotional materials can be better directed towards appropriate market segments utilizing the convenience-installment classification suggested in this article.

Research Design

The results of a mail questionnaire study conducted in a large eastern metropolitan area follow. A random sample of 4,316 credit card holders was drawn from the files of a large commercial bank and a questionnaire mailed to each bank credit card holder. Of the 2,187 returned questionnaires, a total of 1,896 were usable. The initial questionnaire resulted in 1,615 returns, while the follow-up letter and questionnaire resulted in an additional 572 questionnaires. A chi-square analysis indicated that the two samples were not significantly different at the .025 level.

A two-factor index of social position combining occupation and education was used in this study to measure an individual's social class membership.[4] Occupation is presumed to reflect the skill and power individuals possess as they perform the many maintenance functions in society. Education is believed to reflect not only knowledge but also cultural tastes. This instrument, therefore, measures social class without taking income into consideration.

Major Concepts and Definitions

The two-factor social position index divides society into five status structures. The hierarchy ranges from the low status evaluation of unskilled physical labor to the more prestigious use of skill and the manipulation of men.

Lower Class and Lower Middle Class. The lower social classes tend to be oriented locally in outlook and emphasize relatively short horizons and considerations. Immediate gratifications and readiness-to-express impulses are observed. Occupations require little skill and education, for example, taxi drivers, car washers, and janitors.

Middle Class. The middle class is oriented to a functional and pragmatic view. This gives them a larger perspective than found in the lower class and reinforces the importance of deferring gratifications in favor of long-range goals. Included are bookkeepers, small business owners, and minor professionals.

Upper Middle Class and Upper Class. The upper classes embody the intellectual, professional, and managerial personnel, for example, executives, lawyers, and doctors. They tend to integrate a variety of means to satisfy their aims, and concern themselves with individuality and achievement. Such people are highly trained and are responsible for decisions affecting other persons.

Card use was studied by analyzing the bank's credit card records over a 28-month period beginning in 1966. Two classifications of card use were developed. A card holder who elected to pay an amount less than the balance and pay interest charges on the unpaid balance was classified as an *installment* user. A card holder who paid his balance within the billing cycle was considered to be using the card in lieu of cash as a *convenience* finance instrument, and these card holders have been defined as *convenience* users.

Findings

Table 1 presents the basic findings of the study concerning credit card use by social class. The data show that the percentage of installment use from upper class to lower class increases from 52% to 82%. An increase is shown for each class. Thus, members of different social classes exhibit different credit card use patterns. Members of the lower classes tend to use their credit cards for installment financing to a greater extent than upper classes. Lloyd Warner has reported that buying habits of lower-class persons are profoundly different from middle-class persons. What each buys and where he purchases it reflects symbolic as well as economic values.[5] Caplovitz,[6] Rainwater,[7] and Vidich[8] have also supported the relationship between social class and spending-saving behavior.

A consensus of the behavioral consequences of membership in a particular social class has emerged from these studies. One differential consequence of class membership is the individual's ability to defer gratifications. Deferred gratification patterns are one of the major cultural patterns which establish and maintain boundaries between social classes in America.[9] This term was introduced by sociologists Schneider and Lysgaard to describe the phenomenon of "impulse renunciation."[10] Deferred gratification, therefore, refers to the postponement of satisfactions. An important point is the normative character of deferred gratification. Middle class persons feel that they should save money, postpone purchases, and, in short, renounce a variety of gratifications.

A study by Davis and Dollard indicated that "impulse following" was a characteristic of lower class people and that "impulse renunciation" was a characteristic of the middle class.[11] The lower class characteristic of "impulse following" involves *free spending* (buy now, pay later) and a minimum pursuit of education. On the other hand, the middle class characteristic of "impulse renunciation" involves the reverse of these behavioral patterns. The differential pattern with respect to gratification deferment may help to explain the credit card use patterns shown in Table 1.

The data in Table 1 reflect the low classes' low emphasis on saving (even when possible) in favor of expenditures at the moment. For example, the fact that appliances purchased by lower class families were not only predominately new but usually the more expensive models, led Herbert Gans to imply that this class had a low sales resistance and tends to "buy now, pay later."[12] Vidich and Bensman found that "shack people" (lower class people) tend to reject middle class standards in such areas as housing and prefer instead to spend their money on immediate needs and fancies, such as car accessories, flashy clothes, and sporting equipment.[13] Martineau offers an additional example with the record of "an individual earning $200 a month who . . . bought a new Mercury on which the payments were $96 a month."[14]

On the other hand, the upper classes have a greater tendency than the lower classes toward convenience use. This result supports the theory of deferred gratification. That is, while upper classes would not use credit for installment purposes, there is no reason they could not use it for convenience. Thus, there is certainly an indication that the nature of card use is related to social class membership. Different social classes reflect different values, and these differences are manifested in consumer buying behavior.

Acceptable Consumer Goods to Charge with a Commercial Bank Credit Card

One of the most important marketing aspects of a credit service is to determine what merchandise and/or services the consumer considers chargeable. Once a group of goods has been identified as a potential market, the credit-

TABLE 1.   Use of Commercial Bank Credit Cards by Social Class[a]

Social Class	Convenience		Installment		Row Total	
	Number	Per-centage	Number	Per-centage	Number	Per-centage
Upper Class	89	48	97	52	186	100
Upper Middle Class	158	38	263	62	421	100
Middle Class	154	29	381	71	535	100
Lower Middle Class	152	24	492	76	644	100
Lower Class	21	18	89	82	110	100
Totals	574		1,322		1,896	

[a]A chi-square analysis indicates that these findings are significant at the .001 level of confidence.

granting institution has a frame of reference within which to plan and develop its marketing strategies. The data pertaining to which good(s) is acceptable to buy with credit are presented in Figure 1. The data show that the majority of card users favor purchasing goods such as appliances, furniture, clothing, and gifts on credit. Individuals appear to feel that it is acceptable to purchase consumer durable goods, some "necessities," and services, such as education and medical expenses, with credit. Fewer commercial bank credit card users find it acceptable to purchase items like furs, meals in restaurants, vacations, and antiques on credit.

These same people do not feel that an individual need go into debt to purchase "luxury goods." These findings parallel those of George Katona at the University of Michigan. Katona's research shows that the majority of consumers in all social strata consider credit buying a good idea; only about a third indicate that it is a "bad idea."[15]

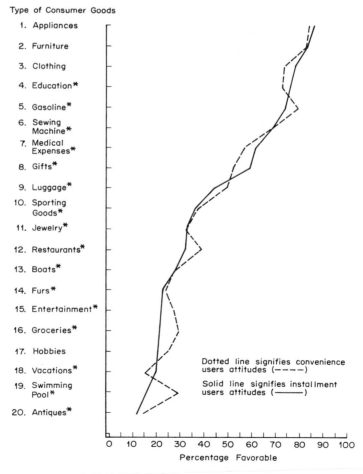

FIGURE 1.   Favorable attitudes toward buying consumer goods on credit.
* Attitudes differ significantly by social class: upper class more favorable.

Figure 1 also shows that some differences in acceptable items to charge were found between convenience and installment users. Convenience card holders felt gasoline, restaurant expenses, luggage, entertainment, groceries, hobbies, and swimming pools were more acceptable goods to charge than installment users. It is readily apparent that except for swimming pools, these are purchases where charging is merely a convenience. Installment users, as might be expected, were overwhelmingly of lower social classes and had a more favorable attitude toward purchasing consumer durable merchandise on credit. In these instances, credit facilitates the acquisition of durable goods.

This study indicates that there are also differences in the acceptability of purchasing specific items on credit, depending on social class. Items marked by an asterisk in Figure 1 indicate those for which the upper classes found it more acceptable to use credit. This is interpreted to mean that the upper classes are generally favorable toward using credit to purchase "luxury goods." Conversely, the lower classes restrict credit use to durable and necessity goods. Rainwater, Coleman, and Handel in *Workingman's Wife* and Vidich and Bensman in *Small Town in Mass Society* all suggest this phenomena.

As previously noted, the higher social classes have a wider range of goods deemed acceptable to buy on credit. It is perhaps appropriate to say that the upper classes' quest for distinction and achievement is a salient factor affecting their credit-buying philosophy. Similarly, these people appeared to have a more favorable attitude toward credit than members of the lower class.[16] It was also found, consistent with Rainwater, Coleman and Handel's studies that installment users had a more favorable attitude toward credit than convenience users. It is how the individual actually uses the card which seems to have the greatest influence on what he considers acceptable to buy on credit, and it is these uses which profoundly reflect the value system that a person has toward credit.

Card Use Patterns

It is the purpose of this section to examine the attitudinal and behavioral components of credit card usage. The overt act of using the card and an individual's attitude toward credit and acceptable goods to buy on credit need not be congruent.

On the basis of the data presented in Figure 2, it appears that attitudes toward credit and actual use of the bank credit card are congruent. That is, convenience users actually use their cards less than installment users. Over the 28-month period for which data was analyzed, approximately 50% of the convenience users concentrated on between one and four separate months, while only 34% of the installment usage took place in the comparable period.

It is necessary to consider the amount charged by card holders as a basis for formulating strategies. Most installment users charge more items than convenience users, but how much do they owe? . . .

Installment users who are predominately members of the middle class and lower-middle classes, have a favorable attitude toward credit and purchasing merchandise with the bank card, and generally use their cards more than convenience users. The tendency to buy new appliances, furniture, and clothes

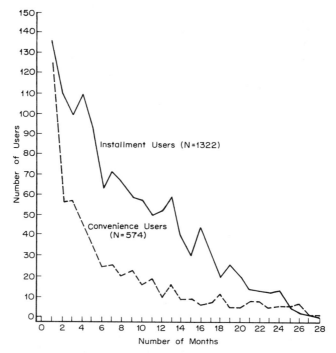

FIGURE 2.   Credit card usage patterns.[a]
N = 1322 for installment users.
N = 574 for convenience users.
[a]A chi-square analysis indicates that these findings are significant at the .01 level of confidence.

on credit is somewhat more marked among those card holders in the installment category than in the convenience user category. The preference for new and more expensive models points toward what has been labeled "compensatory compensation." The value in use of the goods matters, of course, but beyond that the goods evidently express their owners' aspiration for status. The need for credit may explain why the number of installment users extended their repayment schedules over a long period of time. Bridging the gap between current income and extensive needs and aspirations is the credit card that offers an installment payment plan.

The people who are inclined to make their repayments over an extended period of time are likely to charge more than others. They run higher absolute balances and higher average balances than people who use the card for convenience purposes. These intimations are borne out in Figures 3 and 4, which show the relationship between installment and convenience users' balances.

In large part, these findings confirm the previous contention that installment users are buying big ticket items and are using credit cards as a financing device. The fact that convenience users' balances are significantly less than the installment users' lends additional support to our interpretation.

The consumers who buy furniture, T.V. sets or stereophonic phono-

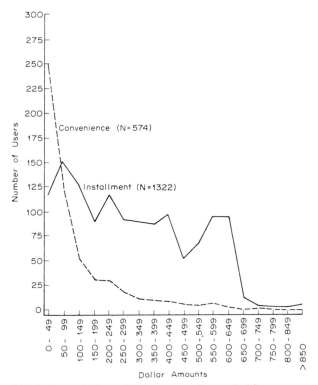

FIGURE 3.   High balance during a 30 day accounting period.[a]
N = 574 and 1322 respectively.
[a]The term balance means the amount owed since the inception of the credit card plan.
For example, 3 installment users had high balances greater than 900 dollars at one time.
A chi-square analysis indicates that these findings are significant at the .01 level of
confidence.

graphs at terms of "a dollar down and a dollar a week," are prepared to pay
the interest charges. These card holders are not concerned with "how much?"
rather they ask the merchant "how much per month?" Their concept of the
pricing systems differs sharply from that of the convenience users who pay their
bills within the normal accounting period.

Summary

Commercial bank credit card holders exhibit different card-use patterns
related to class membership. Members of the lower social classes tend to use
their cards for installment purposes; upper classes, for convenience. The
differences reflect respective social class values, which can be used as a basis for
marketing credit service. Installment credit card holders tend to seek out stores
honoring their cards. Their general attitude toward use of credit is favorable
and is reflected in actual card use.

Convenience users state that they do not seek stores accepting the
bank charge plan. Other alternative charge arrangements seem to be used by

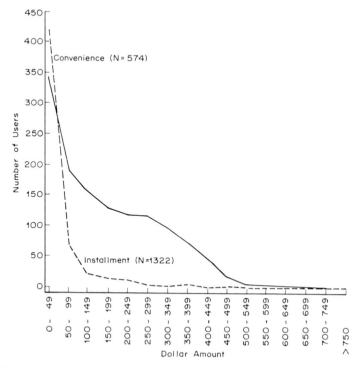

FIGURE 4. Average balance during a 30 day accounting period.[a]
N = 574 and 1322 respectively.
[a] A chi-square analysis indicates that these findings are significant at the .01 level of confidence.

convenience users. It is also possible that because convenience users are using their cards in lieu of cash, they do not want to risk overextending themselves and hesitate to use the card to purchase goods that they consider unchargeable. This pattern bears strong resemblance to the sociological concept of deferring gratifications, which also was found to vary by social class membership.

Notes and References

1. See, for example, John A. Howard, *Marketing Management: Analysis and Planning, Revised Edition* (Homewood, Illinois: Richard D. Irwin, Inc., 1963) and "A Theory of Buyer Behavior" (unpublished manuscript, 1968); Francesco Nicosia, *Consumer Decision Processes* (Englewood Cliffs, New Jersey: Prentice-Hall, Inc., 1966); Philip Kotler, "Behavioral Model for Analyzing Buyers," *Journal of Marketing*, Vol. 29 (October 1965), 37–45, and "Mathematical Models of Individual Buyer Behavior," *Behavioral Science*, Vol. 13 (July 1968), 274–278.

2. Pierre Martineau, "Social Classes and Spending Behavior," *Journal of Marketing*, Vol. 23 (October 1958), 121.

3. Robert Bartels, "Credit Management as a Marketing Function," *Journal of Marketing,* Vol. 28 (July 1964), 59–61, and Philip Klein and Geoffrey Moore, *Quality of Consumer Installment Credit* (New York: National Bureau of Economic Research, Studies in Consumer Installment Financing, 1967).

4. Alfred B. Hollingshead and Frederick C. Redlich, *Social Class and Mental Illness* (New York: John Wiley & Sons, 1958), 398–407.

5. Lloyd Warner, *Democracy in Jonesville* (New York: Harper and Brothers, 1949).

6. David Caplovitz, *The Poor Pay More* (New York: Free Press of Glencoe, 1963).

7. Lee Rainwater, et al., *Workingman's Wife* (New York: Oceana Publishing Co., 1959).

8. Arthur Vidich and Joseph Bensman, *Small Town in Mass Society* (New York: Anchor Books, Inc., 1960).

9. For example, see Murray S. Straus, "Deferred Gratification, Social Class, and the Achievement Syndrome," *American Sociological Review,* Vol. 27 (June 1962), 325–335; Richard P. Coleman, "The Significance of Social Stratification in Selling," in *Marketing: A Mature Discipline*, Martin L. Bell, editor (Chicago, Illinois: American Marketing Association, 1961), 171–184; Harry Beilin, "The Pattern of Postponability and Its Relation to Social Class Mobility," *Journal of Social Psychology,* Vol. 44 (August 1956), 33–48; William Sewell, Archibald Haller, and Murray Straus, "Social Status and Educational and Occupational Aspiration," *American Sociological Review,* Vol. 22 (February 1957), 67–73; and Alfred Hollingshead, *Elmtown's Youth* (New York: John Wiley and Sons, 1949).

10. Louis Schneider and Sverre Lysgaard, "The Deferred Gratification Pattern: A Preliminary Study," *American Sociological Review*, Vol. 18 (March 1953), 142–149.

11. A. Davis and J. Dollard, *Children of Bondage* (Washington, D.C.: American Council on Education, 1948).

12. Herbert Gans, *The Urban Villagers* (New York: The Free Press of Glencoe, 1962).

13. Same reference as footnote 9.

14. Same reference as footnote 2, p. 150.

15. George Katona, *The Powerful Consumer* (New York: The McGraw-Hill Book Company, 1960), 100, and James E. Morgan, "Consumer Credit in Family Financial Management," a speech delivered to the American Home Economics Association (Madison, Wisconsin: October 9, 1967).

16. A Likert-type scale was developed to measure an individual's attitude toward credit. For additional information, see H. Lee Mathews and John W. Slocum, Jr., *Marketing Strategies in the Commercial Bank Credit Card Field* (Chicago, Illinois: Bank Public Relations and Marketing Association, 1968), 30–33.

5.4 Living Room Styles and Social Attributes: The Patterning of Material Artifacts in a Modern Urban Community
EDWARD O. LAUMANN, JAMES S. HOUSE

Over the past seventy years, many writers have commented on the importance of studying the material artifacts with which individuals and families surround themselves, in order to gain insight into the ways by which people express their personalities, facilitate their pursuit of personal and social goals, and symbolize their status position in society. Many theorists have attempted to go beyond the obvious fact that material artifacts typically serve utilitarian or functional needs for individuals and groups to consider why most artifacts seem to be elaborated in design or decoration far beyond the modest dictates of strict utility. Such theorists range from those anthropologists who suggest that certain fundamental panhuman expressive needs for aesthetic expression and aesthetic delight are fulfilled by the embellishment of objects[1] to certain rather more cynical sociologists who emphasize the role that nonutilitarian elaboration of objects plays in facilitating the invidious comparison of individuals and groups, particularly in the more "advanced" societies. With regard to this last point, we might note Veblen's[2] classic work on the theory of the leisure class, which was especially directed to analyzing the significance of the conspicuous consumption of time and goods in interpreting the status behavior of the leisure and working (industrial) classes.

While somewhat oversimplifying the general picture, the subsequent sociological research tradition on material style of life may be characterized as falling into two broad categories or camps.[3] On the other hand, writers in what might be termed the tradition of social commentary and criticism have typically acknowledged their deep indebtedness to Veblen[4] and have updated his commentary. In a society in which leisure and consumption have become increasingly central in the lives of individuals, these writers view style of consumption as a primary means of asserting and/or validating social status and identity. Thus, the style and quality of the exterior and interior of a person's home are viewed as pawns in a Goffmanesque game of impression management.[5] This process has been chronicled in its most extreme forms among those newly arrived in (or still striving for) more prestigious social positions, e.g., the new "suburbanites" or the rising young "organization man."[6]

On the other hand, writers of a more methodologically sophisticated and "objective" bent, such as F. Stuart Chapin and William H. Sewell,[7] have confined their attention to an evaluation of the potential utility of using, let us say, selected living room furnishings to predict the relative socioeconomic status or family income of the household. The possible significance of differences in taste and styles of decor (given comparable economic positions) in serving expressive functions for the individual's personality or in symbolizing the individual's social location and conception of his social position have often been ignored on the grounds of being too "subjective" to sustain rigorous analysis.[8] Thus, the first camp is very rich in social insight and interpretation of contemporary society, but often lacks convincing empirical tests of its propositions; while the second is methodologically more rigorous, but limited in the scope and application of its findings.

In this article we wish to show that it is possible and fruitful to bring more rigorous empirical methods to bear on some of the theoretical speculations of the "social commentary tradition." We will employ for this purpose some new techniques for multivariate statistical analysis. This is thus an exploratory effort at empirical measurement and analysis of one aspect of individuals' "styles of life," which hopefully will suggest both the need for and the difficulty of further research in this area. More specifically, we seek to explore the relationship of social attributes and attitudes (including social status and social mobility) to the manner in which persons furnish their living rooms.

The living room (in addition to the front exterior of the home) is clearly the most appropriate source of data for examining the ways in which individuals express their actual (or desired) social identities in their homes. Goffman[9] makes the distinction between the front (public) and rear (private) regions of behavior in impression management: "The performance of an individual in a front region may be seen as an effort to give the appearance that his activity in the region maintains and embodies certain standards."[10] A crucial part of the front region is the "setting," i.e., "the fixed sign-equipment in such a place."[11] The living room is the area where "performances" for guests are most often given, and hence the "setting" of it must be appropriate to the performance. Thus we expect that more than any other part of the home, the living room reflects the individual's conscious and unconscious attempts to express a social identity. Its decor, in contrast to that of other rooms, is most likely to reflect decisions made on criteria of taste and style, rather than purely economic grounds.

There are at least two points of view as to how the "criteria of taste and style" are acquired or chosen. On the one side is Veblen's notion of the standard-setting function of the leisure class in establishing matters of taste and style in consumption:

> The leisure class stands at the head of the social structure in point of reputability; and its manner of life and its standards of worth therefore affords the norm of reputability for the community. The observance of these standards, in some degree of approximation, becomes incumbent upon all classes lower in the scale. In modern civilized communities the lines of demarcation between social classes have grown vague and transient, and wherever this happens the norm of reputability imposed by the upper class extends its coercive influence with but slight hindrance down through the social structure to the

lowest strata. The result is that the members of each stratum accept as their ideal of decency the scheme of life in vogue in the next higher stratum, and bend their energies to live up to their ideal.[12]

Noteworthy here is the fact that Veblen assumed a monolithic or singular leisure class that effectively monopolized the canons of reputability and enjoy a general consensus on what these canons should be at a particular point in time. His argument would seem to imply that traditionally high-status "persons" should be the ultimate arbiters of taste in home decorations and, therefore, that those striving for or recently arriving in the top status group should eagerly adopt the style of those who are already well-established there. Furthermore, he would expect that innovation in style should be the exclusive province of such a top group.

In contrast, more recent social commentators such as Riesman and Whyte, Jr.,[13] have seen the most transient people (both geographically and socially mobile) as those most sensitive (because of their hypothesized other directedness) to the changes in the canons of consumption. And such canons are in Riesman's view bound to be transient in a modern consumption-oriented society. From this perspective the socially and geographically mobile will shun the life style of the "traditional aristocracy" for one which partakes of the latest fashions and fads. These fashions and fads are set more often by the class of "tastemakers,"[14] i.e., advertising men, designers, etc., rather than the "leisure class." Such as explanation would be consistent with such phenomena as the life style of the so-called "jet set," and the rapid acceptance of pop art.

Given the rich, but diffuse and impressionistic nature of previous theoretical speculation, our empirical effort must be clearly exploratory. Basically our analysis will seek to answer the following questions:

(a) Are clear patterns of decor evident in the living rooms of families in an urban area, and can they be meaningfully characterized?

(b) How are social status and other aspects of social identity (religion, ethnicity, values, etc.) related to style or decor?

(c) Is there a clear upper-class style of life, and how have the canons of this style disseminated themselves through the stratification system (particularly among those who are upwardly mobile)?

Source of Data

During the spring and summer of 1966, interviewers from the University of Michigan Detroit Area Study conducted 85-minute interviews with a probability sample of 1,013 native-born, white men between the ages of 21 and 64, living in the greater metropolitan area of Detroit.[15] Midway through the interview, the respondent was asked to fill out a self-administered questionnaire taking approximately ten minutes to complete. During this interval, the interviewer noted the contents and characteristics of the living room on a 53-item check-list inventory. In most cases the interviewer was merely to check on the list if given objects were to be found in the living room. The objects had to be seen in the living room itself—the fact that the object might be found in some other room in the house did not result in a "check" for present. For example, nearly all households possessed a television set, but it was checked only if it was actually in the living room. As we shall see, the presence of the television set in the living room is associated with relatively low-income households. Many higher-income families put the television set in another room, which often is specially designed for television viewing. In 11.5 percent of the households, the relevant information could not be collected because the interview was conducted in another part of the house and the interviewer did not have an opportunity to observe the living room. Consequently, the results reported below are based on only 897 cases.

Data Analysis

The Smallest Space Analysis (SSA)

First, we wanted to see if certain clusters of objects seemed to occur together more frequently than others in our respondents' living rooms, and whether these clusters constituted meaningful styles of decor. Secondly, we hoped to look at the social correlates of these styles.

We, therefore, coded each object or attribute as present (1) or absent (0) and then correlated these attributes with each other (using the ϕ coefficient). The resulting 53 × 53 matrix of correlations showed the degree to which any given object tended to be found in the same living room with each of the other objects. For example, the presence of modern furniture is highly correlated with the presence of sculpture and abstract painting, indicating that people with modern furniture often have sculpture and abstract paintings in their living rooms as well.

We then used a technique called smallest space analysis to transform the information in the correlation matrix into a graphic representation of how living room characteristics covary.[16] This technique takes account of the whole correlation matrix simultaneously and tries to map the 53 objects into an *m*-dimensional Euclidean space such that the following condition is satisfied: (1) Distance (A,B) ≤ distance (A,C), whenever $r_{ab} \geq r_{ac}$. That is, object A will be nearer to B than it is to C when the correlation of A with B is greater than the correlation of A with C. The higher the positive correlation between two variables the closer they will be in the *m*-dimensional space; the higher the negative correlation the farther apart they will be. [Thus in Figure 1, sculpture, abstract painting and modern furniture appear close together, but far away from antimacassars and French furniture.]

To the extent that condition (1) above is not satisfied in all cases, the geometric portrayal of the correlation matrix is inaccurate. The degree of inaccuracy is expressed by the "coefficient of alienation." Smallest space analysis tries to arrange the points in a space with the smallest possible number of dimensions, while keeping the coefficient of alienation *low*.

In this analysis a good fit was obtained in a five-dimensional space. However, we found that the basic arrangement of the points in the two dimensional space was not greatly altered in the higher dimensionalities. Since it is also easier to visualize and interpret the results in two dimensions, we present data for that solution. Figure 1 shows how our 53 variables arranged themselves

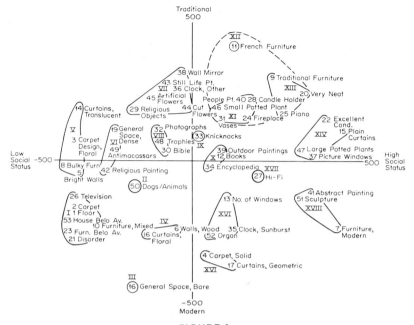

FIGURE 1.

in this space. Clusters of objects which are most often found together are circled and designated by Roman numerals.

Interpretation of the Space

While the coordinate axes in Figure 1 are themselves essentially arbitrary, the configuration of points remains the same no matter where the axes are placed. The coordinates, however, can help us in understanding the underlying dimensions of this configuration of points. Visual inspection of Figure 1 suggests that the ordering of points along the first axis is in terms of social status or family income. More speculatively, the second axis seems to order objects roughly along a dimension of modern vs. traditional style of decor. Thus, French and traditional furniture, wall mirrors, pianos, flowers and vases all appear near the top of this dimension and are generally associated with traditional decor. Likewise, the cluster of modern furniture, sculpture and abstract paintings is near the bottom of the second dimension; along with sunburst clocks and solid carpets—all elements of modern decor.

We tried to validate and extend these intuitions by relating an object's position on these dimensions to the correlation of the presence of that object with other socioeconomic and attitudinal variables. Thus we asked if the presence of objects that are near the positive end of our first dimension is highly positively correlated with measures like income, education and occupation; while the presence of objects near the negative end is negatively correlated with these measures. Likewise, are objects near the top of the second dimension highly correlated with indicators of "traditional" values, like frequency of church attendance or "devotionalism"? Table 1 presents the results of correlating an object's position on each axis with the correlation between this object and socioeconomic or attitudinal measures.

One can readily see from this table that the first axis of the solution is highly related to measures of family income, occupational status, and educational attainment of husband and wife (rows 1–4). Although family income appears to be related quite strongly to the first axis, it is still moderately related to the second axis where high family income, occupational status, and educational attainment tend to be associated with the more "traditional" objects (positive end of the second axis in the 2-space) and lower family income, etc., with "modern" objects.

Clearly, then, the ordering of objects along the first axis is a function of the ability to pay for them. We will contend that the second (vertical) axis orders attributes along a dimension of modern vs. traditional decor. Each quadrant of the space in Figure 1 seems to have an intuitive substantive meaning. Roughly, there appear to be four distinguishable styles of decor: (1) high status-modern (i.e., clusters XVI, XVII, and XVIII); (2) higher status-traditional (i.e., clusters XI, XII, and XIII); (3) low status-traditional (i.e., clusters V, VI, VII, and VIII); and (4) low status-modern (i.e., clusters

TABLE 1. Product-Moment Correlations of the Coordinates of the Best 2-Space Solutions with Selected Socioeconomic and Attitude Characteristics

Characteristics	Smallest Space Coordinates 2-Space		
	First Axis	Second Axis	(Income Partialed) Second Axis
1. Total family income	.846	.468	
2. Occupational status	.798	.437	
3. Educational attainment of respondent	.814	.310	
4. Educational attainment of wife	.749	.315	
5. Religious preference of respondent	.363	.261	.558
6. Religious preference of wife	.287	.243	.441
7. Subjective ethnic identification	.245	.252	.427
8. Frequency of church attendance	.428	.553	.416
9. Devotionalism	.113	.495	.443
10. Preference to marry same religion	.471	.521	.342
11. Political party preference	.681	.386	.000
12. Father-son inter-generational mobility	.534	.466	.205
13. Father-in-law—son-in-law intergenerational mobility	.697	.533	.298
14. Traditionalism in marital role relations	.542	.193	.629

Significance levels (for r and partial r's): $r \geq .273$, $p < .05$; $r \geq .354$, $p < .01$.

I, II, III, and IV). The last pattern seems more the result of impoverish-
ment than real stylistic preference.

Since the second axis is also highly correlated with income, we have
partialed out the effects of income in the third column of Table 1. Here it
becomes very clear that our "traditional" axis is strongly associated with
attitudinal measures of traditionalism in two areas: (1) religion and (2) conceptions of marital roles. "Traditional" objects tend to be found in the homes of
persons who are Catholic, "devotional" (in Lenski's sense of the word) and
frequent church attenders. Hence our notion of "traditionalism" homes are
also highly likely to hold "traditional" views about marriage—to feel that
husbands and wives should stick to masculine and feminine tasks (as traditionally defined), respectively, and not share in household chores or decision-
making. There is also a less marked tendency for traditional decor to be found
in the homes of the upwardly mobile. . . .

Discussion

Veblen posited that the traditional elite would set the consumption
norms for society and would be emulated by those below. Our SSA results
would indicate that generally this is true, especially among those who are
upwardly mobile, Catholic and non-Anglo-Saxon. However, the "nouveaux
riches" of our SSA analysis who are really "making it" for the first time
behave quite differently. Here the notions of Riesman, Whyte and Sapir[17]
seem more illuminating. The *nouveaux riches* have a strong need to validate
their newly found status, yet they are not accepted socially by the traditional
upper classes (cf. Warner, on the lack of association between the "upper
upper" and "lower upper" classes).[18] Since their associations do not clearly
validate their position, they turn to conspicuous consumption. However,
conspicuous consumption must be done with "taste" if it is to validate one's
claims to high status in respects other than mere money. Hence the *nouveaux riches*, in their other-directedness, seek to discover what are the latest
and most *chic* norms of consumption.

Discovery of such norms is easy in a society that possesses a class of
professional taste-makers (e.g., architects, interior decorators, fashion designers) and taste-setting media (ranging from *Better Homes and Gardens*
through the *New Yorker*). Normative consumption trends are also evident in
the styles of decor adopted by business and government for their new offices
and stores. In all cases, the norms today favor modern decor. The *nouveaux
riches*, then, spurn the style of the traditional upper class in favor of the newer
fashions. This serves a double purpose: (1) to establish their tastefulness and
hence status, while (2) symbolically showing their disdain of the "snobby"
traditionals.

The rest of the population does not follow the path of the *nouveaux
riches* partly because status validation may be somewhat less of a problem
for them, and partly because they are less likely to be in touch with the people
or mass media which propagate the latest trends. As the *nouveaux riches* become established, and modern norms of consumption become more clearly
modal, we may expect the upwardly mobile at all levels to adopt modern styles.
But by then the *nouveaux riches* may have moved on to newer styles.

Naturally these speculations and conclusions must be offered very tentatively indeed. Several qualifications (and suggestions for improving subsequent research) arising out of the character of our data and methods of analysis should be noted. First, although we attempted to include many types of objects in our inventory, there remains a fundamental crudity in our categorization of these objects. Our pretesting experience with the inventory of objects revealed that the interviewers were not capable of making very refined distinctions in stylistic and qualitative features of a number of objects without an investment of special training that could not be undertaken given the limited time available. Knickknacks, for example, are highly heterogeneous in stylistic and quality connotations—a Woolworth hobnail milk glass or ten-cent-store figurine (low status traditional) is very different from a Steuben Glass owl or dolphin (high status modern) or from Royal Dalton and Hümmel figures (high status traditional). Such distinctions were often beyond the untutored grasp of our interviewers. It is interesting to note that the crude category "knickknacks" falls between the low and high status traditional clusters and toward the middle of the traditional-modern axis in Figure 1. . . . Future research ought to try to delineate the dimensions along which style differences are of interest (e.g., modern vs. traditional, colorful vs. subdued, ornate vs. functional, etc.) and build a checklist of objects aimed at delineating just such distinctions. This, of course, entails the construction of hypotheses as to why such dimensions of style are important as indicators of social attributes or attitudes.

Secondly, our sample of attributes seems to contain many more indicators of traditional decor than of modern (33 attributes in the upper quadrants vs. 20 in the lower). Furthermore the traditional objects are fairly evenly distributed along the status dimension, while the modern objects are clustered at the upper and lower extremes. This may reflect the realities of middle class decor (in line with our above interpretations), but it may also reflect our failure carefully to select and differentiate the objects in our checklist. The distribution of objects along posited stylistic dimensions should receive greater attention in future studies.

Nevertheless, the techniques appear to yield sufficiently plausible and promising results that further work obtaining more refined and elaborate data would be amply justified. Certainly they afford a means of examining some of the more subtle hypotheses regarding people's life styles with greater objectivity and precision than hitherto has been possible.

Conclusion

We have shown that it is possible to characterize in a meaningful way the styles of interior decoration found in the living rooms of homes in a metropolitan area. The choice of a style of decor is rather strongly related to the achieved and ascribed statuses of the individuals, and to their attitudes and behavior in other areas of life. That is, people with traditional decor are also more traditional in their behavior and attitudes regarding religion and marital role definitions. Finally we have tried to indicate how these data reflect on the theories of Veblen and other social commentators regarding the establishment and dissemination of norms for styles of life and consumption.

Notes

1. For example, Melville J. Herskovits, *Cultural Anthropology: An Abridged Version of Man and his Works* (New York: Alfred A. Knopf, 1955), 234, 266, observes:

   "The search for beauty is universal in human experience. Its innumerable forms have sprung from the play of the creative imagination, and afford some of the deepest satisfactions known to man. To understand how closely integrated with all of life, and how expressive of a way of living art can be, is again not easy for members of the highly specialized societies of Euro-American culture, where we are confronted with the effect of compartmentalization. . . .

   ". . . in all societies the aesthetic impulse finds expression in terms of beauty laid down in the traditions of the people . . . No art . . . is haphazard or chaotic. It is the expression of desire for beauty that finds fulfillment in the application of technical skill through sanctioned form, in terms of the patterned perception and imaginative resources of the artistically endowed members of every society."

   See also, Clyde Kluckhohn, *Mirror for Man* (New York: McGraw-Hill, Premier Books, 1960).

2. Thorstein Veblen, *The Theory of the Leisure Class* (New York: The New American Library, 1953).

3. For a selected bibliography, see Edward Sapir, "Fashion." *Encyclopedia for the Social Sciences,* Vol. VI (December 1931), 139–144; F. Stuart Chapin, *Contemporary American Institutions: A Sociological Analysis* (New York: Harper and Bros. 1935), 373–397; William H. Sewell, *The Construction and Standardization of a Scale for the Measurement of the Socio-economic Status of Oklahoma Farm Families* (Stillwater, Oklahoma: Oklahoma Agricultural and Mechanical College, Agricultural Experimental Station, Technical Bulletin No. 9, 1940); Alfred L. Kroeber and Jane Richardson, "Three Centuries of Women's Dress Fashions, A Qualitative Analysis," Anthropological Records, 2 (no. 2, 1940); Allison Davis, Burleigh B. Gardner, and Mary R. Gardner, *Deep South: A Social Anthropological Study of Caste and Class* (Chicago: University of Chicago Press, 1941); Erving Goffman, "Symbols of Class Status," *British Journal of Sociology*, Vol. 2 (December 1951), 294–304; David Riesman, *The Lonely Crowd* (New York: Doubleday Anchor Books, 1953), 94–102, 141–149, 168–188, 240–246, 260–271, 330–345; Thomas Ford Hoult, "Experimental Measurement of Clothing as a Factor in Some Social Ratings of Selected Men," *American Sociological Review*, Vol. 19 (June 1954), 324–328; Russell Lynes, *The Tastemakers* (New York: Harper and Brothers, 1954); Buford H. Junker, *Room Compositions and Life Styles: A Sociological Study in Living Rooms and Other Rooms in Contemporary Dwellings* (Unpublished doctoral thesis, University of Chicago, 1955); James A. Davis, *Living Rooms as Symbols of Status: A Study in Social Judgment* (Unpublished doctoral dissertation, Harvard University, 1955); William H. Whyte, *The Organization Man* (Garden City, New York: Doubleday Anchor Books, 1956), 295–448; John R. Seeley, R. Alexander Sim, and Elizabeth W. Loosely, *Crestwood Heights: A Study of the Culture of Suburban Life* (New York: Basic Books, 1956), esp. Chapter 3; Jurgen Ruesch and Weldon Kees, *Nonverbal Communication: Notes on the Visual Perception of Human Relations* (Berkeley and Los Angeles: University of California Press, 1956), 132–159; Herbert

J. Gans, *The Urban Villagers: Group and Class in the Life of Italian-Americans* (New York: The Free Press, a Division of the Macmillan Co., 1962), 181–187; James N. Porter, Jr., "Consumption Patterns of Professors and Businessmen: A Pilot Study of Conspicuous Consumption and Status," *Sociological Inquiry,* Vol. 37 (Spring 1967), 255–265.

Of course, as noted above, there is a voluminous anthropological literature, beginning with Franz Boas, cataloging material artifacts of primitive peoples and discussing their significance in understanding the cultures of these peoples. On the whole, however, the issues addressed, such as the diffusion of objects and the determination of culture areas, are not directly of relevance to the concerns of this paper although they do bear some indirect relevance; Herskovits, op. cit.; Clyde Kluckhohn, op. cit.; Frank M. LeBar, "A Household Survey of Economic Goods, on Romanum Island, Truk," in Ward H. Goodenough, Ed., *Explorations in Cultural Anthropology: Essays in Honor of George P. Murdock* (New York: McGraw-Hill Book Co., 1964), 335–350; Horace Miner, "Body Ritual Among the Nacirema," *American Anthropologist*, Vol. 58 (1956), 503–507; Harold E. Driver and Karl Schuessler, "Factor Analysis of Ethnographic Data," *American Anthropologist*, Vol. 59 (August 1957), 655–663.

4. Thorstein Veblen, op. cit., see C. Wright Mills' introduction, vi–xix.

5. Erving Goffman, *The Presentation of Self in Everyday Life* (New York: Anchor Books, 1959).

6. John R. Seeley, et al., op. cit., especially Ch. 3; William H. Whyte, op. cit., especially Part VII.

7. F. Stewart Chapin, op. cit.; William H. Sewell, op. cit.

8. For one exception to this generalization, see Allison Davis, op. cit. Davis had respondents make judgments about the social status and some other attributes of the owners of pictured living rooms, a complementary approach to the problem in this paper. His study is flawed methodologically because 15 of the 23 pictures he used contained people who often provided stronger status cues than the living room itself. His most interesting finding in relation to the present paper was that the ability to judge the status of living rooms (i.e., "sensitivity to generalized status order of symbols") is associated with *expectancy* of change in social context or status, but not necessarily with actual past histories of social mobility. See Allison Davis, op. cit., 113. The lack of association between actual mobility and status sensitivity seems counter to generally accepted beliefs and the findings of this paper. But his findings are still generally consistent with explanations offered for the greater sensitivity of the socially mobile.

9. Erving Goffman, op. cit.

10. Ibid., 107.

11. Ibid., 107.

12. Thorstein Veblen, op. cit., 70.

13. David Riesman, op. cit.; William H. Whyte, op. cit.

14. Russell Lynes, op. cit.

15. A multistage probability sample of dwelling units of that part of the Detroit SMSA that was tracted in 1950 plus some small additions made to take into account recent surburban population growth was drawn. Within each dwelling unit having one or more eligible respondents, one person was drawn at random for interview. A total of 985 actual interviews was obtained, of which 28 have been double-weighted, yielding a final set of 1,013 cases for use in analysis. These 1,013 cases represent 80% of the eligible households sampled. Refusals to grant interviews account for 13.9% of the eligible households (N = 1,271); another 6.4% was lost because none had been found home after 6 calls (5.5%) or for other reasons.

  For further details concerning the sampling design and sample completion rates, the interested reader may write Howard Schuman, Director, Detroit Area Study, University of Michigan, for a copy of Working Paper #1, Project #938, "Sampling Memorandum for 1965–66 Detroit Area Study," January 1967.

16. For a more detailed exposition of the statistical analysis and a description of the available computer programs, see Louis Guttman, "A General Nonmetric Technique for Finding the Smallest Euclidean Space for a Configuration of Points," *Psychometrika*, Vol. 33 (December 1968), 469–506; James C. Lingoes, "New Computer Developments in Patterns Analysis and Nonmetric Techniques," *Uses of Computers in Psychological Research* (Paris: Galthier-Villars, 1966a), 1–22; James C. Lingoes, "An IBM-7090 Program for Guttman-Lingoes Smallest Space Analysis—I," *Behavioral Science,* Vol. 10 (April 1965a), 183–184; James C. Lingoes, "An IBM-7090 Program for Guttman-Lingoes Smallest Space Analysis—II," *Behavioral Science,* Vol. 10 (October 1965), 487; James C. Lingoes, "An IBM-7090 Program for Guttman-Lingoes Smallest Space Analysis—III." *Behavioral Science*, Vol. 11 (January 1966), 75–76: Edward O. Laumann and Louis Guttman, "The Relative Association Contiguity of Occupations in an Urban Setting," *American Sociological Review,* Vol. 31 (April 1966), 169–178, Louis Guttman, "The Development of Nonmetric Space Analysis; A Letter to Professor John Ross," *Multivariate Behavioral Research,* Vol. 2 (January 1967), 71–82.

17. Edward Sapir, op. cit.

18. W. Lloyd Warner, *American Life* (Chicago: University of Chicago Press, 1953).

5.5 Profile in Poverty

LOLA M. IRELAN, ARTHUR BESNER

Currently, in our national concern for the alleviation of poverty and economic dependency, the need to know and understand what life looks like from the bottom of society is a crucial one. We can induce meaningful change only if we understand the situation where we intend it to occur. It is unlikely, for example, that we can change or reduce rates of dependency and poverty without knowing what the conditions of dependence and deprivation mean to people caught up in them. Nor can we bring any class of people into a different relationship to society without knowing the quality of the existing situation.

As yet, knowledge of this sort is fugitive and tenuous. Much needed research has yet to be designed. There are gaps and flaws in the exploratory research which has been done. The findings on hand are suggestive rather than definitive. There is enough known, however, to warrant inventory and judicious application. It behooves us to systematize and use such knowledge as we do have. In the long run, such a step will serve to refine and increase it.

This paper summarizes available findings, largely from studies in the United States, bearing on the approach to life of the poor, the people at the bottom of society's economic ladder. It will discuss the connection between the condition of poverty, the views of man and society which arise there, and the apparent effect of those views on the lower class version of American goals and values.

Life Conditions of the Poor

In our society, a continuously low income is directly associated with certain life situations. Poorer, more crowded living quarters, reduced access to education and recreation, occupational restriction to simpler, manual types of work—these and similar characteristics of the very poor are sufficiently obvious to need no underlining. The result of these circumstances is a set of life conditions which is not so obvious. They consist of four general limitations: (1) comparative simplification of the experience world, (2) powerlessness, (3) deprivation, and (4) insecurity. These limitations are, of course, relative. Indeed, they can be discerned only because of the different extent of their existence at the several levels of society.

1. Limited alternatives. The poor, of all the strata in society, have the slightest opportunity to experience varieties of social and cultural settings. Their own setting is one of the least intricacy and flexibility. Throughout life, they experience a very narrow range of situations and demands. Their repertoire of social roles is limited. They seldom participate in any activity which takes them out of the daily routine. They rarely play roles of leadership, or fill any position calling for specialized functioning. On their jobs they confront less complex situations and have fewer, less diverse standards to meet. Socially, they seldom go beyond the borders of kinship and neighborhood groups—people very like themselves.[1]

2. Helplessness. The position of the poor vis-a-vis society and its institutions is one of impotence. They have practically no bargaining power in

the working world. Unskilled and uneducated, they are the most easily replaced workers. The skills they do have are minimal, of little importance in productive processes. On the job itself, the very poor man can exercise little autonomy and has small opportunity to influence conditions of work. He is close to helpless even to acquire information and training which would change this situation. He has neither the knowledge nor the means to get it.

    3. Deprivation. It is reasonable to suspect that this general condition, almost universally associated with poverty, is felt with particular intensity in American society. Deprivation is, after all, relative. When it is defined as lack of resources relative to felt wants and needs, it is evident that America has one of the greatest gaps between generally accepted goals and the extent to which the lower class can realistically expect to attain them. As a nation, we stress, perhaps inordinately, the value and virtue of high attainment. We expect and applaud efforts at self-improvement and upward social mobility. Commercial advertising attempts to stimulate and increase desire for status achievement. The richness of life in the rest of society is well displayed—on television, in newspapers, on billboards, in store windows, on the very streets themselves. All this, plus awareness that some people have actually succeeded in the strenuous upward move, makes the condition of the unachieving poor one of unremitting deprivation. Their relative deprivation is, perhaps, the condition which more than anything else affects the life-view of the poor. Constant awareness of their own abject status and the "failure" which it rightly or wrongly implies understandably leads to embarrassed withdrawal and isolation.

    4. Insecurity. People of low income are more at the mercy of life's unpredictability than are the more affluent. Sickness, injury, loss of work, legal problems—a range of hazardous possibilities—may overwhelm anyone. But to the poor man they are especially fearful. His resources are more sparse. His savings, if any, are quickly expended in any sizable emergency. Certain conditions of his life make emergencies more likely. His work skills are more expendable, sometimes more dependent on seasonal demands. He is more likely to lose his job on short notice. An emergency expenditure of funds may mean the postponing of rent payments and the fear of eviction. He is unable to secure for himself and his family the regular, preventive health measures which would fend off medical emergencies. He often finds that he cannot successfully navigate the channels involved in using public sources of emergency help, such as clinics and legal aid agencies.[2]

Low-Income View of Man and Society

    Constant, fruitless struggle with these conditions is likely to produce estrangement—from society, from other individuals, even from oneself. The wholeness of life which most of us experience—the conjunction of values, knowledge, and behavior which gives life unity and meaning—is less often felt by the poor. They see life rather as unpatterned and unpredictable, a congeries of events in which they have no part and over which they have no control.

    Conceptualized as "alienation," this view of life is repeatedly found associated with lower social and economic status.[3] It is multifaceted—despair can be generated and felt in many ways. Generally, however, it seems to have four different forms of expression. The alienation of the poor is graphically seen in their feelings of: (1) powerlessness, (2) meaninglessness, (3) anomia, and (4) isolation.

1. Powerlessness.   The objective condition of helplessness in relation to the larger social order leads naturally to the conviction that one cannot control it. The poor are widely convinced that individuals cannot influence the workings of society. Furthermore, they doubt the possibility of being able to influence their own lives. Correspondingly, they are likely to voice such pessimistic views as, "A body just can't take nothing for granted; you just have to live from day to day and hope the sun will shine tomorrow."[4]

2. Meaninglessness.   Powerlessness, the feeling of being used for purposes not one's own, usually is accompanied by conviction of meaninglessness. The alien conditions in which an individual may be caught up tend to be unintelligible. He does not grasp the structure of the world in which he lives, cannot understand his place in it, and never knows what to expect from it. Oriented, by need, to the present, he is relatively insensitive to sequences in time. He often does not understand the continuity of past experience and current ones. And, not only does the poor man feel unable to control future events, he cannot even predict them.

3. Anomia.   The term "anomie" was originally coined to describe situations in which social standards have been broken down, or have no influence upon behavior.[5] It has subsequently been pointed out that this normless condition is a probable result of the failure of prescribed behavior to lead one to expected goals.[6] The life view of individuals caught in such a discrepant situation is likely to be cynical, perhaps fatalistic. For example, the poor man who is taught in many ways that economic success is the most desirable thing in life—and then is barred from legitimate means of achieving it—may come to expect that illegal behavior is necessary to reach approved goals. The situation, moreover, induces people to believe in luck. The poor are in no position to comprehend the whole of society's structure and operation, or to understand its dysfunctions. Since they also have little control over it, its impact on them is frequently fortuitous. Understandably, they are quick to credit their difficulties to fortune and chance.[7]

4. Isolation.   More than any other segment of society, the very lowest economic stratum is socially isolated. The poor man not only fails to comprehend society or his community, he is out of touch with it. He reads fewer newspapers, hears fewer news programs, joins fewer organizations, and knows less of the current life of either the community or the larger world than more prosperous, better educated people do. Nor do the poor associate among themselves more than minimally.[8] Experiencing separation from society and each other, it is natural for them to feel alone and detached. And feeling no identity, even with each other, they view the world as indifferent and distant—"No one is going to care much what happens to you when you get right down to it."[9]

Goals and Values

What are the aims of life in such circumstances? In a situation of relative helplessness, knowing themselves worse off than the rest of society, living on the edge of chronic emergencies, and seeing their own circumstances as formless and unpredictable, how do the poor shape their lives? What values do they hold? What goals do they seek? Essentially, they seek and value the same things as other Americans. Naturally enough, since they are American poor, they absorb characteristic American values and preferences. And just as naturally, the realities of low economic status are visible in the lower class version of American dreams and designs. The result is a constricted but recognizable variant of society-wide goals and standards.

Increased sophistication of research on lower income and deprived groups is correcting a long-held impression that the poor place no value on occupational and educational achievement. While the poor do have a more modest absolute standard of achievement than do those who are better off, they want relatively more improvement in their condition. They value the same material comforts and luxuries. Psychologically, they seek the securities that appeal to other Americans. They hold, with little qualification, to the same proprieties of social conduct.

Interest in improving one's status, however, seems to have different sources at different social levels. To the middle-class youth, the idea of having a better job than his father is appealing, sometimes absorbing. Such achievement is attractive in itself. A lower-class youngster has more urgent, material reasons for wanting an improved future. His present is painfully unsatisfactory. His urge toward better, stabler occupations is not so much drive for achievement as flight from discomfort and deprivation. It is probably stronger for that difference.[10]

Reality—expenses of education and training, lack of resources— usually keeps less well-off high school students from aspiring to the highest level professions. But, more than their middle-class fellows, lower class high school students want better jobs than their fathers'. They are more likely to value increased income. In significantly greater numbers, they are unwilling to enter the same occupations as their fathers.[11]

Although they may not expect to achieve it, most low-income people value advanced education. It has been found that up to 65 percent of parents will say they want a college education for their children.[12]

Materially, the lower classes are not satisfied with poor housing or living conditions. High on their list of desirable improvements are better housing and neighborhoods. Inside their homes, they value the same things as the general run of Americans—comfortable and durable furniture, a television set, an array of electrical appliances, and, to give life grace as well as comfort, a few ornaments and art objects. Tastes in style are definitely American— modern furniture, colored telephones, pole lamps, systematic color schemes.[13] It sometimes happens, as in more affluent circumstances, that materialistic values win out over real human needs. Parents stint on children's clothing to save money for a car. Older children are pressed too early into adult responsibilities because both parents are working away from the home.[14] A woman postpones an operation for herself because the family must have a car or a radio.[15]

In common with other Americans, the lower class enjoys excitement and values the opportunity to escape routines and pressures of day-to-day existence. Spectator sports, television, visiting—all are valued leisure-time pursuits.[16]

Probably the most basic value held by the poor is that of security. Even more than "getting ahead," they value "getting by," avoiding the worsening of an already unstable situation.[17] They are unwilling to take risks, and seek security rather than advancement—also a frequent pattern in economically better-off segments of the population.[18]

The moral code of the very lowest class is a moot subject. It has been said that they have an entirely separate set of moral and ethical values. They have also been described as subscribing so fully to the general American code that they are frustrated by it.[19] The most realistic conception seems to be that which credits them with an adapted version of society's rules of behavior. They value stable marriages, perhaps even more highly than do middle-class Americans. They do not, however, reject out of hand other forms of sex partnership. A sliding scale seems to exist, whereon a good common-law marriage is valued less than legal union, but more than a transient arrangement. Illegitimacy is not devalued to the extent that it is elsewhere. Legitimate families are the ideal, but there is also some merit ascribed to the parent who acknowledges and supports children out of wedlock.[20]

Life Themes

The anomaly of life at the poverty line is evident. When people live in conditions of such obvious helplessness, when they are themselves so aware of their condition as to feel alienated and apart from society, how can they retain, much less implement, the values of that society?

The apparent answer is reinterpretation. Paths to achievement, to security, to any goal—the very quality of the goal itself—are refracted by the lower class view of life. They are interpreted in the light of what the poor man considers to be facts about life. The helplessness which he feels, the insecurity he experiences, the meaninglessness of life—all have their effect upon the way he lives and behaves.

There are four distinctive themes peculiar to lower class behavior, all apparently the result of a deprived, alienated condition: fatalism, orientation to the present, authoritarianism, and concreteness.

The genuine powerlessness experienced by the lower class is the source of persistent fatalistic beliefs. The natural counterpart of feeling helpless is belief in uncontrollable external forces. The attitude is reminiscent of belief in fate. People cannot avoid what is going to happen to them. Resignation is the most realistic approach to life.[21] Even when optimism is expressed, it is likely to be in terms of the working of chance—"A poor person should never give up hope; there's always a chance that a lucky break will put him on top."[22] This attitude acts as a definite brake on occupational and educational aspirations, and retards health care. In various other ways fatalism minimizes efforts to cope with deprivation and its consequences.

Hand in hand with fatalism goes a persistent tendency to think in terms of the present rather than the future. It is, after all, fruitless to pay attention to the distant future or try to plan life when fortune and chance are considered its basic elements. Also, when so much of one's resources must be expended simply to survive the present, little is left over for the future.[23] Results of this ad hoc orientation are pervasive. It handicaps people for the planning required in systematic economic improvement. It works against the frugality and rainy-day planning which could offset economic dependency. In the home, it results in child-training in terms of immediate reward and punishment. Children quickly evince their own present-time thinking. This low concern for future goals has been shown to be related to low academic achievement[24]—and the cycle continues.

The authoritarian theme is a strong underlying factor in interpersonal relationships of the poor. Generally defined, it is the embodiment of belief, more prevalent in the lower classes than elsewhere, in the validity of strength as the source of authority, and in the rightness of existing systems. It seems to arise from simplification of life experiences, in which one learns to prefer simple solutions to problems, and from constant subordination of the poor. Authoritarianism is incarnate in the habit of classifying people as either "weak" or "strong," in belief that deviance or disobedience should be severely punished, and in reliance on authority, rather than reason, as the proper source of decisions. It has traceable effects on family relations, child-rearing patterns, and relation to community institutions—schools, clinics, the police, welfare agencies, even to churches.[25]

Concreteness, stress on material rather than intellectual things, is a believable but little-discussed theme of lower class life. It is natural to people preoccupied by material problems. It shows itself in verbal patterns, in distrust of intellectualism, and in occupational values.

The concrete verbal style of the poor has been well-documented.[26] It is characterized by less abstraction, fewer concepts, more frequent reference to concrete objects and situations, and a less discursive manner. It includes fewer generalizations, relies less on intellectual processes than on observation, and is more tied to the world of immediate happenings and sensations.

Consistent with its patterns of speech, the lower class inclines to withhold its admiration from "eggheads," reserving it instead for the practical, down-to-earth man of action. What counts is not abstract, intellectual pursuits, but the hard tangible products of action. Results are important.[27]

This pragmatic orientation has a vital effect upon the occupational values of the lower classes. They have been found, at as early an age as 10 years, to value occupations for more tangible rewards rather than for intellectual or emotional ones. That is, a boy will aspire to a certain profession because of what it offers in terms of money and prestige rather than the nature of the work itself.[28]

Summary and Implications

Our lower income population is insecure and comparatively powerless in relation to the rest of American society. Realizing their submerged position, they have come to feel apart from society rather than part of it. From their own helplessness, they have generalized to the belief that most of life is uncontrollable. They are convinced of their own impotence so that, while they accept typical American values they are frequently lethargic in trying to attain them.

It would be incautious, in view of the sparseness of our knowledge, to say just what program implications such knowledge has, or what techniques of improvement are most likely to succeed. But it would be irresponsible to close this discussion without underlining the precautions it suggests:

1. The entire life situation of the poor must be considered if any part of it is to be changed. Their attitudes arise in no vacuum but are logical results of real circumstances.
2. Lower class citizens must be brought off the periphery into the structure of the community. Nothing which the community does for them can be durably effective until they are a functioning part of the community.
3. Energetic patience must prevail. The alienated adult cannot be completely reeducated. His children can be somewhat swayed. But it is with his grandchildren that one can really have hope.

Notes and References

1. Dotson, Floyd. "Patterns of Voluntary Association Among Urban Working Class Families," *American Sociological Review,* Vol. 16 (Oct. 1951), 687–693.

2. These four conditions of lower class life were pointed out by Albert K. Cohen and Harold M. Hodges, Jr., in "Characteristics of the Lower-Blue-Collar Class," *Social Problems*, Vol. 10, no. 4 (Spring 1963), 303–334.

3. Bell, Wendell. "Anomie, Social Isolation, and the Class Structure," *Sociometry*, Vol. 20, no. 2 (June 1957), 105–116.
   Simpson, Richard L., and Max Miller. "Social Status and Anomia," *Social Problems,* Vol. 10 (Winter 1963), 256–264.
   Dean, Dwight G. "Alienation: Its Meaning and Measurement," *American Sociological Review*, Vol. 26, no. 5 (Oct. 1961), 753–758.

4. Quoted in Cohen and Hodges, *op. cit.*, p. 322.

5. Durkheim, Emile. *Suicide.* Translated by John A. Spaulding and George Simpson. The Free Press, Glencoe, Ill. (1951), 253.

6. Merton, Robert K. *Social Theory and Social Structure.* The Free Press, Glencoe, Ill. (1949), 128.

7. *Ibid.*, pp. 138, 148–149.

8. Wright, Charles R., and Herbert H. Hyman. "Voluntary Association Memberships of American Adults: Evidence from National Sample Surveys," *American Sociological Review,* Vol. 23 (June 1958), 284–294.
   Leighton, Dorothea, *et al. The Character of Danger.* Basic Books, New York (1963), 384.
   Myers, Jerome, and Bertram Roberts. *Family and Class Dynamics in Mental Illness.* John Wiley, New York (1959), 178–179.

9. Seeman, Melvin. "On the Meaning of Alienation," *American Sociological Review*, Vol. 24, no. 6 (Dec. 1959), 783–791.

Simpson, Richard L., and Max Miller. "Social Status and Social Alienation," paper read at the meetings of the Southern Sociological Society, Miami Beach, Fla., 1961.

10. Gould, Rosalind. "Some Sociological Determinants of Goal Strivings," *Journal of Social Psychology*, Vol. 13 (May 1941), 461–473.

11. Empey, LaMar J. "Social Class and Occupational Aspirations: A Comparison of Absolute and Relative Measurement," *American Sociological Review*, Vol. 21 (Dec. 1956), 703–709.

12. Bell, Robert R. "Lower Class Negro Mothers' Aspirations for Their Children," *Social Forces*, Vol. 43 (May 1965), 493–500.

13. Lewis, Hylan. "Culture, Class, and the Behavior of Low-Income Families," paper read at the Conference on Lower Class Culture, New York City, 1963, 26, 34.

14. *Ibid.*, p. 37.

15. Koos, Earl Loman. *The Health of Regionville.* Columbia University Press, New York (1954), 35.

16. Riessman, Frank. *The Culturally Deprived Child.* Harper and Row, New York (1962), 28.

17. Kahl, Joseph A. *The American Class Structure.* Rinehart and Company, New York (1959), 205–210.

18. Centers, Richard. *The Psychology of Social Classes.* Princeton University Press, Princeton (1949), 62.

19. This controversy is summarized in Hyman Rodman, "The Lower-Class Value Stretch," *Social Forces*, Vol. 42, no. 2 (Dec. 1963), 205–215.

20. Lewis, *op. cit.*, p. 29. The problem of lower-class attitudes toward "deviant" behavior is currently being researched by Dr. Hyman Rodman of the Merrill Palmer Institute (Cooperative Research Project No. 243, Welfare Administration, U.S. Dept. of Health, Education, and Welfare).

21. Miller, Walter. "Lower Class Culture as a Generating Milieu of Gang Delinquency," *Journal of Social Issues*, Vol. 14, no. 3 (1958), 11.
Rainwater, Lee. *And the Poor Get Children.* Quadrangle Books, Chicago (1960), 52.

22. In research supported by the Welfare Administration (Cooperative Research Project No. 125, Leonard Goodman, principal investigator) it has been found that poor people are more likely, by 13 percent, to express "strong agreement" with this statement. At less than the .05 level of confidence, the difference is statistically significant:

Economic level and degree of agreement with the statement, "A poor person should never give up hope; there's always a chance that a lucky break will put him on top."

	Percent indicating—	
Economic level[a]	Strong agreement	Little or no agreement
Poor ($N = 169$)	31	69
Not poor ($N = 166$)	18	82
Percent difference	13	13

[a] According to the measure developed by James Morgan *et al.*, in *Income and Welfare in the United States.* McGraw-Hill, New York (1962), 188–196.

23. LeShan, Lawrence L. "Time Orientation and Social Class," *Journal of Abnormal and Social Psychology*, Vol. 47 (1952), 589–592.

An example of this trait is a recent finding by Leonard Goodman (Welfare Administration Cooperative Research Project No. 125): Economic level and agreement with the statement, "Nowadays a person has to live pretty much for today and let tomorrow take care of itself."

	Percent indicating—	
Economic level	Agreement	Disagreement
Poor ($N = 169$)	48	52
Not poor ($N = 166$)	34	66
Percent difference[a]	14	14

[a] Significant at less than the .05 confidence level.

24. Teahan, John E. "Future Time Perspective, Optimism, and Academic Achievement," *Journal of Abnormal and Social Psychology*, Vol. 57 (Nov. 1958), 379–380.

25. Lipset, Seymour M. *Political Man.* Doubleday and Company, Garden City, N.Y. (1960), 97–130.

26. Bernstein, B. "Language and Social Class," *British Journal of Psychology*, Vol. 11 (Sept. 1960), 271–276.

27. Miller, S. M., and Frank Riessman. "The Working Class Subculture: A New View," *Social Problems*, Vol. 9 (Summer 1961), 86–97.

28. Galler, Enid H. "Influence of Social Class on Children's Choices of Occupations," *Elementary School Journal*, Vol. 51 (April 1951), 439–445.
Morse, Nancy C., and Robert S. Weiss. "The Function and Meaning of Work and the Job," *American Sociological Review*, Vol. 20 (April 1955), 191–198.

6 Culture and Subcultures

Overview

Culture refers to social heritage. It is the distinctive life style of a society, representing its particular adaptation to its environment and its design for living. The noted anthropologist Ralph Linton, in a selection in this chapter, looks upon culture as "... the configuration of learned behavior and results of behavior whose component elements are shared and transmitted by the members of a particular society." E. B. Tylor (1891), often regarded as the father of cultural anthropology, views culture more simply as "... that complex whole which includes knowledge, belief, art, morals, law, customs and any other capabilities and habits acquired by man as a member of society" (p. 1).

The impact of culture on behavior, including consumption behavior, is not always well recognized—perhaps because this impact is so pervasive, yet indirect and difficult to delineate empirically. As Sturdivant (1973) notes, anthropologists have tended to ignore consumption as a distinguishing, researchable feature of a society and have restricted their observations to other rituals, such as marriage, religion, and childrearing. There has also been a tendency on the part of U.S. multinational marketers to lack sufficient sensitivity to cultural factors, since the "American way of life" has been so dominant and widely diffused.

Despite the worldwide diffusion of the artifacts of U.S. culture, U.S. borrowings from other cultures are easily demonstrated. Here is Linton's (1937) account of the American male's early morning routine (cultural change might make a similar account appropriate for the American female):

> Breakfast over, he places upon his head a molded piece of felt, invented by the nomads of Eastern Asia and, if it looks like rain, puts on outer shoes of rubber, discovered by the ancient Mexicans, and takes an umbrella, invented in India . . . . At the station he pauses for a moment to buy a newspaper, paying for it with coins invented in ancient Lydia . . .

he reads the news of the day, imprinted in characters invented by the ancient Semites, by a process invented in Germany, upon a material invented in China. As he scans the latest editorial pointing out the dire results to our institutions of accepting foreign ideas, he will not fail to thank a Hebrew God in an Indo-European language that he is a one hundred percent (decimal system invented by the Greeks) American (from Americus Vespucci, Italian geographer).

Cross-Cultural Analysis

A structural framework for the analysis of world cultures can be based on three major dimensions: distributive, organizational, and normative. A society is located along the *distributive* dimension demographically, in terms of (for example) age, income, and education; along the *organizational* dimension in terms of the structure of its cultural institutions, including social classes and family units; and along the *normative* dimension in terms of its value systems, including economic and religious philosophies.

Distributive Dimension

A favorite pastime of many academicians has been to categorize the cultures of the world. Walter Rostow (1962), for example, endeavored to classify them according to their level of achievement on the distributive dimension. He proposed five stages of economic growth: (1) the traditional society; (2) preconditions for take-off toward industrialization; (3) take-off; (4) the drive to maturity; and (5) the age of mass consumption. India, for example, might be classified as a country in the take-off stage, Russia as in the maturity stage, and the United States as in the age of the mass consumption.

Without necessarily developing a classification scheme, we can simply observe the empirical differences on the distributive dimension. Table 1, for example, shows the diversity of societies in terms of such demographic variables as per capita income, birth rates, and literacy rates.

TABLE 1. Distributive Variables in Selected Countries

	Great Britain	Japan	Italy	Chile	Greece	Ceylon
Population Density (per sq. mile)	475	680	445	29	168	431
Population Growth (%)	0.4	1.0	0.6	2.3	0.9	2.7
Urbanization[a]	66.9	43.1	30.3	46.3	38.4	11.4
Per Capita Income	1684	626	971	483	565	140
Life Expectancy (Years)	74	69	70	52	71	60
Infant Mortality[b]	21	23	35	120	39	52
Literacy (% of Adults)	98	95	87	80	82	70–80

[a] Percent in cities over 20,000.
[b] Per 1000 live births.
Sources: Liander (1967) and Douglas (1971, pp. 40–41).

Organizational Dimension

It is sometimes useful to simplify and think in terms of "ideal types." For example, Robert Redfield (1956), a sociologist, proposes a distinction between *folk society* and *modern industrial society*. In folk society, life centers around the family, and behavior is based on custom and tradition. In modern industrial society, many functions are transferred from the family to other societal institutions, and custom and tradition are not allowed to hinder progress. In general, it appears that traditional (folk) societies are characterized by a fairly extended kinship pattern, whereas modern societies are characterized by a conjugal (father, mother, children) family pattern.

The individual's relationship to a society and its organizational structure may differ quite markedly, with a resulting effect on modes of interaction. Stanley Davis (1969) notes that both a North American and a Latin American possess a strong sense of individuality, but that this means something quite different for each. The North American bases his notion on equality; individuality is considered to have its best chance to flourish when each person has equal rights and opportunities. Says Davis, "Paradoxically, it is his belief in his very sameness, *vis-à-vis* others, that makes him distinct and defines his individuality." The Latin American, in contrast, views individuality in terms of "uniqueness." According to Davis, telling a Latin American that he is the equal of anyone else would be an insult, since he cannot be equal to others if he is unique.

The basic conceptual distinctions noted by Davis lead to differences in group interaction and functioning. In North America, the group is a place where individuality is suppressed and the cooperative spirit is stressed. Teamwork is perceived to be vital to progress, and, as Davis notes, it is felt that "people who do not work well in groups represent a threat to both the stability and progress of our society." In Latin America, the group tends to function as a haven for individuality and exists "as a protective environment, a sanctuary in which the unique identity of each individual is valued, supported, and enhanced, rather than absorbed and assimilated into a single group identity." Davis cites the charter of a group of Latin American students who formed an association. The first sentence stated that they had "come together to act as individuals in forming this association."

In Japan the functioning of groups is different from both North and Latin America. Group activity is seen primarily as a means of sharing responsibility. If anything should go wrong, "the prospect of individual shame is lessened or at least shared by all the members" (Weigand, 1970, p. 27). This is frequently frustrating to U.S. businessmen marketing in Japan, since they have difficulty finding the decision maker when decisions are often shared, and authority and responsibility are somewhat diffuse.

Normative Dimension

The normative dimension takes as its focus the values and beliefs within a culture. In northern Europe, Great Britain, and the United States, people have traditionally been influenced by the "Protestant ethic," which sanctions hard work and frugal living. Thus, Benjamin Franklin advised his readers in *Poor Richard's Almanac:*

How much more than is necessary do we spend in sleep! forgetting that "the sleeping fox catches no poultry, and that there will be sleeping enough in the grave." . . . If we are industrious, we shall never starve: for, "at the working man's house, hunger looks in, but dares not enter" (Franklin, 1806).

Although these thoughts no longer fully represent the contemporary U.S. position, the social heritage handed down to us has been affected by this "Protestant ethic" thesis.

Sirota and Greenwood (1971) examined goal orientations among workers of an international corporation in twenty-five countries and found significant differences among normative variables. Five groupings seemed to emerge:

1. *Anglo* cluster—high on individual goal achievement and low on desire for security.
2. *French* cluster—similar to Anglo but gives greater importance to security and less to challenging work.
3. *Northern European* cluster—less oriented to job advancement and more oriented to job accomplishment.
4. *Latin* cluster—low on individual goal achievement and high on need for security.
5. *Independent* cluster—countries that did not show consistent patterns.

These results are perhaps indicative only of the effect of normative variables and the need for differential personnel strategies in different countries.

Impact of Culture on Consumption

Product Meaning

The culture in which a person lives affects his consumption patterns and also affects his perception of specific products and the meanings which he attaches to them. Although a baseball bat is perceived as an instrument of play in U.S. society, it could just as easily be perceived as a weapon in another culture. Culture, according to Irving White (1959), "places the product in a social context and imbues it with meanings that set the broadest limitations on how it is experienced."

Cultural stereotypes and folklore can be deceiving. Chinese visitors to this country are surprised to learn that we attribute chop suey to the Chinese, just as some Italians express surprise that we consider pizza to be an Italian dish. Dichter (1962) pointed out that only twenty percent of French housewives have discovered perfumed soap, which we refer to as a French type of soap.

The impact of distributive dimension variables (demographics) on product acceptance is noted by J. Douglas McConnell, (1971). He cites the case of a company that wished to introduce margarine to the Spanish market as a substitute for butter. The venture was doomed to failure since butter had a low rate of use in Spain; cooking oil was cheaply obtainable and widely used. A further factor was that few Spaniards owned refrigerators. The economics were simply against margarine's acceptance.

The social meanings attached to shopping in various countries may also affect the types of products purchased. For example, grocery shopping in Britain remains a daily social activity. Perhaps this is an important reason for the acceptance there of small rather than large refrigerators (Goldstucker, 1968). In France, the housewife's daily shopping routine is apparently a reinforcement of group membership. The French housewife is very conscious of how to dress while shopping (Dunn, 1962). An alternative explanation for daily shopping trips, especially in less developed countries is the inability of consumers to finance home inventories, and the lack of funds for large home refrigerators. There are still many countries of the world where *most* of the population buy on a hand-to-mouth basis.

The social meanings attached to a product within a culture are critical points in assessing how likely a product is to be accepted. In Venezuela, for example, it is considered demeaning for higher status people to engage in any form of manual labor (Boyd et al., 1958). Hired laborers are, therefore, common, and the introduction of do-it-yourself products and even appliances meets fairly severe social resistance.

The diversity of world cultures requires close analysis for successful product marketing. Some products may simply not gain much acceptance (margarine in Spain), others may have to possess distinguishable features from the U.S. market (small instead of large refrigerators in Britain), and some products may be marketed multinationally in essentially one form (Coca Cola).

Promotion Within a Culture

It is a cardinal rule of marketing that it is always easier to appeal to existing cultural wants, needs, and expectations than to try to change the culture or to create new needs. Product promotion must be sensitive to the core values of the country and the resulting consumption differences.

Examples of cultural quirks in consumption from country to country are common, and useful for portraying the flavor of multinational marketing problems. McConnell (1971) cites the receptivity of Americans to advertisements for "gleaming white teeth" but notes that this appeal might have negative impact in Southeast Asia where betel chewing is common, and black teeth are admired. Color perceptions frequently vary. A white feather connotes cowardice in England, whereas yellow serves the same purpose in the United States. White represents purity in Western civilization but connotes mourning in much of Asia. McConnell cites a further example of the beer producer who had to add a third white elephant to his label since two were perceived in Africa as unlucky.

The promotion *mix* used should be based on the characteristics of the society. Because of the low literacy levels in Nigeria, print media are scarce, and because of the low levels of income, television is an unimportant medium. Thus, radio, because of its widespread diffusion, and motion picture advertising are major advertising media. Furthermore, personal selling takes on major importance, because Nigerians "enjoy and appreciate the efforts of aggressive salesmen in hotly competitive situations" (Baker, 1965, p. 47).

National advertising in India, according to Westfall and Boyd (1960), is "impossible" because of some fifty-one spoken dialects and the lack of media reaching any large market segment. Advertising to create demand is therefore limited, and personal selling is important. In Yugoslavia, mass media are important, but so too are the trade fairs held throughout the country for individual product categories (Skobe, 1965). In Italy, movie theater advertising predominates, since the government severely limits the amount of advertising on television and sets rigid standards for "taste" (Carson, 1966).

A fascinating commentary on the cultural differences in personal selling is provided by Edward Hall in a selection in this chapter. He examines the cultural differences found in varying concepts of time, space, things, friendship, and agreements. The language of time, for example, is by no means universal. The U.S. businessman expects to be kept waiting no more than a few minutes, and, if he is, he becomes irritated. In Latin America, however, to wait for an hour or more may be typical. Time simply does not have the same meaning in all cultures, and the U.S. businessman must respond accordingly.

Pricing Behavior

Pricing is often bound to a society's economic philosophy and the degree of price control which it exerts on business firms. In Japan, for example, the government is closely involved in pricing, perhaps because of the traditional extended family concept, which is still a cultural mandate. (Japanese business firms, in turn, seem to bear extended responsibility for the "family" of people they employ, and company-subsidized housing, meals, education, and recreation are common.)

The role of price as a means of competition in many countries is not always as important as in the United States. Resale price maintenance, for example, effectively limits the discounting of national brands in Britain. Spain, among many other countries, fixes the prices of raw materials. The pricing of consumer items in Spain also seems fairly rigid. Price competition in Venezuela is uncommon, since it is believed that there is only so much business and low prices will simply ruin the market.

The one-price system is not everywhere as common as in the United States. In fact, bargaining is often an institutionalized and important part of a society's way of life. Fayerweather (1965) illustrates this with reference to a Peruvian woman and her bushel of corn.

> When a visitor offered to buy the whole bushel early in the morning for a relatively high price, she refused. Although she had to earn a living, the satisfaction of spending a day in the market haggling with an assortment of buyers over the purchase of small fractions of her bushel was equally, if not more, important to her (p. 22).

Distribution Structure

An interesting issue is the extent to which retailing serves social needs within a culture; for example, the acceptance of supermarkets in many countries has been slower than expected. In Spain, supermarkets initially tried to appeal to higher income groups, but the women of this income level did not hold jobs outside of the home and welcomed their daily shopping as an opportunity to meet friends (Guerin, 1964). In Britain, buying is still viewed as a social relationship between customers and storekeepers, and therefore British supermarkets, which account for twenty percent of food purchases, tend to be small and cued to individual attention (Goldstucker, 1968). In Latin America, supermarkets are catching on at middle-class levels where customers may actually pay more but are assured of quality (Fayerweather, 1965). There may also be a certain status which goes with shopping at modern supermarkets in Latin America.

Distribution structures tend toward larger scale operations concurrent with economic growth, but this is not always the case. France, for example, has a highly fragmented retail structure. There are separate shops for fish, dairy products, pastries, meat, coffee, and many other food products. This would seem to be influenced by traditional French values. The desire to keep control of the store within the family and to maintain status within the community may be more important than showing much profitability. The storekeeper may also be an important communication channel for the community. Whether these factors will change is difficult to predict, but small French merchants have already shown considerable resilience in resisting the attempts of some entrepreneurs to establish the supermarket concept in France.

Subcultures

Within a complex and heterogeneous culture, such as that of the United States, *subcultures* exist. Their existence is generally predicated upon such recognizable and distinguishable features as language, religion, and race, which supposedly lead to unique and homogeneous patterns of behavior.

The concept of subculture is, however, rather loose, and it is difficult to imagine homogeneous response traits on the part of, for example, Mexican-Americans or black Americans. Furthermore, individuals generally maintain membership in several subcultures, with varying levels of attachment and participation. Thus, while it has been common to discuss the Jewish subculture, the black subculture, or the subculture of poverty, there is some question of whether these are subcultures in any real sense, or merely identifiable groupings adhering to the dominant norms of the mass U.S. culture.

In any strict sense, a subculture would have to possess a distinct social heritage apart from the dominant culture and transmit this heritage inter-generationally, based on socialization of the child. Oscar Lewis (1966), in his analysis of poverty, contends that poverty is a self-sustaining subculture, because a life style and accompanying norms are passed on to the child, who is then ill-equipped to break out of the subculture. In Lewis' words, the culture of poverty is

> a subculture of Western society with its own structure and rationale, a way of life handed down from generation to generation along family lines . . . a culture in the traditional anthropological sense that it provides human beings with a design for living, with a ready-made set of solutions for human problems (p. 19).

Lewis' work has been embraced in some quarters and criticized in others. Lewis himself was not so willing to posit that a subculture of poverty exists in the United States (most of his work was done in Puerto Rico and Cuba), because the U.S. has an advanced technology, high literacy rates, pervasive mass media, and high aspiration levels. Some other researchers, such as Rossi and Blum (1967), have directly disputed the idea of a poverty subculture:

> There is little firm evidence for the existence of a "culture of poverty" which marks off the very poor as distinctively different from SES [socioeconomic status] levels immediately above them. The poor appear to be quantitatively rather than qualitatively different.

These researchers and others such as Valentine (1968) see the behavior of the poor as an adaptation to existing conditions, and not as a result of the transmission of a set of values and a poverty heritage. This position is also taken by Elliot Liebow (1967) in his analysis of street-corner life among lower-class black males. His overall conclusion:

> The street-corner man does not appear as a carrier of an independent cultural tradition. His behavior appears not so much as a way of realizing the distinctive goals and values of his own subculture, or of conforming to its models, but rather as his way of trying to achieve many of the goals and values of the larger society, of failing to do this, and of concealing his failure from others and from himself as best he can (p. 222).

The richness of the subculture notion may thus be lost if we rigorously pursue a formal definition of subcultures based on the transmission of a shared social heritage. For our purposes it will be more valuable if a more open definition is used.

Subcultures: Another View

Gordon (1947) views a subculture as

> a subdivision of a national culture, composed of a combination of factorable social situations such as class status, ethnic background, regional and rural or urban residence, and religious affiliation, but *forming in their combination a functioning unity which has an integrated impact on the participating individual* (p. 41).

This relaxed definition, which is more in line with the popular use of the term, does not necessarily imply a consistent socialization experience from generation to generation. It allows us to speak of a subculture of poverty or a black subculture to the extent that the component elements of that aggregate lead to some consistency of individual behavior. Thus, whether there is a black heritage distinct and separate from the dominant U.S. heritage is debatable, but there does seem to be a black subculture to the extent that a combination of factors exists that leads to some consistent impact on the individual in it—lower income per capita than whites, higher inner-city concentration, etc. Thus, blacks may be a subculture not because of race *as such*, but because of associated factors tied to race.

Black Subculture

Although we may speak of a black subculture, it is extremely difficult to isolate *racial behavior*. Research with U.S. blacks as an ethnic group is complicated by the fact that the U.S. black has no real ties with a "mother culture," as is the case for Italian-Americans, Irish-Americans, or Jews. But even Gans' (1962) study of Italian-Americans in Boston concluded that social class differences were more powerful than ethnic differences in explaining life style. Attempts to generate among U.S. blacks an identification with the African culture have not been very successful, since to the U.S. black the African experience is almost as foreign as it is to his white counterpart.

Despite these difficulties, it has seemed productive to generate research on the Negro market, even though much of it is superficial, and assumes that there is *one* such market, when in fact it is highly segmented along a number of dimensions. What follows is an attempt to review some of the more important findings relevant to black consumption behavior.

Black-White Consumption Differences

A favorite pastime of researchers has been to look for consumption differences between blacks and whites. There are some obvious differences—blacks purchase "Afro combs" but not much suntan lotion. Macroanalysis by Alexis (1962), based on secondary data, reveals that:

- Blacks save more than whites of comparable income levels.
- Blacks spend more for clothing and nonautomobile transportation than whites of comparable income levels but less for food, housing, medical care, and automobile transportation.
- There is no consistent racial difference in expenditures for either recreation or home furnishings at comparable income levels.

It is important to note that these findings are controlled for income level. If income is not held constant, blacks are found to spend, for example, a greater proportion of their income on food, clothing, and other necessities, since the black income profile is downwardly biased.

Some studies have sought to find differences in brand preferences between blacks and whites. Larson (1968), in a Chicago study, found more blacks to own Chevrolets and more whites to own Buicks and Pontiacs; he did not control for income. Blacks were more likely to shop at A & P and whites at Jewel; he did not control for the proportion of each chain's stores in inner-city areas. Larson also found some significant differences in level of consumption for certain product categories. Whites, for example, consume more diet soft drinks. Can we attribute this to race?

Rather than attempt to summarize the host of findings on real or imagined consumption differences between blacks and whites, we include Table 2), from a fairly rigorous study by Stafford et al. (1968), which shows many of the differences found. These authors were able to explain almost all of the variances in consumption in terms of income and other sociodemographic variables. The two notable exceptions were butter and Scotch whiskey, and the authors conclude: "No economically 'rational' explanation exists why Negroes at every income level consume more of these products than do whites. The two most likely reasons . . . are compensatory consumption and status or conspicuous consumption."

Perhaps three main conclusions are in order regarding black-white consumption patterns:

TABLE 2. Percentage of Blacks and Whites Recently Purchasing or Owning Various Household Products

Products	Annual Family Income							
	Less than $3000		$3000–5999		$6000–7999		$8000 or More	
	Whites	Blacks	Whites	Blacks	Whites	Blacks	Whites	Blacks
Food products[a]								
Butter	6.6	23.3	8.0	31.2	7.7	26.9	14.1	45.4
Margarine	58.3	61.6	63.6	72.7	69.8	57.7	69.5	81.8
Frozen vegetables[b]	30.5	31.4	28.0	50.6	39.6	34.6	47.1	54.6
Canned vegetables[c]	20.5	35.6	35.6	44.5	37.9	40.4	40.6	43.2
Dietary soft drinks	7.3	17.4	11.9	23.4	20.8	23.1	25.5	13.6
Nondietary soft drinks	26.5	60.5	55.5	71.4	62.4	23.1	67.1	45.4
Liquor								
All respondents[d]	15.2	26.7	29.7	39.0	39.3	46.2	56.5	54.6
Scotch[e]	3.3	9.3	4.2	22.1	7.7	34.6	19.7	27.3
Bourbon[e]	7.3	15.1	20.3	23.4	29.2	7.7	40.9	40.9
Personal hygiene products[f]								
Shampoo	42.4	41.9	59.3	52.0	74.5	65.4	72.6	50.0
Deodorant	39.7	65.1	56.8	79.2	74.5	92.3	76.6	81.8
Toothpaste	48.3	76.7	75.0	89.6	86.9	88.5	89.1	86.4
Mouthwash	43.7	61.6	58.5	75.3	56.7	88.5	63.5	86.4
Disinfectants	52.3	69.8	56.4	80.5	70.1	61.5	68.6	86.4
Home appliances[g]								
Auto. washing machine	47.4	19.8	57.6	29.9	78.6	50.0	85.5	72.7
Auto. clothes dryer	12.6	5.8	16.5	7.8	34.2	15.4	54.9	27.3
Auto. dishwasher	2.0	—	5.5	—	14.1	3.8	33.8	—
B&W television	87.4	91.8	89.5	98.7	83.7[h]	97.9[h]	—	—
Color television	3.3	0.6	5.7	1.9	24.3[h]	6.2[h]	—	—
Home ownership								
Own home	68.3	39.5	49.4	57.1	70.8	73.0	81.5	77.3

[a] Purchased within the past seven days.
[b] Includes all types of frozen vegetables.
[c] Includes canned corn, peas, green beans, and tomatoes.
[d] Percentage of total respondents purchasing some alcoholic beverages within past 12 months.
[e] Percentage of Scotch and Bourbon purchases among total respondents.
[f] Purchased within past 30 days.
[g] Percentage "having" in the home.
[h] Last two income classes were combined because of small number of respondents.
Source: Stafford et al. (1968).

1. There are, apparently, some "real" racial differences in consumption.
2. Most implied black-white consumption differences are a function of income or some other explanatory variable, rather than race. For example, even the generalization that blacks at any given income level save more money than whites has been questioned, since there are so many other uncontrolled variables—income expectation, age, dependents, education, location, and financial reserves. "The concept of race ... in the assessment of so-called Negro-White savings and consumption patterns, has no more validity than left-handedness, eye pigmentation, or height" (Sawyer, 1962, p. 220).
3. The similarity of black-white consumption patterns far outweighs the differences, especially when income is controlled.

However, although we are minimizing the predictive value of race itself in consumer behavior, we are not denying the existence of a Negro market, whose composite pattern of consumption may be largely a function of other variables associated with race in U.S. society in the 1970s. Thus, income, household size, family structure, urban location, and other such variables have their impact on black consumption modes.

Communicating to the Black Subculture

An important concern in marketing management circles is how to reach the black subculture. Advertising in mass media has in the past depicted few blacks, and when it did so, they were generally in inferior occupational roles. Even now, when blacks appear in advertising, they are seldom shown in equal roles *interacting* with whites. Do annual advertising expenditures of $20 million, depicting a particular form of race relations, retard social change and the integration of blacks in U.S. society? This question poses a social responsibility which must be faced by the marketing community.

A historical analysis of the roles of blacks in U.S. advertising is provided by W. Kassarjian in a selection in this chapter. The occupational roles portrayed by blacks have improved, but few ads treat blacks and whites as equals.

Responses of blacks and whites to particular communication stimuli, including package design and advertising content, have recently been researched. Krugman (1966), for example, studied black-white responses to various designs of cans for malt liquor, using physiological measures (pupil dilation) and conventional rating procedures. He found minimal differences, and the only real differentiating feature seemed to be that whites associated colorfulness with inexpensiveness.

Racial response to advertising format is a subtle and complex topic, and there is not a definitive and well-documented set of results from research in this area. One of the best articles on this topic (Barban, 1969) suggests that whites will accept integrated advertising: "Among the groups of white subjects, the ads with Negro and white models were generally preferred as much or more than the treatments with only white models; least preference was shown for the ads containing only Negro models" (p. 495). Blacks, on the other hand, "tended to evaluate both the integrated ads and the Negro-model ads rather similarly and showed slightly less relative preference for the white-model treatments"

(p. 495). These findings may be indicative of reality, but they must be considered as tenuous until more research is conducted.

Consumption Motivations: Desire for Assimilation

The dominant view in the 1960s of black consumption motivations was that blacks wanted to be like whites, and bought the symbols of the white middle-class way of life. In an early but important article, Bullock (1961) probed consumer motivations in black and white. One of his central theses was the black "search for belongingness" and its impact on consumption.

According to Bullock, the desire to gain admittance to the white kingdom resulted in the belief among blacks that goods and services from white merchants were better and more reliable than goods offered by blacks. He further stated that blacks (as of 1961) "attempt to surround themselves with visible symbols of whiteness," thinking that this will make them "less like themselves—more like white people and the general community norm" (p. 96). This was manifested by ready willingness to buy a house vacated by a white, and the adoption by upper income blacks of "country club ways without a country club."

In research conducted during the 1960s and summarized in a selection in this chapter, Bauer and Cunningham observe behavior similar to Bullock's "search for belongingness." They see blacks "fighting to attain full membership in American society," but constrained by skin color and low levels of assimilation. This leads Bauer and Cunningham to pose the "dilemma of the Negro market":

> Simply expressed, the basic dilemma of the Negro is whether to strive against odds to attain middle-class values (and the benefits which accrue with them), or to forfeit them and give priority to finding immediate gratifications within the boundaries of his own present situation.

This dilemma, as Sturdivant (1973) points out, is stated in a somewhat misleading fashion. It would be more accurate to state that the basic dilemma is whether to strive against odds to attain "material symbols" of middle-class values.

The underlying dimensions of black consumer behavior are portrayed in an article by Bauer et al. (1965). Blacks, for example, are found to have a high degree of involvement with material goods of high symbolic value. Black shoppers are found to manifest great anxiety in shopping situations, according to these authors, because of a desire to avoid mistakes: "Shopping can be an especially serious business for a social group that is moving up in society and very concerned with whether their funds are sufficient for buying the goods to which they aspire" (p. 4).

According to Bauer and his colleagues, fear of making mistakes, especially in purchasing products of high symbolic value, tends to make the black consumer more brand conscious and more deeply involved in brand selection. This fear and involvement is found only for those products perceived to represent white middle-class values. Bauer et al. conclude that, compared to whites, blacks show greater concern, anxiety, and ambivalence over exchanging scarce resources for material goods which are tangible evidence of social achievement.

A final example of the 1960s research tradition is that of Dalrymple, Robertson, and Yoshino (1971). These authors conducted research across subcultures—black, Japanese-American, and white—at comparable social class levels. Their overall explanatory variable was "desired assimilation," and it was felt that higher levels of desired assimilation would be manifested by strong interest in brand names, new products, credit to obtain these items, and prestige retail outlets. These expectations were generally confirmed.

Consumption Motivations: A Reconsideration

The argument for a "dilemma in the Negro market" may not be well supported. One might well argue that it is a false dilemma. The great U.S. American middle-class way of life is promised daily in mass media, and the act of reaching out for it need not be a desire for assimilation with whites but may only represent grabbing for what is there. Feldman and Star (1968), for example, in addressing themselves to Bauer's dilemma, find little evidence for it, and are forced to the same conclusion as many other authors—similarities between black and white shoppers outweigh the differences. Similarly, King and De Manche (1969) are critical of the Bauer and Bullock hypotheses, and found, for example, that blacks buy more private brands than whites, which is hardly an indication of anxiety and insecurity.

The desire for assimilation among blacks should not be dismissed, but apparently the matter is not that simple, and "striving," "search for belonging-ness," and "desired assimilation" are inadequate conceptions to account for the range of black consumption motivations. These variables, posited in the 1960s, are based on the notion that blacks are actively concerned with *moving toward* white middle-class society. Yet, sufficient evidence is available to suggest that a reasonable proportion of black Americans are also interested in *moving away from* white middle-class society and establishing a more legitimate black subculture with its own integrity and uniqueness.

Research and theoretical development in the 1970s must take a new tack and answer a different set of questions regarding consumption motivations in the black subculture. The explanatory model will have to take into account not only desired assimilation, but also desired alienation. The model must be enriched in order to begin to explain the richness of human response patterns in the marketplace.

References

Alexis, M. "Some Negro-White Differences in Consumption." *Amer. J. of Economics and Sociology*, Vol. 21 (Jan. 1962), 11–28.

Baker, R. "Marketing in Nigeria." *J. of Marketing*, Vol. 29 (July 1965), 40–48.

Barban, A. M. "The Dilemma of Integrated Advertising." *J. of Business*, Vol. 42 (Oct. 1969), 477–496.

Bauer, R. A., S. M. Cunningham, and L. H. Wortzel. "The Marketing Dilemma of Negroes." *J. of Marketing*, Vol. 29 (July 1965), 1–6.

Boyd, H. W., Jr., R. M. Clewett, and R. L. Westfall. "The Marketing Structure of Venezuela." *J. of Marketing*, Vol. 22 (April 1958), 391–397.

Bullock, H. A. "Consumer Motivations in Black and White." Part I, *Harvard Business Review*, Vol. 39 (May–June 1961), 89–104. Part II, *Harvard Business Review*, Vol. 39 (July–Aug. 1961), 110–124.

Carson, D. "Marketing in Italy Today." *J. of Marketing*, Vol. 30 (Jan. 1966), 10–16.

Dalrymple, D. J., T. S. Robertson, and M. Y. Yoshino. "Consumption Behavior Across Ethnic Categories." *California Management Review*, Vol. 14 (1971), No. 1, 65–70.

Davis, Stanley M. "U.S. versus Latin America: Business and Culture." *Harvard Business Review*, Vol. 47 (Nov.–Dec. 1969), 88–98.

Dichter, E. "The World Customer." *Howard Business Review*, Vol. 40 (July–Aug. 1962), 113–122.

Douglas, S. P. "Patterns and Parallels of Marketing Structures in Several Countries." *MSU Business Topics*, Vol. 19 (Spring 1971), 38–48.

Dunn, S. W. "French Retailing and the Common Market." *J. of Marketing*, Vol. 29 (Jan. 1962), 19–22.

Fayerweather, J. *International Marketing*. Prentice-Hall, 1965.

Feldman, L. P., and A. D. Star. "Racial Factors in Shopping Behavior." *Proc. AMA*, eds. K. Cox and B. M. Enis, (June 1968), 216–226.

Franklin, B. *The Complete Works of the Late Dr. Benjamin Franklin.* J. Johnson and Company, 1806.

Gans, H. J. *The Urban Villagers.* The Free Press, 1962.

Goldstucker, J. L. "The Influence of Culture on Channels of Distribution." *Proc. AMA*, ed. R. L. King, (1968), 468–473.

Gordon, M. M. "The Concept of the Sub-Culture and Its Application." *Social Forces*, Vol. 26 (Oct. 1947), 40–42.

Guerin, J. R. "Limitations of Supermarkets in Spain." *J. of Marketing*, Vol. 28 (Oct. 1964), 22–26.

King, R. L., and E. R. De Manche. "Comparative Acceptance of Selected Private-Branded Food Products by Low-Income Negro and White Families." *Proc. AMA*, ed. P. R. McDonald, (Aug. 1969), 63–69.

Krugman, H. E. "White and Negro Responses to Package Designs." *J. of Marketing Research*, Vol. 3 (May 1966), 199–200.

Larson, C. M. "Racial Brand Usage and Media Exposure Differentials." *Proc. AMA*, eds. K. Cox and B. M. Enis, (June 1968), 208–215.

Lewis, O. "The Culture of Poverty." *Scientific American*, Vol. 215 (1966), 19–25.

Liander, B. (ed.), *Comparative Analysis for International Marketing.* Allyn and Bacon, 1967.

Liebow, E. *Tally's Corner: A Study of Negro Streetcorner Men.* Little, Brown, 1967.

Linton, R. "One Hundred Per Cent American." *The American Mercury*, Vol. 40 (April 1937),

McConnell, J. D. "The Economics of Behavioral Factors on the Multi-National Corporation." *Proc. AMA,* ed. F. C. Allvine (1971), 262–266.

Redfield, R. *Peasant Society and Culture.* Univ. of Chicago Press, 1956.

Rossi, P. H., and Z. D. Blum. "Social Stratification and Poverty," a paper presented at the Annual Meeting of the Sociological Research Association in San Francisco, 1967.

Rostow, W. W. *The Stages of Economic Growth.* Cambridge Univ. Press, 1962.

Sawyer, B. E. "An Examination of Race as a Factor in Negro-White Consumption Patterns." *Review of Economics and Statistics*, Vol. 44 (May 1962), 217–220.

Sirota, D., and J. M. Greenwood. "Understanding Your Overseas Work Force." *Howard Business Review*, Vol. 49 (Jan.–Feb. 1971), 53–60.

Skobe, M. "Marketing and Advertising in Yugoslavia." *Proc. AMA*, ed. P. D. Bennett, (1965), 96–101.

Stafford, J. E., K. K. Cox, and J. B. Higginbotham. "Some Consumption Pattern Differences Between Urban Whites and Negroes." *Social Science Quarterly*, Vol. 49 (Dec. 1968), 619–630.

Sturdivant, F. D. "Subculture Theory: Poverty, Minorities and Marketing." *Consumer Behavior: Theoretical Foundations*, eds. S. Ward and T. S. Robertson. Prentice-Hall, 1973.

Tylor, E. B. *Primitive Culture.* John Murray, 1891.

Valentine, C. A. *Culture and Poverty.* Univ. of Chicago Press, 1968.

Weigand, R. E. "Department Stores in Japan." *J. of Retailing*, Vol. 39 (Fall 1963), 31–35, 52.

Westfall, R. L., and H. W. Boyd, Jr. "Marketing in India." *J. of Marketing*, Vol. 25 (Oct. 1960), 11–17.

White, I. S. "The Functions of Advertising in Our Culture." *J. of Marketing*, Vol. 24 (July 1959), 8–14.

6.1 The Concept of Culture
RALPH LINTON

The term *culture*, as it is employed in scientific studies, carries none of the overtones of evaluation which attach to it in popular usage. It refers to the total way of life of any society, not simply to those parts of this way which the society regards as higher or more desirable. Thus culture, when applied to our own way of life, has nothing to do with playing the piano or reading Browning. For the social scientist such activities are simply elements within the totality of our culture. This totality also includes such mundane activities as washing dishes or driving an automobile, and for the purposes of cultural studies these stand quite on a par with "the finer things of life." It follows that for the social scientist there are no uncultured societies or even individuals. Every society has a culture, no matter how simple this culture may be, and every human being is cultured, in the sense of participating in some culture or other.

Actually, the work of the social scientist must begin with the investigation of *cultures*, the ways of life which are characteristic of particular societies. *Culture*, as he uses the term, represents a generalization based upon the observation and comparison of a series of *cultures*. It bears much the same relation to these individual cultures that "the spider monkey" of a naturalist's description bears to the innumerable individual spider monkeys who together constitute the species. When the anthropologist says that culture has such and such characteristics, what he really means is that all cultures have these characteristics in common. It is the cultures, each linked to a particular society, which are the organized, functional entities, and it is against the background of a specific culture, not of culture in general, that the individual must be studied....

On the basis of common usage and understanding and with regard to the special interests of students of personality, I will venture the following definition: "A culture is the configuration of learned behavior and results of behavior whose component elements are shared and transmitted by the members of a particular society." Like all definitions, this requires some amplification and explanation. The term *configuration* implies that the various behaviors and results of behavior which compose a culture are organized into a patterned whole. This feature of culture involves a number of problems which need not be dealt with here. *Learned behavior* limits the activities which are to be classed as part of any given culture configuration to those whose forms have been modified by the learning process. This limitation has the sanction of long usage. Neither instinctive behavior nor the basic needs or tensions which provide the ultimate motivations for behavior in the individual have ever been regarded as parts of culture in spite of their obvious influence upon culture. The elimination of these phenomena from the culture concept still leaves it an exceedingly wide scope. Man appears to have very few unconditioned reflexes aside from those connected with his physiological processes. Although his behavior is motivated by his needs, the forms which it assumes are normally conditioned by experience. Thus although eating is a response to the individual's need for nourishment, the way in which he eats depends upon how he has learned to eat. The term *behavior* in the phrase under discussion is to be taken in the broadest sense to include all the activities of the individual, whether overt or covert, physical or psychological. Thus for the purposes of this definition, learning, thinking, and so on are to be considered quite as much forms of behavior as are the coördinated muscular movements involved in technological processes.

The term *results of behavior* refers to phenomena of two quite different orders, psychological and material. The former include those results of behavior which are represented in the individual by psychological states. Thus attitudes, value systems and knowledge would all be included under this head. To class these phenomena as results of behavior may appear a tour de force, but they are unquestionably established in the individual as a result of his interaction with his environment and consequent learning. At the same time, they cannot be classed as learned *behavior*, since they lack the dynamic qualities implied by this term. Like the realities of the external environment, they exercise a directive influence on the development of behavior patterns. Thus when confronted by a new situation the individual will react to it not only in terms of its objective reality but also in terms of the attitudes, values and knowledge which he has acquired as a result of his past experience. The native who meets a white man for the first time may worship him as a god, treat him as an honored guest or attack him on sight, his line of action depending entirely on factors of the sort under discussion.

The inclusion of material results of behavior in the phenomena covered by the culture concept may meet with objections from certain sociologists, but it is sanctioned by anthropological usage as old as the term *culture* itself. The objects habitually made and used by the members of any society have always been known collectively as its "material culture" and regarded as an integral part of the culture configuration. The real problem in this case is whether the objects themselves are to be regarded as a part of culture or whether the content of the culture configuration should be limited to the psychological elements to which the objects correspond. In other words, shall we include the axe or simply the ideas shared by the members of a society as to how an axe should look and what its qualities should be? . . .

The phrase *shared and transmitted* limits the content of culture configurations still further. In the present case *shared* must be taken to mean that a particular pattern of behavior, attitude or piece of knowledge is common to two or more of a society's members. It carries no implications of cooperative activity or joint ownership. Any item of behavior, and so on, which is peculiar to a single individual in a society is not to be considered as a part of the society's culture. However, such individual peculiarities may, in due course of time, become a part of the culture. Actually, all cultural innovations originate either with some one person or with a very small group of persons. Thus a new technique for weaving baskets would not be classed as a part of culture as long as it was known only to one person. It would be classed as a part of culture as soon as it came to be shared by other individuals. . . .

One further qualification with respect to the term *shared* is necessary. It must not be taken to imply that elements which are to be regarded as part of a culture configuration have to be shared by all members of a society either through time or at any particular point in time. Actually, it would be impossible to find any element of culture which had been shared by all members of a society throughout that society's entire duration. Cultures change and grow, discarding certain elements and acquiring new ones in the course of their history. As a result of this process, they may experience an almost complete turnover in content and profound changes in pattern if the associated society endures long enough and is subject to enough vicissitudes. Thus there are many places in the world where, on the basis of physical anthropological evidence, the modern population is a direct descendant of the Neolithic one and where the cultural and social continuity has never been interrupted; yet the life of these moderns has few features in common with that of their Neolithic forebears. Even if we take any social-cultural configuration at a particular point in time, we will find that there are no elements of the culture which are shared by all members of the society. Although some of them may be shared by all adults, even these are not shared by small children, while many adult ideas and activities are shared only by the members of certain groupings within the society, as men, women or specialized craftsmen. Such specialties must none the less be regarded as integral parts of the culture configuration. They are adjusted to other elements within the configuration and contribute to the well-being of the society as a whole.

The term *transmitted* requires little discussion. The sharing of elements of behavior, and so on, is dependent upon their transmission from one individual to another through instruction or imitation. These processes operate through time, and most of the elements which compose culture configurations are transmitted from generation to generation and endure far beyond the life span of any one member of the society. From the point of view of the individual, the culture of the society in which he is reared constitutes his social, as distinct from his biological, heredity. It provides him with a series of adaptations to the environment in which he must live and function. These adaptations, embodied in patterns of behavior, have been developed by earlier members of his society as a result of their experiences and are passed on to him by way of his learning processes. They save him from the necessity of going through many frequently painful experiences in order to make successful adjustments. The transfer of such behavioral adaptations parallels in many respects the transfer of the structural and physiological adaptations developed by the individual's ancestors as a result of mutation and selection. Thus in a West African Negro society the cultural techniques for getting food in the jungle, developed by past generations, will be transmitted to the individual through learning. A high degree of immunity to malaria, also developed by past generations, will be transmitted to him by heredity. Both will be necessary for survival under the local conditions.

It can be seen from the foregoing discussion of culture that the concept includes phenomena of at least three different orders: material, that is, products of industry; kinetic, that is, overt behavior (since this necessarily involves movement); and psychological, that is, the knowledge, attitudes and values shared by the members of a society. . . .

6.2 The Silent Language in Overseas Business
EDWARD T. HALL

With few exceptions, Americans are relative newcomers on the international business scene. Today, as in Mark Twain's time, we are all too often "innocents abroad," in an era when naiveté and blundering in foreign business dealings may have serious political repercussions.

When the American executive travels abroad to do business, he is frequently shocked to discover to what extent the many variables of foreign behavior and custom complicate his efforts. Although the American has recognized, certainly, that even the man next door has many minor traits which make him somewhat peculiar, for some reason he has failed to appreciate how different foreign businessmen and their practices will seem to him.

He should understand that the various peoples around the world have worked out and integrated into their subconscious literally thousands of behavior patterns that they take for granted in each other. (For details, see E. T. Hall. *The Silent Language.* Doubleday, 1959.) Then, when the stranger enters, and behaves differently from the local norm, he often quite unintentionally insults, annoys, or amuses the native with whom he is attempting to do business.

In the United States, a corporation executive knows what is meant when a client lets a month go by before replying to a business proposal. On the other hand, he senses an eagerness to do business if he is immediately ushered into the client's office. In both instances, he is reacting to subtle cues in the timing of interaction, cues which he depends on to chart his course of action.

Abroad, however, all this changes. The American executive learns that the Latin Americans are casual about time and that if he waits an hour in the outer office before seeing the Deputy Minister of Finance, it does not necessarily mean he is not getting anywhere. There people are so important that nobody can bear to tear himself away; because of the resultant interruptions and conversational detours, everybody is constantly getting behind. What the American does not know is the point at which the waiting becomes significant.

In another instance, after traveling 7000 miles, an American walks into the office of a highly recommended Arab businessman on whom he will have to depend completely. What he sees does not breed confidence. The office is reached by walking through a suspicious-looking coffeehouse in an old, dilapidated building situated in a crowded non-European section of town. The elevator, rising from dark, smelly corridors, is rickety and equally foul. When he gets to the office itself, he is shocked to find it small, crowded, and confused. Papers are stacked all over the desk and table tops—even scattered on the floor in irregular piles.

The Arab merchant he has come to see had met him at the airport the night before and sent his driver to the hotel this morning to pick him up. But now, after the American's rush, the Arab is tied up with something else. Even when they finally start talking business, there are constant interruptions. If the American is at all sensitive to his environment, everything around him signals, "What am I getting into?"

Before leaving home he was told that things would be different, but how different? The hotel is modern enough. The shops in the new part of town have many more American and European trade goods than he had anticipated. His first impression was that doing business in the Middle East would not present any new problems. Now he is beginning to have doubts. One minute everything looks familiar and he is on firm ground; the next, familiar landmarks are gone. His greatest problem is that so much assails his senses all at once that he does not know where to start looking for something that will tell him where he stands. He needs a frame of reference—a way of sorting out what is significant and relevant.

That is why it is so important for American businessmen to have a real understanding of the various social, cultural, and economic differences they will face when they attempt to do business in foreign countries. To help give some frame of reference, this article will map out a few areas of human activity that have largely been unstudied.

The topics I will discuss are certainly not presented as the last word on the subject, but they have proved to be highly reliable points at which to begin to gain an understanding of foreign cultures. While additional research will undoubtedly turn up other items just as relevant, at present I think the businessman can do well to begin by appreciating cultural differences in matters concerning the language of time, of space, of material possessions, of friendship patterns, and of agreements.

Language of Time

Everywhere in the world people use time to communicate with each other. There are different languages of time just as there are different spoken languages. The unspoken languages are informal; yet the rules governing their interpretation are surprisingly *ironbound.*

In the United States, a delay in answering a communication can result from a large volume of business causing the request to be postponed until the backlog is cleared away, from poor organization, or possibly from technical complexity requiring deep analysis. But if the person awaiting the answer or decision rules out these reasons, then the delay means to him that the matter has low priority on the part of the other person—lack of interest. On the other hand, a similar delay in a foreign country may mean something altogether different.

In Ethiopia, the time required for a decision is directly proportional to its importance. This is so much the case that low-level bureaucrats there have a way of trying to elevate the prestige of their work by taking a long time to make up their minds. (Americans in that part of the world are innocently prone to downgrade their work in the local people's eyes by trying to speed things up.)

In the Arab East, time does not generally include schedules as Americans know and use them. The time required to get something accomplished depends on the relationship. More important people get fast service from less important people, and conversely. Close relatives take absolute priority; non-relatives are kept waiting.

In the United States, giving a person a deadline is a way of indicating the degree of urgency or relative importance of the work. But in the Middle East, the American runs into a cultural trap the minute he opens his mouth.

"Mr. Aziz will have to make up his mind in a hurry because my board meets next week and I have to have an answer by then," is taken as indicating the American is overly demanding and is exerting undue pressure. "I am going to Damascus tomorrow morning and will have to have my car tonight," is a sure way to get the mechanic to stop work, because to give another person a deadline in this part of the world is to be rude, pushy, and demanding.

An Arab's evasiveness as to when something is going to happen does not mean he does not want to do business; it only means he is avoiding unpleasantness and is side-stepping possible commitments which he takes more seriously than we do.

The Arabs themselves at times find it impossible to communicate even to each other that some processes cannot be hurried, and are controlled by built-in schedules. This is obvious enough to the Westerner but not to the Arab. A highly placed public official in Baghdad precipitated a bitter family dispute because his nephew, a biochemist, could not speed up the complete analysis of the uncle's blood. He accused the nephew of putting other less important people before him and of not caring. Nothing could sway the uncle, who could not grasp the fact that there is such a thing as an *inherent* schedule.

With us the more important an event is, the further ahead we schedule it, which is why we find it insulting to be asked to a party at the last minute. In planning future events with Arabs, it pays to hold the lead time to a week or less because other factors may intervene or take precedence.

Again, time spent waiting in an American's outer office is a sure indicator of what one person thinks of another or how important he feels the other's business to be. This is so much the case that most Americans cannot help getting angry after waiting 30 minutes; one may even feel such a delay is an insult, and will walk out. In Latin America, on the other hand, one learns that it does not mean anything to wait in an outer office. An American businessman with years of experience in Mexico once told me, "You know, I have spent two hours cooling my heels in an executive's outer office. It took me a long time to learn to keep my blood pressure down. Even now, I find it hard to convince myself they are still interested when they keep me waiting."

The Japanese handle time in ways which are almost inexplicable to the Western European and particularly the American. A delay of years with them does not mean that they have lost interest. It only means that they are building up to something. They have learned that Americans are vulnerable to long waits. One of them expressed it, "You Americans have one terrible weakness. If we make you wait long enough, you will agree to anything."

Indians of South Asia have an elastic view of time as compared to our own. Delays do not, therefore, have the same meaning to them. Nor does indefiniteness in pinpointing appointments mean that they are evasive. Two Americans meeting will say, "We should get together sometime," thereby setting a low priority on the meeting. The Indian who says, "Come over and see me, see me anytime," means just that.

Americans make a place at the table which may or may not mean a place made in the heart. But when the Indian makes a place in his time, it is yours to fill in every sense of the word if you realize that by so doing you have crossed a boundary and are now friends with him. The point of all this is that time communicates just as surely as do words and that the vocabulary of time is different around the world. The principle to be remembered is that time has different meanings in each country.

Language of Space

Like time, the language of space is different wherever one goes. The American businessman, familiar with the pattern of American corporate life, has no difficulty in appraising the relative importance of someone else, simply by noting the size of his office in relation to other offices around him.

Our pattern calls for the president or the chairman of the board to have the biggest office. The executive vice president will have the next largest, and so on down the line until you end up in the "bull pen." More important offices are usually located at the corners of buildings and on the upper floors. Executive suites will be on the top floor. The relative rank of vice presidents will be reflected in where they are placed along "Executive Row."

The French, on the other hand, are much more likely to lay out space as a network of connecting points of influence, activity, or interest. The French supervisor will ordinarily be found in the middle of his subordinates where he can control them.

Americans who are crowded will often feel that their status in the organization is suffering. As one would expect in the Arab world, the location of an office and its size constitute a poor index of the importance of the man who occupies it. What we experience as crowded, the Arab will often regard as spacious. The same is true in Spanish cultures. A Latin American official illustrated the Spanish view of this point while showing me around a plant. Opening the door to an 18-by-20-foot office in which 17 clerks and their desks were placed, he said, "See, we have nice spacious offices. Lots of space for everyone."

The American will look at a Japanese room and remark how bare it is. Similarly, the Japanese look at our rooms and comment, "How bare!" Furniture in the American home tends to be placed along the walls (around the edge). Japanese have their charcoal pit where the family gathers in the *middle* of the room. The top floor of Japanese department stores is not reserved for the chief executive—it is the bargain roof!

In the Middle East and Latin America, the businessman is likely to feel left out in time and overcrowded in space. People get too close to him, lay their hands on him, and generally crowd his physical being. In Scandinavia and Germany, he feels more at home, but at the same time the people are a little cold and distant. It is space itself that conveys this feeling.

In the United States, because of our tendency to zone activities, nearness carries rights of familiarity so that the neighbor can borrow material possessions and invade time. This is not true in England. Propinquity entitles you to nothing. American Air Force personnel stationed there complain because they have to make an appointment for their children to play with the neighbor's child next door.

Conversation distance between two people is learned early in life by copying elders. Its controlling patterns operate almost totally unconsciously. In the United States, in contrast to many foreign countries, men avoid excessive touching. Regular business is conducted at distances such as 5 feet to 8 feet; highly personal business, 18 inches to 3 feet—not 2 or 3 inches.

In the United States, it is perfectly possible for an experienced executive to schedule the steps of negotiation in time and space so that most people feel comfortable about what is happening. Business transactions progress in stages from across the desk to beside the desk, to the coffee table, then on to the conference table, the luncheon table, or the golf course, or even into the home—all according to a complex set of hidden rules which we obey instinctively.

Even in the United States, however, an executive may slip when he moves into new and unfamiliar realms, when dealing with a new group, doing business with a new company, or moving to a new place in the industrial hierarchy. In a new country the danger is magnified. For example, in India it is considered improper to discuss business in the home on social occasions. One never invites a business acquaintance to the home for the purpose of furthering business aims. That would be a violation of sacred hospitality rules.

Language of Things

Americans are often contrasted with the rest of the world in terms of material possessions. We are accused of being materialistic, gadget-crazy. And, as a matter of fact, we have developed material things for some very interesting reasons. Lacking a fixed class system and having an extremely mobile population, Americans have become highly sensitive to how others make use of material possessions. We use everything from clothes to houses as a highly evolved and complex means of ascertaining each other's status. Ours is a rapidly shifting system in which both styles and people move up or down.

The Cadillac ad men feel that not only is it natural but quite insightful of them to show a picture of a Cadillac and a well-turned out gentleman in his early fifties opening the door. The caption underneath reads, "You already know a great deal about this man."

Following this same pattern, the head of a big union spends an excess of $100,000 furnishing his office so that the president of United States Steel cannot look down on him. Good materials, large space, and the proper surroundings signify that the people who occupy the premises are solid citizens, that they are dependable and successful.

The French, the English, and the Germans have entirely different ways of using their material possessions. What stands for the height of dependability and respectability with the English would be old-fashioned and backward to us. The Japanese take pride in often inexpensive but tasteful arrangements that are used to produce the proper emotional setting.

Middle East businessmen look for something else—family, connections, friendship. They do not use the furnishings of their office as part of their status system; nor do they expect to impress a client by these means or to fool a banker into lending more money than he should. They like good things, too, but feel that they, as persons, should be known and not judged solely by what the public sees.

One of the most common criticisms of American relations abroad, both commercial and governmental, is that we usually think in terms of material things. "Money talks," says the American, who goes on talking the language of money abroad, in the belief that money talks the *same* language all over the world. A common practice in the United States is to try to buy loyalty with high salaries. In foreign countries, this maneuver almost never works, for money and material possessions stand for something different there than they do in America.

Language of Friendship

The American finds his friends next door and among those with whom he works. It has been noted that we take people up quickly and drop them just as quickly. Occasionally a friendship formed during schooldays will persist, but this is rare. For us there are few well-defined rules governing the obligations of friendship. It is difficult to say at which point our friendship gives way to business opportunism or pressure from above. In this we differ from many other people in the world. As a general rule in foreign countries friendships are not formed as quickly as in the United States but go much deeper, last longer, and involve real obligations.

It is important to stress that in the Middle East and Latin America your "friends" will not let you down. The fact that they personally are feeling the pinch is never an excuse for failing their friends. They are supposed to look out for your interests.

Friends and family around the world represent a sort of social insurance that would be difficult to find in the United States. We do not use our friends to help us out in disaster as much as we do as a means of getting ahead—or, at least, of getting the job done. The United States systems work by means of a series of closely tabulated favors and obligations carefully doled out where they will do the most good. And the least that we expect in exchange for a favor is gratitude.

The opposite is the case in India, where the friend's role is to "sense" a person's need and do something about it. The idea of reciprocity as we know it is unheard of. An American in India will have difficulty if he attempts to follow American friendship patterns. He gains nothing by extending himself in behalf of others, least of all gratitude, because the Indian assumes that what he does for others he does for the good of his own psyche. He will find it impossible to make friends quickly and is unlikely to allow sufficient time for friendships to ripen. He will also note that as he gets to know people better, they may become more critical of him, a fact that he finds hard to take. What he does not know is that one sign of friendship in India is speaking one's mind.

Language of Agreements

While it is important for American businessmen abroad to understand the symbolic meanings of friendship rules, time, space, and material possessions, it is just as important for executives to know the rules for negotiating agreements in various countries. Even if they cannot be expected to know the details of each nation's commercial legal practices, just the awareness of and the expectation of the existence of differences will eliminate much complication.

Actually, no society can exist on a high commercial level without a highly developed working base on which agreements can rest. This base may be one or a combination of three types:

1. Rules that are spelled out technically as law or regulation.
2. Moral practices mutually agreed on and taught to the young as a set of principles.
3. Informal customs to which everyone conforms without being able to state the exact rules.

Some societies favor one, some another. Ours, particularly in the business world, lays heavy emphasis on the first variety. Few Americans will conduct any business nowadays without some written agreement or contract.

Varying from culture to culture will be the circumstances under which such rules apply. Americans consider that negotiations have more or less ceased when the contract is signed. With the Greeks, on the other hand, the contract is seen as a sort of way station on the route to negotiation that will cease only when the work is completed. The contract is nothing more than a charter for serious negotiations. In the Arab world, once a man's word is given in a particular kind of way, it is just as binding, if not more so, than most of our written contracts. The written contract, therefore, violates the Moslem's sensitivities and reflects on his honor. Unfortunately, the situation is now so hopelessly confused that neither system can be counted on to prevail consistently.

Informal patterns and unstated agreements often lead to untold difficulty in the cross-cultural situation. Take the case of the before-and-after patterns where there is a wide discrepancy between the American's expectations and those of the Arab.

In the United States, when you engage a specialist such as a lawyer or a doctor, require any standard service, or even take a taxi, you make several assumptions: (1) the charge will be fair; (2) it will be in proportion to the services rendered; and (3) it will bear a close relationship to the "going rate."

You wait until after the services are performed before asking what the tab will be. If the charge is too high in the light of the above assumptions, you feel you have been cheated. You can complain, or can say nothing, pay up, and take your business elsewhere the next time.

As one would expect in the Middle East, basic differences emerge which lead to difficulty if not understood. For instance, when taking a cab in Beirut it is well to know the going rate as a point around which to bargain and for settling the charge, which must be fixed before engaging the cab.

If you have not fixed the rate *in advance*, there is a complete change and an entirely different set of rules will apply. According to these rules, the going rate plays no part whatsoever. The whole relationship is altered. The sky is the limit, and the customer has no kick coming. I have seen taxi drivers shouting at the top of their lungs, waving their arms, following a redfaced American with his head pulled down between his shoulders, demanding for a two-pound ride ten Lebanese pounds which the American eventually had to pay.

It is difficult for the American to accommodate his frame of reference to the fact that what constitutes one thing to him, namely, a taxi ride, is to the Arab two very different operations involving two different sets of relationships and two sets of rules. The crucial factor is whether the bargaining is done at the beginning or the end of the ride! As a matter of fact, you cannot bargain at the end. What the driver asks for he is entitled to!

One of the greatest difficulties Americans have abroad stems from the fact that we often think we have a commitment when we do not. The second complication on this same topic is the other side of the coin, i.e., when others think we have agreed to things that we have not. Our own failure to recognize binding obligations, plus our custom of setting organizational goals ahead of everything else, has put us in hot water far too often.

People sometimes do not keep agreements with us because we do not keep agreements with them. As a general rule, the American treats the agreement as something he may eventually have to break.

Once, while I was visiting an American post in Latin America, the Ambassador sent the Spanish version of a trade treaty down to his language officer with instructions to write in some "weasel words." To his dismay, he was told, "There are no weasel words in Spanish."

A personnel officer of a large corporation in Iran made an agreement with local employees that American employees would not receive preferential treatment. When the first American employee arrived, it was learned quickly that in the United States he had been covered by a variety of health plans that were not available to Iranians. And this led to immediate protests from the Iranians which were never satisfied. The personnel officer never grasped the fact that he had violated an iron-bound contract.

Certainly, this is the most important generalization to be drawn by American businessmen from this discussion of agreements: there are many times when we are vulnerable *even when judged by our own standards*. Many instances of actual sharp practices by American companies are well known abroad and are giving American business a bad name. The cure for such questionable behavior is simple. The companies concerned usually have it within their power to discharge offenders and to foster within their organization an atmosphere in which only honesty and fairness can thrive.

But the cure for ignorance of the social and legal rules which underlie business agreements is not so easy. This is because:

- The subject is complex.
- Little research has been conducted to determine the culturally different concepts of what is an agreement.
- The people of each country think that their own code is the only one, and that everything else is dishonest.
- Each code is different from our own; and the farther away one is traveling from Western Europe, the greater the difference is.

But the little that has already been learned about this subject indicates that as a problem it is not insoluble and will yield to research. Since it is probably one of the more relevant and immediately applicable areas of interest to modern business, it would certainly be advisable for companies with large foreign operations to sponsor some serious research in this vital field.

A Case in Point

Thus far, I have been concerned with developing the five check points around which a real understanding of foreign cultures can begin. But the problems that arise from a faulty understanding of the silent language of foreign custom are human problems and perhaps can best be dramatized by an actual case.

A Latin American republic had decided to modernize one of its communication networks to the tune of several million dollars. Because of its reputation for quality and price, the inside track was quickly taken by American company "Y."

The company, having been sounded out informally, considered the size of the order and decided to bypass its regular Latin American representative and send instead its sales manager. The following describes what took place.

The sales manager arrived and checked in at the leading hotel. He immediately had some difficulty pinning down just who it was he had to see about his business. After several days without results, he called at the American Embassy where he found that the commercial attaché had the up-to-the-minute information he needed. The commercial attaché listened to his story. Realizing that the sales manager had already made a number of mistakes, but figuring that the Latins were used to American blundering, the attaché reasoned that all was not lost. He informed the sales manager that the Minister of Communications was the key man and that whoever got the nod from him would get the contract. He also briefed the sales manager on methods of conducting business in Latin America and offered some pointers about dealing with the minister.

The attaché's advice ran somewhat as follows:

1. You don't do business here the way you do in the States; it is necessary to spend much more time. You have to get to know your man and vice versa.

2. You must meet with him *several times* before you talk business. I will tell you at what point you can bring up the subject. Take your cues from me. (Our American sales manager at this point made a few observations to himself about "cookie pushers" and wondered how many payrolls had been met by the commercial attaché.)

3. Take that price list and put it in your pocket. Don't get it out until I tell you to. Down here price is only one of the many things taken into account before closing a deal. In the United States, your past experience will prompt you to act according to a certain set of principles, but many of these principles will *not* work here. Every time you feel the urge to act or to say something, look at me. Suppress the urge and take your cues from me. This is very important.

4. Down here people like to do business with men who *are* somebody. In order to be somebody, it is well to have written a book, to have lectured at a university, or to have developed your intellect in some way. The man you are going to see is a poet. He has published several volumes of poetry. Like many Latin Americans, he prizes poetry highly. You will find that he will spend a good deal of business time quoting his poetry to you, and he will take great pleasure in this.

5. You will also note that the people here are very proud of their past

and of their Spanish blood, but they are also exceedingly proud of their liberation from Spain and their independence. The fact that they are a democracy, that they are free, and also that they are no longer a colony is very, very important to them. They are warm and friendly and enthusiastic if they like you. If they don't, they are cold and withdrawn.

6. And another thing, time down here means something different. It works in a different way. You know how it is back in the States when a certain type blurts out whatever is on his mind without waiting to see if the situation is right. He is considered an impatient bore and somewhat egocentric. Well, down here, you have to wait much, much longer, and I really mean *much, much* longer, before you can begin to talk about the reason for your visit.

7. There is another point I want to caution you about. At home, the man who sells takes the initiative. Here, *they* tell you when they are ready to do business. But, most of all, don't discuss price until you are asked and don't rush things.

The Pitch

The next day the commercial attaché introduced the sales manager to the Minister of Communications. First, there was a long wait in the outer office while people kept coming in and out. The sales manager looked at his watch, fidgeted, and finally asked whether the minister was really expecting him. The reply he received was scarcely reassuring, "Oh yes, he is expecting you but several things have come up that require his attention. Besides, one gets used to waiting down here." The sales manager irritably replied, "But doesn't he know I flew all the way down here from the United States to see him, and I have spent over a week already of my valuable time trying to find him?" "Yes, I know," was the answer, "but things just move much more slowly here."

At the end of about 30 minutes, the minister emerged from the office, greeted the commercial attaché with a *doble abrazo,* throwing his arms around him and patting him on the back as though they were long-lost brothers. Now, turning and smiling, the minister extended his hand to the sales manager, who, by this time, was feeling rather miffed because he had been kept in the outer office so long.

After what seemed to be an all too short chat, the minister rose, suggesting a well-known café where they might meet for dinner the next evening. The sales manager expected, of course, that, considering the nature of their business and the size of the order, he might be taken to the minister's home, not realizing that the Latin home is reserved for family and very close friends.

Until now, nothing at all had been said about the reason for the sales manager's visit, a fact which bothered him somewhat. The whole setup seemed wrong; neither did he like the idea of wasting another day in town. He told the home office before he left that he would be gone for a week or ten days at most, and made a mental note that he would clean this order up in three days and enjoy a few days in Acapulco or Mexico City. Now the week had already gone and he would be lucky if he made it home in ten days.

Voicing his misgivings to the commercial attaché, he wanted to know if the minister really meant business, and, if he did, why could they not get together and talk about it? The commercial attaché by now was beginning to show the strain of constantly having to reassure the sales manager. Nevertheless, he tried again:

> What you don't realize is that part of the time we were waiting, the minister was rearranging a very tight schedule so that he could spend tomorrow night with you. You see, down here they don't delegate responsibility the way we do in the States. They exercise much tighter control than we do. As a consequence, this man spends up to 15 hours a day at his desk. It may not look like it to you, but I assure you he really means business. He wants to give your company the order; if you play your cards right, you will get it.

The next evening provided more of the same. Much conversation about food and music, about many people the sales manager had never heard of. They went to a night club, where the sales manager brightened up and began to think that perhaps he and the minister might have something in common after all. It bothered him, however, that the principal reason for his visit was not even alluded to tangentially. But every time he started to talk about electronics, the commercial attaché would nudge him and proceed to change the subject.

The next meeting was for morning coffee at a café. By now the sales manager was having difficulty hiding his impatience. To make matters worse, the minister had a mannerism which he did not like. When they talked, he was likely to put his hand on him; he would take hold of his arm and get so close that he almost "spat" in his face. As a consequence, the sales manager was kept busy trying to dodge and back up.

Following coffee, there was a walk in a nearby park. The minister expounded on the shrubs, the birds, and the beauties of nature, and at one spot he stopped to point at a statue and said: "There is a statue of the world's greatest hero, the liberator of mankind!" At this point, the worst happened, for the sales manager asked who the statue was of and, being given the name of a famous Latin American patriot, said, "I never heard of him," and walked on.

The Failure

It is quite clear from this that the sales manager did not get the order, which went to a Swedish concern. The American, moreover, was never able to see the minister again. Why did the minister feel the way he did? His reasoning went somewhat as follows:

> I like the American's equipment and it makes sense to deal with North Americans who are near us and whose price is right. But I could never be friends with this man. He is not my kind of human being and we have nothing in common. He is not *simpático*. If I can't be friends and he is not *simpático*, I can't depend on him to treat me right. I tried everything, every conceivable situation, and only once did we seem to understand each other. If we could be friends, he would feel obligated to me and this obligation would give me some control. Without control, how do I know he will deliver what he says he will at the price he quotes?

Of course, what the minister did not know was that the price was quite firm, and that quality control was a matter of company policy. He did not realize that the sales manager was a member of an organization, and that the man is always subordinate to the organization in the United States. Next year maybe the sales manager would not even be representing the company, but would be replaced. Further, if he wanted someone to depend on, his best bet would be to hire a good American lawyer to represent him and write a binding contract.

In this instance, both sides suffered. The American felt he was being slighted and put off, and did not see how there could possibly be any connection between poetry and doing business or why it should all take so long. He interpreted the delay as a form of polite brushoff. Even if things had gone differently and there had been a contract, it is doubtful that the minister would have trusted the contract as much as he would a man whom he considered his friend. Throughout Latin America, the law is made livable and contracts workable by having friends and relatives operating from the inside. Lacking a friend, someone who would look out for his interests, the minister did not want to take a chance. He stated this simply and directly.

Conclusion

The case just described has of necessity been oversimplified. The danger is that the reader will say, "Oh, I see. All you really have to do is be friends." At which point the expert will step in and reply:

> Yes, of course, but what you don't realize is that in Latin America being a friend involves much more than it does in the United States and is an entirely different proposition. A friendship implies obligations. You go about it differently. It involves much more than being nice, visiting, and playing golf. You would not want to enter into friendship lightly.

The point is simply this. It takes years and years to develop a sound foundation for doing business in a given country. Much that is done seems silly or strange to the home office. Indeed, the most common error made by home offices, once they have found representatives who can get results, is failure to take their advice and allow sufficient time for representatives to develop the proper contacts.

The second most common error, if that is what it can be called, is ignorance of the secret and hidden language of foreign cultures. In this article I have tried to show how five key topics—time, space, material possessions, friendship patterns, and business agreements—offer a starting point from which companies can begin to acquire the understanding necessary to do business in foreign countries.

Our present knowledge is meager, and much more research is needed before the businessman of the future can go abroad fully equipped for his work. Not only will he need to be well versed in the economics, law, and politics of the area, but he will have to understand, if not speak, the silent languages of other cultures.

6.3 Uses of Common Objects as Indicators of Cultural Orientations
WAYNE DENNIS

If children are asked with regard to each of several objects, "What is it for?" one finds that children's concepts of the functions of identical things vary from society to society. Those functions of common objects which are frequently mentioned by the children of a social group, it is here proposed, are indicative of the activities, interest, and values that prevail in that society. That is, it is held that children value things for the uses to which they may be put, and, conversely, that frequently-mentioned uses are indicative of values. For example, if children in one society often mention boys and girls, cats and dogs, trees and sand, as functioning chiefly in play whereas the children of another group mention them more often in connection with work, these facts suggest that there is a difference between the two groups in regard to work-play emphases. The present paper illustrates the application of this method, The Uses Test, with three groups of children, an American group, a Lebanese group, and a Sudanese group.

If the objects used in questioning children are universally present, this test procedure can be employed in all cultures. Techniques for the study of child behavior that are universally applicable are very small in number. The method employed in the present study is offered as a useful addition to the small stock of tools available for cross-cultural research. It is believed to be particularly useful as an exploratory technique in societies whose patterns of child behavior are but slightly known to the investigator.

Method

The question employed is the simple and probably universal one, "What is————for?" Naturally, this question may be asked in regard to any plant or animal, any class of persons, or any part of the body.

The question, "What is————for?" was chosen because numerous studies indicate that the young child readily thinks in terms of use. He spontaneously asks what things are for, he defines objects in terms of their use, and he seems to presume that every object in the world has a use. No difficulties have been encountered in obtaining answers to the question from hundreds of children between ages five and ten in a variety of cultures. In all likelihood it can be used above and below the age levels represented in this study. The technique is not limited to the particular word list employed here. The objects concerning which children are questioned will vary with the interests and hypotheses of the investigator.

In the present study, the following words were used in the order given: the mouth, the hands, a mother, a father, a boy, a girl, trees, wood, dogs, cats, birds, stones, the sun, sand, rain, and gold. In the case of the American and Lebanese subjects, data were gathered by individual interview. The Sudanese subjects were instructed orally as a group, and they were requested to write their answers.

Although the question put to the child did not ask for more than one use for each object, some children gave more than one. In the present study, responses beyond the first were not included in the analysis of the data, unless specific reference is made to answers beyond the first one.

Subjects

American. These were American children attending the American Community School in Beirut, Lebanon. The majority of these children were born in the United States and spent their pre-school years there. They were in Lebanon in 1955–56 because their parents were temporary residents of that country. Most of the fathers were employed by the University, or American business firms. Nearly all could be classified as belonging to the American middle class. All children between ages 5.0 and 11.0 were tested. These totaled 120 children, approximately equally representing the two sexes and the various ages.

Lebanese. This group consisted of an analytic sample of native-born children in Beirut, Lebanon. The sample was divided into 36 cells, produced by cross classifying in terms of four criteria: sex, private schools vs. public schools, age (5–6 years, 7–8 years, 9–10 years) and religious community (Arab-Christians, Moslems, and Armenians). With 25 children in each cell, the sample comprised 900 subjects in all. All children of appropriate ages were interviewed in each of several schools, the pupils being subsequently assigned to cells. If more than 25 so obtained *S*s fell into a given cell, the number was reduced to 25 by discarding the data from *S*s selected by chance.

Sudanese. This group consisted of 13 girls and 45 boys, all aged 9 and 10, from a private school in Omdurman, the capital of Sudan. Unlike the others, these children gave their answers in writing (in Arabic).

Treatment of Results

For the answers to each question, categories (to be described below) were established to which the majority of replies could be assigned. Each answer was assigned to only one category. Answers that did not fall into any of the defined categories are not represented in the tables of results.

Results

The percentage of each group giving each type of answer to each question is indicated in Table 1. . . .

The major group contrasts in regard to each question will be discussed in the order in which the questions are listed in the table. In general, only group differences high in statistical significance are noted. In statements assessing the significance of differences, A-L refers to an American-Lebanese comparison, L-S refers to a Lebanese-Sudanese comparison and A-S to an American-Sudanese comparison.

TABLE 1.   Major Group Comparisons

Stimulus Words and Use—Categories	Percentage Frequencies of Responses		
	American	Lebanese	Sudanese
Mouth			
Eating	61	74	71
Talking	39	22	14
Drinking	0	0	7
Hands			
Eating	6	23	33
Writing	11	10	16
Working	12	12	12
Playing	4	1	0
Mother			
Providing food	16	51	7
Providing care	62	44	41
Nursing	0	0	19
Father			
Working, earning money	55	76	10
Buying food	1	16	7
Providing care	12	6	16
Assisting family	14	3	29
Boy			
Going to school	16	37	7
Working, helping parents	23	24	17
Future reference	11	20	12
Playing	34	9	0
Girl			
Going to school	12	33	9
Working, helping parents	28	45	34
Future reference	12	11	0
Playing	27	5	0
Trees			
Food	34	69	52
Wood	8	8	10
Shade	10	2	12
Climbing	12	1	0
Dogs			
Guarding, watching	16	66	62
Barking, biting	9	19	0
Hunting	4	8	7
Pets, playing	49	4	3
Cats			
Catching mice	16	63	53
Meowing	6	13	2
Pets, playing	52	6	7
Birds			
Eating	7	37	16
Flying, singing	34	36	36
Enjoying	33	8	2
Stones			
Throwing, hitting	19	13	2
Building	38	73	53

TABLE 1.   Major Group Comparisons

Stimulus Words and Use—Categories	Percentage Frequencies of Responses		
	American	Lebanese	Sudanese
Sun			
Drying	0	9	2
Warming	25	28	9
Light	53	47	67
Sand			
Playing	41	18	2
Building	21	58	26
Rain			
Growing plants	75	46	41
Providing water	19	16	12

The Mouth

According to the subjects, the primary uses of the mouth are eating and talking. These two answers make up 100%, 96%, and 92% of the first responses to question 1 for the three groups respectively.

"Talking" as a response to this question is given more frequently by the Americans than by either of the other groups. . . . Conversely, eating is a response given more often by . . . the Lebanese sample than by the Americans.

The Sudanese are the only *S*s to mention drinking as the *first* response to the question "What is the mouth for?" Not shown by Table 1, because it deals only with first-mentioned uses, is the fact that among the Sudanese children a very common response to the question, "What is the mouth for?" is "eating and drinking." This joint mention of eating and drinking occurred among 50% of the Sudanese, but among only 3% of the Americans (S-A $p <$ .001) and none of the Lebanese. The frequent mention of drinking in Sudan is probably related to the high temperatures prevailing there, which require a high water consumption.

It is noteworthy that many possible uses of the mouth were not mentioned by any child in any of the three groups. Many possible replies were absent not only as first responses but failed to appear among subsequent responses as well. Among such absent responses were singing, chewing, spitting, shouting, biting, pouting, smiling, laughing, crying, coughing, sucking, blowing, whistling, praying, and cursing. It seems likely that in societies other than the three which were investigated one or more of these would be common word associations with the mouth.

Hands

For all three groups of children, the uses of the hands are more diversified than the uses of the mouth. The most common responses to the question, "What are hands for?" are to hold things, to grasp, to work, to carry, to touch with, to eat with, and to write with. Only the frequencies of eating, writing, working, and playing are examined below.

Eating as something for which the hands are used is mentioned much more often by the Lebanese and Sudanese (by 23% and 33% of the respective groups) than by the Americans (6%) (p of A-S and A-L $< .001$). These figures no doubt reflect differences in eating customs among the groups, holding food with the hands being common among some groups of the Lebanese and Sudanese. . . .

In regard to writing and working, the response frequencies of the three major groups are almost identical. Play is mentioned most frequently by the Americans, seldom by the Lebanese, not at all by the Sudanese. Other responses are of such a miscellaneous nature as to be difficult to treat in a comparative manner.

Mother

In all groups, providing food and care for children comprise the major functions of a mother in the eyes of the child. Providing food is most often mentioned among the Lebanese. This response is more common among the younger Lebanese children than among the older, but even among the Lebanese 9–10-year-olds food is mentioned more frequently than by the Americans as a whole. The Sudanese children are unique among the groups in specifically mentioning nursing, 19% of their first-mentioned uses of the mother being to nurse a baby. The complete absence of such responses among the American and Lebanese Ss probably reflects a taboo against making references to the breasts in these groups.

Although the general response, "she takes care of us," was common, in all groups there is an almost complete absence of reference to *specific* motherly acts other than feeding. No child mentioned sweeping, washing dishes, laundering, ironing, sewing, dressing, washing faces, bathing, shopping, putting to bed, arousing, getting off to school, or the superintending of these activities, although some of these would probably have been mentioned if as many responses as was possible had been obtained to each question. Also unmentioned are helping with lessons, moral instruction, reward and punishment, dispensation of justice within the family, love and affection, story-telling, and parent-child play.

Father

If the child's point of view is accepted, the life of a Lebanese father must be a dreary one. He works and earns money in order to support the family. This is the general tenor of all answers. As in the case of the mother, there is no mention of his playing with the child, rewarding or punishing, or of expressing love or hate. So far as the manifest content of the responses are concerned, the Lebanese child seems to have a father who provides for him but who otherwise has little relationship to him. The answers of the American children are similar, but there is a much larger miscellaneous category. In contrast to the Lebanese and the Americans, the Sudanese child mentions the working and earning functions of his father very seldom. Only 10% of the Sudanese answers fall into this category as compared to 55% and 76% of the Americans and Lebanese respectively. Assisting the family and taking care of the family are common answers among the Sudanese but are infrequent in the other two groups.

Boy and Girl

"What is a boy for?" "What is a girl for?" Nearly every answer to these questions can be placed in one of four categories: The function of a boy (or a girl) is (a) to go to school, (b) or to work, help at home, assist mother and father, do chores and run errands, (c) or to grow up in order to do something in the future (become a man or woman, earn money when he grows up, etc.), (d) or to play. . . .

Working (including the helping of parents) stands relatively high in frequency in all groups. In all groups working is mentioned more often as a function of the girl than as a function of the boy. Preparing for future has frequencies roughly equal in all groups, except that among the Sudanese Ss, most of whom were boys, preparation for the future on the part of girls received no mention.

Play seems to be the outstanding function of American children. It is said to be the purpose of a boy in 34% of the instances and of the girl in 27% of the cases. The corresponding Lebanese frequencies are 9% and 5% (p of A-L for boys and girls each $> .001$). . . .

No mention of play occurred in the Sudanese answers to these questions. No supporting data are available, but the rarity of Sudanese references to play strongly suggests either that play is relatively infrequent, or that it is disapproved of, or both, among this group.

Trees

Sixty-nine per cent of the Lebanese Ss state that trees are to provide food. The high proportion of such answers among the Lebanese is no doubt related to the fact that Lebanon has a great variety of food-bearing trees, including olives, almonds, hazel nuts, walnuts, dates, oranges, lemons, grapefruit, bananas, cherries, peaches, plums, and apples. Even pine trees are prized for edible nuts. But American children, living in the same environment, mention the food-producing function of trees only half as often (34%) (A-L $p < .001$). This finding demonstrates again that answers are derived from culture rather than from the physical environment.

The shade-producing function of trees is mentioned more often by the Americans and the Sudanese (10% and 12%) than by the Lebanese (2%) (p of S-L $= .01$, p of A-L $< .001$). Climbing trees, which is a play function, has a frequency of 12% among the Americans, 1% among the Lebanese, and zero among the Sudanese. Again, since American and Lebanese Ss were all living in Beirut, it can be assumed that the differences were not produced by differences in natural environment. . . .

Cats and Dogs

In the Near East and in certain other parts of the world cats and dogs are not pets as they are in Europe and America. In the Near East they are treated in much the same way as are other domestic animals whereas in the Western world they have a special status. The Lebanese and Sudanese answers reflect the fact that if a dog is kept it is for the purpose of guarding the house and warning against intruders. A dog is occasionally used for hunting. In consonance with these adult notions, guarding and hunting make up 62–66% of the Lebanese and Sudanese responses. Among the Lebanese, to play with a dog and to pet a dog are referred to only by the younger children, among whom such answers occur in 4% of the cases. Attitudes towards dogs do not differ as between the Lebanese Moslem and Christian groups.

In contrast, 49% of the American answers indicate that dogs are pets and are to be played with (A-L $p < .001$). Among the Americans such answers are as frequent among the older children as among the younger.

The difference among the groups in regard to cats is similar to that prevailing in reference to dogs. For the Lebanese and Sudanese the primary feline purpose is the catching of mice and rats. Occasionally the catching of insects by cats is mentioned. When specific insects are mentioned, they are usually cockroaches. Reference to cats as animals to play with or to pet occurs infrequently in these groups (6–7%) but 52% of the American answers fall into this class ($p < .001$).

Birds

For some children in all groups, birds are to fly, to sing, and to be put in a cage. But 37% of the Lebanese Ss state that birds are to be killed and eaten. This reflects the Lebanese custom of shooting and eating many birds which Americans do not classify as game birds. The reader may note again the prevalence of responses referring to food on the part of the Lebanese. The Sudanese mention birds as food less frequently (16%) than the Lebanese, but more frequently than the Americans (7%) (A-L $p < .001$).

Stones

In all groups stones are primarily to build with, 38%, 73% and 53% of the answers, respectively, being in this category. This answer is not surprising in countries in which stone has been the most widely used building material for thousands of years.

"Stone" was included in the stimulus list in part because stones can be used aggressively. In this regard only small differences appear among the groups. Using stones for throwing or hitting makes up only 13% of the Lebanese, 19% of the American, and 2% of the Sudanese responses. That the frequency of this answer is low among the Sudanese seems to be due to the greater age of the Sudanese subjects. . . .

The Sun

As might be expected the sun's predominant functions are to provide warmth and light. On this item one of the major group contrasts lies in the fact that the Sudanese Ss referred to the heat-providing function of the sun much less often than the other groups (9% as contrasted to 25–28%) (A-S $p <$

.001). Apparently, the Sudan is ordinarily so hot that the child thinks the sun's contribution is not useful!

Another service provided by the sun is that of drying clothes. This is mentioned by 9% of the Lebanese, 2% of the Sudanese, and none of the Americans. Presumably, more clothes are dried at home in the former groups. . . .

Sand

Because of very extensive building operations which are under way in Beirut, construction work is familiar to all Beirut children. The use of sand in building is mentioned by 58% of the Lebanese. American children living in Beirut mention construction much less often (21%) ($p < .001$).

One of the major group differences in regard to sand involves play. Playing in sand is mentioned by 41% of the Americans, 18% of the Lebanese (A-L $p < .001$), and 2% of the Sudanese. The generally high rating of the Americans on play responses has been noted in connection with several earlier questions. The low play rating of the Sudanese Ss on this particular question is in part due to their ages, since sand play is uncommon at ages 9 and 10. Among the Lebanese, play as a use for sand has a frequency of 30% at ages 5–6 and of only 7% at ages 9–10. It will be noted that the frequency for American children for ages 5–10 combined is higher than the frequency at ages 5–6 among the Lebanese.

Rain

Rain provided no group differences of special interest. In all groups, the most common use attributed to rain is that of aiding the growth of plants. This response is highest among the Americans. The other two groups gave many more answers which fell into the miscellaneous or unclassified category. . . .

Hypotheses Concerning the Lebanese Child

The data have been seen to reveal a considerable number of differences among the three major groups of Ss. It remains to attempt to characterize in a general way the answers of each group. Such a general characterization is warranted only for the Lebanese and the American groups in view of the small size of the Sudanese sample and the fact that it represented only one age level.

It has already been observed that the Lebanese answers seem to show a considerable concern with food. Common answers include the following: mother feeds us, father provides food, the mouth and the hands are used for eating, trees produce food, and birds are to be eaten. The answers taken by themselves do not show why food is so important. There is no reason to believe that the Ss suffered from malnutrition. Actually, the majority of Lebanese children appear to be very well fed. Observations other than those presented here support the tentative suggestion that food preparation and eating have for the Lebanese a pleasure function that is comparable to the positive valuation given by some societies to other activities such as music, conversation, or visual esthetic experiences.

In the second place, the Lebanese responses seem to indicate that industriousness is highly valued. Note the following common answers: father and mother work, girls and boys work, the hands are for work, dogs work by guarding the house, cats work by catching mice and rats. Trees and birds provide food, which may be thought of as a work function. Stones and sand supply building materials. Much of the world seems to be oriented toward utilitarian ends.

Concern for language facility and scholastic performances seems evident, particularly among the private school pupils. The mouth is for talking, the hands for writing, and one of the chief functions of both boys and girls is to go to school.

Few other emphases are observable in the Lebanese answers. There is some mention of play in connection with questions about boys and girls, and the question about sand, but little or no mention of it in reference to parents, hands and mouth, or animals. There is no mention of art, of music, of athletics, or of sensory pleasures other than eating. There is little indication of valuation of emotional life or of group cohesion. There are no references to competitiveness in areas other than school achievement. There is nothing to suggest that religious observances or religious affiliations are highly significant.

Hypotheses Concerning the American Child

The present data, it is important to remember, are restricted to American children in Lebanon, and more specifically, to those attending a specific progressive school. The parents are nearly all college graduates, and most seem to have accepted the doctrine of permissiveness. While many groups of children living in America probably would answer as do the American group in Lebanon, not all groups of children in America would do so.

The Beirut colony of American children (at ages 5–10) may be characterized, from their answers, as being greatly concerned with play. To a much greater extent than among the Lebanese *S*s, the hands are for play, boys and girls have play as their purpose, trees are for shade and climbing, dogs and cats serve as pets and playmates, birds are to be enjoyed, and sand serves a a play function. In contrast to the seriousness of the Lebanese children, life for the American children in Beirut would seem to constitute a perpetual vacation.

Positive mention of play is associated with low frequencies of reference to work and to duties. Going to school, and helping parents are reported as functions of boys and girls much less often by Americans than by the Lebanese. The function of the father as a bread-winner is less frequently cited by the American group. As noted previously, dogs and cats are for fun and are seldom thought of as utilitarian animals. Similarly, the use of stones and sand as building materials is stressed much less by the American group. Apparently the American child sees the world more in terms of pleasure and less in terms of duty and work than does the Lebanese child. . . .

The categories listed in Table 1 include only the most common answers. The responses that are not represented in this Table were given by only a few children. They may therefore reasonably be called individual or unconventional answers, and may represent individuality or originality. If one adds for each question the percentages of Americans and Lebanese giving answers in the categories of Table 1, one finds that to fourteen of the sixteen questions the Lebanese gave a larger proportion of common, or stereotyped answers. The American answers, in general, show more variety. This finding may represent the result of permissiveness, it may point to more varied experiences, or it may be the result of direct encouragement of individual interests and modes of thought. This difference seems to the investigator to be among the more interesting ones revealed by the study.

Summary

A technique for the study of children's concepts of the uses of common objects has been presented which is believed to be universally applicable. Its use has been illustrated with American and Lebanese groups and to a lesser extent with Sudanese Ss. The study has demonstrated that in regard to universally present objects, such as hands and mouth, dogs and cats, sun, sand and stone, children of different cultures differ in their ideas as early as five years of age. It has also demonstrated that the test responses enable one to formulate hypotheses concerning the interests, values, and activities which are being developed in different groups of children. The method is believed to be a useful addition to the research techniques available for the study of cultural differences in child development.

6.4 The Negro Market
RAYMOND A. BAUER AND SCOTT M. CUNNINGHAM

The ways in which Negroes buy and use goods and services are simultaneously a practical business concern and a social issue, with the two interacting with each other. In this overview of the Negro market, we shall find that the spending behavior of Negroes reflects their broader conditions of poverty, lack of education, discrimination, and occupational and social deprivation. We shall see Negroes taking and rejecting cues from the white community on what to buy. We shall find them spending disproportionately on the maintenance of their social facade, and on such items of immediate gratification as tobacco and liquor. We shall also find them willing to buy on credit.

In this overview, we shall (1) outline basic data on the status of the Negro in American life in the 1960's, (2) trace the development of interest in the Negro market, (3) look at the general pattern of Negro spending, and (4) summarize some of the circumstances that offset when, where, how, and what Negroes buy.

In the early 1960's as interest in the Negro market grew, sophisticated marketers asked, "Is there really a Negro market?" The intent of this question was to raise the issue of whether the buying behavior of Negroes was in any way different from the buying pattern of whites of comparable income. One of the inescapable facts of the Negro market is that the income distribution of the Negro portion of the population is considerably lower than that of the whites. This in turn unquestionably accounts for much of the Negroes' buying behavior. Accordingly, there is focus on understanding the extent to which Negroes buy and use goods in a manner comparable to or different from that of whites with equivalent economic status.

However, despite similarities, it is posited that economic status alone does not account for all that can be observed. We shall also come to the conclusion that the Negro market is in several respects socially and psychologically unique.

In the past decade or so, the traditional stereotype of the Negro has been replaced with a new one. The "old" Negro was impoverished, had little taste or discrimination in the products he bought, and generally just was not the type of person on whom a marketer expended any effort. Announcement of the "new" Negro, on the other hand, usually begins with some lofty statement, such as the assertion that the Negro market is as large as the entire Canadian market in dollar volume (which in fact is true).

It is also said that the Negro is an exceedingly discriminating buyer who is interested only in nationally known prestige brands. While examples of this can be found in many sources, following are just two of them:

"Surveys and variety chain experience show the Negro to be extremely brand conscious" (*Variety Store Merchandiser,* 1964).

"The Negro has now become much more brand conscious due to shoddy merchandise pushed off on him in the past" (*Sponsor,* 1964).

In actual fact, the new Negro is closer to being the true Negro, but needless to say the facts are a bit more complicated.

It is true that the Negro market is large, both in numbers and in purchasing power. In 1960, there were almost 19 million Negroes in the United States, comprising almost 11% of our total population, and the number was growing at a rate more rapid than that of the population in general (U.S. Government, 1966). Yet this is still a market composed of disproportionate numbers of people who are poor, undereducated, and generally underprivileged.

Table 1 shows the distribution of family incomes of Negroes and whites in 1965. In that year, 61% of Negro families had incomes under $4,999. This was true of only 29% of the white families. Furthermore, the shape of income

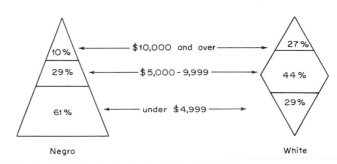

TABLE 1.   Negro vs. white family income.
Source: U.S. Census Bureau Abstract, 1967.

TABLE 2. Illustrative Time Series of Annual Data (Averages for Three-Year Periods) for the Nonwhite (N) and White (W) Population of the United States: 1948–1965

Series		Period					
		1948– 1950	1951– 1953	1954– 1956	1957– 1959	1960– 1962	1963– 1965
School enrollment, percentage of	N	70.7	75.5	83.1	86.2	88.8	92.4[a]
males age 14–17	W	84.5	87.2	89.6	91.7	92.9	94.6[a]
Percentage high school graduates,	N	(NA)	15.1[b]	(NA)	21.7[b]	27.3[b]	32.3[a]
male labor force	W	(NA)	42.1[b]	(NA)	49.4[b]	53.5[b]	56.8[a]
Percentage of male workers with	N	50.2[b]	53.0	55.6[a]	51.3	51.8	55.2[a]
year-round full-time jobs	W	66.8[b]	69.9	68.8[a]	66.0	65.3	67.2[a]
Percentage of employed persons	N	9.6[a]	9.7[b]	12.2[a]	14.0[a]	16.4	18.6
in white-collar jobs	W	39.7[a]	39.8[b]	42.2[a]	45.6[a]	46.8	47.2
Median income of families	N	1,762	2,277	2,529	2,797	3,251	3,758
(dollars)	W	3,329	4,122	4,646	5,370	6,018	6,859
Infant deaths per 1,000 live	N	46.1	45.5	42.6	44.4	41.8	41.3[a]
births	W	28.5	25.4	23.6	23.4	22.5	21.9[a]
Percentage of married women	N	(NA)	16.0	19.6	20.3	19.8	21.0
with husband absent	W	(NA)	4.6[a]	5.0	4.2	4.3	4.4
Percentage of live births illegiti-	N	17.1	18.6	20.2	21.2	22.3	23.6[b]
mate	W	1.8	1.6	1.9	2.1	2.5	3.1[b]
Subfamilies per 100 families	N	12.1	10.1[a]	10.4	9.2	7.4	6.4
	W	6.1	4.4[a]	4.2	3.4	2.8	2.4

[a] Based on data for only two years.
[b] Data for only one year.
NA: Not Available.
Source: Various federal publications; OASDI figures from unpublished calculations of the Office of Research and Statistics, Social Security Administration.

distribution among Negro families is such that one finds increasing proportions at the bottom of the pyramid, whereas among white families the distribution is diamond-shaped, and the mode is closer to the middle of the distribution.

A recent comparison of the status of Negroes to whites in the United States has been made by Otis Dudley Duncan (1967). The major data updated to 1963–1965 are presented in Table 2. Duncan also plots the trends of these various indices of deprivation from the time base of 1948–1950, showing the changes in status of Negroes on these dimensions since World War II.

Only in school enrollment have Negroes achieved approximate equality with whites. One of the most widely discussed facts of the recent American scene is that the equality of educational experience of Negroes is below that of whites, that they drop out of school sooner, and that they have a lower level of achievement at the completion of any given year of schooling. Hence, school enrollment appears to be the least relevant of these indicators.

On all other indicators, it is clear that Negroes continue to lag well behind whites. Median income for Negro families for the years 1963–1965 was $3,758 in comparison with $6,859 for whites. Negroes lag in years of completed education, full-time employment of males, white collar employment, infant survival, presence of husband in the household, complete families, and proportion of legitimate births.

Whether Negroes have progressed relative to whites on these various series is a matter of judgment. Duncan presents an extended discussion of the various bases of comparison that may be used, such as the proportionate increase from a previous base, the relative standing of Negroes and whites over time, the lag between the times at which Negroes reach the same levels that whites had previously attained, and so on. Each method of comparison has its strengths and weaknesses. Suffice it to say that the present level of deprivation is not only considerable, but also that deprivation of this sort tends to become self-perpetuating.

The Black Dilemma

The deprived state of the black population is a function of past discrimination. Thus, even if discrimination were to vanish immediately, a prospect that seems highly unlikely in the fall of 1969, the low level of income and education of Negroes, and the relative weakness of the Negro family, would still constitute a series of handicaps in the raising of their status.

Some conditions may be in part a function of past and present discrimination (e.g., lesser sums spent on vacations and on food outside the home). More often, however, they appear to be a function of deprivation, and more specifically of the disparity between aspiration and opportunity.

As a number of observers have commented, the Negro Revolution is a peculiar one in that most American Negroes are not trying to overthrow the existing order. Instead, they are fighting to obtain full membership in the American society.

The American Negro has already accepted many of the important values of white middle-class society, and illustrations are numerous: the freedom to move about—in housing, in travel, and in admittance to public and private facilities; the freedom of opportunity in private and public employment; the ability to express opinions and have a say in decision-making processes; a belief in the ability of the basic components of the American democratic system to provide parity for all citizens; the power of education; and the desire for the material goods which represent well-being and status for white America.

This is not entirely a new phenomenon in the American society; it has happened before with other minority groups. However, other minority groups, such as the Italian and Irish immigrants of the late 19th century and even the Puerto Ricans of today, have both a "mother culture—mother society" to fall back on and a physical appearance more or less conducive to assimilation. The Negro has neither a mother culture which may offer a refuge (some recent eulogies of African heritage notwithstanding), nor an appearance which allows him to "blend with the crowd." Thus, the Negro has found that, because of his skin color, his chances of being assimilated into the white middle class are impaired.

This was put another way by John Johnson, publisher of *Ebony*, when he said: "Not only is the Negro not melting—he has not been permitted to get into the pot" (*Advertising Age*, 1964).

Simply expressed, the basic dilemma of the Negro is whether to strive against odds to attain middle-class values (and the benefits which accrue with them), or to forfeit them and give priority to finding immediate gratifications within the boundaries of his own present situation.

Perception of Social Status

Deprivation extends well beyond educational and economic opportunities. As one very successful Negro put the matter: "You can get the education. You can get the job. You can get the money. But, you are still a second class citizen!" The extent to which this is felt by Negroes is reflected in their own perception of their social status.

In a study of urban, male Scotch whiskey drinkers with incomes over $5,000, which was conducted for Browne Vintners by Arthur D. Little in 1963, respondents were asked to rate their social status on a seven-point scale ranging from "upper lower" to "upper upper." One might expect that Negroes would use other Negroes as their reference group, and at each income level rate their social status higher than that of whites of comparable income.

Table 3 gives data that show the reverse is true. At each income level, Negro male Scotch drinkers are likely to rate their social status considerably lower than comparable whites.

Since some Negroes with incomes of less than $5,000 were admitted into the sample, one might be tempted to explain the difference in the lowest economic group by this fact. But this cannot explain the data for those persons in the higher income groups.

What these data appear to say is that when asked their social status, Negroes use whites as a reference group, and conclude that even at the same income level they themselves have a lower status. However, since these data are confined to persons in the middle-income and upper-income groups, this generalization may not hold for lower-status Negroes. This does not deprive the generalization of much of its power, because the question is whether relatively well-off Negroes compare themselves with whites or Negroes. Apparently, their reference group—for status purposes—is white.

Beyond deprivation per se, there are other features of the Negro population that are distinctive and may account for marketing behavior that cannot be explained in terms of household income. The average Negro family at any income level is larger than that of comparable whites. As a result, Negro per capita income is even proportionately lower than household income. Seldom

TABLE 3.   Self-Assigned Social Class as a Function of Race and Income

Social Class	$5–$7.5 N	$5–$7.5 W	$7.5–$10 N	$7.5–$10 W	$10–$15 N	$10–$15 W	$15 and Over N	$15 and Over W
Lower or lower middle	64%	34%	24%	14%	15%	3%	13%	0%
Middle-middle	25	53	58	53	43	39	31	14
Upper middle or higher	10	13	19	33	43	57	56	85
(Number)	(100)	(112)	(66)	(205)	(40)	(273)	(16)	(207)

Note: This analysis was done in a more refined fashion, with controls for gross educational level, and for the status of the job—as rated on the NORC scale of job status. The findings were the same except that small samples in some cells caused a good deal of statistical variability.

Source: Arthur D. Little, "Scotch Survey," 1963, done for Browne Vintners. Original data made available to us for secondary analysis.

does anyone have data sufficiently voluminous to permit control for per capita income, and household income must be used as a first approximation.

The Negro population is also comparably younger than the white population, and is reproducing at a more rapid rate. This means that its numerical significance as a market segment will increase. Also, at this point in time, it has a higher proportion of young consumers.

Much has been made of the distinctiveness of the Negro family. There are many more partial families (see Table 2). Moreover, the Negro family is traditionally more matriarchal than the white family. Finally, "non-single" Negro women (e.g., married and living with husband and "all other") are considerably more likely to work.

All of this adds up to the presumption—there seems to be no direct information on this point—that Negro women must play a greater relative role in family buying decisions than do white women.

Development of Interest in the Negro Market

Strictly speaking, interest in the Negro market dates from the moment that someone with something to sell encountered a Negro who had the wherewithal to buy it. Here, however, the concern is with the origins of the more systematic approach to the market that characterizes present-day interest.

While active consideration of this topic dates mainly from the period immediately after World War II, it has some early precursors. As early as 1916, it was reported that a local gas company in Rock Hill, South Carolina, teamed up with the church elders and city fathers to conduct a cooking school for Negro servants. As a result, it was said that the gas company sold 12 ranges (*American Gas Light Journal*, 1916). In 1922, the Fuller Brush Company used four black high school teachers to sell to the Negro population of Tulsa. Great success was reported, with $2,083 worth of brushes sold in the months of June and July (*Printers' Ink*, 1922).

A 1928 article disclosed that there was a disproportionate number of beauty parlors in Harlem, and that Harlem drug stores sold a lot of laxatives and cosmetics (*Advertising and Selling*, 1928). In 1930, one author said that the Negro consumer was responsive to handbills and displays, but not to newspaper ads (*Advertising and Selling*, 1930). He also mentioned that Negroes had distinctive food preferences.

The first approach to the Negro market on a national basis—insofar as determinable—was a study of income and living habits conducted by the National Negro Business League. The survey, which was financed by Montgomery Ward, Lever Brothers, and Anheuser Busch, included information on size of family, amount of money spent on household appliances, media, services, etc., and stressed the overall spending power of this market—$1,650,000,000 (*Sales Management*, 1931).

By 1931, several themes were stated which were to persevere: the use of Negroes to sell to Negroes, the need to display concern for the welfare of the Negro, the differential product usage of Negroes, choice of media, the interest of Negroes in personal-care products, and the amount of their spending power.

In 1932, Paul K. Edwards, a professor of economics at Fisk University, gave systematic attention to the Negro market that was not to be duplicated for some years to come. His article "The Negro Commodity Market," emphasized that Southern Negroes and whites of the same income and occupation had different spending habits. Four years later, he expanded this basic work to include Northern urban Negroes whom he characterized as suffering from the same restrictions and discrimination as Southern rural Negroes, and as restricted to similar occupations. In his thesis, he stressed the interest of the Negro in good quality and brand names, and his concern for personal appearance.

The most solid and encompassing of the continuing academic studies pioneered by Edwards was that of Irwin Friend and Irving B. Kravis (1957) of the Wharton School, using the Bureau of Labor Statistics data for 1950 to compare Negro and white spending habits at each economic level. This study, which firmly establishes the similarities and differences in the spending habits of the two races for broad categories of items, serves as an anchoring point for discussion of these patterns.

By the early 1940's, Negro marketing consultants began to appear, and some companies added Negroes to their staffs, either as salesmen or as marketing advisors. On at least one occasion an official of the Urban League acted as a consultant, advising Bullock's Department Store in Los Angeles on proper advertising directed at Negroes (*Business Week*, 1940).

One thread of advice offered at that time stressed the need to avoid offending Negroes. David Sullivan (1943) cautioned marketers to avoid Negro stereotypes such as minstrels, the name George, incorrect grammar, dialect, Aunt Jemima-type Negroes, watermelon, chicken, crap shooting, pork chops, gin, pickaninny, and Negroes as servants. Additionally, he advised avoidance of exaggerated Negroid facial attributes.

Market Surveys

In the post World War II years, Negro newspapers commissioned a number of market surveys. In 1946, a study was made which covered Milwaukee and Omaha (*Advertising Age*, 1946). A larger study, made at the same time, included a sample of 5,000 families in almost 30 cities (*Printers' Ink*, 1946).

In 1947, a study of 3,000 families in Washington, Baltimore, and Philadelphia was made for the Afro-American News *(Sales Management)*. Income, education, and brand preferences were reported. The total income of American Negroes was then estimated at $12 billion per year (*Journal of Marketing*, 1947).

In 1950, Daniel Starch, in a survey of 1,245 Negro men and women throughout the country for *Ebony* magazine, explored brand preferences. Studies of this sort, serving Negro-oriented media have since grown in volume. They have tended increasingly to be sponsored by magazines, but more recently also by radio stations, chains of stations, and station representatives.

In the mid-1950's, Henry Bullock (1961) conducted an extensive study of the Negro market for a chain of radio stations headed by Jules Paglin. Professor Bullock, subsequent to this study, wrote a general article on the Negro market which proved to be controversial, largely because he turned on the medium that sponsored his research. In it, he reported that Negroes were offended by appeals which distinguish them from other consumers and that their dignity was affronted by jive-talking radio disc jockeys.

Research and market assessments sponsored by radio and other sources have proliferated in the past decade. Major themes have been the increasing urbanization of Negroes and their growing power. In 1939, Negroes were said to have a cash income of $10.29 billion (*Sales Management*, 1945), in 1957, $16 billion, and in 1960, $20 billion (*Printers' Ink*, 1965).

In the late 1950's and early 1960's, articles in trade journals began to stress the brand consciousness and brand loyalty of Negroes. In 1958, for example, the Negro was described as seeking status and prestige through purchasing leading brands, and it was asserted that advertisements should emphasize this need (*Advertising Age*, 1958). An *Amalgamated Publishers, Inc.* (1963) article stated, "Quality is always put ahead of price since the Negro is determined to enjoy the symbols of status whenever he can, whatever the price."

The marketer was also reminded that there are social class distinctions within the Negro community (*Printers' Ink*, 1958). The upper class was reputed to value race, pride, and respectability; the middle class, security and status; and the lower class, conspicuous consumption and splurging.

Also in the late 1950's and early 1960's, numerous commercial surveys of the Negro market were done for the insurance industry, automobile companies, food manufacturers, and personal-care products manufacturers, among others. Parallel in time to these was a series of studies which concentrated on savings *vs.* aggregate spending (Alexis, 1962). Generally, these studies found that blacks saved *more* than whites of comparable income—a finding that violated a well-established stereotype. For a number of reasons, including the difficulty of arriving at an appropriate definition of saving (i.e., does it include investment in durable goods?), this line of inquiry is not pursued, but rather a concentration on the allocation of money among those goods and services which are bought.

Thus, by the mid-1960's, concern with the Negro market was widespread.

General Pattern of Expenditures

Buying behavior can be regarded as the allocation of a scarce resource—money—to various areas of life. As such, it will in part reflect the values of a person making such expenditures. But it will also reflect constraints and pressures of his life situation, his special advantages and disadvantages. In the past two decades, a number of studies have been made of the comparative spending and saving habits of Negroes and whites on a national basis, and sometimes comparative studies on a city-by-city basis. All manner of explanatory principles have been invoked.

Following is a brief outline of the factual information on similarities and differences in Negro-white spending patterns in such general areas as food, housing, medicine, and transportation.

In 1962, Marcus Alexis reviewed and summarized the more important studies of the Negro-white consumer behavior then available. There are some minor differences in findings in some of the city-to-city comparisons which were made from time to time, but these findings—if statistically reliable—are likely to reflect historical local conditions that are no longer relevant.

Of importance are Alexis' overall conclusions:

1. Total consumption expenditures of Negroes are less than for comparable income whites (i.e., Negroes save more out of a given income than do whites with the same incomes).

2. Negro consumers spend more for clothing and non-automobile transportation, and less for food, housing, medical care, and automobile transportation than do comparable-income whites.

3. There is no consistent racial difference in expenditures for either recreation and leisure, or for home furnishings and equipment at comparable income levels.

It should be noted that Alexis' summary includes two findings that are consistent across all studies up to that time, and which are in direct contradiction to well-known stereotypes: Negroes save more than whites of comparable income; Negroes spend less on automobiles than whites of comparable income. The lack of consistent differences in spending for recreation and leisure, and for home furnishings may be due to some definitional problems that we shall take up later.

The most solid and recent of the data on which Alexis' summary relies appears to be the 1950–1951 Bureau of Labor Statistics Cost of Living Survey, analyzed by Friend and Kravis. In Table 4 is their summary comparison of

TABLE 4.   Comparison of Negro-White Consumption Patterns, All Income Groups, Urban, 1950

	Negro	White	Negro as Percentage of White[a]
Number of families in sample	1,294	11,136	
Average after-tax income	$ 2,605	$ 4,051	64.3%
Average expenditure on total consumption	2,614	3,938	66.4
Total consumption	100.0%	100.0%	
Food	31.9	29.5	71.8
Alcoholic beverages	2.3	1.7	92.4[b]
Tobacco	2.1	1.8	81.2[b]
Housing	11.3	11.5	65.3
Fuel, light, etc.	5.0	4.1	82.0
Household operation	4.1	4.7	57.5
Furnishings and equipment	7.2	6.8	69.9
Clothing	13.6	11.3	79.8
Automobile expenses	7.0	11.9	39.1[c]
Other transportation	2.6	1.7	103.0
Medical care	3.7	5.3	46.2[c]
Personal care	3.0	2.2	91.9[b]
Recreation, etc.	4.8	6.0	52.7
Miscellaneous	1.1	1.5	51.7

[a]The percentages in this column are ratios of the dollar figures for Negroes to the corresponding dollar figures for whites. They are *not* the ratio of columns one and two.

[b]Discretionary expenditures.

[c]Unusually low.

Source: Study of Consumer Expenditures (Philadelphia, University of Pennsylvania, 1956).

Negro-white consumption patterns. This table can serve a number of purposes, including giving a more detailed breakdown than Alexis' broad categories, and at the same time illustrating the limitation of making such comparisons without income control.

When Negroes and whites as a total group are compared, Negroes spend proportionately more on food (31.9 to 29.5%), unquestionably as a reflection of Engel's law (Samuelson, 1961) that lower income households spend proportionately more on food.

However, if it is kept in mind that the average Negro expenditure on total consumption is 66.4% of that of white families, there are a number of figures that leap out. Certain categories of discretionary spending (marked [b]) are unusually high. For example, alcoholic beverages, 92.4%; tobacco, 81.2%; personal care, 91.9%. On the other hand, automobile expenses are only 39.1% and medical care 46.2%. The categories of overspending are those which one might label as personal display and immediate gratification.

Friend and Kravis also presented more detailed comparisons for the two income categories in which the bulk of the Negroes fell in the 1950–1951 study. At a minimum, these data of consumption patterns by city class are consistent with Alexis' conclusions when income is controlled. In five out of six circumstances, Negroes spent less on food than whites of comparable income. The exception is in small Southern cities, and may be due to the instability of the small sample of Negroes in that category.

With Alexis' summary and the Friend and Kravis data as a background, the latest comprehensive study available, the 1960–1961 BLS Cost of Living Survey, may be studied. Analyses of these data have been done by the authors and by Dr. Andrew F. Brimmer for the Department of Commerce. The two analyses are different and complementary to each other: the author's analysis looks at the 1960–1961 expenditure patterns; Brimmer makes an interesting study of the changes between 1950–1951 and 1960–1961.

A summary of expenditure patterns is shown in Table 5, which contains a built-in income control in that the *percentage* distribution of expenditures has been averaged across all income categories by thousand dollar intervals from $1,000 to $14,999 for each race. In this manner, the two races have been treated as though they had identical income distributions with equal numbers of persons in each income category.

As far as the overall profile of Negro-white differences is concerned, it remains the same as that for the previous decade with two exceptions: Negroes in 1960–1961 spent as much as whites on housing ("shelter"), and they clearly spent more on household furnishings and equipment.

To summarize the differences between the two groups, Table 6 shows the absolute percentage of "overspending" and "underspending" of Negroes in each expenditure category and the relative proportion of Negro/white spending. (The use of the terms "overspend" and "underspend" with regard to Negro expenditures in comparison with whites is not intended as evaluation, but as relative to the predominant white patterns which serve as the model responses.)

Because some categories (e.g., food and clothing) represent high absolute levels, a fairly large percentage difference makes for a small proportionate difference, whereas the reverse is true with alcoholic beverages which take only a relatively small amount of the total expenditures.

TABLE 5. Negro vs. White Distribution of Family Expenditures for Current Consumption
(Controlled for income: $1,000–$14,999 income inclusive)[a]

Expenditure Category	Average Percentage of Current Consumption	
	White	Negro
Total food expenditures	25.7%[b]	24.4%
Food prepared at home	20.7	20.0
Food away from home	5.1	4.4
Tobacco	1.8	2.0
Alcoholic beverages	1.7	2.3
Shelter	16.1	16.1
Rented dwelling	8.5	11.3
Owned dwelling	7.1	4.7
Other shelter	0.5	0.1
Fuel, light, refrigeration and water	4.8	4.6
Household operations	5.8	6.3
House furnishings and equipment	4.6	5.3
Clothing, material and services	8.9	12.5
Personal care	2.8	3.8
Medical care	7.1	4.5
Recreation	3.5	3.7
Reading	1.0	0.9
Education	0.9	0.5
Transportation	13.1	11.9
Automobiles	11.4	9.5
Other travel and transportation	1.8	2.4
Other expenditure	2.2	1.4
Expenditure for current consumption	100.1%	100.3%
Value items received without expenditure	5.1	4.2
Food	0.5	0.4
Shelter	0.5	2.2
Other	4.1	3.6

[a]Income control was obtained by "averaging averages"—that is, the per cent for each income group was weighted by 1, summed and divided by 8, the number of income categories. Income categories under $1,000 and over $15,000 were excluded from the analysis. Total sample size was *8000* families.

[b]For whites (controlled for income), 25.7% of the total expenditures for current consumption was spent on food.

One way of summarizing these is to note that Negroes and whites allocate about 6.6% of their income differently. The pattern of this difference in allocation is substantially what has been found in the past. Negroes spend more on clothing, personal care, household furnishings, alcoholic beverages, and tobacco. They are practically tied on recreation, housing (also new), and reading. They spend less (in order of magnitude) on medical care, food, transportation, "other," education, and fuel and light.

It is true that these data are controlled only for household income, and, therefore, one might be tempted to interpret some of these differences as a function of the great number of persons in the average Negro household. According to the 1960 census, Negroes averaged about 1.3 times as many persons per household as did whites.

TABLE 6. Summary Comparisons of Negro-White Expenditure Differences (Per Household)

	Percentage Difference Negro minus White	Proportion Negro/White Expenditure
Clothing	3.6%	1.4
Personal care	1.0	1.4
Household furnishings	0.7	1.2
Household operations	0.5	1.1
Alcoholic beverages	0.5	1.4
Tobacco	0.2	1.1
Recreation	0.1	1.0
Total Overspending	+6.6%	
Shelter	0.0	1.0
Fuel and light	−0.2	0.9
Education	−0.4	0.6
Other	−0.8	0.6
Transportation	−1.2	0.9
Food	−1.3	0.9
Medical care	−2.6	0.6
Total Underspending	−6.6%	

However, the number of persons to be fed must impose as severe a constraint as the number of persons to be serviced by any other category of expense. Clothing can be handed down. Household furnishings can be done without, and so on. According to this logic, the mere fact that Negro households are larger would tend to press more for overspending on food than on other items. However, since this does not happen, it must be concluded that differences are due to other factors.

At this point, the pattern shows what early data suggested: some greater amount of spending by Negroes on maintaining appearances and on immediate gratification.

Probably most persons would conclude that the fact that Negroes spend only 60 per cent as much as comparable whites on education and medical care is a misallocation of resources, particularly in the light of certain areas of overspending. But one might with equal justification argue that the overall pattern reflects either the lack of opportunity to spend on education, or in fact the broad life situation of the Negro and his estimation of what pays off for him.

One may then ask if a change in the Negroes' life situation has been or will be reflected in a change in expenditure patterns. This question has been raised both by Friend and Kravis, and by Brimmer.

On one hand, Friend and Kravis compared expenditure patterns of 1950–1951 with those from a 1935–1936 study. They used the $1,250–$1,500 before-tax income group in 1935–1936, and the $2,000–$3,000 after-tax income group for 1950–1951, thus adjusting as well as they could for changes in the value of the dollar. They concluded: "Except for the more rapid rise in the total of Negro income and consumption as compared with white, there is not much evidence that the consumption patterns of Negroes and the rest of the population are closer today than they were in the mid-1930s."

In substance, they found that Negroes of comparable economic status allocated their resources about the same way as their opposite number of 15 years previously.

On the other hand, Brimmer's comparison (1964) of 1950–1951 expenditure patterns with those for 1960–1961 led him to a conclusion different from that of Friend and Kravis for the earlier period. Brimmer computed "the percentage increase between 1950 and 1960–1961 in consumer expenditures for selective categories of goods and services in response to the percentage increase in family incomes after taxes."

This is a rough measure of what the economist calls income elasticity. If a person were to continue to allocate his expenditures in the same pattern after his income increased, all categories would have an index of one. However, as he shifted some of his new dollars disproportionately to any one category it would have an index number of more than one, or if he shifted away, less than one.

Brimmer's analysis is reproduced in Table 7. We can see from this that in the period from 1950–1960/61, blacks tended to invest their new dollars selectively in those categories of goods and services in which they have traditionally spent proportionally less than whites: education, household operation, housing (owned dwelling), automobile, medical care, and housing (rented and owned).

Furthermore, Negroes'.selective emphasis on previous areas of underspending exceed that of whites in all categories except food. And, except for personal care, which had an index number of 1.66, all of the traditional areas of overspending—tobacco, fuel, clothing, and alcoholic beverages—had index numbers of less than one. Brimmer thus concluded:

TABLE 7. Percentage Change in Selected Consumption Expenditures in Response to Percentage Change in After-Tax Income for Negro and White Families, 1950 and 1960–61

Expenditure Item	Negro Families	White Families
1. Education	4.22%	3.06%
2. Household operation	2.39	1.50
3. Housing: owned dwelling	2.25	2.11
4. Automobile	1.93	1.12
5. Medical care	1.80	1.56
6. Housing: rented dwelling	1.74	0.72
7. Personal care	1.66	1.58
8. Food away from home	1.02	0.51
9. Reading	1.00	0.85
10. Tobacco	0.91	0.78
11. Recreation	0.78	0.56
12. Fuel, light, etc.	0.73	1.09
13. Clothing	0.64	0.54
14. Alcoholic beverages	0.49	0.75
15. Transportation (exc. auto)	0.43	0.77
16. House furnishings	0.17	0.13
17. Food (at home)	0.12	0.27
18. Total Consumption	0.80	0.81

Read: 4.22% of each incremental dollar of after-tax income was spent on education.

Negro families will register the strongest demand in those areas associated with overall *upgrading in their standard of living*. There should be a strong market for housing and household operations, automobiles, medical care, and personal care. Those areas which have traditionally received a good share of the Negro's patronage—tobacco, clothing, alcoholic beverages, and food—will probably be characterized by relatively slow growth.

Perhaps Brimmer would have been more accurate if, instead of referring to an "upgrading in their standard of living," he had said that the Negroes' conception of a standard of living was coming closer to the white conception.

If one harks back to the conclusion of Friend and Kravis that the pattern of distribution of expenditures of Negroes had not changed in the decade and a half preceding 1950, it may be that they posed the question incorrectly. They asked, over a period in which income was rising, whether people who were on the same adjusted income level in 1950 were behaving like comparable people in 1935–1936.

However, Brimmer asked, over a period in which the absolute level of Negro income was rising, where the additional income was being allocated. It would appear on the basis of his analysis that as the absolute level of Negro income rose, their expenditure patterns in the decade 1950–1951 to 1960–1961 came closer to those of whites.

One may take this as evidence of the gradual assimilation of Negroes into the overall American life style to the extent that the opportunities exist (e.g., adequate housing on which to spend money), and to the extent that Negroes feel such assimilation is worth the effort.

There is little reason to pontificate on Negro-white differences in expenditure patterns. They reflect the life situation of Negroes and some aspects of Negroes' response to that situation. As one investigates the more detailed aspects of this market segment, however, one finds that within the broad consumer categories, some behaviors classified as similar may be dissimilar on closer inspection.

Thus, high expenditures on clothing may be associated with either a desire for display and immediate "kicks," or with striving toward respectability. And high expenditures on alcoholic beverages may be associated either with retreat from the present world, or with striving for social status.

One overall lesson that can be carried forward from a look at the broad patterns of expenditures is that any propensity to overpatronize one type of product or service necessitates at least a *de facto* strategy to free up discretionary money. Historically, Negroes have done this by underspending on many things that whites have regarded as "necessities," and by overspending on items that give "status."

However, such words as "necessity" and "status" are question begging, since what is at stake is precisely the question of what is seen as necessary and as status-giving.

Why Study the Negro Market?

There is without doubt in some meaningful sense, a "Negro market," and the case should be made that the Negro market is worthy of research for three reasons: (1) as the marketing behavior of Negroes is closely tied to the broad social problem of the Negro revolution; (2) as a practical marketing issue, the Negro market is a large segment of the American market, especially for certain products or brands; and (3) as an exercise in the much propounded doctrine of market segmentation, the study of the Negro market is a promising topic on which to hone our competence.

What does the Negro have to gain from studies of the Negro market? On the most general level, the white community is so deficient in understanding the situation of the Negro one might contend that an increase in comprehension of any sort is a "good thing."

With respect to our insights into the relationship of buying behavior to essential aspects of the Negroes' situation, changes in buying behavior must be assumed to be related to more fundamental changes. This knowledge may be used for diagnosis of changes in the Negroes' situation.

References

Advertising Age. "Ads Must Enhance Negroes' Prestige." (October 6, 1958), 87.

Advertising Age. "Ebony's Survey Reveals Negro Buying Habits." (August 28, 1958), 6.

Advertising Age. "Negroes Get More Brand Conscious as Incomes Rise." (March 19, 1946), 30.

Advertising Age. "Negro Market Will Be Controlling Factor in Profit Margin of Big U.S. Companies in 15 Years." September 21, 1964.

Advertising and Selling. "The Negro as Consumer." (September 3, 1930), 20.

Advertising and Selling. "Selling to Harlem." (October 17, 1928), 17.

Alexis, Marcus. "Some Negro-White Difference in Consumption." *The American Journal of Economics and Sociology,* Vol. 21 (January 1962), 12.

Amalgamated Publishers, Inc. "The Uncommon Market for Food." (1963), 4.

American Gas Light Journal. "Southern Servants Learn to Use Gas Economically." Vol. 104 (1916), 161.

Bullock, Henry. "Consumer Motivations in Black and White: I and II." *Harvard Business Review* (May–June 1961), 89; and (July–August 1961), 110.

Business Week. "Advice on Negroes, Los Angeles League Guides Ads." (April 13, 1940), 47.

Duncan, Otis D. "Discrimination Against Negroes," *The Annals of the American Academy of Political and Social Science.* Vol. 371 (May 1967), 85.

Edwards, Paul K. *Harvard Business School Alumni Association Bulletin.* Vol. 8 (May 1932), 242.

Friend, Irvin, and Irving B. Kravis. "New Light on the Consumer Market," *Harvard Business Review* (January–February 1957), 105.

Journal of Marketing. "Some Aspects of the Negro Market." Vol. 11, No. 299, 401.

Printers' Ink. "Marketing Guide." Fall, 1965.

Printers' Ink. "Methods Found Successful in Selling to Colored Population." (July 27, 1922), 120.

Printers' Ink. "The Negro Market." (April 14, 1958), 29.

Printers' Ink. "158 Negro Newspapers Study Racial Market." Vol. 216 (August 23, 1946), 98.

Sales Management. "Business and Government Leaders to Aid Study of Negro Market." Vol. 28, No. 78, January 10, 1931.

Sales Management. "Don't Do This If You Want to Sell Your Product to Negroes." Vol. 52 (March 1, 1943), 46.

Sales Management. "Negro Incomes and How They Are Spent." (June 14, 1945), 106.

Sales Management. "Negro Market Highlights in Three Cities." (May 20, 1947), 62.

Samuelson, Paul. *Economics.* New York: McGraw-Hill (1961), 132.

Sponsor. "The Negro Consumer." (September 14, 1964), 37.

U.S. Government. Current Population Reports: Population Estimates. Series P-25, No. 345, July 29, 1966.

Variety Store Merchandiser. "Negro Market Seen Changing." (September 1964), 39.

6.5 The Role of Blacks in Mass Media
WALTRAUD M. KASSARJIAN

The mass media in their short history have undergone many drastic changes and increased the importance of their role in society manyfold. One of the most recent and significant changes was not so much brought on by technological advance, as so many have been, but indicates the advent of a social change: a recognition of the existence of over 10 million black citizens and their influence on American life. The mass media began to reckon with blacks at all levels—from ownership through accurate portrayal of the black population and employment of Negroes to the actual consumption of mass media.

In this paper the emphasis is on the Negro as a consumer and the ramification of that for the mass media. It should first be stated that the Negro for almost all of his contacts is locked into a practically all-white media world. None of the 670 television stations in the U.S. are Negro-owned or programmed. Only 13 radio stations are Negro-owned although an additional 116 stations are Negro-programmed.[1] One hundred thirty-three Negro newspapers exist in this country of which only two are dailies.[2] Many of these have extremely limited circulation. In employment within the mass media the picture is hardly different, and data are not easy to come by. What role, then, does the Negro play in the white-dominated communications world?

It seems that it would be profitable to consider the relationship of America's black population with the mass media from more than one point of view. Any kind of a communicative act involves at least three main elements—the communicator, the message or content, and the audience or respondents. Thus we may focus on any one of these areas in an attempt to analyze the extent of the Negro's involvement with the mass media.

By far the least amount of information in the literature deals with the Negro as an audience or receiver of the communication. There is a fair amount of concern about the existence of a specific "Negro market" or the lack of one, but this is usually centered around demographic variables and buying habits of Negroes rather than their consumption of mass media output. It would seem that it would be equally profitable for the communicators to not only provide equal employment opportunities for Negroes in areas like the advertising business but also to be well informed about the consumption habits of Negroes as far as the media are concerned. Do Negroes present different percentages of the recipients of the various media, that is, is the proportion of black television viewers the same as for newspapers or for magazines? Are the same people making up these proportions? Are similar programs preferred by whites and Negroes? Do blacks and whites respond similarly to the same ad? What if the people shown in the ad are an integrated group? There is no end to the questions that need answering. The literature does not provide answers to all these questions. One reason for this is probably the relative recency of interest in the Negro as a consumer.

Cohen, in her survey of the black population's relationship to advertising, discusses in detail the difficulties experienced by blacks at the employment and initiating phase of communication material, and we shall not dwell on it here.[3]

Blacks as Respondents to the Mass Media

Bauer and Cunningham in their historical review of studies on the Negro market mention Bullock's 1961 study of advertising on radio as the earliest such endeavor.[4,5,6] Bullock went beyond the usual market segmentation data and studied Negro advertising receptivity and media consumption. At least at that time white people spent most of their time with television and newspapers (44% and 37% respectively), while blacks spent most time with the radio (39%) and with television and newspapers only 28% and 25% of the time. It was maintained that radio was preferred because it offers freedom to the imagination. Another influential factor may be that there are black-oriented radio stations but not television stations.

A survey of existing studies almost ten years later brings related results.[7] Greenberg and Dervin's studies are of special interest insofar as they not only report for several mass media but contrast three groups of audiences— middle-income whites, poor whites, and poor nonwhites. These researchers report poor blacks to be most exposed to television and radio, next to magazines, though mainly black publications, and least to newspapers. Non-poor whites watch television much less than blacks and use the newspapers considerably more than poor people, both black and white. It should be noted that the content of the reading also varies between nonpoor and poor; the latter limiting themselves very frequently to "headlines, ads and classified section."

Bogart in 1968 reported percentages of whites and Negroes using the three media—newspapers, radio, and television—with various demographic breakdowns for the two groups. He found that whites definitely read newspapers more than Negroes, while the difference in amount of time spent with radio becomes much less pronounced and disappears altogether in television.[8] In a subsequent analysis of more recent data, Bogart still finds the discrepancy in newspaper reading between whites and blacks but reports generally greater amounts of time spent by blacks than whites viewing television.[9] Unfortunately both of the studies are completely lacking in statistical analysis so that it is hard to determine the significance of these findings.

The first investigation of television viewing habits was conducted late in 1963 by Carey including 5,000 families in Illinois of which 10% were blacks.[10] He found differences in program preferences using rank orders for some 75 shows. Negroes preferred individual-centered programs with themes of conflict and loneliness; they showed less desire than whites for variety shows and those portraying families.

Several years later a similar study, but using sixth to twelfth graders of a southern school as subjects, found no significant differences between white and black viewers.[11]

A third study focuses on still another age group and geographic region— the teenager in Philadelphia,[12] and compares the results with those of Fletcher and Carey. Surlin and Dominick support Carey's finding that Negroes do not have a strong interest in family shows. Unfortunately, the study did not indicate how much of the differences could be explained by the variation in age groups and geographic areas sampled.

Greenberg and Dervin were no more successful in distinguishing consistent viewer preferences between blacks and whites.[13] However, blacks listed as their most liked shows programs featuring a black actor or actress.

Judging from the results of these few available studies, those communicators trying to reach the black audience are still lacking more definite guidelines. The picture is no different for the printed media than for television. There is little information on relative readership patterns of magazines and newspapers by blacks and whites. One study by an advertising company reported in *Advertising Age* concludes that advertisers will reach as many or more blacks by advertising in selected white publications than by employing the black media.[14] It appears that many Negro publications have a limited circulation and the one magazine which probably reaches more than one million readers, *Ebony*, seems to appeal to a select group of Negroes. Berkman[15] and Hirsch,[16] who both describe separately the readership of *Ebony*, call it atypical of the black population insofar as it strives toward whiteness and middle-class status, and thus can hardly be considered representative of the Negro population as a whole.

One actual experimental study is reported by Petrof.[17] He interviewed 612 black people after an ad for a local merchant dealing with both blacks and whites was run in the major white and in the only black newspaper in Atlanta, Georgia. The conclusion was that firms catering primarily to blacks can have a more effective impact on their prospective customers by advertising in the black publication. Blacks notice advertisements in their newspaper primarily when the message concerns products or firms used exclusively by them. The advertiser of goods and service for general use can attract more attention from blacks by advertising in the general newspapers. Apparently blacks bought the black paper because it covered local black news more adequately than the white papers.

While the studies just cited are centered on Negro audiences and their preferences, there is another facet of Negro participation in the mass media which requires a closer look not only at Negro but maybe even more so at white audiences or recipients of communication. After all, those involved at the production end of the communications for the longest time were shy in utilizing Negroes for fear of an adverse reaction in their by far more numerous white customers. Some advertisers speak of an expected "white backlash" without providing any evidence of its existence.

Barban and his associates conducted several studies in this area.[18,19,20] Employing the semantic differential technique for measuring reactions to ads using all-white or all-negro models as well as integrated ads, they observed nothing approaching a white backlash response in their middle-class samples. All three kinds of ads were rated favorably by both Negroes and whites. Whites showed greatest preference for integrated ads, then for white ones, and least for all-Negro ads. Negroes rated all-Negro and integrated ads equally favorably, all-white ads somewhat less so. However, Negroes also did not seem to have any difficulty identifying with all-white ads.

In another study, Gould, Sigband, and Zoerner found little evidence that blacks react more favorably to black ads.[21] An experimental study by Muse also found that ads using black models were rated no less favorably than all-white ones by a group of students.[22] However, it is interesting to note that some variations across product categories were obtained. Vodka and beer showed no significant differences in mean rating for the black and white advertisements; black cigarette ads were rated more favorably than white ones; and for feminine napkins the reverse was true.

Stafford, Birdwell, and Van Tassel approached the same problem somewhat differently.[23] They used both verbal responses and measurements with the pupillometer to study responses of 100 white shoppers in New York, Chicago, and Los Angeles to two integrated ads. Their findings were not clear-cut and varied over products and ads, but the expected "white backlash" could not be established. Unstructured verbal questioning indicated little difference in overt reaction to the integrated and nonintegrated ads. The semantic rating scale clearly revealed a preference for integrated ads, especially with regard to a lipstick advertisement, which stands in contrast to Muse's findings,[24] whose subjects preferred all-white ads for a personal item.

Cagey and Cardozo divided white audiences by degree of prejudice as determined by the California "E" Scale and found only highly prejudiced people reacted unfavorably to integrated ads, the others received all the ads similarly.[25] This investigation has been criticized for its lack of generalizability because of the use of students as subjects. The same would hold for the Muse study.

Blacks as Communicators

The foregoing studies were concerned with respondent analyses carried out almost exclusively on television and printed media audiences. However, this is not the whole story. The change suggested at the outset of the paper is probably most clearly seen in the content part of the mass media. Even without conducting an analysis, the layman lately can observe a much greater utilization of the Negro in all the media. But just how great is the impact? Are we overestimating the inroads made by Negroes simply because any change in this area is highly noticeable and somewhat of a surprise?

Probably the earliest study available is that of Shuey, King, and Griffith, who in 1949–1950 examined the frequency of appearance of Negroes in pictures of six nationally distributed magazines, *Life, Time, Saturday Evening Post, Ladies Home Journal,* and *Colliers.*[26] Their findings seem typical of findings by later studies. Only about .5% of the pictures showed a readily identifiable Negro. Of these only 6%, very few indeed, could be classified as holding occupations "above skilled labor," and those were in sports or entertainment. While the whites were often shown idle, the blacks were never at leisure.

This condition seems to continue until the late 1960's when—probably as a result of much social unrest and hard work by civil rights workers—an increase and change in role of the Negro in the mass media occurred.

Boyenton in checking four large metropolitan newspapers and three magazines in 1965 for ads portraying Negroes, found still well under 1%.[27] When Cox surveyed in 1967–1968 the same magazines that Shuey had, the percentage had gone to 2%.[28] The slow increase continued. For 1969, Cox reported about 4% integrated ads in six large circulation newspapers—*New York Times, Washington Post, Los Angeles Times, Philadelphia Inquirer, Chicago Daily News,* and *Houston Post.* The *Houston Post* was quite out of line with the others, with only 1.2%.[29] By that time, Cox found Negro ads in the magazines had gone up to 5.3%.

Kassarjian, in his longitudinal studies of twelve national magazines from 1946 to 1956 to 1965 and finally 1969, surveyed some 150,000 pages of print in search of black ads.[30,31] He also found a definite numerical increase of Negroes in ads, especially in 1969, but only to about 2 or 3%.

Greenberg and Kahn concentrated their analysis on cartoons in *Playboy* magazine.[32] In bi-annual samples from 1956 through 1966 they report less than 1% of the cartoons showed blacks in a contemporary setting. However, after that the percentage started increasing to 3% in 1968 and 4% in the first nine issues of 1969.

Advertising in business magazines, such as *Business Week, Dun's Review, Fortune, Forbes,* and *Nation's Business,* showed similar changes from 1.5% of Negro ads in 1958–1959 to 5.6% in 1968–1969.[33]

We thus can find our general impression of an increase in sheer number of Negroes appearing in print confirmed, but definitely not to the point where they would be found proportionately to their number in the general population and definitely frequently not in real life situations. Several studies stress that a large proportion even of the Negroes appearing in ads in the earlier years are shown as non-Americans or in exotic settings. However, in many of the recent studies another factor, maybe even more important than mere number, seemed to stand out. The role the Negro plays is changing drastically, which is probably a reflection of their general role change in society.

Shuey noted the menial role portrayed by almost all the Negroes in their sample.[34] When Cox endeavored to replicate for 1967–1968 Shuey's study, he still found only 2% of the ads depicting Negroes, but their occupations were just about reversed.[35] In the later study 71% held "above skilled labor" jobs while only 8% appeared in the "below skilled labor" category or the previously stereotyped role of the Negro. This encouraging finding, which seems to bring the Negro closer to the roles depicted by whites in the magazines, appears in more than one study.

As one part of his study, Ferguson sampled two issues a year of five different magazines, *Newsweek, Life, Mademoiselle, Esquire,* and *Business Week* from 1953 to 1969.[36] He reports a gradual increase in Negro and integrated ads from almost nonexistent to close to 5% in 1969. The overall average for Negro ads was only .26% and an additional .84% were integrated. Ten years had no blacks at all. By 1969 the all-Negro ads had increased to 1% and the integrated ads to close to 5%. On the average, blacks were portrayed a surprising 68% of the time as equals to whites (more yet in recent years), 26% as inferior and 5% as superior.

The Kassarjian studies reflected very similar trends.[37,38] In 1946 more than three fourths of the Negroes shown fit into the "service" and "labor" occupational categories. Beginning with 1965 and continued in 1969 the greatest number of Negroes were classified in "professional sports, entertainment" (about two thirds) and about one fourth of all the Negroes were depicted without a specific occupation, also a pronounced change from earlier years and studies. The "service" and "labor" categories together fell to just over 3%. With regard to group composition, mixed nonpeer relationships declined from 63% in 1946 to 9.5% in 1969; mixed peer relationships increased from 6% in 1946 to 45% in 1969. Advertisements portraying black-white work interaction declined from 57% to 18% in 1969, as mixed social interaction rose from 2% in 1946 to 25% in 1969.

Another related finding to the above role changes was reported from a comparison of advertising in *Ebony* for 1960 and 1969.[39] While this magazine caters to the Negro aspiring to white society and the middle-class, even here the type of model used in the ads changed over the years from greater use of light-skinned Negroes in 1960 to more emphasis on dark-skinned, more explicitly Negroid-looking models in 1969. It is hoped that this trend is an indication of higher self-esteem and pride in their race.

The findings presented in the previous section revolve around the printed media. However, comparable results are reported by researchers for the field of television.

The earliest television audit was reported by Schmidt for Los Angeles in 1965 and revealed 2% of the commercials had Negro models, which broke down into .65% with speaking roles and 1.39% with nonspeaking roles.[40] The percentage of shows containing blacks was 12% of which only 3.36% were in speaking roles. These figures increased in subsequent studies, but vary as the investigations never are exact replicas of previous ones.

In 1966 Plotkin audited ads in connection with sports events which often have Negro participants, but he found even here only 5% Negroes in the commercials.[41]

While Shayton speaks of 2.5% Negro commercials in 1967 in connection with the inquiry by the New York City Commission on Human Rights,[42] Dominick and Greenberg observed an increase from 4% in 1967 to 10% in 1969 in prime-time exposures and from 5% to 12% during the day.[43] The latter study also notes that blacks are still not shown in realistic roles.

Wanderer in a study early in 1970 of both network and local stations in Los Angeles reports 9% of the 1,600 commercials viewed were integrated or all-Negro, with no significant differences between day and prime-time programs nor between network and local stations.[44]

An Iowa City television analysis in 1970 by Roberts included regular programs as well as commercials.[45] A Negro appeared on 50% of the shows but only 10% of the commercials.

According to Cox the number of advertisements utilizing Negroes by 1969 had reached 11% on the Houston network channels.[46] This study is of special interest insofar as it is the only survey found which reached over three media—television, newspapers, and magazines. The outstanding finding was that television leads with the highest percentage of Negro commercials, followed by magazines (5.3%), and last the newspapers (3.4%). The highest intra-media fluctuations showed up in magazines, from the *New Yorker* with 3% to *Look* and *Life* with over 8%. As is generally the case, no significant difference in percentages shows up between networks. Of the newspapers, the *Houston Post* with only 1.2% stood out, as reported before. Cox hypothesized about these findings that television is most readily adaptable to incorporating Negro models in commercials and that local advertising, heavily present in newspapers, is less sensitive to social change.

The only other study reaching across media was carried out by Ferguson.[47] The magazine portion was reported earlier. It is of interest to note that while Cox found *Life* to have one of the highest percentages of Negro ads in his sample, Ferguson noted it to be lowest. A second portion of the study centered on an early 1970 network audit in prime-time in Boston. A total of 8% of the commercials observed contained Negro characters, about equally divided between males and females and with no differences between the three networks.

All these percentages do not do justice to absolute numbers of Negroes being used in commercials, as the total number of commercials also increased

50% over the years and more recently many a time more than one Negro appeared in one commercial. On the other hand, complaints have been heard that Negro ads are given shorter exposure time and are not run as frequently as equivalent white commercials.

The relative recency of all these studies probably accounts for the fact that many of these analyses indicate—contrary to the early studies of the printed media—that Negroes are very seldom portrayed on television in the former, stereotyped roles. Thus one study may report a high percentage of Negroes in speaking roles (about 50% of those appearing)[48] another, portrayal of blacks mainly as equals to whites or overrepresented in professional or managerial roles.[49,50,51] The latter seems to hold also for whites.

An interesting hypothesis is presented by Clark who suggests that minorities on television go through four successive stages from nonrecognition through ridicule and regulation to, finally, respect.[52] In 1969 when he was writing, he placed minorities at the regulatory stage, manifested by overemphasis on roles relating to law and order. It comes to mind that this may be true for majorities as well.

Conclusion

In recent years an awakening by the mass media to the existence of the black segment in the American population has taken place. With the explosion of the importance of the mass media in modern life, we can also record a very slowly increasing utilization of black communicators, most notably at first in television, and a heightened interest by the industry in reaching and understanding the black minority. Nonetheless, by no means should we get the mistaken impression that the battle is won for the Negro. A start has been made, but the road to equality and acceptance has only begun.

Notes and References

1. *Advertising Age,* "Black Ownership of Radio Grows—Slowly," Vol. 41 (February 9, 1970), 10.

2. Spaulding, N. W., "Bridging the Color Gap," *Public Relations Journal,* Vol. 25 (April 1969), 8–11.

3. Cohen, Dorothy, "Advertising and the Black Community," *Journal of Marketing,* Vol. 34 (4) (1970), 3–11.

4. Bauer, Raymond A., and Scott Cunningham, "The Negro Market," *Journal of Advertising Research,* Vol. 10 (2) (1970), 3–13.

5. Bullock, Henry Allen, "Consumer Motivations in Black and White—I," *Harvard Business Review,* Vol. 39 (1961), 89–104.

6. ———, "Consumer Motivations in Black and White—II," *Harvard Business Review,* Vol. 39 (1961), 110–124.

7. Greenberg, Bradley S., and Brenda Dervin, *Use of the Mass Media by the Urban Poor,* Praeger, 1970.

8. Bogart, Leo, "Black Is Often White," *Media/scope Magazine,* November 1968.

9. ———, "Negro and White Media Exposure: New Evidence," *Journalism Quarterly.* Vol. 49 (1) (1972), 15–21.

10. Carey, James W., "Variations in Negro-White Television Preferences," *Journal of Broadcasting,* Vol. 10 (3) (1966), 199–212.

11. Fletcher, ALan, "Negro and White Children's Television Program Preferences," *Journal of Broadcasting,* Vol. 13 (4) (1969), 359–366.

12. Surlin, Stuart H., and Joseph R. Dominick, "Television's Function as a 'Third Parent' for Black and White Teenagers," *Journal of Broadcasting,* Vol. 15 (1) (Winter 1970–1971), 55–64.

13. Greenberg and Dervin, *op. cit.*

14. ———, "Negro Media Not Mathematically Necessary to Reach Black Market," *Advertising Age,* August 18, 1969.

15. Berkman, Dave, "Advertising in 'Ebony' and 'Life': Negro Aspirations vs. Reality," *Journalism Quarterly,* Vol. 40 (Winter 1963), 53–64.

16. Hirsch, Paul M., "An Analysis of *Ebony:* The Magazine and Its Readers," *Journalism Quarterly,* Vol. 45 (1968), 261–265.

17. Petrof, John V., "Reaching the Negro Market: A Segregated Versus a General Newspaper," *Journal of Advertising Research,* Vol. 8 (1968), 40–43.

18. Barban, Arnold M., and Edward W. Cundiff, "Negro and White Response to Advertising Stimuli," *Journal of Marketing Research,* Vol. 1 (1964), 53–56.

19. ———, and Werner F. Grunbaum, "A Factor Analytic Study of Negro and White Responses to Advertising Stimuli," *Journal of Applied Psychology,* Vol. 49 (4) (1965), 274–279.

20. ———, "The Dilemma of 'Integrated' Advertising," *The Journal of Business of the University of Chicago,* Vol. 42 (4) (1969), 477–496.

21. Gould, John W., Norman B. Sigband, and Cyril E. Zoener, Jr., "Black Consumer Reaction to Integrated Advertising: An Explanatory Study," *Journal of Marketing,* Vol. 34 (1970), 20–26.

22. Muse, William V., "Product-Related Response to Use of Black Models in Advertising," *Journal of Marketing Research,* Vol. 8 (1971), 107–109.

23. Stafford, James, Al Birdwell, and Charles Van Tassel, "Integrated Advertising—White Backlash?" *Journal of Advertising Research,* Vol. 10 (2) (1970), 15–20.

24. Muse, *op. cit.*

25. Cagley, James W., and Richard N. Cardozo, "White Response to Integrated Advertising," *Journal of Advertising Research,* Vol. 10 (1970), 35–39.

26. Shuey, A. M., M. King, and B. Griffith, "Stereotyping of Negroes and Whites: An Analysis of Magazine Pictures," *Public Opinion Quarterly,* Vol. 17 (1953), 281–287.

27. Boyenton, W. H., "The Negro Turns to Advertising," *Journalism Quarterly,* Vol. 42 (Spring 1965), 227–235.

28. Cox, Keith K., "Changes in Stereotyping of Negroes and Whites in Magazine Advertisements," *Public Opinion Quarterly,* Vol. 33 (Winter 1969–1970), 603–606.

29. ———, "Social Effects of Integrated Advertising," *Journal of Advertising Research,* Vol. 10 (2) (1970), 41–44.

30. Kassarjian, Harold H., "The Negro and American Advertising: 1946–1965," *Journal of Marketing Research,* Vol. 6 (1969), 29–39.

31. ———, "Blacks in Advertising: A Further Comment," *Journal of Marketing Research,* Vol. 8 (1971), 392–393.

32. Greenberg, Bradley, and Sandra Kahn, "Blacks in *Playboy* Cartoons," *Journalism Quarterly,* Vol. 48 (1971), 557–560.

33. Roeder, Richard A., "Integration in Business Advertising," *The Master of Business Administration,* Vol. 5 (1) (1970), 26–29.

34. Shuey, *op. cit.*

35. Cox (1969–1970), *op. cit.*

36. Ferguson, Richard D., Jr., "The Role of Blacks in Magazine and Television Advertising," Unpublished Master's Thesis, Boston University, May 1970.

37. Kassarjian (1969), *op. cit.*

38. Kassarjian, Harold H., "The Negro and American Advertising: An Historical Analysis," Paper read at the Western Psychological Association Meetings in Los Angeles, April 1970.

39. Geizer, Ronald, "Advertising in *Ebony:* 1960 and 1969," *Journalism Quarterly,* Vol. 48 (1) (1971), 131–134.

40. Schmidt, Fred H., "A Guest in the Home: A Survey of Television and the American Negro," Unpublished Paper, Institute of Industrial Relations, UCLA, January 1966.

41. Plotkin, Lawrence, "Report on the Frequency of Appearance of Negroes on Televised Commercials," NAACP Legal Defense and Educational Fund, 1967.

42. Shayon, Robert Lewis, "Commercials in Black and White," *Saturday Review,* (October 5, 1968), 48.

43. Dominick, Joseph R., and Bradley S. Greenberg, "Three Seasons of Blacks on Television," *Journal of Advertising Research,* Vol. 10 (2) (1970), 21–27.

44. Wanderer, Aviva, "The Negro Image in Television Advertising—1970," A Master's Thesis in Theater Arts, UCLA, 1970.

45. Roberts, Churchill, "The Portrayal of Blacks on Network Television," *Journal of Broadcasting,* Vol. 15 (1) (Winter 1970–1971), 45–53.

46. Cox, Keith K., "An Audit of Integrated Advertisements in Television, Magazines, and Newspapers," Paper read at the Western Psychological Association Meeting in Los Angeles, April 1970.

47. Ferguson, *op. cit.*

48. Wanderer, *op. cit.*

49. Ferguson, *op. cit.*

50. DeFleur, Melvin L., "Occupational Roles as Portrayed on Television," *Public Opinion Quarterly,* Vol. 28 (Spring 1964), 57–74.

51. Roberts, *op. cit.*

52. Clark, Cedric, "Television and Social Controls: Some Observations on the Portrayals of Ethnic Minorities," *Television Quarterly,* Vol. 8 (Spring 1969), 19–22.

7 Models of Consumer Decision Making

Overview

Throughout this book a number of conceptions of human behavior and consumer decision making have been presented. It might be useful to distinguish them in terms of their inclusiveness and level of theoretical abstraction.

In some cases reference has been made to *comprehensive formal theories* of behavior, including Freud's psychoanalytic theory, Lewin's field theory, and Hull's learning theory. In other cases *"middle range" theories* of human behavior have been applied to consumer decision processes. The sociologist Merton (1957) has designated middle range theories as those "intermediate to the minor working hypotheses evolved in abundance during the day-to-day routines of research, and the all-inclusive speculations comprising a master conceptual scheme" (pp. 5–6). Such middle range theories include such concepts as cognitive dissonance and diffusion theory. Finally, certain *limited hypothetical concepts* have been presented, including the notions of social character and perceived risk.

Emerging Concerns

There are perhaps three emerging concerns within the field of consumer behavior today worthy of note and discussion. These concerns are (1) the optimum route to predictive and useful theories, (2) the extent of borrowing from the pure behavioral sciences, and (3) the issue of who is served by consumer behavior theory—marketers or consumers.

The *optimum route to theoretical development* in a field is always a difficult matter. The goal is to chart the most reasonable means to improve explanation and prediction of human actions in the marketplace. If anything, the field of consumer behavior has been overburdened with disjointed research on limited hypothetical concepts. That is, replications have been rare and research has insufficiently built on previous research. The knowledge base has undoubtedly increased, but the sum total of that knowledge is sometimes discouraging to contemplate. In this last chapter we present some master models of consumer decision making which offer some promise for integrating and organizing our knowledge in the field and guiding future research and theoretical development.

Consumer behavior is an applied field, and has *borrowed* extensively from the basic behavioral science disciplines. The difficulty is that some of this borrowing has been unsystematic, and perhaps inappropriate when taken out of the context for which it was intended. Wholesale borrowing may also delay the development of concepts specific to the consumption role.

The issue of borrowing is now being confronted within consumer behavior. This is most clearly seen with regard to personality theory—as discussed in the Kassarjian selection in Chapter 2. In essence, much of the discouragement with the value of personality as a determinant of consumer behavior has been due to using personality theories and measures indiscriminately, and administering personality inventories designed to measure schizophrenia or paranoia on the assumption that they will predict whether a person buys Charmin or Scott toilet paper. Consumer behavior researchers are now designing their own personality measures.

We must also confront the issue of *who is served by consumer behavior research.* Is it an instrument for the manipulation and control of consumers by marketers? Is it a means of better determining consumer needs in order to improve the efficiency of the marketing system, with a resulting decline in the cost of marketing and an increase in consumer welfare? Is it a means of improving consumer decision processes through education and public policy, such as unit pricing and standard size requirements for packaging? Consumer behavior theory is being used increasingly, both by consumer advocates such as the Federal Trade Commission and by the marketing community. The promise is for improved and more effective marketing, ultimately in the public interest.

Formal Models of Consumer Decision Processes

An important development within the consumer behavior field has been the emergence of formal models of consumer decision processes. These models represent a departure from the traditional practice of building toward a theory on the basis of specific behavioral concepts. The potential of consumer decision models is that integration of concept-related research and findings may occur more quickly and systematically, and that the gaps in our knowledge may be more readily apparent, thus suggesting research priorities. Formal, integrative models may also encourage better empirical analysis of consumer behavior phenomena, which are usually complex and multivariate.

The models presented in this chapter draw upon the range of theoretical propositions developed in the preceding chapters, and incorporate a diversity of theoretical approaches. They fulfill an integrative and organizational function, and should serve to guide future empirical research on consumer behavior.

Howard-Sheth Model

Researchers Howard and Sheth have rigorously pursued the development of a "theory" of buyer behavior. Howard's early formulation was based on learning theory (1963), but in subsequent elaborations and revisions the model has become highly robust theoretically, and now draws from a considerable range of behavioral areas.

The Howard-Sheth model focuses on repeat buying, and relies on four major components: stimulus inputs, hypothetical constructs, exogenous variables, and response outputs. The *stimulus inputs* emanate from the marketing and social environments. The *hypothetical constructs* represent the buyer's internal state and include perceptual and learning variables. The *exogenous variables,* including social class and culture, influence the hypothetical constructs. Finally, the *response outputs* represent a hierarchical set of possible responses from attention to purchase behavior.

The complete and elaborated account of this very rich model is presented in a book by Howard and Sheth (1969). These authors are now working on the application of their model to public policy decisions as well as to marketing decisions.

Kotler's Review

In the selection following the Howard-Sheth model, Kotler reviews a number of mathematical models of consumer behavior, which again draw heavily from learning theory formulations. The decision problem on which he focuses is how consumers select brands of consumer staples in repeat purchase situations.

In examining models of increasing sophistication, Kotler opts for model complexity in order to best approximate market reality. Yet, as he notes, "simple models have the virtue that data can be found and predictions can be tested." In fact, most comprehensive models of consumer behavior are difficult to test since they are generally characterized by implied relationships, and the concepts and variables used tend to vary in level of abstraction, thus making measurement and analysis exceedingly difficult. These difficulties are aptly demonstrated in an empirical test of the Howard-Sheth model by researchers Farley and Ring (1970). They found that considerable methodological advances are necessary before valid assessment of this very sophisticated model can be made.

Nicosia Model

Nicosia offers a comprehensive model encompassing a number of sets of variables and specification of relationships (Nicosia, 1966). The selection by Nicosia summarizes some of the essential elements of the model. (For a comprehensive account of the model, see Nicosia, 1966, third printing.) Nicosia describes its simplest form in the following sequence:

A first approximation of the structure would consist of the flow: the firm, its advertisement, the consumer's possible exposure to it, the interaction between the advertisement and the consumer's predispositions operating or evoked at the time of exposure, the possible formation of an attitude, the possible transformation of this attitude into a motivation, the possible conversion of this motivation into an act of purchase, and then back to the consumer's predispositions, *and* to the firm.

The Nicosia model is a step toward an encompassing cognitive theory of consumer behavior, and in fact can be considered a model of general human decision-making behavior. The essential idea is that consumer behavior can be seen as a decision-making sequence. This allows the use of simulation and mathematical techniques to explore interrelationships and to better predict decision outcomes. Adaptability to mathematical formulations opens up promising avenues for further research.

Bettman's Information Processing Model

Bettman's model is based on cognitive theory. Basically, the view of the cognitive theorist is not that decisions are purely the end result of stimulus-response sets, but rather that the individual's cognitive structures are involved in information acquisition and processing. Decisions, in essence, are not the result of learning over time, but involve the cognitive reorganization of reality as perceived by the actor. Bettman, for example, argues that "persons often perceive the external world in terms of cue patterns or configurations, rather than in terms of separate cues." This is an important distinction, since in essence the consumer is not exposed to a product stimulus but rather to a configuration of product stimuli, which has important implications for his choice processes.

Bettman develops a flow chart of how a specific individual consumer selects grocery products, using mathematical concepts such as decision networks and Simon's work on an information processing theory of human problem solving. Bettman's selection presents the results of his attempt to computerize the actual decision process and develops a general decision and choice model.

The Bettman and Nicosia models have some similarities in their general approach. Both are grounded in the cognitive theory of consumer behavior, and are capable of employing microanalytic simulation in order to derive decision criteria.

Conclusion

Knowledge of consumer behavior is increasing at a rapid pace. The absolute level of knowledge and the ability to explain and predict consumer actions are, however, still quite limited. The field of consumer behavior has been somewhat fragmented in orientation until now, and has largely borrowed at will from the behavioral sciences without a consistent rationale for theoretical development.

The development of comprehensive models and formulations is a significant step toward the eventual development of a consistent theory of consumer behavior which specifies interrelationships among variables and is capable of explanation and prediction. The rationale for model development is that empirical research can be most meaningful and productive when conducted with some sort of theoretical model in mind. Certain variables can then be isolated for intensive analysis of their interrelationships and effects. Furthermore, empirical knowledge can be integrated in an overall framework as it is conducted.

References

Farley, J. U., and L. W. Ring. "An Empirical Test of the Howard-Sheth Model of Buyer Behavior." *Journal of Marketing Research,* Vol. 7 (November 1970), 427–438.

Howard, J. A., and J. N. Sheth. *The Theory of Buyer Behavior.* Wiley, 1969.

———. *Marketing Management: Analysis and Planning* (revised edition). Irwin, 1963.

Merton, R. K. *Social Theory and Social Structure* (revised edition). The Free Press, 1957.

Nicosia, F. M. *Consumer Decision Processes.* Prentice-Hall, 1966.

7.1 A Theory of Buyer Behavior
JOHN A. HOWARD, JAGDISH N. SHETH

The usual purpose of a theory is to explain empirical phenomena. The empirical phenomenon which we want to explain is the buying behavior of individuals over a period of time. More specifically, our theory is an attempt to explain the *brand choice* behavior of the buyer. We assume that brand choice is not random but systematic, and the task we have undertaken in developing this theory is to formulate a structure that enables us to view it as a system.

To elaborate on our assumption: First, we assume that buying behavior is rational in the sense that it is within the buyer's "bounded rationality" (March and Simon, 1958); that is, his behavior is rational within the limits of his cognitive and learning capacities and within the constraint of limited information. Second, we are attempting to build a positive theory and not a normative theory. Third, if brand choice behavior is assumed to be systematic, then it can be observed in certain standard ways. Later on, we describe a series of measures of the buyer's buying behavior generally labeled purchase behavior, attitude toward a brand, comprehension of the brand, attention to impinging stimuli, and intention to buy a brand. Fourth, if behavior is systematic, it is caused by some event—a stimulus—either in the buyer or in the buyer's environment. This event or stimulus is the input to the system, and purchase behavior is the output. What we must describe then, is what goes on between the input and the output.

A Summary of the Theory

Much buying behavior is more or less repetitive, and the buyer establishes purchase cycles for various products which determine how often he will buy. For some products, such as durable appliances, this cycle is lengthy and purchase is infrequent. For many other products, such as food and personal-care items, the purchase cycle is short and purchase is frequent. Confronted by repetitive brand-choice decisions, the consumer simplifies his task by storing relevant information and establishing a routine in his decision process. Therefore our theory must identify the elements of his decision process, observe the changes that occur in them over time as a result of their repetitive nature, and show how a combination of decision elements affects search processes and the incorporation of information from the buyer's commercial and social environment.

The elements of a buyer's brand-choice decision are (1) a set of motives, (2) several alternative courses of action, and (3) decision mediators by which the motives are matched with the alternatives. Motives are specific to a product class, and reflect the underlying needs of the buyer. The alternatives are the various brands that have the potential of satisfying the buyer's motives.

There are three important notions involved in the definition of alternatives as brands. First, the several brands which become alternatives to the buyer need not belong to the same product class *as defined by the industry.* For example, a person may see Sanka coffee, Ovaltine, and Tetley's tea as three alternatives to satisfy his motives related to beverage consumption. He also may see only two alternatives, such as coffee and beer, both belonging to physically dissimilar product classes. Second, the brands which are alternatives of the buyer's choice decision are generally small in number, collectively called his "evoked set." The evoked set is only a fraction of the brands he is aware of, and a still smaller fraction of the total number of brands actually on the market. Third, any two consumers may have quite different alternatives in their evoked sets.

Decision mediators are the set of rules that the buyer employs to match his motives and his means of satisfying those motives. They serve the function of ordering and structuring the buyer's motives, and then ordering and structuring the various brands based on their potential to satisfy these ordered motives. Decision mediators develop by the buyer's process of learning about the buying situation. They are therefore influenced by information from the buyer's environment, and even more importantly by the actual experience of purchasing and consuming the brand.

When the buyer is just beginning to purchase a product class, he lacks experience; he does not have a set of decision mediators for that product class. To develop them, he *actively seeks information* from his commercial and social environments. The information he actively seeks, or accidentally receives, is subjected to perceptual processes, which not only limit his intake of information (magnitude of information is affected) but modify it to suit his frame of reference (quality of information is affected). These modifications are significant in that they distort the neat "marketing-stimulus consumer-response" relation.

Along with his active search for information, the buyer may to some extent generalize from similar past experience. Such generalization may be due to the physical similarity of a new product class to an old product class. For example, during initial purchases of whisky, a buyer may generalize from his experiences in buying gin. Generalization can also occur when two product classes are physically dissimilar, but have a common meaning deriving from a company brand name. For example, a buyer might generalize from his experience in buying a refrigerator or range to his first purchase of a dishwasher.

Whatever the source, the buyer develops sufficient decision mediators to enable him to choose a brand which seems to have the best potential for satisfying his motives. If the brand proves satisfactory, the potential of that brand to satisfy his motives for subsequent purchases is increased, and the probability of his buying that brand again is likewise increased. With repeated satisfactory purchases of one or more brands, the buyer is likely to manifest a routine decision process in which the sequential steps in buying are so well structured that an event which triggers the process may also complete it. Routine purchasing implies that decision mediators are well established, and that the buyer has strong brand preferences.

The phase of repetitive decision making in which the buyer reduces the complexity of a buying situation with the help of information and experience is called "the psychology of simplification." The more the buyer simplifies his environment, the less is his tendency to engage in active search behavior. The environmental stimuli related to the purchase situation become more meaningful and less ambiguous. Furthermore, the buyer establishes more cognitive consistency among brands as he moves toward routine response, and the incoming information is then screened with regard to its magnitude and quality. He becomes less attentive to stimuli which do not fit his cognitive structure, and he distorts these stimuli when they are forced upon him. These implied mechanisms explain a phenomenon for which there is growing evidence (cf. the work of John Dollard of Yale University): people can be exposed to a television commercial but not perceive it.

A surprising phenomenon occurs in the case of frequently purchased products, such as food and personal-care items. The buyer, after establishing a routine decision process, may begin to feel bored with such repetitive decision making. He may also become satiated, even with a preferred brand. In both cases, he may feel that all existing alternatives—including the preferred brand—are unacceptable, which generates a desire to *complicate* the buying situation by considering new brands. This process can be called "the psychology of complication." Ultimately the buyer identifies a new brand, and begins again to simplify. Thus the continuing process of buying frequently purchased items develops a cycle of information seeking that goes from simplification to complication and back again.

Determining the intensity of a buyer's information-seeking effort at a point in time is obviously important to the marketing manager. For example, if he knows that a substantial group of buyers are at a level of routine decision making where they feel satiated or bored, he can introduce a new brand or innovation which might provide the needed source of change. Similarly, if buyers are engaged in extensive brand-choice problem solving, they are likely to actively seek information. The mass media may therefore prove very effective in communicating information about a brand.

Any theory of human behavior must account for individual differences. However, in order to identify the invariant relations of human behavior, at least under field conditions, it is often necessary to hold interpersonal variability constant by taking into account mediating variables and so classify individuals into homogeneous subgroups. The marketing manager is also interested in differentiated masses of buyers. He wants to understand and separate individual differences so that he can classify or segment the total market in terms of these differences. If we can understand the psychology of the individual buyer, we may achieve this classification.

Depending on the internal state of the buyer, a given stimulus may result in a given response. For example, one buyer who urgently needs a product may respond to an ad for a brand in that product class by buying it; another buyer who does not need the product may simply notice the ad and store the information; a third buyer may ignore the ad altogether. A construct such as "level of motivation" will then explain divergent reactions to the same stimulus. Alternatively, two buyers may both urgently need a product, but they buy two different brands. This can be explained by another construct: "predisposition toward a brand."

Elements of the Theory

Figure 1 represents our theory of buyer behavior. The central rectangular box isolates the various internal variables and processes which, taken together, show the state of the buyer. The inputs to the rectangular box are stimuli from the marketing and social environments. The outputs are a variety of responses which the buyer is likely to manifest, based on the interaction between the stimuli and his internal state.

Besides the inputs and outputs, there are a set of seven influences which affect the variables in the rectangular box. These variables appear at the top of the diagram and are labeled "exogenous" variables. Their function is to provide a means of adjusting for the interpersonal differences discussed above.

(Terminology is difficult in a problem area that cuts across both economics and psychology, because each discipline has often defined its terms differently from the other. We find the economist's definitions of "exogenous," vs. "endogenous," and "theory" vs. "model" more useful than those of the psychologist. The psychologist's distinction of hypothetical constructs and intervening variables, however, provides a helpful breakdown of endogenous variables. Finally, for the sake of exposition, we have often not clearly distinguished here between the theory and its empirical counterparts. Although this practice encourages certain ambiguities, and we lay ourselves open to the charge of reifying our theory, we believe that it simplifies the exposition.)

The variables within the rectangular box are hypothetical constructs, which serve the role of endogenous variables in the sense that changes in them are explained, but they are something less than endogenous variables in that they are not well defined and are not observable. Their values are inferred from relations among the output intervening variables.

Several of the exogenous variables such as personality, social class, and culture have traditionally been treated as endogenous variables. We believe

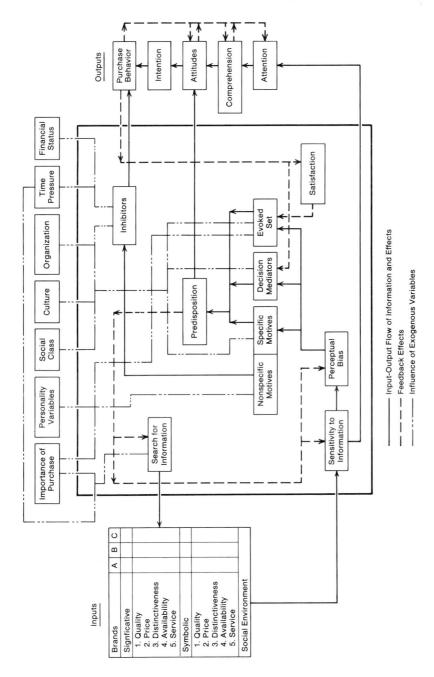

FIGURE 1. A theory of buyer behavior.

that they affect more specific variables, and that, by conceiving their effect via the hypothetical constructs, we can better understand their role.

Our theory of buyer behavior has four major components: stimulus variables, response variables, hypothetical constructs, and exogenous variables. We will elaborate on each of these components below, in terms of both their substances and their interrelationships.

Stimulus Input Variables

At any point in time, the hypothetical constructs which reflect the buyer's internal state are affected by numerous stimuli from his environment. This environment is classified as either commercial or social. The commercial environment consists of the marketing activities of various firms, by which they attempt to communicate to the buyer. From the buyer's point of view, these communications basically come via either the brand objects themselves or some linguistic or pictorial representation of brand attributes. If brand elements such as price, quality, service, distinctiveness, or availability are communicated through brand objects (significates), the stimuli are defined and classified as *significative* stimuli. If, on the other hand, brand attributes represented by linguistic or pictorial symbols are communicated via mass media, billboards, catalogs, salesmen, etc., the stimuli from these commercial sources are classified as *symbolic* stimuli. We view the marketing mix as the optimum allocation of funds between the two major channels of communication to the buyer—significative and symbolic.

Each commercial input variable is hypothesized to be multivariate. The five major dimensions of a brand—price, quality, distinctiveness, availability, and service—probably summarize the various attributes. The same dimensions are present in both the significative and symbolic communication that becomes the input stimuli for the buyer. However, certain dimensions may be more appropriately conveyed by significative rather than symbolic communication, and vice versa. For example, price is easily communicated by both channels; shape may best be communicated by two-dimensional pictures rather than verbal communication. Finally, size may not be easily communicated by any symbolic representation: the physical product (significate) may be necessary.

The third stimulus input variable is the information that the buyer's social environment provides for a purchase decision. The most obvious example is word-of-mouth communication.

The inputs to the buyer's mental state from the three major categories of stimuli are processed and stored through their interaction with a series of hypothetical constructs. The buyer may react to these stimuli immediately, or later.

Hypothetical Constructs

Our hypothetical constructs and their interrelationships are the result of an integration of Hull's (1943, 1952) learning theory, Osgood's (1957[a,b]) cognitive theory, and Berlyne's (1963) theory of exploratory behavior, along with other ideas.

These constructs fall into two classes: (1) those having to do with perception, and (2) those having to do with learning. Perceptual constructs serve the function of information processing; learning constructs serve the function of concept formation. It is interesting that, after years of experience in advertising, Reeves (1961) arrived at a very similar classification: his "penetration" is analogous to perceptual variables, and his "unique selling propositions" are analogous to learning variables. We will first describe learning constructs, since they are the major components of decision making; the perceptual constructs which serve the important role of obtaining and processing information are more complex, and will be described later.

Learning Constructs. The learning constructs are labeled (1) motives—specific and nonspecific, (2) brand-potential of the evoked set, (3) decision mediators, (4) predisposition toward brands, (5) inhibitors, and (6) satisfaction with the purchase of a brand.

Motive is impetus to action. The buyer is motivated by expectation or anticipation, based on learning from the outcome of past purchase of a brand in his evoked set. Motives or goals may be thought of as constituting a means-end chain, and hence as being general or specific, depending upon their position in the chain.

The specific motives—lower level motives in the means-end chain—are very closely anchored to the attributes of a product class; in this way they become purchase criteria. Examples of specific motives are those for buying a dietary product—low calories, nutrition, taste, and value. Similarly, the specific motives in buying an air conditioner might be durability, quietness, cooling power, and design.

Very often, several specific motives are nothing more than indicators of some underlying, more general motive; that is, some motive that is higher in the means-end chain. In the foregoing example, the specific motives of nutrition and low calories might be indicators of the common motive of good health.

Motives also serve the important function of raising the buyer's general motivational state, thereby rousing him to pay attention to environmental stimuli. Probable examples of nonspecific motives are anxiety and fear, the personality variables of authoritarianism, exhibitionism, and aggressiveness, and the social motives of power, status, and prestige. Although they are non-specific, they are not innate but learned, mostly as a result of acculturation. The nonspecific motives also possess a hierarchy within themselves. For example, anxiety is considered to be the source of another motive, that of the need for money (Brown, 1961).

Brand potential of the evoked set is a second learning construct. A buyer who is familiar with a product class has an evoked set of alternatives to satisfy his motives. The elements of his evoked set are some of the brands that make up the product class. This concept is important because the brands in a buyer's evoked set constitute competition for the seller.

A brand is, of course, a class concept, like many other objects or things. The buyer attaches a *word* to this concept—a label or brand name. The brand name conveys certain meanings, including its potential to satisfy his motives. In an advanced economy with relatively careful quality controls, the buyer is generally assured that any one brand object is like another. If quality controls are not adequate, the buyer will probably not summarize the potential of a brand in one word or label, but instead divide it into subclasses.

Various brands in the buyer's evoked set will generally satisfy his goal structure differently. One brand may possess such strong potential that it is an ideal brand for the buyer. Another brand may satisfy his motives barely enough to be part of his evoked set. Through a learning process, the buyer obtains and stores knowledge of each brand's potential, and then ranks them in order of their potential to satisfy his wants. The evoked set, in short, is a set of alternatives to be evaluated. Predisposition represents the buyer's preference ranking of them.

Decision mediators, a third learning construct, are the buyer's mental rules for matching alternatives with motives and ranking them in terms of their want-satisfying capacity. As mental rules, they exhibit reasoning, wherein the cognitive elements related to alternatives and motives are structured. In addition, decision mediators also contain a set of criteria by which the buyer denotatively discriminates between the brands he views as being in a product class, and those brands that are not. The words he uses to describe these criteria are the words he thinks with and finds easy to remember. These criteria are important to the manufacturer, because if he knows them he can deliberately build into his product and its promotion those characteristics which will differentiate his brand from competing brands.

Decision mediators thus represent enduring cognitive rules established by the process of learning, and their function is to establish meaningful and congruent relations among brands, so that the buyer can manifest goal-directed behavior. In view of the fact that decision mediators are learned, principles of learning become crucial in understanding their development and change over time.

There are two broad sources of learning: (1) actual experience, and (2) information. Actual experience can be with either the *same* buying situation in the past, or with a *similar* buying situation. The latter is generally labeled "generalization." Similarly, information as a source of learning can come from either the buyer's commercial or his social environment. Later, we will elaborate on each of these sources of learning.

Predisposition, a fourth construct, is the summary effect of the previous three constructs. It refers to the buyer's preference toward brands in his evoked set. It is, in fact, an aggregate index expressed in attitudes, which in turn can be measured by attitude scales. It might be visualized as the "place" where brands in the evoked set are compared with the mediator's choice criteria, to yield a judgment on the relative contribution of the brands to the buyer's motives. This judgment includes not only an estimate of the value of the brand, but also an estimate of the confidence with which the buyer holds that position. This uncertainty aspect of predisposition can be called "brand ambiguity," in that the more confidently he holds it, the less ambiguous the connotative meaning of the brand is to him and the more likely he is to buy it (G. S. Day, 1967).

Inhibitors, the fifth learning construct, are forces in the environment which create important disruptive influences on the actual purchase of a brand, even when the buyer has reasoned out that that brand will best satisfy his motives. In other words, when the buyer is motivated to buy the product class and is predisposed to buy a particular brand, he may not buy it because certain environmental forces inhibit the purchase act and prevent him from satisfying his preferences.

We postulate at least four types of inhibitors. They are (1) a high price for the brand, (2) lack of availability of the brand, (3) time pressure on the buyer, and (4) the buyer's financial status. The first two are part of the environmental stimuli, and therefore they are part of the input system. The last two come from the two exogenous variables of the same name. Temporary barriers to the purchase of a brand may also be created by social constraints emanating from other exogenous variables.

An essential feature of all inhibitors is that they are *not internalized* by the buyer, because their occurrence is random and strictly situational. However, for a given buyer, some inhibitors may persist systematically over time. If they persist long enough, the buyer is likely to incorporate them as part of his decision mediators, thus permitting them to affect the mental structure of his alternatives and motives. An example of such internalization might be the consequences of the constant time pressure a housewife faces because she has taken a job. Continuation of the time pressure may alter her evoked set as well as her motive structure. Convenience and time saving become important motives, and her evoked set may come to include time-saving brands, such as instant coffee. Similarly, a brand may be withdrawn by a company because of its stage in the product life cycle. The permanent unavailability of that brand will be learned and internalized by buyers, and they will remove that brand from their evoked sets.

Satisfaction, the last of the learning constructs, refers to the degree of congruence between the actual consequences of purchase and consumption of a brand, and what was expected from it by the buyer at the time of purchase. If the actual outcomes are judged by the buyer to be *better than or equal to* the expected, the buyer will feel satisfied; that is,

actual consequences $\geq$ expected consequences.

If, on the other hand, the actual outcomes are judged to be *less than* what he expected, the buyer will feel dissatisfied; that is,

actual consequences $<$ expected consequences.

Satisfaction or dissatisfaction with a brand can be with any one of its different attributes. If the brand proves to be more satisfactory than the buyer expected, the attractiveness of the brand will be enhanced. If it proves less satisfactory than he expected, its attractiveness will diminish. Satisfaction, therefore, affects the ranking of brands in the evoked set for the next buying decision.

We also think that, if a brand purchase proves completely unsatisfactory, the buyer will *remove* the brand from his evoked set. In other words, he will not consider it for future purchases. If the brand has proved extremely satisfactory, the buyer will retain *only* the purchased brand in his evoked set; other brands will have close to zero probability of consideration. In short, *extreme* outcomes are likely to affect the *number* of brands in the evoked set, and reasonable discrepancies between actual and expected outcomes will affect the *ranking* of the brands in the evoked set.

Relations Among Learning Constructs.   Several important notions underlie the concept of predisposition toward a brand and its related variables. The simplest way to describe them is to state that we may classify a decision process as either "extensive problem solving," "limited problem solving," or "routine response behavior," depending on the strength of predisposition toward brands. In the early phases of buying, the buyer does not yet have well-developed decision mediators; specifically, his product-class concept is not well formed and his predisposition is low. As he acquires information and gains experience in buying and consuming a brand, his decision mediators become firm and his predisposition toward that brand is generally high.

In extensive problem solving, predisposition toward a brand is low. None of the brands are sufficiently discriminated on the basis of their decision-mediator criteria for the buyer to show preference for any one brand. At this stage of decision making, brand ambiguity is high, and the buyer actively seeks information from his environment. The more extensive the search for information, the greater is *latency of response*—the time interval between initiation of a decision and its completion. Similarly, deliberation or reasoning is high, since the buyer lacks a well-defined product-class concept—the denotative aspect of his decision mediators. He is also likely to consider many brands as part of his evoked set, and stimuli coming from the commercial environment are less likely to trigger an immediate purchase reaction.

When predisposition toward brands is moderate, the buyer's decision process is one of limited problem solving. Brand ambiguity still exists, since he is not able to discriminate and compare brands to develop a preference for one brand over others. He is likely to seek information, but not to the extent he does for extensive problem solving. More importantly, he seeks information to compare and discriminate various brands more on a relative basis than to compare them absolutely. He thinks and deliberates, since his predispositions are only tentatively defined. His evoked set consists of a small number of brands, and he has about the same degree of preference for each of them.

In routine response behavior, the buyer has accumulated sufficient experience and information to eliminate brand ambiguity, and he has a high level of predisposition toward one or two brands in his evoked set. He is unlikely to actively seek information from the environment, since such information is not needed. Also, insofar as he does admit information, it will tend to be that which supports his current choice. Very often, this congruent information will act as a "triggering cue" to motivate him to manifest purchase behavior.

Much impulse purchase behavior is really the outcome of a strong predisposition and a facilitating commercial stimulus, such as a store display. The buyer's evoked set consists of a few brands, toward which he is highly predisposed. However, he will have greater preference toward one or two brands in his evoked set than toward the others.

As mentioned earlier, predisposition is an aggregate index of how well a brand conforms to the choice criteria contained in a decision mediator. Thus, any changes in these criteria as a result of learning from experience or information imply some change in predisposition. The greater the learning, the stronger is predisposition toward brands in the evoked set. The exact nature of learning will be described later, when we discuss the dynamics of buying behavior. However, there are two other issues which need some attention here.

First, although our focus is on brand choice behavior, the buyer also simplifies the total sequence of behavior necessary to make a purchase—i.e. going to the store, looking at products, paying at the counter, etc.—by reducing the number of steps and ordering them in a definite sequence. The greater is his predisposition, the more will be his simplification of total buying behavior, and therefore the more routine will be his purchase behavior.

Second, if the purchase cycle is very long, as is the case for automobiles and other durable appliances, the buyer may develop firm decision mediators and yet manifest exploratory behavior to a marked degree at each purchase decision, because (1) market conditions invariably change and the buyer may find past experience insufficient, and (2) his decision mediators have become fuzzy, through lack of use and the resultant forgetting.

Perceptual Constructs.   Another set of constructs serves the function of procuring and processing information relevant to a purchase decision. As mentioned earlier, information can come from any one of the three stimulus inputs—significative commercial stimuli, symbolic commercial stimuli, and social stimuli. Here we will describe only the constructs; their use by the buyer will be explained when we discuss the dynamics of buying behavior. The perceptual constructs in Figure 1 are (1) sensitivity to information, (2) perceptual bias, and (3) search for information.

A perceptual phenomenon implies either ignoring a physical event which could be a stimulus, seeing it attentively, or sometimes imagining what is not present in reality. All perceptual phenomena create some change in the quantity or quality of objective information.

Sensitivity to information refers to the opening and closing of sensory receptors which control the intake of information. The manifestation of this phenomenon is generally called "perceptual vigilance" (paying attention) or "perceptual defense" (ignoring information). Sensitivity to information therefore serves primarily as a gatekeeper for information entering the buyer's nervous system, thus controlling the quantity of information input.

Sensitivity to information is a function of two variables, according to Berlyne (1963). One is the degree of stimulus ambiguity. If a stimulus to which the buyer is exposed is very familiar or too simple, its ambiguity is low and the buyer will not pay attention—unless he is predisposed to such information from past learning. Furthermore, if stimulus ambiguity continues to be low, the buyer feels a sense of monotony and actively seeks other information—he can be said to *complicate* his environment. If the stimulus is so complex and ambiguous that the buyer finds it hard to comprehend, he will ignore it by resorting to perceptual defense. Only if the stimulus is moderately ambiguous will the buyer be motivated to pay attention and freely absorb objective information about the brand under consideration.

In response to a single communication, the buyer at first may find the information complex and ambiguous and tend to ignore it. As the information continues to enter his nervous system, he may find it really to be at the medium level of ambiguity, and pay attention. As the process of communication progresses and he pays continuing attention, he may find the information too simple and look for more complex information.

The second variable which governs sensitivity to information is the buyer's predisposition toward the brand which is the subject of that information. The buyer learns to attach connotative meanings to a brand and to the symbols which stand for the brand. Thus, both the *source* of communication and the *content* of communication, as well as the brand itself, can come to have meaning for him. For example, he may have learned in the past to associate *low* credibility with commercial sources and *high* credibility with social sources. Similarly, he may attach connotations of quality to certain attributes of the brand, such as package, color, flavor, and taste. These connotations are part of his predisposition toward the brand.

Predisposition thus acts as a feedback in Figure 1, governing sensitivity to information, and, in turn, the intake of further information. This feedback is his degree of interest. The more pertinent to the brand is the information, the more likely the buyer is to open up his receptors and pay attention to it. Similarly, the more pertinent the source, the greater the attention the buyer is likely to give the communication.

Perceptual bias is the second perceptual construct. The buyer not only selectively attends to information, but he may actually distort it, once it enters his nervous system. In other words, the quality of information can be altered by the buyer. He may distort the cognitive elements contained in information to make them congruent with his own frame of reference, as determined by the amount of information he has already stored. Theories of cognitive consistency have been developed (Feldman, 1966; Fishbein, 1967) to explain how this congruency is established and what its consequences are, in terms of the distortion of information that might be expected. Most qualitative change in information occurs as a result of feedback from various decision components, such as motives, the evoked set, and decision mediators. These relations are too complex, however, to describe in this summary.

The perceptual phenomena described above are likely to be less operative if information is received from the buyer's social environment. This is so because (1) the source of social information (such as a friend) is likely to be favorably regarded by the buyer, and (2) the information itself is modified by the social environment (the friend) so that it conforms to the needs of the buyer; therefore, distorted reception and further modification is less likely.

Search for information is the third perceptual construct. During the total buying phase, which extends over time and involves several repeat purchases of a product class, there are times when the buyer *actively* seeks information. It is very important to distinguish times when he passively receives information from occasions when he actively seeks it. We believe that perceptual bias is less operative in the latter instance, and that a commercial communication at that stage has, therefore, a high probability of influencing the buyer.

Active seeking of information occurs when the buyer senses ambiguity of brand meaning in his evoked set. As we saw earlier, this happens in the extensive problem-solving and limited problem-solving phases of the decision process. Ambiguity of brand meaning exists because the buyer is not certain of the purchase outcome of each brand. In other words, he has not yet learned enough about alternatives to establish an expectancy of brand potential that will satisfy his motives. This type of brand ambiguity is generally confined to initial buying of that brand.

However, ambiguity may exist despite knowledge of relative brand potential. This ambiguity rests in the buyer's inability to discriminate between alternatives. The buyer may be unable to discriminate because his motives are not well structured: he does not know how to order them. He may then seek information to resolve conflict among goals—a resolution implied in his learning of the appropriate product-class aspect of decision mediators, as discussed earlier.

There is yet another stage of buying behavior in which the buyer is likely to seek information. It is when the buyer has established a routine decision process, but he is so familiar and satiated with repeat buying that he feels bored. Then all the existing alternatives in his evoked set, including the more preferred brand, become unacceptable to him. He seeks change or variety in that buying situation. In order to obtain this change, he actively searches for information on other alternatives (brands) that he never considered before. At this stage, he is particularly receptive to any information about new brands. This explains large advertising budgets in a highly stable industry, a phenomenon which has long baffled both the critics and defenders of advertising. New products on the market and buyer forgetfulness are not plausible explanations.

Response Variables

The complexity of buyer behavior extends beyond our hypothetical constructs. Just as there is a variety of inputs, there is also a variety of buyer responses, which become relevant for different areas of marketing strategy. The wide variety of consumer responses can be easily appreciated in the diversity of measures used to evaluate advertising effectiveness. We have attempted to classify and order this diversity of buyer responses in terms of output variables. Most of our output variables are directly related to some, but not other constructs. Each output variable serves different purposes, both in marketing practice and in fundamental research.

Attention.   Attention is related to sensitivity to information. It is a buyer response that indicates the magnitude of his information intake. Attention is measured continuously during the time interval that the buyer is receiving information. There are several psycho-physiological methods of quantifying the degree of attention a buyer pays to a message. Awareness is not an appropriate measure, because it is a stock concept, not a flow concept.

Comprehension.   Comprehension refers to the store of knowledge about a brand that the buyer possesses at any point in time. This knowledge can vary from simple awareness of a single brand's existence, to a complete description of the attributes of a brand. It reflects the denotative meaning of the brand. In that sense it is strictly cognitive, and not included in the motivational aspects of behavior. Simply stated, it is a description of the common denotative elements of the brand in words with which the buyer communicates, thinks, and remembers. Some of the standard measures of advertising effectiveness such as awareness, aided or unaided recall, and recognition may capture different aspects of the buyer's knowledge of a brand.

Attitude Toward a Brand.   Attitude toward a brand is the buyer's evaluation of the brand's potential to satisfy his motives. It therefore includes the connotative aspects of the brand concept; it contains those aspects of the brand which are relevant to the buyer's goals. Attitude is directly related to predisposition, consisting of both the evaluation of a brand in terms of the decision-mediator criteria of choice, and the confidence with which that evaluation is held.

Intention to Buy.   Intention to buy is the buyer's forecast of which brand he will buy. It includes not only the buyer's predisposition toward a brand, but also a forecast of inhibitors. Intention to buy has been used extensively in predicting the purchases of durable goods, with some recent refinements in terms of the buyer's confidence in his own forecast; however, these studies are in terms of broadly defined product classes (Juster, 1964). We may characterize intention to buy as a response short of actual purchase behavior.

Purchase Behavior.   Purchase behavior is the overt manifestation of the buyer's predisposition, in conjunction with any inhibitors that may be present. It differs from attitude to the extent that inhibitors are taken into consideration; and it differs from intention to the extent that it is actual behavior, which the buyer only forecasted in his intention.

What becomes a part of a company's sales, or what the consumer records in a diary as a panel member, is only the terminal act in the sequence of shopping and buying. Very often, it is useful to observe the complete movement of the buyer from his home to the store and his purchase in the store. Yoell (1965), for example, presents several case histories showing that time-and-motion study of consumer purchase behavior has useful marketing implications.

We think that, at times, it may be helpful to go so far as to incorporate the act of consumption into the definition of purchase behavior. We have, for example, used a technique for investigating decision making in which the buyer verbally describes the sequential pattern of his purchase and consumption behavior in a given buying situation. Out of this description, we have obtained a "flow chart" of sequential decision making which reveals the number and structure of the decision rules the buyer employs.

Several characteristics of purchase behavior become useful if we observe the buyer in a repetitive buying situation. These include the incidence of buying a brand, the quantity bought, and the purchase cycle. Several stochastic models of brand loyalty, for example, have been developed (Sheth, 1967). Similarly, we could take the magnitude purchased and compare light buyers with heavy buyers to determine if heavy buyers are more loyal buyers.

The Interrelationships of Response Variables.   In Figure 1 the five response variables are ordered to create a hierarchy, similar to the variety of hierarchies used in practice, such as AIDA (attention, interest, desire, and action); to the Lavidge and Steiner (1961) hierarchy of advertising effectiveness; as well as to the different mental states a person is alleged by anthropologists and sociologists to pass through when he adopts an innovation (Rogers, 1962). There are, however, some important differences which we believe will clarify certain conceptual and methodological issues raised by Palda (1966) and others.

First, a response variable called "attention" has been added, which is crucial because it indicates whether or not a communication is received by the buyer. Second, several different aspects of the cognitive realm of behavior, such as awareness, recall, and recognition, are lumped into one category called "comprehension," to suggest that they are all varying indicators of the buyer's storage of information about a brand. In this way we obtain leverage for understanding buyer innovation. Third, attitude is defined to include its affective and conative aspects, since any attempt to establish causal relations between attitude and behavior must take into account the motivational aspects of attitude. Furthermore, the perceptual and the preference maps of the buyer with respect to brands are separated into "comprehension" and "attitude," respectively. Fourth, another variable, "intention to buy," is added, because properly defined and measured intentions for several product classes in both durable and semidurable goods have proved useful. To the extent that intention incorporates a buyer's forecast of his inhibitors, it might form a basis for marketing strategy designed to remove the inhibitors before actual purchase behavior is manifested.

Finally, and most important, we have incorporated several feedback effects which were described when the hypothetical constructs were discussed. We will now show the relations as direct connections among response variables —although these "outside" relations are merely the reflection of relations among the hypothetical constructs. For example, purchase behavior via satisfaction involves consequences that affect decision mediators and brand potential in the evoked set; any change in mediators and brand potential constitutes a change in predisposition. Attitude is related to predisposition, and therefore it can change in the period from pre-purchase to post-purchase. By incorporating this feedback, we are opening the way to resolving the question of whether attitude causes purchase behavior, or purchase behavior causes attitude. Over a period of time the relation is interdependent, each affecting the other. Similarly, we have a feedback from "attitude" to "comprehension" and "attention," the rationale for which was given when perceptual constructs were described.

The Dynamics of Buying Behavior

We will now explain the changes in hypothetical constructs which occur as a result of learning. Learning constructs are, of course, directly involved in the change that we label "learning." Since some learning constructs indirectly govern perceptual constructs by way of feedback, there is also an indirect effect on the learning constructs themselves. As mentioned earlier, decision mediators, which structure motives and the evoked set, can be learned from two broad sources, (1) past experience, and (2) information. Past experience can be further classified as deriving from buying a specified product or buying a similar product. Similarly, information can come from the buyer's commercial environment or his social environment; if the source is commercial, the information may be significant or symbolic.

We will look at development and change in learning constructs as due to (1) generalization from similar buying situations, (2) repeat buying of the same product class, and (3) information.

Generalization from Similar Purchase Situations

Some decision mediators are often similar across product classes because many motives are common to a wide variety of purchasing activities. For example, a buyer may satisfy his health motive by buying many different product classes. Similarly, he may buy many product classes at the same place; this very often leads to spatial or contiguous generalization. The capacity to generalize allows the buyer to exercise great flexibility in adapting his purchase behavior to the myriad of varying market conditions he faces.

Generalization refers to the transfer of responses from past situations to new situations which are similar, based on the relevance of stimuli. It saves the buyer time and effort otherwise spent in seeking information to resolve the uncertainty inevitable in a new situation. Generalization can occur at any one of the several levels of purchase activity, but we are primarily interested in the generalization of those decision mediators which involve only *brand-choice* behavior, in contrast to choice of store or choice of time and day for shopping.

Two kinds of brand generalization should be distinguished. First, there is *stimulus generalization,* in which the buyer—who has associated a brand purchase with a decision mediator (product class)—associates with the same decision mediator a new brand similar to the old one. For example, suppose a buyer has a decision mediator which calls for the purchase of *double-edged* shaving blades. His purchase response may then be transferred to a new brand of *stainless steel* double-edged blades via the same decision mediator. He may further refine his decision mediator to associate his purchase behavior with only one brand of new stainless steel blades, rather than with all.

Stimulus generalization can occur, not only when two brands are physically similar, but also when two brands are physically dissimilar but possess the same meaning. This is called *semantic generalization.* It is likely to occur when a radically new product is introduced by a company with which the buyer has had satisfactory past experience. The buyer can generalize via the company image. This is especially true of durable appliances, where a brand name is common to different products.

Second, there is *response generalization,* in which the buyer generalizes an *old response* to a *new response,* given the *same stimulus.* It can occur when the buyer, after reading an ad for brand A, goes to the store to buy it, but finds brand B, which is similar to brand A, and switches. In the same fashion, a buyer may "move up" the quality ladder for a particular make of automobile. Finally, he might buy *larger* packages of the same brand product.

Just as we find semantic *stimulus* generalization, we also find semantic *response* generalization. For example, a buyer who is motivated to purchase low-calorie food may generalize his response from skim milk to diet cola.

Repeat Purchase Experiences

Another source of change in learning constructs is the repeated purchase of the same product class over a period of time. In Figure 1 the purchase of a brand involves two types of feedback, one affecting decision mediators and the other affecting brand potential of the evoked set. First, the experience of buying, with all its cognitive aspects of memory, reasoning, etc., has a learning effect on decision mediators. This occurs irrespective of which specific brand the buyer chooses in any one purchase decision, because decision mediators, like motives, are product-specific and not limited to any one brand. Hence, every purchase has an incremental effect in more firmly establishing decision mediators. This is easy to visualize if we remember that buying behavior is a series of mental and motor steps; the actual choice is only its terminal act.

Purchase of a brand creates certain satisfactions for the buyer which he compares with his evaluation of the brand's potential. If the buyer is satisfied, the potential of the brand is enhanced, increasing the probability of repeat purchase. If he is dissatisfied, the potential of the brand is diminished, and the probability of repeat purchase is reduced. Hence the second feedback, from purchase behavior to satisfaction, changes the attractiveness of the brand purchased.

If there are no inhibitory forces influencing the buyer, he will continue to buy a brand which proves satisfactory. In the initial stages of decision making, he may show some tendency to oscillate between brands in order to formulate his decision mediators. In other words, he may learn by trial-and-error at first, then settle on a brand, and thereafter buy it with such regularity as to suggest that he is brand loyal. However, unless a product involves high purchase risk, there is a time limit on this brand loyalty: he may become bored with his preferred brand and look for something new.

Information As a Source of Learning

The third major means by which learning constructs are changed is information received from (1) the buyer's commercial environment, consisting of advertising, promotion, salesmanship, and retail shelf display; and (2) his social environment, consisting of his family, friends, reference groups, and social class.

We will first describe the influence of information as if perceptual constructs were absent. In other words, we will assume that the buyer receives information with perfect fidelity, as it exists in the environment. Also, we will discuss separately information received from commercial and social environments.

The Commercial Environment.   A company communicates its offerings to buyers either by the physical brand itself (significates), or by symbols (pictorial or linguistic) which represent the brand. Significative and symbolic communication are the two major means of interaction between sellers and buyers.

Figure 1 shows the influence of information on motives, decision mediators, the evoked set, and inhibitors. We believe that the influence of commercial information on motives (specific and nonspecific) is limited. The main effect is primarily to *intensify* whatever motives the buyer has, rather than to create new ones. For example, a physical display of the brand may intensify his motives above the threshold level, which, combined with strong predisposition, can result in impulse (unplanned) purchase. A similar reaction is possible when an ad creates sufficient intensity of motive to provide an impetus for the buyer to go to the store. A second way to influence motives is to show the *perceived instrumentality* of the brand, and thereby make it a part of the buyer's defined set of alternatives.

Finally, to a very limited extent, marketing stimuli may change the *content of motives*. This, we believe, is rare. The general conception among both marketing men and laymen is that marketing stimuli do change the buyer's motives. However, on a closer examination it would appear that what is changed is the *intensity* of those motives already provided by the buyer's social environment. Many dormant or latent motives may become stimulated. The secret of success very often lies in identifying the change in motives created by social change and intensifying them, as seems to be the case in the advertising projection of youthfulness for many buying situations.

Marketing stimuli are important in determining and changing the buyer's evoked set. Commercial information tells him of the existence of brands (awareness), their identifying characteristics (comprehension plus brand name), and their relevance to the satisfaction of his needs (decision mediator).

Marketing stimuli are also important in creating and changing the buyer's decision mediators. They become important sources for *creating* (learning) decision mediators when the buyer has no prior experience to rely upon. In other words, when he is in the extensive-problem-solving (EPS) stage, it is marketing and social stimuli which are his important sources of learning. Similarly, when the buyer actively seeks information because all existing alternatives are unacceptable to him, marketing stimuli become important in *changing* his decision mediators.

Finally, marketing stimuli can unwittingly create inhibitors. For example, a company's efforts to emphasize a price-quality association may result in a high-price inhibition in the mind of the buyer. Similarly, in emphasizing the details of usage and consumption of a product, marketing communication might perhaps create inhibition related to time pressure.

The Social Environment.   The social environment of the buyer—family, friends, and reference groups—is another major source of information influencing his buying behavior. Most social input is likely to be symbolic (linguistic), although at times a friend may show the physical product to the buyer.

Information from the social environment also affects the four learning constructs: motives, decision mediators, the evoked set, and inhibitors. However, the effect on these constructs is different than that of the commercial environment. First, information about brands is considerably modified by the social environment before it reaches the buyer. Most of the modifications are likely to be in adding connotative meanings to brands and their attributes, and in the effects of such perceptual variables as sensitivity to information and perceptual bias.

Second, the buyer's social environment will probably strongly influence the content of his motives, and his ordering of them to establish a goal structure. Several research studies have concentrated on such influences (Bourne, 1957; Bush and London, 1960; Gruen, 1960; Laird, 1950; Katz and Lazarsfeld, 1955).

Third, the buyer's social environment may also affect his evoked set. This is particularly true when he lacks experience. Furthermore, if the product class is important to the buyer, and he is not technically competent or he is uncertain in evaluating the consequences of the brand for his needs, he may rely more on the social than on the marketing environment for information. This is well documented by several studies using the perceived risk hypothesis (Bauer, 1960, 1961; Bauer and Wortzel, 1966; Cox, 1962; S. M. Cunningham, 1966; Arndt, 1967).

Information-Processing Effects

As we have said, distortion of stimuli by the perceptual constructs—sensitivity to information, perceptual bias, and search for information—is likely to be much greater for marketing stimuli than for social stimuli. This is so essentially because the buyer attaches greater credibility—competence and trust—to social sources, and because of the ease of two-way communication in social situations. Similarly, the buyer may more actively seek information from his social environment, particularly evaluative information. Thus, the foregoing discussion of the commercial and social environments must be qualified by the perceptual effects inevitable in any information processing.

Exogenous Variables

As mentioned earlier, there are several influences operating on the buyer's decisions which we treat as exogenous; that is, we do not explain their formation and change. Many of these influences come from the buyer's social environment, and we wish to separate those effects of his environment which have occurred in the past and are not related to a specific decision, from those which are current and do directly affect the decisions that occur while the buyer is being observed. The inputs that occur during the observation period provide information to the buyer to help his current decision making. Past influences are already embedded in the values of the perceptual and learning constructs. These exogenous variables are particularly appropriate as market-segmenting variables, because they are causally linked to purchase.

Strictly speaking, there is no need for exogenous variables, since in the social sciences these forces are traditionally left to *ceteris paribus*. We will bring them out explicitly, however, for the sake of research design, so that a researcher may control or take into account the individual differences among buyers that are due to past influence. Incorporating the effects of these exogenous variables reduces the unexplained variance, or error in estimation, which it is particularly essential to control under field conditions. Figure 1 presents a set of exogenous variables which we believe provide the control essential to obtaining satisfactory predictive relations between the inputs and outputs of the system.

Importance of purchase refers to differential degrees of ego-involvement in or commitment to different product classes. It is therefore an entity which must be carefully examined in inter-product studies. Importance of purchase will influence the size of the evoked set and the magnitude of the search for information. For example, the more important the product class, the larger is the evoked set (Howard and Moore, 1963).

Time pressure is a current exogenous variable and therefore specific to a decision situation. When a buyer feels pressed for time, because of any of several environmental influences, he must allocate his time among alternative uses. In this process a reallocation unfavorable to purchasing activity can occur. Time pressure will create inhibition, as mentioned earlier. It will also unfavorably affect the search for information.

Financial status refers to the constraint a buyer may feel because he lacks financial resources. This can affect his purchase behavior by creating a barrier (inhibitor) to purchasing the most preferred brand. For example, a buyer may want to purchase an expensive foreign car, but lacking sufficient financial resource, he will settle for a low-priced American model.

Personality traits are such variables as self-confidence, self-esteem, authoritarianism, and anxiety, which have been researched to identify individual differences. These individual differences are "topic free" and therefore supposedly exert their effect across product classes. We believe their effect is felt on (1) nonspecific motives and (2) the evoked set. For example, the more anxious a person, the greater his motivational arousal; dominant personalities are more likely (by a small margin) to buy a Ford instead of a Chevrolet; the more authoritarian a person, the narrower the category width of his evoked set.

Social and organizational setting involves the group, a higher level of social organization than the individual. It includes informal social organization, such as family and reference groups, which is relevant for *consumer behavior*; and formal organization, which constitutes much of the environment for *industrial purchasing*. Organizational variables are those of small group interaction, such as power, status, and authority. We believe that the underlying processes of intergroup conflict in both industrial and consumer buying behavior are in principle very similar, and that the differences are largely due to the formal nature of industrial activity. Organization, both formal and social, is a crucial variable because it influences most of the learning constructs.

Social class involves a still higher level of social organization, the social aggregate. Several indices are available to classify people socially. Perhaps the most common index is Warner's classification (see Ch. 5, this book). Social class mediates the relation between input and output by influencing (1) specific motives, (2) decision mediators, (3) the evoked set, and (4) inhibitors. The latter influence is important, particularly in the adoption of innovations.

Culture provides a more comprehensive social framework than social class. It consists of patterns of behavior, symbols, ideas, and their attached values. Culture will influence motives, decision mediators, and inhibitors.

Conclusions

In the preceding pages we have summarized a theory of buyer brand choice. It is complex, but we strongly believe that complexity is essential to an adequate description of buying behavior.

We hope that our theory will provide new insights into past empirical data, and guide future research by instilling coherence and unity into current research, which now tends to be atomistic and unrelated. Models can be constructed of the relations between the output intervening variables, and a splendid beginning along these lines has been carried out by Day (1967). Also, as the hypothetical constructs are explored, elements of the constructs will be broken out and better defined, so that these elements can be invested with the operational status of intervening variables. McClelland's work with achievement, for example, has shown how this transformation can occur with motive. In this way our theory suggests specific programs of research.

We are vigorously pursuing a large research program aimed at testing the validity of this theory. The research was designed in terms of the variables specified by the theory, and our preliminary results lead us to believe that it was fruitful to use the theory in this way. Because it specifies a number of relationships, it has clearly been useful in interpreting preliminary findings. Above all, it is a great aid in communication among the researchers and with the companies involved.

Finally, a number of new ideas are set forth in the theory, but we would like to call attention to three in particular. The concept of evoked set provides a means of reducing the noise in many analyses of buying behavior. The product class concept offers a new dimension for incorporating many of the complexities of innovation, and especially for integrating systematically the idea of innovation into a framework of psychological constructs. Anthropologists and sociologists have been generally content to deal with peripheral variables and to omit the psychological constructs which link the peripheral variables to behavior. The habit-perception cycle in which perception and habit respond inversely offers hope for explaining, to a great extent, the phenomenon which has long baffled both critics and defenders of advertising: large advertising expenditures in a stable market, where, on the surface, it would seem that buyers are already sated with information.

References

Arndt, J. "Role of Product-Related Conversations in the Diffusion of a New Product." *J. Marketing Research*, Vol. 4 (Aug. 1967), 291–295.

Bauer, R. A. "Consumer Behavior as Risk Taking." *Proc. AMA* (June 1960), 389–398.

———. "Risk Handling in Drug Adoption: The Role of Company Preference." *Public Opinion Quarterly*, Vol. 25 (Winter 1961), 546–559.

———, and L. H. Wortzel. "Doctor's Choice: The Physician and His Sources of Information About Drugs." *J. Marketing Research*, Vol. 3 (Feb. 1966), 40–47.

Berlyne, D. E. "Motivational Problems Raised by Exploratory and Epistemic Behavior." *Psychology: A Study of a Science*, Vol. 5, ed. S. Koch. McGraw-Hill, 1963.

Bourne, F. S. "Group Influence in Marketing." *Some Applications of Behavioural Research,* ed. R. Likert and S. P. Hayes, Jr. Paris: UNESCO (1957), 208–224.

Brown, J. S. *The Motivation of Behavior.* McGraw-Hill, 1961.

Bush, G., and P. London. "On the Disappearance of Knickers: Hypothesis for the Functional Analysis of Clothing." *J. Social Psychology,* Vol. 51 (1960), 359–366.

Cox, D. F. "The Measurement of Information Value: A Study in Consumer Decision-Making," *Proc. AMA* (Dec. 1962), 413–431.

Cunningham, S. M. "Perceived Risk as a Factor in the Diffusion of New Product Information." *Proc. AMA* (Fall 1966), 698–721.

Day, G. S. "Buyer Attitudes and Brand Choice Behavior." Unpub. Ph.D. dissertation, Graduate School of Business, Columbia Univ., 1967.

Feldman, S. (ed.). *Cognitive Consistency: Motivational Antecedents and Behavioral Consequences.* Academic Press, 1966.

Fishbein, M. (ed.). *Readings in Attitude Theory and Measurement.* Wiley, 1967.

Gruen, W. "Preference for New Products and Its Relationship to Different Measures of Conformity." *J. Applied Psychology*, Vol. 44 (Dec. 1960), 361–366.

Howard, J. A., and C. G. Moore, Jr. "A Descriptive Model of the Purchasing Function." Unpub. paper, Univ. of Pittsburgh, 1963.

Hull, C. L. *Principles of Behavior.* Appleton-Century-Crofts, 1943.

———. *A Behavior System.* Yale Univ. Press, 1952.

Juster, T. F. *Anticipations and Purchases: An Analysis of Consumer Behavior.* Princeton Univ. Press, 1964.

Katz, E., and P. F. Lazarsfeld. *Personal Influence.* The Free Press, 1955.

Laird, D. A. "Customers Are Hard to Change." *Personnel Journal* (1950), 402–405.

Lavidge, R. J., and G. A. Steiner. "A Model for Predictive Measurements of Advertising Effectiveness." *J. Marketing,* Vol. 25 (Oct. 1961), 59–62.

March, J. G., and H. A. Simon. *Organization.* Wiley, 1958.

Osgood, C. E. "Motivational Dynamics of Language Behavior." *Nebraska Symposium on Motivation,* ed. E. R. Jones. Univ. Nebraska Press (1957a), 348–423.

———. "A Behavioristic Analysis of Perception and Cognitive Phenomena." *Symposium on Cognition, University of Colorado, 1955.* Harvard Univ. Press (1957b), 75–119.

Palda, K. S. "The Hypothesis of a Hierarchy of Effects: A Partial Evaluation." *J. Marketing Research,* Vol. 3 (Feb. 1966), 13–24.

Reeves, R. *Reality in Advertising.* Knopf, 1961.

Rogers, E. M. *Diffusion of Innovations.* The Free Press, 1962.

Sheth, J. N. "A Review of Buyer Behavior." *Management Science*, Vol. 13 (Aug. 1967), B718–B756.

Yoell, W. A. "Science of Advertising Through Behaviorism." Unpub. paper, 1965.

7.2 Mathematical Models of Individual Buyer Behavior
PHILIP KOTLER

Buyer behavior has been studied from a variety of theoretical perspectives, resulting in a number of interesting and occasionally incompatible explanations. Depending upon one's scientific predilection, there is the Marshallian buyer, Pavlovian buyer, Freudian buyer, Veblenian buyer, and Hobbesian buyer (Kotler, 1965a). Less grandiose but equally interesting new breeds of buyers can be formulated, such as the Festinger buyer (Festinger, 1957), Riesman buyer (Riesman, Glazer, and Denney, 1956), and Rogerian buyer (Rogers, 1951).

It should be recognized that all these models of buyer behavior are true to some extent, and yet each is incomplete. Buyer behavior, as an aspect of human behavior, is so complex that theory develops in connection with particular aspects of the phenomena. The contemporary effort of behavioral scientists in marketing is to analyze well specific aspects of behavior in the hope that someday someone will put them all together.

The complexity of buyer behavior requires the language of prose to convey all the intricate nuances. Virtually all the classical models of behavior are formulated in prose terms and continue to derive their power through the flexibility and delicious ambiguity of prose. At the same time, the polar viewpoints in behavioral theory are the direct consequence of this ambiguity. This has led an increasing number of scholars to express their behavioral explanations in mathematical terms. Though this involves a high degree of simplification, it promotes increased rigor in the communication and comparison of theories. The development of mathematical behavioral models is a welcome complement to the abundant verbal formulations of individual buyer behavior dynamics.

This is not the place to present a detailed history of mathematical formulations of human behavior, but it would be desirable to highlight a few major works. Some of this work stretches back into the 19th century, when economists such as Edgeworth (1881) and Jevons (1871) first formulated their utility maximization equations of buyer behavior. Early experimental psychologists described many of their findings on learning, memory, and motivation in terms of mathematical relationships between two or more variables. However, it is only recently that whole systems of equations have been developed to describe more comprehensive aspects of human behavior. A significant step in this direction occurred with the mathematical formulation by Herbert Simon (1954) of George Homan's verbal propositions on human interaction. Simon's model related the strength of positive sentiments, the amount of interaction, and the number of common activities of individuals through a series of simultaneous differential equations, each equation showing the change in one of the variables as a function of the others.

Another milestone is represented in the set of papers delivered at a conference on computer simulation and personality theory held at the Educational Testing Service, Princeton University in June 1962 (Tomkins and Messick, 1963). These papers contain impressive speculations and suggestions as to the programming of a computer to duplicate some of the perceptual, cognitive, affective, motivational, and behavioral aspects of homo sapiens. As for representing mathematically the more social interactions of human beings, the recent book by James S. Coleman (1964a) presents an impressive collection of mathematical tools, studies, and possibilities in this area.

With regard to consumer behavior, the literature on mathematical models of individual behavior is scant. A pioneering article by Carman and Nicosia (1965) offers a formulation of buyer decision processes in terms of five simultaneous differential equations. This work is an extention of the Simon approach mentioned earlier (1954). Most of the Markov process articles on consumer brand choice deal with aggregate brand loyalty and switching tendencies rather than with individual consumer behavior. The exceptions are found in the work of Amstutz (1966), Duhamel (1966), Frank (1962), Lipstein (1965), Massy (1965), Montgomery (1966), and Morrison (1966). Germane research of still a different character is found in Guy Orcutt's work (1961) and that of the Simulmatics Corporation (1962). Orcutt has modeled individual persons who are born, age, marry, divorce, save, spend, and die. The Simulmatics Corporation has modeled the media habits of a hypothetical population of 2,944 persons who choose their programs and reading material probabilistically in a way related to their varying social-economic characteristics. As for business and marketing games, hardly any of them have incorporated individual buyers as the modus operandi for determining market response, but instead utilize total market or market segment response functions directly.

This brief review of the existing literature is intended to show that the mathematical formulation of human behavior and particularly consumer behavior is in its infancy. Some would say that it ought to stay there because the concept of mathematizing human behavior is either repugnant, simple-minded, or useless. The hostility aroused by this work justifies some discussion of the possible benefits which might emerge from these mathematical investigations. Among the scientific contributions which might be forthcoming from the development of mathematical models of individual buyer behavior are the following:

1. These models will force a more rigorous statement of the variables operating in buying situations and the nature of their relationships.

2. These models will facilitate the comparison of different theories of buyer behavior. The similarities will show up more clearly and the differences can be subjected to sharper empirical tests. The models will highlight the degree to which the differences are structural, functional, or only parametric.

3. These models will help pinpoint more accurately the data needs of marketing decision makers who seek to understand and to some degree influence consumer behavior.

4. These models will stimulate inferences not ordinarily obvious from verbal formulations, much in the way a set of postulates about points and lines stimulates a large number of theorems about spatial relations.

5. These models will facilitate the construction of microconsumer market simulators. The use of microconsuming units in a simulation permits the study of some important properties overlooked in gross market response models, such as the distribution of preferences, the distribution of delays in response to marketing stimuli, and so forth.

These various contributions will be achieved in different degrees depending upon the buying situation which is being modeled and the resources and imagination of the model builder. Each buying situation makes salient a different set of consumer mechanisms and marketing factors. For example, the problem of brand choice of frequently purchased consumer nondurables (say coffee, bread, and so on) does not involve the consumer's affective or motivational mechanisms (emotions and drives) as much as his perception and learning mechanisms. Thus a model of buyer behavior in this situation is likely to be most explicit on the perception and learning questions. On the other hand, modeling the buying process for a new automobile does require the imputation of strong and conflicting drives, affective feelings, and information seeking.

In short, at the beginning we will have to tolerate a variety of models tailored to specific buying situations. Eventually, they may be forced into higher order abstractions, serving to explain a broader range of buying situations. The beginnings of such a fusion may be found in John Howard's recent verbal model (1963) of the elements describing buying behavior and their interrelationships. By modifying the model in different degrees, one has a flexible framework for examining buying situations ranging from the simple purchase of a staple grocery item (which he classifies as Autonomous Response Behavior), to the purchase of a fountain pen (Limited Problem Solving), to the purchase of a whole computer installation (Extensive Problem Solving). This type of fusion is the ultimate goal of buyer behavior theory. But at the beginning, the most useful mathematical models may be developed for highly specific buying situations.

The Brand Choice Problem for Frequently Purchased Consumer Staples

This paper takes a highly specific buying situation—the weekly shopping for branded staple grocery items—and seeks to describe mathematically the nature of the individual's buying process. This buying situation has been selected for two reasons. First, it is one of the most important and familiar types of buying situations. Second, the type of buying situation has the virtue of being relatively simpler than others in the number and type of psychological processes and marketing factors. It is a good strategy to start with the modeling of simple buying situations and move gradually to more complex ones.

For ease of reference, the brand choice behavior will be thought of as taking place with respect to coffee, a product which has the advantages of familiarity, a wide availability of factual information (See Kotler, 1965b, footnote 15), and several sophisticated analyses of consumer panel data designed to appraise the influence of price and price deals (Massy and Frank, 1965; Duhamel, 1966).

The specific problem will be to formulate a mechanism which will cause a hypothetical consumer to make a weekly selection of a coffee brand from three available brands called A, B, and C. The brands can be thought of as having some differences between them in product and merchandising characteristics which partly contribute to variations in buyer response. The task is one of describing how outside stimuli and internal psychological mechanisms interact to produce individual buyer choice behavior over time.

The problem can be made concrete by viewing consumer brand choice behavior in the larger context of the competitive marketing process. The view which will be taken is illustrated in Exhibit 1. Assume that each week (Box 1) individual consumers go to the supermarket and buy, among other things, a one-pound can of coffee. Three brands are available: A, B, and C. They differ slightly in quality, price, sale promotion features, shelf space and position, and other marketing characteristics. In fact, each week may produce some changes in the marketing characteristics of one or more brands (Box 2). The first buyer enters the store with certain brand predispositions (Box 3) and makes a brand choice (Box 4). Buyers continue to enter the store during the week and make coffee brand choices. After the last buyer has made a purchase (Box 5), brand shares are computed for week *t* (Box 6) and they influence through a feedback process the *marketing strategies* of the three competitors in the following week. This process continues week after week until the simulation is over

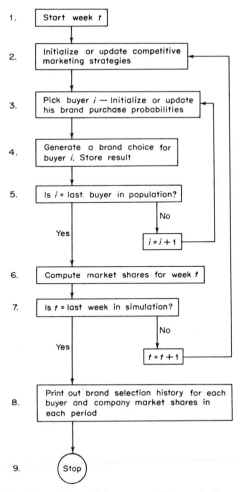

EXHIBIT 1.   Simulation of the competitive marketing process.

(Box 7), at which point the computer program prints out the brand selection history for each individual buyer and also the brand shares in each period (Box 8). These data can be analyzed for various purposes, such as evaluating different competitive marketing strategies (Kotler, 1965b), examining the validity of different statistical techniques now used to develop demand estimates, and other purposes.

The objective of this paper is to review and extend current models that implement the individual buyer brand choice process in Boxes 3 and 4. These models produce simulated individual brand choice histories that hopefully resemble actual consumer panel histories. To the extent that the simulated histories resemble actual histories, they help sharpen the underlying theory.

It is in fact very difficult to proceed the other way, moving from actual consumer brand histories to inferences about the underlying brand decision processes. Some analysts have sought to interpret buyer decision processes on the basis of their individual brand purchase histories. Consider the following ten-week purchase history: AAABAACAA. The most plausible interpretation is that the buyer has a strong preference for Brand A and occasionally tries other brands for sundry reasons but always returns to A. Yet this same purchase history is subject to a variety of interpretations:

1. *Brand loyalty hypothesis.*   The consumer consciously prefers Brand A, feels loyal to it, and buys it at every opportunity. She may occasionally buy another brand for variety but always returns to her favorite brand.

2. *Habit persistence hypothesis.*   The consumer buys Brand A out of habit rather than conscious preference. She gives little thought to brand choice and simply tends to reach for the familiar. Her behavior may be characterized as autonomous response behavior.

3. *Maximization of quality-to-price hypothesis.*   The consumer has no loyalty to any brand and makes her choice strictly on the basis of which current brand gives her the most for her money. She feels that Brand A currently offers the most quality for the price and only buys another brand when it is on sale. If another brand is upgraded in quality or if its price is permanently reduced to a sufficient extent, she will buy the other brand more often.

4. *Shifts in brand availability hypothesis.*   The consumer patronizes a store which is well stocked only in Brand A and this accounts for her choosing A most of the time.

Other hypotheses may also offer a plausible explanation of the observed purchase history. The point is that an actual purchase history gives rise to a multiplicity of hypotheses about the buyer's brand decision processes.

Yet the nature of the brand decision process is the crucial issue. The theory that a firm holds of buyer behavior in its markets will influence and determine its marketing strategy. For example, a view of the consumer as "stimulus prone and highly persuasible" leads to a great reliance on advertising, price deals, and point-of-purchase displays. A view of the consumer as "a creature of habit" leads to some complacency with respect to holding present customers and some despair in attracting new customers. A view of the consumer as "an economic calculating machine" leads to a policy of improving real values (a better ratio of quality or quantity to price) rather than emphasizing brand or company image advertising. A view of the consumer as "fantasy prone" leads to a great reliance on imaginative advertising and packaging.

Given the importance to marketing planning of developing correct interpretations of buyer behavior, we shall now examine a succession of mathematical models describing how the buyer chooses a brand. They are, ranging from the simple to the complex: brand loyalty model; constant brand probability model; last brand purchased model; learning model; variable Markov model; competitive marketing mix model; and total behavior model.

The Brand Loyalty Model

The first model is hardly a model at all, but it offers a good point of departure. The brand loyalty model says that the buyer develops a strong preference or habit for a particular brand and purchases it repeatedly, giving little or no thought to the other brands. This explanation of buyer behavior can be described mathematically in the following way. Let there be three brands on the market, A, B, and C, and let the respective probabilities of their purchase by buyer i be represented by the vector (P_A, P_B, P_C). The latter will be called the *brand purchase probability vector* (*BPPV*). If buyer i has developed a strong and unyielding preference for Brand A, then the brand probability purchase vector for buyer i at time t ($BPPV_{it}$) is:

$$BPPV_{it} = (1.00, 0.0, 0.0) \text{ for all } t.$$

Rationale

That some people display this behavior is incontrovertible, especially in the buying of frequently purchased grocery staples. In the buying of coffee, many consumer panel members report the same brand choice in the last ten or more purchases. It may be hypothesized that these consumers spend very little time thinking about brand choice or seeking brand information. As long as their brand provides the anticipated satisfactions, they are insensitive to cues from other brands and are unlikely to try them.

An important problem not answered by this model is how consumers develop a strong brand preference in the first place. Do they try several brands and then settle on one? Or do they stick with the first one they try? To what extent are they influenced by friends, mass media, and in other ways?

In other words, this model describes the process of being brand loyal rather than becoming brand loyal. A market made up entirely of brand loyal buyers would be highly uninteresting. There would be no shifts in brand share, and merchandising variables such as price deals, advertising, and point-of-purchase displays would be largely wasted. Price deals would only subsidize present customers, and advertising and point-of-purchase displays would mainly sustain present customer loyalties rather than attract away competitors' customers.

In a simulation using a population of hypothetical consumers, programming some fraction of them to behave according to the brand loyalty model may well be warranted. But the behavior of many buyers is not described by this model. The model's main contribution is to describe some buyers and to provide a starting point for further model building.

The Constant Brand Probability Model

The brand purchase histories of many members of consumer panels show brand switching behavior which is inconsistent with the brand loyalty model. The task is to formulate an explanation of brand switching behavior.

Brand switching can be explained as the result of response uncertainty, response change, or some mixture of the two (Coleman, 1964b).

Response uncertainty means that a buyer's behavior is probabilistic rather than certain, and that probabilities are fairly stable. It would be illustrated by the housewife who buys Brand A approximately three out of four times, Brand B one out of four times, and never Brand C. Her next brand choice cannot be perfectly predicted but the average frequency of each brand choice can be predicted quite well.

Response change means that a buyer's behavior is probabilistic and that probabilities undergo systematic change. It would be illustrated by the housewife who grows to like Brand A more and more through time, with the result that Brand A's repurchase probability increases through time.

Now the problem is that observed individual brand switching histories do not immediately suggest whether response uncertainty or response change is at work. Both tend to be confounded in the observed data. Coleman (1964b) has developed interesting techniques for trying to unravel the two. Here, for the sake of systematic theory construction, we shall treat the case of pure response uncertainty first, under the rubric of the constant brand probability model.

This model says that it is not possible to predict exactly the next choice, but that one could predict the average proportion of times each brand will be purchased by the buyer. For example,

$$BPPV_{it} = (.50, .30, .20) \text{ for all } t$$

says that buyer i will purchase Brand A 50% of the time, Brand B 30% of the time, and Brand C 20% of the time.

Through the adoption of more extreme probabilities, one would almost be describing the brand loyalty model subject to a small amount of response uncertainty. This is accomplished, for example, in

$$BPPV_{it} = (.90, .08, .02) \text{ for all } t.$$

The buyer is highly loyal to Brand A but for sundry reasons occasionally buys B and less frequently C.

While it is easy to state this mechanism, it is not easy to provide a plausible psychological explanation of it. Clearly the housewife does not have a random chance device in her head which she spins prior to selecting a brand. About the closest behavioral explanation is that she has some stable pattern of brand preferences such as $A > B > C$ and when she goes to the store, she is subject to a large number of random influences affecting her actual choice: the presence of a point-of-purchase display, an out-of-stock condition, a price deal on an offbrand, an advertisement in the morning newspaper, and so forth. In general, behavior may be described as having a random component when a great many small factors operate in a situation and may affect the normal predisposition of the actor.

Can observed brand switching in the coffee market be explained by a model which postulates constant household brand probabilities? Ronald E. Frank (1962) found that this hypothesis provided a statistically satisfactory explanation of brand choice behavior in the coffee market. It was not necessary to evoke the hypothesis of learning to explain observed brand histories.

If this model is used to describe a hypothetical population of consumers, each having a different but stable brand probability purchase vector, it is possible to derive analytically the long-run implied average market shares. At the same time, the constant brand probability model has a number of short-comings. First, it does little to promote the development of psychologically rich theory in the area of buyer behavior. At the most, it may stimulate the development of better techniques for mapping brand preference rankings or ratings into brand probability vectors and for relating them to individual social-economic-personality characteristics.

Second, it denies the possibility of finding systematic relationships between changing marketing stimuli and consumer response. It treats market-ing stimuli on too implicit and random a level to permit a study of their effects on buyers.

Third, it denies learning, the tendency for a person's predispositions to change with experience. There is much psychological evidence that favorable experiences increase the probability that an individual will respond in a similar way to the next occasion.

Finally, this model is unable to reproduce the serial correlation that is observed in many actual brand histories. Specifically, the data often show various length runs of the same brand purchases, and such runs cannot be explained on the basis of pure random drawings.

For all these reasons, we must formulate a more sophisticated model of the brand choice process, although we may have occasion to revert to this model as a bench mark for judging the more elaborate ones.

The Last Brand Purchased Model

In the previous model, the buyer's brand purchase probability vector remains constant throughout the simulation, a direct denial of learning theory. Learning theory holds that a person's responses to stimuli are determined through experience. If a stimulus leads a person to try something, and if that experience is rewarding, it strengthens the habit connection between stimulus and response so that on the next trial there is a greater probability to respond in the same way. Conversely, if a person is dissatisfied, this reduces the prob-ability that he will respond in the same way to similar cues. In either case, the brand probabilities are likely to change after the purchase.

There are a number of mathematical devices for incorporating or repre-senting the effects of learning. The general problem is to formulate a model which makes

$$BPPV_{i,t+1} = f(BPPV_{i,t}, B_{i,t}),$$

where $B_{i,t}$ is the last brand purchased by buyer i.

A Simple Markov Formulation

As a start, consider the first-order Markov probability transition matrix in Exhibit 2. The original marketing use of this matrix is to represent the aggregate switching and staying tendencies of the market as a whole rather than of the individual buyer. Thus, it may be observed that of those consumers who buy Brand A this period, 70% buy A again, 20% switch to B, and 10% switch to C. The other two rows are similarly interpreted. If these percentages hold from period to period for the market as a whole and if other assumptions are satisfied (Ehrenberg, 1965), then the matrix can be used to derive a number of interesting propositions about the market, including the ultimate level of brand shares and speed of convergence to this level (Maffei, 1960).

$$
\begin{array}{c}
\phantom{\text{From}}\begin{array}{ccc} A_{t+1} & B_{t+1} & C_{t+1} \end{array} \\
\text{From}\ \begin{array}{c} A_t \\ B_t \\ C_t \end{array}
\begin{bmatrix}
.70 & .20 & .10 \\
.50 & .40 & .10 \\
.60 & .20 & .20
\end{bmatrix}
\end{array}
$$

EXHIBIT 2. A First-Order Markov Matrix

The same matrix can be reinterpreted to describe the effect of the last brand choice of an individual buyer on her current brand purchase probabilities. Suppose a housewife purchased Brand A in the last period. Then there is a .70 probability that she will buy A again and some chance that she will buy B and C. Suppose she buys B next time (the chance is .20). Then we would expect the probability of her repurchasing B to go up (assuming satisfaction with B) and the probability of her repurchasing A to decline. Both effects are captured in this matrix. The probability of her buying A (having just bought B) has fallen from .70 to .50, and the probability of her buying B has risen from .20 to .40. (The probability of her buying C has been unaffected in this example. If, however, she buys C in the future, the probability of her repurchasing C will rise from .10 to .20.)

There are however at least two unsatisfactory features in using a first-order Markov matrix to interpret the effects of the last brand purchased on the buyer's future brand probabilities. The first problem is that while the matrix provides for probability modifications when a switch occurs, it does not provide for probability modifications when the same brand is repurchased. Thus, if A was purchased last time with a purchase probability of .70 and is then purchased again, we would expect A's repurchase probability to increase from .70. It doesn't, and therefore this model produces learning only when switching occurs rather than when staying occurs.

A second fault is that the model is static: it builds in only one-period learning. It implies that the buyer is influenced only by the last purchase and not the last *n* purchases. It is static in postulating the same row vector every time the buyer returns to a particular last brand.

A frequent suggestion is to use a two- or more-period Markov matrix to generate period-to-period brand choices (Harary and Lipstein, 1962). But it soon becomes apparent that this is a cumbersome device for expressing the impact of cumulative learning, and that some better mechanism must be found.

The Learning Model

A different way to express the reinforcement effects of past brand choices uses a learning model developed by Bush and Mosteller (1955), and later applied to consumer behavior by Kuehn (1961). This model postulates the existence of a pair of "learning operators" which explicitly alter current brand probabilities on the basis of the last brand choice.

The basic device is illustrated in Exhibit 3. The horizontal axis represents the probability of choosing brand j in period t, and the vertical axis represents the probability of choosing brand j in period $t + 1$. The figure contains a positively sloped 45° line as a norm. The figure also contains two positively sloped lines called the purchase and rejection operators. These operators show how the probability of purchasing brand j is modified from period t to period $t + 1$, depending on whether or not brand j was just purchased.

For example, suppose the probability that a housewife will purchase brand j this period is .60. Suppose this is actually what she buys. What is the probability that she will buy brand j again? This is found by running a dotted line up from the horizontal axis at .60 to the purchase operator line (because brand j was purchased) and going across to the vertical axis and reading the new probability. In this illustration, the new probability is .78. Thus as a result of buying A, the housewife's predisposition toward A has increased from .60 to .78. If she had not purchased A, the dotted line from .60 would have been run up only to the rejection operator and read on the vertical axis. Her probability of buying A next time would have fallen from .60 to .31.

Thus, the prevailing probability of buying brand j is incremented or diminished according to whether brand j is bought. And the amount of increase or decrease depends on the probability of buying brand j in period t. If brand j is purchased three times in a row, starting with a probability of .60, the prob-

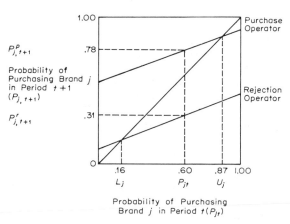

EXHIBIT 3.   The cumulative learning model.

ability increases each time according to the following values: .60, .78, .83, .86 (not shown).

If the consumer continues to buy brand *j* for a long number of trials, the probability of buying brand *j* approaches .87 in the limit. This upper limit is given by the intersection of the purchase operator and the 45° line and represents a phenomenon known as incomplete learning. No matter how much brand *j* is bought, there is still some probability left that the consumer may buy another brand. On the other hand, if the consumer does not buy brand *j* for a long time, the probability of buying this brand falls continuously but never to zero. This is the phenomenon of incomplete extinction. There is always some positive probability that a consumer may buy a previously neglected brand.

The particular rates of brand learning or extinction, as well as their upper and lower limits respectively, depend upon the slopes, intercepts, and curvatures of the two operators. In Exhibit 3, the operators are assumed to be parallel and linear. The parallel condition is required when there are more than two brands in order that the probabilities sum to one. The linearity condition greatly simplifies the estimation problem (Carman, 1966). Yet it is conceivable that the actual learning process for a household is subject to more flexible operators.

Although this model represents an improvement over the last brand purchased model as a way of handling the effects of learning, it presents a number of difficulties. In the first place, the model is couched not in terms of the buyer's brand purchase probability vector but in terms of her probability of buying brand *j*. When her probability of buying brand *j* increases, the total probability of her buying the other two brands must decrease by the same amount. The problem is how to distribute the decrease between B and C. There is no a priori reason that the total decline should be distributed in a proportional way.

Another difficulty is that this model implies that the purchase of a particular brand always increases the probability of repurchasing it. This implies that there are no significant product quality differences and that the only psychological process operating is that of habit formation and habit extinction. This may be a fairly safe assumption for relatively homogeneous products such as coffee, bread, frozen orange juice, cigarettes, and so forth. In other cases, however, product differences are above the just noticeable level. In these cases, it is not the choice of the brand which increases its probability of repurchase but rather the buyer's degree of satisfaction or dissatisfaction. The purchase operator is too rigid in implying inevitable satisfaction with use.

Third, this model, like the previous ones, ignores the effect on brand choice of variations in the marketing mix. It describes the buyers' brand purchase probabilities as being modified solely through past brand choices. This might be remedied through making the slopes and intercepts of the two operators a function of relative brand marketing effort. However, other methods of bringing marketing variables explicitly into the brand choice process will now be considered.

The Variable Markov Model

One of the earliest suggestions was made by Alfred Kuehn and involves a novel interpretation of the probabilities in the Markov matrix (1961). Each cell probability is considered to be made up of the more basic elements shown in Exhibit 4.

This model was formulated by Kuehn to explain aggregate switching and staying behavior, but it can be reinterpreted in terms of the individual consumer. In this case, r_j represents the unadjusted probability that the buyer will choose brand j again. It reflects essentially the buyer's degree of preference for brand j after having used it; a_j represents the relative merchandising attractiveness of brand j. The cell probability that a buyer will switch from B to A is given by

$$(1 - r_B)a_A,$$

that is, the product of the degree to which she is not committed to brand B and the relative merchandising attractiveness of brand A. Similarly, the cell probability that a buyer will repeat her purchase of B is given by

$$r_B + (1 - r_B)a_B,$$

that is, the degree of the buyer's loyalty to brand B (r_B), plus the extent to which her nonloyalty to B is overcome by brand B's relative merchandising attractiveness.

$$
\begin{array}{c}
\begin{array}{ccc}
A_{t+1} & B_{t+1} & C_{t+1}
\end{array} \\
\begin{array}{c} A_t \\ B_t \\ C_t \end{array}
\left[
\begin{array}{ccc}
r_A + (1 - r_A)a_A & (1 - r_A)a_B & (1 - r_A)a_C \\
(1 - r_B)a_A & r_B + (1 - r_B)a_B & (1 - r_B)a_C \\
(1 - r_C)a_A & (1 - r_C)a_B & r_C + (1 - r_C)a_C
\end{array}
\right]
\end{array}
$$

where r_j = the unadjusted repurchase probability $0 \leq r_j \leq 1$.

   a_j = the relative merchandising attractiveness of brand j. $\Sigma a_j = 1$.

EXHIBIT 4. The Variable Markov Model

With this formulation, we need the parameters a_A, a_B, a_C, r_A, r_B, r_C to generate an individual buyer's behavior over time. (Actually one of the a_j terms is redundant since $\Sigma a_j = 1$.)

The a_j terms reflect the current differential attractiveness of competitive marketing policies. For example, $a_A = .5$, $a_B = .3$, $a_C = .2$ would indicate that brand A is the most appealing brand at the time to the average customer, brand B is the next most appealing brand, and brand C is the least appealing brand. Relative brand attractiveness can change from week to week as competitors change their merchandising strategy.

Relative brand attractiveness is not measured directly, but rather represents the result of averaging several dimensions of brand competition. The averaging can be accomplished in a number of ways, one of which is suggested in a later model.

The r_j terms are generally treated as constants in the original model describing aggregate behavior. However, in the application of this model to individual buyer behavior, the r_j terms can be treated as changing each period as a result of the reinforcement effect of last period brand choice. Specifically the probability of repurchasing brand *j* through habit should be increased if *j* was bought last time and reduced if it was not. This can be accomplished readily through linear learning operators.

Thus, it is possible to modify the Markov model in a way which brings in two desirable effects: 1) the effect of brand learning; 2) the effect of company merchandising variables. This approach might prove to be quite fruitful as a framework for developing specific consumer behavior hypotheses and marketing measurement techniques. At the same time, the model over-simplifies the learning phenomenon and also the dimensions of brand competition. It is with this in mind that the writer developed two further models.

The Competitive Marketing Mix Model

The variable Markov model described in the previous section used the device of a_j terms to describe the net effect of competitive merchandising strategies on brand switching behavior. From a marketing point of view, it is desirable to make more explicit the specific effect of each marketing element on the buyer.

Assume that the current marketing characteristics of the different brands can be represented in a matrix called the *competitive marketing mix matrix* at time *t* (M_t). An illustrative competitive marketing mix matrix for three brands and eight marketing variables is shown below:

		Brand		
		A	*B*	*C*
List price	*P*	.31	.33	.36
Price deal	*D*	$.33\frac{1}{3}$	$.33\frac{1}{3}$	$.33\frac{1}{3}$
Premium	*G*	$.33\frac{1}{3}$	$.33\frac{1}{3}$	$.33\frac{1}{3}$
Packaging	*C*	.35	.33	.32
Quality	*Q*	.40	.33	.27
Shelf space	*S*	.20	.50	.30
Advertising	*A*	.25	.42	.33
Point of purchase	*L*	$.33\frac{1}{3}$	$.33\frac{1}{3}$	$.33\frac{1}{3}$

Each row represents the relative attractiveness of the three brands on a particular marketing dimension. The higher the number in a row, the more attractive the brand is on the dimension relative to the other brands. The numbers in each row add to one.

Consider price. Brand C stands at .36, making it the most attractive brand pricewise on the market. This implies that it has the lowest list price. As for price deal, all three brands stand at $.33\frac{1}{3}$, indicating either that there are no price deals or that all the brands have the same deal. Moving to packaging, note that brand A is rated as having the most attractive package, followed by B and C; at the same time, the ratings are quite close. In the case of quality, the ratings are further apart, indicating that A is perceived to be of substantially higher quality than B and C. The brands also differ in shelf space exposure, brand B being the best exposed. Ratings are also available for advertising and point-of-purchase display differences among the three brands.

The competitive marketing mix matrix is used to summarize the average market perception of the three brands along the different dimensions of competition. A sample of consumers is surveyed and asked to rate the three brands on each dimension, in such a way that the ratings add up to one in each case. The ratings of all the consumers on each dimension are averaged and normalized to add to one. It is in this sense that the matrix represents the average market perception of competitive marketing mix differences.

The competitors have the capability of influencing the average market perception through specific marketing actions. A competitor can increase his relative rating on price deals by offering one; he can improve his relative rating on advertising by finding a better message. The efforts of competitors to increase market favor will be reflected in the competitive marketing mix matrix.

In principle, each buyer has his own perception of the marketing mix differences among the brands. But for our purpose, it is more useful to work with the concept of an average perception of the market. Individual variations are assumed to enter in a different manner, specifically in the fact that households vary in the importance they attach to different marketing elements. Their individual differences in response can be expressed through a second construct known as buyer i's *marketing response vector* (W_i):

$$W_i = (P, D, G, C, Q, S, A, L).$$

It represents the relative weights placed by buyer i on the eight marketing variables. The weights in the vector are scaled to add to 1.00. An illustrative marketing response vector for buyer i is:

$$W_i = (.08, .05, .06, .18, .20, .08, .20, .15).$$

This vector shows that buyer i places the most value on quality (.20), advertising (.20), packaging (.18), and point-of-purchase (.15). A possible inference is that this is a middle-class housewife interested mainly in quality and brand image, and uninterested in small price differences.

In a simulation involving a population of buyers, each buyer would face the same competitive marketing mix matrix but would respond differentially according to her individual marketing response vector. Each week the marketing mix matrix would change to reflect the latest competitive marketing actions. But the individual buyer's marketing response vectors would remain constant from week to week. In this way, brand share changes would be due entirely to marketing competition, not to individual buyer changes. In a more elaborate model, the individual buyer's response vector would also change through time as a result of brand usage, learning social influences, and other factors.

The model is set up to yield a brand probability purchase vector for each household in each week $(BPPV_{it})$. For example, the brand probability purchase vector for buyer i at time t is derived by multiplying buyer i's response vector and the marketing mix matrix at time t:

$$W_i M_t = (.08, .05, .06, \\ .18, .20, .08, \\ .20, .15) \begin{bmatrix} .31 & .33 & .36 \\ .33\tfrac{1}{3} & .33\tfrac{1}{3} & .33\tfrac{1}{3} \\ .33\tfrac{1}{3} & .33\tfrac{1}{3} & .33\tfrac{1}{3} \\ .35 & .33 & .32 \\ .40 & .33 & .27 \\ .20 & .50 & .30 \\ .25 & .42 & .33 \\ .33\tfrac{1}{3} & .33\tfrac{1}{3} & .33\tfrac{1}{3} \end{bmatrix}$$

$$= (.32, .36, .32)$$
$$= BPPV_{it}.$$

The resulting brand purchase probability vector will necessarily be a unit vector, because it is the product of a unit vector and a matrix composed of unit row vectors. In effect, the buyer's brand purchase probabilities depend on: a) how attractive the relative brand characteristics are; and b) how much weight the buyer attaches to the different characteristics. In the example, the combination of the relative brand characteristics and buyer i's weights put brand B ahead of the other two brands. Buyer i's brand purchase probabilities would change from week to week as the competitive marketing mix matrix changes.

The simulation task is to derive the brand purchase probability vector for each buyer in the particular week, and use Monte Carlo methods to generate the brand choices. The brand choices of all buyers are totaled each week to derive weekly brand shares.

This conceptual approach requires several refinements before it can satisfy theoretical and operational requirements for a good model. One problem is that the method does not allow for interaction effects among marketing mix variables. Because the model is linear, the effects of different changes in merchandising are treated additively. A second problem is that the brand purchase probabilities cannot fall outside the range of the lowest and highest numbers within each column of the marketing mix matrix. This is because the multiplication operation essentially amounts to taking a weighted average of the columns, which means that the results cannot fall outside the limits. Thus it would take extreme differences in relative marketing ratings to produce extremely low or high brand purchase probabilities. A third problem is that the model as it now stands does not provide for learning. As mentioned earlier, this could be remedied by updating the buyers' response vectors for the effect of recent purchases and experiences. A fourth problem is to develop a meaningful way to scale the different dimensions of competition and to talk about the average perception of the market. One of the benefits of this conceptual approach is the stimulus it gives to finding better ways to scale relative awareness and attitudes toward brand differences.

The Total Behavior Model

All the previous models dealt with one or more effects that belong in a total model for generating consumer choice behavior. At this stage, it would be worthwhile to restate all the effects that ideally should be designed into a model. Five effects can be distinguished:

1. The effect of current attitudes on brand choice (predisposition effect).
2. The effect of interim experiences on brand choice (interim experience effect).
3. The effect of out-of-stock conditions on brand choice (availability effect).
4. The effect of in-store stimuli on brand choice (in-store experience effect).
5. The effect of using a brand on brand choice (usage effect).

The relationships between these effects are illustrated in the flow diagram in Exhibit 5 and explained below.

At periodic intervals, the housewife buys coffee. The first box poses the question of whether it is time for her to buy coffee. In the simplest case, it will be assumed that the answer is yes after a week passes, although a more complex model can be developed which makes interpurchase time a stochastic function

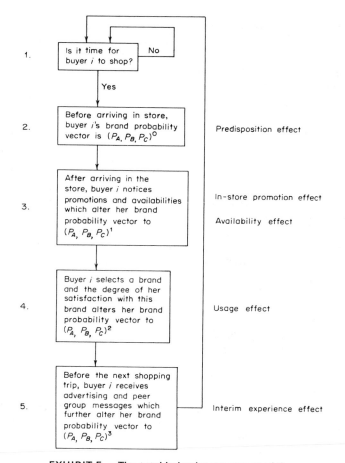

EXHIBIT 5.   The total behavior process model.

of several variables, including the family consumption rate, current inventory level, social occasions, and other variables.

It is then postulated that the housewife goes to the supermarket with a particular predisposition toward the available brands, represented by a brand purchase probability vector.

When she enters the store, her predisposition vector may be altered by in-store experiences, such as price deals, premiums, and point-of-purchase displays. This is accomplished by premultiplying her brand probability purchase vector by an in-store experience matrix.

A further adjustment is made for the chance that particular brands may be out of stock. It is assumed that each competitor spends a specific amount of money on making sure that its brand is in stock—a table is used to indicate the cost of achieving different probabilities that the brand will be in stock. The appropriate probabilities are used in the simulation. A random number is drawn to indicate whether each brand is in stock. If a brand is not in stock, the brand purchase probability vector is rescaled so that the remaining brand probabilities add to one.

The housewife takes home the brand and her experience has some effect on her predisposition vector. If the brand is satisfying, her probability of buying it again increases and of buying the other brands decreases. If the brand is dissatisfying, the reverse consequences take place. The effect of using the brand on future brand purchase probabilities is accomplished by multiplying the latest brand probability purchase vector by a usage effect matrix.

During the week, various events may happen to alter the housewife's brand probability purchase vector. The two main categories of events are impersonal communications such as advertising and personal communications from friends and neighbors.

The simplest way to handle advertising is by assuming that every advertising exposure has a positive effect on the housewife. Her predispositions toward the brands will be altered in proportion to the relative number of brand messages she receives. Later, this can be modified to allow for more subtle effects, such as: 1) the fact of selective perception—that is, she is more likely to notice advertisements of brands she uses than of others; and 2) the effect of differences in advertising quality and scheduling.

The effect of personal communications can be handled by assuming that her brand purchase probabilities are altered according to the number of competing brand messages she hears and whether they are negative or positive. In a simulation of coffee buying behavior, word-of-mouth messages are probably not an important factor in brand choice and can be neglected in the modeling process. In simulations of product markets where word-of-mouth influence is critical, care must be taken to formulate this process. Some progress has been made in modeling word-of-mouth influence in at least two marketing simulations (Amstutz, 1966; Stanfield, Clark, Lin, and Rogers, 1965).

This type of model takes a more comprehensive view of the factors operating in brand choice behavior than the previous models. It is represented today in its most developed form in the work of Arnold Amstutz (1966). He designs operational models in which markets are represented by a representative cross-section of highly specific consumers. Each person is specified in terms of economic-demographic characteristics, present brand ownership status, retailer preferences, attitudes toward different brand characteristics, recall of specific communications regarding product characteristics, advertising media habits, and personal relations with other consumers. Each week each consumer receives new communications, forgets some previous communications, may have some experience with the product, may decide to shop, and if she does, has a specific set of in-store experiences with salesmen and the product that may or may not lead to purchase. All of these events are determined by Monte Carlo draws based on situation-related probabilities. By summing the brand purchases of his sample population over time, Amstutz is able to develop a time series of brand shares and compare them to historical time series in an attempt to validate the model.

In spite of the many points at which this type of comprehensive model is still conjectural, it highlights major challenges facing the theorist and methodologist in this area, along with desirable directions of future work. It reminds us of the many limitations of the previous models in representing the complexity of the brand choice process.

Conclusion

The issue of statistically estimating the parameters of the above models from real data has not been specifically dealt with. This involves a separate and detailed discussion of underlying assumptions, data availability, and alternative estimating procedures. The estimation problems that arise, even in fitting the simple models, are often so tricky that many researchers have shown a bias against more elaborate model construction. Simple models have the virtue that data can be found and predictions can be tested. Complex models, on the other hand, meet the desire for a richer understanding of the phenomenon. The development of both types of models has its place, and the utility of each is to be judged by the purpose it is intended to serve.

References

Amstutz, A. E. *Management use of computerized micro-analytic behavioral simulations.* Working Paper 169–166, Alfred P. Sloan School of Management, M.I.T., March 1966.

Bush, R. R., & Mosteller, F. *Stochastic models of learning.* New York: John Wiley, 1955.

Carman, J. M. Brand switching and linear learning models. *J. Advertising Res.,* Vol. 6 (2) (1966), 23–31.

Carman, J. M., & Nicosia, F. M. Analog experiments with a model of consumer attitude change. In L. G. Smith (Ed.), *Reflections on progress in marketing.* Chicago: American Marketing Association (1965), 246–257.

Coleman, J. S. *Introduction to mathematical sociology.* New York: Macmillan Company, 1964. (a)

Coleman, J. S. *Models of change and response uncertainty.* Englewood Cliffs, N.J.: Prentice-Hall, 1964. (b)

Duhamel, W. F. *The use of variable Markov processes as a partial basis for the determination and analysis of market segments.* Unpublished Ph.D. dissertation, Stanford University, 1966.

Edgeworth, F. Y. *Mathematical psychics.* London: C. K. Paul, 1881.

Ehrenberg, A. S. C. An appraisal of Markov brand-switching models. *J. Marketing Res.,* Vol. 2 (1965), 347–363.

Festinger, L. *A theory of cognitive dissonance.* Stanford: Stanford University Press, 1957.

Frank, R. E. Brand choice as a probability process. *J. Business,* Vol. 35 (1962), 43–56.

Harary, F., & Lipstein, B. The dynamics of brand loyalty: A Markovian approach. *Op. Res.,* Vol. 10 (1962), 19–40.

Howard, J. A. *Marketing management: Analysis and planning* (Rev. ed.) Homewood, Ill.: Richard D. Irwin, 1963.

Jevons, W. S. *The theory of political economy.* New York: Macmillan, 1871.

Kotler, P. Behavioral models for analyzing buyers. *J. Marketing,* Vol. 29 (4) (1965), 37–45. (a)

Kotler, P. The competitive marketing simulator—A new management tool. *California Mgmt. Rev.,* Vol. 7 (3) (1965), 49–60. (b)

Kuehn, A. A. A model for budgeting advertising. In F. M. Bass, et al., (Eds.), *Mathematical models and methods in marketing.* Homewood, Ill.: Richard D. Irwin (1961), 302–356.

Lipstein, B. A mathematical model of consumer behavior. *J. Marketing Res.,* Vol. 2 (1965), 259–265.

Maffei, R. B. Brand preferences and simple Markov processes. *Op. Res.,* Vol. 8 (1960), 210–218.

Massy, W. F. *A dynamic model for monitoring new product adoption.* Working Paper No. 95, Graduate School of Business, Stanford University, March 1965.

Massy, W. F., & Frank, R. E. Short term price and dealing effects in selected market segments. *J. Marketing Res.,* Vol. 2 (1965), 171–185.

Montgomery, D. B. *A probability diffusion model of dynamic market behavior.* Working Paper 205–66, Alfred P. Sloan School of Management, M.I.T., May 1966.

Morrison, D. G. New Models of consumer behavior: Aids in setting and evaluating marketing plans. In P. D. Bennett (Ed.), *Marketing and economic development.* Chicago, Ill.: American Marketing Association (1966), 323–337.

Orcutt, G. H., Greenberger, M., Korbel, J., & Rivlin, Alice. *Microanalysis of socio-economic systems: A simulation study.* New York: Harper Brothers, 1961.

Riesman, D., Glazer, N., & Denney, R. *The lonely crowd* (Abridged ed.). Garden City, N.Y.: Doubleday, 1956.

Rogers, C. *Client-centered therapy.* Boston: Houghton Mifflin, 1951.

Simon, H. A. The construction of social science models. In P. F. Lazarsfeld (Ed.), *Mathematical thinking in the social sciences.* Glencoe, Ill.: Free Press (1954), 430–440.

Simulmatics media-mix: Technical description. New York: The Simulmatics Corporation, October 1962.

Stanfield, J. D., Clark, J. A., Lin, Nan, & Rogers, E. M. *Computer simulation of innovation diffusion: An illustration from a Latin American village.* Paper presented at a joint session of the American Sociological Society, Chicago, August–September 1965.

Tomkins S. S., & Messick, S. (Eds.), *Computer simulation of personality.* New York: John Wiley, 1963.

7.3 Advertising Management, Consumer Behavior, and Simulation
FRANCESCO M. NICOSIA

Past research has uncovered many of the variables that make up the structure of consumer behavior. These efforts have enriched our knowledge by identifying variables that any one researcher, theory, or method may have overlooked. The list we have inherited constitutes our knowledge of the "anatomy" of the structure of consumer behavior.

This list, however, does not tell us how the variables interact among themselves. Past research has isolated relatively few interactions among some variables. Further, in most cases, isolation has been made under the assumption of "all other factors being equal," in the tradition of comparative static analysis. In life, of course, these "other factors" are not equal: they do not remain constant; they change, often together with changes in the very variables whose relations the researcher tries to isolate and assess. One of the pressing needs of advertising research, therefore, is to reconstruct the total picture, to put together the various parts of the economic, psychological, and social mechanisms that govern observable behavior, and to study the interactions over time among the parts of these mechanisms.

To cope with this complexity, we must work in two directions at once. First, we must work toward mapping out the "blueprints" of the total structure that underlies behavior. Second, we must develop the research tools and methodology necessary to carry out this substantive work.

Consider a very simplified illustration of the structure of consumer behavior. Take a hypothetical situation where only two factors operate; (a) a communicator (e.g., a firm) which controls the content and timing of its messages (e.g., advertising, product design, price), and (b) a *type* of consumer (i.e., one individual or a homogeneous market segment) who is exposed to no other stimulus except one of the firm's messages. The message may or may not influence this consumer; in either case, his reaction then influences the firm's subsequent decisions about its future messages. His reaction also influences his own self, so that he becomes a slightly different person. Thus, there are two main circular flows: (a) a "loop" from the firm to the consumer and back to the firm (the firm's loop); and (b) a "loop" from the consumer's social psychological field before the message, to his reaction, and back to his social psychological field (the consumer's loop). (See Flow Chart 1.)

The firm and the consumer are seen as a closed system, and the two loops are the vehicles through which they interact over time. Note that in this structural or systemic view the firm and the consumer determine *each other*. Through time neither is inherently and exclusively the cause or the effect of the other (or independent of, or dependent upon, the other).

In reality, a firm's loop contains many variables and mechanisms (or subloops) that provide for the firm's adjustments to the reactions of the consumer; and a consumer's loop is made up of many subloops that provide for the consumer's adjustments to his own reactions and to those of the firm. All these interact over time in circular system-like ways. Many of the interactions can occur simultaneously or in sequences that are not necessarily time ordered, and these interactions can be described by reference to functional relations among economic, psychological, social, and other variables.

Various research traditions describe some of the interactions in the consumer's loop in seemingly different, and sometimes contradictory, ways. One example of these apparent differences is that between the communication paradigm—where the interactions are described by the temporal sequence of stimulus-attitude-motivation-behavior, and some versions of the cognitive

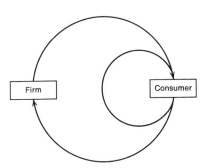

CHART 1.   A simplified structure of consumer behavior.

dissonance paradigm—where the interactions are described by the temporal sequence of behavior-attitude. But, over time, neither sequence will stop at behavior or attitude, respectively. In the communication paradigm, behavior will feed back into the individual and will affect, for example, his attitude; in the second paradigm, a change in attitude will directly or indirectly affect future behavior.

Flow Chart 2 portrays the very simplified structure of a possible consumer decision process. The arrows indicate the functional relations among the variables as follows: C stands for a firm, or a communicator, or a stimulus such as an ad; A is an attitude toward a product class; M is a motivation toward a specific brand in the product class; B is the purchase of a brand in the product class; and t is the time at which our observations on the four variables are collected. Parenthetically, note that the distinction between attitude and motivation above is based on a review of basic and consumer research of several decades—from the early studies of the psychologists of the Wurtzburg group to those of the Hovland group, from studies of political decision processes to those of the consumer (Nicosia, 1966). Briefly, an *attitude* toward an item is a cognitive structure (a) that has a generic scope, i.e., it includes percepts about the product class of which the brand under consideration is a member; and (b) that weakly drives a subject toward this product class. A *motivation* is a cognitive structure (a) that has a specific scope, i.e., it includes only one brand; and (b) that strongly drives a subject toward this particular brand. Of course, the empirical indicators for these two dimensions (scope and driving force) necessarily vary from product class to product class, and from brand to brand.

Again, in the flow chart no variable is inherently dependent or independent; over time they all affect each other. Only the purpose of a specific investigation dictates the treatment of the variables. There may indeed be management questions which can be answered only if research isolates specific parts of the flow chart and excludes the effects of the remaining parts. For example, to assess the effect of advertising C on the act of buying B on the basis of the communication paradigm, we must rewrite the flow chart above so that C is determined exogenously—i.e., it is defined as the independent or experimental variable (in laboratory and field studies we do this by "erasing" arrow 5); while attitude A and motivation M toward a brand are postulated to be intervening or endogenously determined—i.e., they intervene between the independent variable C and the dependent variable B (we do this by "erasing" arrow 3);

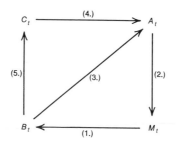

CHART 2.   **A simplified consumer decision process.**

and the act of purchase B is the dependent variable—i.e., it is determined by C as filtered by A and M.

To assess the effect of a past purchase on motivation, we would design our study so that B is the independent variable, C is controlled, A is intervening, and M is the dependent variable.

Both studies are examples of legitimate basic and applied interests; when we carry them out, we obtain the description of the communication paradigm excluding the effects of the dissonance paradigm in the first study, and vice versa in the second. In life, however, both mechanisms may be working concurrently, and there are advertising problems in which this must be taken into account. For example, we may need to study the interaction between the two paradigms by reassessing the effect of C on B while the dissonance paradigm exerts its influence (rather than by controlling it as we did previously by erasing arrow 3). The use of current laboratory and survey research techniques makes it generally possible to attempt the reconstruction which is illustrated by the example.

The structure of consumer behavior, however, is much more complex than that portrayed in Flow Chart 2, and, unfortunately, the above techniques do not allow us to study the dynamics of a structure made up of many variables and many relations among them. Let us look, therefore, at the type of apparatus we need to study such complex structures, namely, simulation techniques.

A Complex Flow Chart of Consumer Decision Processes

Laboratory and, to a lesser degree, survey research have identified relations among variables that in most cases are of the type "X is associated with Y, under certain conditions." Even the more advanced forms of multivariate analysis do not allow us to study interactions among a large number of simple functional relations. Digital computers and programing languages have recently provided one way to satisfy the need to analyze very complex systems of interactions (*American Behavioral Scientist*, 1965). In general, digital computer simulation can handle systems of interactions where none of the many variables alone accounts for much of the variance or has an impact strong enough to determine the state of the system, but where all the variables simultaneously bear upon the state of the system (De Sola Pool, 1964) and its possible time paths. Simulation allows us to handle many variables and many interactions simultaneously, and thus frees us from relying on one-at-a-time approaches, with their restrictive requirement that all other things be held constant.

Although little has been published so far, several advances have been made; for example, computer microanalytic simulation of the U.S. economy (Orcutt, *et al.*, 1961), of the flow of lumber on the West Coast (Balderston and Hoggatt, 1963[a]), of political behavior (McPhee, 1961), of decisions by an investment officer (Clarkson, 1963), and of personality (Tomkins and Messick, 1963; Guetzkow, 1962).

Developments in marketing, especially in the area of micro descriptions of the social and psychological processes underlying consumer decisions, are difficult to assess since almost nothing has been published (for noticeable exceptions, see Claycamp and Amstutz, 1968; Amstutz, 1966; and Wells, 1963). I suspect that what now appears to be a lag may turn to our advantage. Most pioneering studies were handicapped by enthusiasm for the immediate technical advantages of digital simulation and the problem was often not "thought out" first (see Wenkert and Fredrickson, 1962). Simulation is not a substitute for theory; it is only a new way to test theoretical propositions and managerial insights about the dynamics of complex events. To produce meaningful results, it must be guided by some theory that postulates the structure of the decision to be studied.

We have also learned that microanalytic simulations of decision processes call for much more fine-grain data on psychological and social processes than are yet available, and often call for altogether new data. Our situation is characterized by a general unavailability of appropriate laboratory and survey data (for a few and tentative exceptions, see Maloney, 1966, and G. H. Smith, 1965). To obtain such data is of course expensive; besides, the fact that none of us can guarantee sponsors any success generates resistance to investment in this area!

This should not prevent our attempting to integrate what we know so far. From this integration we can derive precise specifications of the psychological, social, and economic variables we need, of the measuring instruments to be used, and of the functional relations we suspect exist among these variables.

Flow Chart 3 of a consumer decision process illustrates the direction in which we should work. It is, of course, only one possible type of integration of our present knowledge. By stating specific variables and their general interdependencies, it offers the necessary guidelines for data collection, and the technical bases for experimental simulations of the psychological, social, and economic processes it describes and of the possible reactions of these processes to different advertising policies. It also offers the necessary background for qualified interpretations of the results of experimental simulations.

The Decision Process

I shall start somewhere in the structure that represents a type of decision process, and describe it step by step. Assume that neither the firm nor the consumer has any history directly relevant to the content of the firm's message; we start at time zero. The firm is introducing a new brand, and the consumer has feelings—i.e., attitude and motivation—neither toward this brand nor toward its product class. A first approximation of the structure would consist of the flow: the firm, its advertisement, the consumer's possible exposure to it, the interaction between the advertisement and the consumer's predispositions operating or evoked at the time of exposure, the possible formation of an attitude, the possible transformation of this attitude into a motivation, the possible conversion of this motivation into an act of purchase, and then back to the consumer's predispositions, *and* to the firm.

In illustrating this cycle, let us take the point of view of a firm that wants to understand the consumer's loop in order to find out *how* its messages reach the consumer and influence his buying behavior. Thus, I shall attend only briefly to the firm's loop; we begin with the firm and proceed to develop in detail the consumer's loop.

A summary of the content of the consumer's loop is given in Flow

Field 1: From the Source of a Message to a Consumer's Attitude

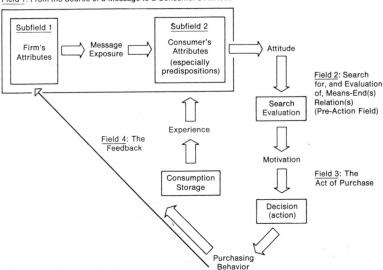

CHART 3. A summary flow-chart structure of consumer behavior.

Chart 3. The chart is basically a computer program that describes an invariant structure of consumer behavior. (This structure reflects a theory of consumer decision making developed elsewhere; see Nicosia, 1966.) More specifically, the structure is made up of four building blocks or "fields" and of their functional relations. The fields are atemporal in character; each should be seen as a subprogram of the overall computer program. A number of invariant cognitive and other psychological activities operate throughout the structure (e.g., physical and cognitive perception, selective exposure). They are sub-routines that may be called to work in any field; e.g., motivated perception operates upon the advice received from friends (Field Two), upon the point-of-purchase display (Field Three), and so on.

Flow Chart 3 pictures *only salient* features of the structure. Beginning with the firm, the first cycle through the process reads as follows: *Field One* encompasses the flow of a message from its source (a firm) to the internalization of the message by a consumer. In particular, *Subfield One* includes the organizational attributes of a firm; and the interaction among these attributes produces a message directed toward a type of consumer, that is, toward a homogeneous market segment. If the consumer is exposed to the message, it becomes an input into *Subfield Two*, the consumer's space. This is made up of all the consumer's attributes, including those relevant to the internalization of the message. Now, internalization implies operations such as physical perception of the stimulus' attributes, environmental attributes prevailing at the moment of perception, and cognitive structures that are evoked and give meaning to the stimulus and its components. The result(s) of these operations are the output of *Subfield Two*. This output may or may not be the formation of an attitude toward the product and brand advertised.

The input into *Field Two* is the attitude that may emerge from Field One. Field Two consists of a search for, and evaluation of, means-ends relations between the attitude toward the advertised product and brand and the number of brands perceived as available. The search may be internal—that is, the subject consciously or unconsciously retrieves the information from his social psychological field that seems to him to concern the advertised brand, the product, the brand's manufacturer and seller, and so forth. External search consists of overt activities that, consciously or unconsciously, purposefully or accidentally, uncover information relevant to the attitude (e.g., self-exposure to advertisements, shopping). The output from Field Two may or may not be the information of a motivation toward the advertised brand.

The motivation that may emerge from Field Two is the input into *Field Three.* This field describes the possible transformation of the motivation into an act of purchase; it is affected by brand availability, in-store factors (e.g., point-of-purchase ads, relative prices and deals, salesmanship), and so forth. The output from it may or may not be the purchase of the advertised brand. The input into *Field Four* is the purchase that may emerge from Field Three. Field Four consists of operations such as storage and consumption (or use) that lead to experience with the brand. The output from it, then, is an experience that in turn becomes the input into Field One, Subfield Two, thus closing the consumer's loop. The output of Field Three—the purchase—is also the input into Field One, Subfield One, and it therefore closes the firm's loop.

Note that the dynamics of the structure are not affected by the choice of a starting point. For instance, we could begin with a consumer's attribute in Field One, Subfield Two, cause the onset of a disequilibrium (e.g., thirst), follow the resolution of this disequilibrium (e.g., purchase), and trace the ensuing feedbacks. Or, if we wanted to experiment with Zeisel's (1957) suggestion of a sequence "from specific to general decision" or with some suggestions offered by cognitive dissonance theory (the forced behavior case, for example), we could begin with Field Three and cause a purchase of a brand, and then follow the eventual effects through the flow chart. For each specific product and brand, changes of details may, of course, be necessary, but the general structure will remain the same.

As this brief description has implied, each of the fields involves a large number of variables and interactions among them. By simulation, each of these interactions can be studied "experimentally" within the dynamics of the whole process and thus without the limitations inherent in laboratory or field designs.

The relevance of this for basic and applied research should be evident. With a computer program describing the structure summarized in Flow Chart 3, and with the relevant survey and laboratory data (especially on cognitive processes), the managerial implications of the recent suggestions by Krugman (1965) concerning the impact of television advertising, can be analyzed. Through this analysis we could identify, for instance, the specific conditions (e.g., type of product and brand, type and size of audience) under which Krugman's ideas operate, and their specific effects on such important variables as recall, liking, comprehension, and repeat purchases. We could identify how the so-called laws which have been isolated one at a time in the field and the laboratory operate simultaneously, and how they might apply to a particular advertising problem.

As another example, consider consumer learning and the development of brand loyalty. Many applications of Markov processes have relied on the assumption that the probability of repurchase is a function of the consumer's previous experience with the brand. But it is clear that several other factors make up a consumer's learning, and that ultimately brand switching is the result of various possible interactions among these factors, and between them and direct experience with the brand. (Data have already strongly suggested that "Customer satisfaction ... may be more a global concept than simply product evaluation," see Cardozo, 1965, p. 249. Further, work has successfully begun in identifying factors other than brand experience, making for the development of loyalty, see Sheth, 1966.) Although isolation in the field and laboratory provides useful information, merely knowing that the factors exist does not give us the knowledge of the structure underlying brand-switching behavior which enables us to see specific targets for appropriate administrative action.

If we can identify various types of consumers, we will have a new perspective from which to approach the question of whether the family or one of its members is a preferable unit of behavior for the study of consumer reactions to mass communications. Moreover, by moving back and forth between micro and macro observations, we can redefine the problem of aggregation of individual members to mean behavior interaction among different types of individuals—family members, families, friends, etc. For example, let us assume that, for a given advertising campaign, consumers affect each other through two channels: (a) verbal communication (e.g., with friends, dealers); and (b) nonverbal communication (e.g., seeing others' behavior). In this case, we could look at our consumer's loop from the point of view of both of these channels. Then we could build other processes with equal and/or different characteristics, hook them together via the variables in (a) and (b), and observe experimentally the interactions among them and with our campaign—e.g., via digital computer simulation.

Despite the need for better laboratory and field data, and despite the need to resolve certain digital simulation problems, preliminary work suggests that the complex structure summarized in Flow Chart 3 provides the background for attacking some of the more pressing needs of management.

A Simple Flow Chart of Consumer Decision Processes

Notice that the overall dynamic properties of the structure in Flow Chart 3 are also presented in Flow Chart 2. The advantage of simulating Flow Chart 3 by digital computer is that we can explain in great depth the structure of a consumer's decision process, and thus be in a better position to predict his behavior when we believe that the structure is not invariant. Although Flow Chart 2 loses much of this explanatory and predictive power, it gains a lot in terms of the immediate availability of data. Most firms have reasonably good data on their advertising expenditures over time (that is, C), and their sales over time (that is, B). Further, many firms have data on brand images, and the like, i.e., data on A and/or M and/or other variables.

The availability of these data allows formal study of the overall dynamic properties, especially feedback, of the structure of consumer behavior in Flow Chart 3. Moreover, by keeping this more detailed flow chart in mind, we can interpret results derived from Flow Chart 2 with the necessary qualifications.

It also gives us direction in gradually increasing the complexity of the simpler flow chart.

Let us reconsider Flow Chart 2. Assume that we are interested in explaining the path through which an advertising campaign may influence behavior, and predicting the ways this behavior may be changed by variations in the dollars spent for the campaign. (For a more rigorous discussion of this and other management problems, see Nicosia, 1966, Ch. 7.) To examine this problem, we will rewrite Flow Chart 2 as shown in Flow Chart 4.

Flow Chart 4 portrays two full cycles of the decision process over time. The value of the variables (B, M, A) are observed at discrete time intervals t_1, t_2, etc. The arrows represent the functional relations among the variables, and the numbers in parentheses refer to equations we could write to translate our chart into a system of differential or difference equations. Eventually, the relations among these variables, including the feedback of B into A, determine changes in their values over time. Because of our stated interest, the value of C is a constant with respect to time. This flow chart and the equations below do not consider explicitly time lags, because these must be estimated for each specific case (e.g., type of stimulus, brand, product class, market segment).

When the forms of the functions and the parameters of our structural model for a specific brand are known, we can "experiment" with our stimulus C by applying it in, say, different intensities and/or times, and observe the consequent impacts on the act of buying. To do this, we can use analog computers, which are especially adept at treating differential equations. Preliminary work in this direction has been reported by Carman and Nicosia (1964).

At this point some questions can be anticipated and answered. First, if the raw data can be treated by difference instead of differential equations, the relevance of the analysis does not change (at worst, it becomes somewhat more cumbersome). The second question concerns whether firms have data for both A and M. Suppose that a firm had data only for A. This means that we should simplify Flow Chart 4 by deleting arrow 2 and by having A feed directly into B. The next question may be about the procedure for estimating empirically the

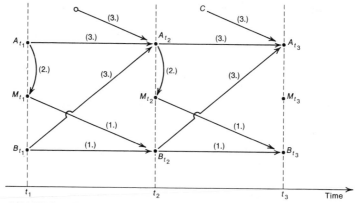

CHART 4. Two cycles of the consumer decision process over time.

forms of the functions relating the variables (B, A, C). This estimate can be made using current routine procedures. For instance, suppose that our chart is translated by the following equations (for $A = M$):

$$\frac{dB(t)}{dt} = -a_1 B(t) + b_1 A(t) \tag{1}$$

$$\frac{dA(t)}{dt} = a_2 B(t) - b_2 A(t) + c_2 C \tag{2}$$

To estimate the parameters in these two equations, current least squares regression techniques can be satisfactorily employed. (For a rigorous discussion of some econometric specifications, see Nicosia, 1967). The values and the changes of the variables in the model can be derived from a firm's internal records (B and C), and from survey data (A), preferably from continuing consumer panels rather than from cross-sectional studies. By keeping the model up to date, timely predictions of purchases can be made, since the model portrays a feedback system. To illustrate, equation (1) tells us that if the quantity $a_1 B(t)$ exceeds $b_1 A(t)$, the time rate of change of $B(t)$ will become negative and $B(t)$ will decrease with the passage of time. The implications of this for developing timely policies affecting the changes in A are clear.

Simulation of Complex versus Simple Structures and Management Strategy

I have already mentioned the unavailability of "fine-grain" data, especially social and psychological. Even those data that are available (e.g., most socioeconomic and demographic attributes) may not be easily used because they may have been collected for other reasons. And when these data come from different studies, they are often not comparable because they use different measuring instruments, or observations are taken at different times or on different subjects. Two more problems should be added to that of unavailability of fine-grain data. First, not only academic research (Hinkle and Wolf, 1966) but also business and government research (Bauer, 1966) badly need data banks. More important, to build a usable data bank, it is necessary not only to have storage hardware, which is available, but also to develop criteria for information storage and retrieval that are oriented toward marketing and advertising problems—and, these criteria are not available (Nicosia, 1966, Ch. 7, Sec. 6).

Further, in simulating complex systems, ". . . what one gains by including more variables [and functional relations] is at least partly offset by the increased difficulty of working with the system that is under study. Notions of equilibrium or optimality, therefore, may become elusive or may vanish altogether as the complexity of the system that is portrayed increases" (Balderston, 1959). Also, "By generating the time path of the model on a digital computer, we observe how these forces interact. However, when this stage has been reached, it is not clear that we understand the model. We find that the problem of deriving the implications from the model is difficult. This is partly because it is constructed from several subsets of variables which are bound together by relations which define submodels within the model" (Balderston, 1963). Finally, simulation of complex systems raises other problems: for example, the determination of the extent to which behavior in the model is sensitive to variations in the many internal parameters (Cyert and March, 1963), or the establishment of the model's viability, i.e., its ability, under plausible initial conditions and parameter settings, to generate adaptive behavior over time (Balderston and Hoggatt, 1963[b], pp. 32–33, and p. 127). In general, the ". . . methodology for testing models that take the form of digital computer programs remains to be developed . . ." (Cyert and March, 1963, p. 97, n. 4, and App. B). (For a suggestion concerning some of these difficulties, see Orcutt, 1960; for a recent review of verification of computer simulation models, see Naylor and Finger, 1967.)

These and other difficulties must be overcome if we want to gain the "engineering" knowledge of consumer behavior that digital simulation can deliver. In the short run, we can avoid them by reducing comprehensive flow charts to their major building blocks, translating the relations among the blocks into mathematical models, and studying these models by analog computers. The discussion of Flow Charts 3 and 4 is an example of this procedure. Analysis of these models may well supply clues about the conditions that future digital simulations of more complex structures must satisfy to be viable (e.g., plausible initial conditions, parameter settings).

These considerations suggest a strategy for consumer research to cope with the increasingly demanding questions posed by advertising management: first, to study relatively simple structures of consumer behavior by analog computer, and then to study progressively more complex structures by digital computers. At present, this strategy is suggested by the unavailability of data, by methodological difficulties, and by the immediate needs of advertising managers. In the future, however, this strategy may, in a sense, be imposed upon us by technological developments: hybrid digital-analog computers are already on the market.

References

Amstutz, A. E. "A Management Oriented Behavioral Theory of Interactions Within Consumer Product Markets." Unpub. Ph.D. dissertation, M.I.T., March 1965.

Amstutz, A. E. "A Management Use of Computerized Micro-Analytic Behavioral Simulations." Unpub. paper, School of Management, M.I.T., March 1966.

Balderston, F. E. "Analytic Models Versus Computer Simulation." *Proc. AMA* (Dec. 1959), 139–151.

———, A. C. Hoggatt. "Simulation Models: Analytic Variety and the Problem of Model Production." *Symposium on Simulation Models,* ed. A. C. Hoggatt and F. E. Balderston, South-Western (1963a), 182–191.

———, and ———. *Simulation of Market Processes.* Institute of Business and Economic Research, Univ. California, Berkeley, 1963b.

Bauer, R. A. "Social Indicators and Sample Surveys." *Public Opinion Quarterly,* Vol. 30 (Fall 1966) 339–352.

Cardozo, R. N. "An Experimental Study of Consumer Effort, Expectation, and Satisfaction." *J. Marketing Research,* Vol. 2 (Aug. 1965), 244–249.

Carman, J. M., and F. M. Nicosia. "Analog Experiments with a Model of Consumer Attitude Change." *Proc. AMA* (Dec. 1964). 246–257.

Clarkson, G. P. E. "A Model of the Trust Investment Process." *Computers and Thought,* ed. E. A. Feigenbaum and J. Feldman. McGraw-Hill (1963), 347–371.

Claycamp, H. J., and A. E. Amstutz. "Behavioral Simulation in Evaluating Alternative Marketing Strategies." *Applications of the Sciences in Marketing Management.* ed. S. M. Bass, *et al.* Wiley, 1968.

Cyert, R. M., and J. G. March. *A Behavioral Theory of the Firm.* Prentice-Hall, 1963.

De Sola Pool, I. "Simulating Social Systems." *International Science & Technology* (March 1964), 62–70.

Guetzkow, H. S. (ed.) *Simulation in Social Science.* Prentice-Hall, 1962.

Hinkle, C. L., and J. S. Wolf. "Academic Research and the Data Drought Dilemma." *J. Marketing Research,* Vol. 3 (May 1966), 196–198.

Krugman, H. E. "The Impact of Television Advertising." *Public Opinion Quarterly,* Vol. 29 (Fall 1965), 349–356.

Maloney, G. C. "Attitude Measurement and Formation." Unpub. paper, 1966.

McPhee, W. N. "Note on a Campaign Simulator." *Public Opinion Quarterly,* Vol. 25 (Summer 1961), 184–193.

Naylor, T. H., and J. M. Finger. "Verification of Computer Simulation Models." *Management Science* (Oct. 1967), 92–101.

Nicosia, F. M. *Consumer Decision Processes.* Prentice-Hall, 1966.

Nicosia, F. M. "On the Structure of Decision Making." Unpub. paper, Univ. California, Berkeley (Aug. 1967).

Orcutt, G. H. "Simulation and Economic Systems." *Amer. Economic Review,* Vol. 50 (Dec. 1960), 893–907.

————, *et al. Microanalysis of Socioeconomic Systems, A Simulation Study.* Harper & Row, 1961.

Sheth, J. N. *A Behavioral and Quantitative Investigation of Brand Loyalty.* Unpub. Ph.D. dissertation, Univ. Pittsburgh, 1966.

Smith, G. H. *Motivation Research in Advertising and Marketing,* McGraw-Hill, 1954.

Smith, G. H. "How GM Measures Ad Effectiveness." *Printers' Ink,* Vol. 290 (May 14, 1965), 19–32.

Tomkins, S. S., and S. Messick (eds.). *Computer Simulation of Personality.* Wiley, 1963.

Wells, W. D. "Computer Simulation of Consumer Behavior." *Harvard Business Review,* Vol. 41 (May-June 1963), 93–98.

Wenkert, R., and R. Fredrickson. *Uses of a University Computer Center.* Survey Research Center, Univ. California, Berkeley, 1962.

Zeisel, H. *Say It with Figures.* Harper & Row, 1957.

7.4 Information Processing Models of Consumer Behavior
JAMES R. BETTMAN

So that better decisions can be made by marketers within the context of marketing systems, decision making by firms and by consumers must be understood. Descriptive models of consumer behavior, one aspect of this problem, are the focus in this paper. These are information processing models of individual consumers' grocery product shopping decisions. Information processing models have been successfully applied to other areas of decision making in economics [4, 8], although such models of the behavior of particular individual consumers have received little research effort (see [1] for a model of shopping for women's clothing, and [9] for a model framework, however).

Following Newell, Shaw, and Simon [10], the models considered in this paper have: (1) a memory consisting of an array of cues; (2) a number of simple processes that operate on the cues and develop mediating constructs; and (3) a network, or discrimination net, which represents rules for combining the cues. A decision process is thus viewed as a net through which an array of cues passes. Alternatives are taken at the choice points in the discrimination net depending upon the value of the cue which that choice point processes. Finally, cues fall into three basic categories: (1) choice object attributes: for example, color, price, weight; (2) external environmental attributes: in order to limit the scope of the modeling process, such complex matters as husband or child preference, use experience with a product, or word of mouth are taken as cues processed by the housewife, but are not explained by a detailed model of their own; (3) internal cues or cognitive variables: the major cue measured here is the degree of risk felt toward a product class [2].

Given this viewpoint, if a model of an individual's processes is desired, how one infers the structure of these processes is an important question. Also, this viewpoint means that one cannot consider many individuals, but rather a few in detail. Finally, procedures for measuring the cues processed must be specified, as in the following section.

Research Method

The researcher followed five housewives(C_1–C_5) with a portable tape recorder as they shopped for grocery products, each over a six to eight-week period. The researcher knew and selected nonrandomly all the housewives, who were encouraged to think aloud as they shopped. For each choice made, the brand, size and number of packages, price, and aisle position were recorded. The data for the choice object and external environment cues come from these records and taped protocols. The only internal cue measured was the degree of risk a housewife perceived in buying a product type. The measurement was ordinal, a rank ordering of product types.[1]

Two consumers, C_1 and C_4, were modeled.[2] Five separate shopping trips were observed for each of these two. The models process the cue array for a given brand and accept or reject that particular brand, given that a product of that type is to be purchased. The models are limited and do not attempt to "menu plan," but take as input that certain product types are to be purchased. Also, the models are restricted by the definition of the external cues. Finally, some of the simple list processing is done external to the model—for example, maintaining the list of products in the store at any given time. These restrictions should give insight into processing of cues and make modeling feasible.

Consumer Behavior Models

Consumer C_1

Consumer C_1 had training in mathematics. She has five children. Her husband recently finished medical school and presently teaches. Her decisions were for the most part based on price, but she let the children have some of their favorites. Her statements emphasize her concern for price:

> I feel I do it [calculate prices] now as a moral obligation, to not be beaten down. . . . And this [buying a family member's preference] is something that I have just started, because I used to do it all by price, whether they liked anything else better or not. . . . It used to take me an hour, an hour and a half to do a week's grocery shopping. Because I did [calculate] everything, and they usually changed price on a good number of things.

The flow chart of consumer C_1's model is in Figure 1. The first branches represent the decision rules for meat, produce, and eggs. For meat and produce, C_1 used the highest justified price (X2) as a learned trigger level for choosing a cut of meat or type of produce, and then processed the primary sensory cues of color, heaviness, and feel (X3, X4, X43, X41). For eggs (X5), the rule shown is one C_2 said she remembered reading in *Consumer Reports* (although the parameter she used, five cents, may not have been accurately remembered).

The nodes X9, X10, and X11 represent C_1's feedback from experience. If it was bad (X10), she would associate risk with that brand and reject it later (X11). (This is not the same as perceived risk, but represents a rejection flag on a particular brand.)

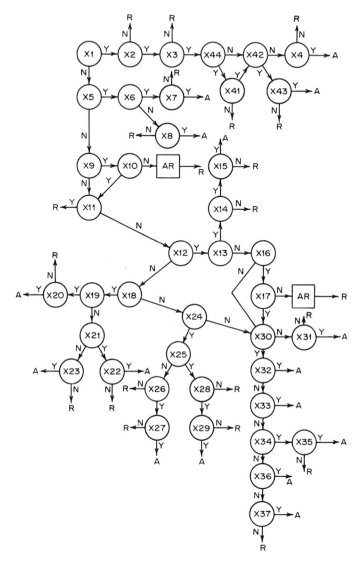

FIGURE 1. The model for consumer C_1.

A major branching point in the model is node X12, the perceived risk cue. For a high risk product class (high on the perceived risk ordering), C_1 checked if her husband or children had a preference (X13), or if the class had generalized health factors (X16; e.g., hexachlorophene soap or sugar-free canned fruit). If so, she bought the cheapest brand which satisfied the preference or health factor (X14, X15, and X17, X30, X31).

For a low risk product, C_1 departed from buying the cheapest only in certain cases, for guests (X18, X19) or the children (X24, X25, X26, X27, X28,

Key to Figure 1

Dictionary

A: Accept
R: Reject
AR: Associate risk (bad experience) with this product
Y: Yes
N: No.

X1: Is this meat or produce?
X2: Is price below justified level?
X3: Is color okay?
X4: Is this the biggest "okay" one?
X5: Is this eggs?
X6: Is the price of extra large over 5 cents more than the price of large?
X7: Is this large size?
X8: Is this extra large size?
X9: Was this product bought last time for this product type?
X10: Was experience with it okay?
X11: Is risk associated with this product (bad experience)?
X12: Is this product class high risk?
X13: Do children or husband have a specific preference?
X14: Is this their preference?
X15: Is it the cheapest size?
X16: Does this class have health (hygiene, diet) factors?

X17: Is this okay on these factors?
X18: Is this for company?
X19: Is the cheapest brand good enough?
X20: Is this the cheapest?
X21: Had a good experience with any brands in this class?
X22: Is this that brand?
X23: Is this the cheapest national brand?
X24: Are children the main users?
X25: Did they state a preference this week?
X26: Have they used this up in the last two weeks?
X27: Is this cheapest size?
X28: Is this that one?
X29: Is this the cheapest size?
X30: Are several "okay" brands cheapest (that they have in stock)?
X31: Is this the cheapest (that they have in stock)?
X32: Have a coupon for this one?
X33: Is this one biggest?
X34: Is there a single national brand?
X35: Is this it?
X36: Have I used this before?
X37: Is this the closest?
X41: Does this feel okay?
X42: Is this for a specific use?
X43: Is this size okay for that?
X44: Is this produce?

X29). She still tried to buy the cheapest within these constraints (X23 and X27 or X29). Otherwise, with no such departures, she bought the cheapest of the "okay" products in stock at the time, in terms of price per unit. This list of products with no associated bad experience (as in X10 or X17) is maintained external to this model.

Since the model for C_1 is largely price-oriented, how she codes products with respect to certain cues (e.g., X18, X24, X13, X16) will determine the number of exceptions to the rule of buying the cheapest. The protocol states:

> I get the, the little tenderized ones [steaks], what are they called? These are the ones, if they get below a dollar (X2).
> By what color it is.... Every picture of watermelon one sees has a picture of pink, quite pink watermelon (X3).
> I picked it because it was the biggest one [pork shoulder] (X4).
> Well, it depends on the price differential. If there's less than what, five cents, I'll get the extra large (X6).
> I've found that these [doesn't buy them], I've got duds, when I get the ones that are supposed to be extra savings (X10, X11).
> The children, I don't, or my husband. They said it was better (X13).
> My daughter ... feels that a deodorant soap or hexachlorophene or

whatever it is is good for her face ... so I got the cheapest deodorant soap (X16, X17, X30).

This part I really can't do without a child to tell me which cereal is in favor this week (X25).

I came last week and divided everything by 14 ounces into 59 and 12 ounces into 49 and so forth and finally figured out which is the best. Now until they change the price on me, I'm all set...

It's a little exhausting by the time you get through (X31).

Consumer C_4

Consumer C_4 presents a vivid contrast to consumer C_1. She is younger and newly married, with no children. She seemed to feel more risk in making product decisions than C_1. She likes to stick with what others had tried and told her to try. Her husband has strong preferences (he didn't like to try something he had not had before) and thus influenced what was bought. Other factors in her decision process were desires for convenience and freshness:

My theory, whatever works. ... If it's something that I like, for two or three times, then I'll keep on getting it rather than change, usually. ... I'd still rather [get] this, because I've used it before [flour]. ... Most of them have only tomatoes, but they have celery and everything in it so you don't have to put anything else in them. ... We like everything very fresh, and we'd rather go and get some more at another time later in the week than buy a larger quantity now. ...

The flow chart of the model for C_4 is in Figures 2 and 3. Figure 2 shows the processes of legitimization and size selection. The outputs of these are then used as mediating cues in the main process shown in Figure 3 (i.e., X14 for size selection and X18 for legitimization are set to Yes or to No in the main model depending upon the outputs in Figure 2).

If in a size decision there is no storage problem (X35) or no recipe or specific use (X36), C_4 bought the smallest size for freshness (X37).

Legitimization is the process by which a product becomes eligible for C_4's consideration. Since she usually did not try brands she did not know, the major cue types are her past experience (X48); word of mouth (X40, X41, X42); trial (X43); or marketing influences (X44, X45, X46). These inputs (except X48) are conditioned, however, by any negative halo effect (X47).

Now consider the main model in Figure 3. Since C_4 bought meat elsewhere, the first branch considers only produce. Here color and feel must be satisfactory (X2 and X6); size is determined by end use (X3, X5) or freshness considerations (X4).

If C_4 has not had any experience that she can recall with a product type (X7), she tries to reduce the perceptual field by using convenience as a filter property (X8, X9): then, if the product itself was visible, she judged by color and size (X10, X11, X14); if it was not visible, she chose by condition of the containers (X12, X13) or price (X15), if size was satisfactory (X14).

If she has had experience with this product class, the next major branching occurs for the perceived risk cue (X16). If a product was low risk

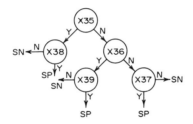

Size Selection

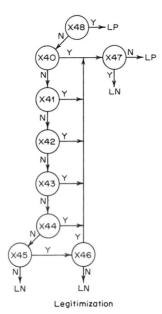

Legitimization

FIGURE 2. Size selection and legitimization models for consumer C_1.

Key to Figure 2

Size selection

N: No
Y: Yes
SP: Size positive
SN: Size negative

X35: Is size a storage problem?
X36: Is this for a recipe or specific use?
X38: Will this size handle it?
X39: Is it the right size for this use?

Legitimization

N: No
Y: Yes

LP: Legitimization decision positive
LN: Legitimization decision negative

X40: Has husband mentioned preference?
X41: Hear about it from parents?
X42: Hear about it from friends?
X43: Tried some before (at friends or sample)?
X44: Like other products from same brand?
X45: Seen ads on television?
X46: Familiar company source of ads?
X47: Had bad experience with other products from this brand?
X48: Used it satisfactorily previously?

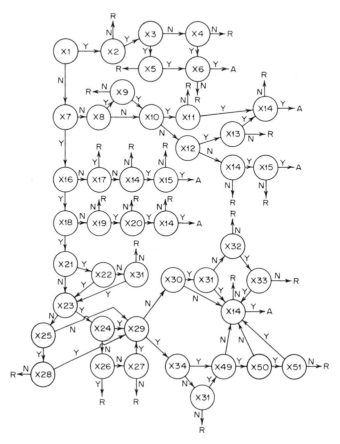

FIGURE 3.   The model for consumer C_1.

and had no stigma of bad experience (X17), then the cheapest one of satisfactory size was selected (X15). However, if a product was high in perceived risk and not legitimized (X18), it was bought only if necessary at that particular time (X20) and the only brand available (X19).

Otherwise, if the product was legitimized, C_1 considered her husband's strong preferences (X21). She next looked for a convenience feature, if necessary (X23, X26, X27), or a freshness factor (X25, X28). If the product passed all these screening cues, the main process of the model is entered, the habit or loyalty process. If the brand was purchased the previous time and is still preferred to others tried before (X29, X34), and no new brands have been legitimized and preferred in a trial (X49, X50, X51), then the brand bought last time is bought again, by size (X14). If the brand was not purchased last time, but the last brand was disliked (X30); the retailer is out of the last brand bought (X31); or if this new brand has been legitimized by trial and is better than the former brand in that trial (X32, X33), then the new brand is purchased by size (X14). Consumer C_1's comments illustrate the processes:

Key to Figure 3

X1: Is this produce?	X22: Is this that brand?
X2: Is the color okay?	X23: Does this product type have a convenience feature?
X3: Is this for a recipe?	
X4: Is it small enough?	X24: Does this one have it?
X5: Is this the right size?	X25: Is there a freshness factor?
X6: Does it feel okay?	X26: Is this factor necessary for this end use?
X7: Had experience with this product type?	
	X27: Is this brand sufficient for this end use?
X8: Is there a convenience type feature?	
X9: Does this have that feature?	X28: Does this have that factor?
X10: Can you see the product itself?	X29: Was this brand bought last time?
X11: Does this have the best color?	X30: Was last brand liked better than others previously tried?
X12: Are packages (cans or boxes) damaged?	
	X31: Are they out of that brand?
X13: Does this have least damage?	X32: Did legitimization of this brand involve trial?
X14: Is size satisfactory?	
X15: Is this the cheapest "okay" one for given size?	X33: Was this one better than the old one in that trial?
	X34: Was this liked better than others previously tried?
X16: Is this high perceived risk?	
X17: Had bad experience with this brand?	X49: Any new brands legitimized since then?
X18: Is this one legitimized?	
X19: Is it the only brand available?	X50: Did this involve trial?
X20: Is it really necessary to have it now?	X51: Was the old one better in this trial?
X21: Does husband have strong preference for brand?	

I get the small kind, because it's got a wide mouth, so you can get all of it out of it, and I have a very small refrigerator, and the bigger bottles don't fit in (X35, X23).

If it's not friends or on television, forget it (X42, X45). We tried some. We were given it free in the supermarket (X43, X32, X50).

This one I'll take because it's solider than the other one, and it's also a good dark green (X1, X2, X6).

First I was looking for Bartlett pears, but they both said Bartlett pears, so then I looked to see, um, if one of them, if all the cans were in good condition in one ... and if one of them, all of them were in good condition, then I'd get that one, over the ones that most of them were bashed in. The third thing I looked for was price, and they were the same price (X7, X12, X13).

I'll get these. By price. We use them up fast, so I might as well get the cheapest thing ... paper products don't matter to me (X16, X17, X15). I'm getting this kind because this is the kind [husband] said he likes (X21, X40).

This time I'll get Brand A [not usual one], because they have everything in it, ... but they don't have any Brand B [usual one] with everything in it (X23, X31). I like this one. We've used it before, and we've had good luck with it (X29, X34).

Consumers C_1 and C_4 have markedly different model behavior styles. This may be partially due to the differing situational and demographic factors involved and to differing degrees of shopping experience. Cox, with his two subjects June and Marsha, found much the same type of contrast in one of his studies [5].

Model Testing

To qualify as an adequate representation of a process, a model must pass the test of output validation. Although not sufficient, it is necessary to test whether a model can replicate reasonably well the decisions actually made. One problem with output validation for a complex process model is that testing all the decision rules imbedded in the model (even seldom-used rules), requires large amounts of data. However, the data collected previously for C_1 involved 226 decisions, but for C_4 only 70, and not all of these could be coded, as discussed further below. Also, some cues specified in the model can be measured only subjectively—i.e., asking the housewife whether her husband or child prefers Product A or whether color was satisfactory.

Despite these difficulties, it was felt that some attempt at output validation had to be made as one way of gaining confidence in the models. As a result, the following methods are a compromise.

The models were programmed in FORTRAN with two sets of data: the original shopping data from which the models were derived and a second set taken especially for validation purposes. For the original data, only those past decisions whose cues could be coded from the tapes were included. Of the 226 original decisions for C_1, 87 were coded; of the 70 for C_1, 50 were coded. This sample (unless specific cases of a product not being purchased were discussed in the protocol) could only test valid positive or false negative judgments.

The second set of choice data, 78 choices for C_1 and 46 for C_4, was collected about four months after the first set: the consumers shopped, a list of the products purchased was made, and the brand, price, and weight of each were recorded. The consumers were then asked questions from the model until enough cues were specified for the model to be able to make a decision. In addition, for most of the products purchased, unchosen alternatives were recorded at the store (to ensure that they were actually in stock), and the procedure above was followed with the subject until the model could make a decision on each of these alternatives. Finally, high and low risk rankings were determined for those product types not ranked in the original 16-product risk ranking.

Tables 1 and 2 present the findings of the study. In Table 1 the perceived risk rankings are given, with one the highest risk, and 16 lowest. Because C_1 did not seem to perceive extreme product risk, the median was used as her dividing line between high and low—Product 8 was high and Product 9 low risk. On the other hand, C_4 seemed to feel very great risk in the shopping situation, so her cutoff point was set at the three-quarters point—Product 12 is high and Product 13 low risk. This cutoff point was verified in the tapes, since C_4 showed that flour was risky and that paper products do not really matter.

Table 2 shows the results of running the models on the data and how well each model matched the actual decisions for each data sample. The diagonal entries represent correct predictions. The percentages of correct predictions for C_1 are thus (a) original data—85.1% ($p = .00$, 6.54σ); (b) validation

TABLE 1. Perceived Risk Rankings for the Consumer Models

Consumer C_1	Consumer C_4
1 Flour	1 Hot dogs
2 Lettuce	2 Ketchup
3 Instant Coffee	3 Frozen Vegetable
4 Tomato Juice	4 Soft Drink (Six Pack)
5 Canned Fruit	5 Canned Vegetable
6 Frozen Orange Juice ⎫	6 Instant Coffee
7 Frozen Vegetable ⎬ Tie	7 Frozen Orange Juice
8 Hot Dogs ⎭	8 Oleomargarine
9 Canned Vegetable ⎫ Tie	9 Canned Fruit
10 Oleomargarine ⎭	10 Tomato Juice
11 Soft Drink (Six pack)	11 Mayonnaise ⎫ Tie
12 Ketchup	12 Flour ⎭
13 Paper Towels	13 Eggs
14 Mayonnaise ⎫ Tie	14 Lettuce ⎫ Tie
15 Eggs ⎭	15 Laundry Bleach ⎭
16 Laundry Bleach	16 Paper Towels

TABLE 2. Results of the Consumer Models

Consumer	Original Data Actual Accept/Reject			Validation Data Actual Accept/Reject		
C_1	Model	Accept	68 0	Model	Accept	32 4
		Reject	13 6		Reject	4 38
C_4	Model	Accept	41 1	Model	Accept	19 3
		Reject	5 3		Reject	3 21

sample—89.7% ($p = .00, 7.02\sigma$); and (c) combined samples—87.2% ($p = .00$, 9.57σ). For C_4 the percentages are (a) original data—88.0% ($p = .00, 5.37\sigma$); (b) validation data—87.0% ($p = .00, 5.01\sigma$); and (c) combined samples—87.5% ($p = .00, 7.35\sigma$). The probabilities listed after each result are those of having that percentage or higher correct, using a normal approximation to the binomial with $p = .5$. The results are significantly better than the expectations under a null hypothesis of guessing accept or reject with equal probability.

Thus the models predict rather well. For behavioral models, process validation is always an important concern. The excerpts from the protocols can be considered a weak Turing's test approach [4, pp. 77–90]. However, the very process of modeling from tape recorded conversations should ensure at least reasonable performance on Turing's test (see [3, pp. 111–224] for new techniques and theoretical approaches).

Implications of the Models

The models for these consumers match their actual decisions with a high level of precision. Three factors contribute to this predictive accuracy: (1) the models do not "menu plan," and hence their task is easier than it might be; (2) the external cues are very general and afford a lower level of explanation than might be wished; and (3) the process of determining cue values, although attempts were made to keep it as objective as possible, still has many subjective elements. Despite these possible objections, the ability of the models to predict accept-reject decisions was very satisfactory.

The major finding of this study is that the product accept-reject decisions of an individual consumer are modeled quite well by a decision net of cues. Such a net has several major subprocesses. The process of cue perception is very important for determining which of these subprocess decision rules are used dominantly. One shortcoming of the present models is that such factors as attitudes and social elements are presumably important in cue encoding, but have not been explicitly dealt with, although some cues deal with these factors implicitly. The models do not explain how product types, for example, are seen as having a convenience or health factor. The models do, however, focus attention on the cue combination process—and the fact that decisions in the consumer models depend upon configurations of cues justifies this focus.

In addition to these broad findings about the structure of the decision process, the models also imply that perceived risk is an important product cue. The difference in risk ratings by C_1 and C_4 implies that a marketer could attempt to assess how his product type's risk ranking varied across the target population for the product. Then he can decide, on the basis of this population distribution, how important it is for his brand to attempt to reduce felt risk.

In conclusion, it is hoped that these findings show that decision process modeling by gathering protocols can lead to better understanding of marketing phenomena. Information processing models of aspects of consumer behavior offer the researcher a very rich field of study. Such models can form the basic data points from which a cognitive theory of consumer behavior can be induced.

Notes

1. A paired comparison questionnaire using 16 product types was used. For every pair of product types A and B, the subject was asked to judge "For which of these two product types would you rather buy a brand you knew nothing about, if you had to buy one of them?" Additional instructions were given to try to ensure a pure choice of the lower perceived risk type—i.e., not a choice of which type is preferred. Finally the 16 product types were ranked according to their scores, with a product type chosen many times a low risk product, and one chosen a few times a higher risk product. For more details, see [3, pp. 36–50]. Also, for a different method of measuring perceived risk, see [7].

2. Models were not constructed for C_3 and C_5 because they moved; C_2 was not modeled because she seemed to have the most trouble articulating while she shopped.

References

1. Marcus Alexis, George H. Haines, and Leonard Simon, "Consumer Information Processing: The Case of Women's Clothing," *Proceedings*, Fall Conference, American Marketing Association, 1968, 197–205.

2. Raymond Bauer, "Consumer Behavior as Risk Taking," in [6], 23–33.

3. James R. Bettman, "Behavioral Simulation Models in Marketing Systems," unpublished Doctoral dissertation, Yale University, 1969.

4. Geoffrey Clarkson, *Portfolio Selection—A Simulation of Trust Investment*, Englewood Cliffs, N.J.: Prentice-Hall, Inc., 1962.

5. Donald F. Cox, "Risk Handling in Consumer Behavior—An Intensive Study of Two Cases," in [6], 34–81.

6. ———, ed., *Risk Taking and Information Handling in Consumer Behavior*, Boston: Graduate School of Business Administration, Harvard University, 1967.

7. Scott M. Cunningham, "The Major Dimensions of Perceived Risk," in [6], 82–108.

8. John A. Howard and William M. Morgenroth, "Information Processing Model of Executive Decisions," *Management Science*, Vol. 14 (March 1968), 416–428.

9. Robert H. King, "A Study of the Problem of Building a Model to Simulate the Cognitive Processes of a Shopper in a Supermarket," in G. H. Haines, ed., *Consumer Behavior: Learning Models of Purchasing*, New York: The Free Press, 1969, 22–67.

10. Allen Newell, J. C. Shaw, and Herbert A. Simon, "Elements of a Theory of Human Problem Solving," *Psychological Review*, Vol. 65 (May 1958), 151–166.

Name Index

Abelson, Robert P. 196, 197, 204, 230, 247, 250–52, 256, 260, 261, 263, 290
Adam, D. 31, 32, 37
Adelson, J. 70, 75
Adler, Alfred 115, 117, 130
Adler, Lee 207, 245, 246
Ahtola, O. T. 179, 187, 261
Ajzen, I. 215–19, 252, 261
Alexis, Marcus 32, 35, 37, 458, 462, 496–98, 503
Allen, Ben M. 128
Allison, Ralph I. 4, 17
Allport, F. H. 85, 86
Allport, Gordon W. 115, 138, 181, 187, 189, 205, 228, 232, 245
Allvine, F. C. 75
Ames, Adelbert, Jr. 17
Amstutz, Arnold E. 53, 542, 557, 558, 563, 570, 571
Anderson, E. E. 64
Anderson, L. K. 197, 205
Anderson, L. R. 219
Andreasen, Alan R. 230
Andrews, P. R. 27, 28, 38
Apple, Valentine 245
Aristotle 105, 375
Arndt, Johan 64, 138, 142, 148, 174, 204, 205, 294, 331, 343, 344, 348, 352, 537, 539
Aronson, Elliot 86, 197, 201, 204, 205, 208, 209, 219, 232, 256, 257, 260, 261, 263
Asch, Solomon E. 198, 205, 297, 298, 315, 324, 325, 330
Axelrod, Joel N. 142

Back 342
Bacon, M. K. 376, 383
Bain, R. 228, 232
Baker, R. 454, 462
Balderston, F. E. 563, 569, 570
Bales, Robert F. 368
Ballachey, E. L. 9, 178, 179, 187, 231, 299

Bandura, A. 128
Barach, Jeffrey A. 139, 142, 143
Barban, Arnold M. 460, 462, 507, 512
Barban, Arnold N. 138, 143
Barnett, N. L. 52, 53
Barry, H., III 376, 383
Bartels, Robert 429
Bass, Frank M. 97, 143, 171, 173, 261
Bass, S. M. 571
Battle, E. S. 71, 74
Bauer, Raymond A. 6, 9, 56, 64, 85, 98, 100, 103, 139, 143, 144, 192, 195, 203, 205, 350, 352, 461, 462, 463, 489, 505, 511, 537, 539, 569, 570, 583
Bavelas 106
Becknell, J. 27, 41
Beilin, Harry 429
Bell, Gerald D. 139, 143
Bell, Martin L. 429
Bell, Robert R. 448
Bem, Daryl J. 191, 192, 198, 199, 205, 295, 296, 374
Bem, Sandra L. 295, 296, 374
Bendix, R. 419
Bennett, P. D. 464, 560
Bensman, Joseph 423, 425, 429
Benson, James 173
Berelson, Bernard 331, 340, 341
Berey, L. A. 369, 373
Berger, C. M. 128
Berger, S. M. 128
Berkman, Dave 507, 512
Berkowitz, Leonard 209, 232, 260, 263, 281
Berlyne, Daniel E. 245, 524, 529, 539
Bernstein, B. 449
Besner, Arthur 441
Bettelheim, B. 118
Bettman, James R. 518, 572, 583
Bharadwaj, Lakschmi 367, 368
Bilkey, Warren J. 111
Birdwell, Al E. 136, 143, 507, 513

Bither, Stewart W. 179, 183, 220, 231, 282
Blackwell, Roger D. 38, 153, 188, 206
Blackwood, James E. 280
Blake, R. 252, 262
Blalock, A. B. 209
Blalock, H. M. 209
Blood, Robert O. 353, 354, 367
Blum, Z. D. 457, 464
Boas, Franz 439
Bogart, Leo 506, 512
Boone, Louis E. 135, 143
Borden, Neil 98, 103
Borgatta, E. F. 137, 207
Boring, R. A. 42
Bourne, Francis S. 309, 314, 325, 331, 536, 539
Bower, Gordon H. 7, 9, 145
Boyd, H. W., Jr. 454, 462, 465
Boyenton, W. H. 508, 513
Bramel, D. 256, 260
Brehm, Jack W. 181, 187, 194, 196, 197, 205, 245, 256, 257, 260, 264, 269, 326, 330, 331
Brim, O. G., Jr. 296, 298
Brimmer, Andrew F. 498, 500–502
Broadbent, D. E. 100, 103
Brock, Timothy C. 205, 258, 260, 280
Brody, Robert P. 134, 143, 153, 156, 162
Broom, L. 394, 399
Broome, C. 28, 42
Brown, F. E. 25, 26, 38
Brown, J. F. 109
Brown, J. S. 128, 525, 539
Brown, M. P. 53
Brown, R. 253, 260, 377, 383
Brown, Roger L. 373
Brown, S. E. 86
Brown, William F. 112
Bruce, Grady D. 134, 143, 309, 314
Bruner, J. S. 26, 38, 201, 203, 209
Bucklin, L. P. 400
Bullock, Henry Allen 461–63, 495, 503, 505, 511
Burger, Philip C. 162
Burgess, Ernest W. 353, 367

Burke 105
Burnight, Robert G. 394
Burstein, E. 249, 260, 263
Bush, G. 536, 539
Bush, R. R. 86, 87, 97, 105, 550, 558
Buzzell, R. D. 53

Cagley, James W. 508, 513
Calder, Bobby J. 180, 247, 252, 259, 260
Campbell, D. T. 38, 104, 205, 228, 231
Canon, L. K. 198, 206
Cantril, Hadley 2, 3, 10, 15, 17, 228, 231
Caplovitz, David 397, 399, 422, 429
Cardozo, Richard N. 53, 508, 513, 567, 571
Carey, James W. 139, 143, 506, 512
Carlsmith, James Merrill 197, 201, 205, 206, 259, 261, 281
Carlson, A. R. 215, 216, 218
Carlson, E. R. 231, 251, 260
Carman, J. M. 542, 551, 558, 568, 571
Carmone, F. J. 5, 9, 49, 53, 54
Carr, H. L. 70, 75
Carson, D. 455, 463
Carter, R. 259, 261
Cartwright, D. 106, 248, 261, 330
Centers, Richard 138, 143, 392, 393, 399, 448
Chaffee, Steven 373
Chaney, David C. 373
Chapanis, Alphonse 264, 269, 280
Chapanis, Natalia P. 264, 269, 280
Chapin, F. Stuart 430, 438, 439
Chapman, D. W. 300, 308
Child, I. L. 376, 383
Cialdini, R. 252, 262
Clark, Cedric 511, 514
Clark, J. A. 557, 560
Clark, Ronald 245
Clarkson, Geoffrey P. E. 563, 571, 583
Clausen, J. A. 298

Claycamp, Henry J. 134, 144, 153, 206, 563, 571
Clewett, R. M. 463
Cocanougher, A. Benton 309
Cohen, Albert K. 447
Cohen, Arthur R. 196, 197, 205, 210, 218, 245, 256, 258–60, 264, 269, 282, 290
Cohen, Dorothy 505, 511
Cohen, Joel B. 131, 140, 144, 153, 156, 162, 179, 181, 182, 186, 187, 261, 270, 280
Coleman, James S. 341, 343, 352, 542, 547, 558, 559
Coleman, Richard P. 395, 396, 399, 425, 429
Collins, B. E. 200, 201, 204, 208, 256, 261
Cook, S. W. 189, 206
Coombs, C. H. 206
Cooper, P. 32, 33, 35, 38
Corso, J. 38
Courtney, Alice E. 295, 384
Cox, Donald F. 6, 9, 139, 142, 144, 153, 338, 342, 537, 539, 580, 583
Cox, Keith K. 463, 464, 508–10, 513, 514
Crandall, V. J. 377, 383
Crane, Edgar 245
Crespi, Irving 207, 245, 246
Crutchfield, R. S. 9, 177–79, 187, 231, 299
Cundiff, Edward W. 136, 145, 512
Cunningham, Scott M. 53, 56, 64, 134, 143, 153, 156, 162, 461, 463, 489, 505, 511, 537, 540, 583
Cyert, R. M. 570, 571

Dalrymple, D. J. 295, 462, 463
Darden, William R. 168, 173, 174
Davis, Allison 404, 405, 408, 423, 429, 438, 439
Davis, H. 208
Davis, Harry L. 295, 353
Davis, James A. 438
Davis, Stanley M. 452, 463
Day, George S. 179, 180, 182, 188, 192, 199, 204, 206, 526, 538, 540

Day, R. I. 50, 54
Dean, Dwight D. 447
de Beauvoir, Simone 245
DeFleur, Melvin L. 204, 208, 217, 220, 514
Della Bita, A. 28, 38
De Manche, E. R. 462, 463
Dembroski, Theodore M. 128
Denney, R. 541, 560
Dennis, Wayne 480
Dervin, Brenda 506, 512
De Sola Pool, I. 563, 571
Deutsch, Morton 2, 9, 218, 258, 261, 298, 341
DeVries, D. L. 215, 218
Dewey, John 303
Dichter, Ernest 144, 453, 463
Dixon, T. 218
Dodge, N. D. 378, 383
Doehlert, D. H. 49, 53
Dolich, Ira J. 136, 144, 183, 282
Dollard, John 81, 85, 86, 131, 228, 408, 423, 429, 521
Dominick, Joseph R. 506, 510, 512, 514
Donnelly, James H., Jr. 144
Donohew, L. 259, 261
Doob, A. 259, 261
Doob, L. W. 228, 232
Dornbusch, Sanford M. 138, 144
Dotson, Floyd 447
Douglas, S. P. 451, 463
Driver, Harold E. 439
Duhamel, W. F. 542, 543, 559
Dulany, D. E. 211–13, 215, 218, 219
Duncan, Otis Dudley 491, 503
Dunn, S. W. 454, 463
Durkheim, Emile 447

Eagly, A. H. 201, 206
Ebbesen, E. B. 194, 209
Ebbinghaus, H. 99, 103
Edgeworth, F. Y. 541, 559
Edwards, Allen L. 140, 153, 156, 245
Edwards, Paul K. 494, 495, 503
Eells, K. 400

Ehrenberg, A. S. C. 549, 559
Ehrlich, D. 256, 258, 261, 269
Ehrlich, Howard J. 153, 219
Elinson, Jack 367
Elms, A. C. 261
Emery, F. 29, 34, 38
Empey, LaMar J. 448
Engel, James F. 38, 153, 188, 206, 257, 261
England, L. 137, 144
Enis, B. M. 27, 38, 64, 463, 464
Estes, W. K. 86, 87, 97, 105
Evans, Franklin B. 133, 134, 141, 144, 147, 153, 162, 169, 174, 190, 206, 231
Evans, Richard I. 126, 128
Eysenck, H. J. 137, 144

Farber, Bernard 353, 367
Faricy, J. H. 65, 71, 75
Farley, J. U. 517, 519
Farnsworth, Paul R. 281
Fayerweather, J. 455, 456, 463
Feigenbaum, E. A. 571
Feldman, J. 571
Feldman, L. P. 462, 463
Feldman, S. 206, 208, 281, 530, 540
Ferber, Robert 187, 325, 326, 331, 354, 367
Ferguson, Richard D., Jr. 509, 510, 513, 514
Feshbach, S. 114, 118
Festinger, Leon 103, 106, 181, 187, 196, 197, 206, 217, 219, 230, 245, 246, 255, 261, 263, 264, 268–70, 281, 298, 342, 348, 352, 541, 559
Fillenbaum, Samuel 153
Finger, J. M. 570, 571
Fishbein, Martin 179, 191, 206, 210, 212, 215, 216, 218–20, 246, 252, 261, 530, 540
Fiske, D. W. 196, 206
Flanagan, J. C. 377, 383
Fleischer, L. 249, 262
Fletcher, Alan 506, 512
Foote, Nelson N. 232, 299, 367
Form, W. H. 393, 399
Fothergill, J. 206

Fouilhé, P. 31, 32, 38
Fourt, L. A. 84, 86
Fowler, H. 196, 206
Fox, Wayne 154
Frank, Ronald E. 95–97, 133, 134, 146, 154, 542, 543, 548, 559
Franklin, Benjamin 452, 453, 463
Fredrickson, R. 564, 572
Freedman, J. 198, 201, 207, 259, 261
French 106
Freud, Sigmund 115, 117, 129, 130, 515
Friedan, B. 383
Friedman, L. 24, 39
Friend, Irwin 495, 497, 498, 500–502, 504
Fromm, Erich 115, 117, 130
Fruchter, Benjamin 153, 154

Gabor, A. 24, 25, 31, 32, 34, 35, 39
Galanter, E. 260
Galler, Enid H. 449
Gans, Herbert J. 423, 429, 438, 439, 458, 463
Gardner, Burleigh B. 130, 135, 145, 404, 408, 438
Gardner, D. 27, 28, 39
Gardner, David M. 75, 187
Gardner, Mary R. 404, 408, 438
Gaudet, Hazel 331, 340, 341
Geizer, Ronald 513
Gerard, H. B. 210, 219, 249, 262, 298
Ginsberg, E. 408
Ginzberg, E. 23, 24, 39
Glass, D. 198, 207
Glazer, N. 541, 560
Glick, I. O. 397, 399, 416, 419
Goethe 302
Goffman, Erving 430, 438, 439
Golby, C. 53
Goldberg, Marvin E. 182, 258, 259, 261, 270
Goldberg, Philip 375, 376, 383
Goldberg, S. 383
Golden, L. L. 67, 75
Goldman, R. 119, 121

Goldstucker, Jac L. 174, 175, 245, 454, 456, 463
Gonsior, M. H. 42
Good, Walter S. 168, 174
Goodenough, Ward H. 439
Goodman, C. 38
Goodman, Leonard, 448, 449
Gordon, A. 119, 121
Gordon, Leonard V. 157, 162
Gordon, M. M. 457, 463
Gottesman, I. I. 379, 384
Gottleib, Morris J. 154
Gottlieb, David 397, 399
Gould, John W. 507, 512
Gould, Rosalind 448
Graham, Elaine 146
Granbois, D. H. 373
Granger, C. 24–26, 31, 32, 34, 35, 39
Grant, Don 389
Grathwohl, Harrison L. 136, 145
Green, Paul E. 5, 9, 44, 49, 53, 54, 204, 207
Greenberg, Bradley S. 506, 508, 510, 512–14
Greenberg, M. 192, 207
Greenberger, M. 560
Greenwald, A. G. 205
Greenwood, J. M. 453, 464
Greyser, Stephen A. 192, 205, 342, 352
Griffith, B. 508, 513
Grinker, R. R. 307, 308
Gross, L. 73, 74, 118, 121
Grubb, Edward L. 136, 145
Gruen, Walter 138, 145, 154, 536, 540
Grunbaum, Werner F. 512
Guerin, J. R. 455, 463
Guerrero, J. 259, 261
Guetzkow, H. S. 563, 571
Guralnick, L. 394
Guthrie, E. R. 103
Guthrie, W. E. 100
Guttman, I. 256, 261, 269
Guttman, Louis 440
Guttmen, L. 222, 231

Haas, Raymond M. 64, 246, 352

Haberman, Paul W. 367
Haddock, R. 39
Haines, G., Jr. 37
Haines, George H. 582, 583
Haire, Mason 185–87
Hall, Calvin S. 115, 118, 142, 145
Hall, Edward T. 220, 455, 468
Haller, Archibald 429
Halloran, James D. 368, 373
Hamm, B. Curtis 136, 145
Hancock, R. S. 64, 205
Handel 425
Hansen, Flemming 179, 232, 246
Harary, F. 109, 112, 248, 261, 549, 559
Harburg, E. 262
Hartley, E. L. 100, 101, 103
Hastorf, Albert H. 2, 3, 10
Hayes, S. P., Jr. 331, 539
Heer, David M. 353, 354, 367
Heider, Fritz 180, 247–49, 253, 262
Heller, H. E. 193, 207
Heller, N. 85, 86
Helson, H. 34, 39
Henderson, P. L. 85, 86
Henry, W. E. 407, 409
Herbst, G. 353, 365, 367
Herskovits, Melville J. 438, 439
Hess, E. H. 189, 207, 260
Hickman, Lauren C. 138, 144
Hicks, Lou E. 169, 174
Higginbotham, J. B. 464
Hilden, Arnold H. 314
Hilgard, Ernest R. 7, 9, 76, 78, 84–86, 145
Hill, C. R. 186, 187
Hill, M. 408
Hill, Reuben 366, 367
Hind, J. F. 86
Hinkle, C. L. 569, 571
Hippocrates 129
Hirsch, Paul M. 507, 512
Hobhouse, L. T. 401, 408
Hochman, Leonard 155
Hodge, R. W. 396, 399
Hodges, Harold M., Jr. 447
Hoffman, L. W. 128, 384
Hoffman, Martin L. 128, 384
Hoggatt, A. C. 563, 570

Hollander, Edwin P. 314
Hollingshead, Alfred B. 399, 429
Holloway, R. J. 197, 205
Homans, George C. 297, 299, 342, 352, 541
Horney, Karen 115, 117, 130, 131
Horowitz, E. L. 228, 232
Horowitz, Miriam 143
Horton, D. 218
Hoult, Thomas Ford 438
House, James S. 430
Hovland, C. I. 41, 104, 199, 203, 207, 209, 231, 263
Hovland, Carl I. 145, 146, 246, 290, 291
Hovland, Carl T. 99, 103, 138
Howard, John A. 8, 75, 131, 188, 199, 207, 230, 325, 331, 428, 517, 519, 537, 540, 543, 559, 583
Huber, J. 393, 399
Hughes, E. C. 306, 308
Hull, C. L. 7, 76, 78, 86, 105, 115, 131, 515, 524, 540
Hunt, Raymond G. 314
Hunt, W. 38
Hupp, Gregg 136, 145
Husted, Thomas P. 171, 174, 207
Hyman, Herbert H. 299, 300, 308, 410, 419, 447

Inkster, James A. 182, 264
Insko, Chester A. 201, 204, 207, 252, 253, 259, 260, 262, 263, 281
Irelan, Lola M. 399, 441
Ito, Rikuma 232
Izard, C. 262

Jackman, Arnold 153
Jacobson, Eugene 135, 145
Jacoby, Jacob 27, 39, 117, 137, 141, 145, 149, 154
Jahoda, M. 326, 331
James, William 15, 135, 306
Janis, Irving L. 114, 118, 145, 146, 246, 290
Janowitz, M. 307, 309
Jeffries, V. 392, 393, 399
Jevons, W. S. 541, 559

Johnston, Donald 135, 148
Jones, E. R. 540
Jones, Mary Gardiner 125, 128
Jones, R. 231
Jordan, N. 249, 262
Jung, Carl 115
Junker, Buford H. 438
Juster, T. F. 532, 540

Kagan, J. 377, 384
Kahl, Joseph A. 395, 399, 448
Kahn, Sandra 508, 513
Kamen, Joseph M. 34, 35, 39, 134, 145, 154
Kanouse, David E. 114, 118
Kanth, A. K. 220
Kassarjian, Harold H. 104, 117, 129, 138, 143, 146, 153, 181, 185–87, 314, 352, 508, 509, 513, 516
Kassarjian, Waltraud M. 8, 70, 74, 138, 143, 146, 460, 504
Katona, George 85, 86, 246, 424, 429
Katz, Daniel 179, 187, 201, 202, 207, 222, 231
Katz, Elihu 100, 204, 207, 291, 294, 299, 332, 336, 340, 341, 343, 352, 536, 540
Kees, Weldon 438
Kelley, Harold H. 68, 74, 106, 246, 291, 310, 314
Kelman, H. C. 190, 207, 330, 331
Kenkel, W. 294, 299
Kernan, Jerome B. 123, 143, 146, 155–57, 160, 162
Kerrick, J. 255, 262
Kiesler, C. A. 200, 201, 204, 208
Kilpatrick, F. P. 16, 17
King, Charles W. 261, 352
King, M. 508, 513
King, R. I. 53
King, R. L. 462, 463
King, Robert H. 583
Kitt, A. 300, 309
Klahr, D. 43, 44, 47–49, 54
Klapp, Orrin E. 128
Klapper, Joseph T. 103, 203, 208, 246, 294, 299

Klein, Philip   429
Klineberg, O.   232
Kluckhohn, Clyde   438, 439
Knox, Robert E.   182, 264
Koch, S.   104, 205, 207, 231
Kohn, M. L.   393, 399
Kollat, David T.   38, 153, 188, 206
Komarovsky, M.   295, 299
Koos, Earl Loman   448
Koponen, Arthur   133, 134, 140, 146, 154, 162
Korbel, J.   560
Kossoff, Jerome   135, 145
Kotler, Philip   428, 517, 541, 543, 545, 559
Krauss, Robert M.   2, 9, 258, 261, 341
Kravis, Irving B.   495, 497, 498, 500–502, 504
Krech, D.   1, 2, 9, 177–79, 187, 222, 231, 292, 299
Kroeber, Alfred L.   438
Krugman, Herbert E.   8, 9, 54, 98, 103, 131, 195, 208, 460, 464, 566, 571
Kruskal, J. B.   47, 48, 54
Kuehn, Alfred A.   8, 50, 54, 84, 86, 87, 90, 95, 97, 133, 142, 146, 550–52, 559

Ladwig, G. W.   71, 74
Laird, D. A.   536, 540
Lambert   125
Lambert, R.   262
Lambert, W. W.   207
Lambert, Z.   27, 39
Landauer, T.   259, 261
Landgrebe, L.   304, 308
Landy, E.   210, 219
Langer, Susan   135
LaPlaca, P.   40
Larson, C. M.   458, 464
Lasater, Thomas M.   128
Laumann, Edward O.   430, 440
Lavidge, R. C.   195, 208
Lavidge, Robert J.   230, 532, 540
Lazarsfeld, Paul F.   204, 207, 294, 299, 309, 331, 332, 340, 341, 536, 540, 560

Lazarus, R. S.   114, 118
Lazer, William   146
Leavitt, H.   26, 27, 40
LeBar, Frank M.   439
Lee, Dorothy   153
Lefcourt, H. M.   71, 74
LeFleur, M.   (*See* DeFleur)
Lehmann, Stanley   146
Leighton, Dorothea   447
LeShan, Lawrence L.   449
Lessig, V. Parker   146
Levin, H.   376, 384
Levine, D.   74
Levinger, George   367
Levy, Sidney J.   3, 4, 9, 130, 135, 145, 146, 397, 399, 409, 414, 416, 417, 419
Lewin, Kurt   8, 106, 108, 109, 111, 112, 115, 255, 515
Lewis, Hylan   448
Lewis, M.   376, 383
Lewis, N.   38
Lewis, Oscar   456, 464
Liander, B.   451, 464
Liddy, L. E.   206
Liebow, Elliot   457, 464
Light, L.   257, 261
Likert, Rensis A.   106, 184, 188, 222, 231, 331, 539
LiLollo, V.   128
Lin, Nan   557, 560
Linder, S. B.   196, 208
Lindzey, Gardner   115, 118, 142, 145, 208, 209, 219, 232, 245
Lingoes, James C.   440
Linton, Harriet   146
Linton, Ralph   450, 464, 465
Lippman   228
Lipset, Seymour M.   419, 449
Lipstein, B.   84, 86, 542, 549, 559
Little, Arthur D.   493
Locke, Harvey J.   353, 367
Lockeretz, Sarah W.   295, 384
Lodahl, Thomas M.   133, 134, 146, 154
London, P.   536, 539
Longstreth, L. E.   123, 128
Lonsdale, Richard T.   143, 171, 173
Loosely, Elizabeth W.   438
LoSciuto, L.   25, 42

Low, J. O. 408, 409
Lumsdaine, Arthur 291
Lunn, J. A. 189, 193, 208
Lunt, P. S. 403, 407–9
Lynes, Russell 438, 440
Lysgaard, Sverre 422, 429

Macaulay, J. 255, 263
McCandless, J. L. 17
McCann, Glen C. 367
McClelland 538
Maccoby, E. E. 118, 128, 376, 384
Maccoby, Nat 100, 103
McConnell, J. Douglas 27, 29, 35, 40, 453, 454, 464
McDavid, J. W. 377, 384
McDonald, P. R. 463
McDougall, G. 40
McGuire, William J. 189, 190, 193, 196, 198, 202, 204, 208, 217, 219, 228, 232, 246, 260, 263, 281–83, 287, 291
McLeod, Jack 373
McNeal, James U. 314
McNemar, Olga 281
McNemar, Quinn 281
McPhee, William N. 341, 563, 571
McQuitty, Louis L. 360, 366, 367
Maddi, S. R. 196, 206
Maffei, R. B. 549, 559
Maheshwari, A. 54
Maloney, G. C. 564, 571
Maloney, J. C. 191, 208
Mandelbaum, D. G. 309
Mandler, G. 260
Manis, M. 201, 206
Mannes, Marya 296, 299, 389
March, J. G. 519, 540, 570, 571
Marcus, Alan S. 146, 350, 352
Marcus, Alexis 582
Marden, Parker G. 394
Martineau, Pierre D. 130, 146, 396, 399, 421, 423, 428
Maslow, Abraham H. 115, 116, 118, 135, 136
Massy, William F. 54, 133, 134, 146, 154, 542, 543, 559
Mathews, H. Lee 396, 421, 430

Mead, G. H. 302, 306–9
Meeker, M. 400
Menzel, Herbert 341, 343, 352
Merton, Robert K. 300, 309, 447, 515, 519
Messick, S. 541, 560, 563, 572
Mikol, Bernard 154
Miller, George A. 246
Miller, Herman P. 394
Miller, Max 447, 448
Miller, N. E. 81, 85, 86, 131, 179, 201, 204, 208
Miller R. 40
Miller, S. M. 449
Miller, Stephen J. 220, 228, 231
Miller, Walter 448
Mills, C. Wright 439
Mills, Judson 84, 86, 256, 258, 259, 261, 262, 269, 284, 291
Milton, G. A. 377, 384
Miner, Horace 439
Minturn, A. L. 38
Misra, H. K. 220
Mizerski, R. W. 70, 71, 75
Moinpour, Reza 114, 122
Monroe, Kent B. 4, 23, 28, 31, 32, 34, 40
Montgomery, D. B. 542, 559
Moore, C. G., Jr. 537, 540
Moore, Geoffrey 429
Morgan, J. N. 85, 86
Morgan, James E. 429, 449
Morgan, James T. 354, 368
Morgan, N. 54
Morgenroth, William M. 583
Morris, C. W. 308
Morris, R. T. 392, 393, 399
Morrison, D. G. 542, 560
Morse, Nancy C. 449
Mosteller, F. 86, 87, 97, 105, 550, 558
Mott, Paul 353, 368
Moyer, Reed 230
Mulaik, S. 252, 262
Murashima, F. 201, 207
Murchison, C. 205, 232
Murphy, Joseph R. 147
Murray, Henry A. 115–18, 133, 246
Muse, William V. 507, 508, 512, 513

Myers, James H.   134, 135, 147, 149, 154
Myers, Jerome   447
Myers, John G.   137, 147, 154, 342, 344, 352

Nakanishi, M.   117, 118
Naylor, T. H.   570, 571
Nebergall, R. E.   199, 200, 208
Nell, Elaine B.   183, 282
Nelson, Alan R.   168, 169, 171, 172, 174
Neugarten, B.   414, 419
Newcomb, T. N.   204, 260, 262, 263
Newell, Allen   572, 583
Newman, D.   27, 41
Newman, Joseph W.   147, 148
Nicosia, Francesco M.   188, 208, 230, 428, 517–19, 542, 558, 560, 562, 565, 568, 569, 571
Nisbett, Richard E.   73, 74, 114, 118, 121
Norman, R. Z.   109, 112
Norris, E.   255, 263
Novak, Edwin G.   153

O'Connell, D. C.   215, 219
O'Keefe, Garrett   373
Olander, F.   26, 35, 41
Olson, J.   39
Orcutt, G. H.   542, 560, 563, 571
Osgood, Charles E.   100, 184, 188, 191, 208, 230, 232, 246, 253, 255, 262, 524, 540
Oshikawa, S.   258, 262
Ostrom, T. M.   205

Paglin, Jules   495
Painter, John J.   132, 133, 148, 155, 157, 162
Palda, Kristian S.   37, 41, 230–32, 246, 532, 540
Palmgreen, P.   259, 261
Papageorgis, Demetrios   282, 283, 287, 291
Parsons, Talcott   302, 309, 365, 368
Patton, Arch   291

Pavlov, I.   131
Peak, Helen   231
Peizer, D.   263
Pennington, Allan A.   137, 147
Pepitone, A.   196, 208
Perry, Michael   139, 147
Pessemier, Edgar A.   33, 41, 137, 147, 162, 168, 171, 174, 207, 246, 261
Peterson, Robert A.   29, 35, 41, 137, 147
Peterson, W.   414, 419
Petrof, John V.   507, 512
Phares, E. J.   71, 74
Plotkin, Lawrence   510, 514
Plummer, Joseph T.   170, 171, 174
Pollay, R. W.   369, 373
Popielarz, D. T.   63
Porter, James N., Jr.   439
Postman, L.   38, 307, 309
Powell, Fredric A.   154
Preston, Lee E.   230
Price, K.   262
Proshansky, Harold   314
Purnell, J. M.   54
Pyron, Bernard   154
Pyszka, R.   259, 261

Rabson, A.   377, 383
Rainwater, Lee   130, 411, 420, 422, 425, 429, 448
Rao, K. S.   220
Rao, V. R.   28, 29, 41, 54
Raven, B. H.   191, 206
Ray, Michael L.   114, 118, 122, 123, 127, 128
Rebhun, Martin T.   154
Redfield, Robert   302, 309, 452, 464
Redlich, Frederick C.   429
Reeves, R.   525, 540
Reisman, S.   263
Reynolds, Fred D.   168, 173, 174
Richards, L. G.   398, 399
Richardson, Jane   438
Riesman, David   137, 138, 432, 436, 438, 440, 541, 560
Riesman, Frank   448, 449
Riezler, K.   301, 304, 309
Ring, L. W.   517, 519

Rivlin, Alice 560
Roberts, Bertram 447
Roberts, Churchill 510, 514
Roberts, Harry V. 144, 231, 232
Robertson, Thomas S. 134, 135, 147, 149, 153, 154, 195, 208, 294, 296, 299, 314, 342, 350, 352, 462, 463
Robinson, H. 86
Robinson, P. J. 5, 9, 54
Rodman, Hyman 448
Rodrigues, A. 262
Roeder, Richard A. 513
Rogers, Carl 135, 560
Rogers, Everett M. 294, 299, 340, 342, 532, 540, 541, 557, 560
Rohrer, J. H. 309
Rokeach, Milton 104, 137, 152–54, 192, 208, 246
Roselius, Ted 6, 55
Rosenau, N. 258, 261
Rosenberg, Milton J. 196, 204, 205, 212, 219, 223, 224, 230, 231, 247, 249–52, 255, 256, 260–63, 281
Ross, John 440
Ross, M. 252, 259, 260
Rossi, P. H. 399, 457, 464
Rossiter, John R. 350, 352
Rostow, W. W. 451, 464
Roth, E. 41
Rothman, L. J. 54
Rotter, J. B. 71, 72, 74
Rozelle, Richard M. 128
Ruch, Dudley M. 147
Ruesch, Jurgen 438
Runkel, P. 263

Saiyadain, M. 201, 207
Salmon, W. J. 53
Samuelson, Paul 498, 504
Sandage, C. H. 138, 143
Sapir, Edward 302, 309, 436, 438, 440
Sawyer, B. E. 460, 464
Scanzoni, John 354, 368
Schachter, S. 73, 74, 118, 119, 121, 128
Schmidt, Fred H. 510, 514
Schneider, H. 394, 400

Schneider, Louis 422, 429
Schonbach, P. 256, 261, 269
Schopler, J. 252, 253, 262
Schramm, Wilbur 341
Schuessler, Karl 439
Schuetz, A. 304, 309
Schuman, Howard 440
Schwartz, S. 215, 220
Scitovsky, T. 26, 35, 41
Sears, David O. 198, 207, 259, 261, 284, 291
Sears, R. R. 376, 384
Seeley, John R. 438, 439
Seeman, Melvin 447
Seigel, P. M. 399
Selltiz, C. 189, 206
Selznick, P. 394, 399
Settle, Robert B. 7, 64, 65, 67, 68, 70, 71, 75
Sewell, William H. 429, 430, 438, 439
Shanmugam, A. V. 220
Shapiro, B. 27, 35, 41
Sharp, Harry 353, 368
Shaw, J. C. 572, 583
Shaw, Marvin E. 314
Shayon, Robert Lewis 510, 514
Sherif, C. W. 31, 36, 41, 199, 200, 208, 209
Sherif, M. 41, 100, 199, 200, 208, 209, 228, 231, 297–300, 309, 325, 331
Sheth, Jagdish N. 64, 131, 188, 199, 207, 230, 263, 517, 519, 532, 540, 567, 571
Shibutani, Tomatsu 293, 299
Shils, E. A. 307, 309
Shoemaker, F. F. 294, 299
Shuchman, Abe 139, 147
Shuey, A. M. 508, 509, 513
Siedenberg, Bernard 314
Siegel, S. 266, 270
Sigband, Norman B. 507, 512
Silk, Alvin J. 42, 208
Sim, R. Alexander 438
Simon, Herbert A. 519, 540, 541, 560, 572, 583
Simon, Leonard 37, 582
Simpson, George 447
Simpson, Richard L. 447, 448

Sinha, A. K. P. 220
Sirota, D. 453, 464
Skinner, B. F. 7, 131
Skobe, M. 455, 464
Slocum, John W., Jr. 396, 421, 430
Smith, E. 28, 42
Smith, Ewart E. 281
Smith, George H. 185, 188, 199, 209, 564, 571, 572
Smith, Janet 389
Smith, L. G. 558
Smith, M. B. 190, 201, 203, 204, 209
Smith, M. E. 377, 384
Social Research, Inc. (SRI) 410, 412–14, 416–18, 420
Sommers, Montrose S. 136, 143, 147, 314
Sowter, A. 34, 39
Sparks, David L. 117, 155
Spaulding, John A. 447
Spaulding, N. W. 511
Spence, Homer E. 114, 122
Spence, K. W. 76, 78, 87, 131
Spiegel, J. P. 307, 308
Stafford, James E. 27, 38, 64, 309, 314, 458, 459, 464, 507, 513
Stanfield, J. D. 557, 560
Stapel, J. 34, 42
Star, A. D. 462, 463
Starch, Daniel 495
Stefflre, Volney 4, 9, 42–46, 48–52, 55
Steiner, Gary A. 147, 154, 195, 208, 230, 532, 540
Steiner, I. D. 219, 220
Sticht, Thomas G. 154
Stoetzel, J. 31, 42
Stonequist, E. V. 306, 309
Stotland, E. 201, 207, 222, 231
Stouffer 300
Straits, B. 259, 263
Straus, Murray S. 429
Strauss, Paul S. 155
Stroebe, W. 263
Sturdivant, Frederick D. 397, 398, 400, 450, 461, 464
Stuteville, John R. 122, 128
Suchand, Otto 168, 174

Suci, George J. 184, 188, 191, 208, 230, 246, 253, 262
Sullivan, David 495
Sullivan, Harry Stack 115, 307, 309
Sullivan, P. 70, 75
Sultan, R. G. 53
Summers, John O. 137, 148, 168, 174, 345, 350, 352
Surlin, Stuart H. 506, 512
Swanson, C. E. 399

Tajfel, H. 42
Talarzyk, W. 263
Tanaka, Y. 220
Tannenbaum, Percy H. 184, 188, 191, 204, 208, 209, 230, 246, 253, 255, 260–63
Tarrant, Mollie 137, 144
Taylor, B. 42
Taylor, J. R. 197, 205
Teach, Richard D. 41, 246
Teahan, John E. 449
Tharp, Roland C. 367, 368
Thomas 301
Thompson, V. 263
Thorndike, E. L. 131
Thrall, R. M. 97
Tigert, Douglas J. 118, 137, 143, 147, 148, 162, 167, 168, 171, 173, 174
Tipton, Leonard 373
Tollefson, John O. 146
Tom, S. 259, 261
Toman, R. 34, 35, 39
Tomkins, S. S. 541, 560, 563, 572
Tompkins, S. 262
Torrance, E. P. 377, 384
Treiman, D. J. 396, 399
Triandis, H. C. 211, 220
Troldahl, Verling C. 333, 337, 341
Tucker, William T. 117, 132, 133, 148, 155, 157, 162
Tull, D. S. 26, 27, 42, 204, 207
Turner, J. A. 201, 205
Turner, J. S. 209
Turner, Ralph 293, 299
Tylor, E. B. 450, 464

Udell, J. G.   64
Udry, J. Richard   394
Uhl, J.   33, 35, 42
Uhl, Kenneth P.   4, 17
Upshaw, H. S.   204, 209

Vacchiano, Ralph B.   155
Valentine, C. A.   457, 464
Valenzi, E. R.   27, 28, 38
Van Dam, Robert   337, 341
Van Tassel, Charles   507, 513
Veblen, Thorstein   430–32, 436–40
Venkatesan, M.   40, 64, 118, 139,
   148, 297, 309, 314, 325
Vernon, Philip E.   245
Vidich, Arthur   422, 423, 425, 429
Vitz, Paul C.   135, 148
Volkmann, J.   300, 308
Von Pechmann, F.   186, 188

Wackman, Daniel B.   295, 368, 373,
   374
Walker, H. J.   409
Walster, E.   258, 263, 281
Walters, R. H.   128
Wanderer, Aviva   510, 514
Ward, Scott   295, 368, 373, 374
Warner, L. G.   217, 220
Warner, W. Lloyd   391, 392, 400,
   403, 407, 408, 409, 422, 429, 436,
   440, 538
Warren, G. T.   65, 75
Webb, E.   42
Webster, F. E.   186, 188
Weigand, R. E.   452, 464
Weiss, Robert S.   449
Weiss, W.   204, 209
Wells, William D.   25, 42, 137, 139,
   141, 148, 162, 172, 174, 192, 209,
   563, 572
Wendell, Bell   447
Wenkert, R.   564, 572
Wensberg, Peter   389
Westfall, R. L.   454, 463, 465
Westfall, Ralph   134, 148, 155, 162,
   169, 175

Wheatley, John J.   128
Wheeler, G. C.   408
White, Irving S.   453, 465
White, R. W.   201, 203, 209
Whyte, William H., Jr.   330, 331,
   432, 436, 438–40
Wicker, A. W.   204, 209, 217, 220
Wilkening, Eugene A.   367, 368
Wilkie, William L.   114, 118, 122,
   123, 127, 128, 141, 148
Wills, G.   42
Wilson, Clark C.   168, 175
Wilson, Clark L.   148
Wilson, M. O.   309
Winer, B. J.   281, 291
Winick, Charles   148, 231
Witt, Robert E.   134, 143, 309, 314
Wolf, J. S.   569, 571
Wolfe, Donald M.   353, 354, 367
Wolgast, Elizabeth H.   354, 366, 368
Woodlock, J. W.   86
Woodside, Arch G.   138, 148
Woolf, Myra   137, 144
Wortzel, L. H.   463, 537, 539
Wright, Charles R.   447
Wright, Jack M.   314
Wright, John S.   174, 175, 245
Wrightsman, L.   70, 75

Yankelovich, Daniel, Inc.   374
Yaryan, Ruby B.   281
Yoell, W. A.   532, 540
Yoshino, M. Y.   462, 463

Zagona, Salvatore V.   155
Zajonc, R. B.   106, 181, 188, 212,
   220, 230–32, 248, 249, 263
Zaltman, Gerald   155
Zander, A.   330
Zeisel, H.   566, 572
Zerega, Virginia   17
Zielske, Herbert A.   99, 103
Ziff, Ruth   169, 175
Zimbardo, P. G.   194, 196, 201, 209
Zoerner, Cyril E., Jr.   507, 512
Zurcher, Louis A.   155

Subject Index

Absolute price thresholds 29–32
Acculturation 525
Achieved status 390, 437
Action, distortion of 320
Activities, interests, and opinions (AIO) 162–76; portraits, 172; scale, 169–70
Adaptation-level theory 34–35
Adopters of a new product 334; early, 334; late, 334; nonadopters, 334; pioneers, 334
Advertising 77, 416–19, 460; copy, 51; economic effects of, 98; television, 98–104
Aggressive types 131
Aggressiveness 525
Agreements, language of 473–75
Alienation 442–43
American child 488–89
Anomia 443
Anthropomorphism 105
Anticipatory socialization 296
Anxiety 149, 538; learned, 123; stimulation of, 122–24, 126
Anxiety-arousing communications 123–24
Aristotelian concepts 105
Art 450
Ascribed (inherited) status 390, 437
Aspirations of consumer 309–14
Assimilation 492, 502
Assimilation effect 199–200
Association, word 185
Attention 531
Attitude change 101, 183, 188–89, 220, 221, 285; theories of, 193–203 (see also Attitudes, Information processing, Process models, Cognitive consistency, Cognitive dissonance, Social judgment, Involvement discrepancy controversy, and Functional theories)
Attitude formation 220, 221
Attitude immunization, generality of 283; techniques of, 282–91
Attitude organization 199

Attitude scales 183–84, 526
Attitude specificity 192–93
Attitude structure 191–92
Attitudes 16, 177–82, 188–209, 233, 292, 310, 431, 466, 526, 533, 564; and action tendency, 179; affective component of, 179, 191–92, 210, 222; toward a brand, 532; changes in (see Attitude change); cognitive component of, 179, 191, 210, 222; and cognitive consistency (see Cognitive consistency); conative component of, 192, 210, 222; feeling component of, 191–92; functional approach to, 179–80, 201–3 (see also Functional theories of attitude); intentions component of, 192; interpersonal, 411–12; multidimensional nature of, 222; multiplex, 178–79; perceptual component of, 191; and search for consistency, 210–20; structural approach to, 179; about women, 375
Attractiveness 190
Attributes, of brands 273–74; social, 430–40; value, 15
Attribution theory 6–7, 64–75; information dependence and, 67–69; promotion and, 66–67
Attributional validation and personality 69–71
Authoritarianism 216, 445, 525, 538
Authority 538
Avant-garde 376

Balance 180
Balance theory 247–53
Baptist 393
Behavior, model of 555–58; political, 393; racial, 458; supermarket shopping, 118–21; theories, 515, 519–40
Behavioral act 213
Behavioral intention 211

Beliefs 177–78, 212, 270, 284, 292, 297, 375, 450
Biological factors 379
Biological need systems 113–14
Black dilemma 492
Black subcultures 458–62
Blacks' role in mass media 504–14
Brand ambiguity 526, 530–31
Brand appeal 225–28; instrumentality and, 226–27; value index and, 225–27
Brand attributes 273–74
Brand availability shift hypothesis 545
Brand choice 87–97, 519, 534, 543
Brand identification 17–23; blind test, 18–19; influence on overall ratings, 20–22; influence on specified characteristics, 22
Brand image 57, 62
Brand loyalty 55, 57; hypothesis, 545; model, 546
Brand name 51
Brand perceptions 46–48
Brand potential 533
Brand preferences 521; cognitive theory view of, 220–32
Brand purchase sequences 90–92; *see also* Last brand purchased model
Brand switching 48–51, 149; model of, 89–95
Bush-Mosteller learning model 84, 86, 87, 89, 105, 550
Buy-response function 32

California Personality Inventory 134–35, 156
Canonical analysis 155–60
Cattell's 16-Personality Factor Inventory 137
Causality 6–7
Chicago Tribune Consumer Panel 90
Child, American 488–89; Lebanese, 487–88; rearing, 410, 450
Children's purchase influence attempts 368–74
Christian Science 393
Cigarette smoking 133

Class, hierarchy 390; leisure, 432; status, 457; system, 400–401; *see also* Social class
Closed-mindedness 137
Cluster analysis 160–61
Cognitive consistency 180, 195–99, 247–63, 521; search for, 210–20
Cognitive dissonance 180–82, 196–98, 255–59; postdecision, 264–70; and postdecision product evaluation, 270–82
Cognitive map 2
Cognitive structure 223
Cognitive theory 8, 518; brand preference, 220–32
Communication, arousing anxiety 123–24; channels, 303–5, 307; effects, 195; interpersonal, 368; significative, 535; symbolic, 535; two-step flow of, 294, 331–42
Comparisons, paired 184; social, 298
Competitive marketing mix model 553–55
Complex flow chart of consumer decision processes 563–64
Compliant types 131
Complication 521
Comprehension 531, 533
Conformity 325–31
Congruity 180
Congruity theory 253–55
Consistency 103
Conspicuous consumption 430, 496
Constant brand probability model 547–48
Consumer aspirations and reference groups 309–14
Consumer choice behavior, experimental approach to 232–47; models of, 517, 541–60
Consumer credit 421
Consumer economics 129
Consumer purchase frequencies 92–94
Consumer Reports 6, 253, 255
Consumer testing 51
Consumption role 296–97
Contract 474

Contrast effect 199–200

Control, internal-external locus of 71–73; theory of propositional, 211–15

Counterarguments 283

Covariance of cause and effect 64

Creativity 150

Credibility 67, 190

Credit card usage 421–30

Cue 76–77

Cultural orientations 480–89

Cultural stereotypes 453

Culture 450–56, 522, 538; configuration, 466; definition of, 465–67; transmitted, 467

Culture dimensions 451; distributive, 451; normative, 451–53; organizational, 451–52

Customary pricing 23

Customs 16, 450

Decision making models 515–19; formal, 516–19

Decision mediation 520, 526, 536; processes, flowchart, 563–64; roles, 358–61

Decoding 221, 228

Deferred gratification 422–23

Dependence 377; *see also* Independence

Deprivation 441–42, 444, 489

Depth interviews 184

Detached types 131

Differential perception 10–17; *see also* Semantic differential *and* Selective perception

Differential price thresholds 30, 32–36

Discrepant information 284

Discretionary income, 114

Discrimination 81–82, 489

Dissonance theory; *see* Cognitive dissonance

Distortion of judgments 315–24

Distribution structure 455–56

Dogmatism 149

Dominance 379

Drive 76–78, 83

Drive-reduction 77

Dunnette Adjective Checklist 137

Economic dependency 441

Education 489

Edwards Personal Preference Schedule (EPPS) 133–34

Ego-defensive function 180, 203

Encoding of stimuli 221, 228, 229

Endogenous variables 522

Endorsements 56, 70

Energy 109–10

Environment 2

Episcopal 393

Esteem needs 115

Ethnic background 457

Ethnocentrism 70

Evoked set 520, 536–37

Exhibitionism 525

Exogenous variables 522

Expenditure patterns in the Negro market 496–502

Expert information 68

Expressed dissonance 273

Expressive function 180, 202–3

Extensive problem solving 528, 536

Extinction 81; incomplete, 551

Factor theory 132–35

Fads 432

Faith 177

Family 535–36, 538; role structure, 353; roles, 294–95

Fashions 432

Fatalism 445

Fear 114, 129

Fear appeals 122–28

Field theory 104–12; ahistorical approach, 107–8; constructive method, 106–7; Lewinian, 8

Financial status 538

Folk society 452

Folklore 453

Force 110–11

Formal groups 293

Formal theories of behavior 515

Frame of reference 100–101, 303

Free sample 57, 62

Friendship, language of 473

Functional theories of attitude 179–80, 201–3; ego-defensive (externalization) function, 180, 203; expressive (self-realizing) function, 180, 202–3; knowledge function, 180, 202; utilitarian (adaptive) function, 179–80, 202

Galileian concepts 106

Generalization 77, 81–83, 526, 534

Geographic environment 2

Gestalt theory 106

Ghetto consumer 397–98

Goal object 77–78

Goals 233

Gordon Personal Inventory 132–33

Graphology 186

Gregariousness 294

Group cohesion 345

Group conformity 297–98

Group norms 310, 327; *see also* Norms

Group pressure 315–24

Habit persistence hypothesis 545

Habits 221; extinction of, 551; formation of, 551; strength of, 78, 83

Helplessness 441–42

Hierarchy, of communication effects 195; of responses, 77; resultant, 77

Hunger 118–21

Hypotheses, of consumer behavior 545; of habit persistence, 545; of information flow, 294, 331–42

Hypothetical concepts 516; constructs, 522, 524–31, 533

Ideology 292, 297, 342

Immunization; *see* Attitude immunization

Impulse buying 120

Impulse renunciation 422–23

Incentive 77; potential, 78, 83

Income elasticity 501

Inconsistency, modes of resolving 197–98; *see also* Consistency

Independence 319, 325–31; *see also* Dependence

Individual differences 319–20

Individuality 376–83

Industrial purchasing 538; *see also* Purchasing

Influence, interpersonal flow of 332; social, 129

Informal groups 293; and innovative behavior, 342–52

Information, search for 530–31; and social influence, 298; sensitivity to, 529–30; sources, 68

Information dependence, attribution and 67–69; personality and, 70

Information processing, models 572–83; theory, 193–95

Inhibitors 526–27, 536

Initial hierarchy of responses 77; *see also* Responses

Initiating drive 78

Innate drives 76

Inner-other-directedness 70

Innovation 129, 345; effect of informal group upon, 342–52; and personality, 149–55

Institute of Human Relations at Yale University 131

Instrumentality, and brand appeal 226–27; perceived, 233, 235, 536

Instrumentality-value analysis 223

Intention to buy 532–33

Interaction 342; intrafamily, 368–69; male-female, 386

Internal-external locus of control 71–73

Interpersonal attitudes 411–12

Interpersonal communication 368

Interpersonal flow of influence 332

Intervening variables 221, 522, 538

Intrafamily interaction 368–69

Involvement, role of 200

Involvement-discrepancy controversy 200–201

I-O Social Preference Scale 70

Judgment, social   199–200
"Just noticeable difference" (JND)
   30

Knowledge   177, 450, 466; function,
   180, 202

Language in overseas business   468–
   79; of agreements, 473–75; of
   friendship, 473; of money, 473; of
   space, 471–72; of things, 472–73;
   of time, 469–71
Last brand purchased model   548–50
Latency of response   528
Latent learning   101
Laws   16, 450
Learned anxiety   123
Learned drives   76
Learning   7–9, 75–87, 533; con-
   structs, 525–29; incomplete, 551; la-
   tent, 101; model, 550–51 (*see also*
   Bush-Mosteller learning model);
   over-, 100; without involvement,
   98–104
Lebanese child, 487–88
Leisure class   432
Lewinian field theory   8
Life space   108–9; style, 136–37,
   410, 431–32, 450
Life-style research   163
Likert scale   184
Limited problem solving   528
Living room styles   430–40
Locus of control, internal-external
   71–73; and race, 71
Long-term memory   100
Love needs   115

McClosky Personality Inventory   137
Majority effect   316
Majority fallacy   50
Male-female interaction   386
Marital roles   353–68
Market segment   409, 494, 502, 537;
   share, 51; structure analysis, 42–51
Markov chain analyses   91
Markov process   84

Markov matrix   549
Markov model, variable   551–53
Mass media, Blacks as communicators
   508–11; Blacks as respondents,
   505–8; role of Blacks in, 504–14
Mass societies   307–8
Material culture   466
Material possessions   472
Mathematical models of consumer
   behavior   517, 541–60; *see also*
   specific models
Mathematical psychology   129
Maximization of quality-to-price hy-
   pothesis   545
Maximum likelihood estimates   89
Media   416
Media choice   129
Memory   100
Middle range theories of behavior
   515
Miller Attitude Toward Any Occupa-
   tion Test   310
Misanthropy   70
Models of consumer behavior   517,
   541–60; *see also specific models*
Modern norms   342
Modern societies   452
Molecular data   107
Money, language of   473
Morals   450
Mores   16
Mormons   393
Motivation   113–16, 564
Motivation research (MR)   83, 104,
   117, 162–63
Motives   525, 535–36
Multidimensional scaling   47
Multiplex attitudes   178–79

Needs, biological   113–14; psycho-
   logical, 114–16; social, 75
Negative reference groups   293
Negotiating agreements   473
Negotiations   474
Negro audiences   507
Negro market   461, 489–505; devel-
   opment of interest in, 494–95; ex-
   penditures in, 496–502

Negro revolution   503

New product development, methodology for   44–51; preference and perception measures in, 42–55

New products   77; adopters of, 334; two-step flow in diffusion of, 331–42

Nonconscious ideology   374–84

Non-taste attributes of brands   273–74

Nonunanimous majorities, effect of   320–24

Normative belief   213

Normative social influence   298

Normative theory   519

Norms   292, 297, 310, 342, 345; *see also* Group norms

Nouveaux riches   436

Novelty   149

Obesity   118–21

Objective reality   70; world, 108

Occupational deprivation   489; prestige, 391

Odd pricing   23–24

Open-ended questions   184

Open-mindedness   137, 150

Opinion   177; leaders, 294, 331–32, 335; leadership, 129, 334, 345; scales, 183–84

Output variable   531

Overlearning   100

Overprivilegedness   396

Overseas business, language in; *see* Language in overseas business

Package   51

Paired comparisons   184

Parameter estimates   89

Parental yielding   368–74

Passivity   377

Perceived instrumentality   233, 235, 536

Perceived risk   6, 149, 343, 345; *see also* Risk

Perception   1–7; distortion of, 320; and new product development, 42–55; personal factors in, 2–3; selective (*see* Selective perception); of self, 412–14; of social status, 493–94; stimulus factors in, 1–2

Perceptual bias   539

Perceptual constructs   529–31

Perceptual defense   529

Perceptual field   303

Perceptual map   5, 47–48; mapping, 4–6

Perceptual space   47

Perceptual stimuli   229

Perceptual vigilance   529

Personal factors in perception   2–3

Personal influence   298

Personality   113, 116–17, 129–48, 522, 538; attributional validation and, 69–71; information dependence and, 70; innovation proneness and, 149–55; multivariate analysis of, 155–62; theories of, 116–17

Persuasibility   138–39

Persuasion   284; resistance to, 282, 284

Phenomonological field   108

Physiological needs   113–15

Political behavior   393

Political propaganda   123

Political science   129

Poor   25, 490

Positive theory   519

Positivism, radical   229

Possessions, material   472

Postdecision conflict   181

Postdecision dissonance; *see* Cognitive dissonance

Postdecision product evaluation   270–82

Poverty   441–49, 457, 489; subculture of, 397–98

Power   190, 323, 525, 538

Powerlessness   443

Predisposition toward a brand   522, 525–26, 533, 564

Preference in new product development   42–55

Prejudice   221
Prestige   390, 391, 525
Price consciousness   24–26
Price perception   23–42; assimilation-contrast effects on, 35–36
Price-quality mapping   29
Price-quality relationship   26–29, 536
Price thresholds   4
Pricing   23–24, 455; standard, 35
Pride   496
Primary needs   75
Prisoner's Dilemma Game   215–17
Problem solving   528, 536
Process models of behavior   195
Products   51; and claims credibility, 67; dissonance model in postdecision evaluation of, 270–82; life cycle of, 282; meaning of, 453–54; promotion of, 454–55; promotion and attribution of, 66–67; use of, 155–62
Projective techniques   185–86
Promotion   66–67, 454–55
Propaganda, political   123
Propositional control, theory of   211–15
Protestant ethic   403, 452
Psychoanalytic theory   129–30
Psychographic research   163
Psychological field   8, 108–9
Psychological needs   114–16
Psychological pricing   23–24
Psychological salience   101, 178
Psychological world   108
Psychology of complication   521
Psychology of simplification   521
Psychophysics   30
Purchasing behavior   129, 532; cycles of, 520; and decisions, 273; in industry, 538; and risk, 535

Q-methodology   311–12
Quality-to-price maximization hypothesis   545

Race   496

Racial behavior   458
Radical positivism   229
Radio stations   505
Rank order technique   184
Reactance   326
Reaction potential   78
Readiness to respond   189
Reality   70
Reference frame   100–101, 303
Reference groups   292–93, 299–309, 313, 326, 493, 535–36, 538; and consumer aspirations, 309–14
Referent individual   313
Reinforcement   76–77
Reliability   186–87
Religion   450
Religious affiliation   457
Repetitive decision making   521
Republicans   393
Resistance to persuasion   282, 284
Responses   76; change of, 547; generalization of, 534; initial hierarchy of, 77; latency of, 528; readiness, 189; uncertainty of, 547
Resultant hierarchy   77
Reward   77, 101
Risk, perceived   6, 149, 343, 345; reduction methods, 55–64; reliever, 55, 60–63; taking, 129
Rituals   16
Role theory   293–96
Roles, consensus in, 354, 361–64; integration of, 295; marital, 353–68; of Blacks in mass media, 504–14; perception of, 354; portrayed by women, 384–89; segregation of, 295; training in, 376–77
Rorschach ink blot test   186
Rosenzweig Picture Frustration Test   186
Routine response behavior   528
Rural sociology   129

Safety needs   115
Salience, psychological   101, 178
Security   115, 496
Segmentation   129
Selective exposure   283–84

Selective perception 2, 301–3, 308; in brand identification, 17–23; differential, 10–17

Self, theory of 135–36

Self-actualization needs 115

Self-concept 270; theory of, 135–36

Self-confidence 538

Self-esteem 413, 538

Self-fulfillment 376–83

Self-perceptions 412–14

Semantic differential 184, 234

Semantic generalization 534

Sensitivity to information 529–30

Sentence completion technique 186

Sex-role training 376–77

Shifts in brand availability hypothesis 545

Short-term memory 100

Significative communication 535

Significative stimuli 524, 529

Similarity data 50

Similarity judgments 43, 47

Similarity measurement 45–46

Similarity perceptions 48–50

Simplification 521

Simulation 560–72; of consumer brand choice, 94–95

Sleeper effects 101

Smallest Space Analysis (SSA) 433–36

Smoking 133

Soap opera 407

Social anthropology 129

Social attributes 430–40

Social changes 404

Social character 70, 137–38

Social class 390–400, 409–20, 522, 535, 538; in America, 400–409; credit card usage and, 421–30

Social comparison processes 298

Social deprivation 489

Social environment 2

Social heritage 450

Social influence 129

Social integration 345

Social judgment 199–200

Social mobility 390, 431

Social needs 75

Social opposition 323

Social pressure 320

Social prestige 390

Social processes 292–99

Social psychology 129

Social reality 70

Social status 431, 493; perception of, 493–94

Social stimuli 529

Social stratification 390–93

Social support 323

Social theorists 130–31

Social worlds 303–5

Socialization 296, 307, 377, 378

Socioeconomic status 25–26, 457

Sociology, rural 129

Space, language of 471–72

Standard of living 502

Standard price 35

Status 496, 502, 525, 538; achievement of, 442; order, 404; perception of, 493–94; social, 431, 493; symbols, 300; system, 408

Stereotypes 221, 228, 490; cultural, 453; of women, 384

Stimuli, significative 524, 529; social, 529; symbolic, 524, 529

Stimulus ambiguity 529

Stimulus factors in perception 1–2

Stimulus generalization 82, 534

Stimulus input variables 524

Stimulus intensity 83

Stimulus-intensity dynamism 78

Stimulus-response theory 7–8, 76–81, 131–32

Stochastic learning models 84, 105; *see also* Bush-Mosteller learning model

Store image 57, 62

Strong Vocational Interest Blank 137

Subcultures 456–62; Black, 458–62; of poverty, 397–98

Submission 320

Submissiveness 379

Supermarket shopping behavior 118–21

Symbolic commercial stimuli 529

Symbolic communication 535

Symbolic meaning 3–4

Symbolic stimuli 524

Tastemakers 432, 436
Television advertising 98–104
Television stations 505
Tension 109
Thematic Apperception Test 116, 186
Theoretical development 515
Theories of consumer behavior 519–40; *see also specific topics*
Things, language of 472–73
Thurstone Temperament Schedule 134
Time, language of 469–71
Time pressure 537
Total behavior model 555–58
Traditional norms 342
Trait theory 132–35
Transmitted culture 467
Trustworthiness 70
Two-step flow of communication 294, 331–42
Two-step flow in diffusion of new product 331–42
Two-step hypothesis 294

Underprivilegedness 490
Utilitarian function 179–80, 202
Utility in economic theory 79–80, 104

Validity 187
Value attribute 15
Value importance 233
Value index and brand appeal 225–27
Value questionnaire 224–25
Values 178, 223, 229, 233–34, 292, 297, 310, 376, 410–11, 441, 457, 466, 480
Variable Markov model 551–53
Variables, intervening 221, 522, 538
Vector 110–11

Weber-Fechner law 31–32
Weber's law 30–31, 33–34
Women, attitudes about 375; roles portrayed by, 384–89; stereotypes of, 384
Word association 185
Word of mouth 57, 62, 334–40
World, objective 108; psychological, 108; social, 303–5

Yankee City 401–2
Yielding 319–20; parental, 368–74